Seventh Workshop on Fact Extraction and VERification (FEVER 2024)

Miami, Florida, USA
15 November 2024

ISBN: 979-8-3313-0845-2

Printed from e-media with permission by:

Curran Associates, Inc.
57 Morehouse Lane
Red Hook, NY 12571

Some format issues inherent in the e-media version may also appear in this print version.

Association for Computational Linguistics
209 N. Eighth Street
Stroudsburg, Pennsylvania 18360

Phone: 1-570-476-8006
Fax: 1-570-476-0860

acl@aclweb.org

Additional copies of this publication are available from:

Curran Associates, Inc.
57 Morehouse Lane
Red Hook, NY 12571 USA
Phone: 845-758-0400
Fax: 845-758-2633
Email: curran@proceedings.com
Web: www.proceedings.com

FEVER 2024

The Seventh Fact Extraction and VERification Workshop

Proceedings of the Workshop

November 15, 2024

The FEVER organizers gratefully acknowledge the support from the following sponsors.

Supported by

Google

Order copies of this and other ACL proceedings from:

Association for Computational Linguistics (ACL)
317 Sidney Baker St. S
Suite 400 - 134
Kerrville, TX 78028
USA
Tel: +1-855-225-1962
acl@aclweb.org

Introduction

With billions of web pages covering nearly every topic, we should be able to collect facts that answer a wide range of questions. However, only a small portion of this information is structured (e.g., Wikidata and Freebase), limiting our ability to convert free-form text into structured knowledge. Additionally, the rise of false information from unreliable sources — both human and NLP systems like large language models — has garnered significant attention.

To ensure accuracy, this content must be verified, but the sheer volume makes human moderation impractical. Therefore, it is crucial to explore automated methods for verifying the accuracy and consistency of online information and systems (such as Question Answering, Search, and Digital Personal Assistants) that depend on it.

The seventh edition of the FEVER workshop collocated with EMNLP 2024 aims to continue promoting ongoing research in above area, following on from the first five collocated with EMNLP 2018, EMNLP 2019, ACL 2020, EMNLP 2021, ACL 2022, and EACL 2023, and three shared tasks in 2018, 2019, and 2021. This year's workshop consists of 3 oral and 14 poster presentations of accepted papers (63% overall acceptance rate), 5 poster presentations from EMNLP Findings papers, and presentations from 4 invited speakers. FEVER 2024 also hosts the AVeriTeC shared task on real-world fact-checking, which consists of an additional 5 oral and 10 poster presentations. The workshop is held in hybrid mode with in-person and virtual poster sessions, as well as live-streamed oral presentations and invited talks.

The organisers would like to thank the authors of all submitted papers, the reviewers, and the invited speakers for their efforts, and we are looking forward to next year's edition.

Best wishes,
The FEVER organisers

Organizing Committee

Workshop Organisers

Michael Schlichtkrull, Queen Mary University of London
Yulong Chen, University of Cambridge
Chenxi Whitehouse, University of Cambridge
Zhenyun Deng, University of Cambridge
Mubashara Akhtar, King's College London
Rami Aly, University of Cambridge
Rui Cao, University of Cambridge
Zhijiang Guo, Huawei
Christos Christodoulopoulos, Amazon
Oana Cocarascu, King's College London
Arpit Mittal, Meta
James Thorne, KAIST
Andreas Vlachos, University of Cambridge

Program Committee

Program Committee

Yasuo Ariki, Kobe University
Anab Maulana Barik, National University of Singapore
Tobias Braun, Technische Universität Darmstadt
Yupeng Cao, Stevens Institute of Technology
Julius Cheng, University of Cambridge
Svetlana Churina, National University of Singapore
Jin Liu, Karlsruher Institut für Technologie
Christopher Malon, NEC Laboratories America
Shrikant Malviya, Durham University
Tomáš Mlynář, Czech Technical Univeresity in Prague
Sandip Modha, University of Milan - Bicocca
Mohammad Ghiasvand Mohammadkhani, Amirkabir University of Technology
Yuki Momii, Kobe University
Adjali Omar, CEA
Paolo Papotti, Eurecom
Kunwoo Park, Soongsil University
Heesoo Park, Dunamu
Parth Patwa, Amazon and University of California, Los Angeles
Mark Rothermel, Technische Universität Darmstadt
Diksha Saxena, State University of New York at Buffalo
Özge Sevgili, Universität Hamburg
Harish Sista, Stevens Institute of Technology
Ieva Staliunaite, University of Cambridge
Dominik Stammbach, Princeton University
Junhao Tang, Hong Kong University of Science and Technology
Herbert Ullrich, Czech Technical Univeresity in Prague
Nicolò Urbani, University of Milan - Bicocca
Mahmud Elahi Akhter, Queen Mary University of London
Karman Chan, Internet Initiative Japan Inc.
Jan Drchal, Czech Technical Univeresity in Prague, Czech Technical University of Prague
Rajvi Kapadia, Google
Pride Kavumba, Tohoku University
Jongmo Kim, King's College London
Neema Kotonya, Dataminr
Amrith Krishna, Learno
Anjishnu Kumar, Amazon AGI
Clément Lefebvre, EPFL - EPF Lausanne
Pietro Lesci, University of Cambridge
Xiangci Li, University of Texas at Dallas
Irene Li, University of Tokyo
Iffat Maab, University of Tokyo
Pranav Mani, Abridge AI
Mira Moukheiber, Massachusetts Institute of Technology
Wolfgang Otto, GESIS
Vatsal Raina, University of Cambridge
Allen G Roush, Oracle

Takehito Utsuro, University of Tsukuba
Francielle Vargas, University of Southern California
Amelie Wuehrl, University of Stuttgart, Universität Stuttgart
Menglin Xia, Microsoft
Paul Youssef, Phillips-Universität Marburg
Moy Yuan, University of Cambridge
Bohui Zhang, King's College London

Invited Speakers

Omar Khattab, Stanford University
Rada Mihalcea, University of Michigan
Peter Cunliffe-Jones, University of Westminster and AfricaCheck
Chris Bregler, Google

Table of Contents

Program

Friday, November 15, 2024

09:00 - 09:45 *Opening Remarks & Shared Task Overview*

09:45 - 10:30 *Keynote Talk: Omar Khattab*

10:30 - 11:00 *Coffee break*

11:00 - 12:00 *Poster Session*

Multi-hop Evidence Pursuit Meets the Web: Team Papelo at FEVER 2024
Christopher Malon

Retrieving Semantics for Fact-Checking: A Comparative Approach using CQ (Claim to Question) & AQ (Answer to Question)
Nicolò Urbani, Sandip Modha and Gabriella Pasi

RAG-Fusion Based Information Retrieval for Fact-Checking
Yuki Momii, Tetsuya Takiguchi and Yasuo Ariki

UHH at AVeriTeC: RAG for Fact-Checking with Real-World Claims
Özge Sevgili, Irina Nikishina, Seid Muhie Yimam, Martin Semmann and Chris Biemann

Improving Evidence Retrieval on Claim Verification Pipeline through Question Enrichment
Svetlana Churina, Anab Maulana Barik and Saisamarth Rajesh Phaye

Dunamu-ml's Submissions on AVERITEC Shared Task
Heesoo Park, Dongjun Lee, Jaehyuk Kim, ChoongWon Park and Changhwa Park

FZI-WIM at AVeriTeC Shared Task: Real-World Fact-Checking with Question Answering
Jin Liu, Steffen Thoma and Achim Rettinger

Zero-Shot Learning and Key Points Are All You Need for Automated Fact-Checking
Mohammad Ghiasvand Mohammadkhani, Ali Ghiasvand Mohammadkhani and Hamid Beigy

Friday, November 15, 2024 (continued)

Friday, November 15, 2024 (continued)

DAHL: Domain-specific Automated Hallucination Evaluation of Long-Form Text through a Benchmark Dataset in Biomedicine
Jean Seo, Jongwon Lim, Dongjun Jang and Hyopil Shin

Detecting Misleading News Representations on Social Media Posts
Satoshi Tohda, Naoki Yoshinaga, Masashi Toyoda, Sho Cho and Ryota Kitabayashi

Evidence Retrieval for Fact Verification using Multi-stage Reranking
Shrikant Malviya and Stamos Katsigiannis

Generating Media Background Checks for Automated Source Critical Reasoning
Michael Schlichtkrull

DYNAMICQA: Tracing Internal Knowledge Conflicts in Language Models
Sara Vera Marjanović, Haeun Yu, Pepa Atanasova, Maria Maistro, Christina Lioma and Isabelle Augenstein

Zero-Shot Fact Verification via Natural Logic and Large Language Models
Marek Strong, Rami Aly and Andreas Vlachos

Do We Need Language-Specific Fact-Checking Models? The Case of Chinese
Caiqi Zhang, Zhijiang Guo and Andreas Vlachos

12:00 - 12:35 *Contributed Shared Task Talks*

InFact: A Strong Baseline for Automated Fact-Checking
Mark Rothermel, Tobias Braun, Marcus Rohrbach and Anna Rohrbach

HerO at AVeriTeC: The Herd of Open Large Language Models for Verifying Real-World Claims
Yejun Yoon, Jaeyoon Jung, Seunghyun Yoon and Kunwoo Park

AIC CTU system at AVeriTeC: Re-framing automated fact-checking as a simple RAG task
Herbert Ullrich, Tomáš Mlynář and Jan Drchal

	Dunamu-ml's Submissions on AVERITEC Shared Task Heesoo Park, Dongjun Lee, Jaehyuk Kim, ChoongWon Park and Changhwa Park
	Multi-hop Evidence Pursuit Meets the Web: Team Papelo at FEVER 2024 Christopher Malon
12:35 - 14:00	*Lunch Break*
14:00 - 14:45	*Keynote Talk: Rada Mihalcea*
14:45 - 15:30	*Keynote Talk: Peter Cunliffe-Jones*
15:30 - 16:00	*Coffee break*
16:00 - 16:30	*Contributed Workshop Talks*
	Enhancing Fact Verification with Causal Knowledge Graphs and Transformer-Based Retrieval for Deductive Reasoning Fiona Anting Tan, Jay Desai and Srinivasan H. Sengamedu
	Contrastive Learning to Improve Retrieval for Real-World Fact Checking Aniruddh Sriram, Fangyuan Xu, Eunsol Choi and Greg Durrett
	FactGenius: Combining Zero-Shot Prompting and Fuzzy Relation Mining to Improve Fact Verification with Knowledge Graphs Sushant Gautam and Roxana Pop
16:30 - 17:15	*Keynote Talk: Chris Bregler*
17:15 - 17:30	*Closing Remarks*

The Automated Verification of Textual Claims (AVeriTeC) Shared Task

Michael Schlichtkrull[1,2], Yulong Chen[2], Chenxi Whitehouse[2,5], Zhenyun Deng[2], Mubashara Akhtar[4], Rami Aly[2], Zhijiang Guo[2], Christos Christodoulopoulos[3], Oana Cocarascu[4], Arpit Mittal[5], James Thorne[6], Andreas Vlachos[2]

[1]Queen Mary University of London, [2]University of Cambridge,
[3]Amazon AGI, [4]King's College London, [5]Meta, [6]KAIST

m.schlichtkrull@qmul.ac.uk, {yc632,cj507,zd302,rmya2,zg283,av308}@cam.ac.uk
chrchrs@amazon.co.uk, {mubashara.akhtar,oana.cocarascu}@kcl.ac.uk
thorne@kaist.ac.kr, arpitmittal@meta.com

Abstract

The Automated Verification of Textual Claims (AVERITEC) shared task asks participants to retrieve evidence and predict veracity for real-world claims checked by fact-checkers. Evidence can be found either via a search engine, or via a knowledge store provided by the organisers. Submissions are evaluated using the AVERITEC score, which considers a claim to be accurately verified if and only if both the verdict is correct and retrieved evidence is considered to meet a certain quality threshold. The shared task received 21 submissions, 18 of which surpassed our baseline. The winning team was TUDA_MAI with an AVERITEC score of 63%. In this paper we describe the shared task, present the full results, and highlight key takeaways from the shared task.

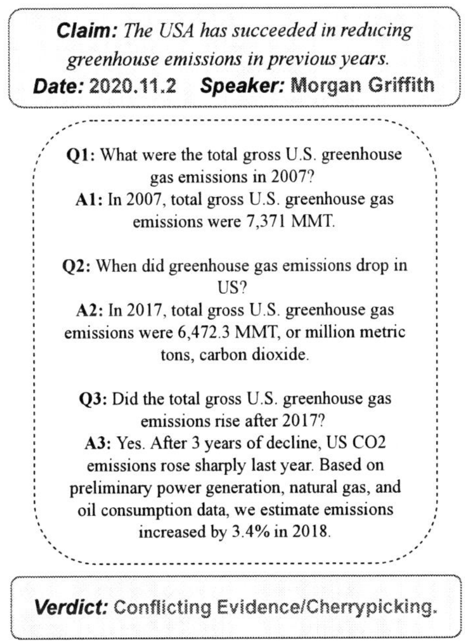

Figure 1: Example instance from AVERITEC. Given a claim and associated metadata, participating systems must first retrieve appropriate evidence. Then, they must output a verdict for the claim given that evidence.

1 Introduction

Automated fact-checking (AFC) has been proposed as an assistive tool for beleaguered fact-checkers (Cohen et al., 2011; Vlachos and Riedel, 2014), whose work is crucial for limiting misinformation (Lewandowsky et al., 2020). This has inspired applications in journalism (Miranda et al., 2019; Dudfield, 2020; Nakov et al., 2021) and other domains, e.g. science (Wadden et al., 2020). Substantial progress has been made on common benchmarks, such as FEVER (Thorne et al., 2018a) and MultiFC (Augenstein et al., 2019). Nevertheless, existing resources have recently come under criticism. Many datasets (for example, Thorne et al. (2018a); Schuster et al. (2021); Aly et al. (2021)) contain purpose-made claims derived e.g. from Wikipedia, and are thus not representative of real-world use cases. Datasets that *do* contain real-world claims either lack evidence annotation (Wang, 2017), or suffer issues resulting from superficial automated evidence annotation (Glockner et al., 2022).

The AVERITEC dataset was constructed to overcome these limitations (Schlichtkrull et al., 2023a). AVERITEC combines real-world claims with evidence from the web. The process of evidence retrieval is broken down into question generation and answering, providing a structured representation of the evidential reasoning process. The annotation process for AVERITEC was designed to ensure (1) that claims are understandable independently of the fact-checking articles they were sourced from, (2) that the evidence given is sufficient to support the verdicts, and (3) that all evidence used would have been available on the web before the claim was made. This avoids common problems found in previous datasets (Ousidhoum et al., 2022; Glockner et al., 2022).

Proceedings of the Seventh Fact Extraction and VERification Workshop (FEVER), pages 1–26
November 15, 2024 ©2024 Association for Computational Linguistics

AVERITEC consists originally of 4,568 examples, collected from 50 fact-checking organizations using the Google FactCheck Claim Search API[1]; itself based on ClaimReview[2]. To ensure that systems are evaluated on unseen data, we expanded the (hidden) test set with a further 1,215 claims for the shared task, bringing the total dataset size to 5,783. We furthermore released a "knowledge store" containing, for each claim in the training, development, and test splits, documents which can be used as evidence for that claim. This was done to prevent participants from being limited by the prohibitive cost of the search API we used for evidence retrieval in the original paper (Schlichtkrull et al., 2023a). We also developed an updated version of the baseline for the shared task, which uses the knowledge store. Participants in the shared task were allowed to use evidence from the knowledge store, use a search engine on their own, or combine the two options. Our dataset and baseline are available under a CC-BY-NC-4.0 license at `https://fever.ai/dataset/averitec.html`.

This paper presents a description of the task and dataset, the final test phase leaderboard. We also summarise the submitted system description papers, drawing out commonalities, differences, and lessons. We furthermore carry out additional analysis of the shared task results, including human evaluation. Finally, we reflect on the task, deriving lessons for future work – and further shared tasks – on automated fact-checking. The shared task received 21 submissions. The winning team, TUDA_MAI, achieved a score of 63%, a very significant improvement on the 11% achieved by the baseline system. Nevertheless, there are still plenty of opportunities for further improvement. During the process, we identified an issue with the evidence set provided for participants, which for some claims in the second half of the dataset contained fact-checking articles written by humans about those claims. We release an updated knowledge store at `https://fever.ai/dataset/averitec.html`, where these articles have been removed. We leave open an evaluation page corresponding to the *new* knowledge store[3] so that future work can build upon the advances made in this shared task.

[1]`https://toolbox.google.com/factcheck/apis`, available under a CC-BY-4.0 license.

[2]`https://www.claimreviewproject.com/`

[3]Also available at `https://fever.ai/dataset/averitec.html`

2 Task Description

Participants are given claims and associated metadata, such as the publication date (see Figure 1). Based on this, they must retrieve *evidence* for or against the claims. In the gold annotation, this evidence is broken down into question-answer pairs, naturally enabling multi-hop reasoning. We do not restrict participants to providing evidence in this format, although given the METEOR-based evaluation setup most participants found it beneficial to follow it. When submitting test set predictions, we also required participants to include a URL to an external website for each piece of evidence, corresponding to a webpage providing *backing*. Finally, based on the evidence, participants must predict whether a veracity label from the set *supported, refuted, not enough evidence*, or *conflicting evidence/cherrypicking*. Unlike the original AVERITEC dataset, we did not require participants to submit a justification for the verdict.

2.1 Dataset

Participants are asked to use the public AVERITEC data for training and validating their systems. To ensure a fairer and more robust evaluation, we constructed a new test set consisting of 1,215 claims, which temporally succeed the original claims, in addition to the original 1000 hidden test set claims of AVERITEC. Like the original test set, these will remain hidden so as to enable future work on the dataset.

Annotation of New Test Set We first collect 2,000 real-world fact-checking articles online from ClaimReview, same source as AVERITEC. Then, we follow the same 5-phase annotation guideline of Schlichtkrull et al. (2023a).

First, given a fact-checking article, an annotator identifies its main claim, collects metadata about it and normalizes the claim by enriching it with necessary context, making it context-independent. Second, given the normalized claim, another annotator generates questions and answers (QAs) with the help of the fact-checking article and the web, and gives a verdict label for the claim. Third, given only the QAs as evidence, a different annotator selects a verdict label for the claim and provides a justification for their choice. At this point, we compare the verdict labels annotated by different annotators. If the labels match, we consider the evidence is sufficient for predicting the veracity; otherwise, we repeat the last two phases as our

Split	Train	Dev	Test (old)	Test (new)
Claims	3,068	500	1,000	1,215
Question / Claim	2.60	2.57	2.57	2.89
Re-annotated (%)	28.1	24.4	25.1	20.0
End date	25-08-2020	31-10-2020	22-12-2021	13-08-2023
Labels (S/R/C/N)	27.6/56.8/6.4/9.2	24.4/61.0/7.6/7.0	25.5/62.0/6.3/6.2	17.3/66.5/4.1/12.1
Types (PS/NC/EPC/QV/CC)	7.8/33.7/57.8/9.6/11.5	5.8/23.8/61.4/13.8/10.8	7.0/21.9/69.8/7.7/11.9	3.5/24.3/71.9/5.2/16.1
Strategies (WE/NCP/FR/EC/SS)	78.8/30.6/6.6/29.9/3.6	88.6/19.0/7.4/27.4/2.0	88.0/19.2/7.7/29.6/1.8	82.4/22.6/10.0/37.6/4.0

Table 1: Statistics for the new test set. For better comparison, we present the statistics for the original dataset. The Labels (%) are Supported (S), Refuted (R), Conflicting Evidence/Cherry-picking (C), and Not Enough Evidence (N). The Claim Types (%) are Position Statement (PS), Numerical Claim (NC), Event/Property Claim (EPC), Quote Verification (QV), and Causal Claim (CC). The Fact-checker strategies (%) are Written Evidence (WE), Numerical Comparison (NCP), Fact-checker Reference (FR), Expert Consultation (EC) and Satirical Source (SS). Note that we for simplicity omitted very low-frequent fact-checker strategies, e.g., Geo-location (0.3%).

fourth and fifth phases, respectively. If the labels given by the fourth and fifth annotators still do not match, we discard this instance. In this way, we obtain 1,215 new instances. Each is annotated with a normalized claim, meta-data, QA pairs as evidence, a verdict label and a justification for it. For the detailed annotation guidelines and procedures, please refer to Schlichtkrull et al. (2023a).

To ensure high quality, we train our annotators before formal annotation. For each phase, annotators are first asked to annotate 10 instances. We then provide feedback and highlight their most frequent and common mistakes. They are then asked to annotate another 10 instances. We select qualified annotators based on their performance on 3 tasks: (1) claim type and fact-checking strategies over 70%+ F-1 scores; (2) 2+ QA pairs per claim; (3) veracity prediction over 50%+ accuracy. These criteria are based on empirical consideration from the earlier AVERITEC annotation (Schlichtkrull et al., 2023a). Finally, we selected 12 qualified annotators from 34 participants.

Comparison between Original and New Test Sets Table 1 presents the statistics of our new test set in comparison with the original AVERITEC dataset. Our new test set (with claims up to 2023) is temporally further removed from the training set (ending in 2020). As such, there can be a domain shift between new and old data, regarding the fact-checking content. However, the majority (66.5%) of claim labels are *refuted*, which is consistent with previous data. Additionally, the distributions of claim labels, claim types and fact-checking strategies are largely similar in terms of their proportions. The new test set has slightly more questions per claim compared to the original one, indicating that the annotation process was at least as thorough.

2.2 Knowledge Store

As mentioned in Schlichtkrull et al. (2023a), reliance on the Google search API made the original baseline prohibitively expensive. Thus, to mitigate the cost, we released a *knowledge store* along with the shared task. The knowledge store contains a collection of potentially useful evidence documents for each claim, obtained via Google search.

We collected the knowledge store using a process inspired by our original baseline. We extracted a variety of search queries using ChatGPT[4], based on the claim, gold questions, and gold answers. We further used *distractor queries* created by changing entities, dates, and events in the claim, in order to add plausible – but irrelevant – documents to the knowledge store. All queries can be seen in Appendix A. For each query, we collected every URL returned on the first page of the Google Search API. We used the same temporal restrictions as in Schlichtkrull et al. (2023a), ensuring that the included documents would have been available on the web before the claim was made. We also included the annotator-selected evidence documents selected for each claim. We deduplicated and shuffled the documents corresponding to each claim.

We provided the URL for each document, as well as a text version scraped using `trafilatura` (Barbaresi, 2021). The knowledge store includes text scraped from PDF URLs, a step omitted in Schlichtkrull et al. (2023a). Furthermore, for the train and development splits (but not test), we made available the specific Google search query used for each document, as well as the category (see Table 11). The average claim has 955 associated documents, each of which have on average of 6,095 tokens. The most common URL

[4]We used `gpt-3.5-turbo-0125`.

domains for knowledge store documents are, in order, the National Center for Biotechnology Information (NCBI), Wikipedia, Quora, the New York Times, and CNN.

The knowledge store allowed participants to compete without access to a paid search engine. Further, it allowed inexpensive experimentation with a variety of different retrieval strategies. Our construction process for the knowledge store relies on information not available normally to participants, such as the gold question-answer pairs. We found that these were necessary to ensure that good, relevant evidence was included. At the same time, relying on the knowledge store complicates the finding of alternative evidence paths to the one used by our annotators. Exploring alternative evidence paths was easier for systems which directly integrated their own search engine. As such, there were upsides to both strategies.

2.3 Baseline

Our baseline closely follows the approach described in Schlichtkrull et al. (2023a), with the main difference being that, instead of requiring direct access to the paid Google Search API, we use the aforementioned knowledge store. This adjustment aims to reduce the costs of participating in the Shared Task.

Our baseline consists of the following steps. (1) We parse the scraped text into sentences and rank their similarity to the claim using BM25 (Robertson and Zaragoza, 2009), retaining the top 100 sentences per claim. (2) Questions-answer (QA) pairs are generated for these top 100 sentences using BLOOM,[5] with the 10 most similar claim-QA pairs from the training set used as in-context examples. (3) The QA pairs are then re-ranked using a pretrained BERT model as described in Schlichtkrull et al. (2023a). (4) Finally, using the top-3 QA pairs as evidence, we predict the veracity label of the claim with another pretrained BERT model, as detailed in Schlichtkrull et al. (2023a).

The baseline results are shown in Table 2. We note that on both the development set, the old test set, and the new test set, the shared task baseline and the baseline from Schlichtkrull et al. (2023a) perform similarly. Further details regarding the implementation, knowledge store, and pretrained BERT models are available at `https://huggingface.co/chenxwh/AVeriTeC`.

[5]We used `bigscience/bloom-7b1`.

2.4 Evaluation

The primary evaluation metric for the shared task is AVeriTeC score, discussed in depth in Schlichtkrull et al. (2023a). We first compute results for question generation and question-answer generation using Hungarian METEOR score. That is, we use the Hungarian Algorithm (Kuhn, 1955) to find an optimal matching of generated text to reference text in terms of METEOR score. Formally, let $X : \hat{Y} \times Y \rightarrow \{0, 1\}$ be a boolean function denoting the assignment between the first 10 generated question-answer pairs (or questions only) $\hat{Y}$ and the reference question-answer pairs (or questions only) Y. Then, the Q + A score (or Q only score) u is calculated as:

$$u_f(\hat{Y}, Y) = \frac{1}{|Y|} \max \sum_{\hat{y} \in \hat{Y}} \sum_{y \in Y} f(\hat{y}, y) X(\hat{y}, y) \tag{1}$$

where the pairwise scoring function $f : S \times S \rightarrow \mathbb{R}$ is METEOR score (Banerjee and Lavie, 2005) using the NLTK implementation (Bird et al., 2009).

To compute the AVeriTeC score, we applied a cutoff of $u_f(\hat{Y}, Y) \geq 0.25$ to determine whether adequate evidence has been retrieved, using the Q + A Hungarian METEOR score. Any claim for which this score is lower then 0.25 receives an AVeriTeC score of 0. For claims where the evidence score is higher than 0.25, the AVeriTeC score is defined as the accuracy of the predicted verdict (veracity). As also discussed in Schlichtkrull et al. (2023a), both for Q only, Q+A, and AVeriTeC score, if a system provided more than 10 QA pairs, all pairs after the 10th were discarded. We note that QA pairs beyond the 10th can still be input to veracity prediction components, and may as such still be useful to some systems.

3 Results

The overall results for the shared task can be seen in Table 2. Each of the 21 participating teams were invited to submit a paper to be reviewed in the FEVER workshop – detailed descriptions for each system can be found in the corresponding papers. 15 system description papers were submitted to the workshop (with a 16th submitted and withdrawn). We analyse the model components discussed in each paper – see Table 3. Below, we present our general observations on the techniques used by participants, as reported in their respective system description papers.

Rank	Team Name	Q only	Q + A	AVERITEC @ .25
1	TUDA_MAI (Rothermel et al., 2024)	0.45	0.34	**0.63**
2	HUMANE (Yoon et al., 2024)	0.48	**0.35**	0.57
3	CTU AIC (Ullrich et al., 2024)	0.46	0.32	0.50
4	Dunamu-ml (Park et al., 2024)	**0.49**	**0.35**	0.50
5	Papelo (Malon, 2024)	0.44	0.30	0.48
6	UHH (Sevgili et al., 2024)	0.48	0.32	0.45
7	SynApSe (Churina et al., 2024)	0.41	0.30	0.42
8	arioriAveri (Momii et al., 2024)	0.38	0.29	0.39
9	Data-Wizards (Singhal et al., 2024)	0.35	0.27	0.33
10	MA-Bros-H (Mohammadkhani et al., 2024)	0.38	0.24	0.27
11	mitchelldehaven	0.27	0.23	0.25
12	SK_DU (Malviya and Katsigiannis, 2024)	0.40	0.26	0.22
13	UPS (Omar, 2024)	0.31	0.27	0.21
14	FZI-WIM (Liu et al., 2024b)	0.32	0.21	0.20
15	KnowComp (Liu et al., 2024a)	0.32	0.21	0.18
16	IKR3-UNIMIB (Urbani et al., 2024)	0.32	0.24	0.18
17	ngetach	0.37	0.21	0.14
18	VGyasi	0.38	0.22	0.12
19	*Baseline*	*0.24*	*0.20*	*0.11*
20	InfinityScalers!	0.26	0.19	0.08
21	AYM	0.13	0.12	0.06
22	Factors	0.20	0.14	0.05

Table 2: Overall results for the AVERITEC shared task. Performance is evaluated on the total of 2214 hidden test set examples. Scores are given in Hungarian METEOR for question-only and question-answer performance, and in AVERITEC-score at evidence cutoff 0.25 for total performance (see Schlichtkrull et al. (2023a)).

Knowledge Source Papelo, SynApSe, and KnowComp relied on the Google Search API as knowledge source, while the remaining systems all used our knowledge store. Participants identified shortcomings in both approaches: the knowledge store is guaranteed to include the gold evidence and can be searched with highly performant embedding methods, whereas the search API allows for more freedom in what information can be retrieved (i.e., if generating questions for a different evidence path than the one our annotators used, the knowledge store may not be able to answer those questions). As evidenced by the strong results of Team Papelo, despite the predominance of systems relying on the knowledge store, the Google Search API (with which the knowledge store itself was built) remained a competitive option (see Table 2).

One issue identified by several participants was the scraper we used for the knowledge store, based on Trafilatura (Barbaresi, 2021). Papelo identified how, in 297 out of 500 development examples, at least one gold document was not correctly scraped. Dunamu-ML similarly discussed how the scraper did not correctly handle evidence from PDFs and videos. In their submission, Dunamu-ML extended the scraper to extract text and transcripts from PDFs and YouTube videos, and noted that this helped performance. When constructing AVERITEC, our annotators filtered out claims requiring multimodal reasoning; all claims in the dataset are textual and can be verified through exclusively textual evidence. Nevertheless, the helpfulness of video transcripts suggests that multimodal evidence can be useful even for that scenario.

Question Generation & Retrieval Most systems employed an LLM-based question generation strategy. That is, they generated questions or queries, and then retrieved evidence based on those questions. Generating questions, rather than simply searching for the claim, was noted by many top-scoring systems to be essential for good retrieval performance. This supports our hypothesis from Schlichtkrull et al. (2023a) that question generation (or query expansion (Mao et al., 2021)) is a key avenue for further gains in retrieval.

Team Name	Evidence	QG	Retrieval	QA	Veracity
TUDA_MAI	KS	GPT-4o	gte_base_en_v1.5	GPT-4o	GPT-4o
HUMANE	KS	Llama-3-8b	BM25 SFR-embedding-2 Llama-3.1-70b	-	Llama-3.1-70b
CTU AIC	KS	GPT-4o	mxbai-large-v1	GPT-4o	GPT-4o
Dunamu-ML	KS	GPT-4	BM25	GPT-4	GPT-4
Papelo	Google	T5-large GPT-4o	-	GPT-4o	GPT-4o
UHH	KS	GPT-4o-mini	BM25 gte_base_en_v1.5	GPT-4o-mini	Mixtral-8x7B
SynApSe	Google	GPT-4o	all-MiniLM-L6-v2	GPT-4o	GPT-4o GPT-3.5 Mistral-7B
aioriAveri	KS	GPT-4o	stella_en_400M_v5	GPT-4o	GPT-4o
Data-Wizards	KS	Phi-3-medium	stella_en_1.5B_v5	Mixtral-8x22B	Mixtral-8x22B
MA-Bros-H	KS	Llama-3-70B	BM25	Llama-3-70B	Llama-3-70B
SK_DU	KS	GPT-4o	BM25 ms-marco-MiniLM-L-12-v2	-	deberta-v3-base
UPS	KS	T5-large	BM25 BERT	-	BERT
FZI-WIM	KS	Llama-3-70B	ms-marco-MiniLM-L-12-v2	Llama-3-70B bart-large-mnli	Llama-3-70B
KnowComp	Google	Llama-3-8b	-	Llama-3-8b	Llama-3-8b
IKR3-UNIMIB	KS	-	BM25 ColBERT	GPT-3.5	BERT

Table 3: Components used by systems that submitted description papers. Systems are ordered based on AVeriTeC-score (see Table 2). - indicates, respectively, that a system directly used claims and nothing else for search queries, that retrieval was done only through a search API with no reranking, and that the answer used was the entire retrieved passage.

Question generation was typically implemented using large-scale LLMs, such as GPT-4o or Llama-3.1-70b. Some systems based on smaller model – HUMANE with Llama-3-8b, UHH with GPT-4o-mini, Data-Wizards with Phi-3-medium, and Papelo with T5 (for the first question only) – also achieved a high question-only score. This suggests that smaller models can be competitive on search query generation.

Several teams – Papelo, SynApSe, and IKR3 – mentioned that they saw benefits from modeling the retrieval task as multi-hop retrieval. That is, instead of retrieving all documents at once, their systems used multiple rounds of retrieval with each round conditional on previous rounds. The benefits of this strategy were also documented in previous FEVER shared tasks, e.g., Malon (2021). Team Papelo further expanded on this strategy, showing that the use of different components at different retrieval steps – T5 for the first question and GPT-4o for subsequent questions – yielded higher performance than using a single-question generation model.

As can be seen in Table 5, high-performing systems tended to generate and submit a high number of questions. This may be a consequence of our evaluation setup – there is no brevity penalty (other than documents past the 10th being ignored), so submitting more evidence documents means a higher chance of recalling the gold evidence. Several teams also noted that even duplicates of the same question could slightly increase their score.

We tested this, and observed baseline performance increase by 2 points QA score and 0.5 points AVERITEC score when including two additional duplicates of each question. There are two reasons this might happen. First, some generated QA pairs may be the best match for multiple gold QA pairs (i.e. because they are very long, or because other QA pairs are irrelevant to the claim). Duplicating QA pairs means the generated pair can be matched to multiple gold pairs when computing the Hungarian algorithm, marginally increasing overall performance. Second, Hungarian METEOR is computed by averaging over gold question-answer

Team Name	Text	PDF	Table	Metadata	Audio	Video	Image	Other	1 doc	2 docs	3+ docs
TUDA_MAI	**0.34**	0.35	0.36	0.31	0.31	**0.33**	0.32	0.33	0.39	0.35	0.31
HUMANE	**0.34**	**0.36**	0.38	**0.32**	**0.34**	0.32	0.33	**0.38**	**0.41**	0.35	0.31
CTU AIC	0.31	0.33	0.36	0.30	0.26	0.30	0.32	0.35	0.33	0.33	0.29
Dunamu-ml	**0.34**	**0.36**	**0.39**	0.31	0.24	**0.33**	**0.34**	0.37	0.40	**0.36**	**0.32**
Papelo	0.3	0.31	0.32	0.27	0.22	0.29	0.29	0.3	0.35	0.3	0.27
UHH	0.31	0.34	0.36	0.29	0.23	0.31	0.31	0.37	0.37	0.32	0.28
SynApSe	0.29	0.31	0.32	0.25	0.25	0.28	0.28	0.31	0.38	0.32	0.22
arioriAveri	0.28	0.29	0.32	0.26	0.21	0.27	0.27	0.32	0.34	0.29	0.25
Data-Wizards	0.26	0.26	0.28	0.23	0.17	0.27	0.25	0.27	0.36	0.29	0.19
MA-Bros-H	0.23	0.25	0.28	0.22	0.16	0.23	0.22	0.27	0.3	0.26	0.19
mitchelldehaven	0.22	0.23	0.24	0.18	0.19	0.22	0.2	0.22	0.28	0.23	0.19
SK_DU	0.25	0.26	0.27	0.22	0.17	0.25	0.24	0.27	0.34	0.28	0.18
UPS	0.26	0.29	0.31	0.25	0.23	0.27	0.28	0.31	0.29	0.27	0.25
FZI-WIM	0.2	0.22	0.24	0.18	0.12	0.18	0.19	0.21	0.27	0.22	0.15
KnowComp	0.2	0.22	0.23	0.18	0.05	0.18	0.19	0.22	0.29	0.23	0.14
IKR3-UNIMIB	0.23	0.24	0.26	0.19	0.13	0.23	0.21	0.25	0.31	0.25	0.16
ngetach	0.21	0.22	0.23	0.18	0.15	0.19	0.2	0.23	0.24	0.23	0.18
VGyasi	0.21	0.22	0.24	0.2	0.11	0.22	0.2	0.24	0.27	0.24	0.17
Baseline	*0.19*	*0.2*	*0.23*	*0.17*	*0.14*	*0.19*	*0.19*	*0.21*	*0.24*	*0.21*	*0.14*
Factors	0.19	0.19	0.21	0.16	0.21	0.18	0.16	0.17	0.24	0.2	0.15
InfinityScalers!	0.11	0.11	0.1	0.08	0.07	0.11	0.1	0.09	0.22	0.12	0.06
AYM	0.13	0.13	0.13	0.1	0.05	0.12	0.11	0.13	0.26	0.14	0.06
Average	0.25	0.26	0.28	0.22	0.18	0.24	0.24	0.26	0.31	0.26	0.2

Table 4: Retrieval results in terms of Q+A Hungarian METEOR, broken down according to 1) the document type of the gold evidence, and 2) the number of gold evidence QA pairs for the claim. The overall best performance on retrieval was achieved by Dunamu-ML.

pairs. If there are more gold pairs than generated pairs, some gold pairs will be *unmatched*. These will receive a score of 0, as the "matched" evidence is the empty string, dragging down the average. Effectively, systems are heavily penalised for generating too *few* questions, and may benefit slightly from generating too *many*.

For evidence retrieval, vector-based dense retrieval systems (Karpukhin et al., 2020) were common, along with BM25 (Robertson and Zaragoza, 2009). Several teams – HUMANE, UHH, SK_DU – proposed hybrid systems where coarse retrieval with BM25 was followed by reranking with a vector-based approach. For vector-based retrievers, the *gte* (Li et al., 2023; Zhang et al., 2024) family of models were popular, and noted by participants to perform well on the task; this includes Stella[6], an MRL (Kusupati et al., 2022) approach based on *gte*. Several teams noted that their *gte*- or Stella-based retrievers were chosen as they, at the time of the competition, were top performers on the MTEB (Muennighoff et al., 2023) leaderboard.

[6]https://huggingface.co/dunzhang/stella_en_400M_v5

The overall best performing retrieval system was Dunamu-ML, closely followed by HUMANE. In Table 4, we break down performance on retrieval according to which document type the *gold* evidence originated from. We see that Dunamu-ML do have top performance on PDFs and videos (for which they added a custom scraper), but tie respectively with HUMANE and TUDA_MAI on these categories. On the other hand, Dunamu-ML perform better than other systems on tabular and image evidence, while HUMANE is the top performer on Metadata, Audio, and "Other" evidence (used by participants mostly for social media posts, as well to link to external web tools, such as a calculator in support of numerical reasoning).

In Table 4, we also break down retrieval performance by the number of gold evidence question-answer pairs per claim. HUMANE performs the best on claims with only one gold document, narrowly followed by Dunamu-ML. As the number of claims increases, Dunamu-ML takes the lead. With an average of 2.74 questions per claim in the test set, this may explain why Dunamu-ML achieved the overall highest retrieval performance.

Team name	QV	N	E/P	C	PS	S	R	NEE	CE/C	Avg. # Docs
TUDA_MAI	**0.64**	**0.58**	**0.64**	**0.64**	**0.58**	0.64	**0.73**	0.12	0.19	9.3
HUMANE	0.59	0.57	0.58	0.55	0.46	**0.76**	0.62	0.01	0.12	10.0
CTU AIC	0.57	0.49	0.51	0.52	0.38	0.58	0.58	0.1	0.01	9.89
Dunamu-ml	0.44	0.49	0.5	0.55	0.4	0.69	0.5	**0.31**	0.12	12.41
Papelo	0.51	0.38	0.5	0.51	0.45	0.45	0.59	0.0	0.0	9.95
UHH	0.46	0.43	0.46	0.48	0.39	0.47	0.54	0.0	0.0	10.0
SynApSe	0.45	0.39	0.43	0.43	0.36	0.42	0.5	0.02	**0.21**	4.26
arioriAveri	0.44	0.37	0.39	0.4	0.29	0.45	0.44	0.09	0.06	8.98
Data-Wizards	0.37	0.3	0.34	0.32	0.29	0.44	0.36	0.05	0.04	3.0
MA-Bros-H	0.29	0.3	0.26	0.25	0.19	0.4	0.27	0.08	0.0	3.74
mitchelldehaven	0.24	0.26	0.25	0.25	0.16	0.4	0.25	0.0	0.0	5.0
SK_DU	0.27	0.3	0.21	0.15	0.14	0.36	0.22	0.01	0.11	3.0
UPS	0.29	0.18	0.22	0.2	0.21	0.17	0.24	0.08	0.14	10.0
FZI-WIM	0.21	0.25	0.18	0.16	0.21	0.31	0.18	0.12	0.02	2.52
KnowComp	0.16	0.19	0.19	0.15	0.13	0.27	0.19	0.0	0.01	2.55
IKR3-UNIMIB	0.21	0.22	0.17	0.17	0.15	0.28	0.19	0.01	0.05	3.0
ngetach	0.16	0.13	0.14	0.17	0.09	0.0	0.22	0.0	0.0	4.25
VGyasi	0.16	0.11	0.13	0.11	0.10	0.1	0.12	0.22	0.03	3.46
Baseline	*0.14*	*0.16*	*0.11*	*0.10*	*0.06*	*0.17*	*0.12*	*0.0*	*0.04*	*3.0*
InfinityScalers!	0.04	0.10	0.09	0.08	0.08	0.24	0.04	0.04	0.10	3.52
AYM	0.07	0.06	0.06	0.03	0.10	0.11	0.05	0.0	0.0	1.0
Factors	0.04	0.05	0.05	0.05	0.04	0.13	0.03	0.04	0.01	1.0
Average	0.31	0.29	0.29	0.29	0.24	0.36	0.32	0.06	0.06	5.63

Table 5: We compute separate results based on claim type (QV = Quote Verification, N = Numerical, E/P = Event/Property, C = Causal, PS = Position Statement). We also compute results separated by gold verdict (S = Supported, R = Refuted, NEE = Not Enough Evidence, CE/C = Conflicting Evidence / Cherrypicking). Finally, we report the average number of evidence documents submitted per claim. We note that if a team submitted more than 10 documents for a claim, only the first 10 were used to compute retrieval scores for evaluation.

Veracity Prediction Veracity prediction was also dominated by LLM-based approaches, including GPT-4o, Llama 3.1, and Mixtral. Teams HUMANE and SynApSe note that some fine-tuning was necessary for good performance on veracity prediction. Various teams saw improvements both from full fine-tuning of all the weights, and from fine-tuning with LORA (Hu et al., 2022). Interestingly, one team – Papelo – chose to prevent their veracity prediction system from predicting Not Enough Evidence and Conflicting Evidence, arguing that their prompting-based model too frequently chose these rarer labels. This may explain why calibration was especially helpful for this task.

We note that top-scoring systems tended to use very large models for veracity prediction, such as GPT-4o, Llama-3.1-70b, or Mixtral-8x7b. The superior reasoning capabilities of these cutting-edge models appear especially critical to this stage of the pipeline, unlike for question generation.

Types & Verdicts In Table 5, we provide a detailed breakdown of the results based on claim type (quote verification, numerical claims, event/property claims, causal claims, position statements) and verdict (supported, refuted, conflicting evidence/cherrypicking, not enough evidence). For each category, we report AVERITEC scores on the corresponding subset of the test set.

Systems performed slightly better on quote verification, slightly worse on position statements, and approximately equally well on other claims. This is interesting, as quote verification and position statements are relatively similar tasks. In the former, systems must verify if a person has uttered a quote verbatim; in the latter, systems must verify if a person or organisation holds a specific position (e.g., supporting a policy), but not necessarily verbatim. Verifying position statements often required abductive reasoning, which LLMs are known to struggle with (Dougrez-Lewis et al., 2024).

Among the top performing systems, performance is frequently lower on numerical statements (along with position statements) compared to other claims. This suggests that the gap is smaller for numerical reasoning than other forms of reasoning. As top performers often use very large LLMs, that is suggestive of the type of reasoning gains accomplished by scaling up these models.

In terms of performance across the different labels, there is significant variation. First, systems often have different calibration to predict supported versus refuted claims. As refuted claims dominate (making up approximately two-thirds of the dataset), this yields a significant advantage for some participants. We note that a common strategy among participants was to ignore the rarer veracity labels – not enough evidence, and conflicting evidence. As mentioned e.g. by team Papelo in their system description paper, large language models tend to overpredict these rarer classes. Nevertheless, many top performers, including the winning system, made significant gains on these classes.

Quality Controls on Test Submissions To ensure the reliability of submitted systems, we conducted quality control on our submissions. Here, *reliability* refers to the evidence (QA pairs) being grounded and supported by their retrieved documents. Typically, participants returned answers generated based on retrieved documents; although some systems generated answers e.g. with an LLM, and subsequently matched the answer to a "backing document".

We first used an automatic method to evaluate the entailment between the answers and the retrieved documents. Specifically, we applied a DeBERTa-large-based NLI model (He et al., 2020)[7] on all submissions, taking each answer as hypothesis and its corresponding document as premise. Generally, we find that most teams see a small proportion of entailment labels and a large proportion of neutral labels (80%). This can be because the NLI model cannot perform well on out-of-distribution data in a zero-shot setting, in particular when the retrieved document is much longer than the standard NLI premise (e.g., the average document length in words in TUDA_MAI's submission is over 4,000, while it is around 50 in ANLI (Mishra et al., 2021)).

[7] https://huggingface.co/MoritzLaurer/DeBERTa-v3-large-mnli-fever-anli-ling-wanli, which demonstrates the best performance on NLI tasks amongst Hugging Face models.

Therefore, we further investigated submissions via manual evaluation. In particular, we focused on instances which the NLI model identified as either *neutral* or *contradiction*, and on the top-4 performing systems (i.e.: TUDA_MAI, HUMANE, CTU AIC and Dunamu-ml). We randomly selected 20 neutral or contradicting instances from each submission, and then performed human evaluation. Given an instance with its corresponding QA pairs and retrieved documents, we identified whether the answers were entailed by the retrieved documents.

Generally, we found that all systems were mostly reliable, with the evidence they generate being supported by the retrieved documents. All answers from TUDA_MAI were extractive from source documents and thus entailed. The answers from the other three systems were more abstractive. Although the answers can contain some hallucination (e.g., generating answers that contradict the retrieved documents by mistake), our manual evaluation found the answers were mostly (HUMANE: 19/20; CTU AIC: 17/20; Dunamu-ml: 12/20) entailed by their associated documents. Errors were typically due to mistakes by the question-answering components, such as taking a snippet from the associated document out of context. Thus, we conclude that the systems evaluated were reliable and find relevant documents that provide useful information for predicting veracity.

4 Human Evaluation of Evidence

Following the approach taken in the first FEVER shared task (Thorne et al., 2018b), we conducted human evaluation of the evidence retrieved by the systems participating in the shared task, motivated by two concerns. First, the incompleteness of the gold evidence annotation, since it is often the case that adequate evidence to determine the verdict for a claim can be found in multiple webpages, as shown in the inter-annotation agreement study of Schlichtkrull et al. (2023a). Second, the inaccuracies of automatic evaluation metrics of textual evaluation, especially in the case of token-matching metrics such as METEOR (Banerjee and Lavie, 2005) used here, but also of more recent neural ones such as FactScore (Min et al., 2023). Thus we can gain a deeper understanding of the quality of the retrieved evidence, and assess how well the AVERITEC scores assigned to the retrieved evidence aligns with human judgements.

Evaluation Process We conducted human evaluation in collaboration with the participating teams. Sixteen top-performing teams were invited to participate in the evaluation. However, teams Dunamu-ml, mitchelldehaven, and KnowComp did not take part. Each of the remaining thirteen participating teams manually evaluated thirty evidence samples from other participants. Out of these, five were gold-labeled, which were included to assist in the post-processing of the collected annotations and to assess their quality. The evidence samples were randomly selected and evenly distributed across all submitted systems, representing both high- and low-scoring systems, as shown in Table 5.

Figures in Appendix B depict the evaluation form and the instructions provided to human annotators during evaluation. As a first step, we asked annotators to assess whether "at least some part of the evidence" was "non-empty, understandable, and related to the claim." If so, it was considered eligible for further rating. In addition to assigning a verdict label, we asked annotators to rate retrieved evidence in comparison to provided reference evidence[8]. Annotators rated the evidence on a scale from 1 to 5 across five dimensions:

(1) **Coverage**: Measures how much of the reference evidence is covered by the predicted evidence, ensuring that the content, meaning, entities, and other key elements of the reference are fully represented in the retrieved evidence.

(2) **Coherence**: Captures whether the retrieved evidence is coherent, i.e., if all sentences are connected sensibly and the evidence makes sense as a whole.

(3) **Repetition**: Evaluates whether the retrieved evidence exhibits repetition of its content.

(4) **Consistency**: Assesses whether the retrieved evidence is semantically consistent and does not contain conflicting information. Unlike coherence, which focuses on how well the information is structured, consistency evaluates whether the arguments presented in the evidence for or against a claim are sound and aligned.

(5) **Relevance**: Measures how relevant the retrieved evidence is to the content of the claim.

Insights Gained The annotation process resulted in a total of 389 annotations. After filtering out evidence samples that were labeled by evaluators as entirely empty (1%), not understandable (1.8%), or completely irrelevant to the given claim (9.4%), we were left with 344 valid annotations. Among these, 66 annotations corresponded to gold-labeled samples. Excluding the gold-labeled samples, resulted in a final set of 278 evidence annotations.

Label/Pred	CE/C	NEE	Refuted	Supported
CE/C	35.7	3.6	53.6	7.1
NEE	5.9	22.1	60.3	11.8
Refuted	3.9	4.9	85.4	5.8
Supported	7.6	0	16.5	76.0

Table 6: Overview of verdict **label**led by human evaluators (rows) versus system **pred**ictions (columns).

Before labeling the system-retrieved evidence, participants were first asked to label the verdict of the retrieved evidence. Table 6 provides an overview of the matching between system-predicted labels (columns) and human-labeled verdicts (rows). While human annotators generally agreed with evidence labeled as refuted or supported, there was less overlap for evidence labeled as NEE and CE/C by the submitted systems.

Analyzing human judgments across the five evaluated dimensions (see Table 10), we find that the majority of predicted evidence was labeled as very coherent, consistent, relevant, and containing limited repetition. However, in the dimension of semantic coverage, approximately 15% of the evidence received a rating of 0, indicating that "the predicted evidence covers none of the reference evidence." Additionally, around 20% received a rating of 1, meaning that "very little of the reference evidence is covered." This does not necessarily mean that the evidence is false – low coverage can also occur if the retrieved evidence uses different information, arguments, or sources than the reference evidence. Ideally, we aim for an evidence evaluation that can fairly assess evidence even when it differs from the reference and has low coverage.

To assess the relationship between human scoring and the Hungarian METEOR (see Sec 2.4), we computed both the Spearman correlation coefficient (ρ (Spearman, 1987)) and the Pearson correlation coefficient (r (Pearson, 1896)) as shown in Table 8. Correlations were calculated using both the entire evidence text and the question text only. In both cases, we observed a low correlation between the Hungarian Meteor and the assessed dimensions, with the highest correlation seen in the category of "repetition" (see Table 8). While the results show a similar ranking of participating systems compared

[8]We provide the exact instruction for rating each criteria in the appendix.

Rating	COV	COV %	COH	COH %	REP	REP %	CON	CON %	REL	REL %
1	42	15.16	4	1.44	23	8.27	6	2.17	4	1.44
2	59	21.30	42	15.11	51	18.35	35	12.64	26	9.35
3	59	21.30	64	23.02	61	21.94	57	20.58	51	18.35
4	71	25.63	81	29.14	71	25.54	82	29.60	83	29.86
5	46	16.61	87	31.29	72	25.90	97	35.02	114	41.01

Table 7: Overview of ratings for Semantic **Cov**erage, **Coh**erence, **Rep**etition, **Con**sistency, and **Rel**evance. For each evaluation dimension, the first column depicts the absolute number of annotations for a specific score (from 1 to 5) and the second column the percentages.

Dimension	ρ	r
Coverage	.005	-.024
Coherence	.076	.057
Repetition	.117	.025
Consistency	.039	.024
Relevance	.008	.003

Table 8: Correlation between Q + A scores (Hungarian METEOR) and human-rated subset of evidence. We calculate correlation using the Spearman (ρ) and Pearson (r) correlation coefficients.

to human evaluations on the subset, further work is needed to develop scoring methods that align more closely with human assessments of evidence. With that said, overall, the top-ranked teams (based on AVERITEC score) also perform well on human evaluation, while the lower-ranked teams remain similarly positioned, with only minor shifts in their order.[9] It is important to note that this evaluation was solely based on a small sample of system predictions, and that the results should therefore be taken with a grain of salt.

Human evaluation of evidence predictions offers valuable insights into the limitations of the AVERITEC score, and suggests directions for future research. A notable observation is the discrepancy between human evaluation and the AVERITEC score for some of the highest-ranked samples, such as the examples provided in Table 12 in the appendix. For instance, in row three, the predicted evidence directly contradicts the reference evidence by providing different numbers, yet it receives a high AVERITEC score due to similar wording. Similarly, for the first two rows in Table 12, the semantic coverage score is rated with the second lowest score 1, whereas the average score across all examples is 3, indicating misalignment between the predicted and reference evidence.

[9]See Table 10 in the appendix.

Certain low-ranked examples highlight different challenges (see Table 13). For example, the predicted evidence in the first row received a low AVERITEC score despite receiving the highest score of 5 across all categories in human evaluation. Despite both sets of evidence reaching the same conclusion, the large disparity in answer length and wording leads to a much lower AVERITEC score. The example in the second row, also ranks low according to AVERITEC score, even though it scores high in all categories except for coverage, where it scores 3. Here, both the reference and predicted evidence reach the same verdict, but the predicted evidence supports the claim with different information and wording, resulting in low semantic coverage and a low AVERITEC score.

5 Lessons Learned

Providing a knowledge store rather than requiring participants to rely on a search engine API made the task more accessible. Given the cost of API access, this allowed substantial analysis and work by participants on retrieval. We note that most submissions – 13 of 16 system description papers – used the knowledge store. Nevertheless, because of the size of the knowledge store and the inclusion of distractor documents, the knowledge store did not trivialise the task, and systems relying on search remain competitive and provide unique advantages. Several participants, such as team FZI-WIM, commented on how the two are complementary, and suggested hybrid systems using *both* as a potentially fruitful extension of their systems.

AVERITEC presupposes a strong focus on evidence retrieval. The overall score, as in FEVER (Thorne et al., 2018a), is determined *both* by retrieval performance *and* by veracity prediction performance. In the AVERITEC shared task, participant systems innovated across the pipeline, and all of the top-scoring systems suggest improvements to multiple subtasks of fact-checking.

Team name	0-1000	1000-2215
TUDA_MAI	**0.61**	**0.64**
HUMANE	0.55	0.58
CTU AIC	0.45	0.55
Dunamu-ml	0.5	0.5
Papelo	0.49	0.46
UHH	0.41	0.48
SynApSe	0.41	0.43
arioriAveri	0.35	0.42
Data-Wizards	0.32	0.34
MA-Bros-H	0.22	0.31
mitchelldehaven	0.22	0.27
SK_DU	0.2	0.25
UPS	0.15	0.25
FZI-WIM	0.19	0.2
KnowComp	0.19	0.18
IKR3-UNIMIB	0.16	0.2
ngetach	0.12	0.16
VGyasi	0.12	0.12
Baseline	*0.11*	*0.12*
InfinityScalers!	0.1	0.07
AYM	0.06	0.06
Factors	0.06	0.04
Average	0.27	0.3

Table 9: AVERITEC scores for different subsections of the dataset. We compute results for the initial test set of 1000 examples collected by Schlichtkrull et al. (2023a), and for the additional 1215 test examples collected for this shared task.

When submitting test set predictions, we required participants to include a field ("*scraped_text*") for each piece of evidence in their submission, corresponding to the webpage providing backing for that piece of evidence. This enabled us to carry out manual and automatic quality control evaluation verifying that systems do indeed ground their evidence in external sources (see Section 3). This enabled us to detect, for example, if some systems were hallucinating evidence; we did not see any evidence of hallucinated evidence, but we consider guardrails against this crucial. Unfortunately, the inclusion of this field made some submissions substantial in size, as entire webpages were included – up to 2.3gb for the largest submission. Our submission portal, eval.ai, was not able to handle these large files, blocking the portal for all participants during the last few days of the competition. We extended the deadline to compensate.

The scraper we used for the knowledge store (same as in Schlichtkrull et al. (2023a)) to retrieve evidence turned out to be a significant weakness. As some participants noticed, many knowledge store documents are empty. The submission with the best retrieval performance, Dunamu-ml, used a custom scraper, and may have derived significant gains from that choice. We suggest that this may be an interesting area for further research.

During the competition, we identified an issue with the knowledge store data for the last 1215 test examples. Due to an error with date formats, for some claims, web pages published after the claim were included in the knowledge store. This included fact-checking articles, as also mentioned by CTU AIC in their system description paper. As the first 1000 examples were not affected, we computed performance on the first 1000 and last 1215 test examples separately – see Table 9.

As can be seen, the ranking of participants on the two splits is roughly the same – and, indeed, roughly the same as for the entire test set. The second half *was* easier, and many systems perform slightly better there. Somewhat surprisingly, some systems which relied on Google search – specifically, SynApSe – *also* saw a performance gain when measured only on the second split. As such, we do not believe this issue majorly impacted any subset of participants, such as those not relying on the knowledge store. We release an updated knowledge store along with our shared task paper, accessible at `https://fever.ai/dataset/averitec.html`. We have re-compiled the knowledge store with the correct date cutoff, and removed any fact-checking articles that snuck through from the evidence base.

6 Conclusions & Future Work

The AVERITEC shared task attracted submissions from 21 teams, 18 of which outperformed our baseline. The leaderboard was dominated by systems relying on large language models, especially GPT-4o; nevertheless, especially for question generation and retrieval, smaller models – such as LLama-3-8b – also achieved top performance. The winner of the shared task was team TUDA_MAI, which achieved an AVERITEC-score of 63%. In this paper we have analysed the shared task, highlighting aspects of the 16 submitted system description papers, as well as key takeaways from the shared task itself.

The strong performance of the participating teams establishes a firm foundation for automating aspects of real-world fact-checking. The results furthermore indicate clear directions for future work. First, most participating systems – especially for veracity prediction – relied on very large models, such as GPT-4. Further, many of these are blackbox models. These models may be prohibitively expensive for some real-world use cases, e.g., assisting smaller fact-checking organisations (Schlichtkrull et al., 2023b). Given that, we suggest that getting smaller, more efficient models to reach the performance of their larger counterparts may be a fruitful direction for further research. Similarly, we note that performance for most top-scoring systems was much higher on supported and refuted claims, compared to conflicting evidence and not enough evidence. We suggest that leveling this gap is another clear avenue for future improvements.

7 Limitations & Ethics

The datasets and models described in this paper are not intended for truth-telling, e.g. for the design of fully automated content moderation systems. The evidence selection and veracity labels provided in the AVERITEC dataset relate only to the evidence recovered by annotators, and as such are subject to the biases of annotators and journalists. Participant systems, which sought to maximize performance on AVERITEC, may replicate those biases. We furthermore note that shared task leaderboards are a limited representation of real-world task needs, not the least because the test set is static. Acting on veracity estimates arrived at through biased means, including automatically produced ranking decisions for evidence retrieval, risks causing epistemic harm (Schlichtkrull et al., 2023b).

Acknowledgments

Michael, Yulong, Chenxi, Zhenyun, and Andreas received funding from the European Research Council (ERC) under the European Union's Horizon 2020 Research and Innovation programme grant AVeriTeC (Grant agreement No. 865958). Rui is funded by a grant from the Alan Turing Institute and DSO National Laboratories (Singapore). Rami Aly was supported by the Engineering and Physical Sciences Research Council Doctoral Training Partnership (EPSRC). The annotation of the new test set was conducted by a donation from Google.

References

Rami Aly, Zhijiang Guo, Michael Sejr Schlichtkrull, James Thorne, Andreas Vlachos, Christos Christodoulopoulos, Oana Cocarascu, and Arpit Mittal. 2021. The fact extraction and VERification over unstructured and structured information (FEVEROUS) shared task. In *Proceedings of the Fourth Workshop on Fact Extraction and VERification (FEVER)*, pages 1–13, Dominican Republic. Association for Computational Linguistics.

Isabelle Augenstein, Christina Lioma, Dongsheng Wang, Lucas Chaves Lima, Casper Hansen, Christian Hansen, and Jakob Grue Simonsen. 2019. MultiFC: A real-world multi-domain dataset for evidence-based fact checking of claims. In *Proceedings of the 2019 Conference on Empirical Methods in Natural Language Processing and the 9th International Joint Conference on Natural Language Processing (EMNLP-IJCNLP)*, pages 4685–4697, Hong Kong, China. Association for Computational Linguistics.

Satanjeev Banerjee and Alon Lavie. 2005. METEOR: An automatic metric for MT evaluation with improved correlation with human judgments. In *Proceedings of the ACL Workshop on Intrinsic and Extrinsic Evaluation Measures for Machine Translation and/or Summarization*, pages 65–72, Ann Arbor, Michigan. Association for Computational Linguistics.

Adrien Barbaresi. 2021. Trafilatura: A web scraping library and command-line tool for text discovery and extraction. In *Proceedings of the 59th Annual Meeting of the Association for Computational Linguistics and the 11th International Joint Conference on Natural Language Processing: System Demonstrations*, pages 122–131, Online. Association for Computational Linguistics.

Steven Bird, Ewan Klein, and Edward Loper. 2009. *Natural language processing with Python: analyzing text with the natural language toolkit.* " O'Reilly Media, Inc.".

Svetlana Churina, Anab Maulana Barik, and Saisamarth Rajesh Phaye. 2024. Improving evidence retrieval on claim verification pipeline through question enrichment. In *Proceedings of the Seventh Workshop on Fact Extraction and VERification (FEVER)*. Association for Computational Linguistics.

Sarah Cohen, Chengkai Li, Jun Yang, and Cong Yu. 2011. Computational journalism: A call to arms to database researchers. In *5th Biennial Conference on Innovative Data Systems Research (CIDR)*.

John Dougrez-Lewis, Mahmud Elahi Akhter, Yulan He, and Maria Liakata. 2024. Assessing the reasoning abilities of chatgpt in the context of claim verification. *Preprint*, arXiv:2402.10735.

Andy Dudfield. 2020. How we're using AI to scale up global fact checking. `https://fullfact.org/`

blog/2020/jul/afc-global/. Accessed: 2023-01-17.

Max Glockner, Yufang Hou, and Iryna Gurevych. 2022. Missing counter-evidence renders NLP fact-checking unrealistic for misinformation. In *Proceedings of the 2022 Conference on Empirical Methods in Natural Language Processing*, pages 5916–5936, Abu Dhabi, United Arab Emirates. Association for Computational Linguistics.

Pengcheng He, Xiaodong Liu, Jianfeng Gao, and Weizhu Chen. 2020. Deberta: Decoding-enhanced bert with disentangled attention. *arXiv preprint arXiv:2006.03654*.

Edward J Hu, yelong shen, Phillip Wallis, Zeyuan Allen-Zhu, Yuanzhi Li, Shean Wang, Lu Wang, and Weizhu Chen. 2022. LoRA: Low-rank adaptation of large language models. In *International Conference on Learning Representations*.

Vladimir Karpukhin, Barlas Oguz, Sewon Min, Patrick Lewis, Ledell Wu, Sergey Edunov, Danqi Chen, and Wen-tau Yih. 2020. Dense passage retrieval for open-domain question answering. In *Proceedings of the 2020 Conference on Empirical Methods in Natural Language Processing (EMNLP)*, pages 6769–6781, Online. Association for Computational Linguistics.

H. W. Kuhn. 1955. The hungarian method for the assignment problem. *Naval Research Logistics Quarterly*, 2(1-2):83–97.

Aditya Kusupati, Gantavya Bhatt, Aniket Rege, Matthew Wallingford, Aditya Sinha, Vivek Ramanujan, William Howard-Snyder, Kaifeng Chen, Sham Kakade, Prateek Jain, et al. 2022. Matryoshka representation learning. In *Advances in Neural Information Processing Systems*.

Stephan Lewandowsky, John Cook, Ullrich Ecker, Dolores Albarracin, Michelle Amazeen, Panayiota Kendeou, Doug Lombardi, Eryn Newman, Gordon Pennycook, Ethan Porter, David G. Rand, David N. Rapp, Jason Reifler, Jon Roozenbeek, Philipp Schmid, Colleen M. Seifert, Gale M. Sinatra, Briony Swire-Thompson, Sander van der Linden, Emily K. Vraga, Thomas J. Wood, and Maria S. Zaragoza. 2020. Debunking Handbook 2020. https://sks.to/db2020.

Zehan Li, Xin Zhang, Yanzhao Zhang, Dingkun Long, Pengjun Xie, and Meishan Zhang. 2023. Towards general text embeddings with multi-stage contrastive learning. *Preprint*, arXiv:2308.03281.

Jiayu Liu, Junhao Tang, Hanwen Wang, Baixuan Xu, Haochen Shi, Weiqi Wang, and Yangqiu Song. 2024a. GProofT: A multi-dimension multi-round fact checking framework based on claim fact extraction. In *Proceedings of the Seventh Workshop on Fact Extraction and VERification (FEVER)*. Association for Computational Linguistics.

Jin Liu, Steffen Thoma, and Achim Rettinger. 2024b. FZI-WIM at averitec shared task: Real-world fact-checking with question answering. In *Proceedings of the Seventh Workshop on Fact Extraction and VERification (FEVER)*. Association for Computational Linguistics.

Christopher Malon. 2021. Team papelo at FEVEROUS: Multi-hop evidence pursuit. In *Proceedings of the Fourth Workshop on Fact Extraction and VERification (FEVER)*, pages 40–49, Dominican Republic. Association for Computational Linguistics.

Christopher Malon. 2024. Multi-hop evidence pursuit meets the web: Team papelo at FEVER 2024. In *Proceedings of the Seventh Workshop on Fact Extraction and VERification (FEVER)*. Association for Computational Linguistics.

Shrikant Malviya and Stamos Katsigiannis. 2024. SK_DU team: Cross-encoder based evidence retrieval and question generation with improved prompt for the AVeriTeC shared task. In *Proceedings of the Seventh Workshop on Fact Extraction and VERification (FEVER)*. Association for Computational Linguistics.

Yuning Mao, Pengcheng He, Xiaodong Liu, Yelong Shen, Jianfeng Gao, Jiawei Han, and Weizhu Chen. 2021. Generation-augmented retrieval for open-domain question answering. In *Proceedings of the 59th Annual Meeting of the Association for Computational Linguistics and the 11th International Joint Conference on Natural Language Processing (Volume 1: Long Papers)*, pages 4089–4100, Online. Association for Computational Linguistics.

Sewon Min, Kalpesh Krishna, Xinxi Lyu, Mike Lewis, Wen-tau Yih, Pang Koh, Mohit Iyyer, Luke Zettlemoyer, and Hannaneh Hajishirzi. 2023. FActScore: Fine-grained atomic evaluation of factual precision in long form text generation. In *Proceedings of the 2023 Conference on Empirical Methods in Natural Language Processing*, pages 12076–12100, Singapore. Association for Computational Linguistics.

Sebastião Miranda, Andreas Vlachos, David Nogueira, Andrew Secker, Afonso Mendes, Rebecca Garrett, Jeffrey J Mitchell, and Zita Marinho. 2019. Automated fact checking in the news room. In *The Web Conference 2019*, pages 3579–3583, United States. Association for Computing Machinery (ACM). 2019 World Wide Web Conference, WWW 2019 ; Conference date: 13-05-2019 Through 17-05-2019.

Anshuman Mishra, Dhruvesh Patel, Aparna Vijayakumar, Xiang Lorraine Li, Pavan Kapanipathi, and Kartik Talamadupula. 2021. Looking beyond sentence-level natural language inference for question answering and text summarization. In *Proceedings of the 2021 Conference of the North American Chapter of the Association for Computational Linguistics: Human Language Technologies*, pages 1322–1336, Online. Association for Computational Linguistics.

Mohammad Ghiasvand Mohammadkhani, Ali Ghiasvand Mohammadkhani, and Hamid Beigy. 2024. Zero-shot learning and key points are all you need for automated fact-checking. In *Proceedings of the Seventh Workshop on Fact Extraction and VERification (FEVER)*. Association for Computational Linguistics.

Yuki Momii, Tetsuya Takiguchi, and Yasuo Ariki. 2024. RAG-fusion based information retrieval for fact-checking. In *Proceedings of the Seventh Workshop on Fact Extraction and VERification (FEVER)*. Association for Computational Linguistics.

Niklas Muennighoff, Nouamane Tazi, Loic Magne, and Nils Reimers. 2023. MTEB: Massive text embedding benchmark. In *Proceedings of the 17th Conference of the European Chapter of the Association for Computational Linguistics*, pages 2014–2037, Dubrovnik, Croatia. Association for Computational Linguistics.

Preslav Nakov, David Corney, Maram Hasanain, Firoj Alam, Tamer Elsayed, Alberto Barrón-Cedeño, Paolo Papotti, Shaden Shaar, and Giovanni Da San Martino. 2021. Automated fact-checking for assisting human fact-checkers. In *Proceedings of the Thirtieth International Joint Conference on Artificial Intelligence, IJCAI-21*, pages 4551–4558. International Joint Conferences on Artificial Intelligence Organization. Survey Track.

Adjali Omar. 2024. Exploring retrieval augmented generation for real-world claim verification. In *Proceedings of the Seventh Workshop on Fact Extraction and VERification (FEVER)*. Association for Computational Linguistics.

Nedjma Ousidhoum, Zhangdie Yuan, and Andreas Vlachos. 2022. Varifocal question generation for fact-checking. In *Proceedings of the 2022 Conference on Empirical Methods in Natural Language Processing*, pages 2532–2544, Abu Dhabi, United Arab Emirates. Association for Computational Linguistics.

Heesoo Park, Dongjun Lee, Jaehyuk Kim, ChoongWon Park, and Changhwa Park. 2024. Dunamu-ml's submissions on AVeriTeC shared task. In *Proceedings of the Seventh Workshop on Fact Extraction and VERification (FEVER)*. Association for Computational Linguistics.

Karl Pearson. 1896. Vii. mathematical contributions to the theory of evolution.—iii. regression, heredity, and panmixia. *Philosophical Transactions of the Royal Society of London. Series A, containing papers of a mathematical or physical character*, (187):253–318.

Stephen Robertson and Hugo Zaragoza. 2009. The probabilistic relevance framework: Bm25 and beyond. *Foundations and Trends® in Information Retrieval*, 3(4):333–389.

Mark Rothermel, Tobias Braun, Marcus Rohrbach, and Anna Rohrbach. 2024. InFact: A strong baseline for automated fact-checking. In *Proceedings of the Seventh Workshop on Fact Extraction and VERification (FEVER)*. Association for Computational Linguistics.

Michael Schlichtkrull, Zhijiang Guo, and Andreas Vlachos. 2023a. Averitec: A dataset for real-world claim verification with evidence from the web. In *Advances in Neural Information Processing Systems*, volume 36, pages 65128–65167. Curran Associates, Inc.

Michael Schlichtkrull, Nedjma Ousidhoum, and Andreas Vlachos. 2023b. The intended uses of automated fact-checking artefacts: Why, how and who. In *Findings of the Association for Computational Linguistics: EMNLP 2023*, pages 8618–8642, Singapore. Association for Computational Linguistics.

Tal Schuster, Adam Fisch, and Regina Barzilay. 2021. Get your vitamin C! robust fact verification with contrastive evidence. In *Proceedings of the 2021 Conference of the North American Chapter of the Association for Computational Linguistics: Human Language Technologies*, pages 624–643, Online. Association for Computational Linguistics.

Özge Sevgili, Irina Nikishina, Seid Muhie Yimam, Martin Semmann, and Chris Biemann. 2024. UHH at AVeriTeC: RAG for fact-checking with real-world claims. In *Proceedings of the Seventh Workshop on Fact Extraction and VERification (FEVER)*. Association for Computational Linguistics.

Ronit Singhal, Pransh Patwa, Parth Patwa, Aman Chadha, and Amitava Das. 2024. Evidence-backed fact checking using RAG and few-shot in-context learning with LLMs. In *Proceedings of the Seventh Workshop on Fact Extraction and VERification (FEVER)*. Association for Computational Linguistics.

C. Spearman. 1987. The proof and measurement of association between two things. *The American Journal of Psychology*, 100(3/4):441–471.

James Thorne, Andreas Vlachos, Christos Christodoulopoulos, and Arpit Mittal. 2018a. FEVER: a large-scale dataset for fact extraction and VERification. In *Proceedings of the 2018 Conference of the North American Chapter of the Association for Computational Linguistics: Human Language Technologies, Volume 1 (Long Papers)*, pages 809–819, New Orleans, Louisiana. Association for Computational Linguistics.

James Thorne, Andreas Vlachos, Oana Cocarascu, Christos Christodoulopoulos, and Arpit Mittal. 2018b. The fact extraction and VERification (FEVER) shared task. In *Proceedings of the First Workshop on Fact Extraction and VERification (FEVER)*, pages 1–9, Brussels, Belgium. Association for Computational Linguistics.

Herbert Ullrich, Tomáš Mlynář, and Jan Drchal. 2024. AIC CTU system at AVeriTeC: Re-framing automated fact-checking as a simple RAG task. In *Proceedings of the Seventh Workshop on Fact Extraction and VERification (FEVER)*. Association for Computational Linguistics.

Nicolò Urbani, Sandip Modha, and Gabriella Pasi. 2024. Retrieving semantics for fact-checking: A comparative approach using CQ (claim to question) & aq (answer to question). In *Proceedings of the Seventh Workshop on Fact Extraction and VERification (FEVER)*. Association for Computational Linguistics.

Andreas Vlachos and Sebastian Riedel. 2014. Fact checking: Task definition and dataset construction. In *Proceedings of the ACL 2014 Workshop on Language Technologies and Computational Social Science*, pages 18–22, Baltimore, MD, USA. Association for Computational Linguistics.

David Wadden, Shanchuan Lin, Kyle Lo, Lucy Lu Wang, Madeleine van Zuylen, Arman Cohan, and Hannaneh Hajishirzi. 2020. Fact or fiction: Verifying scientific claims. In *Proceedings of the 2020 Conference on Empirical Methods in Natural Language Processing (EMNLP)*, pages 7534–7550, Online. Association for Computational Linguistics.

William Yang Wang. 2017. "liar, liar pants on fire": A new benchmark dataset for fake news detection. In *Proceedings of the 55th Annual Meeting of the Association for Computational Linguistics (Volume 2: Short Papers)*, pages 422–426, Vancouver, Canada. Association for Computational Linguistics.

Yejun Yoon, Jaeyoon Jung, Seunghyun Yoon, and Kunwoo Park. 2024. The herd of open llms for verifying real-world claims. In *Proceedings of the Seventh Workshop on Fact Extraction and VERification (FEVER)*. Association for Computational Linguistics.

Xin Zhang, Yanzhao Zhang, Dingkun Long, Wen Xie, Ziqi Dai, Jialong Tang, Huan Lin, Baosong Yang, Pengjun Xie, Fei Huang, Meishan Zhang, Wenjie Li, and Min Zhang. 2024. mgte: Generalized long-context text representation and reranking models for multilingual text retrieval. *Preprint*, arXiv:2407.19669.

A Search Queries for Knowledge Store Generation

When creating the knowledge stores for the train, development, and test set, we used a series of search query generation strategies. An overview can be seen in Table 11. We note that some of these rely on information not available normally to participants, such as the gold question-answer pairs. We note that, despite this, systems not relying on the knowledge store, such as Papelo, were competitive.

B Human Evaluation

We carried out human evaluation of the submitted test set predictions. Below in Figures 2-9, we include screenshots of the interface used by annotators. We also include, in Tables 12 and 13, instructive examples from the human evaluation.

Source	Score Coverage
CTU AIC	4.1
TUDA_MAI	4.1
SynApSe	3.8
Dunamu-ML	3.5
MA-Bros-H	3.4
Factors	3.3
Data-Wizards	3.2
UHH	3.2
mitchelldehaven	3.1
SK_ DU	3.1
IKR3-UNIMIB	3.1
FZI-WIM	2.9
InfinityScalers!	2.9
arioriAveri	2.9
HUMANE	2.8
Papelo	2.8
KnowComp	2.8
UPS	2.4
VGyasi	2.3
AYM	2.3
ngetach	2.0

Table 10: Average scores assigned to evidence samples from different participating teams for the semantic coverage category, based on human evaluation.

Query type	Description
Generated questions	*Questions are generated with gpt-3.5-turbo based on the claim. Three claim-question pairs from the training set are used as in-context examples.*
Generated background queries	*Queries are generated with gpt-3.5-turbo based on the claim. The prompt focuses on background information, such as details about entities in the claim. Three manually constructed claim-query pairs are used as in-context examples.*
Generated provenance queries	*Queries are generated with gpt-3.5-turbo based on the claim. The prompt focuses on information necessary to establish provenance, such as whether the claim source is a satire site. Three manually constructed claim-query pairs are used as in-context examples.*
Claim named entities	*Named entities from the claim are extracted and used as search queries. One query for each entity is constructed, along with one query containing all entities.*
Most similar gold evidence	*The most similar paragraph in the gold evidence document is selected using BM25, and used as a search query.*
Gold URL generated questions	*Queries are generated with gpt-3.5-turbo based on the URL of the gold evidence. The prompt tried to generate questions that would retrieve the URL in question. Three manually constructed URL-query pairs are used as in-context examples.*
Different event same entity	*Queries are generated with gpt-3.5-turbo based on the named entities in the claim. The prompt focuses on different events involving some of the same entities. Results are used as distractors to make the retrieval task harder.*
Similar entities	*Queries are generated with gpt-3.5-turbo based on the claim. The prompt replaces entities in the claim with other similar entities, such as changing one city to another. Results are used as distractors to make the retrieval task harder.*
Gold questions	*Gold questions used verbatim as search queries.*
Claim + gold question	*Gold questions used verbatim as search queries. The claim is prepended, processed as in Schlichtkrull et al. (2023a).*
Rephrased gold questions	*Gold questions are rephrased using gpt-3.5-turbo, and then input as search queries.*
Gold answers	*Gold questions used verbatim as search queries.*
Rephrased gold answers	*Gold answers are rephrased using gpt-3.5-turbo, and then input as search queries.*

Table 11: Queries input to the Google Search API for each claim in order to build the knowledge store. Following Schlichtkrull et al. (2023a), we restrict search results to documents published before the claim. For each claim, we also extend the knowledge store with the corresponding gold evidence documents.

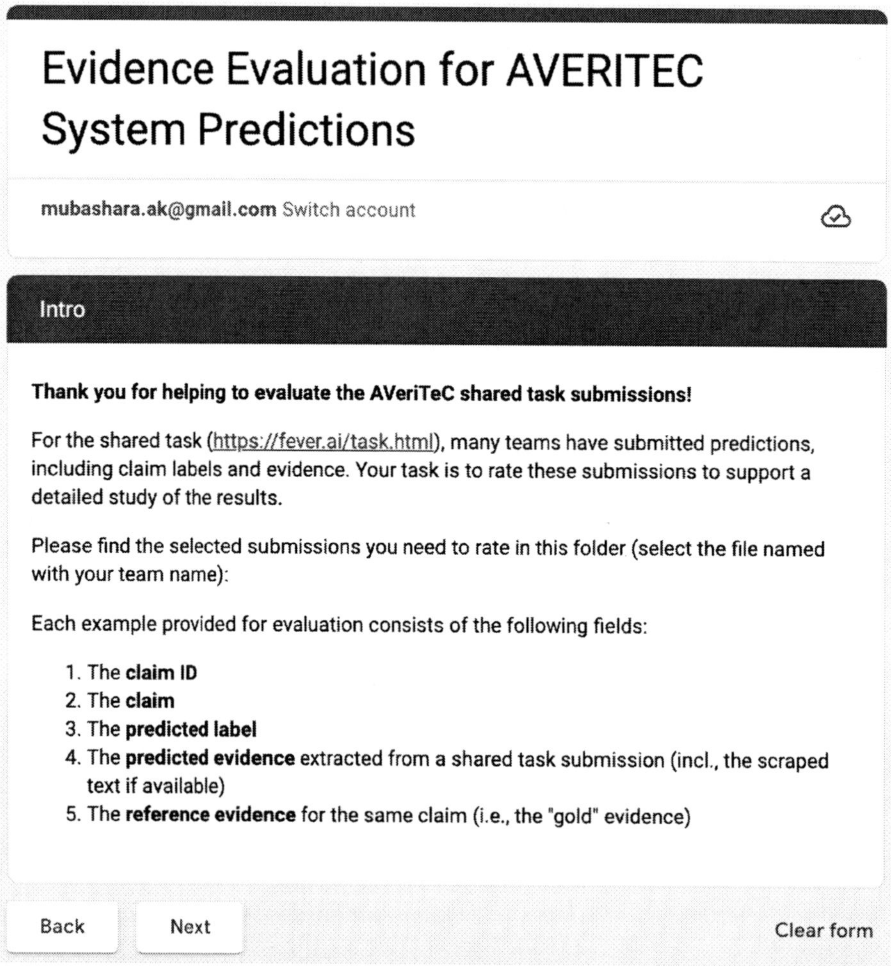

Figure 2: Platform for human evaluation of retrieved evidence from participating systems.

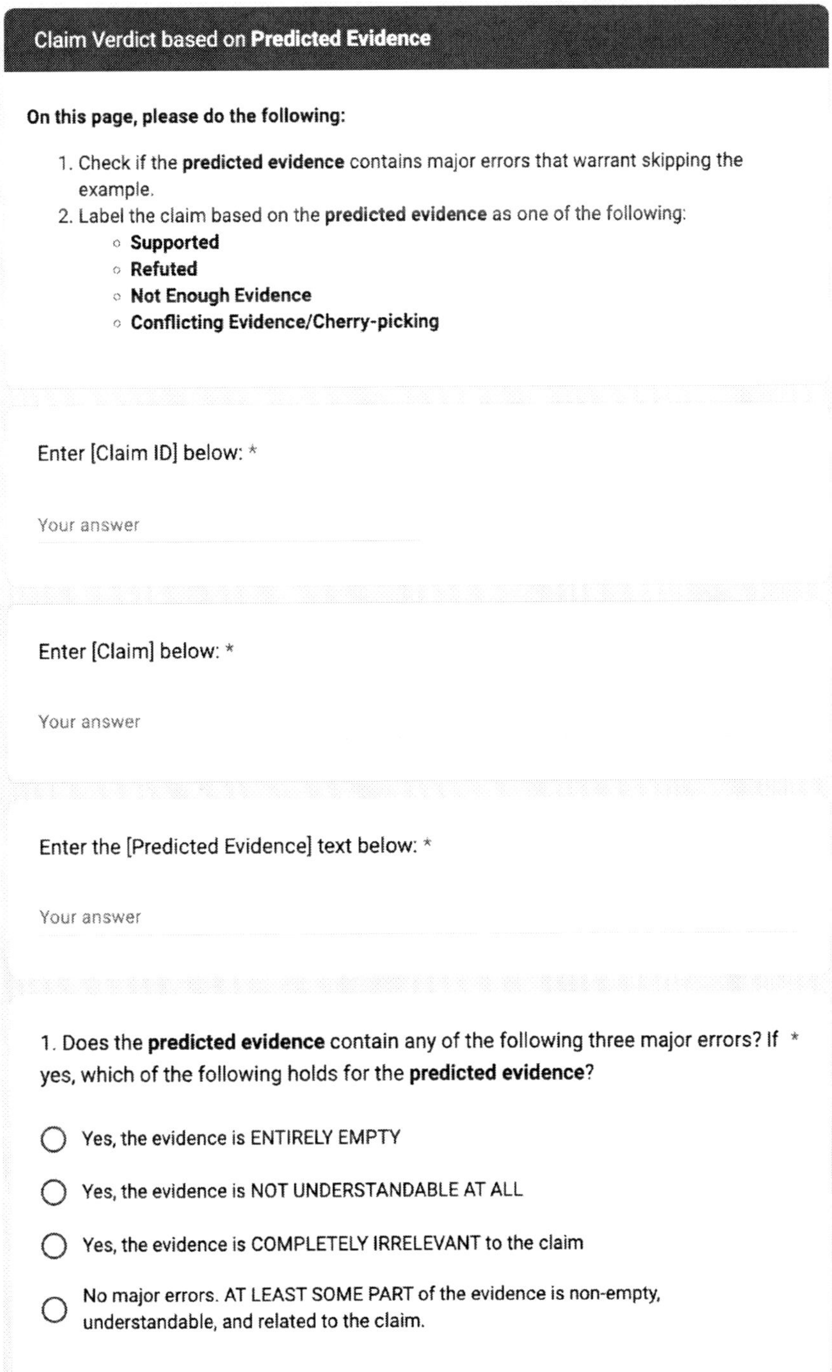

Claim Verdict based on **Predicted Evidence**

On this page, please do the following:

1. Check if the **predicted evidence** contains major errors that warrant skipping the example.
2. Label the claim based on the **predicted evidence** as one of the following:
   - **Supported**
   - **Refuted**
   - **Not Enough Evidence**
   - **Conflicting Evidence/Cherry-picking**

Enter [Claim ID] below: *

Your answer

Enter [Claim] below: *

Your answer

Enter the [Predicted Evidence] text below: *

Your answer

1. Does the **predicted evidence** contain any of the following three major errors? If yes, which of the following holds for the **predicted evidence**? *

- Yes, the evidence is ENTIRELY EMPTY
- Yes, the evidence is NOT UNDERSTANDABLE AT ALL
- Yes, the evidence is COMPLETELY IRRELEVANT to the claim
- No major errors. AT LEAST SOME PART of the evidence is non-empty, understandable, and related to the claim.

Figure 3: Platform for human evaluation of retrieved evidence from participating systems.

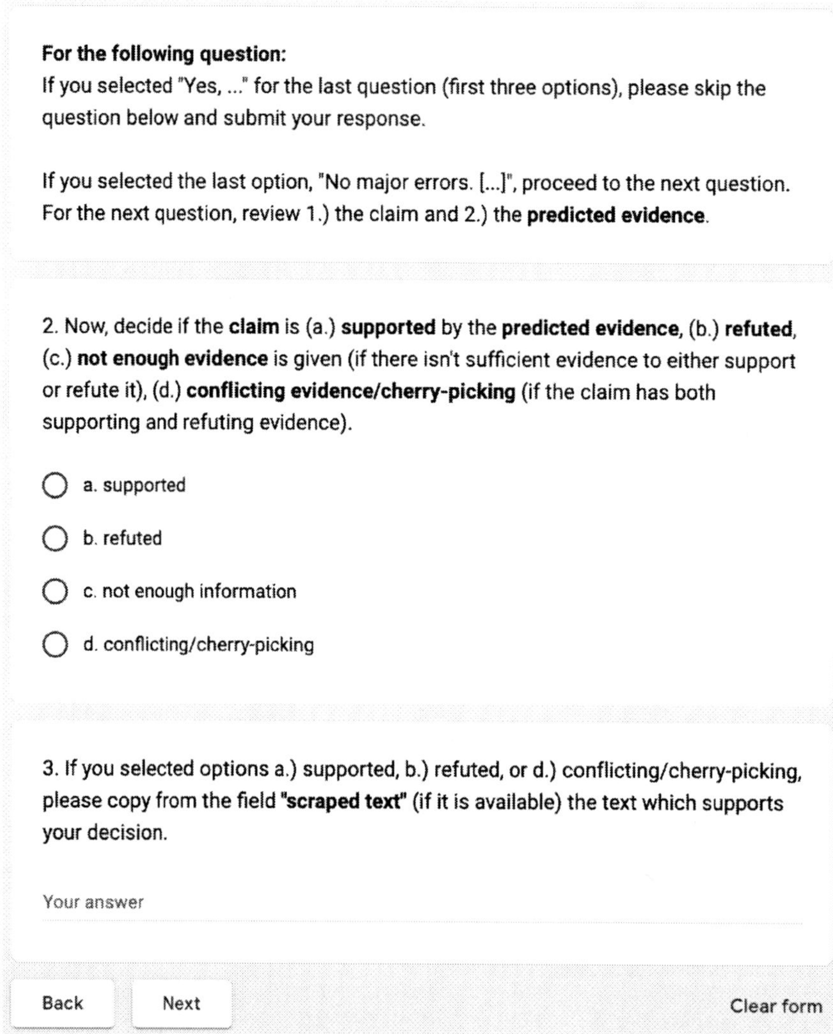

For the following question:
If you selected "Yes, ..." for the last question (first three options), please skip the question below and submit your response.

If you selected the last option, "No major errors. [...]", proceed to the next question. For the next question, review 1.) the claim and 2.) the **predicted evidence**.

2. Now, decide if the **claim** is (a.) **supported** by the **predicted evidence,** (b.) **refuted,** (c.) **not enough evidence** is given (if there isn't sufficient evidence to either support or refute it), (d.) **conflicting evidence/cherry-picking** (if the claim has both supporting and refuting evidence).

- a. supported
- b. refuted
- c. not enough information
- d. conflicting/cherry-picking

3. If you selected options a.) supported, b.) refuted, or d.) conflicting/cherry-picking, please copy from the field **"scraped text"** (if it is available) the text which supports your decision.

Your answer

Back Next Clear form

Figure 4: Platform for human evaluation of retrieved evidence from participating systems.

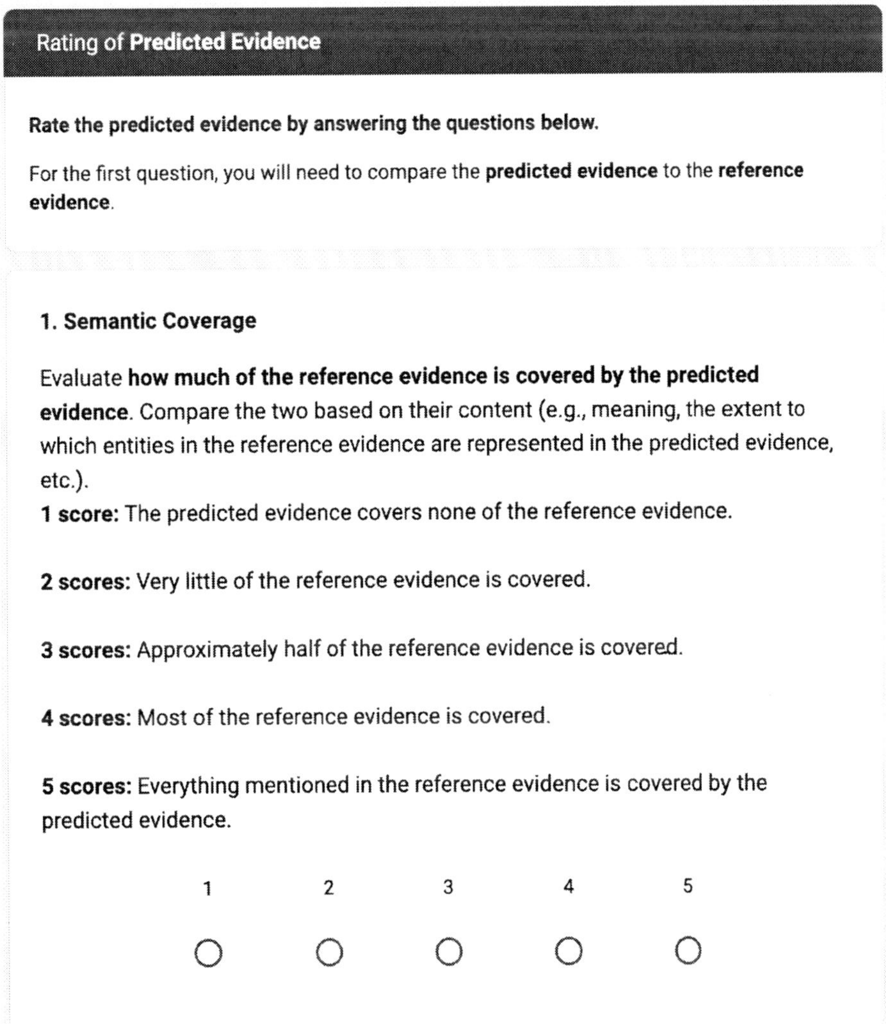

Figure 5: Platform for human evaluation of retrieved evidence from participating systems.

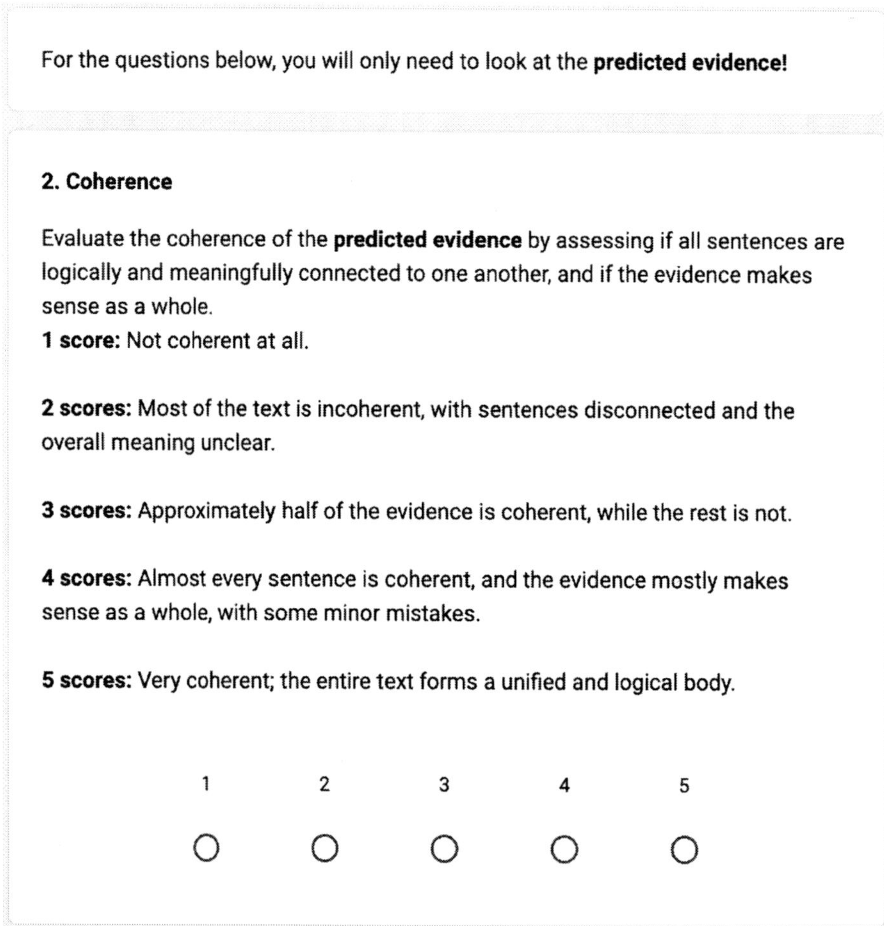
For the questions below, you will only need to look at the **predicted evidence!**

2. Coherence

Evaluate the coherence of the **predicted evidence** by assessing if all sentences are logically and meaningfully connected to one another, and if the evidence makes sense as a whole.
1 score: Not coherent at all.

2 scores: Most of the text is incoherent, with sentences disconnected and the overall meaning unclear.

3 scores: Approximately half of the evidence is coherent, while the rest is not.

4 scores: Almost every sentence is coherent, and the evidence mostly makes sense as a whole, with some minor mistakes.

5 scores: Very coherent; the entire text forms a unified and logical body.

1 2 3 4 5

Figure 6: Platform for human evaluation of retrieved evidence from participating systems.

3. Repetition

Evaluate the **predicted evidence** for any repetition.
1 score: A lot of repetition; most of the evidence text is redundant.

2 scores: A significant portion of the text repeats the same information.

3 scores: Approximately half of the text is repeated content.

4 scores: Minor repetitions in the text.

5 scores: No repetition at all.

1 2 3 4 5

○ ○ ○ ○ ○

Figure 7: Platform for human evaluation of retrieved evidence from participating systems.

4. Consistency

Evaluate the consistency of the **predicted evidence** in the information it provides.
1 score: Not consistent at all; contains a lot of conflicting and/or illogical information.

2 scores: Most of the evidence is inconsistent, with major parts that conflict or are illogical.

3 scores: Approximately half of the evidence is consistent, but there are significant conflicts or illogical information.

4 scores: The evidence is mostly consistent, with a few minor issues such as confusion of dates, names, or other details.

5 scores: The evidence is very consistent, with no conflicting or illogical information.

1 2 3 4 5

○ ○ ○ ○ ○

Figure 8: Platform for human evaluation of retrieved evidence from participating systems.

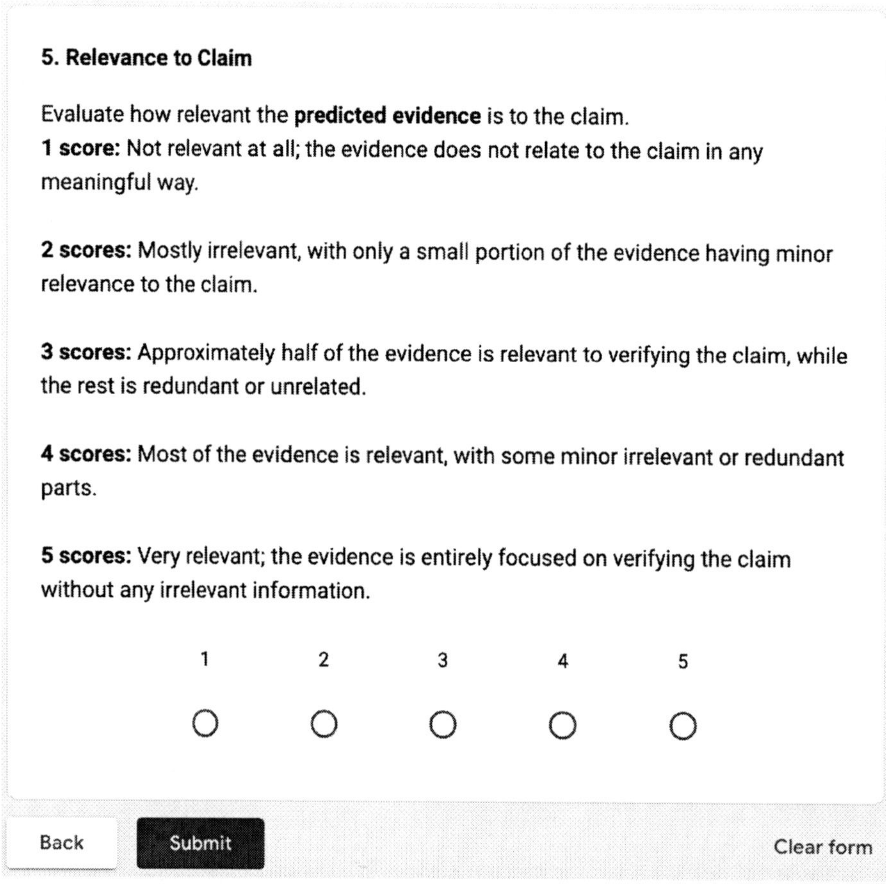

5. Relevance to Claim

Evaluate how relevant the **predicted evidence** is to the claim.
1 score: Not relevant at all; the evidence does not relate to the claim in any meaningful way.

2 scores: Mostly irrelevant, with only a small portion of the evidence having minor relevance to the claim.

3 scores: Approximately half of the evidence is relevant to verifying the claim, while the rest is redundant or unrelated.

4 scores: Most of the evidence is relevant, with some minor irrelevant or redundant parts.

5 scores: Very relevant; the evidence is entirely focused on verifying the claim without any irrelevant information.

1 2 3 4 5

Back Submit Clear form

Figure 9: Platform for human evaluation of retrieved evidence from participating systems.

	claim	predicted evidence	label human eval	semantic coverage	coherence	redundancy	consistency	relevance	predicted label	reference evidence
1	New changes to the Highway Code in Great Britain states drivers should give five feet when overtaking cyclists.	Question: Should drivers give five feet when overtaking bicyclists? Answer: No answer could be found. Question: What is the Highway Code in Great Britain? Answer No answer could be found.	not enough information	1	5	1	5	5	Not Enough Evidence	Question: What is 5 feet in metres? Answer: 1.5 metres. Question: What is the new overtaking distance between drivers and cyclists in the Highway Code? Answer: leave at least 1.5 metres when overtaking cyclists. Question: At what maximum speed is the new 1.5-distance rule applicable? Answer: at speeds of up to 30mph. Question: Should drivers leave more space if driving faster? Answer: Yes. On a PDF for the 'Table of Changes to the Highway Code' it states, "Give them more space when overtaking at higher speeds."
2	Tweet portrays Ravish Kumar targeting AAP ahead of Punjab elections	Question: When were the Punjab elections? Answer: No answer could be found. Question: When was the tweet made? Answer: The tweet was allegedly made by Ravish Kumar in the midst of the Punjab election. Question: Is Ravish Kumar an AAP supporter? Answer: No answer could be found.	not enough information	1	2	5	3	2	Supported	Question: What does Ravish Kumar think of the AAP? Answer: No answer could be found. Question: Did Ravish Kumar tweet about the AAP? Answer: No answer could be found. Question: Has Ravish Kumar been misquoted on political matters? Answer: Senior Congress leader Digvijaya Singh apologised to NDTV anchor Ravish Kumar today after sharing a video on Twitter that incorrectly suggested the latter had abused Prime Minister Narendra Modi in a public speech on Wednesday.
3	In 2010, a newly qualified teacher's salary in the UK was £21,500 and in 2018 it was £22,000.	Question: What was the starting salary for a newly qualified teacher in 2010? Answer: £21,500. Question: What was the starting salary for a newly qualified teacher in 2018? Answer: £22,000. Question: What was the starting salary for a newly qualified teacher in 2010 in 2018 prices? Answer: £25,400 Question: What was the starting salary for a newly qualified teacher in 2018 in 2010 prices? Answer: £23,000.	supported	5	4	1	2	4	Supported	Question: What was the salary of a newly qualified teacher in the UK in 2010? Answer: £21,588. Question: What was the salary of a newly qualified teacher in the UK in 2018? Answer: £23,720. Question: What was the salary of new teachers outside of London in 2010? Answer: £21,588. Question: What was salary of new teachers outside of London in 2018? Answer: Minimum starting salaries for classroom teachers will increase by between £653 (rest of England) and £816 (inner London). This means the minimum starting salary for a qualified teacher in 2019/20 will rise from £23,720 to £24,373 outside of London and from £29,664 to £30,480 in inner London.

Table 12: Examples for system predictions which are highly-ranked by the Averitec score.

	claim	predicted evidence	label human eval	semantic coverage	coherence	redundancy	consistency	relevance	predicted label	reference evidence
1	The reporting environment for foreign correspondents in China is open and free. Communication channels between foreign journalists in China and competent Chinese authorities are open and unfettered.	Question: What is the working environment for foreign journalists in China? Answer: Foreign correspondents in China have reported higher levels of concern about surveillance and invasion of privacy, as well as greater pressure by overseas Chinese officials on media organization headquarters. Nearly half of surveyed correspondents said they experienced interference, harassment, and physical violence. [...]	refuted	5	5	5	5	5	Refuted	Question: Does the Chinese government place restrictions on journalist content? Answer: Yes. The Propaganda Department of the Chinese Communist Party sends a detailed notice to all media every day that includes editorial guidelines and censored topics.
2	Philippines Senator Panfilo Lacson changes his opinion and says he sees the sense in the Department of National Defense's (DND) unilateral termination of its 1989 accord with the University of the Philippines (UP).	Question: What was Philippines Senator Panfilo Lacson's previous stance on the Department of National Defense's (DND) termination of its 1989 accord with the University of the Philippines (UP)? Answer: Philippines Senator Panfilo Lacson's previous stance on the Department of National Defense's (DND) termination of its 1989 accord with the University of the Philippines (UP) was critical. [...]	supported	3	5	5	5	4	Supported	Question: What was his initial view on the DND and University of the Philippines longstanding arrangement? Answer: There's sense in the move taken by the President and Sec. Lorenzana because during our red-tagging hearings in the Senate, it was established that—not only UP in particular, other universities—talagang 'yung recruitment nanggagaling dun sa mga estudyante up to the point that they're being killed in encounters, he told ANC's Headstart.

Table 13: Examples for system predictions which are low-ranked by the Averitec score.

Multi-hop Evidence Pursuit Meets the Web: Team Papelo at FEVER 2024

Christopher Malon
NEC Laboratories America
Princeton, NJ 08540
malon@nec-labs.com

Abstract

Separating disinformation from fact on the web has long challenged both the search and the reasoning powers of humans. We show that the reasoning power of large language models (LLMs) and the retrieval power of modern search engines can be combined to automate this process and explainably verify claims. We integrate LLMs and search under a *multi-hop evidence pursuit* strategy. This strategy generates an initial question based on an input claim using a sequence to sequence model, searches and formulates an answer to the question, and iteratively generates follow-up questions to pursue the evidence that is missing using an LLM. We demonstrate our system on the FEVER 2024 (AVeriTeC) shared task. Compared to a strategy of generating all the questions at once, our method obtains .045 higher label accuracy and .155 higher AVeriTeC score (evaluating the adequacy of the evidence). Through ablations, we show the importance of various design choices, such as the question generation method, medium-sized context, reasoning with one document at a time, adding metadata, paraphrasing, reducing the problem to two classes, and reconsidering the final verdict. Our submitted system achieves .510 AVeriTeC score on the dev set and .477 AVeriTec score on the test set.

1 Introduction

Since 2018, the FEVER shared task has challenged natural language processing systems to verify claims using a corpus and provide evidence that witnesses these verdicts. It has evolved from a simple combination of natural language inference (NLI) and entailment (Thorne et al., 2018) to a challenge involving adversarially constructed claims (Thorne et al., 2019), to a challenge to verify complex, multi-hop claims using a combination of tables and free text (Aly et al., 2021). In the current task, it finally arrives at combating real-life disinformation on the web (Schlichtkrull et al., 2023).

Systems are challenged to classify claim texts as supported, refuted, not enough evidence, or conflicting evidence/cherrypicking. In addition to classifying the claim, the systems must submit a list of questions and answers about a claim as evidence, with each answer derived from information on the open web and cited with a URL. Credit is given only when both the classification matches the ground truth and the evidence is adequate. The AVeriTeC score determines evidence adequacy by thresholding an average of METEOR scores between each gold QA pair and the corresponding submitted QA pair in the best assignment of QA pairs.

This task may involve retrieval and reasoning skills at a level for which professional journalists are sometimes employed. The reasoning may involve quote verification, stance detection, or numerical comparisons. The retrieval challenge goes beyond previous political fact-checking tasks (Ostrowski et al., 2021; Alhindi et al., 2018) and even beyond previous FEVER tasks in advancing from a closed corpus (Wikipedia) to the open web.

Whereas previous FEVER shared tasks needed to be solved by researcher-trained models, the current shared task allows the use of commercial API components. The winning team in FEVEROUS based their retriever on fitting a Dense Passage Retriever (Karpukhin et al., 2020) to the FEVEROUS data (Bouziane et al., 2021), but the training data for FEVER 2024 is quite limited, consisting of only 3,068 claims, and a retriever trained on user feedback from worldwide search queries should easily be more powerful. Additionally, an external web search engine such as Google Search may provide additional query understanding features not found in DPR, as a recent feature (not in the API

Proceedings of the Seventh Fact Extraction and VERification Workshop (FEVER), pages 27–36
November 15, 2024 ©2024 Association for Computational Linguistics

we used) applies generative AI to search[1]. Even though the gold evidence documents are guaranteed to appear in the knowledge store provided by the contest organizers, the snippets may not be extracted successfully. We found that 297 of the 500 claims in the dev set included gold documents with empty extracted text. In contrast, web search provides at least some text even from pages that the provided web scraper is blocked from accessing. Therefore, we chose to incorporate web search into our system.

Relying on a large language model (LLM) such as GPT-4o (OpenAI, 2024) for reasoning lets us leverage skills that could not be learned from 3,068 heterogenous claims, and go beyond the simple semantic comparison of an NLI model. Beyond simple NLI, ChatGPT and GPT-4 have been utilized to detect hallucinations in text summaries (Luo et al., 2023), as multi-faceted evaluators that score generated text (Zheng et al., 2023), and for critiques and corrections of generated text (Lin et al., 2024).

Though there are many ways of using a search engine and LLM within a fact-checking system, our main contribution is to show the power of combining them in a strategy of *multi-hop evidence pursuit*, which formulates additional questions only after searching and formulating answers to previous questions. In the following sections, we also investigate the impact of many choices of how the questions could be generated, the nature and size of context for generating answers, handling of multiple search results, metadata, paraphrasing, reducing the problem to two classes, and reconsidering the final verdict.

2 Related work

Retrieval-augmented generation (RAG) (Lewis et al., 2020) provides a general paradigm for enabling an LLM to answer questions that surpass the knowledge encoded in the LLM parameters, which is a task somewhat isomorphic to verifying claims (Demszky et al., 2018).

A growing body of work utilizes LLMs as high-level reasoning controllers that can solve tasks by querying agents to provide information or solve subproblems (Xi et al., 2023; Wu et al., 2023a). An early example for fact-checking an LLM's own output was LLM-Augmenter (Peng et al., 2023), which called an open retrieval pipeline as an agent action to iteratively improve an LLM response. Chan et al. (2024) uses an LLM to rewrite, decompose, and disambiguate queries before searching, and these steps are made into a hierarchy of agents in Chen et al. (2024). Wang et al. (2024) used a combination of Google search and GPT-4 with a single hop to fact-check claims in the FacTool-KB, FELM-WK, and HaluEval datasets. Behind a closed API, SearchGPT has been launched in beta to a few users as a service to provide access to a search-empowered OpenAI LLM.[2]

FEVER 2024 presents a multi-hop, open corpus fact verification challenge. In the multi-hop shared task of FEVEROUS, all but two contestants collected all the needed evidence up front, after only reading the claim (Aly et al., 2021). Later top performers (DCUF, UniFee, SEE-ST) addressed evidence interaction with graph-based methods but still did not address evidence that might be missed by the initial document retrieval (Hu et al., 2022, 2023; Wu et al., 2023b). Malon (2021) established an iterative paradigm for fact verification that retrieves further documents, sentences, and table cells by generating follow-up queries that are formulated after considering only the first retrieval, which we follow in the present system, in *multi-hop evidence pursuit*.

In medical question answering, Xiong et al. (2024) contemporaneously has proposed "iterative RAG for medicine" which uses an LLM to generate follow-up questions considering previous retrievals. In our algorithm, the relevance of each question is assured by generating it only upon a failure to verify the claim as true or false based on the existing evidence. Their method may generate irrelevant questions after an answer could already be obtained, simply because the fixed numbers of questions are not achieved, resulting in lower evidence relevance and higher computational cost. Our system can stop as soon as a verdict is clear, and if our system is configured to generate additional questions by paraphrasing, their relevance is assured by their similarity to the original questions.

3 Methodology

3.1 Overall architecture

Pseudocode outlining the overall system is given in Algorithm 1, with the main loop shown in Figure 1. At the core of the system are question generation functions $GetFirstQuestion$ and $GetNextQuestion$, for which we consider

[1] https://blog.google/products/search

[2] openai.com/index/searchgpt-prototype/

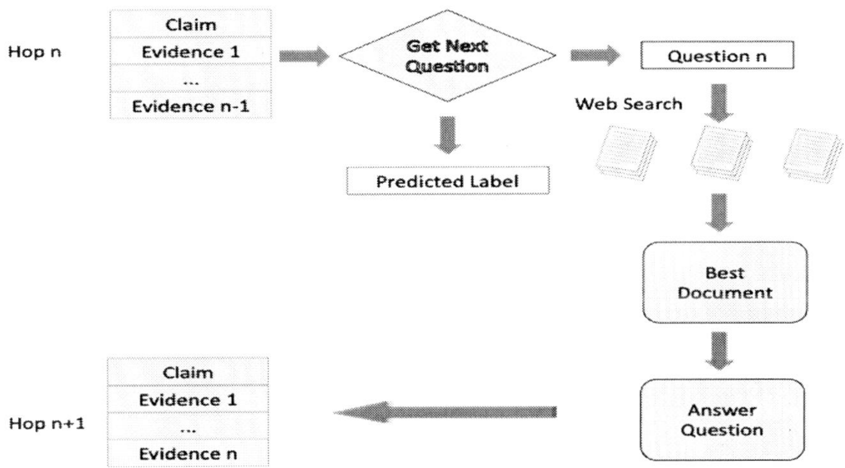

Figure 1: Pursuing additional evidence by generating follow-up questions.

implementations either by sequence-to-sequence encoder-decoder transformers such as T5 (Raffel et al., 2020), or by an LLM. The $GetAnswer$ function (Algorithm 2) prompts an LLM to implement $LLMBestDoc$ and $LLMAnswer$ to answer the generated questions. The final verdict is also chosen by prompting an LLM with the generated questions and answers, in $LLMVerdict$.

Algorithm 1. Claim verification

Input: Claim c, max questions n
Initialize QA list $Q = \emptyset$
Let $q = GetFirstQuestion(c)$
while $|Q| < n$ and $q \neq True$ and $q \neq False$
  Let $a = GetAnswer(q, c)$
  Append (q, a) to Q
  Let $q = GetNextQuestion(c, Q)$
  # $GetNextQuestion$ outputs True or False
  # if next question not needed
Let $k = |Q|$
while $|Q| < n$
  Let $i = |Q|$
  Let $q = Paraphrase(q_{i \bmod k})$
  Let $a = GetAnswer(q, c)$
  Append (q, a) to Q
Output: $v = LLMVerify(Q, c)$ and Q

Algorithm 2. Function $GetAnswer(q, c)$

Input: Question q, claim c
Let $s = c + q$ concatenation
Let $G = WebSearch(s)$
if $G = \emptyset$:
  Let $G = WebSearch(NamedEntities(s))$
$G = \{(url_0, quote_0), \ldots, (url_9, quote_9)\}$
Let $i = LLMBestDoc(G, q)$
Let $d = FullDocument(url_i)$
Let $e = AlignContext(d, quote_i, 5)$
Output: $a = LLMAnswer(q, e)$

Unlike the baseline system (Schlichtkrull et al., 2023), our system does not generate questions on a *post hoc* basis after finding evidence, but generates questions before web searches, playing a key role in steering the verification process. Rather than assuming all evidence can be found up front with a single search query, we review the current set of evidence and generate text (in our case, a question) that provides a query to search for what is still missing and needed after each hop, like the followup queries introduced in Malon (2021). Whereas the queries in Malon (2021) were generated by training a sequence to sequence model to predict what the missing evidence would look like, our system prompts an LLM to ask a question that the missing evidence answers.

The generation of evidence QA pairs temporarily stops when $GetNextQuestion$ thinks it can classify the claim as supported or refuted without asking another followup question (see Appendix B). After that point, the already generated questions are paraphrased using an LLM and corresponding answers are found until the desired number of QA pairs is obtained. Finally, an LLM uses all QA pairs to decide the final classification for the claim.

3.2 Question generation

We consider two variants for the functions $GetFirstQuestion$ and $GetNextQuestion$. In the **Seq** version, we finetune a sequence-to-sequence encoder-decoder transformer model. For $GetFirstQuestion$, the input is the claim, and the output is the first question. For $GetNextQuestion$, the input is the claim concatenated with all previous question-answer pairs, in the format

Claim: *claim* Question: $question_0$ Answer: $answer_0$ Question: $question_1$ Answer: $answer_1 \ldots$

and the output is the next question to be generated. These input strings are prefixed with the string "question: ". Details of the fine-tuning procedure are in Appendix A. Question-answer pairs from the gold data in the training set are used for this fine-tuning.

The other variant is the **LLM** version, in which we prompt the LLM with similar inputs. The prompts are given in Appendix B. Because LLM output is often verbose and may contain unnecessary explanations, we sentence split the output and use only the first sentence containing a question mark. If this is impossible, we use the whole output.

If an adequate number of questions and answers has been generated and the verdict is clear, the model has the opportunity to output a *True* or *False* verdict to stop the question generation.

As a further ablation, we consider a more traditional technique of generating all the questions at once, given the claim. The function *AllAtOnce* (prompt in Appendix B) replaces $GetFirstQuestion$ to generate a set of questions, and the **while** loop in Algorithm 1 is replaced by a loop over the generated questions, calling $GetAnswer$ but not $GetNextQuestion$.

3.3 Evidence selection

Here we describe the function $GetAnswer$, displayed in Algorithm 2, which retrieves evidence and uses it to answer the generated questions. Prompts for its LLM helper functions are given in Appendix B.

The generated question is concatenated to the claim to form a web search query, and the top ten search results are obtained, including their URL, the short snippet displayed in the search results, and usually the page title, site name, and publication date. When the web search returns no results, we retry the search using only the named entities (and other capitalized words after the first word) from the initial search query, following the supplemental queries which improved retrieval by Wikipedia page title lookups in Malon (2018).

By prompting, $LLMBestDoc$ is used to choose one document that best answers the question from the set of ten web search hits. We attempt to retrieve and scrape the text of that document using its URL (function $FullDocument$). This is implemented using the `scrape_text_from_url` function provided in the AVeriTeC baseline (Schlichtkrull et al., 2023), which uses the Python *trafilatura* library.[3] If the scraping succeeds, we look for a small window of text (five sentences in our experiments) that best overlaps the web search snippet (function $AlignContext$). Specifically, all five-sentence windows of the document that include more than 70% of the words in the web search snippet are recorded in order, and the middle such window is taken. Using this window as the document excerpt provides more background and context to the text that web search found to be relevant, while avoiding prompting with the overwhelming amount of text that might be found in the full web page. If the scraping fails, we continue to the next stage using only the web search snippet as document text.

Because $LLMBestDoc$ depends on parsing LLM output, it may fail to choose a best document. If a best document is chosen and the scraping succeeds, the LLM is prompted to answer the question using the selected five-sentence window of the best document in $LLMAnswer$. If the best document is chosen and the scraping fails, $LLMAnswer$ is run using the text of the web search snippet only. If a best document was not chosen in $LLMBestDoc$, we use the full text of the LLM response in that function as the answer and the web search result page itself as the evidence.

In $LLMBestDoc$ and $LLMAnswer$, the prompt includes not only the text for each document, but metadata including the page title, site name, and publication date, when this metadata appears in web search results. This metadata may occasionally be useful in assessing the credibility or relevance of the information to the question.

[3] github.com/adbar/trafilatura

3.4 Reconsideration and Classification

The *Paraphrase* function asks the LLM for paraphrases of the existing questions. In practice, multiple paraphrases of each question are requested at once to avoid repeated calls, even though they are used one at a time. Although these paraphrases may not be logically necessary once *GetNextQuestion* has determined a verdict, sometimes they provide a chance to reconsider the same questions using multiple sources. The variations in wording also improve the AVeriTec score, as discussed in section 4.

The *LLMVerdict* function is called after all question-answer pairs are collected, to choose the predicted label for each example. Using additional QA pairs, it may override the decision that stopped the QA generation process. Table 1 shows the distribution of labels in the training and development sets. "Not Enough Evidence" and "Conflicting evidence / cherrypicking" are minority classes, and we were unable to predict them with good F1 score. We obtained a higher score by limiting *LLMVerdict* to predicting "Supports" or "Refutes."

Class	Train	Dev
Supported	27.7%	24.4%
Refuted	56.8%	61.0%
NEI	9.2%	7.0%
Conflicting	6.4%	7.6%

Table 1: Distribution of class labels.

4 Experiments

We implement Algorithm 1 using GPT-4o (`gpt-4o-2024-05-13`, seed 42) as the LLM, T5 (`t5-large`) (Raffel et al., 2020) as the sequence-to-sequence model, and Google as the web search engine, and consider various ablations. For a faster development cycle and reduced monetary cost, Table 2 reports the performance of each of our systems only on the first 200 examples of the development set.

4.1 Question formation

Recall from Section 3.2 that in Algorithm 1, the functions *GetFirstQuestion* and *GetNextQuestion* could be implemented either by **Seq** or **LLM**, or instead of Algorithm 1, the questions could be generated *AllAtOnce*. Whichever question generation approach is used, at most five questions are taken from the question generator and the paraphrase loop of Algorithm 1 extends the list to five questions. The submitted system follows Algorithm 1 using **Seq** for *GetFirstQuestion*, and **LLM** for *GetNextQuestion* (Seq+LLM).

The lower performance of the *AllAtOnce* alternative indicates that this task requires followup searches considering the evidence already retrieved, with searches that cannot be anticipated using the claim alone. It validates our choice to use a *multi-hop evidence pursuit* strategy (Malon, 2021).

The LLM+LLM alternative shows that performance worsens if we generate the first question using GPT-4o. An inspection of the data revealed that the gold first questions were usually simple rephrasings of the claims, which T5 can learn well, whereas GPT-4o often tried to generate something more complicated.

The Seq+Seq alternative shows that performance worsens if we generate the subsequent questions using T5. Subsequent gold questions often reflected deeper reasoning using the obtained answers, which we suspect are beyond the capabilities of simple sequence to sequence models.

4.2 Label prediction

We have implementations of *LLMVerdict* that use a four-class prompt, or eliminate the "Not Enough Evidence" (NEI) and "Conflicting Evidence / Cherrypicking" classes to decide only between "Supported" and "Refuted." The 4-class result (otherwise the same as the main system) shows very low F1 scores for the NEI and Conflicting classes. As NEI claims form only 7.0% of the dev set and Conflicting claims form only 7.6%, we decided that it is always best to guess another label.

Another variant, "No late verdict," calls *LLMVerdict* only if the **while** loop is not terminated by predicting True or False, and maintains that early decision even after the paraphrases are added. (If True is obtained, "Supported" is predicted and if False is obtained, "Refuted" is predicted.) The difference in label accuracy shows it is sometimes useful to consider the whole question and answer chain from the beginning when forming a verdict.

4.3 Answer formation

The submitted system uses *FullDocument* and *AlignContext* to obtain longer document contexts

System	Supp F1	Ref F1	NEI F1	Conf F1	Acc	AVeriTec 0.25
$AllAtOnce$	.591	.813	0	0	.705	.340
LLM+LLM	.644	.821	0	0	.720	.385
Seq+Seq	.638	.816	0	0	.715	.370
4 class	.486	.593	**.148**	**.069**	.415	.245
No late verdict	.643	.811	0	0	.705	.450
No long doc	.577	.819	0	0	.705	.465
Multi-doc	.673	.837	0	0	.735	.460
No metadata	.575	.810	0	0	.700	.410
No paraphrase	.701	.839	0	0	.745	.225
Repeat not para	.624	.813	0	0	.710	.340
Algorithm 1	**.716**	**.841**	0	0	**.750**	**.495**

Table 2: Results on the first 200 examples of the dev set

Data	Submission	Supp F1	Ref F1	NEI F1	Conf F1	Acc	AVeriTec 0.25
Dev	Algorithm 1	.698	.853	0	0	.754	.486
Dev	Inflated to 10	.698	.853	0	0	.754	.510
Test	Algorithm 1	—	—	—	—	—	.445
Test	Inflated to 10	—	—	—	—	—	.477

Table 3: Final results on full datasets

for prompting $LLMAnswer$. The "No long doc" ablation uses only the original web search snippet as context for $LLMAnswer$. The close performance in AVeriTeC score shows that while longer context is helpful, it is often unnecessary. Scraping web pages to obtain this longer context has become difficult as many sites seek to restrain robots, so relying on snippets is convenient. In cases where our scraping fails, the original snippet is returned by $FullDocument$ anyway.

The "Multi-doc" ablation calls $LLMAnswer$ using all ten search hits and their snippets, without calling $LLMBestDoc$ to focus on one. It is very close to our system in label accuracy. Although it narrows the depth and context of information presented to $LLMAnswer$, it may have advantages in presenting multiple possible perspectives.

Metadata for each document context is usually presented to $LLMAnswer$ in the form

$$\text{Document}\, i : (\mathit{title}, \text{from}\, \mathit{site}, \text{published}\, \mathit{date})$$

The lower label accuracy and AVeriTeC score of the "No metadata" variant show that knowing where evidence came from is helpful to the LLM.

4.4 Evidence length

When the label is predicted correctly for an example, the AVeriTeC score thresholds an example score, which is computed as the sum of the METEOR scores between gold QA pairs and best matching predicted QA pairs, divided by the number of gold QA pairs. Whenever fewer QA pairs are predicted than gold QA pairs, those gold QA pairs contribute zero to this average. Therefore, to optimize the AVeriTec score, it is important to predict at least as many QA pairs as the number of gold pairs, even if the some predicted pairs match poorly.

A system could submit up to ten QA pairs for each example. However, only 5% of examples had more than five gold QA pairs in the development set. Since the ultimate objective is optimizing human evaluation rather than AVeriTeC score and reading more than five QA pairs may be frustrating for a human, we initially applied our systems to produce five QA pairs per question.

For many examples, Algorithm 1 could reach decisions of $q = True$ or $q = False$ in its first loop of $GetFirstQuestion$ and $GetNextQuestion$ using fewer than five QA pairs. We compared the score obtained by *repeating* QA pairs, or by asking the LLM to *paraphrase* the existing questions in the second loop of Algorithm 1, until five QA pairs were obtained. In the case of *paraphrase*, new answers are sought for the rewritten questions. Besides improving the AVeriTeC score, the new answers may be used to reconsider the final verdict.

The "No paraphrase" ablation has a minimal effect on label accuracy, but since fewer QA pairs are generated, AVeriTec score is less than half the score of the submitted system. "Repeat not paraphrase" to get five QA pairs can recover some of the AVeriTeC score, but the paraphrases help the METEOR score of the best assignment much more than duplicates.

Ten QA pairs is the upper limit, and submitting additional QA pairs up to ten can only improve the score of the best assignment between submitted pairs and gold pairs. We took our five generated QA pairs from Algorithm 1 ($GetFirstQuestion$, $GetNextQuestion$, and paraphrasing) and duplicated them to submit ten. Naturally, repeating can be helpful if one generated QA pair addresses points raised in multiple gold QA pairs. The effect of inflating the QA pairs on our full dev set and test set performance is shown in Table 3.

5 Conclusion

The AVeriTeC shared task is a realistic fact-checking challenge on actual web disinformation. The best large language models offer the deep reasoning power needed to pursue missing evidence to verify claims, and the best web search engines provide the vast document indices and retrieval capabilities needed to find it.

We have contributed a multi-hop evidence pursuit framework which combines the strengths of sequence to sequence models with LLMs to generate first question and subsequent questions separately, considering the present information; to stop pursuit once the answer is clear; and to embellish evidence by paraphrasing before considering the whole evidence chain to make the final verdict. Ablations indicate the importance of each design choice. Multi-hop evidence pursuit outperforms trying to generate all questions in one step. Reducing the number of classes, and using metadata and multi-sentence context from one best document, were important in obtaining our best performance.

The fact checking system presented may be useful to expedite the work of human fact checkers or provide a more rapid preliminary response to disinformation. Its full explainability could mitigate the effect of misclassifications, if the explanations were read and considered by a human. Over a history of many claims, ratings of disinformation from our system and/or human fact checkers could be used to rate the credibility of an information source.

Limitations

When "Not Enough Evidence" (NEI) is an option, an LLM tends to select it too often. Our system was unable to predict either NEI or "Conflicting Evidence / Cherrypicking" with acceptable accuracy. Considering this, and the fact the overall label accuracy is only .754, humans should be cautious in trusting this system's output to verify a claim without reading the rationale.

LLMs have insufficient information to judge the overall credibility of a website, and currently just the site name is given for the LLM's consideration. Metadata including the site name helps (to give an example from the dev set, GPT-4o was aware or discovered through its searches that Scoopertino was a satirical website), but generally, misinformation that is corroborated elsewhere on the web may fool our fact checking system.

Although the LLM is always prompted to answer questions "based on the above information" quoted from retrieved documents or its previous answers, there is no guarantee that the LLM does not apply other, untraceable knowledge in forming its answers. We use a date filter to ensure that all web searches return documents only from before each claim date, but we use an LLM whose training cutoff is after the claim dates.

Novel information first reported, which has no basis in existing documents, can never be fact-checked with the techniques of this system (for example, the first report that a presidential candidate was shot). That kind of fact checking requires judgments of plausibility, credibility, and consistency that are out of scope for this system.

References

Tariq Alhindi, Savvas Petridis, and Smaranda Muresan. 2018. Where is your evidence: Improving fact-checking by justification modeling. In *Proceedings of the First Workshop on Fact Extraction and VERification (FEVER)*, pages 85–90, Brussels, Belgium. Association for Computational Linguistics.

Rami Aly, Zhijiang Guo, Michael Sejr Schlichtkrull, James Thorne, Andreas Vlachos, Christos Christodoulopoulos, Oana Cocarascu, and Arpit Mittal. 2021. The fact extraction and VERification over unstructured and structured information (FEVEROUS) shared task. In *Proceedings of the Fourth Workshop on Fact Extraction and VERification (FEVER)*, pages 1–13, Dominican Republic. Association for Computational Linguistics.

Mostafa Bouziane, Hugo Perrin, Amine Sadeq, Thanh Nguyen, Aurélien Cluzeau, and Julien Mardas. 2021. FaBULOUS: Fact-checking based on understanding of language over unstructured and structured information. In *Proceedings of the Fourth Workshop on Fact Extraction and VERification (FEVER)*, pages 31–39, Dominican Republic. Association for Computational Linguistics.

Chi-Min Chan, Chunpu Xu, Ruibin Yuan, Hongyin Luo, Wei Xue, Yike Guo, and Jie Fu. 2024. Rq-rag: Learning to refine queries for retrieval augmented generation. *Preprint*, arXiv:2404.00610.

Zehui Chen, Kuikun Liu, Qiuchen Wang, Jiangning Liu, Wenwei Zhang, Kai Chen, and Feng Zhao. 2024. Mindsearch: Mimicking human minds elicits deep ai searcher. *Preprint*, arXiv:2407.20183.

Dorottya Demszky, Kelvin Guu, and Percy Liang. 2018. Transforming question answering datasets into natural language inference datasets. *Preprint*, arXiv:1809.02922.

Nan Hu, Zirui Wu, Yuxuan Lai, Xiao Liu, and Yansong Feng. 2022. Dual-channel evidence fusion for fact verification over texts and tables. In *Proceedings of the 2022 Conference of the North American Chapter of the Association for Computational Linguistics: Human Language Technologies*, pages 5232–5242, Seattle, United States. Association for Computational Linguistics.

Nan Hu, Zirui Wu, Yuxuan Lai, Chen Zhang, and Yansong Feng. 2023. UnifEE: Unified evidence extraction for fact verification. In *Proceedings of the 17th Conference of the European Chapter of the Association for Computational Linguistics*, pages 1150–1160, Dubrovnik, Croatia. Association for Computational Linguistics.

Vladimir Karpukhin, Barlas Oguz, Sewon Min, Patrick Lewis, Ledell Wu, Sergey Edunov, Danqi Chen, and Wen-tau Yih. 2020. Dense passage retrieval for open-domain question answering. In *Proceedings of the 2020 Conference on Empirical Methods in Natural Language Processing (EMNLP)*, pages 6769–6781, Online. Association for Computational Linguistics.

Patrick Lewis, Ethan Perez, Aleksandra Piktus, Fabio Petroni, Vladimir Karpukhin, Naman Goyal, Heinrich Küttler, Mike Lewis, Wen-tau Yih, Tim Rocktäschel, Sebastian Riedel, and Douwe Kiela. 2020. Retrieval-augmented generation for knowledge-intensive nlp tasks. In *Advances in Neural Information Processing Systems*, volume 33, pages 9459–9474. Curran Associates, Inc.

Zicheng Lin, Zhibin Gou, Tian Liang, Ruilin Luo, Haowei Liu, and Yujiu Yang. 2024. Criticbench: Benchmarking llms for critique-correct reasoning. *Preprint*, arXiv:2402.14809.

Zheheng Luo, Qianqian Xie, and Sophia Ananiadou. 2023. Chatgpt as a factual inconsistency evaluator for text summarization. *Preprint*, arXiv:2303.15621.

Christopher Malon. 2018. Team papelo: Transformer networks at FEVER. In *Proceedings of the First Workshop on Fact Extraction and VERification (FEVER)*, pages 109–113, Brussels, Belgium. Association for Computational Linguistics.

Christopher Malon. 2021. Team papelo at FEVEROUS: Multi-hop evidence pursuit. In *Proceedings of the Fourth Workshop on Fact Extraction and VERification (FEVER)*, pages 40–49, Dominican Republic. Association for Computational Linguistics.

OpenAI. 2024. Gpt-4 technical report. *Preprint*, arXiv:2303.08774.

Wojciech Ostrowski, Arnav Arora, Pepa Atanasova, and Isabelle Augenstein. 2021. Multi-hop fact checking of political claims. In *Proceedings of the Thirtieth International Joint Conference on Artificial Intelligence, IJCAI-21*, pages 3892–3898. International Joint Conferences on Artificial Intelligence Organization. Main Track.

Baolin Peng, Michel Galley, Pengcheng He, Hao Cheng, Yujia Xie, Yu Hu, Qiuyuan Huang, Lars Liden, Zhou Yu, Weizhu Chen, and Jianfeng Gao. 2023. Check your facts and try again: Improving large language models with external knowledge and automated feedback. *Preprint*, arXiv:2302.12813.

Colin Raffel, Noam Shazeer, Adam Roberts, Katherine Lee, Sharan Narang, Michael Matena, Yanqi Zhou, Wei Li, and Peter J. Liu. 2020. Exploring the limits of transfer learning with a unified text-to-text transformer. *Journal of Machine Learning Research*, 21(140):1–67.

Michael Schlichtkrull, Zhijiang Guo, and Andreas Vlachos. 2023. Averitec: A dataset for real-world claim verification with evidence from the web. In *Advances in Neural Information Processing Systems*, volume 36, pages 65128–65167. Curran Associates, Inc.

James Thorne, Andreas Vlachos, Oana Cocarascu, Christos Christodoulopoulos, and Arpit Mittal. 2018. The fact extraction and VERification (FEVER) shared task. In *Proceedings of the First Workshop on Fact Extraction and VERification (FEVER)*, pages 1–9, Brussels, Belgium. Association for Computational Linguistics.

James Thorne, Andreas Vlachos, Oana Cocarascu, Christos Christodoulopoulos, and Arpit Mittal. 2019. The FEVER2.0 shared task. In *Proceedings of the Second Workshop on Fact Extraction and VERification (FEVER)*, pages 1–6, Hong Kong, China. Association for Computational Linguistics.

Yuxia Wang, Revanth Gangi Reddy, Zain Muhammad Mujahid, Arnav Arora, Aleksandr Rubashevskii, Jiahui Geng, Osama Mohammed Afzal, Liangming Pan, Nadav Borenstein, Aditya Pillai, Isabelle Augenstein, Iryna Gurevych, and Preslav Nakov. 2024. Factcheck-bench: Fine-grained evaluation benchmark for automatic fact-checkers. *Preprint*, arXiv:2311.09000.

Qingyun Wu, Gagan Bansal, Jieyu Zhang, Yiran Wu, Beibin Li, Erkang Zhu, Li Jiang, Xiaoyun Zhang, Shaokun Zhang, Jiale Liu, Ahmed Hassan Awadallah, Ryen W White, Doug Burger, and Chi Wang. 2023a. Autogen: Enabling next-gen llm applications via multi-agent conversation. *Preprint*, arXiv:2308.08155.

Zirui Wu, Nan Hu, and Yansong Feng. 2023b. Enhancing structured evidence extraction for fact verification. In *Proceedings of the 2023 Conference on Empirical Methods in Natural Language Processing*, pages 6631–6641, Singapore. Association for Computational Linguistics.

Zhiheng Xi, Wenxiang Chen, Xin Guo, Wei He, Yiwen Ding, Boyang Hong, Ming Zhang, Junzhe Wang, Senjie Jin, Enyu Zhou, Rui Zheng, Xiaoran Fan, Xiao Wang, Limao Xiong, Yuhao Zhou, Weiran Wang, Changhao Jiang, Yicheng Zou, Xiangyang Liu, Zhangyue Yin, Shihan Dou, Rongxiang Weng, Wensen Cheng, Qi Zhang, Wenjuan Qin, Yongyan Zheng, Xipeng Qiu, Xuanjing Huang, and Tao Gui. 2023. The rise and potential of large language model based agents: A survey. *Preprint*, arXiv:2309.07864.

Guangzhi Xiong, Qiao Jin, Xiao Wang, Minjia Zhang, Zhiyong Lu, and Aidong Zhang. 2024. Improving retrieval-augmented generation in medicine with iterative follow-up questions. *Preprint*, arXiv:2408.00727.

Lianmin Zheng, Wei-Lin Chiang, Ying Sheng, Siyuan Zhuang, Zhanghao Wu, Yonghao Zhuang, Zi Lin, Zhuohan Li, Dacheng Li, Eric Xing, Hao Zhang, Joseph E Gonzalez, and Ion Stoica. 2023. Judging llm-as-a-judge with mt-bench and chatbot arena. In *Advances in Neural Information Processing Systems*, volume 36, pages 46595–46623. Curran Associates, Inc.

A Fine-tuning

A `t5-large` model was fine-tuned for three epochs with batch size 4, maximum source length 64 or 256 for $GetFirstQuestion$ or $GetNextQuestion$, and maximum target length 64. For the AdamW optimizer, default Huggingface values of 5×10^{-5} were used for the learning rate, $\beta_1 = 0.9$, and $\beta_2 = 0.999$. The model was prompted with the prefix "question: " followed by the inputs. Only gold data from AVeriTeC was used for the fine-tuning of each model.

B Prompts

GetFirstQuestion. For the LLM variant, the prompt is:

> We are trying to verify the following claim by *speaker* on *date*. Claim: *claim* We aren't sure whether this claim is true or false. Please write one or more questions that would help us verify this claim, as a JSON list of strings. Keep the list short.

The JSON is parsed and only the first string in the list is used.

AllAtOnce. For the $AllAtOnce$ variant, we use the same prompt as $GetFirstQuestion$ to get the questions, but we keep the entire list.

GetNextQuestion. For the LLM variant, the prompt is:

> We are trying to verify the following claim by *speaker* on *date*. Claim: *claim* So far we have asked the questions: Question 0: $question_0$ Answer: $answer_0$ Question 1: $question_1$ Answer: $answer_1 \ldots$ Based on these questions and answers, can you verify whether the claim is true or false? Please answer `[[True]]` or `[[False]]`, or ask one more question that would help you verify.

The response is searched for `[[True]]` or `[[False]]`. If neither is found, then the response is sentence tokenized with the `sent_tokenize` function of NLTK 3.8.1 and the first sentence that includes a question mark is returned.

LLMBestDoc. The prompt is:

> We searched the web and found the following information. Document 0 (*title*$_0$, from *site*$_0$, published *date*$_0$): *snippet*$_0$ Document 1 (*title*$_1$, from *site*$_1$, published *date*$_1$): *snippet*$_1$ ... Document 9 (*title*$_9$, from *site*$_9$, published *date*$_9$): *snippet*$_9$ Based on the above information, please answer the following question, referring to the one document that best answers the question. $question$

Note that the original claim is not used in this prompt. The response is searched with a regex for the first instance of `Document\s+([0-9])` / or `Documents[ 0-9,]+and ([0-9]+)` and the corresponding numbered document is taken. If the regex search fails, the search result page itself is used as context for answering the question, and the full response is used as the answer.

LLMAnswer. Unlike $LLMBestDoc$, this is called with context from one document. The prompt is:

> We searched the web and found the following information. Document (*title*, from *site*, published *date*): *context* Based on the above information, please answer the following question. *question*

The entire response is used as the answer.

Paraphrase. The prompt is:

> Please give four ways to rephrase the following question. Give your answer as a JSON list of strings, each string being one question. Question: *question*

LLMVerify. The prompt is:

> We are trying to verify the following claim: *claim* Based on our web searches, we resolved the following questions. 0. $question_0$ $answer_0$ ... k. $question_k$ $answer_k$ Is the claim (A) fully supported by the evidence, or (B) contradicted by the evidence? Please respond in the format `[[A]]` or `[[B]]`.

We search the response for `[[A]]` or `[[B]]`. For the four class variant, the end of the prompt is:

> Is the claim (A) fully supported by the evidence, (B) contradicted by the evidence, (C) insufficient information, or (D) conflicting evidence? Please respond in the format `[[A]]`, `[[B]]`, `[[C]]`, or `[[D]]`.

Multi-hop Evidence Pursuit Meets the Web: Team Papelo at FEVER 2024

Christopher Malon
NEC Laboratories America
Princeton, NJ 08540
malon@nec-labs.com

Abstract

Separating disinformation from fact on the web has long challenged both the search and the reasoning powers of humans. We show that the reasoning power of large language models (LLMs) and the retrieval power of modern search engines can be combined to automate this process and explainably verify claims. We integrate LLMs and search under a *multi-hop evidence pursuit* strategy. This strategy generates an initial question based on an input claim using a sequence to sequence model, searches and formulates an answer to the question, and iteratively generates follow-up questions to pursue the evidence that is missing using an LLM. We demonstrate our system on the FEVER 2024 (AVeriTeC) shared task. Compared to a strategy of generating all the questions at once, our method obtains .045 higher label accuracy and .155 higher AVeriTeC score (evaluating the adequacy of the evidence). Through ablations, we show the importance of various design choices, such as the question generation method, medium-sized context, reasoning with one document at a time, adding metadata, paraphrasing, reducing the problem to two classes, and reconsidering the final verdict. Our submitted system achieves .510 AVeriTeC score on the dev set and .477 AVeriTec score on the test set.

1 Introduction

Since 2018, the FEVER shared task has challenged natural language processing systems to verify claims using a corpus and provide evidence that witnesses these verdicts. It has evolved from a simple combination of natural language inference (NLI) and entailment (Thorne et al., 2018) to a challenge involving adversarially constructed claims (Thorne et al., 2019), to a challenge to verify complex, multi-hop claims using a combination of tables and free text (Aly et al., 2021). In the current task, it finally arrives at combating real-life disinformation on the web (Schlichtkrull et al., 2023).

Systems are challenged to classify claim texts as supported, refuted, not enough evidence, or conflicting evidence/cherrypicking. In addition to classifying the claim, the systems must submit a list of questions and answers about a claim as evidence, with each answer derived from information on the open web and cited with a URL. Credit is given only when both the classification matches the ground truth and the evidence is adequate. The AVeriTeC score determines evidence adequacy by thresholding an average of METEOR scores between each gold QA pair and the corresponding submitted QA pair in the best assignment of QA pairs.

This task may involve retrieval and reasoning skills at a level for which professional journalists are sometimes employed. The reasoning may involve quote verification, stance detection, or numerical comparisons. The retrieval challenge goes beyond previous political fact-checking tasks (Ostrowski et al., 2021; Alhindi et al., 2018) and even beyond previous FEVER tasks in advancing from a closed corpus (Wikipedia) to the open web.

Whereas previous FEVER shared tasks needed to be solved by researcher-trained models, the current shared task allows the use of commercial API components. The winning team in FEVEROUS based their retriever on fitting a Dense Passage Retriever (Karpukhin et al., 2020) to the FEVEROUS data (Bouziane et al., 2021), but the training data for FEVER 2024 is quite limited, consisting of only 3,068 claims, and a retriever trained on user feedback from worldwide search queries should easily be more powerful. Additionally, an external web search engine such as Google Search may provide additional query understanding features not found in DPR, as a recent feature (not in the API

Proceedings of the Seventh Fact Extraction and VERification Workshop (FEVER), pages 37–46
November 15, 2024 ©2024 Association for Computational Linguistics

we used) applies generative AI to search[1]. Even though the gold evidence documents are guaranteed to appear in the knowledge store provided by the contest organizers, the snippets may not be extracted successfully. We found that 297 of the 500 claims in the dev set included gold documents with empty extracted text. In contrast, web search provides at least some text even from pages that the provided web scraper is blocked from accessing. Therefore, we chose to incorporate web search into our system.

Relying on a large language model (LLM) such as GPT-4o (OpenAI, 2024) for reasoning lets us leverage skills that could not be learned from 3,068 heterogenous claims, and go beyond the simple semantic comparison of an NLI model. Beyond simple NLI, ChatGPT and GPT-4 have been utilized to detect hallucinations in text summaries (Luo et al., 2023), as multi-faceted evaluators that score generated text (Zheng et al., 2023), and for critiques and corrections of generated text (Lin et al., 2024).

Though there are many ways of using a search engine and LLM within a fact-checking system, our main contribution is to show the power of combining them in a strategy of *multi-hop evidence pursuit*, which formulates additional questions only after searching and formulating answers to previous questions. In the following sections, we also investigate the impact of many choices of how the questions could be generated, the nature and size of context for generating answers, handling of multiple search results, metadata, paraphrasing, reducing the problem to two classes, and reconsidering the final verdict.

2 Related work

Retrieval-augmented generation (RAG) (Lewis et al., 2020) provides a general paradigm for enabling an LLM to answer questions that surpass the knowledge encoded in the LLM parameters, which is a task somewhat isomorphic to verifying claims (Demszky et al., 2018).

A growing body of work utilizes LLMs as high-level reasoning controllers that can solve tasks by querying agents to provide information or solve subproblems (Xi et al., 2023; Wu et al., 2023a). An early example for fact-checking an LLM's own output was LLM-Augmenter (Peng et al., 2023), which called an open retrieval pipeline as an agent action to iteratively improve an LLM response. Chan et al. (2024) uses an LLM to rewrite, decompose, and disambiguate queries before searching, and these steps are made into a hierarchy of agents in Chen et al. (2024). Wang et al. (2024) used a combination of Google search and GPT-4 with a single hop to fact-check claims in the FacTool-KB, FELM-WK, and HaluEval datasets. Behind a closed API, SearchGPT has been launched in beta to a few users as a service to provide access to a search-empowered OpenAI LLM.[2]

FEVER 2024 presents a multi-hop, open corpus fact verification challenge. In the multi-hop shared task of FEVEROUS, all but two contestants collected all the needed evidence up front, after only reading the claim (Aly et al., 2021). Later top performers (DCUF, UniFee, SEE-ST) addressed evidence interaction with graph-based methods but still did not address evidence that might be missed by the initial document retrieval (Hu et al., 2022, 2023; Wu et al., 2023b). Malon (2021) established an iterative paradigm for fact verification that retrieves further documents, sentences, and table cells by generating follow-up queries that are formulated after considering only the first retrieval, which we follow in the present system, in *multi-hop evidence pursuit*.

In medical question answering, Xiong et al. (2024) contemporaneously has proposed "iterative RAG for medicine" which uses an LLM to generate follow-up questions considering previous retrievals. In our algorithm, the relevance of each question is assured by generating it only upon a failure to verify the claim as true or false based on the existing evidence. Their method may generate irrelevant questions after an answer could already be obtained, simply because the fixed numbers of questions are not achieved, resulting in lower evidence relevance and higher computational cost. Our system can stop as soon as a verdict is clear, and if our system is configured to generate additional questions by paraphrasing, their relevance is assured by their similarity to the original questions.

3 Methodology

3.1 Overall architecture

Pseudocode outlining the overall system is given in Algorithm 1, with the main loop shown in Figure 1. At the core of the system are question generation functions $GetFirstQuestion$ and $GetNextQuestion$, for which we consider

[1]https://blog.google/products/search

[2]openai.com/index/searchgpt-prototype/

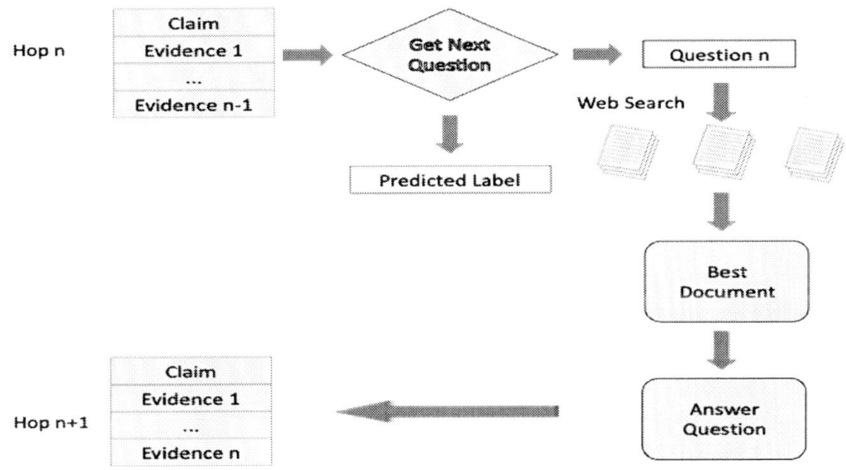

Figure 1: Pursuing additional evidence by generating follow-up questions.

implementations either by sequence-to-sequence encoder-decoder transformers such as T5 (Raffel et al., 2020), or by an LLM. The $GetAnswer$ function (Algorithm 2) prompts an LLM to implement $LLMBestDoc$ and $LLMAnswer$ to answer the generated questions. The final verdict is also chosen by prompting an LLM with the generated questions and answers, in $LLMVerdict$.

Algorithm 1. Claim verification
Input: Claim c, max questions n
Initialize QA list $Q = \emptyset$
Let $q = GetFirstQuestion(c)$
while $|Q| < n$ and $q \neq True$ and $q \neq False$
  Let $a = GetAnswer(q, c)$
  Append (q, a) to Q
  Let $q = GetNextQuestion(c, Q)$
  # $GetNextQuestion$ outputs True or False
  # if next question not needed
Let $k = |Q|$
while $|Q| < n$
  Let $i = |Q|$
  Let $q = Paraphrase(q_{i \bmod k})$
  Let $a = GetAnswer(q, c)$
  Append (q, a) to Q
Output: $v = LLMVerify(Q, c)$ and Q

Unlike the baseline system (Schlichtkrull et al., 2023), our system does not generate questions on a *post hoc* basis after finding evidence, but generates questions before web searches, playing a key role in steering the verification process. Rather than

Algorithm 2. Function $GetAnswer(q, c)$
Input: Question q, claim c
Let $s = c + q$ concatenation
Let $G = WebSearch(s)$
if $G = \emptyset$:
  Let $G = WebSearch(NamedEntities(s))$
$G = \{(url_0, quote_0), \ldots, (url_9, quote_9)\}$
Let $i = LLMBestDoc(G, q)$
Let $d = FullDocument(url_i)$
Let $e = AlignContext(d, quote_i, 5)$
Output: $a = LLMAnswer(q, e)$

assuming all evidence can be found up front with a single search query, we review the current set of evidence and generate text (in our case, a question) that provides a query to search for what is still missing and needed after each hop, like the followup queries introduced in Malon (2021). Whereas the queries in Malon (2021) were generated by training a sequence to sequence model to predict what the missing evidence would look like, our system prompts an LLM to ask a question that the missing evidence answers.

The generation of evidence QA pairs temporarily stops when $GetNextQuestion$ thinks it can classify the claim as supported or refuted without asking another followup question (see Appendix B). After that point, the already generated questions are paraphrased using an LLM and corresponding answers are found until the desired number of QA pairs is obtained. Finally, an LLM uses all QA pairs to decide the final classification for the claim.

3.2 Question generation

We consider two variants for the functions $GetFirstQuestion$ and $GetNextQuestion$. In the **Seq** version, we finetune a sequence-to-sequence encoder-decoder transformer model. For $GetFirstQuestion$, the input is the claim, and the output is the first question. For $GetNextQuestion$, the input is the claim concatenated with all previous question-answer pairs, in the format

Claim: *claim* Question: $question_0$ Answer: $answer_0$ Question: $question_1$ Answer: $answer_1 \ldots$

and the output is the next question to be generated. These input strings are prefixed with the string "question: ". Details of the fine-tuning procedure are in Appendix A. Question-answer pairs from the gold data in the training set are used for this fine-tuning.

The other variant is the **LLM** version, in which we prompt the LLM with similar inputs. The prompts are given in Appendix B. Because LLM output is often verbose and may contain unnecessary explanations, we sentence split the output and use only the first sentence containing a question mark. If this is impossible, we use the whole output.

If an adequate number of questions and answers has been generated and the verdict is clear, the model has the opportunity to output a *True* or *False* verdict to stop the question generation.

As a further ablation, we consider a more traditional technique of generating all the questions at once, given the claim. The function *AllAtOnce* (prompt in Appendix B) replaces $GetFirstQuestion$ to generate a set of questions, and the **while** loop in Algorithm 1 is replaced by a loop over the generated questions, calling $GetAnswer$ but not $GetNextQuestion$.

3.3 Evidence selection

Here we describe the function $GetAnswer$, displayed in Algorithm 2, which retrieves evidence and uses it to answer the generated questions. Prompts for its LLM helper functions are given in Appendix B.

The generated question is concatenated to the claim to form a web search query, and the top ten search results are obtained, including their URL, the short snippet displayed in the search results, and usually the page title, site name, and publication date. When the web search returns no results, we retry the search using only the named entities (and other capitalized words after the first word) from the initial search query, following the supplemental queries which improved retrieval by Wikipedia page title lookups in Malon (2018).

By prompting, $LLMBestDoc$ is used to choose one document that best answers the question from the set of ten web search hits. We attempt to retrieve and scrape the text of that document using its URL (function $FullDocument$). This is implemented using the `scrape_text_from_url` function provided in the AVeriTeC baseline (Schlichtkrull et al., 2023), which uses the Python *trafilatura* library.[3] If the scraping succeeds, we look for a small window of text (five sentences in our experiments) that best overlaps the web search snippet (function $AlignContext$). Specifically, all five-sentence windows of the document that include more than 70% of the words in the web search snippet are recorded in order, and the middle such window is taken. Using this window as the document excerpt provides more background and context to the text that web search found to be relevant, while avoiding prompting with the overwhelming amount of text that might be found in the full web page. If the scraping fails, we continue to the next stage using only the web search snippet as document text.

Because $LLMBestDoc$ depends on parsing LLM output, it may fail to choose a best document. If a best document is chosen and the scraping succeeds, the LLM is prompted to answer the question using the selected five-sentence window of the best document in $LLMAnswer$. If the best document is chosen and the scraping fails, $LLMAnswer$ is run using the text of the web search snippet only. If a best document was not chosen in $LLMBestDoc$, we use the full text of the LLM response in that function as the answer and the web search result page itself as the evidence.

In $LLMBestDoc$ and $LLMAnswer$, the prompt includes not only the text for each document, but metadata including the page title, site name, and publication date, when this metadata appears in web search results. This metadata may occasionally be useful in assessing the credibility or relevance of the information to the question.

[3] `github.com/adbar/trafilatura`

3.4 Reconsideration and Classification

The *Paraphrase* function asks the LLM for paraphrases of the existing questions. In practice, multiple paraphrases of each question are requested at once to avoid repeated calls, even though they are used one at a time. Although these paraphrases may not be logically necessary once *GetNextQuestion* has determined a verdict, sometimes they provide a chance to reconsider the same questions using multiple sources. The variations in wording also improve the AVeriTec score, as discussed in section 4.

The *LLMVerdict* function is called after all question-answer pairs are collected, to choose the predicted label for each example. Using additional QA pairs, it may override the decision that stopped the QA generation process. Table 1 shows the distribution of labels in the training and development sets. "Not Enough Evidence" and "Conflicting evidence / cherrypicking" are minority classes, and we were unable to predict them with good F1 score. We obtained a higher score by limiting *LLMVerdict* to predicting "Supports" or "Refutes."

Class	Train	Dev
Supported	27.7%	24.4%
Refuted	56.8%	61.0%
NEI	9.2%	7.0%
Conflicting	6.4%	7.6%

Table 1: Distribution of class labels.

4 Experiments

We implement Algorithm 1 using GPT-4o (`gpt-4o-2024-05-13`, seed 42) as the LLM, T5 (`t5-large`) (Raffel et al., 2020) as the sequence-to-sequence model, and Google as the web search engine, and consider various ablations. For a faster development cycle and reduced monetary cost, Table 2 reports the performance of each of our systems only on the first 200 examples of the development set.

4.1 Question formation

Recall from Section 3.2 that in Algorithm 1, the functions *GetFirstQuestion* and *GetNextQuestion* could be implemented either by **Seq** or **LLM**, or instead of Algorithm 1, the questions could be generated *AllAtOnce*. Whichever question generation approach is used, at most five questions are taken from the question generator and the paraphrase loop of Algorithm 1 extends the list to five questions. The submitted system follows Algorithm 1 using **Seq** for *GetFirstQuestion*, and **LLM** for *GetNextQuestion* (Seq+LLM).

The lower performance of the *AllAtOnce* alternative indicates that this task requires followup searches considering the evidence already retrieved, with searches that cannot be anticipated using the claim alone. It validates our choice to use a *multi-hop evidence pursuit* strategy (Malon, 2021).

The LLM+LLM alternative shows that performance worsens if we generate the first question using GPT-4o. An inspection of the data revealed that the gold first questions were usually simple rephrasings of the claims, which T5 can learn well, whereas GPT-4o often tried to generate something more complicated.

The Seq+Seq alternative shows that performance worsens if we generate the subsequent questions using T5. Subsequent gold questions often reflected deeper reasoning using the obtained answers, which we suspect are beyond the capabilities of simple sequence to sequence models.

4.2 Label prediction

We have implementations of *LLMVerdict* that use a four-class prompt, or eliminate the "Not Enough Evidence" (NEI) and "Conflicting Evidence / Cherrypicking" classes to decide only between "Supported" and "Refuted." The 4-class result (otherwise the same as the main system) shows very low F1 scores for the NEI and Conflicting classes. As NEI claims form only 7.0% of the dev set and Conflicting claims form only 7.6%, we decided that it is always best to guess another label.

Another variant, "No late verdict," calls *LLMVerdict* only if the **while** loop is not terminated by predicting True or False, and maintains that early decision even after the paraphrases are added. (If True is obtained, "Supported" is predicted and if False is obtained, "Refuted" is predicted.) The difference in label accuracy shows it is sometimes useful to consider the whole question and answer chain from the beginning when forming a verdict.

4.3 Answer formation

The submitted system uses *FullDocument* and *AlignContext* to obtain longer document contexts

System	Supp F1	Ref F1	NEI F1	Conf F1	Acc	AVeriTec 0.25
AllAtOnce	.591	.813	0	0	.705	.340
LLM+LLM	.644	.821	0	0	.720	.385
Seq+Seq	.638	.816	0	0	.715	.370
4 class	.486	.593	**.148**	**.069**	.415	.245
No late verdict	.643	.811	0	0	.705	.450
No long doc	.577	.819	0	0	.705	.465
Multi-doc	.673	.837	0	0	.735	.460
No metadata	.575	.810	0	0	.700	.410
No paraphrase	.701	.839	0	0	.745	.225
Repeat not para	.624	.813	0	0	.710	.340
Algorithm 1	**.716**	**.841**	0	0	**.750**	**.495**

Table 2: Results on the first 200 examples of the dev set

Data	Submission	Supp F1	Ref F1	NEI F1	Conf F1	Acc	AVeriTec 0.25
Dev	Algorithm 1	.698	.853	0	0	.754	.486
Dev	Inflated to 10	.698	.853	0	0	.754	.510
Test	Algorithm 1	—	—	—	—	—	.445
Test	Inflated to 10	—	—	—	—	—	.477

Table 3: Final results on full datasets

for prompting $LLMAnswer$. The "No long doc" ablation uses only the original web search snippet as context for $LLMAnswer$. The close performance in AVeriTeC score shows that while longer context is helpful, it is often unnecessary. Scraping web pages to obtain this longer context has become difficult as many sites seek to restrain robots, so relying on snippets is convenient. In cases where our scraping fails, the original snippet is returned by $FullDocument$ anyway.

The "Multi-doc" ablation calls $LLMAnswer$ using all ten search hits and their snippets, without calling $LLMBestDoc$ to focus on one. It is very close to our system in label accuracy. Although it narrows the depth and context of information presented to $LLMAnswer$, it may have advantages in presenting multiple possible perspectives.

Metadata for each document context is usually presented to $LLMAnswer$ in the form

$$\text{Document}\, i : (title, \text{from}\, site, \text{published}\, date)$$

The lower label accuracy and AVeriTeC score of the "No metadata" variant show that knowing where evidence came from is helpful to the LLM.

4.4 Evidence length

When the label is predicted correctly for an example, the AVeriTeC score thresholds an example score, which is computed as the sum of the METEOR scores between gold QA pairs and best matching predicted QA pairs, divided by the number of gold QA pairs. Whenever fewer QA pairs are predicted than gold QA pairs, those gold QA pairs contribute zero to this average. Therefore, to optimize the AVeriTec score, it is important to predict at least as many QA pairs as the number of gold pairs, even if the some predicted pairs match poorly.

A system could submit up to ten QA pairs for each example. However, only 5% of examples had more than five gold QA pairs in the development set. Since the ultimate objective is optimizing human evaluation rather than AVeriTeC score and reading more than five QA pairs may be frustrating for a human, we initially applied our systems to produce five QA pairs per question.

For many examples, Algorithm 1 could reach decisions of $q = True$ or $q = False$ in its first loop of $GetFirstQuestion$ and $GetNextQuestion$ using fewer than five QA pairs. We compared the score obtained by *repeating* QA pairs, or by asking the LLM to *paraphrase* the existing questions in the second loop of Algorithm 1, until five QA pairs were obtained. In the case of *paraphrase*, new answers are sought for the rewritten questions. Besides improving the AVeriTeC score, the new answers may be used to reconsider the final verdict.

The "No paraphrase" ablation has a minimal effect on label accuracy, but since fewer QA pairs are generated, AVeriTec score is less than half the score of the submitted system. "Repeat not paraphrase" to get five QA pairs can recover some of the AVeriTeC score, but the paraphrases help the METEOR score of the best assignment much more than duplicates.

Ten QA pairs is the upper limit, and submitting additional QA pairs up to ten can only improve the score of the best assignment between submitted pairs and gold pairs. We took our five generated QA pairs from Algorithm 1 ($GetFirstQuestion$, $GetNextQuestion$, and paraphrasing) and duplicated them to submit ten. Naturally, repeating can be helpful if one generated QA pair addresses points raised in multiple gold QA pairs. The effect of inflating the QA pairs on our full dev set and test set performance is shown in Table 3.

5 Conclusion

The AVeriTeC shared task is a realistic fact-checking challenge on actual web disinformation. The best large language models offer the deep reasoning power needed to pursue missing evidence to verify claims, and the best web search engines provide the vast document indices and retrieval capabilities needed to find it.

We have contributed a multi-hop evidence pursuit framework which combines the strengths of sequence to sequence models with LLMs to generate first question and subsequent questions separately, considering the present information; to stop pursuit once the answer is clear; and to embellish evidence by paraphrasing before considering the whole evidence chain to make the final verdict. Ablations indicate the importance of each design choice. Multi-hop evidence pursuit outperforms trying to generate all questions in one step. Reducing the number of classes, and using metadata and multi-sentence context from one best document, were important in obtaining our best performance.

The fact checking system presented may be useful to expedite the work of human fact checkers or provide a more rapid preliminary response to disinformation. Its full explainability could mitigate the effect of misclassifications, if the explanations were read and considered by a human. Over a history of many claims, ratings of disinformation from our system and/or human fact checkers could be used to rate the credibility of an information source.

Limitations

When "Not Enough Evidence" (NEI) is an option, an LLM tends to select it too often. Our system was unable to predict either NEI or "Conflicting Evidence / Cherrypicking" with acceptable accuracy. Considering this, and the fact the overall label accuracy is only .754, humans should be cautious in trusting this system's output to verify a claim without reading the rationale.

LLMs have insufficient information to judge the overall credibility of a website, and currently just the site name is given for the LLM's consideration. Metadata including the site name helps (to give an example from the dev set, GPT-4o was aware or discovered through its searches that Scoopertino was a satirical website), but generally, misinformation that is corroborated elsewhere on the web may fool our fact checking system.

Although the LLM is always prompted to answer questions "based on the above information" quoted from retrieved documents or its previous answers, there is no guarantee that the LLM does not apply other, untraceable knowledge in forming its answers. We use a date filter to ensure that all web searches return documents only from before each claim date, but we use an LLM whose training cutoff is after the claim dates.

Novel information first reported, which has no basis in existing documents, can never be fact-checked with the techniques of this system (for example, the first report that a presidential candidate was shot). That kind of fact checking requires judgments of plausibility, credibility, and consistency that are out of scope for this system.

References

Tariq Alhindi, Savvas Petridis, and Smaranda Muresan. 2018. Where is your evidence: Improving fact-checking by justification modeling. In *Proceedings of the First Workshop on Fact Extraction and VERification (FEVER)*, pages 85–90, Brussels, Belgium. Association for Computational Linguistics.

Rami Aly, Zhijiang Guo, Michael Sejr Schlichtkrull, James Thorne, Andreas Vlachos, Christos Christodoulopoulos, Oana Cocarascu, and Arpit Mittal. 2021. The fact extraction and VERification over unstructured and structured information (FEVEROUS) shared task. In *Proceedings of the Fourth Workshop on Fact Extraction and VERification (FEVER)*, pages 1–13, Dominican Republic. Association for Computational Linguistics.

Mostafa Bouziane, Hugo Perrin, Amine Sadeq, Thanh Nguyen, Aurélien Cluzeau, and Julien Mardas. 2021. FaBULOUS: Fact-checking based on understanding of language over unstructured and structured information. In *Proceedings of the Fourth Workshop on Fact Extraction and VERification (FEVER)*, pages 31–39, Dominican Republic. Association for Computational Linguistics.

Chi-Min Chan, Chunpu Xu, Ruibin Yuan, Hongyin Luo, Wei Xue, Yike Guo, and Jie Fu. 2024. Rq-rag: Learning to refine queries for retrieval augmented generation. *Preprint*, arXiv:2404.00610.

Zehui Chen, Kuikun Liu, Qiuchen Wang, Jiangning Liu, Wenwei Zhang, Kai Chen, and Feng Zhao. 2024. Mindsearch: Mimicking human minds elicits deep ai searcher. *Preprint*, arXiv:2407.20183.

Dorottya Demszky, Kelvin Guu, and Percy Liang. 2018. Transforming question answering datasets into natural language inference datasets. *Preprint*, arXiv:1809.02922.

Nan Hu, Zirui Wu, Yuxuan Lai, Xiao Liu, and Yansong Feng. 2022. Dual-channel evidence fusion for fact verification over texts and tables. In *Proceedings of the 2022 Conference of the North American Chapter of the Association for Computational Linguistics: Human Language Technologies*, pages 5232–5242, Seattle, United States. Association for Computational Linguistics.

Nan Hu, Zirui Wu, Yuxuan Lai, Chen Zhang, and Yansong Feng. 2023. UnifEE: Unified evidence extraction for fact verification. In *Proceedings of the 17th Conference of the European Chapter of the Association for Computational Linguistics*, pages 1150–1160, Dubrovnik, Croatia. Association for Computational Linguistics.

Vladimir Karpukhin, Barlas Oguz, Sewon Min, Patrick Lewis, Ledell Wu, Sergey Edunov, Danqi Chen, and Wen-tau Yih. 2020. Dense passage retrieval for open-domain question answering. In *Proceedings of the 2020 Conference on Empirical Methods in Natural Language Processing (EMNLP)*, pages 6769–6781, Online. Association for Computational Linguistics.

Patrick Lewis, Ethan Perez, Aleksandra Piktus, Fabio Petroni, Vladimir Karpukhin, Naman Goyal, Heinrich Küttler, Mike Lewis, Wen-tau Yih, Tim Rocktäschel, Sebastian Riedel, and Douwe Kiela. 2020. Retrieval-augmented generation for knowledge-intensive nlp tasks. In *Advances in Neural Information Processing Systems*, volume 33, pages 9459–9474. Curran Associates, Inc.

Zicheng Lin, Zhibin Gou, Tian Liang, Ruilin Luo, Haowei Liu, and Yujiu Yang. 2024. Criticbench: Benchmarking llms for critique-correct reasoning. *Preprint*, arXiv:2402.14809.

Zheheng Luo, Qianqian Xie, and Sophia Ananiadou. 2023. Chatgpt as a factual inconsistency evaluator for text summarization. *Preprint*, arXiv:2303.15621.

Christopher Malon. 2018. Team papelo: Transformer networks at FEVER. In *Proceedings of the First Workshop on Fact Extraction and VERification (FEVER)*, pages 109–113, Brussels, Belgium. Association for Computational Linguistics.

Christopher Malon. 2021. Team papelo at FEVEROUS: Multi-hop evidence pursuit. In *Proceedings of the Fourth Workshop on Fact Extraction and VERification (FEVER)*, pages 40–49, Dominican Republic. Association for Computational Linguistics.

OpenAI. 2024. Gpt-4 technical report. *Preprint*, arXiv:2303.08774.

Wojciech Ostrowski, Arnav Arora, Pepa Atanasova, and Isabelle Augenstein. 2021. Multi-hop fact checking of political claims. In *Proceedings of the Thirtieth International Joint Conference on Artificial Intelligence, IJCAI-21*, pages 3892–3898. International Joint Conferences on Artificial Intelligence Organization. Main Track.

Baolin Peng, Michel Galley, Pengcheng He, Hao Cheng, Yujia Xie, Yu Hu, Qiuyuan Huang, Lars Liden, Zhou Yu, Weizhu Chen, and Jianfeng Gao. 2023. Check your facts and try again: Improving large language models with external knowledge and automated feedback. *Preprint*, arXiv:2302.12813.

Colin Raffel, Noam Shazeer, Adam Roberts, Katherine Lee, Sharan Narang, Michael Matena, Yanqi Zhou, Wei Li, and Peter J. Liu. 2020. Exploring the limits of transfer learning with a unified text-to-text transformer. *Journal of Machine Learning Research*, 21(140):1–67.

Michael Schlichtkrull, Zhijiang Guo, and Andreas Vlachos. 2023. Averitec: A dataset for real-world claim verification with evidence from the web. In *Advances in Neural Information Processing Systems*, volume 36, pages 65128–65167. Curran Associates, Inc.

James Thorne, Andreas Vlachos, Oana Cocarascu, Christos Christodoulopoulos, and Arpit Mittal. 2018. The fact extraction and VERification (FEVER) shared task. In *Proceedings of the First Workshop on Fact Extraction and VERification (FEVER)*, pages 1–9, Brussels, Belgium. Association for Computational Linguistics.

James Thorne, Andreas Vlachos, Oana Cocarascu, Christos Christodoulopoulos, and Arpit Mittal. 2019. The FEVER2.0 shared task. In *Proceedings of the Second Workshop on Fact Extraction and VERification (FEVER)*, pages 1–6, Hong Kong, China. Association for Computational Linguistics.

Yuxia Wang, Revanth Gangi Reddy, Zain Muhammad Mujahid, Arnav Arora, Aleksandr Rubashevskii, Jiahui Geng, Osama Mohammed Afzal, Liangming Pan, Nadav Borenstein, Aditya Pillai, Isabelle Augenstein, Iryna Gurevych, and Preslav Nakov. 2024. Factcheck-bench: Fine-grained evaluation benchmark for automatic fact-checkers. *Preprint*, arXiv:2311.09000.

Qingyun Wu, Gagan Bansal, Jieyu Zhang, Yiran Wu, Beibin Li, Erkang Zhu, Li Jiang, Xiaoyun Zhang, Shaokun Zhang, Jiale Liu, Ahmed Hassan Awadallah, Ryen W White, Doug Burger, and Chi Wang. 2023a. Autogen: Enabling next-gen llm applications via multi-agent conversation. *Preprint*, arXiv:2308.08155.

Zirui Wu, Nan Hu, and Yansong Feng. 2023b. Enhancing structured evidence extraction for fact verification. In *Proceedings of the 2023 Conference on Empirical Methods in Natural Language Processing*, pages 6631–6641, Singapore. Association for Computational Linguistics.

Zhiheng Xi, Wenxiang Chen, Xin Guo, Wei He, Yiwen Ding, Boyang Hong, Ming Zhang, Junzhe Wang, Senjie Jin, Enyu Zhou, Rui Zheng, Xiaoran Fan, Xiao Wang, Limao Xiong, Yuhao Zhou, Weiran Wang, Changhao Jiang, Yicheng Zou, Xiangyang Liu, Zhangyue Yin, Shihan Dou, Rongxiang Weng, Wensen Cheng, Qi Zhang, Wenjuan Qin, Yongyan Zheng, Xipeng Qiu, Xuanjing Huang, and Tao Gui. 2023. The rise and potential of large language model based agents: A survey. *Preprint*, arXiv:2309.07864.

Guangzhi Xiong, Qiao Jin, Xiao Wang, Minjia Zhang, Zhiyong Lu, and Aidong Zhang. 2024. Improving retrieval-augmented generation in medicine with iterative follow-up questions. *Preprint*, arXiv:2408.00727.

Lianmin Zheng, Wei-Lin Chiang, Ying Sheng, Siyuan Zhuang, Zhanghao Wu, Yonghao Zhuang, Zi Lin, Zhuohan Li, Dacheng Li, Eric Xing, Hao Zhang, Joseph E Gonzalez, and Ion Stoica. 2023. Judging llm-as-a-judge with mt-bench and chatbot arena. In *Advances in Neural Information Processing Systems*, volume 36, pages 46595–46623. Curran Associates, Inc.

A Fine-tuning

A `t5-large` model was fine-tuned for three epochs with batch size 4, maximum source length 64 or 256 for $GetFirstQuestion$ or $GetNextQuestion$, and maximum target length 64. For the AdamW optimizer, default Huggingface values of 5×10^{-5} were used for the learning rate, $\beta_1 = 0.9$, and $\beta_2 = 0.999$. The model was prompted with the prefix "question: " followed by the inputs. Only gold data from AVeriTeC was used for the fine-tuning of each model.

B Prompts

GetFirstQuestion. For the LLM variant, the prompt is:

> We are trying to verify the following claim by *speaker* on *date*. Claim: *claim* We aren't sure whether this claim is true or false. Please write one or more questions that would help us verify this claim, as a JSON list of strings. Keep the list short.

The JSON is parsed and only the first string in the list is used.

AllAtOnce. For the $AllAtOnce$ variant, we use the same prompt as $GetFirstQuestion$ to get the questions, but we keep the entire list.

GetNextQuestion. For the LLM variant, the prompt is:

> We are trying to verify the following claim by *speaker* on *date*. Claim: *claim* So far we have asked the questions: Question 0: $question_0$ Answer: $answer_0$ Question 1: $question_1$ Answer: $answer_1 \ldots$ Based on these questions and answers, can you verify whether the claim is true or false? Please answer `[[True]]` or `[[False]]`, or ask one more question that would help you verify.

The response is searched for `[[True]]` or `[[False]]`. If neither is found, then the response is sentence tokenized with the `sent_tokenize` function of NLTK 3.8.1 and the first sentence that includes a question mark is returned.

LLMBestDoc. The prompt is:

> We searched the web and found the following information. Document 0 ($title_0$, from $site_0$, published $date_0$): $snippet_0$ Document 1 ($title_1$, from $site_1$, published $date_1$): $snippet_1$ ... Document 9 ($title_9$, from $site_9$, published $date_9$): $snippet_9$ Based on the above information, please answer the following question, referring to the one document that best answers the question. $question$

Note that the original claim is not used in this prompt. The response is searched with a regex for the first instance of `Document\s+([0-9])` / or `Documents[ 0-9,]+and ([0-9]+)` and the corresponding numbered document is taken. If the regex search fails, the search result page itself is used as context for answering the question, and the full response is used as the answer.

LLMAnswer. Unlike $LLMBestDoc$, this is called with context from one document. The prompt is:

> We searched the web and found the following information. Document (*title*, from *site*, published *date*): *context* Based on the above information, please answer the following question. *question*

The entire response is used as the answer.

Paraphrase. The prompt is:

> Please give four ways to rephrase the following question. Give your answer as a JSON list of strings, each string being one question. Question: *question*

LLMVerify. The prompt is:

> We are trying to verify the following claim: *claim* Based on our web searches, we resolved the following questions. 0. $question_0$ $answer_0$ ... k. $question_k$ $answer_k$ Is the claim (A) fully supported by the evidence, or (B) contradicted by the evidence? Please respond in the format `[[A]]` or `[[B]]`.

We search the response for `[[A]]` or `[[B]]`. For the four class variant, the end of the prompt is:

> Is the claim (A) fully supported by the evidence, (B) contradicted by the evidence, (C) insufficient information, or (D) conflicting evidence? Please respond in the format `[[A]]`, `[[B]]`, `[[C]]`, or `[[D]]`.

RAG-Fusion Based Information Retrieval for Fact-Checking

Yuki Momii, Tetsuya Takiguchi, Yasuo Ariki
Graduate School of System Informatics, Kobe University
235x075x@gsuite.kobe-u.ac.jp, {takigu, ariki}@kobe-u.ac.jp

Abstract

Fact-checking involves searching for relevant evidence and determining whether the given claim contains any misinformation. In this paper, we propose a fact verification system based on RAG-Fusion. We use GPT-4o to generate questions from the claim, which helps improve the accuracy of evidence retrieval.

Additionally, we adopt GPT-4o for the final judgment module and refine the prompts to enhance the detection accuracy, particularly when the claim contains misinformation. Experiment showed that our system achieved an AVeriTeC Score of 0.3865 on the AVeriTeC test data, significantly surpassing the baseline score of 0.11.

1 Introduction

In recent years, misinformation has become easier to spread online (Guo et al., 2022). Consequently, to prevent its spread, the demand for automated fact-checking, which automatically detects unreliable information has significantly increased (Nakov et al., 2021). Fact-checking involves searching for information necessary for verification (evidence) from reliable external databases, and determining the truthfulness of given claim based on that information (Zhou et al., 2019).

There are various fact-checking datasets, with unstructured data like text (Thorne et al., 2018; Schuster et al., 2021) and structured data like tables (Wenhu Chen and Wang, 2020; Aly et al., 2021) or knowledge graphs (Kim et al., 2023). Generally, these datasets include a claim, the evidence that needs to be searched to verify the claim, and a label indicating the judgment.

For example, in FEVER (Thorne et al., 2018), claims need to be classified into three labels: "Supported", "Refuted", or "Not Enough Information". Numerous systems have been proposed (DeHaven and Scott, 2023; Krishna et al., 2022; Liu et al., 2020), and the accuracy of this three-class classification has reached nearly 0.8[1]. However, the claims included in these datasets are created from sources like Wikipedia for specific purposes, and they differ from the claims that journalists actually verify. There is a dataset that include real-world data (Wang, 2017), but they face the issue of not providing sufficient evidence necessary for judgment (Schlichtkrull et al., 2023).

In this Shared Task, AVeriTeC(Schlichtkrull et al., 2023) has been newly created. In AVeriTeC, the evidence is based on information collected from the web and is provided in a Question-Answer pair format by human annotators. The judgment labels are: "Supported", "Refuted", "Not Enough Evidence (NEE)", and "Conflicting Evidence/Cherry-picking". Additionally, for each claim, the reasons why annotators assign the judgment labels are annotated.

The system needs to extract evidence from documents obtained through web searches or from documents provided by the organizers as web search results, and then predicts the claim label. The claim is considered correctly judged only if the necessary evidence is appropriately retrieved, and the final judgment label is correctly predicted.

In this paper, we designed the system shown in Figure 1 to improve the AVeriTeC baseline. The baseline system primarily used BM25 (Robertson and Zaragoza, 2009) for evidence collection, but this method does not allow for searching based on the meaning of the claim or web document. Therefore, we perform searches using embedding vectors with stella_en_400M_v5[2]. We generate embedding vectors for the claim and the document, and collect 50 documents related to the claim based on their similarity.

Next, inspired by RAG-Fusion (Rackauckas,

[1] https://competitions.codalab.org/competitions/18814

[2] https://huggingface.co/dunzhang/stella_en_400M_v5

Proceedings of the Seventh Fact Extraction and VERification Workshop (FEVER), pages 47–54
November 15, 2024 ©2024 Association for Computational Linguistics

2024), we use GPT-4o to generate three questions from the claim that are needed to search for the evidence. For each of these generated questions, we select three answer sentences from the previously collected 50 documents. These Question-Answer pairs collected through this procedure are input into GPT-4o along with the claim for the final judgment in verdict inference.

The proposed fact-checking system achieved an AVeriTec score of 0.3865 on the test data.

2 System Description

The system we developed is structured in three phases similar to (Gi et al., 2021): Document Retrieval, Question Generation and Sentence Retrieval and Verdict Inference. **Document Retrieval**: Since the document set provided by the organizers is vast, this phase selects documents related to the claim. **Question Generation and Sentence Retrieval**: Referring to the RAG-Fusion method, questions for information retrieval are generated using GPT-4o from the claim. Subsequently, the sentences that answer these generated questions are retrieved from the sentences contained within the documents selected in the Document Retrieval phase. **Verdict Inference**: Using GPT-4o, which has high inferential capabilities, a judgment is made based on the obtained Question-Answer pairs and the claim. We use GPT-4o via OpenAI API[3].

2.1 Document Retrieval

The AVeriTec dataset provides an average of 999.3 documents per claim, and splitting them into sentences would require extensive resources. Therefore, the target of this phase is to narrow down the candidates at the document level.

In the baseline system, all documents related to a claim were split into sentences, and relevant sentences for each claim were retrieved primarily using BM25. However, this approach doesn't account for paraphrasing or semantic similarity, limiting its search performance. Therefore, we use stella_en_400M_v5 to perform searches for the related documents using embedding vectors. At the time of writing this paper, stella_en_400M_v5 was the highest-performing model under 1B on the MTEB leader-board[4]. Given the vast amount of document to be processed in this dataset, a lightweight model was chosen. Each claim and the documents provided for that claim are converted into embedding vectors, and relevant documents are selected based on similarity. (The prompt used for embedding claim was *s2p_query* (sentence to passage query). When we use stella_en_400M_v5 for embedding search sentence, we can select *s2p_query* or *s2s_query* (sentence to sentence query) depending on our purpose).

[3]https://openai.com/api/

[4]https://huggingface.co/spaces/mteb/leaderboard

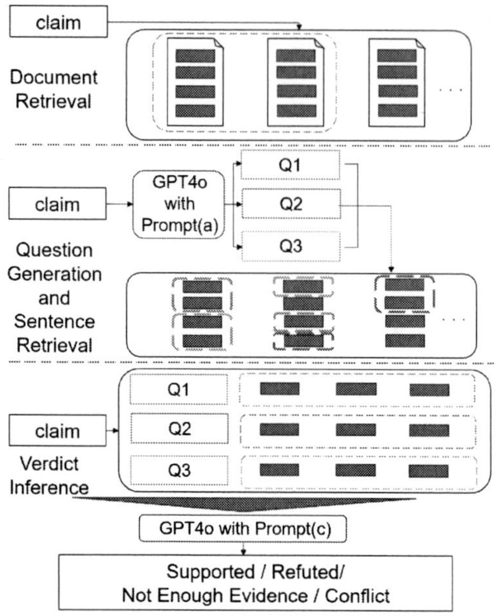

Figure 1: System Overview: Document Retrieval, Question generation and Sentence Retrieval, and Verdict inference. In Document Retrieval, 50 documents are searched. In Sentence Retrieval, up to 3 questions are generated, and for each question, 3 candidate answers are retrieved.

2.2 Question Generation and Sentence Retrieval

After narrowing down documents with Document Retrieval, the document is split into sentences to search for more critical information. The URL of each sentence remains the same as that of the original document before splitting.

The simplest approach is to convert both the claim and each sentence into embedding vectors then retrieve the most similar sentences. On the other hand, a method called RAG-Fusion (Rackauckas, 2024) has been proposed. RAG is a system that searches for relevant information in response to a user's input and uses both the input and the retrieved information to generate a response through

(a) Prompt for question generation from claim

You will be given a text. Your task is to generate up to 3 questions that are necessary to verify the accuracy of the information contained in the text.

Example:
Text: Why should you pay more taxes than Donald Trump pays? And that's a fact. $750. Remember what he said when that was raised a while ago, how he only pays... He said, 'Because I'm smart. I know how to game the system.'
Questions: 1. What was Trump's tax return in 2017
2. When did Trump say he was smart for not paying taxes

(b) Prompt for question generation from answer sentence

I will give you a sentence. Create a question for which this sentence could be the answer.
Output only the question.

Example:
Sentence: Trump Paid $750 in Federal Income Taxes in 2017
Question: What was Trump's tax return in 2017

(c) Prompt for verdict inference with 3 questions

Classify the given claim into four labels: "Supported", "Refuted", "Not Enough Evidence" or "Conflicting Evidence/Cherrypicking".
Your predictions must be based on the given evidence.
The evidence includes questions and three pieces of related information for each question.
If there is even the slightest possibility that it is incorrect, output "Refuted".

Output Format:
"Supported", "Refuted", "Not Enough Evidence" or "Conflicting Evidence/Cherrypicking"

(d) Prompt for verdict inference

Classify the given claim into four labels: "Supported", "Refuted", "Not Enough Evidence" or "Conflicting Evidence/Cherrypicking".
Your predictions must be based on the given evidence.
If there is even the slightest possibility that it is incorrect, output "Refuted".

Output Format:
"Supported", "Refuted", "Not Enough Evidence" or "Conflicting Evidence/Cherrypicking"

(e) Prompt for inferring whether the information is sufficient

```
We are collecting evidence to determine whether
the following claim contains incorrect
information.
Determine if enough information has already been
gathered or if further information is needed.

Output Format:
    "Enough Evidence", "Need More Evidence"
```

Figure 2: Prompts designed for GPT-4o. In our final system, we use (a) and (c). The other prompts are used only for performance evaluation purposes.

a language model (Gao et al., 2024). The concept of retrieving relevant information and using it in subsequent processing is similar to fact-checking.

RAG-Fusion is a method proposed to enhance the retrieval performance of RAG. Instead of directly searching with the user's input, it conducts the search using multiple questions generated from user's input by LLMs (Large Language Models) and re-ranks the external information based on the search results. This approach allows for a broader perspective in the search process compared to searching directly with the user's input, potentially improving search accuracy.

In this study, we focus on RAG-Fusion's ability to retrieve diverse information through search using multiple questions. Using the prompt shown in Figure 2(a), three questions were generated from the claim using GPT-4o to search for information necessary for judgment. At this time, the claim most similar to the target claim was retrieved from the training data (using stella_en_400M_v5), and questions were copied from the evidence annotated to that claim to as the one-shot example included in the prompt. (When experimenting with validation data (500 claims), the claim is retrieved from the training data (3068 claims); when experimenting with test data (2215 claims), it's retrieved from both the training and validation data.)

For each question, three appropriate answers were retrieved, just as before, using stella_en_400M_v5. However, when stella is used to search for similar claims to generate questions, it is set to *s2s_query*; when searching for answers, it is set to *s2p_query*.

2.3 Verdict inference

In the final judgment, based on the created Evidence (Question and Answer), the system must classify the claim into one of four categories: "Supported", "Refuted", "Not Enough Evidence" or "Conflicting Evidence/Cherry-picking". We used GPT-4o for this judgement. In Fact-checking, the most critical error to avoid is mistakenly classifying a "Refuted" claim as another label. Therefore, the prompt includes the instruction: "If there is even the slightest possibility that it is incorrect, output 'Refuted'." The prompt is shown in Figure 2(c).

3 Result

In this chapter, we explain the results at each phase of the system. To consider improving search accuracy, we report the experimental results using a validation dataset (containing 500 claims) where the correct evidence has been distributed. Additionally, when using GPT-4o, the temperature is set to 0 to ensure the reproducibility of the experiments.

3.1 Document Retrieval Result

To verify how many documents could be retrieved necessary for judgment, we utilize the annotated URLs. We counted the number of claims for which the search was successful by comparing the URLs of documents annotated as the necessary sentences for judgment with the URLs of the documents retrieved through embedding vectors (up to a maximum of 500 claims in the validation data). The verification is conducted under two settings: when all the correct URLs are retrieved (All) and when at least one correct URL is retrieved (Easy).

We compared two document retrieval methods: one that uses embedding vectors of claims and documents as described in 2.1, and another that uses the questions generated by the method described in 2.2. The questions generated in 2.2 can also be used for document retrieval. Therefore, each question is converted into an embedding vector and used for document retrieval. We compared whether it is better to use the claim itself or the question generated from the claim for document retrieval.

The search results are shown in Table 1. In the table, "top k" refers to the top k results for each question in the **question-based** search. In other words, the top 25 for each question retrieves the same number of documents as the top 75 in the **claim-based** search (25×3=75). However, in the baseline system of (Schlichtkrull et al., 2023), documents were divided into sentences before the search, so a comparison at this stage cannot be made.

The comparison between the top 75 in claim-based search and the top 25 in question-based search in Table 1 shows that claim-based search yields higher accuracy. Of course, if we increase the top k, search accuracy improves naturally. However, considering computational costs, we decided to retrieve the top 50 documents in claim-based search for this time.

Method	Top k	Easy	All
Claim	Top 75	283	90
	Top 50	247	78
	Top 25	187	54
Question	Top 75	313	115
	Top 50	295	100
	Top 25	242	72

Table 1: Document Retrieval Result

Method	Top k	Easy	All
Base	Top 10	51	14
	Top 3	33	8
	Top 1	17	4
Claim	Top 10	94	27
	Top 3	50	15
	Top 1	26	8
Question	Top 10	143	36
	Top 3	79	19
	Top 1	44	13

Table 2: Sentence Search Result

Method	Q	A	Q+A
Claim (Top 3)	0.3063	0.1814	0.2258
Question (Top 1)	0.3898	0.1699	0.2436

Table 3: Evidence evaluation score of Sentence Search Result

3.2 Sentence Retrieval Results

We compare the performance of sentence retrieval using BM25 at the baseline and retrieval using embedding vectors. In the original baseline, a re-ranker was employed, but the results before introducing the re-ranker are shown for performance comparison. For retrieval using embedding vectors, we employ two methods: one based on the RAG-Fusion method explained in 2.2 and another based on the claim-based retrieval method. Similar to the comparison in 3.1, the top k retrieval results using the question correspond to the number of documents retrieved in the top 3k using the claim.

For evaluation, we report scores based on whether all correct URLs were retrieved or at least one correct URL was retrieved, using the URLs obtained from the retrieved sentences and the correct URLs. The results are shown in Table 2.

When comparing the top 1 in the question-based retrieval and the top 3 in the claim-based retrieval, the retrieval performance is nearly equivalent. Both methods yield higher scores than the baseline. Of course, this evaluation simply calculates the score based on URLs, so there might be cases where an unrelated sentence from the same document as the correct answer is retrieved. Therefore, we also report the evidence evaluation score used in this Shared Task. The evidence evaluation score is calculated as following:

$$u_f(\hat{Y}, Y) = \frac{1}{|Y|} \max \sum_{\hat{y} \in \hat{Y}} \sum_{y \in Y} f(\hat{y}, y) X(\hat{y}, y) \tag{1}$$

Here, X is a boolean function denoting the assignment: $\hat{Y} \times Y \rightarrow \{0,\ 1\}$. $\hat{Y}$ is generated se-

Method	Q	Q+A	Label Accuracy	AVeriTec Score (.1, .2, .25)		
Claim (Top 3)	0.3063	0.2258	0.568	0.528	0.336	0.198
Question (Top 1)	0.3898	0.2436	0.612	0.588	0.384	0.264
Question (Top 3)	0.3898	0.2757	0.692	0.676	0.524	0.38
Gold Evidence	1.0	1.0	0.858	0.858	0.858	0.858

Table 4: Results of claim-based method and question-based method on the validation dataset. AVeriTec Scores are conditioned on correct evidence (Q+A) at λ=(0.1, 0.2, 0.25)

quences and Y is the reference sequences. f is a pairwise scoring function: $\hat{Y} \times Y \rightarrow \mathbb{R}$.

In the Shared Task, two scenarios are evaluated: one where only the question from the QA pair provided as necessary information for the judgment is used, and another where the combination of the question and the answer is used. In this paper, to compare performance in more detail, we also included the scenario where only the answer is used.

In retrieval with the claim and the baseline, the relevant sentences associated with the claim have been retrieved at this point. Consequently information corresponding to the answer has been retrieved. However, the part corresponding to the question has not yet been created. Therefore, we used GPT-4o to generate a question that would match the retrieved sentence as an answer. In this way, we created Question-Answer pairs in the same format as the correct evidence provided for the judgment. The prompt used is shown in Figure 2(b), and the scores are shown in Table 3.

The comparison between claim-based and question-based approaches shows that the pre-creation of questions yields higher Question scores, which in turn improves the Question+Answer scores. On the other hand, the score for the answer alone is slightly higher when using the approach of retrieving with the claim alone and then generating the question afterward. Since this evaluation metric only assesses sequence match, it is difficult to determine superiority at this point. Therefore, we decided to calculate the performance of both methods in the next Verdict Inference and select the approach with higher accuracy.

3.3 Verdict Inference Result

For the final evaluation, we employed GPT-4o. Using the prompt shown in Figure 2(d), we compare the results of Question Top 1 and Claim Top 3.

In the Shared Task, a judgment was considered correct only when the evidence evaluation score (Eq. (1)) exceeded a certain threshold and the final judgment was correct (AVeriTeC Score). However,

Example Evidence of for verdict inference with 3 questions

{'**question**': 'Did Sean Connery write a letter to Steve Jobs?',
'**answer**': "This is a letter Sean Connery wrote didn't write in response to Steve Jobs after being asked to appear in an Apple ad.",
{'**question**': '',
'**answer**': 'First, the bad news. Sean Connery never actually sent a typewritten letter to Steve Jobs in 1998 refusing to be in an Apple ad}
{'**question**': '',
'**answer**': 'Pingback: Did Sean Connery Write an Angry Letter to Steve Jobs? | wafflesatnoon.com'}

Figure 3: Example of increasing the number of possible answers to a question to three. For each claim, three evidences are created that are the same as the following QA pairs.

the AVeriTeC Score is solely based on sequence matching and does not account for the meaning of the sentences. Moreover, it is possible to retrieve information useful for judgment outside of the correct evidence. This indicates that the evidence retrieval may not have been adequately evaluated by AVeriTeC Score.

Therefore, in addition to the AVeriTeC Score, we compared how well the four-class classification of final judgments was performed using Label Accuracy, ignoring the Evidence evaluation score. Since the Label Accuracy is expected to be higher when the necessary evidence for judgment is retrieved, it can be considered an indicator of how well the evidence retrieval was performed. Additionally, since no comparison with the correct Evidence is required, the problem with AVeriTeC Score, where useful information must be retrieved from sources other than the correct evidence, does not become an issue (though there is a possibility of accidentally making the correct judgment based on inappropriate evidence).

The experimental results are shown in Table 4. A comparison of the first and second rows of this table shows that the Label Accuracy for Question Top 1 is higher than the Label Accuracy for Claim Top 3. This suggests that with the current Evidence evaluation score, a small difference in Answer scores

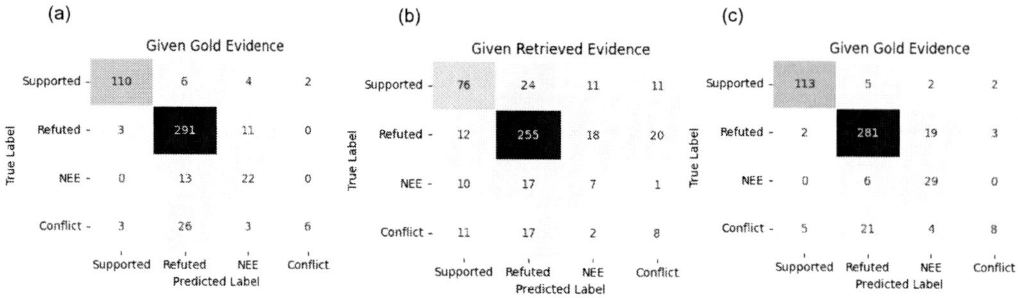

Figure 4: Confusion Matrix of verdict result of GPT-4o. (a) Given gold evidence with prompt Figure 2(d), (b) Given Retrieved evidence with prompt Figure 2(c), (c) Given gold evidence with removing "If there is even the slightest possibility that it is incorrect, output "Refuted"" from prompt Figure 2(d)

of around 0.1, as observed in Table 3, cannot be conclusively interpreted as a decline in retrieval performance.

To further improve the score,we considered the top 3 search results for each question (i.e., when a total of 9 sentences were retrieved). Then we included the Top 3 sentences as Evidence, noting the increase in URL hit rate (Table 2). However, if there are three answers for each question, each question will be reused three times. In this case, if an appropriate question can be created, there is concern that the evidence evaluation score may be unfairly high. Therefore, as shown in Figure 3, we used only the QA pair for the Top 1 answer, leaving the Question field empty for the Top 2 and Top 3 answers, and including them as evidence. In competitions using this dataset, participants can use up to 10 QA pairs. By following this limitation, we select the Top 3 answer sentence. This approach allowed for a fair evaluation of the AVeriTeC Score. The prompt given to GPT-4o in this case is shown in Figure 2(c). The judgment results are shown in the third row of Table 4, where both the Evidence score and judgment score improved by considering more Evidence.

Based on these results on validation dataset, the final form of the system was determined to involve searching based on RAG-Fusion, including three candidate answers in the questions, and making the final judgment using GPT-4o. The scores on the test data were Q 0.3774, Q+A 0.2851, and AVeriTeC Score 0.3865, with a rank of 8 on the leader-board.

4 Error Analysis

Figure 4(a)(b) shows the confusion matrix when the correct data or retrieved data using a RAG-Fusion-based search is provided. It can be seen that when the correct label is "NEE (Not Enough Evidence)" or "Conflict", there is a tendency to predict it as "Refuted". This is likely due to the instruction included in the prompt: "If there is even the slightest possibility that it is incorrect, output 'Refuted'." However, in Fact-checking, to accurately predict "Refuted" claims as Refuted is the most important. Since it is crucial not to provide the user with incorrect information, it is undesirable to remove this instruction from the prompt.

Figure 4(c) shows the confusion matrix when this instruction is removed and the correct evidence is provided, revealing an increased risk of failing to detect Refuted claims, even when the information is complete.

To address this, adopting the concept of Corrective Retrieval Augmented Generation (CRAG) (Yan et al., 2024) could be considered for "NEE". In CRAG, a new module is introduced to determine whether the retrieved document is necessary or not. If we incorporate the module into our system, we could first determine whether the information is enough or not. If the information is not enough, the system would classify it as "NEE". If the information is enough, the system would proceed to classify the remaining three classes using the similar prompt as in 2(d). By adopting this new module, we will be able to improve the performance of "NEE".

As a test, using GPT-4o, we performed a two-class classification—whether the information was complete—using the prompt from Figure 2(e) with the correct data provided. In this task, "Supported", "Refuted", and "Conflict" were considered as having complete information, while "NEE" was considered as lacking information. The accuracy rates were 90% for "Supported", 86% for "Refuted", 60% for "NEE", and 78% for "Conflict". Therefore, further prompt improvements are needed to adapt GPT-4o to this two-stage approach. Fine-tuning BERT should also be considered.

The "Conflict" class is difficult to render a verdict on, so further improvements will be necessary.

5 Another Approach

In this section, we will introduce a classification approach that we experimented with but did not yield satisfactory results. Although the performance did not exceed that of GPT-4o's 4-class classification, we will present it here in the hope that it may contribute to future efforts by other participants.

We considered fine-tuning BERT as the final classifier for 4-class classification. However, the dataset exhibits a bias in the classification labels (in the training data: "Supported" 27.6%, "Refuted" 56.8%, "Not Enough Evidence (NEE)" 6.4%, "Conflicting Evidence/Cherry-picking" 9.2%). In particular, the "NEE" and "Conflict" labels are underrepresented. To address this, we devised two separate classifiers: one for "Supported" and another for "Refuted". These classifiers perform binary classification, with the Supported classifier determining whether a claim is "Supported" or not, and the "Refuted" classifier determining whether a claim is "Refuted" or not. The final prediction label for the claim is then determined based on the results of these classifiers.

If the Supported classifier predicts True and the Refuted classifier predicts False, the final prediction is "Supported". Conversely, if the Supported classifier predicts False and the Refuted classifier predicts True, the final decision is "Refuted". If both classifiers predict False, the decision is "NEE", and if both predict True, it is "Conflict". This approach can mitigate the issue of label imbalance. For example, in the Supported classifier, claims that are annotated as "Supported" are used as positive examples, while "Refuted" and "NEE" claims are used as negative examples. This allows for similar treatment of "Refuted" and "NEE" labels.

We fine-tuned bert-base-uncased[5] for both a 4-class classifier and the combined two-classifier approach (batch size=32, learning rate=1e-5, with the training data split 9:1 and used for fine-tuning). The label accuracy on the validation data, when provided with correct evidence, was 0.536 for the 4-class classifier and 0.60 for the combined two-classifier approach. These results indicate that combining the two classifiers yields higher accuracy. However, as shown in the fourth row of Table 4, simply using GPT-4o for 4-class classification achieves a sufficiently high accuracy of 0.858, so this approach was not adopted for our system. We also conducted experiments where GPT-4o was assigned the task of the two classifiers, but the Refuted classifier did not perform well. We believe the issue arises because the difference between being "Refuted" and lacking the evidence to determine if it is "Refuted" has become unclear.

6 Conclusion

This paper discusses a method for solving the AVeriTeC Task. The proposed system, inspired by RAG Fusion, pre-generates questions for information retrieval. This approach allows for a greater amount of information to be used in searches compared to using only the claims. The Label Accuracy and AVeriTec Score showed that pre-generating questions resulted in higher accuracy.

Proposing an evaluation metric that can consider information beyond the currently accepted evidence when making judgments may lead to more appropriate progress in future research and development. Given the rapid advancement of LLMs, there is also a need to conduct research on adopting LLMs for the evaluation of evidence validity.

Limitation

In this system, the search for answers to questions is conducted using embedding vectors. This approach carries the risk of reducing the validity of the Question-Answer pairs compared to the method where the relevant sentences are searched first and the question is generated afterward. However, as shown in Table 4 of the current dataset, the approach of generating the question first and then searching for the answer yields higher accuracy, indicating that the validity of the Question-Answer pairs has not been compromised. Nonetheless, when the search for answers is more challenging, such as in highly specialized domains like medicine or biology, it is necessary to carefully verify the validity of the QA pairs.

While the current system primarily uses GPT-4o, further experiments with other models are necessary to verify its generalizability.

[5] https://huggingface.co/google-bert/bert-base-uncased

Acknowledgments

This work was supported in part by JSPS KAKENHI (Grant No. JP23K20733).

References

Rami Aly, Zhijiang Guo, Michael Sejr Schlichtkrull, James Thorne, Andreas Vlachos, Christos Christodoulopoulos, Oana Cocarascu, and Arpit Mittal. 2021. The fact extraction and VERification over unstructured and structured information (FEVEROUS) shared task. In *Proceedings of the Fourth Workshop on Fact Extraction and VERification (FEVER)*, pages 1–13, Dominican Republic. Association for Computational Linguistics.

Mitchell DeHaven and Stephen Scott. 2023. BEVERS: A general, simple, and performant framework for automatic fact verification. In *Proceedings of the Sixth Fact Extraction and VERification Workshop (FEVER)*, pages 58–65, Dubrovnik, Croatia. Association for Computational Linguistics.

Yunfan Gao, Yun Xiong, Xinyu Gao, Kangxiang Jia, Jinliu Pan, Yuxi Bi, Yi Dai, Jiawei Sun, Meng Wang, and Haofen Wang. 2024. Retrieval-augmented generation for large language models: A survey. *Preprint*, arXiv:2312.10997.

In-Zu Gi, Ting-Yu Fang, and Richard Tzong-Han Tsai. 2021. Verdict inference with claim and retrieved elements using RoBERTa. In *Proceedings of the Fourth Workshop on Fact Extraction and VERification (FEVER)*, pages 60–65, Dominican Republic. Association for Computational Linguistics.

Zhijiang Guo, Michael Schlichtkrull, and Andreas Vlachos. 2022. A survey on automated fact-checking. *Transactions of the Association for Computational Linguistics*, 10:178–206.

Jiho Kim, Sungjin Park, Yeonsu Kwon, Yohan Jo, James Thorne, and Edward Choi. 2023. FactKG: Fact verification via reasoning on knowledge graphs. In *Proceedings of the 61st Annual Meeting of the Association for Computational Linguistics (Volume 1: Long Papers)*, pages 16190–16206, Toronto, Canada. Association for Computational Linguistics.

Amrith Krishna, Sebastian Riedel, and Andreas Vlachos. 2022. ProoFVer: Natural logic theorem proving for fact verification. *Transactions of the Association for Computational Linguistics*, 10:1013–1030.

Zhenghao Liu, Chenyan Xiong, Maosong Sun, and Zhiyuan Liu. 2020. Fine-grained fact verification with kernel graph attention network. In *Proceedings of the 58th Annual Meeting of the Association for Computational Linguistics*, pages 7342–7351, Online. Association for Computational Linguistics.

Preslav Nakov, David Corney, Maram Hasanain, Firoj Alam, Tamer Elsayed, Alberto Barrón-Cedeño, Paolo Papotti, Shaden Shaar, and Giovanni Da San Martino. 2021. Automated fact-checking for assisting human fact-checkers. In *Proceedings of the Thirtieth International Joint Conference on Artificial Intelligence, IJCAI-21*, pages 4551–4558. International Joint Conferences on Artificial Intelligence Organization. Survey Track.

Zackary Rackauckas. 2024. Rag-fusion: A new take on retrieval augmented generation. *International Journal on Natural Language Computing*, 13(1):37–47.

Stephen Robertson and Hugo Zaragoza. 2009. The probabilistic relevance framework: Bm25 and beyond. *Foundations and Trends in Information Retrieval*, 3:333–389.

Michael Sejr Schlichtkrull, Zhijiang Guo, and Andreas Vlachos. 2023. Averitec: A dataset for real-world claim verification with evidence from the web. In *Thirty-seventh Conference on Neural Information Processing Systems Datasets and Benchmarks Track*.

Tal Schuster, Adam Fisch, and Regina Barzilay. 2021. Get your vitamin C! robust fact verification with contrastive evidence. In *Proceedings of the 2021 Conference of the North American Chapter of the Association for Computational Linguistics: Human Language Technologies*, pages 624–643, Online. Association for Computational Linguistics.

James Thorne, Andreas Vlachos, Christos Christodoulopoulos, and Arpit Mittal. 2018. FEVER: a large-scale dataset for fact extraction and VERification. In *Proceedings of the 2018 Conference of the North American Chapter of the Association for Computational Linguistics: Human Language Technologies, Volume 1 (Long Papers)*, pages 809–819, New Orleans, Louisiana. Association for Computational Linguistics.

William Yang Wang. 2017. "liar, liar pants on fire": A new benchmark dataset for fake news detection. In *Proceedings of the 55th Annual Meeting of the Association for Computational Linguistics (Volume 2: Short Papers)*, pages 422–426, Vancouver, Canada. Association for Computational Linguistics.

Jianshu Chen Yunkai Zhang Hong Wang Shiyang Li Xiyou Zhou Wenhu Chen, Hongmin Wang and William Yang Wang. 2020. Tabfact : A large-scale dataset for table-based fact verification. In *International Conference on Learning Representations (ICLR)*, Addis Ababa, Ethiopia.

Shi-Qi Yan, Jia-Chen Gu, Yun Zhu, and Zhen-Hua Ling. 2024. Corrective retrieval augmented generation. *Preprint*, arXiv:2401.15884.

Jie Zhou, Xu Han, Cheng Yang, Zhiyuan Liu, Lifeng Wang, Changcheng Li, and Maosong Sun. 2019. GEAR: Graph-based evidence aggregating and reasoning for fact verification. In *Proceedings of the 57th Annual Meeting of the Association for Computational Linguistics*, pages 892–901, Florence, Italy. Association for Computational Linguistics.

UHH at AVeriTeC: RAG for Fact-Checking with Real-World Claims

Özge Sevgili, Irina Nikishina, Seid Muhie Yimam, Martin Semmann, Chris Biemann

Language Technology Group, Dept. of Informatics &
Hub of Computing and Data Science,
Universität Hamburg
Germany
{oezge.sevgili.ergueven,irina.nikishina,seid.muhie.yimam,
martin.semmann,chris.biemann}@uni-hamburg.de

Abstract

This paper presents UHH's approach developed for the AVeriTeC shared task. The goal of the challenge is to verify given real-world claims with evidences from the Web. In this shared task, we investigate a Retrieval-Augmented Generation (RAG) model, which mainly contains retrieval, generation, and augmentation components. We start with the selection of the top 10k evidences via BM25 scores, and continue with two approaches to retrieve the most similar evidences: (1) to retrieve top 10 evidences through vector similarity, generate questions for them, and rerank them or (2) to generate questions for the claim and retrieve the most similar evidence, again, through vector similarity. After retrieving the top evidences, a Large Language Model (LLM) is prompted using the claim along with either all evidences or individual evidence to predict the label. Our system submission, **UHH**, using the first approach and individual evidence prompts, ranks 6th out of 23 systems.

1 Introduction

Fact-checking is a process to (automatically) assess the truthfulness of a claim, which is an important task for some domains, e.g. journalism (Guo et al., 2022; Thorne et al., 2018; Thorne and Vlachos, 2018; Vlachos and Riedel, 2014). The AVeriTeC shared task[1](Schlichtkrull et al., 2023) aims at dealing with the challenge of verifying real-world claims with pieces of evidence from the Web, as shown in Figure 1.

Recently, Retrieval-Augmented Generation (RAG) provides a remedy for some issues of Large Language Models (LLMs), e.g. hallucination, while increasing the performance of especially knowledge-intensive tasks, including fact-checking (Gao et al., 2024). Motivated by this, we investigate how to effectively leverage such a method in this shared task.

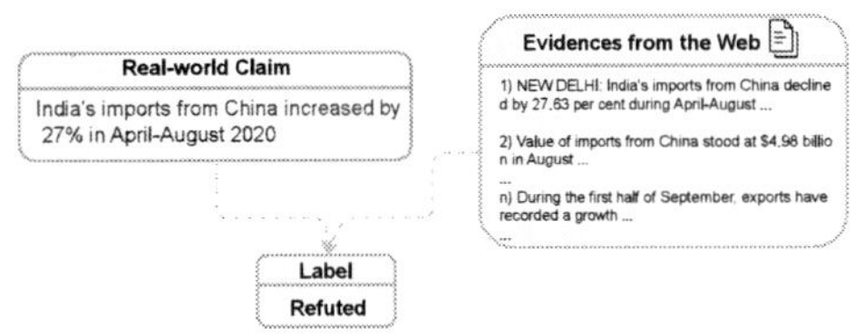

Figure 1: An example claim and several example evidences for this claim provided by organizers.

Our submission's pipeline is as follows; evidences (in the form of short texts like sentences[2]) per claim provided by task organizers are ranked using BM25 (Robertson and Zaragoza, 2009) and the top 10k evidences are selected. For retrieving the most relevant evidences, we consider two approaches: (1) **Retrieve-Question:** retrieving the most similar 10 evidences using vector similarity and generating questions for these evidences. Then, evidences are reranked again based on vector similarity with evidences in the form of question-answer.; (2) **Question-Retrieve:** generating questions for a claim, inspired from Chen et al. (2022), where they see an improvement for the retrieval with decomposed questions. We retrieve the single-best evidence per a question using vector similarity. The two approaches perform competitively in the development set. In the last step, we prompt LLM with the retrieved evidences to predict the label. We experiment to prompt with either all evidences or one evidence at a time. In our experiments, prompting with individual evidence can reach higher scores. Note that our pipeline resembles the steps conducted in the organizer's baseline (Schlichtkrull et al., 2023), especially in the Retrieve-Question approach, for more details see Section 4.

The contributions of this paper as follows:

- We investigate the use of RAG in the fact-

[1] https://fever.ai/task.html

[2] Thus, we use evidence and sentence, interchangeably.

Proceedings of the Seventh Fact Extraction and VERification Workshop (FEVER), pages 55–63
November 15, 2024 ©2024 Association for Computational Linguistics

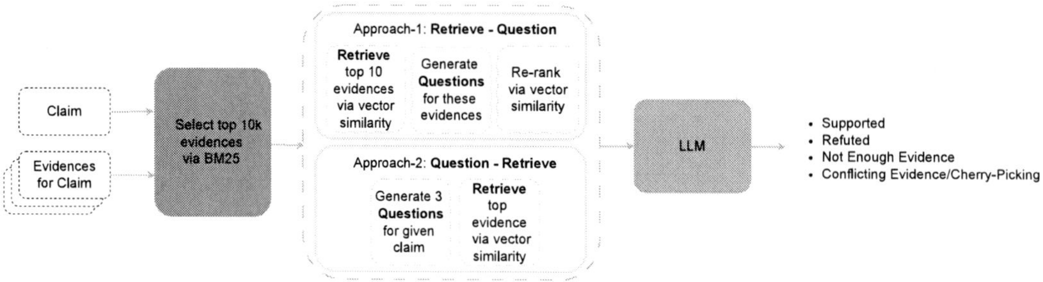

Figure 2: Inputs are the claim and evidences for this claim provided by task organizers. Top 10k evidences are selected with BM25 scores. Top question-sentence pairs are retrieved with Approach-1 (Retrieve-Question) or Approach-2 (Question-Retrieve). An output label is generated with LLM, prompted with either all pairs or individual pair.

checking task with real-world claims and evidences from the Web.

- We increase the baseline AVeriTeC score by more than three times, from 0.11 to 0.45, ranking 6th among 23 systems.

Considering the fact that our method is highly similar to the baseline, we also provide a list of main differences and/or improvements:

- We use top-10 evidences instead of top-3;
- We select 10K sentences with BM25 instead of 100 in baseline;
- Our Approach 2 is different than their pipeline;
- For veracity prediction, we rely on RAG-based predictions, i.e. incorporate evidence(s) into the prompt, while they use a finetuned BERT-large model.

Our code[3] is publicly available. The remainder of the paper is structured as follows. We continue with the background, and then the methodology is explained in detail. In subsequent sections, we present the experimental setup and discuss the results. And finally, conclusions, future work, and limitations are discussed.

2 Background

Retrieval-Augmented Generation LLMs have shown good performance on many tasks with their emergent abilities, e.g. in-context learning (Zhao et al., 2023). Yet, they still have some issues, e.g. hallucination. To resolve such issues, RAG integrates external information into LLMs (Fan et al., 2024; Gao et al., 2024; Li et al., 2024). Recently, many techniques have been developed for RAG in many aspects, for example, RaLLe (Hoshi et al., 2023) provides a framework for the evaluation of RAG approaches. Additionally, RAG has been applied to many tasks, e.g. question answering, fact checking, etc. We refer the readers to surveys, e.g. by Fan et al. (2024); Gao et al. (2024), for more information.

Fact-Checking It is a challenging task to automate a fact-checking process (Guo et al., 2022; Thorne and Vlachos, 2018), with different issues, for example, Chen et al. (2022) discuss the challenges of complex political claims. Many datasets have been developed for this task, e.g. the FEVER (Thorne et al., 2018) dataset from Wikipedia sources. In the AVeriTeC shared task, the dataset contains real-world claims, as shown in Figure 1, annotated with question-answer pairs.

3 Methodology

Overview The pipeline used in our solution is shown in Figure 2. Evidences per claim provided by task organizers are first ranked using BM25 (Robertson and Zaragoza, 2009). The highest-ranked 10k evidences to an input claim are selected. We have experimented two approaches to select the most similar evidences: (1) retrieving top 10 evidences first and then generating questions from evidences (Retrieve-Question), or (2) generating questions for a claim and retrieving the most similar evidence per question (Question-Retrieve). After the most similar evidences to a claim are retrieved, they are used to prompt LLM together with a claim.

[3]https://github.com/uhh-hcds/UHH-at-AVeriTeC

```
From the sentence below, please
formulate 1 question that could be
answered with this question. This
question and answer should help to do
the fact checking for the claim that
is also given. Which question would be
asked to get this asnwer given that we
need to know whether the claim is true?
Examples:
claim: ...
answer: ...
question: ...
...
```

Figure 3: Prompt for Retrieve-Question Approach

Based on an LLM response, one of the labels, `Supported`, `Refuted`, `Not Enough Evidence`, `Conflicting Evidence/Cherrypicking`, is assigned.

3.1 Selecting Evidences via BM25

The task organizers provide a document collection in the form of short text for each claim. First, we make all sentences unique by keeping url references, to reduce the computation time and keep provenance. We apply BM25 to rank these evidences per claim. Then, the top 10K closest evidences to a given claim are selected.

3.2 Approach-1: Retrieve-Question

In this approach, vector representations for a claim and 10k sentences are created. Vector similarities between each sentence and claim are computed. The most similar 10 sentences to a claim are retrieved. Next, we generate a question using LLM for each of these top 10 sentences with the prompt, which is shown in Figure 3.

The vector representations for question + answer and claim are created. Evidences are reranked based on similarity of claim and each evidence in the form of question and answer. We experiment with {3,5,7,10} evidences for the next step.

3.3 Approach-2: Question-Retrieve

First, 3 questions are generated for each claim using the prompt in Figure 4. For each question, the most similar sentence is selected using the similarity between vectors of 10K sentences and the question and claim vector.

```
From the sentence below, please
formulate up to 3 questions to help
to do the fact-checking. What do we
need to know to check whether the
claim is true? "Decompose" the claim
into subquestions. Generate as few
questions as possible.
Example:
claim: ...
questions: ...
...
```

Figure 4: Prompt for Question-Retrieve Approach

3.4 LLM Strategies

In the typical RAG (Gao et al., 2024), all selected documents and claims are combined into a prompt. We experiment two ways, either as in the common RAG or to utilize one retrieved document at a time and then based on individual predictions, assign one label, inspired from the baseline (Schlichtkrull et al., 2023). The prompt[4] that we use in our experiments for the first alternative is shown in Figure 5.

```
<s>[INST]
Classify the claim into “Supported”,
“Refuted”, “Not Enough Evidence”, or
“Conflicting Evidence/Cherrypicking”
based on list of evidences.
No Explanation, No Note! Your respond
should be in JSON format containing
`“label”` key-value pair without any
further information. For instance,
```json
{
“label”: “Supported”
}
```
User Claim: ...
Evidences: [...]
Class: [/INST]
```

Figure 5: Prompt for a label with all evidences

The prompt for the second option also includes a prediction of a score, as shown in Figure 6. The score prediction is only used to assign a label `Not Enough Evidence`. If LLM has no pre-

[4]We use as a reference: `https://www.pinecone.io/learn/mixtral-8x7b/`

diction of Refuted or Supported (or it generates something different or more), and the score is smaller than or equal to 0.5, then Not Enough Evidence is assigned. Therefore, a smaller score is used for the Not Enough Evidence label. We have two strategies to assign a final label from individual evidence labels. In the first one, similar to the baseline, if all labels from evidences are the same, this label is assigned, otherwise Conflicting Evidence/Cherrypicking. In the other one, again if there is only one label, the predicted label will be assigned; if there are only two different labels from evidences, then the majority is assigned. Otherwise, Conflicting Evidence/Cherrypicking is assigned.

LLM might generate different texts than only the label output, in these cases, we assign Refuted, as it is the most common label in the training set[5].

```
<s>[INST]
Classify the claim into "Supported" or
"Refuted" based on list of evidences.
Produce a score for the class label.
No Explanation, No Note! Your respond
should be in JSON format containing
`"label"` key-value pair without any
further information. For instance,
```json
{
"label": "Supported"
"score": 0.7
}
```
User Claim: ...
Evidence: ...
Class: [/INST]
```

Figure 6: Prompt for a label with individual evidence

4 Experimental Setup

4.1 Data, Evaluation, and Baseline

Data The task organizers provide real-world claim files for training, development, and testing that contain 3068, 500, 2215 samples, respectively. They also provide document collections for each claim from the Web, and we leverage these given document collections.

Evaluation Evaluation is done by organizers and based on the agreement between predicted evidences and gold ones with the scoring function of METEOR (Banerjee and Lavie, 2005), computing for question-only pairs (Q) or question and answer pairs (Q+A). If this evidence score is higher than a cutoff value of 0.25, then veracity predictions are evaluated, referred to as Veracity@25 or AVeriTeC score, in this paper. For more information, we refer to the paper by Schlichtkrull et al. (2023).

Baseline The pipeline in the baseline, provided by organizers, starts with collecting evidences from the Web by searching via Google Search API for each claim. Our Retrieve-Question approach pipeline is similar to their pipeline. For example, the next step in the AVeriTeC approach is to filter top 100 sentences using BM25, and then to generate a question for each sentence using BLOOM (Workshop et al., 2023). The question-answer pairs are reranked with a fine-tuned BERT-large model (Devlin et al., 2019). The number of top evidences and models differ in our experiments. For final step of the veracity prediction, AVeriTeC leverages a fine-tuned BERT-large model for an individual question-answer pair prediction with a label of supporting, refuting, or irrelevant. If all labels are Supported or Refuted, the respective one is assigned, else if there are both labels, Conflicting Evidence/CherryPicking is assigned. If no label is assigned based on these two conditions, then Not Enough Evidence is assigned. Our LLM strategy with individual prompt (Figure 6) along with the first strategy is similar to their veracity prediction.

4.2 Implementation Details

For the computation of vectors, we use the model Alibaba-NLP/gte-base-en-v1.5[6] (Li et al., 2023; Zhang et al., 2024), which is available in Hugging Face (Wolf et al., 2020), using sentence-transformers (Reimers and Gurevych, 2019). We choose this model from Hugging Face's MTEB leaderboard[7] by using the "Retrieval" task and the "FEVER" data, as we consider this task and data are relevant to the shared task. This model was ranked 2nd in the leaderboard[8];

[5]For the best model with unique sentences (with veracity score, 0.40) in Table 1, we assigned Refuted for 1573 evidences over 5000 evidences, while for test submission 6767 over 22150 evidences were assigned Refuted.

[6]https://huggingface.co/Alibaba-NLP/gte-base-en-v1.5

[7]https://huggingface.co/spaces/mteb/leaderboard

[8]checked on a date - 08.07.2024

LLM	Retrieval Approach	LLM prompt	top-n	unique sentences	Q	Q+A	Veracity@0.25
Mixtral-8x7B-Instruct-v0.1 (quantized 4bit)	Question-Retrieve	1	3	✔	0.37	0.24	0.19
Mixtral-8x7B-Instruct-v0.1 (quantized 4bit)	Retrieve-Question	1	3	✔	0.40	0.24	0.19
Mixtral-8x7B-Instruct-v0.1 (quantized 4bit)	Retrieve-Question	1	5	✔	0.44	0.27	0.23
Mixtral-8x7B-Instruct-v0.1 (quantized 4bit)	Retrieve-Question	1	7	✔	0.46	0.28	0.27
Mixtral-8x7B-Instruct-v0.1 (quantized 4bit)	Retrieve-Question	1	10	✔	0.48	0.30	0.30
Mixtral-8x7B-Instruct-v0.1 (quantized 4bit)	Retrieve-Question	2-1	10	✔	0.48	0.30	0.19
Mixtral-8x7B-Instruct-v0.1 (quantized 4bit)	Retrieve-Question	2-2	10	✔	**0.48**	**0.30**	**0.40**
Mixtral-8x7B-Instruct-v0.1 (quantized 4bit)	Retrieve-Question	2-2	10	✘	**0.49**	**0.31**	**0.42**
Meta-Llama-3.1-8B-Instruct (quantized 4bit)	Retrieve-Question	2-2	10	✔	0.48	0.30	0.26
GPT-4o-mini	Retrieve-Question	2-2	10	✔	0.48	0.30	0.38
Baseline					0.24	0.19	0.09

Table 1: Results of different approaches on the development for Q, Q+A, Veracity@0.25 scores are shown. Baseline is provided by task organizers. **LLM:** name of LLM model, used in the generation step. **Retrieval Approach:** either Retrieve-Question (first retrieve sentences with vector similarity, generate questions for sentences, and rerank with vector similarity, including questions) or Question-Retrieve (generate questions for a claim and retrieve a sentence based on vector similarity, including questions). **LLM prompt:** either all evidences at once (1) or one by one (2) - (2-1, 2-2) used strategy 1 or 2 for a final label assignment. **top-n:** number of evidences used for the prompt. **unique sentence:** either to make sentences unique before BM25 or not.

however, we preferred it over the first-ranked model due to a lower dimension size of 768.

For question generation, we experiment with `GPT-4o-mini` LLM from OpenAI. For the LLM in the generation step, we have experimented with `mistralai/Mixtral-8x7B-Instruct-v0.1`, `Meta-Llama-3.1-8B-Instruct`[9] with 4-bit quantized, also available in Hugging Face and `GPT-4o-mini`. For BM25, we use the rank-25 library[10], as used in the baseline system, and we use the NLTK library (Bird et al., 2009) to tokenize claims and evidences.

5 Results

We report Q, Q+A, and Veracity@0.25 scores in Table 1, for the development set. According to the results, the veracity scores for Question-Retrieve and Retrieve-Question for the top 3 are the same, however, we continue with Retrieve-Question since the Q score is slightly higher. Although the difference is not that much, we continue with the higher one. Leveraging the top 10 evidences reaches best among top {3, 5, 7, 10} evidences. Prompting LLM with all evidences (LLM prompt 1 – Figure 5), is better than prompting individually with labeling strategy 1 (LLM prompt 2-1 – Figure 6), however, strategy - 2 (LLM prompt 2-2 – Figure 6) reaches higher score. As explained in Section 3.1, we make sentences unique to reduce the computation time, yet for the development set we have also experimented without applying this, as marked with a cross in the "unique sentence" field in Table 1 and observed an improvement. However, since the number of evidences is larger in the test set, we rather prefer to compute with unique sentences for efficiency. We also experiment with two different LLMs, namely `Meta-Llama-3.1-8B-Instruct` and `GPT-4o-mini` with the same prompt, the latter one is competitive with the `Mixtral-8x7B-Instruct-v0.1`.

[9]https://huggingface.co/mistralai/Mixtral-8x7B-Instruct-v0.1, https://huggingface.co/meta-llama/Llama-3.1-8B-Instruct with pipeline parameters top_k=50 and repetition_penalty=1.204819277108434 by referencing Hoshi et al. (2023), and do_sample=False and max_new_tokens=32

[10]https://pypi.org/project/rank-bm25/

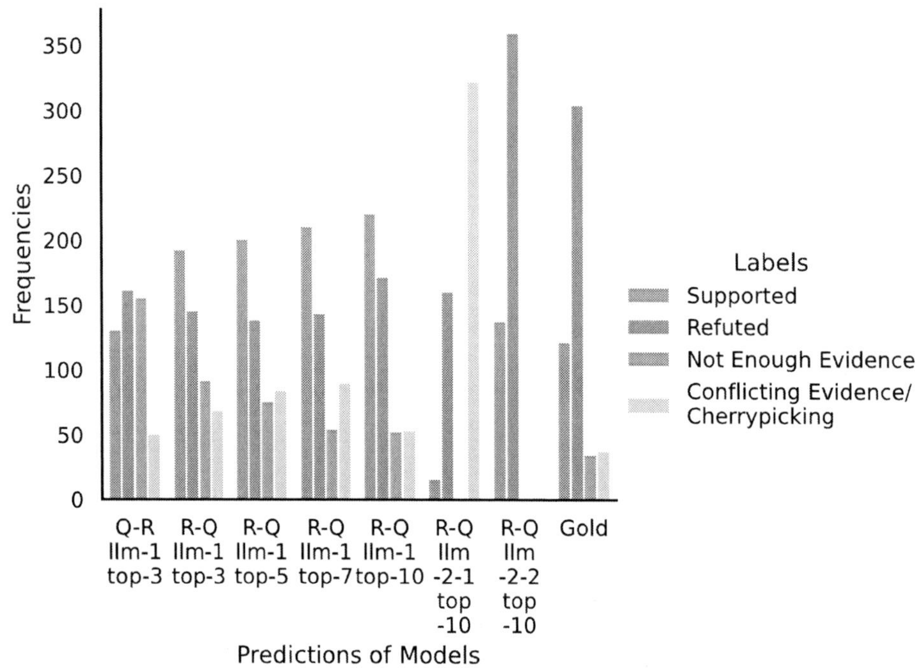

Figure 7: The frequencies of the predicted labels for different model configurations and gold labels on the development set are shown. **Q-R/R-Q:** Question-Retrieve or Retrieve-Question approach. Other configurations are the same as in Table 1.

Rank	Participant Team	Q	Q+A	AVeriTeC
1	TUDA_MAI	0.45	0.34	**0.63**
2	HUMANE	0.48	**0.35**	0.57
3	CTU AIC	0.46	0.32	0.50
4	Dunamu-ml	**0.49**	**0.35**	0.50
5	Papelo	0.44	0.30	0.48
6	**UHH**	0.48	0.32	0.45
20	Baseline	0.24	0.20	0.11

Table 2: Results of baseline and models ranked above our system, UHH, on the test computed and provided by task organizers for Q, Q+A, AVeriTeC scores are displayed.

Table 2 shows the test set results provided by task organizers. We display the systems results that ranked above us and the baseline scores, however in total there are 23 results in the leaderboard[11]. Our approach improves the baseline score and is ranked 6th. Our Q score is in the top 3 and the AVeriTeC score is more than quadrupled as compared to baseline.

[11]https://eval.ai/web/challenges/challenge-page/2285/leaderboard/5655

5.1 Analysis

To analyze the results, we first built a class distribution of the predicted results with all our approaches and compared them with the gold standard label distribution. From Figure 7, we can see that the `Refuted` class has the highest frequency, making it the most common label. In contrast, all models tend to predict `Supported` or `Not Enough Evidence` labels more frequently than `Refuted`, leading to a significant mismatch between the models' predictions and the gold standard. For `Conflicting Evidence/Cherrypicking`, all models predict it

Claim ID - Claim	Individual Predictions	Evidences	Final Prediction	Gold Label
217 - Nigeria's current population exceeds 200 million.	Refuted	**Q:** What is Nigeria's current estimated population? **A:** With a population of roughly 200 million people, Nigeria's	Supported	Supported
	Supported	**Q:** What is the current population estimate for Nigeria? **A:** Nigeria's population is projected to reach 262.9 and 401.3 million people in 2030 and 2050, respectively.		
	Refuted	**Q:** What is the current estimated population of Nigeria? **A:** The population of Nigeria is currently estimated at 198 million, with an annual		
	Supported	**Q:** What is Nigeria's estimated population in comparison to 200 million? **A:** With over 220 million people, Nigeria is the most populated country in Africa and the sixth in the world.		
	Refuted	**Q:** What is the estimated population of Nigeria? **A:** Nigeria has a population of 180 million people (seventh largest in the world) and an economy worth more than $500 billion (21st in the world).		
	Refuted	**Q:** Is Nigeria currently the most populous country in Africa? **A:** Nigeria is the most populous country in Africa and the eighth most populous country in the world, with approximately 162 million people.		
	Supported	**Q:** What was Nigeria's population in 2021? **A:** - The population of Nigeria in 2021 was 213,401,323, a 2.44% increase from 2020.		
	Supported	**Q:** What was Nigeria's population in 2022? **A:** - The population of Nigeria in 2022 was 218,541,212, a 2.41% increase from 2021.		
	Supported	**Q:** What was Nigeria's population in 2020? **A:** Nigeria had a population of 206.14 million people (2020) with an annual population growth rate of 2.5%.		
	Supported	**Q:** What was Nigeria's population as of 2008? **A:** Nigeria is a West African country with about 152 million people (as of 2008). It is by far		
327 - Carlos Gimenez approved a 67% pay raise for himself and increased his own pension.	Refuted	**Q:** Did Carlos Gimenez approve a pay raise for himself? **A:** The amount of money that employees are voluntarily putting into their own pension funds has more than doubled and 70% of employees say they've paid off debt.	Refuted	Supported
	Refuted	**Q:** Did Carlos Gimenez approve a pay raise for himself and increase his pension? **A:** to accrue benefits under the defined benefit pension arrangements, net of his own contributions.		
	Refuted	**Q:** What changes did Carlos Gimenez make to his pay and pension? **A:** subsequently increased the monthly pension rate above what had		
	Refuted	**Q:** Did Carlos Gimenez approve a pay raise for himself and increase his pension? **A:** Gimenez gets a pension of about $120,000 a year from the city of Miami, and has caught heat from labor for opposing the salary hikes for county employees.		
	Refuted	**Q:** What changes to retirement age and pension plans were approved under Carlos Gimenez? **A:** retirement age will gradually increase to 67 by the year 2027, and		
	Refuted	**Q:** What was Carlos Gimenez's salary before the pay raise? **A:** By jacking his own salary up $100,000 for the last two years to $250,000, he significantly improves that average.		
	Refuted	**Q:** What significant changes did Carlos Gimenez implement regarding pay and pensions upon taking office? **A:** huge boost when Carlos Gimenez came into the office		
	Supported	**Q:** What percentage of pay increase did Carlos Gimenez approve for himself? **A:** Read related: Termed out Mayor Carlos Gimenez gives self undeserved 70% pay raise		
	Supported	**Q:** Did Carlos Gimenez authorize a pay raise for himself while making budget cuts in Miami-Dade? **A:** In his time in office, Giménez gave himself a 67% pay raise, and kept a taxpayer funded Mercedes while cutting $400 million in Miami-Dade jobs and investment.		
	Refuted	**Q:** What actions did Carlos Gimenez take regarding pay raises and pensions during his tenure as mayor? **A:** Remember, former Mayor Carlos Alvarez gave big raises to his inner circle also before he was recalled so that Gimenez — or Carlos II, as some have taken to call him — could be elected.		
421 - The CDC recommended wearing only certain beard styles to help prevent the spread of coronoavirus.	Supported	**Q:** Did the CDC recommend wearing only certain beard styles to help prevent the spread of coronavirus? **A:** The CDC recommends shaving beards to protect against the virus	Refuted	Refuted
	Refuted	**Q:** What does the CDC say about beard styles in relation to preventing the spread of coronavirus? **A:** The CDC did not, and does not, recommend that men shave their beards to protect against the SARS-CoV-2 virus.		
	Refuted	**Q:** What does the CDC recommend regarding beard styles in relation to preventing the spread of coronavirus? **A:** To recap, CDC beard advice is not to shave your beard. Coronavirus prevention is best done by washing your hands and practicing social distancing while wearing a cloth face covering.		
	Refuted	**Q:** Did the CDC recommend specific beard styles for preventing the spread of coronavirus? **A:** It's advice about which beards block respirators. The CDC has not said anything about shaving beards for this Coronavirus.		
	Refuted	**Q:** Is the CDC recommending specific beard styles to prevent the spread of coronavirus? **A:** And while facial hair could interfere with respirator masks, the CDC has not recommended people shave their beards to ward off the virus.		
	Refuted	**Q:** What does the CDC say about beard styles and their impact on preventing the spread of coronavirus? **A:** A headline claims that the CDC recommends men shave their beards to protect against coronavirus.		
	Refuted	**Q:** Did the CDC issue guidelines regarding facial hair styles for preventing the spread of coronavirus? **A:** Social media users sharing a CDC infographic showing various styles of facial hair have suggested that the agency is instructing people to shave beards and mustaches to prevent the coronavirus.		
	Refuted	**Q:** What does the CDC say about facial hair styles in relation to the use of respirators? **A:** While the Centers for Disease Control and Prevention (CDC) recommends against certain facial hair stylings for workers who wear tight-fitting respirators, it has not recommended shaving as a precaution to prevent COVID-19.		
	Refuted	**Q:** What guidelines has the CDC provided regarding personal hygiene related to the spread of coronavirus? **A:** The CDC has touted basic personal hygiene like avoiding touching your face and washing your hands since the coronavirus outbreak started, and the same type of cleanliness can be applied to beards.		
	Supported	**Q:** What does the CDC recommend regarding beard styles for effective mask use? **A:** The CDC says to shave your beard into one of a few acceptable styles so you can ensure a snug fit for a mask, if needed.		

Table 3: Some examples on the development set, where we leverage the majority choices based on Retrieve-Question approach along with LLM 2-2, top-10 evidences from unique sentences, and with Mixtral model.

less frequently, aligning with its lower occurrence in the gold standard but still under-predicting it relative to the gold standard's distribution.

Our major concern of the pipeline is "majority voting". One of the hypothesis is that many of the lower-level evidences are unrelated to the claim, making it easier for the LLM to determine that this claim is `Refuted`. In this case, majority voting is also likely to be `Refuted`. To check this, we manually analyze some samples with a majority and demonstrate the examples of different cases in Table 3. For example, the claim "Nigeria's current population exceeds 200 million" has `Refuted` label predictions at the top of the list, however, due to the majority vote, the correct label `Supported` is selected. If we counted only top 5 evidence into account, the final answer could be either `Refuted` (majority vote) or `Conflicting` (both labels are presented, no evident winner). Regarding the second example, we can see that the claim was refuted due to the majority of the retrieved evidence being classified as refuted. However, the majority vote in this case led to an incorrect classification. Regarding the third example, we can see the majority class `Refuted` is coherent with the correct answer, even though the top 1 evidence is classified as `Supported`.

From these examples, we can see that the higher-ranked evidences' labels are not coherent with the golden labels always, the top-10 retrieved evidences provide either correct or incorrect labels regardless the lower-ranked arguments.

6 Conclusion

We have described our UHH system that is submitted to the AVeriTeC shared task. We have explored the use of RAG in this task and have used different LLMs in different steps, with a different number of evidences - top {3, 5, 7, 10}. Top 10 evidences using `Mixtral-8x7B-Instruct-v0.1` (quantized 4-bit) model by prompting individual evidence (strategy 2-2) in the Retrieve-Question approach are ranked 6th in the shared task. In future work, we would like to investigate using a vector database. We have used the evidences as provided by organizers, and we also plan to experiment with different granularity of texts from these evidences.

Limitations

For the creation of unique sentences before BM25 ranking, we used the "set" operation that might change the order of sentences and this might affect the reproducibility regarding the same order of sentences. Additionally, we leverage LLMs, and it could produce different responses every time that might affect the results if reproducing the approach from scratch. However, we have saved the predictions that are used for the task submission. Thus, these predictions can be used to reproduce the results. It is important to note that the computation time for the LLM when predicting a label using strategy 2 is longer than that for strategy 1, as strategy 2 involves prompting individually for each piece of evidence.

Acknowledgements

This research was funded by the "Hamburgische Investitions- und Förderbank" in the project FaktenFassenKI.

References

Satanjeev Banerjee and Alon Lavie. 2005. METEOR: An automatic metric for MT evaluation with improved correlation with human judgments. In *Proceedings of the ACL Workshop on Intrinsic and Extrinsic Evaluation Measures for Machine Translation and/or Summarization*, pages 65–72, Ann Arbor, Michigan. Association for Computational Linguistics.

Steven Bird, Ewan Klein, and Edward Loper. 2009. *Natural Language Processing with Python*. O'Reilly Media Inc.

Jifan Chen, Aniruddh Sriram, Eunsol Choi, and Greg Durrett. 2022. Generating Literal and Implied Subquestions to Fact-check Complex Claims. In *Proceedings of the 2022 Conference on Empirical Methods in Natural Language Processing*, pages 3495–3516, Abu Dhabi, United Arab Emirates. Association for Computational Linguistics.

Jacob Devlin, Ming-Wei Chang, Kenton Lee, and Kristina Toutanova. 2019. BERT: Pre-training of deep bidirectional transformers for language understanding. In *Proceedings of the 2019 Conference of the North American Chapter of the Association for Computational Linguistics: Human Language Technologies, Volume 1 (Long and Short Papers)*, pages 4171–4186, Minneapolis, Minnesota. Association for Computational Linguistics.

Wenqi Fan, Yujuan Ding, Liangbo Ning, Shijie Wang, Hengyun Li, Dawei Yin, Tat-Seng Chua, and Qing Li. 2024. A Survey on RAG Meeting LLMs: Towards Retrieval-Augmented Large Language Models. *Preprint*, arXiv:2405.06211.

Yunfan Gao, Yun Xiong, Xinyu Gao, Kangxiang Jia, Jinliu Pan, Yuxi Bi, Yi Dai, Jiawei Sun, Meng Wang, and

Haofen Wang. 2024. Retrieval-Augmented Generation for Large Language Models: A Survey. *Preprint*, arXiv:2312.10997.

Zhijiang Guo, Michael Schlichtkrull, and Andreas Vlachos. 2022. A Survey on Automated Fact-Checking. *Transactions of the Association for Computational Linguistics*, 10:178–206.

Yasuto Hoshi, Daisuke Miyashita, Youyang Ng, Kento Tatsuno, Yasuhiro Morioka, Osamu Torii, and Jun Deguchi. 2023. RaLLe: A framework for developing and evaluating retrieval-augmented large language models. In *Proceedings of the 2023 Conference on Empirical Methods in Natural Language Processing: System Demonstrations*, pages 52–69, Singapore. Association for Computational Linguistics.

Mahei Manhai Li, Irina Nikishina, Özge Sevgili, and Martin Semmann. 2024. Wiping out the limitations of large language models – a taxonomy for retrieval augmented generation. *Preprint*, arXiv:2408.02854.

Zehan Li, Xin Zhang, Yanzhao Zhang, Dingkun Long, Pengjun Xie, and Meishan Zhang. 2023. Towards general text embeddings with multi-stage contrastive learning. *Preprint*, arXiv:2308.03281.

Nils Reimers and Iryna Gurevych. 2019. Sentence-BERT: Sentence embeddings using Siamese BERT-networks. In *Proceedings of the 2019 Conference on Empirical Methods in Natural Language Processing and the 9th International Joint Conference on Natural Language Processing (EMNLP-IJCNLP)*, pages 3982–3992, Hong Kong, China. Association for Computational Linguistics.

Stephen Robertson and Hugo Zaragoza. 2009. The Probabilistic Relevance Framework: BM25 and Beyond. *Foundations and Trends® in Information Retrieval*, 3(4):333–389.

Michael Schlichtkrull, Zhijiang Guo, and Andreas Vlachos. 2023. AVeriTeC: A Dataset for Real-world Claim Verification with Evidence from the Web. In *Advances in Neural Information Processing Systems*, volume 36, pages 65128–65167. Curran Associates, Inc.

James Thorne and Andreas Vlachos. 2018. Automated Fact Checking: Task Formulations, Methods and Future Directions. In *Proceedings of the 27th International Conference on Computational Linguistics*, pages 3346–3359, Santa Fe, New Mexico. Association for Computational Linguistics.

James Thorne, Andreas Vlachos, Christos Christodoulopoulos, and Arpit Mittal. 2018. FEVER: a large-scale dataset for fact extraction and VERification. In *Proceedings of the 2018 Conference of the North American Chapter of the Association for Computational Linguistics: Human Language Technologies, Volume 1 (Long Papers)*, pages 809–819, New Orleans, Louisiana. Association for Computational Linguistics.

Andreas Vlachos and Sebastian Riedel. 2014. Fact Checking: Task definition and dataset construction. In *Proceedings of the ACL 2014 Workshop on Language Technologies and Computational Social Science*, pages 18–22, Baltimore, Maryland. Association for Computational Linguistics.

Thomas Wolf, Lysandre Debut, Victor Sanh, Julien Chaumond, Clement Delangue, Anthony Moi, Pierric Cistac, Tim Rault, Remi Louf, Morgan Funtowicz, Joe Davison, Sam Shleifer, Patrick von Platen, Clara Ma, Yacine Jernite, Julien Plu, Canwen Xu, Teven Le Scao, Sylvain Gugger, Mariama Drame, Quentin Lhoest, and Alexander Rush. 2020. Transformers: State-of-the-Art Natural Language Processing. In *Proceedings of the 2020 Conference on Empirical Methods in Natural Language Processing: System Demonstrations*, pages 38–45, Online. Association for Computational Linguistics.

BigScience Workshop, :, Teven Le Scao, Angela Fan, Christopher Akiki, Ellie Pavlick, Suzana Ilić, Daniel Hesslow, Roman Castagné, Alexandra Sasha Luccioni, François Yvon, Matthias Gallé, and et. al. 2023. BLOOM: A 176B-Parameter Open-Access Multilingual Language Model. *Preprint*, arXiv:2211.05100.

Xin Zhang, Yanzhao Zhang, Dingkun Long, Wen Xie, Ziqi Dai, Jialong Tang, Huan Lin, Baosong Yang, Pengjun Xie, Fei Huang, Meishan Zhang, Wenjie Li, and Min Zhang. 2024. mGTE: Generalized Long-Context Text Representation and Reranking Models for Multilingual Text Retrieval. *Preprint*, arXiv:2407.19669.

Wayne Xin Zhao, Kun Zhou, Junyi Li, Tianyi Tang, Xiaolei Wang, Yupeng Hou, Yingqian Min, Beichen Zhang, Junjie Zhang, Zican Dong, Yifan Du, Chen Yang, Yushuo Chen, Zhipeng Chen, Jinhao Jiang, Ruiyang Ren, Yifan Li, Xinyu Tang, Zikang Liu, Peiyu Liu, Jian-Yun Nie, and Ji-Rong Wen. 2023. A Survey of Large Language Models. *Preprint*, arXiv:2303.18223.

Improving Evidence Retrieval on Claim Verification Pipeline through Question Enrichment

Svetlana Churina[*a], **Anab Maulana Barik**[*ab], **and Saisamarth Rajesh Phaye**[*]
[a] Centre for Trusted Internet and Community, National University of Singapore
[b] School of Computing, National University of Singapore

Abstract

The AVeriTeC shared task introduces a new real-word claim verification dataset, where a system is tasked to verify a real-world claim based on the evidence found in the internet. In this paper, we proposed a claim verification pipeline called QECV which consists of two modules, Evidence Retrieval and Claim Verification. Our pipeline collects pairs of <Question, Answer> as the evidence. Recognizing the pivotal role of question quality in the evidence efficacy, we proposed question enrichment to enhance the retrieved evidence. Specifically, we adopt three different Question Generation (QG) technique, muti-hop, single-hop, and Fact-checker style. For the claim verification module, we integrate an ensemble of multiple state-of-the-art LLM to enhance its robustness. Experiments show that QECV achieves 0.41, 0.29, and 0.42 on Q, Q+A, and AVeriTeC scores. Code is available here.

1 Introduction

Claim Verification has become critical in the past few years due to the widespread of false information. This highlight the needs for robust automated system for claim verification. To advance the research area, benchmark datasets and challenges such as FEVER (Thorne et al., 2018) and FEVEROUS (Aly et al., 2021) have been introduced and subsequent systems (Zhou et al., 2019; Liu et al., 2020; Zhong et al., 2020; Barik et al., 2022; Chen et al., 2022; Bouziane et al., 2021; Gi et al., 2021) have demonstrated progress in claim verification. Nevertheless, given the artificial claims and structured Wikipedia evidence in FEVER and FEVEROUS, those systems have been optimized primarily under this condition. Verifying real-world claim such as news claim still poses a significant challenge due to the complexity of sources, varying contexts, and the potential for misleading or evolving information.

Recently, a new claim verification benchmark on real-world called AVeriTeC (Schlichtkrull et al., 2024) was introduced. In this benchmark, the system is required to retrieve relevant document from articles across the internet and extract essential information from the articles that can debunk the claim. Then, the system must classify the claim as Supported, Refuted, Not Enough Evidence, or Conflicting Evidence/Cherrypicking.

Compare with previous datasets that relies on synthetic claims derived from Wikipedia, AVeriTeC focused on real-world claims. Additionally, question-answer pairs have been introduced to capture reasoning steps and include annotations for conflicting evidences, offering a more nuanced approach to claim verification.

In this dataset, question generation is a structured process aimed at deconstructing the reasoning used in fact-checking. Annotators identify key aspects of a claim that require verification by reading original claim, relevant fact-checking source(s) and original source of the claim. They have been tasked to generate questions that would help break verification into the smaller steps. These questions need to be designed to extract specific pieces of evidences that would be required to verify claim.

In this paper, we propose Question Enrichment Claim Verification (QECV) consisting of 2 modules, Evidence Retrieval and Claim Verification. To enhance the quality of the retrieved evidence, we adopt three different question generation approaches; multi-hop, single-hop, and fact-checker style. Single-hop aims to retrieve more general evidence to verify the claim, while multi-hop targets more detailed evidence for each component of the claim. Fact-checker style mimic how human fact-checker generate questions by conditioning on both the claim and the content article. In contrast, single-hop and multi-hop solely rely on the claim for

[*]All authors have contributed equally.
Correspondence emails: *churinas@nus.edu.sg* *anabmaulana@u.nus.edu*

Proceedings of the Seventh Fact Extraction and VERification Workshop (FEVER), pages 64–70
November 15, 2024

question generation. Our claim verification module combine two different approaches: evidence-level verifier and claim-level verifier. The former classify intermediate label to individual piece of evidence, which are subsequently aggregated to determine the claim label. Conversely, the latter directly classifies the claim label based from all the retrieved evidence. To leverage the strength of each approach, we employ a voting-based ensemble model to aggregate the output and obtain the final label. Our pipeline achieves 0.41, 0.29, and 0.42 on Q, Q+A, and AVeriTeC scores respectively, which outperforms the baseline model with a substantial margin.

2 Pipeline

As shown in Figure 1, our pipeline consists of two modules: Evidence Retrieval and Claim Verification. The input claim first passes through our three variants of evidence retrieval to retrieve relevant pairs of <Question, Answer>. Each variant generate questions from the claim and retrieve relevant articles through Faiss: a library for efficient similarity search (Douze et al., 2024). Then, it outputs list of <Question, Answer> which later combined to become the retrieved evidence. Thereafter, the claim sentence and the retrieved evidence are fed to the claim verification module to predict the final label. The detail of each module will be elaborated in subsequent subsections.

2.1 Evidence Retrieval

The evidence retrieval module processes a claim sentence through a sequential of sub-modules to extract relevant pairs of <Question, Answer> evidence.

2.1.1 Question Generation

Crafting effective questions is crucial in the question generation process, especially for claim verification. The quality of the questions can significantly influence the verification outcome, guiding it towards uncovering the truth or leading to ambiguity. Therefore, we place great importance on designing these questions carefully. Specifically, we propose three different question generation strategies: multi-hop, claim as a question, and FC-style question generation.

Multi-hop Question Generation Following QACheck methodologies (Pan et al., 2023), we employ two different question types in this strategy, initial question and follow-up question. The initial question serves as the starting point for verification. Here is the prompt structure for generating initial question:

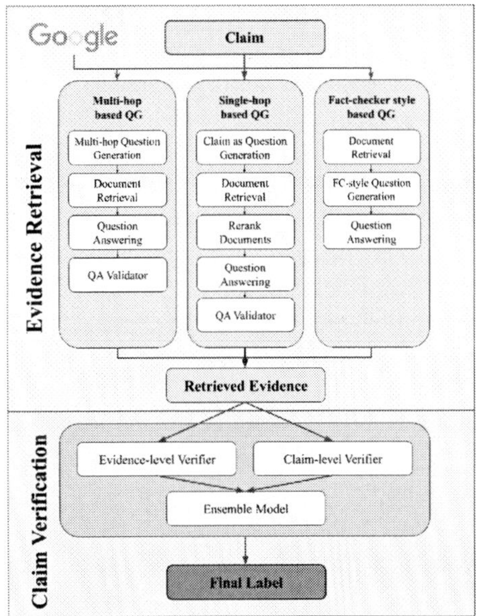

Figure 1: QECV Pipeline

```
Claim = CLAIM
What kind of question need to be
asked to start fact checking
process?
```

Follow-up questions build on the initial question and any previous responses to further validate the claim. Here is the prompt structure for generating follow-up questions:

```
Claim = CLAIM
We already know the following:
CONTEXT = Prev. QA Pairs
Given a claim and previous
questions, what follow-up
question need to be asked to
verify the claim?
```

Claim as Question Generation Unlike the multi-hop question, this strategy leverages the entire claim as a question to better grasp the overall context and nuances of the claim. Specifically, a question "Is it true that CLAIM?" is manually constructed and subsequently paraphrased using OpenAI's GPT4o.

Fact-checker Style Question Generation

After manually reviewing the questions generated by annotators, we discovered that most of these questions are more sophisticated than those based solely on the claim. Generating such sophisticated questions requires additional knowledge, including details from the source text, information about where the claim was published, and the nature of the publishing company. Often, this information might not seem directly connected to the claim at first glance.

To generate these types of questions, we need to provide more comprehensive information to the model and tailor the question generation process accordingly.

Here is the prompt structure for generating fact-checker style questions:

```
Claim = CLAIM

Article text = TEXT Is this
article relevant to our claim?
If yes - what question need to
be asked based on the article
text that will be required to
verify claim?
```

By systematically asking well-structured questions, our system aims to facilitate a thorough and accurate verification process.

2.1.2 Document Retrieval

This module accepts a question as input to extract relevant documents. We leverage the provided document collections from the dataset provided in the challenge. However, given the substantial proportion of empty documents (exceeding 50%) within these collections, we augmented more documents by querying the claim itself with Google API. We also scraped a few hundred URLs manually for which document-text field was empty.

To match any question with the corresponding documents, we tried multiple techniques. In summary, we create an embedding vector for each document and also the question, using the Sentence Transformer library (Reimers and Gurevych, 2019). Considering the resource constraints, we used "all-MiniLM-L6-v2" model to get the encodings. We found that Faiss yields fast indexing and best similarity results even for extremely long texts, partly due to the quality of encodings by Sentence Transformers. We get the 20 best matches with the question and pass it to the Reranking module which is described below.

2.1.3 Rerank Documents

In our manual analysis, we noticed that some of the URLs could be from inauthentic sources, and could include wrong information. However, the gold labeled URLs in training data seemed to have authentic information. To leverage this, we devise a simple reranking algorithm, based on the training data's Gold standard websites (retrieved from the URLs). We calculate the frequency based weighting for the training data's ground truth websites which are of type "gold", and also for the rest, which we call "normal" website weight. Now, for the test stage, we check every URL's Faiss score, and multiply it with the corresponding website weight. Gold websites are always prioritised above the normal weighted websites. This reranking multiplication considers only the top 20 documents and not all, because considering all URLs could result in dissimilar documents being at the top.

Post-reranking, we take the top 5 documents retrieved and pass them to the Question Answering stage, which is described below. This reranking stage yielded us best results for Claim-as-question generation. However, it didn't yield significantly better results for the Multi-hop based QG. By adding URL weightings (and using no claim-as-questions yet) on the development dataset, our Q and Q+A score slightly go down from 31.35 and 21.67 to 30.64 and 20.32 respectively. Our hypothesis for this observation is that, multiple questions retrieve multiple documents. As a result, those retrieved documents already cover a number of authentic websites. Hence, URL weighting might hinder more than help in multi-hop stage.

2.1.4 Question Answering

Once we retrieve the five most relevant documents, the first step is to generate a summary tailored to the question at hand. For summary generation, we utilize OpenAI's GPT4o, providing it with the question, the claim, and the text of the document as input.

Since the summary is generated with the specific goal of addressing the question based on the document's content, it is subsequently treated as the answer in the following modules. The prompt used for generating the summary is as follows:

```
Claim = CLAIM

Question= QUESTION

Text = TEXT
```

```
Provide a brief summary of the
text, focusing on information
relevant to the question. The
summary should aim at answering
the question.
```

2.1.5 QA Validator

The QA Validator module plays a crucial role in our fact-checking system, as it determines the direction of subsequent verification processes. Given that some questions may yield conflicting answers (which could lead to cherry-picking the final label), it is essential to determine differences in answers before proceeding. To address this, we assign individual labels to each QA pair based on their content.

Each QA pair can be assigned one of three labels: *Supported*, *Refuted*, or *Not Enough Evidence*. Once each QA pair is labeled, we group them based on these three categories. The logic for handling the labels is as follows:

- If a question has both *Supported* and *Not Enough Evidence* pairs, we only consider the *Supported* pairs.
- If a question has both *Refuted* and *Not Enough Evidence* pairs, we only consider the *Refuted* pairs.
- If a question has both *Supported* and *Refuted* pairs, we retain both and generate follow-up questions based on these two paths.
- If a question only has *Not Enough Evidence* pairs, we proceed with that label.

After selecting the pairs to continue with, we must choose the best QA pair within each category. Using OpenAI's GPT4o, we analyze each QA pair and select the one that provides the most informative response to the question.

2.2 Claim Verification

The claim verification module is given a claim sentence and evidence as input, it tasked to classify the label of the claim. The module is a combination of two claim verification system variants, namely Evidence-level verifier and Claim-level verifier.

Evidence-level Verifier In this variant, the model was trained to independently classify the label of a claim w.r.t a piece of evidence. The evidence is a concatenation of a question and an answer following this format: *"Question: [Question]. Answer: [Answer]"*. Claims are classified as Supported, Refuted, or Not Enough Evidence, constituting a fine-grained label. Ultimately, the claim label was determined through applying deterministic function to the fine-grained labels:

- **Supported**: If all the fine-grained labels are Supported.
- **Refuted**: If all the fine-grained labels are Refuted.
- **Conflicting Evidence/Cherrypicking**: If both Supported and Refuted are presents in the fine-grained labels
- **Not Enough Evidence**: Otherwise

Claim-level Verifier In this variant, we follow a conventional claim verification model, in which, the model is tasked to classify the label of the claim given all pieces of evidence. The evidence is the concatenation of questions and answers following this format: Question-1: *[Question-1]. Answer-1: [Answer-1]. ... Question-N: [Question-N]. Answer-N: [Answer-N]*. The claim is classified either Supported, Refuted, Not Enough Evidence, or Conflicting Evidence/Cherrypicking.

For each variant, we experimented with different LLMs as the backbone and we combine the output of these models through a voting-based ensemble model to obtain the final claim label. A comprehensive description of each LLM is presented in the next section.

2.2.1 Training Detail

We fine-tuned five LLMs: (1) flan-t5-Large (Chung et al., 2024), (2) Mistral-7B-Instruct-v0.1 (Jiang et al., 2023), (3) Mixtral-8x7B-Instruct-v0.1 (Jiang et al., 2024), (4) gpt-3.5-turbo-0125, and (5) gpt-4o-mini. For T5, Mistral, and Mixtral, we set the learning rate to $1e-4$ and fine-tuned it for 2 epochs. We use LoRA with rank, alpha, and dropout are set to 8, 32, and 0.05. Meanwhile, for GPT3.5 and GPT4, we use 4 epochs. We set the other hyperparameters as default.

Evidence-level Verifier: to obtain the training data for this variants, we first filter out all claims with label $Conflicting\ Evidence/Cherrypicking$. Then, quadruplets of <claim, question, answer, label> are obtained from the training set. For **Claim-level Verifier**, we collect quadruplets of <claim, list of

Model	Q	Q+A
baseline	0.24	0.19
Single	0.23	0.16
Single+Multi	0.39	0.27
Single+Multi+FC	**0.44**	**0.31**

Table 1: Evidence Retrieval Result on Development Set. Comparison of results from different question generation types.

questions, list of answers, label> from the whole training set.

We employ majority voting for the ensemble models. Based from the experiments on the dev set, our final claim verification is an ensemble of 4 different models: GPT4 on Evidence-level verifier and Mistral, GPT3.5, and GPT4 on Claim-level verifier.

3 Results

3.1 Evidence Retrieval

Table 1 reports the results evidence retrieval performance of QECV compared to the baseline models on the development set. Among the investigated Question Generation style, the single-hop approaches yield the lowest score among other variants. This shows that claim as question is not sufficient to retrieve enough evidence to verify the claim. Nevertheless, the claim as question is competitive with the baseline models. Augment the evidence through multi-hop question led to a substantial improvement, which improves 0.13 on Q and 0.11 on Q+A. This suggest that Q+A effectively capture more detailed and relevant evidence. Finally, adding FC-style question improve additional performance gain by 0.5 on Q and 0.4 on Q+A, emphasizing the efficacy of this approach to collect evidence that are hardly mention by the claim.

3.2 Claim Verification

Table 2 reports the Evidence-level Verifier, and Table 3 reports the Claim-level Verifier on the development set using various fine-tuned LLM.

Effect on LLMs size: Through the experiments, we can see that on evidence-level verifier, bigger model such as mixtral, GPT3.5, and GPT4 outperforms smaller models on AVeriTeC score. Meanwhile on claim-level verifier, mistral, GPT3.5 and GPT4 outperforms smaller models on AVeriTeC score. Moreover, GPT3.5 and GPT4 are consistently achieved the highest performance across both variants.

Effect on Different Variants: Experimental results demonstrate that claim-level verifier are superior than the evidence-level verifier, both in macro F1 and AVeriTeC score. The under performance of evidence-level is attributed to the deterministic function. For instance, for a "Supported" claim "*Amy Coney Barrett was confirmed as US Supreme Court Justice on October 26, 2020.*", our evidence retrieval retrieves 7 evidence and the evidence-level verifier predicts 6 out of the 7 evidence as "Supported". The last evidence stated that "*The summarized information does not provide the exact date of Amy Coney Barrett's confirmation to the US Supreme Court. It only states that she has been confirmed.*", which the verifier predicts as Not Enough Evidence. Finally, the final claim label is Not Enough Evidence due to the deterministic function. Nevertheless, evidence-level verifier is superior in identifying Not Enough Evidence label, achieving 0.28 F1 score compared to 0.16 F1 score for claim-level verifier.

Impact of using different LLMs: Experimental results indicate that different models exhibit varying strength. In claim-level verifier, GPT3.5 and GPT4 are superior on Supported and Refuted labels, whereas Mistral and Mixtral excel on Not Enough Evidence and Conflicting labels. Conversely, in the evidence-level verifier, GPT3.5 and GPT4 are the most effective on Not Enough Evidence and Conflicting labels, meanwhile Mixtral excels on Refuted and BART on Supported. This suggest that each LLM possesses it's own strength depending on the verifier variant. Consequently, combining the strength of these models across different variants can enhance the robustness of the verifier.

3.3 Full Pipeline

For our final pipeline, we use the best performance for the evidence retrieval, which is a combination Single+Multi+FC-style based QG. For the claim verification, we ensemble GPT4 on evidence-level verifier and Mistral, GPT3.5, and GPT4 on claim-level verifier to gain benefit the strength of different variants. Table 4 indicates that our final pipeline significantly outperforms the baseline on every metrics, by 0.17 on Q, 0.10 in Q+A, and 0.31 in AVeriTeC score.

Model	AVeriTeC	F1				
		Sup	Ref	Nee	Conf	Macro
baseline (BART_large)	0.09	**0.43**	0.71	0.00	0.09	0.32
T5	0.33	0.28	0.78	0.27	**0.14**	0.36
Mistral	0.32	0.19	0.78	0.24	0.10	0.33
Mixtral	0.36	0.33	**0.81**	0.16	0.09	0.35
GPT3.5	0.35	0.24	0.79	**0.28**	0.13	0.36
GPT4	**0.37**	0.40	0.80	0.22	**0.14**	**0.39**

Table 2: Evidence-level verifier results on the development set. "Sup" denotes "Supported," "Ref" stands for "Refuted," "Nee" represents "Not Enough Information," and "Conf" corresponds to "Conflicting" or "Cherrypicking" label types.

Model	AVeriTeC	F1				
		Sup	Ref	Nee	Conf	Macro
T5	0.39	0.42	0.79	0.11	0.14	0.37
Mistral	0.44	**0.61**	0.82	0.09	**0.20**	**0.43**
Mixtral	0.38	0.46	0.82	**0.16**	0.16	0.40
GPT3.5	**0.46**	**0.61**	**0.84**	0.12	0.16	**0.43**
GPT4	0.44	0.59	**0.84**	0.08	0.18	0.42

Table 3: Claim-level Verifier Result on Development Set, where "Sup" - Supported, "Ref" - Refuted, "Nee" - Not Enough Information, "Conf" - Conflicting/Cherrypicking type of labels.

	Development Set			Test Set		
Model	Q	Q+A	AVeriTeC	Q	Q+A	AVeriTeC
baseline	0.24	0.19	0.09	0.24	0.20	0.11
ours	**0.44**	**0.31**	**0.46**	**0.41**	**0.30**	**0.42**

Table 4: Result on Full Pipeline compare with baseline results, where "Q" - question-based retrieval performance, "Q+A" - question + answer retrieval performance

4 Conclusion

In this paper, we introduced the QECV, a pipeline for verifying real-world claims. Improving the evidence retrieval through question enrichment enable the framework to cover more evidence for verifying the claim, thus achieves 0.41 and 0.30 for the Q and Q+A performance on the test set. Additionally, our pipeline combines across various claim verifier variants and LLMs to leverage their unique strengths, resulting in more robust verification process and an 0.42 AVeriTeC score on the test set.

5 Limitations

We believe one of the major limitations of this pipeline is relevance of documents we retrieve for each question. We have tried to address this by introducing multi-hop QG, claim-as-question module, and emphasising fact-checking styled documents. However, there is definitely scope of further improvement here.

Despite the ability of our question enrichment methods on the evidence retrieval, the hallucination remains, particularly in the question answering stage. Moreover, our claim verification models rely solely on the ground truth data for training. Given that the previous works demonstrate the effectiveness of adding noise for claim verification on synthethic claim, it is worthwhile to investigate whether a similar approach can be applied to the real-world claims.

References

Rami Aly, Zhijiang Guo, Michael Sejr Schlichtkrull, James Thorne, Andreas Vlachos, Christos Christodoulopoulos, Oana Cocarascu, and Arpit Mittal. 2021. FEVEROUS: Fact extraction and VERification over unstructured and structured information.

Anab Maulana Barik, Wynne Hsu, and Mong Li Lee. 2022. Incorporating external knowledge for evidence-based fact verification. In *Companion Pro-*

ceedings of the Web Conference 2022*, pages 429–437.

Mostafa Bouziane, Hugo Perrin, Amine Sadeq, Thanh Nguyen, Aurélien Cluzeau, and Julien Mardas. 2021. Fabulous: fact-checking based on understanding of language over unstructured and structured information. In *Proceedings of the Fourth Workshop on Fact Extraction and VERification (FEVER)*, pages 31–39.

Jiangjie Chen, Qiaoben Bao, Changzhi Sun, Xinbo Zhang, Jiaze Chen, Hao Zhou, Yanghua Xiao, and Lei Li. 2022. Loren: Logic-regularized reasoning for interpretable fact verification. In *Proceedings of the AAAI Conference on Artificial Intelligence*, volume 36, pages 10482–10491.

Hyung Won Chung, Le Hou, Shayne Longpre, Barret Zoph, Yi Tay, William Fedus, Yunxuan Li, Xuezhi Wang, Mostafa Dehghani, Siddhartha Brahma, et al. 2024. Scaling instruction-finetuned language models. *Journal of Machine Learning Research*, 25(70):1–53.

Matthijs Douze, Alexandr Guzhva, Chengqi Deng, Jeff Johnson, Gergely Szilvasy, Pierre-Emmanuel Mazaré, Maria Lomeli, Lucas Hosseini, and Hervé Jégou. 2024. The faiss library.

In-Zu Gi, Ting-Yu Fang, and Richard Tzong-Han Tsai. 2021. Verdict inference with claim and retrieved elements using roberta. In *Proceedings of the Fourth Workshop on Fact Extraction and VERification (FEVER)*, pages 60–65.

Albert Q Jiang, Alexandre Sablayrolles, Arthur Mensch, Chris Bamford, Devendra Singh Chaplot, Diego de las Casas, Florian Bressand, Gianna Lengyel, Guillaume Lample, Lucile Saulnier, et al. 2023. Mistral 7b. *arXiv preprint arXiv:2310.06825*.

Albert Q Jiang, Alexandre Sablayrolles, Antoine Roux, Arthur Mensch, Blanche Savary, Chris Bamford, Devendra Singh Chaplot, Diego de las Casas, Emma Bou Hanna, Florian Bressand, et al. 2024. Mixtral of experts. *arXiv preprint arXiv:2401.04088*.

Zhenghao Liu, Chenyan Xiong, Maosong Sun, and Zhiyuan Liu. 2020. Fine-grained fact verification with kernel graph attention network. In *Proceedings of the 58th Annual Meeting of the Association for Computational Linguistics*, pages 7342–7351.

Liangming Pan, Xinyuan Lu, Min-Yen Kan, and Preslav Nakov. 2023. Qacheck: A demonstration system for question-guided multi-hop fact-checking. In *Proceedings of the 2023 Conference on Empirical Methods in Natural Language Processing: System Demonstrations*, pages 264–273.

Nils Reimers and Iryna Gurevych. 2019. Sentence-bert: Sentence embeddings using siamese bert-networks. In *Proceedings of the 2019 Conference on Empirical Methods in Natural Language Processing*. Association for Computational Linguistics.

Michael Schlichtkrull, Zhijiang Guo, and Andreas Vlachos. 2024. Averitec: A dataset for real-world claim verification with evidence from the web. *Advances in Neural Information Processing Systems*, 36.

James Thorne, Andreas Vlachos, Christos Christodoulopoulos, and Arpit Mittal. 2018. Fever: a large-scale dataset for fact extraction and verification. In *Proceedings of the 2018 Conference of the North American Chapter of the Association for Computational Linguistics: Human Language Technologies, Volume 1 (Long Papers)*, pages 809–819.

Wanjun Zhong, Jingjing Xu, Duyu Tang, Zenan Xu, Nan Duan, Ming Zhou, Jiahai Wang, and Jian Yin. 2020. Reasoning over semantic-level graph for fact checking. In *Proceedings of the 58th Annual Meeting of the Association for Computational Linguistics*, pages 6170–6180.

Jie Zhou, Xu Han, Cheng Yang, Zhiyuan Liu, Lifeng Wang, Changcheng Li, and Maosong Sun. 2019. Gear: Graph-based evidence aggregating and reasoning for fact verification. In *Proceedings of the 57th Annual Meeting of the Association for Computational Linguistics*, pages 892–901.

Dunamu-ml's Submissions on AVERITEC Shared Task

Heesoo Park, Dongjun Lee, Jaehyuk Kim, ChoongWon Park, Changhwa Park
Dunamu Inc.
{belle, tonny, loki, elvie, dexter}@dunamu.com

Abstract

This paper presents the Dunamu-ml's submission to the AVERITEC shared task of the 7th the Fact Extraction and VERification (FEVER) workshop. The task focused on discriminating whether each claim is a fact or not. Our method is powered by the combination of an LLM and a non-parametric lexicon-based method (i.e. BM25). Essentially, we augmented the list of evidences containing the query and the corresponding answers using an powerful LLM, then, retrieved the relative documents using the generated evidences. As such, our method made a great improvement over the baseline results, achieving 0.33 performance gain over the baseline in AveriTec score.

1 Introduction

The rise in misinformation has led to a greater need for fact-checking, which involves determining the accuracy of a claim through evidence. Consequently, research on methods that automatically detect whether specific claims are true or false is being conducted actively. (Vlachos and Riedel, 2014; Thorne et al., 2018a) As part of this effort, the shared task Fact Extraction and VERification (FEVER) [1] is held regularly (Thorne et al., 2018b, 2019; Wang et al., 2021; Aly et al., 2021).

Fact-checking requires large-scale retrieval. Large-scale retrieval involves retrieving the most relevant documents from a vast collection containing millions to billions of entries in response to a text query. Over the past ten years, deep representation learning techniques have become essential for large-scale retrieval, transitioning from traditional Bag-of-Words (BoW) (Mikolov et al., 2013) methods to Pre-trained Language Models (PLMs) (Devlin et al., 2019). The latest advancements in LLMs offer a quicker path to achieve zero-shot retrieval by enhancing a query with potential answers obtained from the LLMs (Gao et al., 2023).

In this paper, we introduce our approach to the FEVER 2024 Share Task named AveriTeC shared tasks (Schlichtkrull et al., 2023). We aim to build our model powered by the generation and retrieval ability of recent LLMs (Achiam et al., 2023). Our method is inspired by (Shen et al., 2023) which utilize a non-parametric lexicon-based method (such as BM25 (Robertson et al., 2009)) as the retrieval component to directly measure the similarity between the query and document and boost the query using powerful LLM.

First, we generated initial question and answer pairs without any documents retrieved. Then, we retrieved relevant documents and fix the initial answers using it. Finally, we infer the final answer using the given evidences. Our approach significantly enhanced the baseline outcomes, securing a 0.33 increase in performance compared to the baseline according to the AveriTec score. For evaluation, we used the given system[2].

2 Task Description

The AVeriTeC challenge (Schlichtkrull et al., 2023) aims to evaluate the ability of systems to verify real-world claims with evidence from the Web.

- The systems need to find evidence that either supports or contradicts a claim, based on the claim itself and its accompanying metadata. This evidence can be sourced from the Web or from the collection of documents provided by the organizers.
- Based on the evidence gathered, classify the claim as either `Supported` or `Refuted`, or categorize it as `Not Enough Evidence` if there is insufficient evidence to make a determination. If the evidence presents conflicting view-

[1] `https://fever.ai/index.html`

[2] `https://eval.ai/web/challenges/challenge-page/2285/overview`

Proceedings of the Seventh Fact Extraction and VERification Workshop (FEVER), pages 71–76
November 15, 2024 ©2024 Association for Computational Linguistics

points or appears selective, label the claim as `Conflicting Evidence/Cherry-picking`.

- For a response to be deemed accurate, both the label assigned and the quality of evidence provided must be correct. Since evaluating evidence retrieval can be challenging to automate, participants will be requested to assist in manually evaluating it to ensure a fair assessment of the systems.

The output format of each claim should be:

- $claim\_id$: The ID of the sample.
- $claim$: The claim text itself.
- $pred\_label$: The predicted label of the claim.
- $evidence$: A list of QA pairs. Each set consists of dictionaries with four fields.
  - $question$: The text of the generated question.
  - $answer$: The text of the answer of the generated question.
  - url: The source url for the answer.
  - $scraped\_text$: The text scraped from the url.

2.1 AVERITEC Corpus

The AVeriTeC dataset, as described in the study by (Schlichtkrull et al., 2023), comprises 4,568 examples sourced from 50 fact-checking organizations using the Google FactCheck Claim Search API[3], which is built on ClaimReview[4]. AVeriTeC is distinguished as the initial AFC dataset to offer question-answer decomposition along with justifications, while also addressing challenges related to context dependence, evidence insufficiency, and temporal leaks. Additional details about AVeriTeC can be found on the project's GitHub repository: `https://github.com/MichSchli/AVeriTeC`.

2.2 Evaluation metric

The AVeriTeC score is based on adjustments made to the FEVER scorer (Thorne et al., 2018a). While FEVER relies on a closed evidence source such as Wikipedia, AVERITEC is tailored to handle evidence sourced from the open web. Since identical evidence may be found across multiple sources, precise matching for scoring retrieved evidence is impractical. Hence, AVERITEC utilizes approximate matching and utilizes the Hungarian Algorithm to determine the most suitable match between the provided evidence and the annotated evidence.

$$u_f(\widehat{Y}, Y) = \frac{1}{|Y|} \max \sum_{\hat{y} \in \hat{Y}} \sum_{y \in Y} f(\hat{y}, y) X(\hat{y}, y) \tag{1}$$

During the evaluation process, the system employed the METEOR (Banerjee and Lavie, 2005) implementation from NLTK (Bird et al., 2009) as the scoring function f, known for its strong correlation with human assessments of similarity (Fomicheva and Specia, 2019). They do not utilize a precision metric to prevent penalizing systems for posing extra relevant information-seeking questions. Nevertheless, all systems are constrained to a maximum of $k = 10$ question-answer pairs. We assess the accuracy of truthfulness predictions and supporting evidence by applying a threshold of $f(\hat{y}, y) >= \lambda$ to ascertain the retrieval of accurate evidence (using combined questions and answers). Claims with lower evidence scores are assigned veracity and justification scores of 0.

3 System Overview

In this section, we firstly provide a brief description of how we pre-processed the given knowledge store and present our approach to the task.

3.1 Data crawling and preprocessing

As we mentioned in Section 2.1, the pre-googled knowledge store, which includes web urls and their scraped text for each claim, is provided by the organizers. However, in the case that the url corresponds to either a YouTube video or a PDF document, the scraped text field is left blank, even if it includes crucial evidence for verifying the claim. To address this, we extract the transcripts from YouTube videos and parse the text from PDF documents, subsequently saving them in the data store. In addition, we segment all the documents into segments comprising 10 sentences each, not containing an excessive amount of information.

3.2 Model configuration

Our approach to the task consists of three steps, as depicted in Figure 1.

Step 1: Generate initial question and answer pairs without any documents retrieved. In order to verify the veracity of claims, it is essential to

[3]`https://toolbox.google.com/factcheck/apis`
[4]`https://www.claimreviewproject.com/`

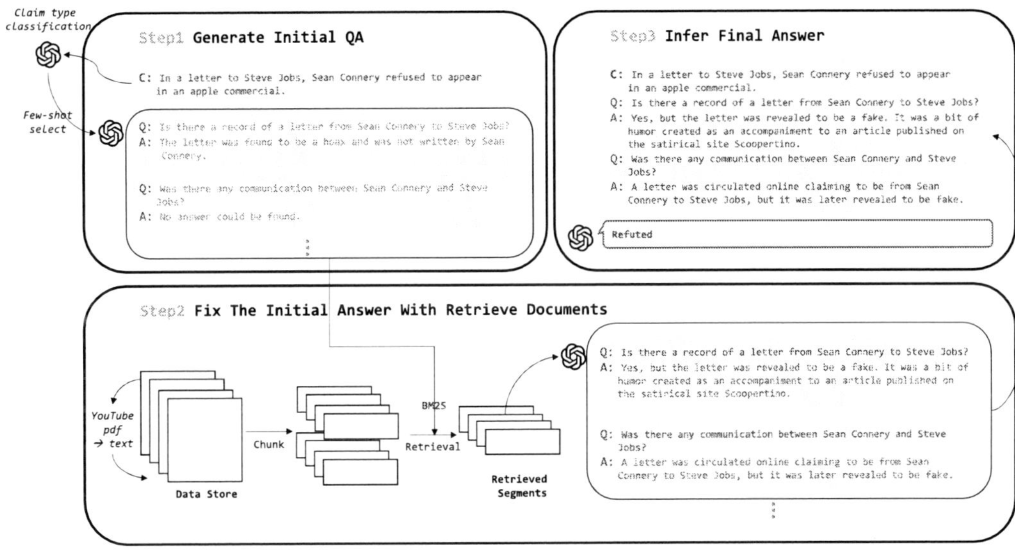

Figure 1: A diagram illustrating the three steps of our method for AVERITEC shared task. The text generated by GPT-4 is in green in Step 1 and in red in Step2. In Step 3, the predicted answer by GPT-4 is enclosed in a red box.

formulate questions that can be answered based on reliable documents retrieved from the knowledge store. Research has shown that utilizing artificially generated answers in the search, as opposed to using the questions alone, can enhance document retrieval performance. (Gao et al., 2023) As a result, a decision has been made to concurrently generate both questions and answers for use in the search process. This approach aims to improve the efficiency and effectiveness of information retrieval for fact-checking purposes.

Initially, we categorize each claim using GPT-4 with few shots which consist of pairs of (1) each claim and (2) its corresponding claim type. We classify each claim using the following prompt:

```
Every claim belongs to at least one of the
categories below.
It may also belong to multiple categories.
Return one or more categories to which the
claim belongs. The majority of claims belong
to only one category.
{'Numerical Claim', 'Causal Claim', 'Quote
Verification', 'Event/Property Claim',
'Position Statement'}

<few shots>
<claim>
```

Next, in training dataset, we extract samples corresponding to the predicted claim category. We then create total 20 few-shot samples by randomly selecting four samples labeled as "supported" or "refuted," respectively and six samples from the other two labels, respectively. Each few-shot sample consists of (1) claim, (2) claim label and (3) its evidence list. Finally, we have gpt-4 to generate initial evidence list, question and answer pairs, using these few shots with following prompt:

```
The given claim falls into one of the following
four categories.
1. Supported
2. Refuted
3. Not Enough Evidence (if there isn't
sufficient evidence to either support or refute
it)
4. Conflicting Evidence/Cherry-picking (if the
claim has both supporting and refuting evidence)

Classify each claim into four categories
and provide evidence for the classification.
If there are not enough evidences, you should
list the evidence that needs to be supported
or refuted.

<few shots>
<claim>
```

Step 2: Retrieve relevant documents and fix the initial answers using it. In the second step, we revise the initial answers for each question we generate in Step 1. Initially, for each generated question answer pair, we retrieved reliable document segments. Then, we also retrieved similar questions with each generated question for few shots. We construct each few-shot sample with (1) the retrieved questions, (2) their corresponding answers and (3) gold documents segments. For both retrieval, we leveraged ranked bm25 package which built on the algorithm taken from (Trotman et al., 2014). Using those few shots and retrieved document segments, we fix the initial answer with following prompt:

```
Given the context, you should find the answer
for each question.
When answering, try to use as many words from
the passage as possible.
But if you cannot find the answer, say "No
answer could be found." without extra words.

<few shots>
<claim>
<retrieved document segments>
<generated question>
```

Step 3: Infer the final answer using the given evidences. In the last step, we infer the final answer. We re-used the same samples as a few-shot in Step 1 (used in the second prompt). While in Step 1 we utilized a sequence the claim, evidence list, and label for one few-shot, in this step, we employed a sequence including (1) the claim, (2) evidence list, (3) justification, and (4) label. The justification text describes the reason why the claim is supported and refuted (Wei et al., 2022). Using gpt-4, we predict final answer with the following prompt:

```
The given claim falls into one of the following
four categories.
1. Supported
2. Refuted
3. Not Enough Evidence (if there isn't
sufficient evidence to either support or refute
it)
4. Conflicting Evidence/Cherry-picking (if the
claim has both supporting and refuting evidence)

Classify each claim into four categories
and provide evidence for the classification.
If there are not enough evidences, you should
list the evidence that needs to be supported
or refuted.

<few shots>
<claim>
<generated evidence>
```

4 Experiment

In this section, we present our experimental setup, the tools we used and the final task results.

Implementation Details The library used to obtain Youtube transcripts is youtube-transcript-api [5], and the library used for PDF parsing is PyMuPDF [6]. We used GPT-4 as an LLM and the LLM model used GPT-4, and BM25 was implemented through the langchain library [7]. For GPT-4 we use $T = 0.7$ without top-k truncation and $N = 5$, then select the last answer by majority voting (Wang et al., 2022).

Model	Q only	Q+A	AveriTeC
TUDA_MAI_0	0.45	0.34	**0.63**
HerO	0.48	**0.35**	0.57
AIC System	0.46	0.32	0.50
papelo-ten-r773	0.44	0.30	0.48
dun-factchecker	**0.49**	**0.35**	0.50

Table 1: The systems ranked in the top 5 in the AVERITEC leaderboard during the test phase. The system "dun-factchecker" is ours.

Baseline The baseline model that has been fine-tuned on BLOOM (Schlichtkrull et al., 2023) can be referred to in (Le Scao et al., 2023).

Main Results Table 1 presents the evaluation results in test phase. We have the following observations:

- Our method achieved SOTA in Q and Q+A humeteor scores, indicating that the few-shot sampling method following classification in Step 1 was effective.
- We observed that although our scores in evidence generation were higher or equal to those of the TUDA_MAI_0 and HerO systems, there was a slight drop in the performance when it comes to the final label prediction.
- It appears that utilizing generated questions and answers for retrieval was quite effective, but there are some limitations of the final prediction in the Step 3 that need to be addressed in the future.

5 Conclusion

In this work, we described the Dunamu-ml's submission to the AVERITEC shared tasks of the FEVER 2024. By integrating a language model (LLM) with a non-parametric lexicon-based method (BM25), our approach bolstered the evidence list by integrating the query and associated answers using a robust LLM. This strategy allowed us to pinpoint pertinent documents based on the

[5] https://pypi.org/project/youtube-transcript-api/

[6] https://github.com/pymupdf/PyMuPDF

[7] https://github.com/langchain-ai/langchain

generated evidence, resulting in a notable improvement over the baseline outcomes with a 0.33 performance gain in the AVeriTeC score.

References

Josh Achiam, Steven Adler, Sandhini Agarwal, Lama Ahmad, Ilge Akkaya, Florencia Leoni Aleman, Diogo Almeida, Janko Altenschmidt, Sam Altman, Shyamal Anadkat, et al. 2023. Gpt-4 technical report. *arXiv preprint arXiv:2303.08774*.

Rami Aly, Zhijiang Guo, Michael Schlichtkrull, James Thorne, Andreas Vlachos, Christos Christodoulopoulos, Oana Cocarascu, and Arpit Mittal. 2021. Feverous: Fact extraction and verification over unstructured and structured information. *arXiv preprint arXiv:2106.05707*.

Satanjeev Banerjee and Alon Lavie. 2005. METEOR: An automatic metric for MT evaluation with improved correlation with human judgments. In *Proceedings of the ACL Workshop on Intrinsic and Extrinsic Evaluation Measures for Machine Translation and/or Summarization*, pages 65–72, Ann Arbor, Michigan. Association for Computational Linguistics.

Steven Bird, Ewan Klein, and Edward Loper. 2009. *Natural language processing with Python: analyzing text with the natural language toolkit.* " O'Reilly Media, Inc.".

Jacob Devlin, Ming-Wei Chang, Kenton Lee, and Kristina Toutanova. 2019. Bert: Pre-training of deep bidirectional transformers for language understanding. In *Proceedings of the 2019 Conference of the North American Chapter of the Association for Computational Linguistics: Human Language Technologies, Volume 1 (Long and Short Papers)*, pages 4171–4186.

Marina Fomicheva and Lucia Specia. 2019. Taking MT evaluation metrics to extremes: Beyond correlation with human judgments. *Computational Linguistics*, 45(3):515–558.

Luyu Gao, Xueguang Ma, Jimmy Lin, and Jamie Callan. 2023. Precise zero-shot dense retrieval without relevance labels. In *Proceedings of the 61st Annual Meeting of the Association for Computational Linguistics (Volume 1: Long Papers)*, pages 1762–1777, Toronto, Canada. Association for Computational Linguistics.

Teven Le Scao, Angela Fan, Christopher Akiki, Ellie Pavlick, Suzana Ilić, Daniel Hesslow, Roman Castagné, Alexandra Sasha Luccioni, François Yvon, Matthias Gallé, et al. 2023. Bloom: A 176b-parameter open-access multilingual language model.

Tomas Mikolov, Kai Chen, Greg Corrado, and Jeffrey Dean. 2013. Efficient estimation of word representations in vector space. *arXiv preprint arXiv:1301.3781*.

Stephen Robertson, Hugo Zaragoza, et al. 2009. The probabilistic relevance framework: Bm25 and beyond. *Foundations and Trends® in Information Retrieval*, 3(4):333–389.

Michael Sejr Schlichtkrull, Zhijiang Guo, and Andreas Vlachos. 2023. Averitec: A dataset for real-world claim verification with evidence from the web. In *Thirty-seventh Conference on Neural Information Processing Systems Datasets and Benchmarks Track*.

Tao Shen, Guodong Long, Xiubo Geng, Chongyang Tao, Tianyi Zhou, and Daxin Jiang. 2023. Large language models are strong zero-shot retriever. *arXiv preprint arXiv:2304.14233*.

James Thorne, Andreas Vlachos, Christos Christodoulopoulos, and Arpit Mittal. 2018a. FEVER: a large-scale dataset for fact extraction and VERification. In *Proceedings of the 2018 Conference of the North American Chapter of the Association for Computational Linguistics: Human Language Technologies, Volume 1 (Long Papers)*, pages 809–819, New Orleans, Louisiana. Association for Computational Linguistics.

James Thorne, Andreas Vlachos, Oana Cocarascu, Christos Christodoulopoulos, and Arpit Mittal. 2018b. The fact extraction and VERification (FEVER) shared task. In *Proceedings of the First Workshop on Fact Extraction and VERification (FEVER)*, pages 1–9, Brussels, Belgium. Association for Computational Linguistics.

James Thorne, Andreas Vlachos, Oana Cocarascu, Christos Christodoulopoulos, and Arpit Mittal. 2019. The FEVER2.0 shared task. In *Proceedings of the Second Workshop on Fact Extraction and VERification (FEVER)*, pages 1–6, Hong Kong, China. Association for Computational Linguistics.

Andrew Trotman, Antti Puurula, and Blake Burgess. 2014. Improvements to bm25 and language models examined. In *Proceedings of the 19th Australasian Document Computing Symposium*, ADCS '14, page 58–65, New York, NY, USA. Association for Computing Machinery.

Andreas Vlachos and Sebastian Riedel. 2014. Fact checking: Task definition and dataset construction. In *Proceedings of the ACL 2014 workshop on language technologies and computational social science*, pages 18–22.

Nancy X. R. Wang, Diwakar Mahajan, Marina Danilevsky, and Sara Rosenthal. 2021. SemEval-2021 task 9: Fact verification and evidence finding for tabular data in scientific documents (SEM-TAB-FACTS). In *Proceedings of the 15th International Workshop on Semantic Evaluation (SemEval-2021)*, pages 317–326, Online. Association for Computational Linguistics.

Xuezhi Wang, Jason Wei, Dale Schuurmans, Quoc Le, Ed Chi, Sharan Narang, Aakanksha Chowdhery, and Denny Zhou. 2022. Self-consistency improves chain of thought reasoning in language models. *arXiv preprint arXiv:2203.11171*.

Jason Wei, Xuezhi Wang, Dale Schuurmans, Maarten Bosma, Fei Xia, Ed Chi, Quoc V Le, Denny Zhou, et al. 2022. Chain-of-thought prompting elicits reasoning in large language models. *Advances in neural information processing systems*, 35:24824–24837.

FZI-WIM at AVeriTeC Shared Task: Real-World Fact-Checking with Question Answering

Jin Liu[1,2], Steffen Thoma[1], and Achim Rettinger[1,3]

[1]FZI Research Center for Information Technology, Karlsruhe, Germany
[2]Karlsruhe Institute of Technology, Karlsruhe, Germany
[3]Trier University, Trier, Germany
{jin.liu, thoma, rettinger}@fzi.de

Abstract

This paper describes the FZI-WIM system at the AVeriTeC shared Task, which aims to assess evidence-based automated fact-checking systems for real-world claims with evidence retrieved from the web. The FZI-WIM system utilizes open-source models to build a reliable fact-checking pipeline via question-answering. With different experimental setups, we show that more questions lead to higher scores in the shared task. Both in question generation and question-answering stages, sampling can be a way to improve the performance of our system. We further analyze the limitations of current open-source models for real-world claim verification. Our code is publicly available[1].

1 Introduction

Disinformation is a major concern in digital times as recent advances in generative artificial intelligence, i.e., large language models (LLMs), enable humans to create fake information on a large scale. Meanwhile, LLMs have also been integrated into automated fact-checking (AFC) systems (Chen and Shu, 2024), which have drawn lots of attention. Guo et al. (2022) summarize three stages of an AFC system: claim detection, evidence retrieval, and claim verification. Various evidence-based fact-checking datasets have been proposed for testing the systems (Thorne et al., 2018; Wadden et al., 2020; Jiang et al., 2020; Aly et al., 2021). The AVeriTeC shared task aims to fact-check real-world claims. Compared to previous fact-checking datasets, the AVeriTeC dataset (Schlichtkrull et al., 2023) utilizes question-answer (QA) pairs to tackle the complex reasoning task for real-world claims. Questioning is a natural step in the fact-checking process. The following steps involve retrieving corresponding answers and making inferences based on the QA pairs to validate the claims. Fan et al. (2020) have introduced the QABRIEF dataset, which was collected via crowdsourcing. They demonstrate that generating questions and then answering questions using open-domain question-answering can increase the accuracy and efficiency of fact-checking. With the ClaimDecomp dataset, Chen et al. (2022) show that questions to the claim can help identify relevant evidence and verify the claim with their answers.

The FZI-WIM system is composed of three stages, namely, question generation, question-answering, and claim verification. All components in the system are designed with open-source models. Given the claim and its meta information, the system first generates critical questions. A retrieval augmented generation (RAG) system is utilized to answer the generated questions with context information from the provided knowledge store. The generated QA pairs are fact-checked and filtered to tackle the potential hallucination problem. The selected QA pairs are utilized to verify the claim. We summarize our findings regarding this shared task as follows:

- More sets of distinct questions lead to better performance.
- The sampling strategy can compensate for the deficits of open-source LLMs.
- Fact-checking the RAG system is critical for getting reliable grounded answers.
- Compared to open-source models, proprietary models show significantly better performance regarding context understanding and reasoning capabilities for answering questions.

2 Background

The AVeriTeC dataset (Schlichtkrull et al., 2023) is a continuation of the previous evidence-based fact-checking dataset FEVER (Thorne et al., 2018)

[1]https://github.com/jens5588/FZI-WIM-AVERITEC

Proceedings of the Seventh Fact Extraction and VERification Workshop (FEVER), pages 77–85
November 15, 2024 ©2024 Association for Computational Linguistics

and FEVEROUS (Aly et al., 2021). The dataset contains real-world claims from various sources. The number of claims in the train, dev, and test set are 3068, 500, and 2215 respectively. There are five types of claims in the dataset, namely position statement, numerical claim, event/property claim, quote verification, and causal claim. The corresponding evidence has been collected from internet websites. Different from the previous dataset, which uses sentences from documents as evidence, the evidence of the AVeriTeC dataset has been formulated as QA pairs. On average, each claim in the train and dev sets has 2.6 questions. The answers can be classified into four types, boolean, abstractive, extractive, and unanswerable. Based on the QA pairs, the verification labels of the claims can be classified into supported, refuted, not enough evidence, and conflicting evidence/cherry-picking. Figure 1 shows an example from the dataset.

Claim: Donald Trump has kept his promises to voters.
Claim type: Event/Property Claim
Speaker: None
Claim date: 24-8-2020

Question 1: What promises did Donald Trump make to voters?
Answer 1 (Extractive & Abstractive): During the 2016 campaign, Donald Trump made more than 280 promises, though many were contradictory or just uttered in a single campaign event. By 2020 Trump had made a number of promises, 6 of which he had not fulfilled, including ...
Question 2: Of the promises Donald Trump made, did he fulfil any of them?
Answer 2 (Boolean): Yes.
Question 3: Has President Donald Trump kept his campaign promises to voters?
Answer 3 (Abstractive): President Trump has only kept a few of his promises.

Verification: Conflicting Evidence/Cherrypicking
Justification: QA pairs state promises kept and not kept. Claim does not state he kept all promises.

Figure 1: An example from the AVeriTeC dataset, which includes the claim, meta information, questions, answers (answer types), verification label, and justification

3 System Description

Figure 2 illustrates the three-stage pipeline of the FZI-WIM system for the AVeriTeC shared task in the test phase. In the following, we will describe the key components of each stage. The technical implementation details are presented in Appendix A.1.

3.1 Question Generator

As mentioned by (Chen et al., 2022), questions can help to identify relevant evidence. As the first component of the pipeline, raising the right questions about the claim can be critical for the final verification. Similar to the AVeriTeC dataset, the ClaimDecomp dataset (Chen et al., 2022) contains in total 1200 claims in the training, validation, and test sets while, on average, each claim has 2.7 questions. We integrate both datasets and create an instruction-tuning dataset. Besides the claim and questions, we also include the relevant meta information, such as the speaker and claim date, in the instruction dataset. We show an example of the instruction dataset in Appendix A.2.

We apply Low-rank adaption (LORA) (Hu et al., 2022), one of the parameter-efficient fine-tuning methods for LLMs, to fine-tune the existing LLM, Llama-3-70B-Instruct (AI@Meta, 2024). The concept of LORA assumes that the updates to the weights have a low intrinsic rank during the adaption of LLMs for downstream tasks. The parameter updates ΔW for a pre-trained matrix W_0 can be formulated as

$$W_0 + \Delta W = W_0 + BA, \tag{1}$$

where $B \in \mathbb{R}^{d \times r}$, $A \in \mathbb{R}^{r \times k}$ and $r \ll \min(d, k)$ (Hu et al., 2022). Given the instruction x and target output $\{y_1, y_2, ..., y_m\}$, i.e., questions, the loss function of the training can be formulated as

$$L = \sum_{i=1}^{m} - \log(p_\theta(y_i|x, y_1, ..., y_{i-1})), \tag{2}$$

where θ represents W_0, B, A and only B and A are trainable.

With the instruction-tuned model, we first generate for each claim one set of questions greedily. With the greedy generation strategy, the model selects the token with the highest probability as its next token[2]. We further sample five sets of questions for each claim with a temperature of 0.7. With an embedding model, all-mpnet-base-v2[3] (Reimers and Gurevych, 2019), we iteratively select 2 sets from 5 sampled sets, which are most distinct from the greedy set based on the cosine similarity. Finally, each claim has three sets of questions, one greedy set, and two sampled sets.

[2]https://huggingface.co/blog/how-to-generate

[3]https://huggingface.co/sentence-transformers/all-mpnet-base-v2

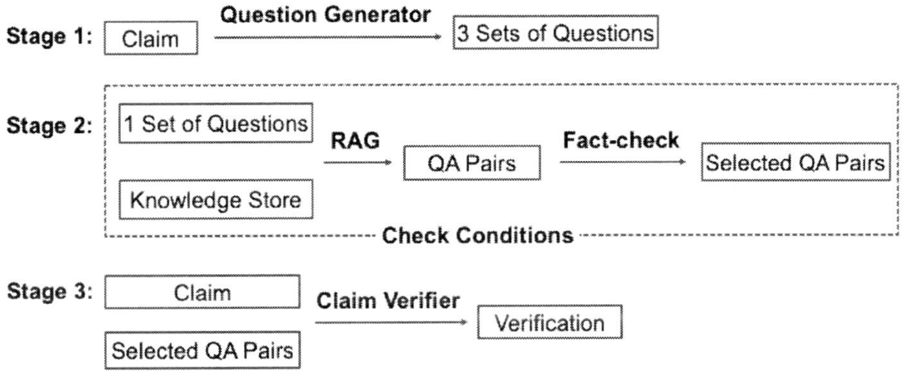

Figure 2: FZI-WIM system pipeline for the test phase in stages. In Stage 1, we first generate three sets of questions for each claim. One set of questions can contain multiple questions. Given questions and the knowledge store, our system utilizes an RAG system to generate answers to the questions. With an entailment model, the generated QA pairs are filtered. The selected QA pairs have a further conditional check. If conditions are not fulfilled, the steps in stage 2 are then repeated with another set of questions, a maximum of two repeats. Finally, an instruction-tuned claim verifier verifies the claim based on the aggregated QA pairs.

3.2 Question Answering

After generating questions for each claim, stage 2 answers these generated questions. Beginning with the greedy set of questions, the questions are answered with a retrieval augmented generation (RAG) system. We further fact-check and select answered QA pairs. We check whether the selected QA pairs fulfill the predefined conditions. If not, we then repeat the process with another sampled question set. The process is repeated at most two times.

3.2.1 RAG-based QA

Retriever After generating questions for the claims, we retrieve relevant evidence in the provided knowledge store to answer these questions. Our system only uses the provided knowledge store without querying further documents with the Google search engine. For each claim, the relevant documents are provided in the knowledge store. Various retrieval methods have been applied for documents and sentence retrieval in evidence-based fact-checking, including TF-IDF (Thorne et al., 2018), BM25 (Schlichtkrull et al., 2023), bi-encoder (Karisani and Ji, 2024), ColBERT (Khattab et al., 2021), cross-encoder (Soleimani et al., 2020), etc. Due to the limited number of relevant documents for each claim in the knowledge store, we directly apply a cross-encoder, ms-marco-MiniLM-L-12-v2[4] (Reimers and Gurevych, 2019), to select relevant evidence. Concretely, for each generated question, we concatenate it with the claim as the query. We then iteratively split each document into chunks so that the total length of the query and chunk pair does not exceed the maximum length of the cross-encoder, 512 tokens. Figure 3 illustrates the input of the cross-encoder. We rank the chunks based on the relevance scores predicted by the cross-encoder. For each question, we select the top 3 chunks for answering the question.

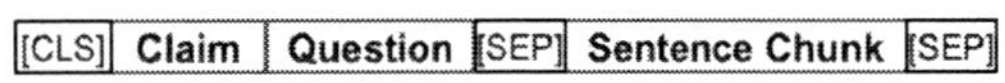

Figure 3: Input of the cross-encoder. The document is split into multiple sentence chunks so that the total length of the combination doesn't exceed 512 tokens. A sentence chunk includes about 400 to 500 tokens.

Generator With the retrieved top 3 chunks for each question, we utilize a fine-tuned LLM, Llama3-ChatQA-1.5-70B (Liu et al., 2024), to generate answers given the question and corresponding top chunks as the context. Besides the greedy generation, we sample 10 further answers with temperature 0.7 to increase the probability that the generator correctly answers the question. We show the prompt for answer generation in Appendix A.3. The candidate pool for the answer is initialized with the greedy answer. Further distinct answers from sampling are iteratively added to the candidate pool based on the similarity scores with an embedding model, all-mpnet-base-v2 (Reimers and Gurevych,

[4]https://huggingface.co/cross-encoder/ms-marco-MiniLM-L-12-v2

2019). In this step, one question can have multiple distinct answers. This design choice is based on our observation from experiments, that the correct answer to the question can not always be generated with the greedy decoding strategy by our generator.

3.2.2 Fact-check QA Pairs

Hallucination is a common problem of current RAG systems and it can lead to the problem that generated answers are not entailed in the source chunks. Therefore, we further add an entailment check step for generated answers. We first use few-shot learning to convert QA pairs into statements. The prompt is shown in Appendix A.4. A pre-trained natural language inference (NLI) model, bart-large-mnli[5] (Lewis et al., 2019), is used to check whether the statement is entailed in the corresponding sentence chunks. The pre-trained NLI model has three labels for (premise, hypothesis) pairs, namely refuted, not enough information (NEI), and entailed. Each statement corresponds to three sentence chunks. As soon as the statement is entailed in one sentence chunk, the corresponding QA pair will be selected. Since one question can have multiple entailed answers, i.e., statements, we select the answer with the largest entailment probability. We observe that our NLI model cannot correctly handle the entailment relationship for statements like *No information regarding ... could be found.*, which are often classified as NEI despite being entailed (supported) in the sentence chunks. So if a question has no entailed answer and there are NEI answers like *There is no information...*, *Sorry, I cannot find the answer based on the context*, etc., we also select the question with a uniform answer *No answer could be found.* for further processing. The questions that have neither entailed answers nor NEI answers are dropped.

3.2.3 Check Conditions & Aggragate

Since the fact-checking step has filtered some QA pairs, it can make the verification step difficult. We introduce two conditions to check the completeness of answers to a set of questions, namely $\frac{\#questions\ answered}{\#questions} > 0.8$ and $\frac{\#question\ answered\ with\ NEI}{\#questions\ answered} < 0.3$, where $\#questions\ answered$ represents for the number of answered questions and includes both the entailed answer and the NEI answer. If the conditions are not fulfilled, we repeat the steps in stage 2 with another set of questions.

After the maximal two times repeat, we aggregate all QA pairs for each claim. Each claim can have from one to three rounds of question answering. There can be duplicated QA pairs after aggregation. We first rank the QA pairs with a cross-encoder model based on their relevance to the claim. The QA pairs are iteratively selected with a further embedding model so that the to-be-selected pair does not exceed the similarity threshold to selected pairs. Some claims do not have any entailed or NEI answer after the third question answering round. For these claims, we use the greedy set of questions and assign *No answer could be found.* as the answer.

3.3 Claim Verification

We verify the claims with the aggregated QA pairs. Similar to the question generation process, we utilize the train and dev set to instruction-tune a pre-trained LLM, Llama-3-70B-Instruct (AI@Meta, 2024), with LORA. We show an example of the instruction dataset in Appendix A.5. We also include the justification in the target output before the verification label so that the model not only generates the verification label but also the justification. This mimics the chain-of-thought idea (Wei et al., 2022). Studies (Wang et al., 2023; Liu and Thoma, 2024) show that sampling instead of greedy decoding can improve the reasoning performance of LLMs. We sample 40 verifications for each claim and apply majority voting to derive the final verification label.

4 Evaluation

In this section, we show the performance of our proposed systems for the shared task. Besides the system in the test phase, the FZI-WIM Test, we also include the improved version in the after competition phase, FZI-WIM After Compet., for comparison. With the FZI-WIM After Compet. setup, each claim has three sets of distinct questions without conditional check described in Section 3.2.3.

4.1 Evaluation Metrics

For the shared task, both retrieved evidence and veracity predictions are evaluated. For the evidence evaluation, generated questions and answers are compared to the reference (gold questions and answers). The pairwise scoring function is defined as $f : S \times S \rightarrow \mathbb{R}$, where S is the set

[5]https://huggingface.co/facebook/bart-large-mnli

System	Q	Q+A	AVeriTeC Score
FZI-WIM Test	0.32	0.21	0.20
FZI-WIM After Compet.	0.40	0.27	0.33
Baseline	0.24	0.20	0.11
Best scores	0.49	0.35	0.63

Table 1: Overview of our systems compared to the baseline system and best scores in each category. FZI-WIM Test is our proposed system in the test phase. We further improve the system in the after competition phase with the system FZI-WIM After Compet..

of sequence tokens. The scoring function adopts the METEOR (Banerjee and Lavie, 2005) metric. The Hungarian Algorithm (Kuhn, 1955) is applied to find an optimal match between generated sequences and reference sequences (Schlichtkrull et al., 2023). A boolean function X is defined as $X : \hat{Y} \times Y \rightarrow \{0, 1\}$ to denote the assignment between the generated sequences $\hat{Y}$ and the reference sequences Y. The final score u is calculated (Schlichtkrull et al., 2023) as:

$$u_f(\hat{Y}, Y) = \frac{1}{|Y|} \max \sum_{\hat{y} \in \hat{Y}} \sum_{y \in Y} f(\hat{y}, y) X(\hat{y}, y) \quad (3)$$

The evaluation of veracity prediction uses the accuracy metric. A cut-off of $f(\hat{y}, y) \geq \lambda$ has been applied to determine whether correct evidence (concatenation of questions and answers) has been retrieved. Claims with an evidence score lower than the cut-off score λ receive veracity scores of 0. The AVeriTeC score in the shared task has a λ value of 0.25 (Schlichtkrull et al., 2023).

4.2 Results

Table 1 shows the performance of our proposed systems compared to the baseline system and the best scores in each category. After the competition, we further improved our system with more questions (FZI-WIM After Compet.). Concretely, we remove the conditional check step and further repeat stage 2 twice for every claim. This means each claim has three sets of questions and three rounds of question answering. With more questions, we can observe significant performance improvement regarding three metrics. In the following, we give a detailed analysis of our system regarding question generation & answering and claim verification.

4.3 QA Analysis

Table 2 shows the statistics of three different setups for selecting QA pairs. In the Greedy setup, the selected QA pairs for each claim are aggregated only with the greedy set of questions. In the FZI-WIM Test setup, with the conditional check, 1405 claims have utilized one set of questions, 365 claims with 2 sets of questions, and 445 claims with three sets of questions to select QA pairs. In the FZI-WIM After Compet. setup all 2215 claims have three sets of questions to select QA pairs. From the results, we can observe that more sets of different questions improve the scoring of both question and QA pairs. This is partly because we have not retrieved extra documents outside the knowledge store, which can cause questions to be not properly answered. There are various ways to ask critical questions for each claim, i.e., various reasoning possibilities. More sets of different questions can increase the probability of matching the gold questions. In the following, we give a further analysis regarding each component in our question-answering pipeline, with a focus on the deficits that cause errors.

Retriever We have directly applied a cross-encoder model to select relevant chunks from the document corpus. Compared to other methods, e.g., TF-IDF, dual-encoder, etc., the advantage of the cross-encoder is the retriever performance, and the disadvantage is the computing time. Another limitation of the cross-encoder model is the input length, in our case a maximum of 512 tokens. The incomplete context information can lead to misleading answers, especially adversarial information, i.e., misinformation or satire exists in the context.

Generator We have utilized Llama3-ChatQA-1.5-70B (Liu et al., 2024) from Nvidia to generate answers with a zero-shot setup. For a question, the corresponding context combined of the top 3 sentence chunks, normally includes around 1500 tokens. Hallucination and insufficient understanding of questions and contexts are two major reasons leading to wrong answers. We observe that with the greedy generation, the model cannot always come to the correct answer. We further sample 10 answers with a temperature of 0.7 for each question. Table 3 shows the distribution of answer sources. The statistics show the necessity of sampling besides the greedy generation.

Fact-check The difference between the number of total questions and answered questions in Table 3 reflects the number of dropped questions under

Setup	#Total Questions	#Selected QA	NEI (%)	Q	Q+A
Greedy Set of Questions	5004	3846	17.57	0.28	0.18
FZI-WIM Test	8212	5574	16.02	0.32	0.20
FZI-WIM After Compet.	16696	10048	18.68	0.40	0.27

Table 2: Comparison of different setups for QA pairs selection, including the numbers of total generated questions and selected QA pairs, percentage of the NEI answer in selected QA pairs, and the resulting question scores, question + answer scores.

Setup	#Total Questions	#Answered	Greedy / Sampling (%)
Greedy Set of Questions	5004	4381	74.30 / 25.70
FZI-WIM Test	8212	7004	69.20 / 30.80
FZI-WIM After Compet.	16696	14512	68.54 / 31.46

Table 3: Distribution of answers, including entailed and NEI answers, among greedy generation and sampling under different setups.

System	Greedy	Sampling
FZI-WIM Test	0.1991	0.1959
FZI-WIM After Compet.	0.3314	0.3336

Table 4: Comparison of AVeriTeC scores under greedy generation and sampling strategies for claim verification. The same QA pairs are used for each system with two strategies.

each setup. The dropped questions have neither entailed answers nor NEI answers, which shows the necessity of fact-checking the RAG system in the pipeline. We have utilized a pre-trained discriminative NLI model, bart-large-mnli (Lewis et al., 2019), with a maximum input length of 1024 tokens. Existing pre-training datasets for NLI, i.e., MNLI, SNLI, etc., have normally short contexts. Given the trend of growing context length in the current RAG systems, reliable entailment-check at the document level can be interesting for future research.

4.4 Claim Verification

The claim is verified with an instruction-tuned model. In the submitted systems, we have sampled 40 verifications for each claim and applied majority voting to select the final label. With the same instruction-tuned model and QA pairs, we generate the verification greedily for comparison. Table 4 shows the verification performance of greedy generation and sampling. The performance difference regarding the AVeriTeC score is negligible between the two strategies. This can be partly attributed to the final AVeriTeC scoring function. We can only conclude the greedy generation and sampling for claims, whose corresponding QA pairs compared to gold QA pairs have exceeded the cut-off threshold of 0.25, make a small difference. For claims with QA scores smaller than 0.25, which are not necessarily wrong, the effect of sampling compared to the greedy generation is not reflected in the AVeriTeC scores.

4.5 Open-source VS Proprietary Models

We have observed the current bottleneck of our pipeline lies in the generator, which utilizes an open-source LLM Llama3-ChatQA-1.5-70B (Liu et al., 2024) as the backbone to answer questions. We conduct further experiments and replace the open-source LLM with a proprietary model, namely GPT4-Turbo from OpenAI [6]. Concretely we apply the same question generator, retriever, and claim verifier as shown in Figure 2. Only the generator is replaced with GPT4-Turbo. Due to the budget constraint, we evaluate the model only on the dev set and generate the answers greedily (temperature 0) without sampling. We have not fact-checked (entailment check) the answers from GPT4-Turbo, which is generally wordy compared to the open-source generator and makes the entailment check difficult. We have utilized maximal two sets of distinct questions. For comparison, we select the FZI-WIM After Compet. system, which utilizes three sets of distinct questions for each claim. The results are shown in Table 5. The Q+A scores in the table demonstrate significantly better performance of GPT4-Turbo than the open-source generator. Our manual investigation shows also that GPT4-Turbo has better context understanding and reasoning capabilities, especially in adversarial cases.

[6] https://openai.com

Setup	#Selected QA	Q	Q+A	AVeriTeC Score
FZI-WIM After Compet.	2266	0.41	0.26	0.29
GPT4-Turbo (1 Set Questions)	1096	0.32	0.22	0.24
GPT-4 Turbo (2 Sets Questions)	2372	0.42	0.30	0.45

Table 5: Comparison between open-source and proprietary LLMs as the generator for answering questions on the dev dataset. FZI-WIM After Compet. utilizes all three sets of questions.

5 Conclusion & Outlook

In this paper, we have described the FZI-WIM system for the AVeriTeC shared task, which aims to tackle the real-world claim verification problem. The complex reasoning problem in fact-checking is tackled via question-answering. For each claim, we first generate relevant critical questions. Based on the provided knowledge store, the questions are answered with an RAG system. Considering the hallucination problem in RAG systems, we fact-check the generated QA pairs to ensure the answers are entailed in the source texts. We show that more questions, i.e., more question-answering rounds, lead to better model performance. The claim verification is based on the selected QA pairs.

Generally, our current systems need a large amount of computing. The improvement of the efficiency with open-source models is needed for the real-world scenario. Compared to proprietary models, our generator in the RAG system is not robust enough against adversarial contexts, e.g., misinformation, satire, etc. Further enhancement of the robustness can be a promising research direction.

6 Acknowledgments

This work was carried out with the support of the German Federal Ministry of Education and Research (BMBF) within the project "DeFaktS" (Grant 16KIS1524K). This work was performed on the HoreKa supercomputer funded by the Ministry of Science, Research and the Arts Baden-Württemberg and by the Federal Ministry of Education and Research.

Limitations

Due to the limited time for developing the systems in the test phase, our systems have only used the provided knowledge store without searching for extra relevant documents related to our questions. Extra search can make a big difference for certain steps, e.g., the repeated processes in stage 2. With extra search, the times of repeats can be reduced. To achieve the best performance our current systems have always selected better-performed open-source models, e.g., cross-encoder, LLMs, etc., which normally have a larger size. This leads to the fact that our systems require a large amount of computing. In the future, we will focus on the trade-off of performance and efficiency for real-world fact-checking systems.

References

AI@Meta. 2024. Llama 3 model card.

Rami Aly, Zhijiang Guo, Michael Sejr Schlichtkrull, James Thorne, Andreas Vlachos, Christos Christodoulopoulos, Oana Cocarascu, and Arpit Mittal. 2021. The fact extraction and VERification over unstructured and structured information (FEVEROUS) shared task. In *Proceedings of the Fourth Workshop on Fact Extraction and VERification (FEVER)*, pages 1–13, Dominican Republic. Association for Computational Linguistics.

Satanjeev Banerjee and Alon Lavie. 2005. METEOR: An automatic metric for MT evaluation with improved correlation with human judgments. In *Proceedings of the ACL Workshop on Intrinsic and Extrinsic Evaluation Measures for Machine Translation and/or Summarization*, pages 65–72, Ann Arbor, Michigan. Association for Computational Linguistics.

Canyu Chen and Kai Shu. 2024. Combating misinformation in the age of llms: Opportunities and challenges. *AI Magazine*.

Jifan Chen, Aniruddh Sriram, Eunsol Choi, and Greg Durrett. 2022. Generating literal and implied subquestions to fact-check complex claims. In *Proceedings of the 2022 Conference on Empirical Methods in Natural Language Processing*, pages 3495–3516, Abu Dhabi, United Arab Emirates. Association for Computational Linguistics.

Angela Fan, Aleksandra Piktus, Fabio Petroni, Guillaume Wenzek, Marzieh Saeidi, Andreas Vlachos, Antoine Bordes, and Sebastian Riedel. 2020. Generating fact checking briefs. In *Proceedings of the 2020 Conference on Empirical Methods in Natural Language Processing (EMNLP)*, pages 7147–7161, Online. Association for Computational Linguistics.

Zhijiang Guo, Michael Schlichtkrull, and Andreas Vlachos. 2022. A survey on automated fact-checking. *Transactions of the Association for Computational Linguistics*, 10:178–206.

Edward J Hu, Yelong Shen, Phillip Wallis, Zeyuan Allen-Zhu, Yuanzhi Li, Shean Wang, Lu Wang, and Weizhu Chen. 2022. LoRA: Low-rank adaptation of large language models. In *International Conference on Learning Representations*.

Yichen Jiang, Shikha Bordia, Zheng Zhong, Charles Dognin, Maneesh Singh, and Mohit Bansal. 2020. HoVer: A dataset for many-hop fact extraction and claim verification. In *Findings of the Association for Computational Linguistics: EMNLP 2020*, pages 3441–3460, Online. Association for Computational Linguistics.

Payam Karisani and Heng Ji. 2024. Fact checking beyond training set. In *Proceedings of the 2024 Conference of the North American Chapter of the Association for Computational Linguistics: Human Language Technologies (Volume 1: Long Papers)*, pages 2247–2261, Mexico City, Mexico. Association for Computational Linguistics.

Omar Khattab, Christopher Potts, and Matei Zaharia. 2021. Baleen: Robust multi-hop reasoning at scale via condensed retrieval. In *Advances in Neural Information Processing Systems*.

H. W. Kuhn. 1955. The hungarian method for the assignment problem. *Naval Research Logistics Quarterly*.

Mike Lewis, Yinhan Liu, Naman Goyal, Marjan Ghazvininejad, Abdelrahman Mohamed, Omer Levy, Veselin Stoyanov, and Luke Zettlemoyer. 2019. Bart: Denoising sequence-to-sequence pre-training for natural language generation, translation, and comprehension. *arXiv preprint arXiv:1910.13461*.

Jin Liu and Steffen Thoma. 2024. FZI-WIM at SemEval-2024 task 2: Self-consistent CoT for complex NLI in biomedical domain. In *Proceedings of the 18th International Workshop on Semantic Evaluation (SemEval-2024)*, pages 1269–1279, Mexico City, Mexico. Association for Computational Linguistics.

Zihan Liu, Wei Ping, Rajarshi Roy, Peng Xu, Chankyu Lee, Mohammad Shoeybi, and Bryan Catanzaro. 2024. Chatqa: Surpassing gpt-4 on conversational qa and rag. *arXiv preprint arXiv:2401.10225*.

Nils Reimers and Iryna Gurevych. 2019. Sentence-bert: Sentence embeddings using siamese bert-networks. In *Proceedings of the 2019 Conference on Empirical Methods in Natural Language Processing*. Association for Computational Linguistics.

Michael Sejr Schlichtkrull, Zhijiang Guo, and Andreas Vlachos. 2023. AVeritec: A dataset for real-world claim verification with evidence from the web. In *Thirty-seventh Conference on Neural Information Processing Systems Datasets and Benchmarks Track*.

Amir Soleimani, Christof Monz, and Marcel Worring. 2020. Bert for evidence retrieval and claim verification. In *Advances in Information Retrieval*, pages 359–366, Cham. Springer International Publishing.

James Thorne, Andreas Vlachos, Christos Christodoulopoulos, and Arpit Mittal. 2018. FEVER: a large-scale dataset for fact extraction and VERification. In *Proceedings of the 2018 Conference of the North American Chapter of the Association for Computational Linguistics: Human Language Technologies, Volume 1 (Long Papers)*, pages 809–819, New Orleans, Louisiana. Association for Computational Linguistics.

David Wadden, Shanchuan Lin, Kyle Lo, Lucy Lu Wang, Madeleine van Zuylen, Arman Cohan, and Hannaneh Hajishirzi. 2020. Fact or fiction: Verifying scientific claims. In *Proceedings of the 2020 Conference on Empirical Methods in Natural Language Processing (EMNLP)*, pages 7534–7550, Online. Association for Computational Linguistics.

Xuezhi Wang, Jason Wei, Dale Schuurmans, Quoc V Le, Ed H. Chi, Sharan Narang, Aakanksha Chowdhery, and Denny Zhou. 2023. Self-consistency improves chain of thought reasoning in language models. In *The Eleventh International Conference on Learning Representations*.

Jason Wei, Xuezhi Wang, Dale Schuurmans, Maarten Bosma, brian ichter, Fei Xia, Ed H. Chi, Quoc V Le, and Denny Zhou. 2022. Chain of thought prompting elicits reasoning in large language models. In *Advances in Neural Information Processing Systems*.

Yanli Zhao, Andrew Gu, Rohan Varma, Liang Luo, Chien-Chin Huang, Min Xu, Less Wright, Hamid Shojanazeri, Myle Ott, Sam Shleifer, Alban Desmaison, Can Balioglu, Pritam Damania, Bernard Nguyen, Geeta Chauhan, Yuchen Hao, Ajit Mathews, and Shen Li. 2023. Pytorch FSDP: experiences on scaling fully sharded data parallel. *Proc. VLDB Endow.*, 16(12):3848–3860.

A Appendix

A.1 Implementation details

Instruction-tuning We have applied Fully Shared Data Parallel (FSDP) from Meta AI (Zhao et al., 2023) for the instruction-tuning of question generation and claim verification models. The training script is based on llama-recipes[7] with two 4×Nvidia-H100 nodes. The dev sets are included for fine-tuning to make predictions on the final test set. For question generation, we have fine-tuned for 5 epochs and claim verification for 3 epochs.

Model inference We have applied transformers library[8] for inference. For the greedy generation, we set the parameter *do_sample* as false. For sampling, we set *temperature* as 0.7 and *top_k* as 50.

A.2 Example for instruction-tuning question generator

Figure 4 shows an example of the instruction-tuning dataset for the question generator.

[7]`https://github.com/meta-llama/llama-recipes`

[8]`https://github.com/huggingface/transformers`

You are a fact-checker and your task is to generate critical questions for verifying the following claim.
Claim date: 25-8-2020
Claimer: Pam Bondi
Claim: Hunter Biden had no experience in Ukraine or in the energy sector when he joined the board of Burisma.
Questions: Did Hunter Biden have any experience in the energy sector at the time he joined the board of the Burisma energy company in 2014? Did Hunter Biden have any experience in Ukraine at the time he joined the board of the Burisma energy company in 2014?

Figure 4: An example of the instruction dataset for fine-tuning an LLM to generate questions. The prompt ends with "Questions: ". The questions are the target output for fine-tuning the LLM.

A.3 Prompt for question-answering

Figure 5 shows the prompt for question-answering.

System: This is a chat between a user and an artificial intelligence assistant. The assistant gives helpful, detailed, and polite answers to the user's questions based on the context. The assistant should also indicate when the answer cannot be found in the context.

GSK does not own Pfizer and or the Wuhan biological laboratory You have sent us an Instagram message with these and other misleading and false relation ...

Disclosure: The Open Society Foundations and Bill and Melinda Gates Foundation are among Africa Check's funders, which together provided 21% of our income in 2019 ...

Rumor – Facts list shows that the Wuhan Laboratory is owned by Glaxo, Pfizer, has connections with foreign companies and receives money from George Soros and Bill Gates ...

User: Please give a full and complete answer for the question. **Who owns GlaxoSmithkline?**

Assistant:

Figure 5: Prompt template for answering the question given the top 3 chunks, adopted from Liu et al. (2024). The top 3 chunks in the context are ordered reversely.

A.4 Few-shot prompt for converting QA pairs to statements

Figure 6 shows the few-shot examples to convert QA pairs to statements.

A.5 Example for instruction-tuning claim verifier

Figure 7 shows an example of the instruction dataset for the claim verification.

Your task is to convert question answer pairs into statements. In the following there are some example showing how to convert question answer pairs into statements.

Question: What resolutions did Biden support in favor of US intervention in Iraq?
Answer: He supported the H.J.Res.114 - Authorization for Use of Military Force Against Iraq Resolution of 2002 107th Congress (2001-2002)
Statement: Joe Biden supported the H.J.Res.114 - Authorization for Use of Military Force Against Iraq Resolution of 2002 107th Congress (2001-2002)

Question: How much of their national budget did the Kenyan judiciary receive in 2021?
Answer: Budget speeches for 2020/21 show the judiciary received 0.6% of the national budget.
Statement: Budget speeches for 2020/21 show the Kenyan judiciary received 0.6% of the national budget.

Question: Should counties be chasing the 10% spending target or should it be done at a national level?
Answer: No answer could be found.
Statement: No answer could be found regarding whether counties should be chasing the 10% spending target or if it should be done at a national level.

Question: Did Hunter Biden have any experience in the energy sector at the time he joined the board of the Burisma energy company in 2014
Answer: No
Statement: Hunter Biden didn't have any experience in the energy sector at the time he joined the board of the Burisma energy company in 2014.

Figure 6: Few-shot prompt for converting QA pairs to statements.

Your task is to verify the claims based on the context information in format of question answer pairs. Verify the claim with justification using the following labels: Supported, Refuted, Not Enough Evidence, Conflicting Evidence/Cherrypicking.

Claim: Hunter Biden had no experience in Ukraine or in the energy sector when he joined the board of Burisma.
Question 1: Did Hunter Biden have any experience in the energy sector at the time he joined the board of the Burisma energy company in 2014
Answer 1: No
Question 2: Did Hunter Biden have any experience in Ukraine at the time he joined the board of the Burisma energy company in 2014
Answer 2: No

Justification: No former experience stated.
Label: Supported

Figure 7: An example of the instruction dataset for fine-tuning an LLM to verify the claims. The prompt ends with "Answer 2: No ". The justification and label are the target output.

Zero-Shot Learning and Key Points Are All You Need for Automated Fact-Checking

Mohammad Ghiasvand Mohammadkhani[1], **Ali Ghiasvand Mohammadkhani**[2]
Hamid Beigy[3]
[1]Amirkabir University of Technology, [2]Shahid Soltani 4 High School
[3]Sharif University of Technology
mohammad.ghiasvand@aut.ac.ir, aghiasvandm@gmail.com, beigy@sharif.edu

Abstract

Automated fact-checking is an important task because determining the accurate status of a proposed claim within the vast amount of information available online is a critical challenge. This challenge requires robust evaluation to prevent the spread of false information. Modern large language models (LLMs) have demonstrated high capability in performing a diverse range of Natural Language Processing (NLP) tasks. By utilizing proper prompting strategies, their versatility—due to their understanding of large context sizes and zero-shot learning ability—enables them to simulate human problem-solving intuition and move towards being an alternative to humans for solving problems. In this work, we introduce a straightforward framework based on ***Zero-Shot Learning*** and ***Key Points*** (ZSL-KeP) for automated fact-checking, which despite its simplicity, performed well on the AVeriTeC shared task dataset by robustly improving the baseline and achieving 10th place.[1]

1 Introduction

The AVeriTeC task (Schlichtkrull et al., 2024) is designed to encourage the development of advanced frameworks for automated fact-checking, a critical task in NLP. With the rapid spread of information and misinformation online, automated fact-checking is increasingly important. Given the time-consuming nature of manual fact-checking, building an effective neural language model-based framework is valuable for saving time and costs, improving performance, and supporting human judgment. Significant efforts are being made to automate this process within digital tools or LLMs (Nakov et al., 2021).

LLMs with billions of parameters offer extensive knowledge and strong reasoning capabilities that can be customized for various tasks. Designing effective and appropriate prompts is crucial in this customization process. Recent utilization of LLMs can mainly be divided into two categories: fine-tuning and In-Context Learning (ICL). Given the enormous size of LLMs and the high computational cost associated with fine-tuning them, utilizing ICL through zero-shot or few-shot prompting is much more efficient.

Explaining the reasoning behind a decision is crucial for user trust in automated fact-checking, as users need to understand the evidence behind the model's verdict (Guo et al., 2022). This work employs Large Language Models (LLMs) with Zero-Shot Learning (ZSL), which offer advantages over simpler, classification-based models due to their long context windows and high reasoning capabilities. Besides using powerful LLMs and effective prompting, accurate retrieval of relevant information is vital. This involves hierarchical, step-by-step prompting and decomposition-based retrieval methods (Zhang and Gao, 2023). This paper describes the novel approach implemented by our team, **MA-Bros-H**, for the AVeriTeC shared task, which integrates ZSL and key point utilization within a unified and straightforward framework.

2 Related Works

To highlight a few recent research efforts in automated fact-checking, it is notable that (Kotonya and Toni, 2020) provided explainability through summarization, and (Lee et al., 2020) utilized the internal knowledge of pretrained language models such as BERT (Devlin, 2018) within their framework. Additionally, (Lee et al., 2021) employed few-shot prompting for fact-checking, (Zhang and Gao, 2023) introduced a hierarchical, step-by-step prompting method that involves claim decomposition followed by step-by-step reasoning to predict the final verdict, and (Kim et al., 2024) proposed

[1]Code and data released at https://github.com/mghiasvand1/ZSL-KeP

Proceedings of the Seventh Fact Extraction and VERification Workshop (FEVER), pages 86–90
November 15, 2024 ©2024 Association for Computational Linguistics

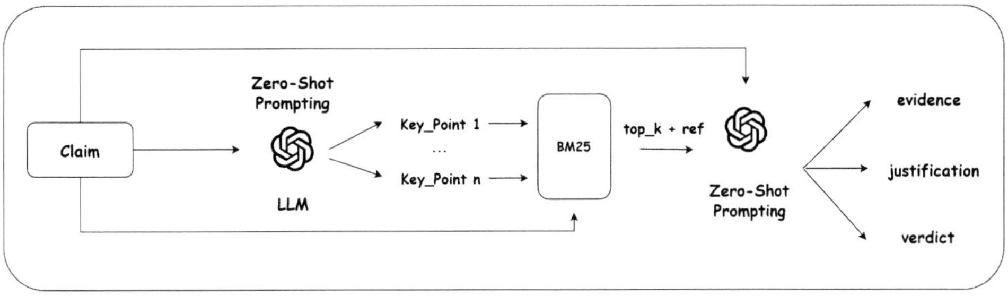

Figure 1: ZSL-KeP Framework Illustration

a multi-agent debate strategy for explainable fact-checking.

3 Methodology

This section provides a detailed overview of the problem definition of AVeriTeC task, as well as the operational procedure of our ZSL-KeP model, as outlined in Figure 1.

3.1 Problem Definition

Since our method is explicitly based on zero-shot prompting, we use only the test data to execute our framework, ignoring the train and validation datasets. For each data point in the test dataset, a claim is provided, and a verdict must be predicted from the labels "*Supported*", "*Refuted*", "*Not Enough Evidence*", and "*Conflicting Evidence/Cherry-Picking*". Additionally, for each claim, a JSON file called a knowledge store is provided. This file contains numerous URLs with scraped texts, including some gold documents that assist in selecting the accurate label. The expected output includes a verdict for the input claim and adequate, yet non-redundant, evidence, preferably in the form of question-answer pairs, along with the corresponding URL and scraped text for each pair to justify the source of each proposed question-answer pair. It is noteworthy that the answer type for each question can be "*Extractive*", "*Abstractive*", "*Boolean*" or "*Unanswerable*".

3.2 ZSL-KeP Framework

Our ZSL-KeP framework is a procedure that contains multiple steps detailed below. However, compared to the baseline method proposed in (Schlichtkrull et al., 2024), our method is much more straightforward, containing fewer steps than the baseline, does not require any fine-tuning, and is simpler to implement.

3.2.1 Zero-Shot Key Points Construction

In the first step, we receive the claim as input and aim to construct key points based on the received claim using ZSL with our chosen LLM. The primary objective of forming key points is that even a simple claim can contain several key points. When searching and retrieving information from the knowledge store, more extensive retrieval typically yields more comprehensive information. A claim might not return many helpful documents when queried directly, but by constructing diverse key points from it, we can obtain more relevant and diverse information. As shown in the prompting template in Appendix A, we limit the number of primitive key points to four. For these distinct key points, we ask the LLM to identify and return pairs of key points whose combinations result in valuable and richer key points. This process aims to construct an extensive set of key points based on the input claim, facilitating more divergent retrieval in the next step.

3.2.2 Extensive Retrieval with References

As mentioned, for each claim, we have a large knowledge store consisting of various URLs with their scraped texts, among which the gold documents for selecting the best and correct verdict are present. In the previous step, we constructed several key points for each claim, either of a normal type or paired, as explained earlier. If the number of constructed key points is n, we treat these key points as a list of queries. We append the main input claim to this list and use BM25 (Robertson et al., 2009) to retrieve results for each of the $n + 1$ queries with a different *top_k* parameter for each query. For each selected retrieval result, since each JSON file contains many URLs and each URL has several scraped texts, we construct an ID by concatenating the URL index within the JSON file

Method	Q only	Q + A	AVeriTeC score
AVeriTeC Baseline (Schlichtkrull et al., 2024)	0.24	0.20	0.11
ZSL-KeP (Ours)	0.38	0.24	0.27

Table 1: Main results include retrieval scores for both questions alone and for questions with answers, as well as the AVeriTeC score for the baseline and our proposed method.

with an underscore, followed by the index of the scraped text within the list. For each retrieval document, we attach the text "<ID>" (where ID is the constructed corresponding ID) to the document. After retrieving and appending all these documents for each query, we separate them with a newline character. Finally, we concatenate all groups of retrievals, separating them with two newline characters and several dashes in between, to form a unified retrieval string for the input claim.

3.2.3 Zero-Shot Prediction

In this stage, which is the final step of our framework, we use ZSL to generate evidence, followed by a justification and, finally, a verdict. We pass the original claim along with the unified retrieval string formed in the previous step as input, exactly as shown in Appendix A; However, due to the limited context window of the LLM we are using, errors may arise. In such cases, we reduce the number of documents in the unified retrieval string and prompt the LLM again with a shorter input length. The reason we include only the retrievals in the unified retrieval string and omit the key points is that we want to avoid influencing the evidence construction process—specifically, the creation of question-answer pairs—in our strategy. We aim to keep this process dynamic, based on the available selected knowledge and the claim's purpose.

Since the number of adequate question-answer pairs available as evidence for any claim may vary, we limit the LLM to providing at most 4 pairs to avoid penalties from additional, non-essential question-answer pairs in our prompt. The justification is needed to reason about the verdict based on the evidence and to directly write the predicted verdict afterward. Since the task requires the URL and scraped text for each item of evidence, we instruct the LLM to provide the citation ID when answering questions. This ensures that we can show the source for our verdict and each question-answer pair.

4 Experiments and Results

4.1 Experimental Setup

In this work, we utilized the *Llama-3-70B model* for both steps described in Sections 3.2.1 and 3.2.3, using the Groq API[2]. Additionally, we set the *temperature* to 0 to ensure reproducibility and *top_p* to 0.8. For key point construction, we set *max_length* to 512, and for zero-shot prediction, we set it to 1024. In the retrieval step using BM25, we set *top_k* to 70 for the original claim and to 12 for other queries, which include key points from both normal and combined forms. For zero-shot prediction, which is the third step of the strategy, if a rate limit occurs due to input length limitations, we retain only the first 55 documents for the original claim and 9 documents for key point retrievals.

4.2 Evaluation Metrics

The AVeriTeC scoring follows a similar approach to FEVER (Thorne et al., 2018) and considers the correctness of the verdict label conditioned on the correctness of the evidence retrieved. The label will only be considered correct if it mathches with the gold label and the Hungarian meteor score between the predicted evidence and the gold evidence is at least 0.25. However, Unlike in FEVER using a closed source of evidence such as Wikipedia, AVERITEC is intended for use with evidence retrieved from the open web. Since the same evidence may be found in different sources, we cannot rely on exact matching to score retrieved evidence. As such, the shared task evaluation strategy instead rely on approximate matching. Specifically, the Hungarian Algorithm (Kuhn, 1955) is used to find an optimal matching of provided evidence to annotated evidence.

4.3 Main Results

Despite our framework's straightforward procedure, which does not require any fine-tuning and only utilizes ZSL, as depicted in Table 1, it robustly improves the baseline in both retrieval

[2]https://groq.com/

scores—calculated for questions alone and for questions with answers—and the AVeriTeC score. This includes improvements of 0.14, 0.04, and 0.16 in retrieval scores for questions only, retrieval scores for questions with answers, and the AVeriTeC score, respectively. Based on these results, by using an open-source LLM, our framework has achieved a 10th rank among all 23 system result submissions.

5 Conclusion

In this paper, we introduced ZSL-KeP, an effective yet straightforward framework for automated fact-checking. We utilized the ZSL capability of LLMs and constructed key points for extensive retrieval to generate evidence in a question-and-answer pairs format, along with a final verdict. By relying solely on the ICL capability of LLMs, our strategy operates without requiring any fine-tuning and is more straightforward compared to the baseline. Our framework sets a new benchmark, indicating promising avenues for future research in related topics.

6 Limitations

While our work shows strong performance, it has some limitations that suggest areas for future research. Our method improves diversity by using zero-shot key points for retrieval, but the limited input length of our LLM, constrained by time and budget limitations, prevented us from retrieving a larger document set. Additionally, a more powerful LLM could enhance accuracy in generating evidence and verdicts. Addressing these issues could significantly improve our framework's results.

References

Jacob Devlin. 2018. Bert: Pre-training of deep bidirectional transformers for language understanding. *arXiv preprint arXiv:1810.04805*.

Zhijiang Guo, Michael Schlichtkrull, and Andreas Vlachos. 2022. A survey on automated fact-checking. *Transactions of the Association for Computational Linguistics*, 10:178–206.

Kyungha Kim, Sangyun Lee, Kung-Hsiang Huang, Hou Pong Chan, Manling Li, and Heng Ji. 2024. Can llms produce faithful explanations for fact-checking? towards faithful explainable fact-checking via multi-agent debate. *arXiv preprint arXiv:2402.07401*.

Neema Kotonya and Francesca Toni. 2020. Explainable automated fact-checking for public health claims. In *Proceedings of the 2020 Conference on Empirical Methods in Natural Language Processing (EMNLP)*, pages 7740–7754.

Harold W Kuhn. 1955. The hungarian method for the assignment problem. *Naval research logistics quarterly*, 2(1-2):83–97.

Nayeon Lee, Yejin Bang, Andrea Madotto, and Pascale Fung. 2021. Towards few-shot fact-checking via perplexity. In *Proceedings of the 2021 Conference of the North American Chapter of the Association for Computational Linguistics: Human Language Technologies*, pages 1971–1981.

Nayeon Lee, Belinda Z Li, Sinong Wang, Wen-Tau Yih, Hao Ma, and Madian Khabsa. 2020. Language models as fact checkers? *ACL 2020*, page 36.

P Nakov, D Corney, M Hasanain, F Alam, T Elsayed, A Barron-Cedeno, P Papotti, S Shaar, G Da San Martino, et al. 2021. Automated fact-checking for assisting human fact-checkers. In *IJCAI*, pages 4551–4558. International Joint Conferences on Artificial Intelligence.

Stephen Robertson, Hugo Zaragoza, et al. 2009. The probabilistic relevance framework: Bm25 and beyond. *Foundations and Trends® in Information Retrieval*, 3(4):333–389.

Michael Schlichtkrull, Zhijiang Guo, and Andreas Vlachos. 2024. Averitec: A dataset for real-world claim verification with evidence from the web. *Advances in Neural Information Processing Systems*, 36.

James Thorne, Andreas Vlachos, Christos Christodoulopoulos, and Arpit Mittal. 2018. Fever: a large-scale dataset for fact extraction and verification. In *Proceedings of the 2018 Conference of the North American Chapter of the Association for Computational Linguistics: Human Language Technologies, Volume 1 (Long Papers)*, pages 809–819.

Xuan Zhang and Wei Gao. 2023. Towards llm-based fact verification on news claims with a hierarchical step-by-step prompting method. In *Proceedings of the 13th International Joint Conference on Natural Language Processing and the 3rd Conference of the Asia-Pacific Chapter of the Association for Computational Linguistics (Volume 1: Long Papers)*, pages 996–1011.

A Prompt Templates

This section provides all of the prompting templates used within the strategy. Figure 2 illustrates the full prompts for section 3.2.1, while the prompts for section 3.2.3 are shown in Figure 3. It is noteworthy that in the user messages, the tags "*<claim>*" and "*<retrieval>*" are replaced by the original claim and the unified retrieval string, respectively.

[System]
You're a helpful assistant with expertise in understanding the concepts of a given claim and writing subclaims that decompose the main claim well.

[User]
Based on the given claim, your task is to extract several distinct key points (2 to 4, depending on the claim's length and complexity) without paraphrasing, in the format of short sentences. Focus on key points that support the main intent of the claim, rather than unnecessary details. Then, only if the number of key points is more than two, identify the pairs of key points whose combination leads to new and richer key points, and return a single coherent short text as a representation of each combination without paraphrasing. Provide your response explicitly in the format of {"key_points": [], "combined_key_points": []}.

Claim: <claim>

Figure 2: The Prompts for Zero-Shot Key Points Construction

[System]
You are a helpful assistant with expertise in creating evidence through suitable question-answer pairs based on a given claim and the available key points within the retrieved knowledge, and in providing an accurate verdict for that claim.

[User]
Your task is to accurately determine a correct verdict for a given claim from the labels "Refuted", "Supported", "Not Enough Evidence", or "Conflicting Evidence/Cherry-Picking". You need to provide 1 to 4 necessary and helpful question-answer (QA) pairs. Each QA pair should be well-constructed, focusing on different important parts of the claim and utilizing the retrieved knowledge effectively to guide accurate decision-making. Therefore, you need to break down the claim into its distinct and most important subclaims, focusing on these individual components, as well as considering direct questions related to the main claim if the retrieved knowledge is sufficient. Your answers can only be in the forms of extractive (preferred), abstractive, or unanswerable. Extractive answers are those directly pulled from the text, while abstractive answers summarize or infer information based on the text. Unanswerable type is very rare, and in this case, set the answer to "No answer could be found." and the citation_id to "". Each piece of text in the retrieved knowledge has a <citation_id> at its end, where the placeholder is replaced by the main citation ID. For each proposed answer to all answerable questions in your evidence, you must include exactly one citation ID (if there are multiple citation_id, select only one) solely within the "citation_id" field. After providing evidence, you must also provide a concise justification explaining how the evidence and the retrieved knowledge support the selected label for the claim. Provide your answer explicitly in the following format without any other change or additional feedback:

```
{
  "evidence": [
    {
      "question": "question",
      "answer": "answer",
      "citation_id": "<citation_id>"
    },
    ...
  ],
  "justification": "justification",
  "pred_label": "pred_label"
}
```

Claim:
<claim>

Retrieved Knowledge:
<retrieval>

Figure 3: The Prompts for Zero-Shot Prediction

Evidence-backed Fact Checking using RAG and Few-Shot In-Context Learning with LLMs

Ronit Singhal[1], Pransh Patwa[2], Parth Patwa[3], Aman Chadha[4,5*], Amitava Das[6],

[1]IIT Kharagpur, India, [2]Aditya English Medium School, India, [3]UCLA, USA,
[4]Stanford University, USA, [5]Amazon GenAI, USA, [6]University of South Carolina, USA
[1]ronit@kgpian.iitkgp.ac.in, [2]pransh.patwa@aemspune.edu.in, [3]parthpatwa@g.ucla.edu
[4,5]hi@aman.ai, [6]amitava@mailbox.sc.edu

Abstract

Given the widespread dissemination of misinformation on social media, implementing fact-checking mechanisms for online claims is essential. Manually verifying every claim is very challenging, underscoring the need for an automated fact-checking system. This paper presents our system designed to address this issue. We utilize the Averitec dataset (Schlichtkrull et al., 2023) to assess the performance of our fact-checking system. In addition to veracity prediction, our system provides supporting evidence, which is extracted from the dataset. We develop a Retrieve and Generate (RAG) pipeline to extract relevant evidence sentences from a knowledge base, which are then inputted along with the claim into a large language model (LLM) for classification. We also evaluate the few-shot In-Context Learning (ICL) capabilities of multiple LLMs. Our system achieves an 'Averitec' score of 0.33, which is a 22% absolute improvement over the baseline. Our Code is publicly available on https://github.com/ronit-singhal/evidence-backed-fact-checking-using-rag-and-few-shot-in-context-learning-with-llms.

1 Introduction

The proliferation of fake news and misinformation on social media platforms has emerged as a significant contemporary issue (Panke, 2020). False online claims have, in some cases, incited riots (Lindsay and Grewar, 2024) and even resulted in loss of life (Kachari, 2018). This problem is particularly amplified during critical events such as elections (Bovet and Makse, 2019) and pandemics (Karimi and Gambrell, 2020; Bae et al., 2022; Morales et al., 2021). Given the vast volume of online content, manually fact-checking every claim is impractical. Therefore, the development of an automated fact verification system is imperative. Moreover, simply assigning a veracity label is inadequate; the prediction must be supported by evidence to ensure the system's transparency and to bolster public trust. Although recent solutions have been proposed (Patwa et al., 2021a; Capuano et al., 2023), the problem remains far from resolved and requires further research efforts.

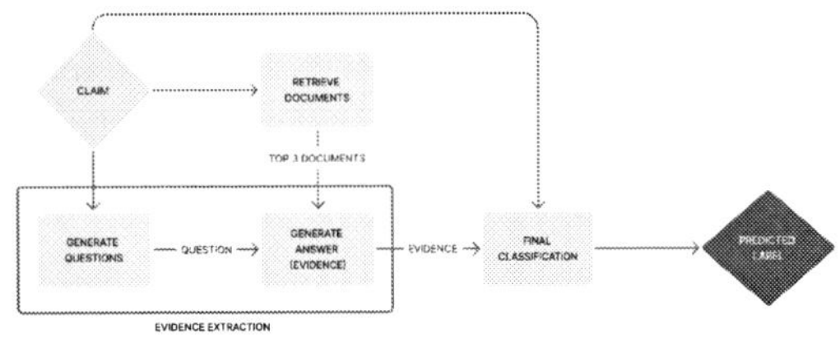

Figure 1: Overview diagram of our system. First, the claim is used to retrieve the top 3 relevant documents. Next, evidence is extracted from these documents using questions and answers generated by an LLM. Finally, the evidence is used for veracity prediction via few-shot ICL.

In this paper, we present our system for automated fact verification. Our system classifies a given textual claim into one of four categories: Supported, Refuted, Conflicting Evidence/Cherrypicking, or Not Enough Evidence. Additionally, it provides supporting evidence for the classification. Our approach leverages recent advancements in Large Language Models (LLMs), specifically Retrieval-Augmented Generation (RAG) and In-Context Learning (ICL), to produce evidence-backed veracity predictions. Given a claim and a collection of documents, our system first employs a RAG pipeline to retrieve the three most relevant documents and extract evidence from them. Subsequently, we utilize ICL to determine the veracity of the claim based on the extracted evidence. Figure 1 provides a high-level overview of our system. We evaluate our system on the Averitec dataset (Schlichtkrull et al., 2023), where it outper-

*Work does not relate to position at Amazon.

Proceedings of the Seventh Fact Extraction and VERification Workshop (FEVER), pages 91–98
November 15, 2024 ©2024 Association for Computational Linguistics

forms the official baseline by a large margin. Our key contributions are as follows:

- We develop a system for automated fact verification that integrates RAG with ICL to provide evidence-based classifications.
- Our proposed system requires only a minimal number of training samples, thereby eliminating the need for a large manually annotated dataset.
- We conduct experiments with various recent LLMs and provide a comprehensive analysis of the results.

The remainder of this paper is structured as follows: Section 2 provides a literature review of related works, while Section 3 describes the dataset. In Section 4, we outline our methodology, followed by a detailed account of the experimental setup in Section 5. Section 6 presents and analyzes our results, and finally, we conclude in Section 7.

Class	**Train**	**Dev**
Supported	847	122
Refuted	1743	305
Conflicting evidence/Cherrypicking	196	38
Not enough evidence	282	35
Total	3068	500

Table 1: Class-wise distribution of train and dev set of the dataset. The data is skewed towards the Refuted class.

Figure 2: Word cloud of the claims. We can see that Politics and COVID-19 are common topics in the claims.

2 Related Work

Recently, there has been increased research interest in fake news detection and fact checking. Glazkova et al. (2021) proposed an ensemble of BERT (Devlin et al., 2019) for Covid fake news (Patwa et al., 2021b) detection. Harrag and Djahli (2022) employed deep learning techniques for fact checking in Arabic (Baly et al., 2018). (Song et al., 2021) tackled the problem of fake news detection using graph neural networks. The factify tasks (Mishra et al., 2022; Suryavardan et al., 2023b) aimed to detect multi-modal fake news. However, these systems only provide the veracity prediction without any evidence.

On the FEVER dataset (Thorne et al., 2018), Krishna et al. (2022) designed a seq2seq model to generate natural logic-based inferences as proofs, resulting in SoTA performance on the dataset. Schuster et al. (2021) released the VitaminC dataset and propose contrastive learning for fact verification. Hu et al. (2022) proposed a DRQA retriever (Chen et al., 2017) based method for fact checking over unstructured information (Aly et al., 2021). These systems provide evidence or explanation to back their predictions but they test the veracity of synthetic claims whereas we test real claims.

Some researchers have also used LLMs to tackle the problem. Kim et al. (2024) leveraged multiple LLMs as agents to enhance the faithfulness of explanations of evidence for fact-checking. Zhang and Gao (2023) designed a hierarchical prompting method which directs LLMs to separate a claim into several smaller claims and then verify each of them progressively.

There have also been attempts to solve the problem using RAG. Khaliq et al. (2024) utilized multimodal LLMs with a reasoning method called chain of RAG to provide evidence based on text and image. Deng et al. (2024) proposed a method to decrease misinformation in RAG pipelines by reranking the documents during retrieval based on a credibility score assigned to them. Similar to these systems, we also use RAG and LLMs in our solution.

For more detailed surveys, please refer to Thorne and Vlachos (2018); Kotonya and Toni (2020); Guo et al. (2022).

3 Data

We utilize the Averitec dataset (Schlichtkrull et al., 2023) for fact-checking purposes. This dataset comprises claims accompanied by a knowledge store (a collection of articles). Each claim is annotated with question-answer pairs that represent the evidence, a veracity label, and a justification for the label. The veracity label can be one of

Convert the following claim to one neutral question. Do not miss out anything important from the claim. Question the claim, not the fact.
Claim: Donald Trump has stated he will not contest for the next elections
Incorrect Question: "What did Donald Trump state for the next elections?"
Correct Question: "Did Donald Trump state that he will not contest for the next elections?"
Claim: [another claim]
Incorrect Question: [example of an incorrect question]
Correct Question: [expected correct question]
Given claim: In a letter to Steve Jobs, Sean Connery refused to appear in an Apple commercial.
Generated question: "Is it true that Sean Connery wrote a letter to Steve Jobs refusing to appear in an Apple commercial?"

Figure 3: The prompt used for generating questions. Some manually created correct and incorrect examples are given to guide the LLM.

Your task is to extract a portion of the provided text that directly answers the given question. The extracted information should be a conclusive answer, either affirmative or negative, and concise, without any irrelevant words. You do not need to provide any explanation. Only return the extracted sentence as instructed. You are strictly forbidden from generating any text of your own.
Question: Is it true that Sean Connery wrote a letter to Steve Jobs refusing to appear in an Apple commercial?
Document text: [entire text of one of the retrieved documents]
Generated answer: "No, it is not true that Sean Connery wrote a letter to Steve Jobs refusing to appear in an Apple commercial. The letter was a fabrication created for a satirical article on Scoopertino."

Figure 4: The prompt used for generating answers. This prompt is repeated for each of the top three documents.

the following: Support (S), Refute (R), Conflicting Evidence/Cherrypicking (C), or Not Enough Evidence (N). A claim is labeled as C when it contains both supporting and refuting evidence. The data distribution, as shown in Table 1, indicates a class imbalance favoring the R class, while the C and N classes have relatively few examples. The final testing is conducted on 2,215 instances (Schlichtkrull et al., 2024). For further details on the dataset, please refer to Schlichtkrull et al. (2023, 2024).

On average, each claim consists of 17 words. Figure 2 (word cloud of the claims) reveals that most claims are related to politics and COVID-19.

4 Methodology

Given a claim and a knowledge store, our system is comprised of three key components: relevant document retrieval, evidence extraction from the documents, and veracity prediction based on the extracted evidence. The first two components form our Retrieval-Augmented Generation (RAG) pipeline.

4.1 Document Retrieval Using Dense Embeddings

In the document retrieval phase, it is essential to match claims with relevant documents from a knowledge store (in our case, the knowledge store consists of documents provided in the dataset, though it could be replaced with documents retrieved via a search engine). To facilitate this, all documents are first transformed into dense vector embeddings using an embedding model. Since our knowledge store is static, this transformation is a one-time process. The claim in question is then converted into embeddings using the same model.

Once the claim is embedded, we utilize FAISS (Facebook AI Similarity Search) (Douze et al., 2024) to conduct a nearest-neighbor search within the knowledge store. FAISS is an efficient library for similarity search and clustering of dense vectors. We configure FAISS to retrieve the top three documents most relevant to the claim. These documents are then used in the subsequent evidence extraction and veracity prediction steps.

4.2 Evidence Extraction Using LLMs

After identifying the top three relevant documents, the next step involves extracting evidence supported by these documents. This process consists of two steps:

Question Generation: The claim is transformed into a question challenging its validity using an LLM. We employ In-Context Learning, which enables the model to generate responses based on a few provided examples, aiding in the creation of nuanced and contextually appropriate questions.

Classify the given claim based on provided statements into one of:
1. 'Supported' if there is sufficient evidence indicating that the claim is legitimate. 2. 'Refuted' if there is any evidence contradicting the claim.
3. Not Enough Evidence' If you cannot find any conclusive factual evidence either supporting or refuting the claim.
4. 'Conflicting Evidence/Cherrypicking' if there is factual evidence both supporting and refuting the claim.
Claim: [claim]
Statements: [statements related to claim]
Class: [ground truth class]
Claim: [claim]
Statements: [statements related to claim]
Class: [ground truth class]
Given Claim: New Zealand's new Food Bill bans gardening.
Given Statements: ["The Food Bill does not impose restrictions on personal horticultural activities, such as growing vegetables and fruits at home.", "Gardening is not banned in New Zealand.", "There are no laws against people having gardens, or sharing food that they've grown at home, said a spokesperson for New Zealand's Ministry for Primary Industries."]
Generated class: Refuted

Figure 5: A prompt similar to the one used for generating the final prediction. The actual prompt has some more instructions which are omitted here in the interest of space. two annotated train examples are provided for the LLM to learn from.

The prompt is designed to ensure that the generated question challenges the claim's veracity rather than simply seeking a factual answer. An example prompt is provided in Figure 3.

Answer Generation: After generating the question, we provide a single document to an LLM and pose the question. The LLM is prompted to deliver concise and definitive answers derived directly from the content of the document. This process is repeated for each of the three documents, resulting in three distinct answers for each claim. These answers collectively constitute our evidence. It is important to note that in our experiments, the LLM used for answer generation does not necessarily need to be the same as the one used for question generation. The prompt utilized in this step is similar to the one depicted in Figure 4.

4.3 Few-Shot ICL for Final Classification

For the final veracity prediction, we use an LLM to classify a claim based on the three pieces of evidence extracted earlier. The LLM is prompted to choose one out of the four possible classes. The prompt is designed to guide the model through the classification process, ensuring that it correctly interprets the relationship between the claim and the evidence. An example prompt is given in Figure 5.

Our methodology aligns with recent advancements in retrieval-augmented generation (RAG) pipelines which alleviate hallucination and ICL methods, which have been shown to improve the accuracy of LLMs. The integration of these state-of-the-art methods is an attempt to ensure that the extracted evidence is both relevant and contextually appropriate for validating the claims accurately.

5 Experiments

To convert documents into dense embeddings, we utilize the `dunzhang/stella_en_1.5B_v5` model[1]. This model is chosen because, at the time of our experiments, it was ranked first on the Massive Text Embedding Benchmark (MTEB) leaderboard (Muennighoff et al., 2022), and holds the second position at the time of writing this paper.

For all LLMs used in our experiments, we employ their 4-bit quantized versions via Ollama[2]. This quantization enables us to load larger LLMs onto our GPUs.

For question generation, we use the Phi-3-medium model (Abdin et al., 2024). The temperature is set to 0, and greedy decoding is used to ensure that the answers are as factual as possible and to minimize hallucinations.

For answer generation and final classification, we experiment with multiple LLMs of varying sizes, including InternLM2.5 (Cai et al., 2024), Llama-3.1 (Dubey et al., 2024), Phi-3-medium (Abdin et al., 2024), Qwen2 (Yang et al., 2024), and Mixtral (Jiang et al., 2024). These models are selected based on their performance on the Open LLM Leaderboard (Fourrier et al., 2024) and their availability through Ollama.

We utilize an A40 GPU for Mixtral, while all other models are run on an A100 GPU. Our best-performing model, Mixtral, requires an average of 2 minutes for evidence extraction and final prediction. Our code is publicly available on https://github.com/ronit-singhal/evidence-backed-fact-checking-using-rag-and-few-shot-in-context-

[1]`https://huggingface.co/dunzhang/stella_en_1.5B_v5`

[2]`https://github.com/ollama/ollama`

Model	Size	Q+A ↑	Averitec ↑	Acc ↑
InternLM2.5	7B	0.278	0.194	0.374
Llama3.1	8B	0.259	0.224	0.538
Phi-3-Medium	14B	0.259	0.28	0.654
Llama 3.1	70B	0.272	0.328	**0.662**
Qwen2	72B	0.285	0.33	0.61
Mixtral	8*22B	**0.292**	**0.356**	0.636

Table 2: Results of various models on the dev set. Performance improves as the model size increases. Acc refers to accuracy. Q+A and Averitec scores are described in Section 5.1.

System	Q ↑	Q+A ↑	Averitec ↑
Official Baseline	0.24	0.2	0.11
Mixtral (ours)	**0.35**	**0.27**	**0.33**

Table 3: Results on the test set. Our system which uses Mixtral for final prediction outperforms the official baseline in all metrics. For more details of the metrics, please refer to section 5.1.

learning-with-llms.

5.1 Evaluation Metrics

The evaluation metrics used ensure that credit for a correct veracity prediction is given only when the correct evidence has been identified.

To evaluate how well the generated questions and answers align with the reference data, the pairwise scoring function METEOR (Banerjee and Lavie, 2005) is used. The Hungarian Algorithm (Kuhn, 1955) is then applied to find the optimal matching between the generated sequences and the reference sequences. This evidence scoring method is referred to as Hungarian METEOR. The system is evaluated on the test set using the following metrics:

- **Q only:** Hungarian METEOR score for the generated questions.
- **Q + A:** Hungarian METEOR score for the concatenation of the generated questions and answers.
- **Averitec Score:** Correct veracity predictions where the Q+A score is greater than or equal to 0.25. Any claim with a lower evidence score receives a score of 0.

6 Results and Analysis

Table 2 provides a summary of the performance of various models on the development set. The Mixtral 8*22B model (Jiang et al., 2024) achieves the highest Averitec score, while the Llama 3.1 model (Dubey et al., 2024) attains the highest accuracy. These findings indicate that model performance generally improves with increasing model size. Moreover, the relative rankings of these models on the development set differ from their positions on the Open LLM leaderboard (Fourrier et al., 2024), suggesting that superior performance on the Open LLM leaderboard does not necessarily correlate with better performance in the fact verification task.

Given that Mixtral achievs the highest Averitec score on the development set, we select it for evaluation on the test set. Table 3 provides a comparison of our system and the official baseline (Schlichtkrull et al., 2023) on the test set. The baseline model utilizes Bloom (Scao et al., 2023) for evidence generation, followed by re-ranking of the evidence using a finetuned BERT-large model and finally a finetuned BERT-large model veracity prediction. Unlike the baseline, which uses finetuned models, we only use a few train examples via ICL. Despite that, our system outperforms the baseline across all three evaluation metrics. Notably, our Averitec score of 0.33 is a 22% absolute improvement over the baseline.

Model	S	R	N	C	Macro
Mixtral	0.605	0.780	0.126	0.117	**0.47**
Qwen2	**0.620**	0.754	**0.157**	**0.153**	0.42
Llama 3.1 70b	0.613	**0.809**	0.022	0	0.361

Table 4: Class-wise F1 scores of our top three LLMs on the dev set. Classes are Supported (S), Refuted (R), Not enough evidence (N), and conflicting evidence/cherrypicking. Macro-averaged F1 score is also reported.

6.1 Class-wise Performance

Table 4 presents the class-wise performance of our top three models on the development set. Across all models, the Refuted class emerges as the easiest to predict, while the "Not Enough Evidence" and "Conflicting Evidence/Cherrypicking" classes present greater challenges. Notably, no single model excels across all classes. Although Mixtral achieves the highest macro F1 score, it is not the top-performing model for any individual class. Qwen2 surpasses the other models in performance across all classes except Refuted. This suggests that exploring ensemble techniques could be a valu-

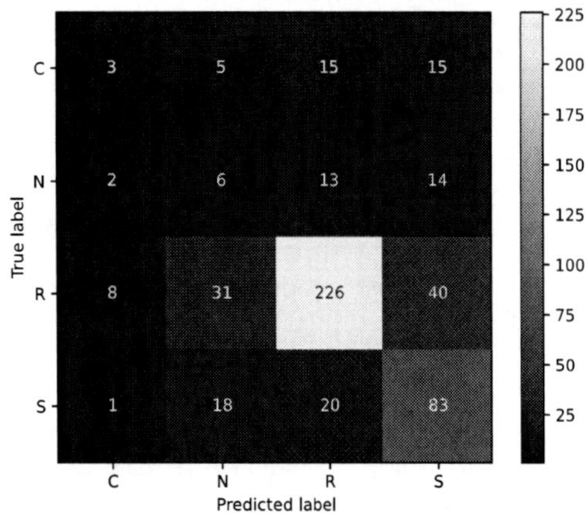

Figure 6: Confusion matrix of Mixtral on the development set, illustrating the model's performance across four classes (C, N, R, S). While class R is mostly accurately classified, classes C and N are often mis-predicted as R or N.

able direction for future research.

Figure 6 illustrates the confusion matrix of Mixtral 8*22B on the development set. It reveals that both the N and C classes are equally likely to be misclassified as the R and S classes. Additionally, there is significant confusion between the S and R classes, highlighting the inherent difficulty of fact verification.

7 Conclusion and Future Work

In this paper, we introduced our system for evidence-supported automated fact verification. Our system - based on RAG and ICL - requires only a minimal number of training examples to extract relevant evidence and make veracity predictions. We observed that all LLMs demonstrate sub-optimal performance on the "Conflicting Evidence/Cherrypicking" and "Not Enough Evidence" categories, which emphasizes the inherent challenges of these categories. Additionally, no single LLM consistently outperforms others across all categories. Our system achieved an Averitec score of 0.33, highlighting the complexity of the problem and indicating a substantial potential for future improvement.

Future research could involve fine-tuning the LLM using parameter-efficient fine-tuning (PEFT) techniques (Liu et al., 2022; Patwa et al., 2024) and improving performance through the use of ensemble techniques (Mohammed and Kora, 2022). Extending the system to include multi-modal fact verification (Patwa et al., 2022; Suryavardan et al., 2023a) also represents an interesting direction for further investigation.

8 Limitation

As we are using few-shot ICL, our system cannot make use of large annotated datasets if available, because of the limitation of the prompt size. Furthermore, we assume the availability of high-quality LLMs, which might not be the case for some low-resource languages.

9 Ethical Statement

LLMs are prone to hallucination. In our case, the extracted evidence could be incorrect due to hallucination. Furthermore, the prompts can be tweaked to intentionally generate wrong evidence or predictions. We caution the reader to be aware of such issues and to not misuse the system.

References

Marah Abdin, Sam Ade Jacobs, Ammar Ahmad Awan, Jyoti Aneja, et al. 2024. Phi-3 technical report: A highly capable language model locally on your phone. *Preprint*, arXiv:2404.14219.

Rami Aly, Zhijiang Guo, Michael Sejr Schlichtkrull, James Thorne, Andreas Vlachos, Christos Christodoulopoulos, Oana Cocarascu, and Arpit Mittal. 2021. The fact extraction and VERification over unstructured and structured information (FEVEROUS) shared task. In *Proceedings of the Fourth Workshop on Fact Extraction and VERification (FEVER)*, pages 1–13, Dominican Republic. Association for Computational Linguistics.

Joseph Bae, Darshan Gandhi, Jil Kothari, Sheshank Shankar, Jonah Bae, Parth Patwa, Rohan Sukumaran, Aviral Chharia, Sanjay Adhikesaven, Shloak Rathod, Irene Nandutu, Sethuraman TV, Vanessa Yu, Krutika Misra, Srinidhi Murali, Aishwarya Saxena, Kasia Jakimowicz, Vivek Sharma, Rohan Iyer, Ashley Mehra, Alex Radunsky, Priyanshi Katiyar, Ananthu James, Jyoti Dalal, Sunaina Anand, Shailesh Advani, Jagjit Dhaliwal, and Ramesh Raskar. 2022. Challenges of equitable vaccine distribution in the covid-19 pandemic. *Preprint*, arXiv:2012.12263.

Ramy Baly, Mitra Mohtarami, James Glass, Lluís Màrquez, Alessandro Moschitti, and Preslav Nakov. 2018. Integrating stance detection and fact checking in a unified corpus. *arXiv preprint arXiv:1804.08012*.

Satanjeev Banerjee and Alon Lavie. 2005. METEOR: An automatic metric for MT evaluation with improved correlation with human judgments. In *Proceedings of the ACL Workshop on Intrinsic and Ex-*

trinsic Evaluation Measures for Machine Translation and/or Summarization, pages 65–72, Ann Arbor, Michigan. Association for Computational Linguistics.

Alexandre Bovet and Hernán A. Makse. 2019. Influence of fake news in twitter during the 2016 us presidential election. *Nature Communications*, 10(1):7.

Zheng Cai, Maosong Cao, Haojiong Chen, Kai Chen, et al. 2024. Internlm2 technical report. *Preprint*, arXiv:2403.17297.

Nicola Capuano, Giuseppe Fenza, Vincenzo Loia, and Francesco David Nota. 2023. Content-based fake news detection with machine and deep learning: a systematic review. *Neurocomputing*, 530:91–103.

Danqi Chen, Adam Fisch, Jason Weston, and Antoine Bordes. 2017. Reading wikipedia to answer open-domain questions. *Preprint*, arXiv:1704.00051.

Boyi Deng, Wenjie Wang, Fengbin Zhu, Qifan Wang, and Fuli Feng. 2024. Cram: Credibility-aware attention modification in llms for combating misinformation in rag. *Preprint*, arXiv:2406.11497.

Jacob Devlin, Ming-Wei Chang, Kenton Lee, and Kristina Toutanova. 2019. BERT: Pre-training of deep bidirectional transformers for language understanding. In *Proceedings of the 2019 Conference of the North American Chapter of the Association for Computational Linguistics: Human Language Technologies, Volume 1 (Long and Short Papers)*, pages 4171–4186, Minneapolis, Minnesota. Association for Computational Linguistics.

Matthijs Douze, Alexandr Guzhva, Chengqi Deng, Jeff Johnson, Gergely Szilvasy, Pierre-Emmanuel Mazaré, Maria Lomeli, Lucas Hosseini, and Hervé Jégou. 2024. The faiss library. *Preprint*, arXiv:2401.08281.

Abhimanyu Dubey, Abhinav Jauhri, Abhinav Pandey, Abhishek Kadian, et al. 2024. The llama 3 herd of models. *Preprint*, arXiv:2407.21783.

Clémentine Fourrier, Nathan Habib, Alina Lozovskaya, Konrad Szafer, and Thomas Wolf. 2024. Open llm leaderboard v2. `https://huggingface.co/spaces/open-llm-leaderboard/open_llm_leaderboard`.

Anna Glazkova, Maksim Glazkov, and Timofey Trifonov. 2021. *g2tmn at Constraint@AAAI2021: Exploiting CT-BERT and Ensembling Learning for COVID-19 Fake News Detection*, page 116–127. Springer International Publishing.

Zhijiang Guo, Michael Schlichtkrull, and Andreas Vlachos. 2022. A survey on automated fact-checking. *Transactions of the Association for Computational Linguistics*, 10:178–206.

Fouzi Harrag and Mohamed Khalil Djahli. 2022. Arabic fake news detection: A fact checking based deep learning approach. *ACM Trans. Asian Low-Resour. Lang. Inf. Process.*, 21(4).

Nan Hu, Zirui Wu, Yuxuan Lai, Xiao Liu, and Yansong Feng. 2022. Dual-channel evidence fusion for fact verification over texts and tables. In *Proceedings of the 2022 Conference of the North American Chapter of the Association for Computational Linguistics: Human Language Technologies*, pages 5232–5242, Seattle, United States. Association for Computational Linguistics.

Albert Q. Jiang, Alexandre Sablayrolles, Antoine Roux, Arthur Mensch, et al. 2024. Mixtral of experts. *Preprint*, arXiv:2401.04088.

Panjuri Kachari. 2018. Death by 'fake news': social media-fuelled lynchings shock india. *France24*.

Nasser Karimi and Jon Gambrell. 2020. Hundreds die of poisoning in iran as fake news suggests methanol cure for virus. *Times of Israel*.

M Abdul Khaliq, P Chang, M Ma, Bernhard Pflugfelder, and F Miletić. 2024. Ragar, your falsehood radar: Rag-augmented reasoning for political fact-checking using multimodal large language models. *arXiv preprint arXiv:2404.12065*.

Kyungha Kim, Sangyun Lee, Kung-Hsiang Huang, Hou Pong Chan, Manling Li, and Heng Ji. 2024. Can llms produce faithful explanations for fact-checking? towards faithful explainable fact-checking via multi-agent debate. *Preprint*, arXiv:2402.07401.

Neema Kotonya and Francesca Toni. 2020. Explainable automated fact-checking: A survey. *arXiv preprint arXiv:2011.03870*.

Amrith Krishna, Sebastian Riedel, and Andreas Vlachos. 2022. ProoFVer: Natural logic theorem proving for fact verification. *Transactions of the Association for Computational Linguistics*, 10:1013–1030.

H. W. Kuhn. 1955. The hungarian method for the assignment problem. *Naval Research Logistics Quarterly*, 2(1-2):83–97.

Martin Lindsay and Calum Grewar. 2024. Social media misinformation 'fanned riot flames'. *BBC*.

Haokun Liu, Derek Tam, Mohammed Muqeeth, Jay Mohta, Tenghao Huang, Mohit Bansal, and Colin Raffel. 2022. Few-shot parameter-efficient fine-tuning is better and cheaper than in-context learning. *Preprint*, arXiv:2205.05638.

Shreyash Mishra, S Suryavardan, Amrit Bhaskar, Parul Chopra, Aishwarya N Reganti, Parth Patwa, Amitava Das, Tanmoy Chakraborty, Amit P Sheth, Asif Ekbal, et al. 2022. Factify: A multi-modal fact verification dataset. In *DE-FACTIFY@ AAAI*.

Ammar Mohammed and Rania Kora. 2022. An effective ensemble deep learning framework for text classification. *Journal of King Saud University-Computer and Information Sciences*, 34(10):8825–8837.

Manuel Morales, Rachel Barbar, Darshan Gandhi, Sanskruti Landage, Joseph Bae, Arpita Vats, Jil Kothari, Sheshank Shankar, Rohan Sukumaran, Himi Mathur, Krutika Misra, Aishwarya Saxena, Parth Patwa, Sethuraman T. V., Maurizio Arseni, Shailesh Advani, Kasia Jakimowicz, Sunaina Anand, Priyanshi Katiyar, Ashley Mehra, Rohan Iyer, Srinidhi Murali, Aryan Mahindra, Mikhail Dmitrienko, Saurish Srivastava, Ananya Gangavarapu, Steve Penrod, Vivek Sharma, Abhishek Singh, and Ramesh Raskar. 2021. Covid-19 tests gone rogue: Privacy, efficacy, mismanagement and misunderstandings. *Preprint*, arXiv:2101.01693.

Niklas Muennighoff, Nouamane Tazi, Loïc Magne, and Nils Reimers. 2022. Mteb: Massive text embedding benchmark. *arXiv preprint arXiv:2210.07316*.

Stefanie Panke. 2020. Social media and fake news. *aace*.

Parth Patwa, Mohit Bhardwaj, Vineeth Guptha, Gitanjali Kumari, Shivam Sharma, Srinivas PYKL, Amitava Das, Asif Ekbal, Md Shad Akhtar, and Tanmoy Chakraborty. 2021a. Overview of constraint 2021 shared tasks: Detecting english covid-19 fake news and hindi hostile posts. In *Combating Online Hostile Posts in Regional Languages during Emergency Situation*, pages 42–53, Cham. Springer International Publishing.

Parth Patwa, Simone Filice, Zhiyu Chen, Giuseppe Castellucci, Oleg Rokhlenko, and Shervin Malmasi. 2024. Enhancing low-resource LLMs classification with PEFT and synthetic data. In *Proceedings of the 2024 Joint International Conference on Computational Linguistics, Language Resources and Evaluation (LREC-COLING 2024)*, pages 6017–6023, Torino, Italia. ELRA and ICCL.

Parth Patwa, Shreyash Mishra, S Suryavardan, Amrit Bhaskar, Parul Chopra, Aishwarya Reganti, Amitava Das, Tanmoy Chakraborty, Amit Sheth, Asif Ekbal, and Chaitanya Ahuja. 2022. Benchmarking multimodal entailment for fact verification. In *Proceedings of De-Factify: Workshop on Multimodal Fact Checking and Hate Speech Detection*. CEUR.

Parth Patwa, Shivam Sharma, Srinivas Pykl, Vineeth Guptha, Gitanjali Kumari, Md Shad Akhtar, Asif Ekbal, Amitava Das, and Tanmoy Chakraborty. 2021b. Fighting an infodemic: Covid-19 fake news dataset. In *Combating Online Hostile Posts in Regional Languages during Emergency Situation*, pages 21–29, Cham. Springer International Publishing.

Teven Le Scao, Angela Fan, Christopher Akiki, Ellie Pavlick, et al. 2023. Bloom: A 176b-parameter open-access multilingual language model. *Preprint*, arXiv:2211.05100.

Michael Schlichtkrull, Yulong Chen, Chenxi Whitehouse, Zhenyun Deng, Mubashara Akhtar, Rami Aly, Zhijiang Guo, Christos Christodoulopoulos, Oana Cocarascu, Arpit Mittal, James Thorne, and Andreas Vlachos. 2024. The automated verification of textual claims (averitec) shared task. In *Proceedings of the Seventh Workshop on Fact Extraction and VERification (FEVER)*.

Michael Sejr Schlichtkrull, Zhijiang Guo, and Andreas Vlachos. 2023. Averitec: A dataset for real-world claim verification with evidence from the web. In *Thirty-seventh Conference on Neural Information Processing Systems Datasets and Benchmarks Track*.

Tal Schuster, Adam Fisch, and Regina Barzilay. 2021. Get your vitamin C! robust fact verification with contrastive evidence. In *Proceedings of the 2021 Conference of the North American Chapter of the Association for Computational Linguistics: Human Language Technologies*, pages 624–643, Online. Association for Computational Linguistics.

Chenguang Song, Kai Shu, and Bin Wu. 2021. Temporally evolving graph neural network for fake news detection. *Information Processing & Management*, 58(6):102712.

S Suryavardan, Shreyash Mishra, Megha Chakraborty, Parth Patwa, Anku Rani, Aman Chadha, Aishwarya Reganti, Amitava Das, Amit Sheth, Manoj Chinnakotla, Asif Ekbal, and Srijan Kumar. 2023a. Findings of factify 2: Multimodal fake news detection. *Preprint*, arXiv:2307.10475.

S Suryavardan, Shreyash Mishra, Parth Patwa, Megha Chakraborty, Anku Rani, Aishwarya Reganti, Aman Chadha, Amitava Das, Amit Sheth, Manoj Chinnakotla, et al. 2023b. Factify 2: A multimodal fake news and satire news dataset. *arXiv preprint arXiv:2304.03897*.

James Thorne and Andreas Vlachos. 2018. Automated fact checking: Task formulations, methods and future directions. *arXiv preprint arXiv:1806.07687*.

James Thorne, Andreas Vlachos, Christos Christodoulopoulos, and Arpit Mittal. 2018. FEVER: a large-scale dataset for fact extraction and VERification. In *Proceedings of the 2018 Conference of the North American Chapter of the Association for Computational Linguistics: Human Language Technologies, Volume 1 (Long Papers)*, pages 809–819, New Orleans, Louisiana. Association for Computational Linguistics.

An Yang, Baosong Yang, Binyuan Hui, Bo Zheng, et al. 2024. Qwen2 technical report. *Preprint*, arXiv:2407.10671.

Xuan Zhang and Wei Gao. 2023. Towards llm-based fact verification on news claims with a hierarchical step-by-step prompting method. *Preprint*, arXiv:2310.00305.

SK_DU Team: Cross-Encoder based Evidence Retrieval and Question Generation with Improved Prompt for the AVeriTeC Shared Task

Shrikant Malviya and **Stamos Katsigiannis**
Department of Computer Science, Durham University, UK
{shrikant.malviya,stamos.katsigiannis}@durham.ac.uk

Abstract

As part of the AVeriTeC shared task, we developed a pipelined system comprising robust and finely tuned models. Our system integrates advanced techniques for evidence retrieval and question generation, leveraging cross-encoders and large language models (LLMs) for optimal performance. With multi-stage processing, the pipeline demonstrates improvements over baseline models, particularly in handling complex claims that require nuanced reasoning, by improved evidence extraction, question generation and veracity prediction. Through detailed experiments and ablation studies, we provide insights into the strengths and weaknesses of our approach, highlighting the critical role of evidence sufficiency and context dependency in automated fact-checking systems. Our system secured a competitive rank, 7th on the development and 12th on the test data, in the shared task, underscoring the effectiveness of our methods in addressing the challenges of real-world claim verification.

1 Introduction

Fact-checking has become an essential tool in the fight against misinformation, which can have far-reaching impacts on public opinion and policy. Manual fact-checking is a resource-intensive process, requiring skilled analysts to meticulously scrutinise claims and verify their authenticity. This necessity has driven the development of automated fact-checking (AFC) systems designed to assist human fact-checkers by efficiently processing large volumes of information and detecting false claims. (Nakov et al., 2021; Guo et al., 2022). The effectiveness of AFC systems depends significantly on the quality of the datasets used to train and evaluate them. Common datasets, such as FEVER (Thorne et al., 2018), FEVEROUS (Aly et al., 2021) and MultiFC (Augenstein et al., 2019), have been instrumental in advancing AFC research, but come with limitations, including the reliance on artificially constructed claims and inadequate evidence annotations (Schlichtkrull et al., 2023).

In response to these limitations, the 2024 AVeriTeC (Automated VERIfication of TExtual Claims) task was specifically designed to address the challenges of real-world claim verification (Schlichtkrull et al., 2023). AVeriTeC comprises 5,783 claims sourced from 50 fact-checking organisations, collected via the Google FactCheck Claim Search API. Each claim in the dataset is meticulously annotated with question-answer pairs, supported by online evidence, and accompanied by textual justifications explaining how the evidence leads to a verdict. This structured annotation approach ensures that the dataset supports robust AFC model training and evaluation (Schlichtkrull et al., 2023). This advancement aligns the dataset more closely with real-world scenarios, potentially enhancing the generalisation ability of the developed models and facilitating the creation of more robust approaches. The diversity of the data presents unique challenges, necessitating a deeper understanding of the data and the development of effective reasoning strategies. Our method (SK_DU) achieved the 12th Rank in the AVeriTeC shared task during the testing phase[1], providing valuable insights into the strengths and weaknesses of our pipeline and highlighting areas for further improvement.

In this paper, we aim to describe the design of our proposed fact verification pipeline and to share the insights we gained on the AVeriTeC dataset (Schlichtkrull et al., 2023) during the workshop competition. The paper introduces a comprehensive approach to real-world claim verification, leveraging the AVeriTeC dataset to develop and evaluate a sophisticated pipeline for automated fact-checking. The proposed system incorporates cutting-edge models and techniques,

[1]https://eval.ai/web/challenges/challenge-page/2285/leaderboard/5655

Proceedings of the Seventh Fact Extraction and VERification Workshop (FEVER), pages 99–107
November 15, 2024 ©2024 Association for Computational Linguistics

including cross-encoders for precise evidence retrieval/reranking (Humeau et al., 2019) and large language models (LLMs) for effective question generation (Schlichtkrull et al., 2023), and Cross-Encoder based natural language inference (NLI) for veracity prediction (Li et al., 2022). By focusing on multi-stage processing—ranging from the selection of evidence to nuanced reasoning for claim validation, the work addresses the complexities of real-world data, emphasising the importance of context and evidence sufficiency in fact-checking processes. Our code is released to the public for further exploration[2].

In short, the contributions of this paper are the following:

- The paper presents a detailed pipeline that integrates cross-encoders for evidence retrieval and LLMs for question generation, improving the overall accuracy of claim verification.
- Showing a pretrained Cross-Encoder model performs better than a fine-tuned BERT model on evidence extraction and reranking tasks.
- The paper provides in-depth ablation studies and performance analysis, offering insights into the strengths and weaknesses of the proposed approach.
- The model's competitive performance in the AVeriTeC shared task highlights its practical applicability and potential for real-world deployment in automated fact-checking systems.

2 Dataset Insights

AVeriTeC consists of 5,783 claims sourced from 50 reputable fact-checking organisations, where 4,568 claims' data were released earlier, while 1,215 were released during the testing phase of the AVeriTeC Shared Task[3]. Each claim is annotated with detailed question-answer (QA) pairs as evidence, a veracity label, and a textual justification, ensuring a robust foundation for training and evaluating AFC systems (Schlichtkrull et al., 2023). Additionally, the meta-data information, e.g., speaker, date, URL, location, etc., provides contextual details to the claim to support questions, answers, and justifications. This structured and meticulous approach aims to bridge the gap between academic research and practical application in building systems for misinformation detection.

[2]https://github.com/skmalviya/AVeriTeC_SKDU

[3]https://fever.ai/task.html

Property	Stats
Avg questions per claim	2.60
Avg answers per question	1.07
Questions with extractive answer	53%
Questions with abstractive answer	26%
Questions with boolean answer	17%
Questions with no answer	4%

Table 1: Dataset statistics.

As the claims in AVeriTeC are also annotated with date, the dataset is split temporally (ordered by date) into training, validation, and test sets, having 500, 3,068, and 2,215 claims data, respectively. Table 1 illustrates some properties of the AVeriTeC dataset. Claims contain an average of 2.60 questions each, with questions averaging 1.07 answers each. Most answers are extractive (53%), followed by abstractive (26%), and boolean (17%), with 4% being unanswerable. The dataset is somewhat unbalanced, with the majority of claims being refuted, reflecting the focus of journalists on false or misleading claims.

Reasoning about evidence is structured through a question-and-answer format, allowing for multiple answers to reflect potential disagreements. Multi-hop reasoning is also allowed by referring to previous questions, and all answers must be backed by source URLs. In the AVeriTeC dataset, the veracity of claims is predicted into typical classes: Supported, Refuted, and Not Enough Evidence. AVeriTeC also introduces a fourth class: Conflicting evidence/Cherry-picking, which includes conflicting evidence and technically true claims that mislead by omitting crucial context. This addition addresses real-world scenarios where sources may legitimately disagree on interpretations.

One of the primary challenges is *context dependence*. Many claims cannot be accurately verified without additional context that is not always available in the fact-checking articles. This lack of context can lead to incorrect or incomplete verification outcomes. Another major challenge is *evidence sufficiency*. Ensuring that the evidence provided is comprehensive enough to support or refute claims is crucial, as incomplete evidence can skew the verification results. *Temporal leakage* is another critical challenge, where evidence published after the claim date may inadvertently influence the verification process. This can result in biased or inaccurate conclusions, undermining the integrity of the dataset. Additionally, the diverse nature of the data from various sources and the wide range of claim types introduce complexity in data annotation and processing, making it difficult to maintain consistency and accuracy across the dataset.

3 System Description

3.1 AVeriTeC Baseline

The baseline model for AVeriTeC employs a sophisticated approach to automate the fact-checking process, leveraging state-of-the-art natural language processing (NLP) techniques. Specifically, it utilises transformer-based models, such as BERT (Bidirectional Encoder Representations from Transformers) (Devlin et al., 2019) and its variants, which have proven highly effective in understanding and processing natural language. These models are fine-tuned on the AVeriTeC dataset to optimise their performance in various stages of the fact-checking pipeline, including claim representation, evidence retrieval, and veracity prediction.

The *evidence retrieval* component of the baseline model is designed to efficiently retrieve relevant evidence from a vast pool of sentences scrapped from Google Search API. The baseline applies BM25 (Robertson and Zaragoza, 2009) as a coarse filter to select the top 100 sentences to keep relevant evidence pinpointed and presented for evaluation in further stages in the pipeline.

Further, during the *question generation* stage, each evidence is paired with a question generated by an LLM based on few-shot prompting, where the QA pairs as few-shot examples are extracted from the training data using BM25. Baseline utilises BLOOM (Workshop et al., 2023) for this task. It is empirically shown that a 10-shot setting consistently outperforms other configurations, such as 1, 3, or 5-shot prompting, in generating accurate and contextually appropriate questions. To further refine the generated QA pairs, a fine-tuned BERT-large model (Devlin et al., 2019) is employed to *rerank* the outputs, ultimately selecting the top $N = 3$ evidence sets that best support or refute the claim.

The final stage of the baseline model is *veracity prediction*, where the selected evidence as QA pairs are used to determine the truthfulness of the claim. This step involves integrating the claim-evidence pairs into a coherent representation and feeding it into a classification model that assigns a veracity label. The labels typically include categories such as "supported" or "refuted", "not enough evidence" or "conflicting evidence/cherry-picking". The baseline uses a fine-tuned BERT-large model, fine-tuned on annotated examples from the AVeriTeC dataset, learning to weigh the evidence and make informed decisions about the claim's veracity (Schlichtkrull et al., 2023).

3.2 Our Pipeline

Similar to AVeriTeC, our pipeline consists of several models integrated into a multi-stage process, offering a comprehensive solution framework for real-world claim verification. Figure 1 depicts our pipeline, showing various components for a specific task. Each pipeline stage is crucial for accurate claim verification, from retrieving relevant evidence to predicting the claim's veracity. Below, we outline the models utilised in our pipeline. We make use of the evidence collection (knowledge store) retrieved through the Google Search API, as provided in the AVeriTeC shared task.

3.2.1 Evidence Selection

For *evidence retrieval*, we employ a Cross-Encoder to extract evidence sentences from the knowledge store. (Humeau et al., 2019) has shown that cross-encoders typically outperform bi-encoders on sentence-scoring tasks by enabling rich interactions between the claim and candidate evidence. We also compared the retrieval results with those of BM25, TF-IDF, and Bi-Encoder to evaluate their effectiveness. Similar to the baseline, we keep only the top 100 sentences based on the score predicted by the Cross-Encoder. The Cross-Encoder takes the pair of claim $\mathbf{c}$ and evidence $\mathbf{e}$ and processes it through a transformer model, e.g. RoBERTa (Liu et al., 2019):

$$\mathbf{h}_{\text{[CLS]}} = \text{RoBERTa}([\mathbf{c}; \mathbf{e}]) \quad (1)$$

where $\mathbf{h}_{\text{[CLS]}}$ is the final hidden state corresponding to the special [CLS] token. The score $s(\mathbf{c}, \mathbf{e})$ for the (claim, evidence) pair is then computed by applying a linear layer followed by a sigmoid activation function as:

$$s(\mathbf{c}, \mathbf{e}) = \sigma(\mathbf{W} \cdot \mathbf{h}_{\text{[CLS]}} + b) \quad (2)$$

where $\mathbf{W}$ and $\mathbf{b}$ are the linear layer's weight matrix and bias term, and σ is the sigmoid function.

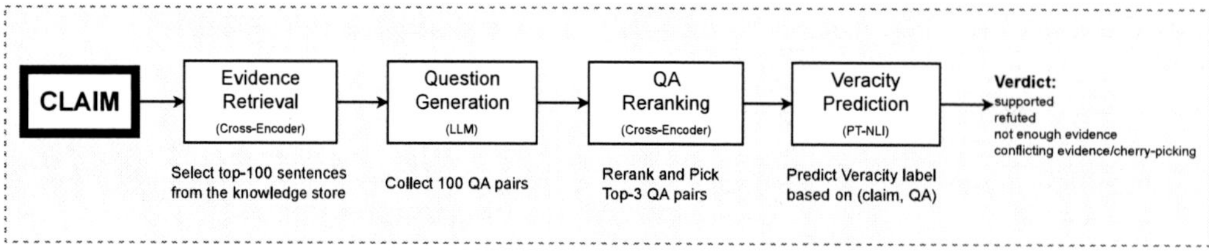

Figure 1: Overview of the pipelined Evidence-Retrieval and Verdict Prediction for a given claim.

```
Evidence:...
Question answered:...

Evidence:...
Question answered:...

...

Evidence:...
Question answered:
```

(a) Prompt1

```
Outrageously, example['speaker'] Claim:...
with Evidence:...
as an answer to the Question:...

Outrageously, example['speaker'] Claim:...
with Evidence:...
as an answer to the Question:...

...

Outrageously, example['speaker'] Claim:...
with Evidence:...
as an answer to the Question:...
```

(b) Prompt2

Figure 2: Prompts used by an LLM for question generation task.

This strategy ensures that the most pertinent evidence is identified (relevance) and made computationally feasible (top-100) for further stages in the verification pipeline.

3.2.2 Question Generation

To generate questions for the extracted evidence sentences from the previous step, we conducted experiments on two fronts: 1) Prompt Engineering, and 2) Utilisation of Various Large Language Models (LLMs).

Prompt Engineering We experimented with two prompt configurations for few-shot learning:

- Prompt1: A straightforward pair of evidence and questions.
- Prompt2: A more descriptive prompt that includes a triplet of claim, answer, and question.

Figure 2 illustrates the prompt configurations employed in our study. In "Prompt2", if a sample lacks a 'speaker' field or is set to NULL, we substitute it with "Speaker" to maintain consistency across the prompts.

In line with baseline criteria for question generation, we adopt a 10-shot approach for prompt construction. Additionally, we explored using the Bi-Encoder model to identify the 10 most relevant examples from the training set for prompting. The Bi-Encoder, based on a transformer architecture, is effective in retrieving in-context examples, enhancing the quality of few-shot prompting. An ablation study in the results section compares the effectiveness of these approaches.

Utilisation of Various Large Language Models (LLMs) With the GPU resources at our disposal, we conducted question-generation experiments using LLMs with up to 8 billion parameters. We evaluated leading open-source models such as BLOOM (Workshop et al., 2023) and Meta-Llama-3-8B (Dubey et al., 2024). Additionally, we tested the recently released Meta-Llama-3.1-8B for the generation task. For comparison, we also utilised the ChatGPT API[4] with the 'OpenAI-GPT-4o' model.

3.2.3 Question-Answer Reranking

After retrieving the initial set of evidence, we apply a reranking process to ensure that the most relevant pieces are selected for the claim verification task. This reranking is essential for identifying specific question-answer (QA) pairs that directly support or refute the claim, thereby sharpening the focus

[4]https://platform.openai.com/docs/api-reference/introduction

on the most pertinent information. To achieve this, we again utilise a Cross-Encoder model, which is particularly effective in capturing nuanced relationships between the claim and the evidence. At this stage, the input format changes to (claim, QA), allowing the model to evaluate the alignment between the claim and the concatenated question-answer (QA) pairs as:

$$\mathbf{h}_{[\text{CLS}]} = \text{RoBERTa}([\mathbf{c}; \mathbf{q} \cdot \mathbf{a}]) \quad (3)$$

the final hidden state $\mathbf{h}_{[\text{CLS}]}$ is then processed through a linear layer followed by a sigmoid activation function (as in Equation 2) to obtain a score $s(\mathbf{c}, \mathbf{qa})$ for the (claim, QA) pair.

By carefully selecting the most relevant evidence, the system significantly reduces noise and enhances the precision of the information used in the final verification step. This meticulous approach ensures that the verification process is not only accurate but also efficient, ultimately leading to more reliable outcomes in automated fact-checking.

3.2.4 Veracity Prediction

Veracity prediction is the final and most critical stage in the automated fact-checking pipeline. In this stage, the model classifies a claim based on the evidence retrieved (e.g., Top 3 QA pairs) and selected in previous stages to predict its veracity into four classes. Unlike the baseline approach using a BERT-Large model, we fine-tune a Cross-Encoder—a smaller, transformer-based model—through supervised natural language inference (NLI) training. This approach is computationally less expensive and well-suited for entailment tasks, where it infers the relationship between pairs of sentences (premise and hypothesis) (Li et al., 2022)

We use the Cross-Encoder with a text classification head for the task. Similar to Equation 3, the claim $\mathbf{c}$ and evidence pair $\mathbf{q} \cdot \mathbf{a}$ are inputted to the model to obtain an encoded input representation $\mathbf{h}_{[\text{CLS}]} = \text{RoBERTa}([\mathbf{c}; \mathbf{q} \cdot \mathbf{a}])$. The hidden state $\mathbf{h}_{[\text{CLS}]}$ is then passed through a linear layer (classification head) followed by a softmax activation function to produce a probability distribution $\mathbf{p}$ over the possible veracity labels (e.g., supported, refuted, insufficient evidence, conflicting/cherry-picking) as:

$$\mathbf{p} = \text{softmax}(\mathbf{W} \cdot \mathbf{h}_{[\text{CLS}]} + b) \quad (4)$$

where $\mathbf{W}$ is the weight matrix and $\mathbf{b}$ is the bias term of the linear layer. The output $\mathbf{p}$ is a vector of probabilities corresponding to each veracity class.

The model is trained using a cross-entropy loss function, which measures the difference between the predicted probability distribution and the true distribution. If $\mathbf{y}$ is the true label (encoded as a one-hot vector) and $\mathbf{p}$ is the predicted probability distribution, the loss function $\mathcal{L}$ is given by:

$$\mathcal{L} = -\sum_{k=1}^{K} y_k \log(p_k) \quad (5)$$

where K is the number of veracity classes, y_k is the true label for class k, and p_k is the predicted probability for class k. The model parameters are optimised to minimise this loss, thereby improving the accuracy of veracity prediction.

4 Experiments

4.1 Evaluation Metrics

In the evaluation of the AVeriTeC dataset and the associated automated fact-checking (AFC) systems, several metrics are employed to assess the performance at various stages of the pipeline. These stages consist of evidence retrieval, evidence selection, and veracity prediction. The metrics are designed to comprehensively measure the effectiveness and accuracy of each component, ensuring robust evaluation and comparison.

Unlike the FEVER dataset and others that use a closed source of evidence like Wikipedia, AVeriTeC is designed to retrieve evidence from the open web. This approach can result in finding the same evidence across multiple sources, making exact matching impractical for scoring purposes. Therefore, a Hungarian algorithm-based pairwise scoring function $f : S \times S \to \mathbb{R}$ is utilised to evaluate how well a set of generated sequences, such as questions or answers, aligns with the reference sequences of tokens. The Hungarian algorithm provides the solution as a boolean function $X : \hat{Y} \times Y \to \{0, 1\}$, maximising the assignment problem between the generated sequences $\hat{Y}$ and the reference sequences Y (Crouse, 2016). This metric, referred to as the Hungarian METEOR (Hu-METEOR) score s_f and is then calculated between $\hat{Y}$ and Y as:

$$s_f(\hat{Y}, Y) = \frac{1}{|Y|} \max \sum_{\hat{y} \in \hat{Y}} \sum_{y \in Y} f(\hat{y}, y) X(\hat{y}, y) \quad (6)$$

where f denotes METEOR, a pointwise scoring function, and X is a boolean function optimised as a linear sum assignment problem. The Final Hu-METEOR score is estimated as the mean of scores between all pairs of generated and reference sequences. The Hu-METEOR is used twice to evaluate questions-only sequences and concatenated question-answer (QA) pairs.

AVeriTeC Score is an accuracy metric utilised to compare the overall performance of the system. The metric considers veracity prediction True for a given claim if the Hu-METEOR score between generated and reference evidence is above a certain threshold ($\lambda > 0.25$):

$$\text{AVeriTeC\_Score} = \frac{1}{|C|}\sum_{c \in C}(c_{\text{pred\_label}} == c_{\text{true\_label}}, \; f(c_{\hat{y}}, c_y) > (\lambda = 0.25)) \tag{7}$$

where, $c_{\text{pred\_label}}$, $c_{\text{true\_label}}$ denotes predicted and true labels, respectively, and $c_{\hat{y}}$ and c_y are the generated and reference evidence sets of the claim.

4.2 Implementation Details

Table 2 provides a comprehensive overview of the models used within the various components of our pipeline, including specific details and the corresponding checkpoints.

In the evidence retrieval step, we extracted sentences from the provided knowledge store using three models: 1) BM25 (AVeriTeC baseline), 2) Bi-Encoder, and 3) Cross-Encoder, for comparison. For the Bi-Encoder, we employed the standard BERT model with a hidden size of 768. For the Cross-Encoder, we utilised a smaller transformer model with a hidden size of 384, fine-tuned specifically for reranking tasks such as MS-Marco Passage reranking (Nguyen et al., 2016). We set the batch size to 32 for both Bi-Encoder and Cross-Encoder. The average time in scoring 1,000 sentences by BM25, Cross-Encoder, and Bi-Encoder are 10.9, 31.9, and 80.3 milliseconds, respectively.

For the *question generation* task, we leverage several large language models (LLMs), including BLOOM, Meta-Llama-3-8B, and Meta-Llama-3.1-8B. For comparison, ChatGPT's GPT-4o model is accessed through its API. Due to financial restrictions, the questions are generated only for the top 25 evidence with ChatGPT. The average time to generate a single question varies across the models, with BLOOM taking 8.9 seconds, Meta-Llama-3-8B taking 3.1 seconds, and Meta-Llama-3.1-8B taking 3.6 seconds. This performance data highlights the efficiency of the Meta-Llama models, particularly in resource-constrained environments. For prompting, BM25 and Bi-Encoder are considered for selecting the 10 most relevant examples from the training set for prompting.

For the *Question-Answer reranking*, Cross-Encoder with 'ms-marco-MiniLM-L-12-v2' checkpoint is utilised instead of the baseline's BERT-large model. It requires no training and is computationally less expensive due to its smaller size, leading to 5 times faster performance. For each claim, it takes approx 40 ms to reorder the QA pairs.

The final stage *verdict prediction* involves training a supervised NLI model as an entailment task. The model takes a pair of a claim and concatenated QA as input and predicts a veracity label. With a cross-encoder setting, we fine-tune a DeBERTa-NLI model on examples from train/development data using Adam (Kingma and Ba, 2017) with a learning rate of 2e-5 and a batch size of 16 for four epochs.

All the experiments were conducted on an NVIDIA RTX 6000 Ada 48GB type GPUs.

5 Results

The proposed pipeline's evaluation involved a comprehensive analysis of performance across various stages, including evidence retrieval, evidence selection, and veracity prediction. The results highlight the effectiveness of the proposed approach in handling the complexities of real-world claim verification and the challenges encountered during the process.

5.1 Evidence Selection

In the evidence retrieval step, we extract the top-100 evidence sentences for each claim from a vast pool of a knowledge store. Table 3 shows the Hu-METEOR based retrieval score by various methods, i.e. BM25, TF-IDF, Bi-Encoder and Cross-Encoder. The Cross-Encoder model demonstrated strong performance in identifying pieces of evidence that were most relevant to the claims. The model's ability to consider both the claim and the evidence sentence jointly allowed it to capture nuanced relationships, leading to improved evidence selection effectively. Additionally, its lightweight architecture makes it comparable to Bi-Encoder.

Models	Checkpoint	Hidden Size	#Parameters	Task
Cross-Encoder	ms-marco-MiniLM-L-12-v2[5]	384	22.7M	Evidence-Retr, QA Reranking
Bi-Encoder	bert-base-uncased[6]	768	109.5M	Evidence-Retr, 10-Shot Prompt
BLOOM	bloom-7b1[7]	4096	7B	Q-Generation
Meta-3	Meta-Llama-3-8B[8]	4096	8B	Q-Generation
Meta-3.1	Meta-Llama-3.1-8B[9]	4096	8B	Q-Generation
ChatGPT	Openai-GPT-4o[10]	–	–	Q-Generation
DeBERTa-NLI	deberta-v3-base[11]	768	82M	Veracity Prediction

Table 2: The details for models used for various tasks in the pipeline.

Models	A only @ (3 / 5 / 10 / 50 / 100)				
BM25 (baseline)	0.1027	0.1207	0.1452	0.2049	0.2338
TF-IDF	0.1062	0.1237	0.1474	0.2077	0.2382
Bi-Encoder	0.1311	0.1521	0.1787	0.2474	0.2753
Cross-Encoder	**0.1413**	**0.1624**	**0.1913**	**0.2614**	**0.2907**

Table 3: Results of evidence selection in terms of Hu-METEOR on the development set.

Prompt Setting	Few-Shot Selection	Q only @ (3 / 5 / 10 / 100)				QA only @ (3 / 5 / 10 / 100)			
Prompt1	Bi-Encoder	0.21	0.25	0.30	0.43	0.22	0.25	0.28	0.36
Prompt1	BM25	0.23	0.27	0.33	0.46	0.22	0.25	0.28	0.36
Prompt2	Bi-Encoder	0.24	0.29	0.34	0.48	**0.23**	**0.26**	**0.29**	0.37
Prompt2	**BM25**	**0.26**	**0.30**	**0.36**	**0.49**	**0.23**	**0.26**	**0.29**	**0.38**

Table 4: Influence of Prompt setting on question generation. `bigscience/bloom-7b1` is used as LLM for generation.

5.2 Question Generation

We consider various LLMs for the question generation task based on the extracted evidence, i.e. bloom-7b1, Meta-Llama-3-8B, Meta-Llama-3.1-8B, and Openai-GPT-4o. We also experimented with sparse, e.g. BM25, and dense, e.g. Bi-Encoder, methods for selecting few-shot examples during prompt construction. The result on prompt construction is shown in Table 4 with both few-shot selection methods under prompt-setting Prompt1 and Prompt2. We found that a descriptive prompt can generate relevant questions in the context of given claims and evidence pairs. This shows BM25's superiority to Bi-Encoders for few-shot example selection in prompting due to its emphasis on exact term matching and robustness in low data scenarios.

[5]https://huggingface.co/cross-encoder/ms-marco-MiniLM-L-12-v2

[6]https://huggingface.co/google-bert/bert-base-uncased

[7]https://huggingface.co/bigscience/bloom-7b1/tree/main

[8]https://huggingface.co/meta-llama/Meta-Llama-3-8B

[9]https://huggingface.co/meta-llama/Meta-Llama-3.1-8B

[10]https://platform.openai.com/docs/models/gpt-4o

[11]https://huggingface.co/microsoft/deberta-v3-base

LLM	Q only @ (3 / 5 / 10 / 100)				QA only @ (3 / 5 / 10 / 100)			
bloom-7b1	0.26	0.30	0.36	0.49	0.23	0.26	0.29	0.38
Meta-Llama-3-8B	0.28	0.32	0.37	0.49	0.23	0.26	0.29	0.38
Meta-Llama-3.1-8B	0.28	0.32	0.37	0.49	0.23	0.26	0.30	0.38
Openai-GPT-4o	**0.41**	**0.45**	**0.49**	–	**0.25**	**0.29**	**0.32**	–

Table 5: Influence of using various LLMs on question generation task. Few-shot selection is done by BM25. Openai-GPT-4o has been used to generate questions for only the first 25 sentences.

Reranking Models	LLM	Q only @3	A only @3	QA @3
BERT-Dual Encoder (baseline)	Meta-Llama-3-8B	0.2799	0.1173	0.2032
	Meta-Llama-3.1-8B	0.2832	0.1199	0.2069
	Openai-GPT-4o	0.4023	0.1392	0.2464
Cross-Encoder	Meta-Llama-3-8B	0.2991	0.1360	0.2341
	Meta-Llama-3.1-8B	0.3018	0.1323	0.2334
	Openai-GPT-4o	**0.4122**	**0.1374**	**0.2584**

Table 6: Results of post-QA reranking Hu-METEOR score @3 through BERT-Dual Encoder (baseline) and Cross-Encoder.

Table 5 depicts the influence of using various LLMs for question generation. It shows Meta models are better than BLOOM due to their bigger architecture and being trained on more diverse and high-quality data (Dubey et al., 2024). ChatGPT-based Openai-GPT-4o model has shown a 0.13 jump in Hu-METEOR score on Q only @3, achieving an overall high performance on AVeriTeC task.

5.3 QA Reranking

In the *question-answer reranking* stage, a pre-trained Cross-Encoder is utilised to select top QA pairs achieving higher Hu-METEOR scores than the baseline's BERT-large, which requires explicit fine-tuning on the training data. Table 6 presents the Hu-METEOR scores for questions only (Q), answers only (A), and combined question-answer (QA) across various LLMs, including Meta-Llama-3-8B, Meta-Llama-3.1-8B, and OpenAI-GPT-4o. The Cross-Encoder based reranking consistently outperforms the baseline in question generation.

LLM	Development set				Test set			
	Q Only	A Only	QA	A.S	Q Only	A Only	QA	A.S
Official Baseline	0.24	–	0.19	0.09	0.24	–	0.20	0.11
Meta-Llama-3-8B	0.2992	0.1360	0.2342	0.1780	0.2976	–	0.2409	0.1986
Meta-Llama-3.1-8B	0.3018	0.1323	0.2334	0.1900	0.2978	–	0.2405	0.1937
Openai-GPT-4o	**0.4122**	**0.1374**	**0.2584**	**0.2240**	**0.3961**	–	**0.2613**	**0.2239**

Table 7: Performance on the development set and test set. A.S is the AVeriTeC score, and Q Only, A Only, and QA are the Hu-METEOR scores of question, answer and question-answer, respectively.

5.4 Overall results: Veracity Prediction

The veracity prediction stage was crucial for determining the final classification of the claims. We fine-tuned a transformer-based classification model, DeBERTa-NLI, on the AVeriTeC dataset, achieving strong results in classifying claims into the predefined categories: supported, refuted, insufficient evidence, and conflicting/cherry-picking. The model's performance was evaluated using metrics Q Only, A Only, QA, and A.S (AVeriTeC Score), where the Q Only, A Only, QA scores are Hu-METEOR scores of the retrieved evidence and A.S is a special metric that considers veracity prediction true for a given claim if the Hu-METEOR is above a certain threshold ($\lambda = 0.25$) as shown in Table 7. We observe that under the same pipeline models, Meta LLMs outperform the baseline by 0.9 to 0.10 AVeriTeC score through obtaining improved QA evidence. Openai-GPT-4o shows a remarkable improvement in question generation, which leads to achieving a higher overall AVeriTec score on both development and test data.

6 Conclusion

In this paper, we presented a comprehensive pipeline for real-world claim verification tailored to the AVeriTeC dataset. Our approach, which integrates cross-encoders for evidence retrieval and LLMs for question generation, has shown to be effective in improving the accuracy of automated fact-checking systems. We show that the cross-encoder performs better than the baseline on both evidence extraction and reranking. The results of our experiments highlight the importance of multi-stage processing and the careful selection of evidence to support or refute claims. Our model's performance in the AVeriTeC shared task demonstrated its potential in real-world applications, particularly in scenarios requiring detailed reasoning and context understanding. Although our system has made significant strides in addressing the complexities of real-world claim verification, further improvements are necessary, particularly in handling ambiguous claims and ensuring the completeness of evidence.

7 Limitations

Despite the promising results, our approach has several limitations. First, we rely on the knowledge store provided by the shared task; therefore, retrieving evidence from scratch from Google with better scrapping and parsing methods may provide a better knowledge space. Secondly, the reliance on cross-encoders, while effective, is computationally expensive, which may hinder scalability in real-time applications. Additionally, advanced reranking models, such as HLATR (Zhang et al., 2023), HybRank (Zhang et al., 2022), and M-ReRank (Malviya and Katsigiannis, 2024) can further enhance evidence retrieval. Thirdly, "the performance of our question generation model, though robust, can be affected by the quality and diversity of few-shot examples used for prompting.

Additionally, our system's ability to handle claims with insufficient or conflicting evidence remains a challenge, often leading to less accurate veracity predictions. Finally, the dataset's temporal dependency introduces potential biases, as evidence published after the claim date could influence the verification process. Addressing these limitations will be crucial for enhancing our system's robustness and generalisability in future work.

Acknowledgements

The authors in this project have been funded by UK EPSRC grant "AGENCY: Assuring Citizen Agency in a World with Complex Online Harms" under grant EP/W032481/2.

References

Rami Aly, Zhijiang Guo, Michael Schlichtkrull, James Thorne, Andreas Vlachos, Christos Christodoulopoulos, Oana Cocarascu, and Arpit Mittal. 2021. FEVEROUS: Fact Extraction and VERification Over Unstructured and Structured information. *Proceedings of the Neural Information Processing Systems Track on Datasets and Benchmarks*, 1. 1

Isabelle Augenstein, Christina Lioma, Dongsheng Wang, Lucas Chaves Lima, Casper Hansen, Christian Hansen, and Jakob Grue Simonsen. 2019. MultiFC: A Real-World Multi-Domain Dataset for Evidence-Based Fact Checking of Claims. In *Proceedings of the 2019 Conference on Empirical Methods in Natural Language Processing and the 9th International Joint Conference on Natural Language Processing (EMNLP-IJCNLP)*, pages 4685–4697, Hong Kong, China. Association for Computational Linguistics. 1

David F. Crouse. 2016. On implementing 2D rectangular assignment algorithms. *IEEE Transactions on Aerospace and Electronic Systems*, 52(4):1679–1696. 5

Jacob Devlin, Ming-Wei Chang, Kenton Lee, and Kristina Toutanova. 2019. BERT: Pre-training of Deep Bidirectional Transformers for Language Understanding. In *Proceedings of the 2019 Conference of the North American Chapter of the Association for Computational Linguistics: Human Language Technologies, Volume 1 (Long and Short Papers)*, pages 4171–4186, Minneapolis, Minnesota. Association for Computational Linguistics. 3

Abhimanyu Dubey, Abhinav Jauhri, Abhinav Pandey, Abhishek Kadian, and Others. 2024. The Llama 3 Herd of Models. 4, 7

Zhijiang Guo, Michael Schlichtkrull, and Andreas Vlachos. 2022. A Survey on Automated Fact-Checking. *Transactions of the Association for Computational Linguistics*, 10:178–206. 1

Samuel Humeau, Kurt Shuster, Marie-Anne Lachaux, and Jason Weston. 2019. Poly-encoders: Architectures and Pre-training Strategies for Fast and Accurate Multi-sentence Scoring. In *International Conference on Learning Representations*. 2, 3

Diederik P. Kingma and Jimmy Ba. 2017. Adam: A Method for Stochastic Optimization. 6

Shuang Li, Xuming Hu, Li Lin, and Lijie Wen. 2022. Pair-Level Supervised Contrastive Learning for Natural Language Inference. In *ICASSP 2022 - 2022 IEEE International Conference on Acoustics, Speech and Signal Processing (ICASSP)*, pages 8237–8241. 2, 5

Yinhan Liu, Myle Ott, Naman Goyal, Jingfei Du, Mandar Joshi, Danqi Chen, Omer Levy, Mike Lewis, Luke Zettlemoyer, and Veselin Stoyanov. 2019. RoBERTa: A Robustly Optimized BERT Pretraining Approach. 3

Shrikant Malviya and Stamos Katsigiannis. 2024. Evidence Retrieval for Fact Verification using Multi-stage Reranking. In *ACL Rolling Review - June 2024*. 8

Preslav Nakov, David Corney, Maram Hasanain, Firoj Alam, Tamer Elsayed, Alberto Barrón-Cedeño, Paolo Papotti, Shaden Shaar, and Giovanni Da San Martino. 2021. Automated Fact-Checking for Assisting Human Fact-Checkers. In *Twenty-Ninth International Joint Conference on Artificial Intelligence*, volume 5, pages 4551–4558. 1

Tri Nguyen, Mir Rosenberg, Xia Song, Jianfeng Gao, Saurabh Tiwary, Rangan Majumder, and Li Deng. 2016. MS MARCO: A Human-Generated MAchine Reading COmprehension Dataset. 6

Stephen Robertson and Hugo Zaragoza. 2009. The Probabilistic Relevance Framework: BM25 and Beyond. *Foundations and Trends® in Information Retrieval*, 3(4):333–389. 3

Michael Schlichtkrull, Zhijiang Guo, and Andreas Vlachos. 2023. AVeriTeC: A Dataset for Real-world Claim Verification with Evidence from the Web. *Advances in Neural Information Processing Systems*, 36:65128–65167. 1, 2, 3

James Thorne, Andreas Vlachos, Christos Christodoulopoulos, and Arpit Mittal. 2018. FEVER: A Large-scale Dataset for Fact Extraction and VERification. In *Proceedings of the 2018 Conference of the North American Chapter of the Association for Computational Linguistics: Human Language Technologies, Volume 1 (Long Papers)*, pages 809–819, New Orleans, Louisiana. Association for Computational Linguistics. 1

BigScience Workshop, Teven Le Scao, Angela Fan, Christopher Akiki, and Others. 2023. BLOOM: A 176B-Parameter Open-Access Multilingual Language Model. 3, 4

Yanzhao Zhang, Dingkun Long, Guangwei Xu, and Pengjun Xie. 2022. HLATR: Enhance Multi-stage Text Retrieval with Hybrid List Aware Transformer Reranking. 8

Zongmeng Zhang, Wengang Zhou, Jiaxin Shi, and Houqiang Li. 2023. Hybrid and Collaborative Passage Reranking. In *Findings of the Association for Computational Linguistics: ACL 2023*, pages 14003–14021, Toronto, Canada. Association for Computational Linguistics. 8

InFact: A Strong Baseline for Automated Fact-Checking

Mark Rothermel* **Tobias Braun*** **Marcus Rohrbach** **Anna Rohrbach**
TU Darmstadt & hessian.AI, Germany

Abstract

The spread of disinformation poses a global threat to democratic societies, necessitating robust and scalable Automated Fact-Checking (AFC) systems. The AVeriTeC Shared Task Challenge 2024 offers a realistic benchmark for text-based fact-checking methods. This paper presents *Information-Retrieving Fact-Checker (*InFact*)*, an LLM-based approach that breaks down the task of claim verification into a 6-stage process, including evidence retrieval. When using GPT-4o as the backbone, InFact achieves an AVeriTeC score of 63 % on the test set, outperforming all other 20 teams competing in the challenge, and establishing a new strong baseline for future text-only AFC systems. Qualitative analysis of mislabeled instances reveals that InFact often yields a more accurate conclusion than AVeriTeC's human-annotated ground truth.

1 Introduction

The weaponization of disinformation poses a critical threat to global stability. The World Economic Forum, in its January report (World Economic Forum, 2024), identified mis- and disinformation as the most significant global risk for the next 24 months, surpassing even extreme weather events and military conflicts. As such, the development and deployment of Automated Fact-Checking (AFC) is essential in safeguarding the integrity of democratic societies worldwide.

Schlichtkrull et al. (2023) introduced the *Automated VERIfication of TExtual Claims* (AVeriTeC) benchmark, consisting of 4,568 real-world claims subject to fact-checks by 50 organizations. AVeriTeC classifies each claim as either Supported, Refuted, NEI (**N**ot **E**nough **I**nformation) or C/CP if there is **c**onflicting evidence or the claim is technically true but misleading due to the exclusion of important context (**c**herry-**p**icking). The benchmark expects the fact-check to be structured as a set of questions and answers, comparing them against the gold QA pairs using the Hungarian METEOR metric in order to ensure that the predicted veracity is sufficiently justified. It further provides a Knowledge Base (KB), a collection of scraped web pages. Each claim is associated with the resources used to fact-check it (gold evidence) and ca. 1,000 unrelated resources to simulate open web search.

Several early works suggest that LLMs and LLM prompting techniques such as Chain-of-Thought could be used for AFC (Geng et al., 2024; Khaliq et al., 2024; Zhang and Gao, 2023; Wei et al., 2024; Zhou et al., 2024). Following these works, we present an approach that is customized for the AVeriTeC challenge (Schlichtkrull et al., 2024) and incorporates intermediate question generation and evidence retrieval to provide answers.

We propose **In**formation-Augmented **Fact**-Checker (InFact), an AFC system with the capability of retrieving evidence. InFact achieves an AVeriTeC score of 62.6% on the test set and yields an accuracy of 72.4% on the development dataset. Qualitative analysis shows that our method's retrieval process and reasoning capabilities provide a powerful baseline for text-only AFC. Further details will be provided on https://github.com/multimodal-ai-lab/InFact.

2 The InFact System

Open-domain, text-only claim verification requires world and commonsense knowledge and some degree of reasoning. Due to their remarkable success in both of these skills, we chose to drive the fact-check by an LLM, supplemented with a custom evidence retrieval module. While our approach is agnostic to the choice of the LLM, the LLM's abilities influence the quality and accuracy of the resulting fact-check. Since the task of fact-checking

*These authors contributed equally to this work.

Proceedings of the Seventh Fact Extraction and VERification Workshop (FEVER), pages 108–112
November 15, 2024

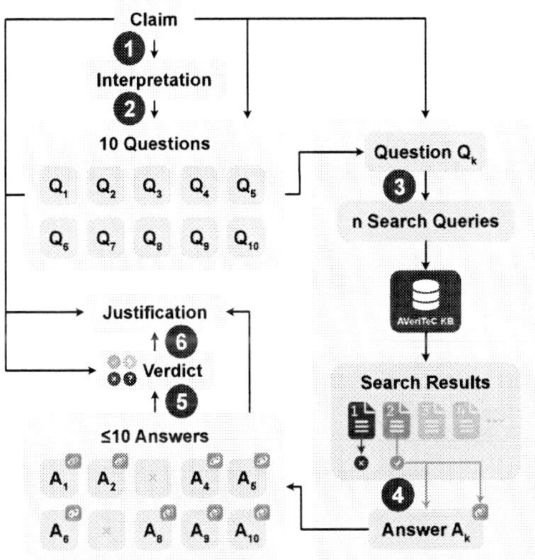

Figure 1: The **InFact System**. (1) Interpret the claim, (2) pose 10 questions, (3) for each question individually, generate search queries and retrieve potentially relevant evidence from the AVeriTeC Knowledge Base, (4) answer the corresponding question using the found evidence, (5) after completing all questions, predict a verdict and (6) generate a justification.

is broad and complex, we subdivide the process into six stages, as shown in Figure 1.

In short, InFact addresses the task with a static, single-pass pipeline that poses critical questions which are answered through evidence retrieved from the AVeriTeC KB. Each of the six stages corresponds to an engineered prompt, applying prompting best practices including Chain-of-Thought (Wei et al., 2022) and In-Context Learning (Min et al., 2021), whenever applicable.

Stage 1: Interpret the Claim. The pipeline begins with an augmentation of the claim text with its author, date, and origin URL. Subsequently the LLM is prompted to reformulate the claim, considering the supplied metadata. This step is helpful when the time frame is unclear as in *"Joe Biden's income has increased recently."* We also expect the interpretation to help when the claim misses context as in *"Tourism, lockdown key to deep New Zealand recession."*

Stage 2: Pose Questions. Next, InFact produces a list of 10 questions that it deems essential for fact-checking. To facilitate the question generation, we provide the LLM with manually selected in-context examples. Furthermore, the instructions are inspired by fact-checking best practices from Silverman (2014).

Stage 3: Retrieve Evidence. For each generated question, InFact iteratively retrieves a list of evidence resources. InFact approaches this by letting the LLM propose one or multiple search queries, which are submitted to the AVeriTeC KB, yielding a list of 5 search results per query.

The AVeriTeC KB contains a collection of about $1,000$ resources per claim. A resource is a scraped URL, ranging from news articles over social media posts to PDF documents. We decided to use the AVeriTeC KB over open-web search for two main reasons: First, it guarantees to contain the gold evidence (possibly erased from the open web) and, second, it yields reproducible results (in contrast to open-web search).

To retrieve the most relevant resources from the KB, we implement a semantic search mechanism. For each resource, we compute its document-level embedding by employing a text embedding model. We chose `gte-base-en-v1.5` (Alibaba-NLP, 2024) due to its competitive FEVER score at time of the challenge given its manageable size. We compute the query's text embedding and use it to perform k-nearest neighbor search w.r.t. the Euclidean Distance in the document embedding space. This outputs a list of the semantically closest 5 resources. We drop resources that were found in previous searches and end up with a list of $\leq 5n$ evidences per question. We found this approach qualitatively superior to the common BM25 ranking method.

Stage 4: Answer Questions. Taking all the search results, InFact iterates from the semantically most similar to the least similar, instructing the LLM to either answer the question using the information from the result or respond with `NONE` if the result is deemed unhelpful. If the LLM returned an answer to the question, InFact saves the answer along with the evidence URL, and the Q&A process continues with the next question. However, if the LLM returned `NONE` for all search results, the question is dropped for the remainder of the fact-check.

Stage 5: Predict a Verdict. Once all the questions are processed, the LLM judges the claim's veracity based on the recorded QA pairs in a single prompt as follows: First, it summarizes the key insights from the Q&A. Second, it identifies any pending, missing information. Third, it writes a brief conclusion, including the final verdict.

Stage 6: Justify the Verdict. In this last stage, InFact generates a brief justification for the verdict through summarization of the previous findings.

System	METEOR Q-Only	METEOR Q&A	AVERITEC Score
INFACT (Ours)	45	34	**63**
HERO	48	**35**	57
AIC	46	32	50
DUN-FACTCHECKER	**49**	**35**	50
PAPELO-TEN	44	30	48
Challenge Baseline	24	20	11

Table 1: Top-5 systems and the baseline on the AVERITEC challenge test set, ranked by AVERITEC score (in %) as defined in Schlichtkrull et al. (2023).

The LLM takes the claim, all the QA pairs, the verdict, and any in-between reasoning (e.g., from stage 5) and creates a summary, focusing on the main reasons for the verdict. This stage is not required by the AVERITEC task and does not affect any of the metrics.

3 Experimental Results

Experimental Setup. We evaluate INFACT on the development set which consists of 305 ✖ `Refuted`, 122 ✔ `Supported`, 35 ❓ `NEI` and 38 `C/CP` claims, 500 claims in total. As our LLM backbone, we test three models: (a) the open-source LLAMA 3 (70B), (b) the closed-source GPT-4O MINI, and (c) the more expensive GPT-4O model. We use the models without any finetuning and set the temperature to 0.01 and top-p to 0.9. Additionally, we truncate each resource to about 8 k tokens, which is the maximum input length of the embedding model. We compare INFACT with the following baseline and ablations: The *Naive* baseline instructs the LLM to predict the verdict right away in a single prompt, skipping evidence retrieval entirely and relying solely on the LLM's parametric knowledge; the *No Interpretation* ablation omits stage 1; *No Evidence* answers the questions by leaving out stage 3 (evidence retrieval); *No Q&A* generates search queries based on the claim instead of a Q&A, gathers 10 results and proceeds to make a verdict based on those; *No Query Generation* skips the step of query generation by using the question as the search query directly.

Challenge Results. Table 1 presents the top-5 entries from the challenge leaderboard, sorted by the AVERITEC score on the test set. INFACT achieves the best score with a significant margin to the second-best system. Yet, it is not the best in terms of the retrieval metrics.

Metric	LLAMA 3	GPT-4O MINI	GPT-4O	Naive	No Interpret.	No Evidence	No Q&A	No Query Gen.	INFACT
AVERITEC Score	✓			-	42.4	40.8	-	40.4	40.2
		✓		-	48.2	36.4	-	41.6	47.2
			✓	-	**59.8**	53.0	-	56.4	58.8
Accuracy	✓			67.0	63.2	67.0	52.9	65.0	61.8
		✓		36.2	61.6	56.8	54.8	59.6	60.2
			✓	52.6	71.8	71.0	68.8	70.2	**72.4**
Q-Only METEOR	✓			-	39.5	41.8	-	37.8	39.6
		✓		-	43.0	44.3	-	42.1	43.3
			✓	-	**46.2**	45.7	-	44.3	45.8
Q&A METEOR	✓			-	29.6	28.7	-	28.4	29.5
		✓		-	31.2	29.1	-	30.9	31.5
			✓	-	**33.5**	32.0	-	32.8	33.2

Table 2: Results in % on the AVERITEC development dataset, showing four metrics for INFACT and the five ablation variants, all tested with three different LLMs.

Analysis. The ablation comparison is shown in Table 2. GPT-4O almost consistently outperforms both other LLMs. INFACT and *No Interpretation* score best in terms of AVERITEC score and accuracy. Their similarity hints at a potential redundancy of the interpretation step in the case of AVERITEC. While our experiments show that generating search queries is superior to searching the literal question, the optimal value for the number of queries per question n remains unknown. Moreover, and surprisingly, leaving out all evidence does not lead to a drastic decline of the METEOR scores, showing its insensitivity to generated (thus potentially hallucinated) evidence vs. actually retrieved evidence.

Judging by the confusion matrices (cf. Fig. 2, the most distinct confusion for LLAMA 3 and GPT-4O MINI happens between ❓ `NEI` (predicted) and ✖ `Refuted` (true), which is less critical than confusion between ✔ `Supported` and ✖ `Refuted`. At the same time, GPT-4O predicts much fewer ❓ `NEI` in favor of ✖ `Refuted`, which could be attributed to its stronger reasoning capabilities.

Surprisingly, in the *Naive* setting, LLAMA 3 outperforms the GPT models by a large margin. As opposed to the GPT models, LLAMA 3 commits more often to either ✔ `Supported` or ✖ `Refuted` rather than choosing ❓ `NEI`, showing a "self-confident" behavior despite having little evidence. In the *No Evidence* variant, the GPT models

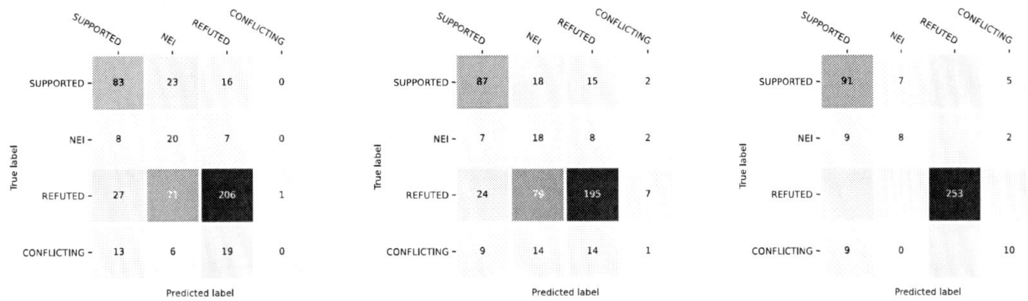

(a) LLAMA 3 (b) GPT-4O MINI (c) GPT-4O

Figure 2: Confusion matrices of INFACT on the AVERITEC development set for three different LLMs.

achieve a higher accuracy and predict ❓NEI much less, while still having no access to any external information. This indicates that structured reasoning elevates GPT models' confidence, regardless of the knowledge source.

Qualitative analysis of 20 failure cases reveals that, in more than half of the cases, the ground truth was at least debatable or INFACT delivered a valid alternative fact-check. E.g., the ground truth of "While serving as Town Supervisor on Grand Island, Nebraska, US Nate McMurray voted to raise taxes on homeowners" is ✅Supported, however McMurray served on Grand Island, **New York**. In two cases, the gold fact-check considered a *different* claim than the one presented. E.g., the claim: "Scientific American magazine warned that 5G technology is not safe" is about the magazine issuing a warning about 5G. However, the gold fact-check analyzed the safety of 5G itself.

In only 6 of the analyzed 20 failure cases, the cause for the mislabeling can be clearly attributed to INFACT. The cases include the usage of unreliable evidence sources, misinterpretations of the claim, the missing ability to process non-textual evidence, and the confusion between clearly refuted and merely unsupported claims. In a nutshell, the analysis implies that the model performs better than the metrics might reflect.

4 Discussion & Conclusion

INFACT establishes a robust baseline for information-augmented fact-checking without requiring fine-tuning. Its LLM-agnostic design ensures that it benefits from advancements in the reasoning capabilities of LLMs, making it adaptable to future developments. Additionally, INFACT provides justifications, enhancing interpretability and trust in its outputs. However, INFACT also has limitations. The inclusion of closed-source models limits transparency, reproducibility, and incurs high cost with about \$ 0.46 per claim when using GPT-4O. While GPT-4O MINI is much cheaper (about \$ 0.01 per claim), it exhibited lower performance. The open-source alternative LLAMA 3 resulted in 8 times longer computation times and reduced effectiveness. Also the number of retrievals was relatively high (7 searches per claim). Increasing INFACT's efficiency by reducing searches and skipping and/or combining steps in the pipeline are a great opportunity for future work. All LLMs evaluated in this study were pre-trained on datasets that extend into 2023, likely covering many of AVERITEC's claims and evidence available online.

Moreover, the AVERITEC dataset comes with its own limitations. The wording of the QA pairs is crucial when using the METEOR score to evaluate them against gold-standard QA pairs. The automated comparison method is limited in capturing semantically similar statements, and it is infeasible to provide an exhaustive list of all potentially relevant evidence. Moreover, we found many questionable ground truth answers, cf. Section 3. We suspect that these inaccuracies stem from layperson annotations. Addressing these limitations and refining the dataset/metric will benefit measuring progress in this challenging task.

Acknowledgements

The research was partially funded by a LOEWE-Start-Professur (LOEWE/4b//519/05.01.002-(0006)/94), LOEWE-Spitzen-Professur (LOEWE/4a//519/05.00.002-(0010)/93) and an Alexander von Humboldt Professorship in Multimodal Reliable AI, sponsored by Germany's Federal Ministry for Education and Research.

References

Alibaba-NLP. 2024. Gte base en v1.5. Accessed: 2024-08-14.

Jiahui Geng, Yova Kementchedjhieva, Preslav Nakov, and Iryna Gurevych. 2024. Multimodal large language models to support real-world fact-checking. *arXiv:2403.03627*.

M. Abdul Khaliq, P. Chang, M. Ma, B. Pflugfelder, and F. Miletić. 2024. Ragar, your falsehood radar: Rag-augmented reasoning for political fact-checking using multimodal large language models. *Preprint*, arXiv:2404.12065.

Sewon Min, Mike Lewis, Luke Zettlemoyer, and Hannaneh Hajishirzi. 2021. Metaicl: Learning to learn in context. *CoRR*, abs/2110.15943.

Michael Schlichtkrull, Yulong Chen, Chenxi Whitehouse, Zhenyun Deng, Mubashara Akhtar, Rami Aly, Zhijiang Guo, Christos Christodoulopoulos, Oana Cocarascu, Arpit Mittal, James Thorne, and Andreas Vlachos. 2024. The automated verification of textual claims (averitec) shared task. In *Proceedings of the Seventh Workshop on Fact Extraction and VERification (FEVER)*. Association for Computational Linguistics (ACL). To appear.

Michael Schlichtkrull, Zhijiang Guo, and Andreas Vlachos. 2023. AVeriTeC: A Dataset for Real-world Claim Verification with Evidence from the Web. *arXiv preprint*. ArXiv:2305.13117 [cs].

Craig Silverman, editor. 2014. *Verification Handbook: A Definitive Guide to Verifying Digital Content for Emergency Coverage*. European Journalism Centre, Maastricht, the Netherlands. Copyeditor: Merrill Perlman, The American Copy Editors Society (ACES).

Jason Wei, Xuezhi Wang, Dale Schuurmans, Maarten Bosma, Ed H. Chi, Quoc Le, and Denny Zhou. 2022. Chain of thought prompting elicits reasoning in large language models. *CoRR*, abs/2201.11903.

Jerry Wei, Chengrun Yang, Xinying Song, Yifeng Lu, Nathan Hu, Dustin Tran, Daiyi Peng, Ruibo Liu, Da Huang, Cosmo Du, and Quoc V. Le. 2024. Long-form factuality in large language models. *arXiv preprint*. ArXiv:2403.18802 [cs].

World Economic Forum. 2024. The global risks report 2024. Page 18.

Xuan Zhang and Wei Gao. 2023. Towards llm-based fact verification on news claims with a hierarchical step-by-step prompting method. *Preprint*, arXiv:2310.00305.

Xinyi Zhou, Ashish Sharma, Amy X. Zhang, and Tim Althoff. 2024. Correcting misinformation on social media with a large language model. *arXiv preprint*. ArXiv:2403.11169 [cs].

Exploring Retrieval Augmented Generation For Real-world Claim Verification

Omar Adjali
Université Paris-Saclay
Gif-sur-Yvette, France

Abstract

Automated Fact-Checking (AFC) has recently gained considerable attention to address the increasing misinformation spreading in the web and social media. The recently introduced AVeriTeC dataset alleviates some limitations of existing AFC benchmarks. In this paper, we propose to explore Retrieval Augmented Generation (RAG) and describe the system (UPS participant) we implemented to solve the AVeriTeC shared task. Our end-to-end system integrates retrieval and generation in a joint training setup to enhance evidence retrieval and question generation. Our system operates as follows: First, we conduct dense retrieval of evidence by encoding candidate evidence sentences from the provided knowledge store documents. Next, we perform a secondary retrieval of question-answer pairs from the training set, encoding these into dense vectors to support question generation with relevant in-context examples. During training, the question generator is optimized to generate questions based on retrieved or gold evidence. In preliminary automatic evaluation, our system achieved respectively 0.198 and 0.210 AVeriTeC scores on the dev and test sets.

1 Introduction

With the unprecedented growing of fake news in the web and on social media, several research efforts have been supported in the recent years to combat online misinformation. While manual fact-checking is the most reliable method for verifying information, the large-scale amount of daily published and shared content has made the development of automated fact-checking solutions crucial to assist in the manual fact checking process. Following such initiatives, the recently introduced AVeriTeC (Automated VERIfication of TExtual Claims) dataset (Schlichtkrull et al., 2024) contributes to address the aforementioned challenges, and serves as a benchmark for the AVeriTeC shared task. In this paper, we report our findings in addressing the AVeriTeC shared task and describe the proposed system which is evaluated on its ability of verifying real-world claims with evidence from the Web. In contrast to other fact-checking datasets such as FEVER (Thorne et al., 2018), VITAMINC (Schuster et al., 2021) and FEVEROUS (Aly et al., 2021), AVeriTeC focuses on realistic scenarios where real-world claims are derived from the web rather than Wikipedia. In this context, systems are required to retrieve evidence that either supports or refutes a given claim, using sources from either the Web or a document collection scrapped from the web and provided by the organizers. Based on this evidence, systems must categorize the claim as *Supported, Refuted, Not Enough Evidence* (when there is insufficient evidence to make a determination), or *Conflicting Evidence/Cherry-picking* (when both supporting and refuting evidence are present). A response is considered correct only if it includes both the accurate label and sufficient supporting evidence. Due to the complexity of evaluating evidence retrieval automatically, a manual evaluation process will be conducted to ensure a fair assessment of the participant systems.

2 AVeriTeC baseline

The AVeriTeC shared task organizers proposed a pipeline system which comprises the following steps: 1) Given a claim c, it is used as a query input of a search engine (Google API) to obtain relevant URLs which are parsed into sentences. The collection of sentences serves for evidence retrieval. 2) For each claim c, only the top 100 sentences $\{s_i\}_{i=1}^{100}$ are kept based on the BM25 similarity between each s_i and c. 3) For each of the top 100 sentence s_i, BLOOM (Le Scao et al., 2023) allows to generate QA pairs which are used as evidence for veracity prediction. To allow more in-context examples for QA pairs generation, the 10 closest

Proceedings of the Seventh Fact Extraction and VERification Workshop (FEVER), pages 113–117
November 15, 2024 ©2024 Association for Computational Linguistics

claim-QA pairs are retrieved from the training set using the BM25 similarity between s_i and each answer included in a claim-QA pair of the training set. 4) The top 3 generated QA pairs are kept as evidence using a pre-trained BERT-based re-ranker (Devlin et al., 2019). 5) Finally, a claim c and its 3 generated QA evidence pairs are input in another pre-trained BERT model to predict the veracity label.

3 Proposed system

Following the baseline pipeline, we propose a simpler end-to-end integrated system (see Figure 1) which relies on the Retrieval Augmented Generation (RAG) framework to solve the AVeriTeC challenge where retrieval and generation complement each other using joint training. At the first stage, we perform evidence dense retrieval after encoding all potential evidence sentences retrieved from the provided knowledge store documents. Then, we perform a second retrieval of question-answer pairs from the training set (encoder into dense vectors) to support question generation with in-context examples. During training, the question generator learns to generate question given retrieved/gold evidence by jointly updating both generator and evidence/answer encoder using the RAG loss (Lewis et al., 2020). Finally, a veracity prediction model is employed to label the retrieved evidence.

3.1 Evidence retrieval

Using the searched documents provided by the search engine, we similarly keep the top 100 sentences as potential evidence using BM25. We then encode each sentence s_i into dense vector representations using a Bert-base encoder $\mathbf{E_s}(\cdot)$. We represent each sentence using the 768-d pooled vector of the [CLS] special token. Given a dataset $\mathcal{D}$ of N claims, instead of encoding all sentences into a $(N \times 100 \times 768)$ matrix, we rather encode the top 100 potential sentence evidence of each claim $c_i \in \mathcal{D}$ into one $(N \times 100 \times 768)$ matrix. This allows to reduce the search space during evidence retrieval since the relevant evidence sentences of claim c_i are likely to be found in its corresponding top-100 retrieved sentence set. Thus, we build N Faiss indexes (Johnson et al., 2019) for each $c_i \in \mathcal{D}$ where each of them, maps evidence sentences to dense vectors. These enable us to perform fast exact maximum inner product search (MIPS). Formally, given a claim c_i, and its top-100 evidence sentence set $S_i = \{s_j\}_{j=1}^{100}$, we compute the inner product between its dense vectors and all $s_j \in S_i$ as follows :

$$s(c_i, s_j) = \mathbf{E_s}(c_i)\mathbf{E_s}(s_j) \tag{1}$$

In this way, given an input claim c_i, we retrieve the top-K most relevant sentence using the highest relevance scores $s(\cdot)$.

3.2 In-context QA pairs retrieval

Similar to (Schlichtkrull et al., 2024), in order to provide the generator in-context examples for question-answer pair generation, we retrieve the top L QA-pairs from the training set which serve for building the final prompt. Given a retrieved sentence s_i obtained after the first step, we encode it using the same pre-train BERT-base encoder $\mathbf{E_s}(\cdot)$. Similar to the baseline system, the top L QA-pairs are selected according to the semantic similarity between answers in the QA pair training set and the retrieved evidence sentences. We therefore perform maximum inner product search for each sentence s_i after encoding and indexing all the answers in the training set as follows:

$$s(s_i, a_j) = \mathbf{E_s}(s_i)\mathbf{E_s}(a_j) \tag{2}$$

Similar to the sentence retrieval stage, we select the top-L QA pairs whose answers achieve the highest retrieval scores.

3.3 Question generation

In this step, given a claim c_i, we generate a question for each sentence retrieved in the first stage. Note that the top-L retrieved QA pairs (in-context examples) are used in the same way as in (Schlichtkrull et al., 2024) to build the prompt. Given a generated question q_i and a retrieved sentence s_i, we consider (q_i, s_i) as a QA evidence pair for c_i.

3.4 Veracity prediction

Given a claim c_i, its top-K QA generated pairs as evidence, we followed the baseline system to predict the veracity label which relies on a pre-trained BERT sequence classification model.

3.5 Training and inference

During training, given a claim c_i, we use its ground-truth QA evidence pairs provided in the training set to build the question generation prompt as well as generation labels. More precisely, given a set of ground truth QA pairs, we use the question of the

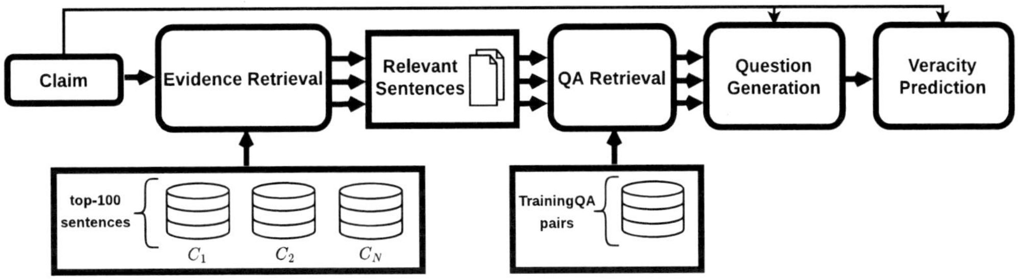

Figure 1: Our proposed pipeline system overview.

first QA pair as the generation target while the remaining pairs are used as in-context QA examples to build the final prompt. Experiments showed that using ground-truth QA pairs to build the prompt during training showed better performance than using retrieved ones. Thus, evidence retrieval and in-context QA pairs retrieval are only performed at inference time. In this setting, the sentence encoder and the question generator are jointly trained on the following RAG loss (Lewis et al., 2020):

$$\mathcal{L}_{\text{RAG}} = -\sum_{i=1}^{N} (\log(s(c_i, a^*) \cdot p_\Phi(q^*|pt(c_i), a^*))) \tag{3}$$

where N is the number of claims in the dataset, q^* is the ground truth question, a^* is the ground truth answer and $p_\Phi(q^*|pt(c_i), a^*)$ is the probability distribution of generating the question q^* given the built prompt $pt(c_i)$ and a^*, and Φ is the generator's parameters. $s(c_i, a^*)$ is the similarity score between the claim c_i and the ground truth answer. This learning objective allows to condition the generated questions on the retrieved evidence since the gradients are propagated through both the sentence encoder and the generator. At inference time, more relevant evidence sentences are expected to be retrieved thanks to the generator feedback signals during training while improved retrieval will contribute to generate more accurate questions.

4 Experiments

4.1 Evaluation

Systems are evaluated on their ability to retrieve evidence and to predict veracity labels. Note that veracity predictions are considered correct only when correct evidence has been found. The Hungarian METEOR metric (Schlichtkrull et al., 2024) is used to score retrieved questions and retrieved questions + answers. Furthermore, systems are ranked according to the Averitec score (METEOR) conditioned on correct evidence retrieved at a cutoff value of 0.25.

4.2 Implementation details

We initialized the pre-trained BERT-base model used for evidence retrieval and in-context QA retrieval with an answer encoder trained on TriviaQA (Joshi et al., 2017). For question generation, we experiment with the T5-large (738M parameters) (Raffel et al., 2020) pre-trained generator. The batch size is set to 2 due to GPU memory limit. We trained our system using a 2e-5 learning rate for 20 epochs. At inference time, we decode using beam-search with 2 beams. We selected the model checkpoints based on the validation performance. All experiments needed only one Nvidia A100 (80G) GPU. Our implementation is based on PyTorch (Paszke et al., 2017). Pretrained models are obtained using Hugginface and Transformers (Wolf et al., 2020). The Faiss library (Johnson et al., 2019) is used for MIPS search and vector indexing.

5 Results

Table 1 reports the performance results of our approach and baseline systems evaluated on the AVeriTeC shared task for the dev and test splits. Models are evaluated based on their ability to: 1) retrieve evidence in two settings: Question only (Q only), Question and Answer (Q+A). 2) Verifying veracity of claims using the AVeriTeC score for different cutoff values. Overall, our system with 955M parameters (BERT encoder + T5-large) significantly outperforms the AVeriTeC-BLOOM-7b baseline on both evidence retrieval and veracity checking across all the metrics suggesting that LLM's parametric memory is not sufficient to solve knowledge-intensive tasks such as fact-checking.

Model	split	Q only	Q+A	Veracity@0.2	Veracity@0.25	Veracity@0.3
AVeriTeC-BLOOM-7b	dev	0.240	0.185	0.186	0.092	0.050
AVeriTeC-BLOOM-7b	test	0.248	0.185	0.176	0.109	0.059
Ours (UPS)	dev	0.280	0.250	0.280	0.198	0.092
Ours (UPS)	test	0.310	0.270	-	0.210	-

Table 1: Averitec shared task results

Claim Type	Veracity score
Event/Property Claim	0.131
Position Statement	0.168
Causal Claim	0.118
Numerical Claim	0.144
Quote Verification	0.123

Table 2: Averitec scores by type @0.25 of our best performing system for dev set.

Veracity Label	F1
Supported	0.292
Refuted	0.653
Not Enough Evidence	0.160
Conflicting Evidence/Cherrypicking	0.166

Table 3: Veracity prediction dev set F1 results for each veracity label.

At inference time, we achieved the best performance with the number of retrieved evidence K=10, while higher values decreases both evidence retrieval and veracity checking. Regarding the number of retrieved in-context examples L, we found that building the prompt using only L=3 is sufficient for the question generation model to reach our best performing system. We assume that our BERT-base retrieval provides more useful in-context examples in the top retrieved QA pairs and does not need to re-rank evidence compared to the baseline model which relies on BM25 to retrieve evidence. Indeed, while we do not perform evidence retrieval during training, we still update the BERT retrieval encoder parameters using the claim-evidence similarity scores with the RAG loss. This latter allows to learn retrieving more relevant evidence for the target question using the feedback from the question generator.

We reports in Table 2 the veracity scores of our best performing system for each claim type. We note that there is no substantial performance gap between claim types, even if our system struggles more with *causal* and *Quote Verification* claims. Analysing these results need more investigations in future work.

Table 3 shows the F1 scores for each veracity label. We employed the provided checkpoint for veracity prediction which failed to predict the *Conflicting Evidence/Cherrypicking* label even with gold evidence (Schlichtkrull et al., 2024). Veracity prediction performs better on this label using our system however predictions are worse for the *Supported* label which suggests that improving evidence retrieval plays an important role to achieve the best fact-checking performance.

6 Conclusion

We presented in this paper our participant system (UPS) at the AVeriTeC shared task on verifying real-world claims with evidence from the Web. In preliminary automatic evaluation, our system achieved respectively 0.198 and 0.210 AVeriTeC scores on the dev and test sets, and was ranked 13 out of 23 participant teams. In terms of limitations, our proposed system relies solely on the AVeriTeC training set which is relatively small size. We believe that our RAG approach would benefit from more training data. Moreover, experimenting with larger generator models may improve the quality of generated questions and thus the overall fact-checking performance.

References

Rami Aly, Zhijiang Guo, Michael Schlichtkrull, James Thorne, Andreas Vlachos, Christos Christodoulopoulos, Oana Cocarascu, and Arpit Mittal. 2021. FEVEROUS: Fact Extraction and VERification Over Unstructured and Structured information. *arXiv preprint*. ArXiv:2106.05707 [cs].

Jacob Devlin, Ming-Wei Chang, Kenton Lee, and Kristina Toutanova. 2019. BERT: Pre-training of deep bidirectional transformers for language understanding. In *Proceedings of the 2019 Conference of the North American Chapter of the Association for Computational Linguistics: Human Language Technologies, Volume 1 (Long and Short Papers)*, pages 4171–4186, Minneapolis, Minnesota. Association for Computational Linguistics.

Jeff Johnson, Matthijs Douze, and Hervé Jégou. 2019. Billion-scale similarity search with gpus. *IEEE Transactions on Big Data*, 7(3):535–547.

Mandar Joshi, Eunsol Choi, Daniel Weld, and Luke Zettlemoyer. 2017. Triviaqa: A large scale distantly supervised challenge dataset for reading comprehension. In *Proceedings of the 55th Annual Meeting of the Association for Computational Linguistics (Volume 1: Long Papers)*, pages 1601–1611, Vancouver, Canada. Association for Computational Linguistics.

Teven Le Scao, Angela Fan, Christopher Akiki, Ellie Pavlick, Suzana Ilić, Daniel Hesslow, Roman Castagné, Alexandra Sasha Luccioni, François Yvon, Matthias Gallé, et al. 2023. Bloom: A 176b-parameter open-access multilingual language model.

Patrick Lewis, Ethan Perez, Aleksandra Piktus, Fabio Petroni, Vladimir Karpukhin, Naman Goyal, Heinrich Küttler, Mike Lewis, Wen-tau Yih, Tim Rocktäschel, et al. 2020. Retrieval-augmented generation for knowledge-intensive nlp tasks. *Advances in Neural Information Processing Systems*, 33:9459–9474.

Adam Paszke, Sam Gross, Soumith Chintala, Gregory Chanan, Edward Yang, Zachary DeVito, Zeming Lin, Alban Desmaison, Luca Antiga, and Adam Lerer. 2017. Automatic differentiation in pytorch. In *NIPS 2017 Workshop on Autodiff*, Long Beach, CA, USA. MIT Press.

Colin Raffel, Noam Shazeer, Adam Roberts, Katherine Lee, Sharan Narang, Michael Matena, Yanqi Zhou, Wei Li, and Peter J. Liu. 2020. Exploring the limits of transfer learning with a unified text-to-text transformer. *Journal of Machine Learning Research*, 21(140):1–67.

Michael Schlichtkrull, Zhijiang Guo, and Andreas Vlachos. 2024. Averitec: A dataset for real-world claim verification with evidence from the web. *Advances in Neural Information Processing Systems*, 36.

Tal Schuster, Adam Fisch, and Regina Barzilay. 2021. Get your vitamin c! robust fact verification with contrastive evidence. *arXiv preprint arXiv:2103.08541*.

James Thorne, Andreas Vlachos, Christos Christodoulopoulos, and Arpit Mittal. 2018. Fever: a large-scale dataset for fact extraction and verification. *arXiv preprint arXiv:1803.05355*.

Thomas Wolf, Lysandre Debut, Victor Sanh, Julien Chaumond, Clement Delangue, Anthony Moi, Pierric Cistac, Tim Rault, Remi Louf, Morgan Funtowicz, Joe Davison, Sam Shleifer, Patrick von Platen, Clara Ma, Yacine Jernite, Julien Plu, Canwen Xu, Teven Le Scao, Sylvain Gugger, Mariama Drame, Quentin Lhoest, and Alexander Rush. 2020. Transformers: State-of-the-art natural language processing. In *Proceedings of the 2020 Conference on Empirical Methods in Natural Language Processing: System Demonstrations*, pages 38–45, Online. Association for Computational Linguistics.

GProofT: A Multi-dimension Multi-round Fact Checking Framework Based on Claim Fact Extraction

Jiayu Liu*, **Junhao Tang***, **Hanwen Wang***,
Baixuan Xu, Haochen Shi, Weiqi Wang, Yangqiu Song
Department of Computer Science and Engineering, HKUST, Hong Kong SAR, China
{jliufv, jtangay, hwangfs}@connect.ust.hk

Abstract

In the information era, the vast proliferation of online content poses significant challenges, particularly concerning the trustworthiness of these digital statements, which can have profound societal implications. Although it is possible to manually annotate and verify the authenticity of such content, the sheer volume and rapid pace of information generation render this approach impractical, both in terms of time and cost. Therefore, it is imperative to develop automated systems capable of validating online claims, ensuring that users can use the wealth of information available on the Internet effectively and reliably. Using primarily ChatGPT and the Google search API, GProofT fact checking framework generates question-answer pairs to systematically extract and verify the facts within claims. Based on the outcomes of these QA pairs, claims are subsequently labeled as *Supported*, *Conflicted Evidence/Cherry-Picking*, or *Refuted*. Shown by extensive experiments, GProofT Retrieval generally performs effectively in fact-checking and makes a substantial contribution to the task. Our code is released on `https://github.com/HKUST-KnowComp/GProofT`.

1 Introduction

With the chaotic nature of information on the Internet, it appears to be challenging to determine the credibility of claims on the web. This poses difficulties on Large Language Models (LLMs) such as ChatGPT (OpenAI, 2023) to conduct fact checking as the hallucination (Huang et al., 2023; Ji et al., 2022; Chan et al., 2024a) of them can produce seemingly feasible but fake information. Though time-consuming and tedious when performed manually, fact-checking is rather crucial to ensure the trustworthiness of information, especially for the fact-sensitive industry such as journalism and science. In the explosion of information, it's far from adequate to solely rely on manual check to eliminate the rumor and misinformation, while remain difficult to be detected simply with commonsense knowledge (Fang et al., 2021b,a; Shi et al., 2023; Lu et al., 2024). Therefore, it's pivotal to develop a trustworthy automatic process to complete fact-checking efficiently and accurately. Recent advancements in LLMs have showcased remarkable performance in tasks involving text comprehension and generation (OpenAI et al., 2024; Wang et al., 2023b; He et al., 2023). However, the application of LLMs in automatic fact-checking has remained a persistent challenge, undergoing continuous exploration and development (Hang et al., 2024; Kim et al., 2024). Current LLMs can only memorize the knowledge embedded in their pretrain data, which makes them struggle with fact-checking when the event is out of their pretrain corpus, namely, out of their knowledge domain. Under this circumstance, it is necessary and crucial to incorporate real-time online search engine to provide LLMs with real-time facts information to assist its reasoning. However, the chaotic nature of internet could imply that the knowledge provided from the search engine could result in misinformation to the LLMs, hindering its reasoning process. Hence, a consistent framework for multi-dimension, multi-round fact checking needs to be proposed to generate stable and trustworthy fact checking result.

To solve the limitation, we propose GProofT fact checking framework to crawl and analyze web evidence based on Google Search API and ChatGPT. As demonstrated in Figure 1, For each given textual claim, we incorporate three stages to retrieve the pertinent evidence from the Internet and a final step to attribute a label based on the retrieved evidence. As suggested in the shared task, our retrieved evidence is in the format of QA pair. The retrieval procedure includes Claim Split, Question Generation, Answer Generation and Expansion. More information could be found in Section 3.1. Overall,

*First three authors make equal contribution to this paper.

Proceedings of the Seventh Fact Extraction and VERification Workshop (FEVER), pages 118–129
November 15, 2024 ©2024 Association for Computational Linguistics

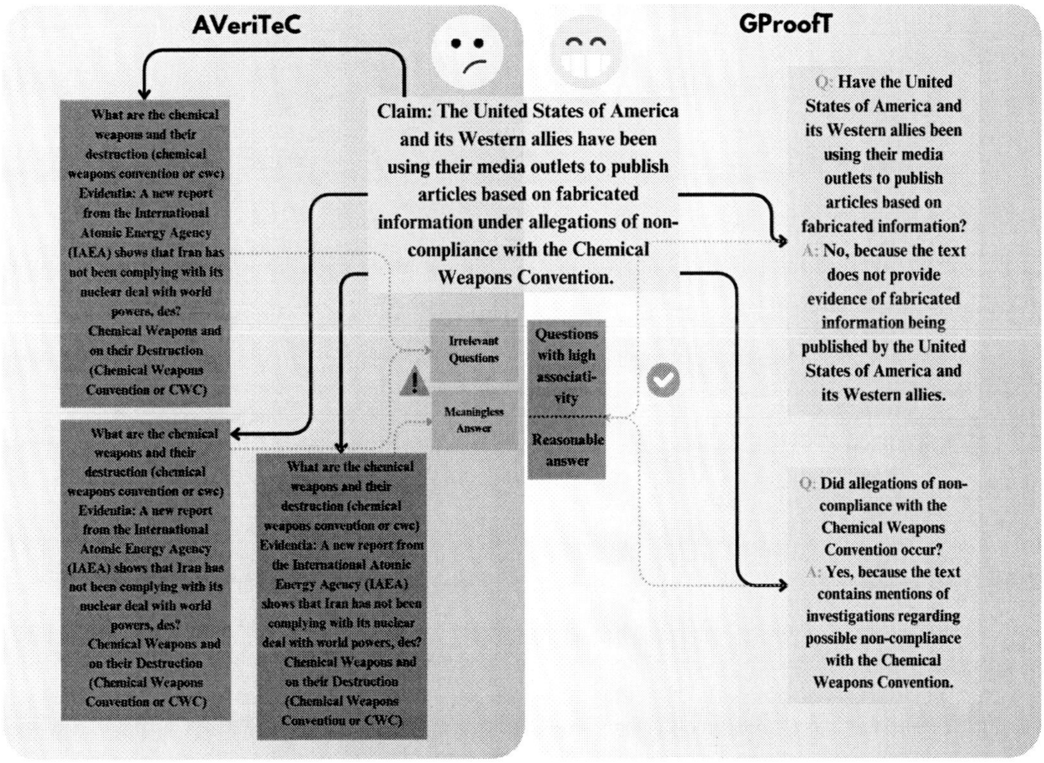

Figure 1: An overview structure of GProofT retrieval

our framework could be decomposed into 3 stages:

1. Claim Split: It focuses on the decomposition of the claim for the following question generation.

2. Question Generation: Based on the resulted subclaims in Claim Split, binary questions are generated respectively to validate the claim.

3. Answer Generation: Google Search API is employed to search for the questions in Question Generation and 9 relevant snippets are saved in the search results. ChatGPT is then adopted to determine whether they are supporting or refuting the original claim and generate the rationale.

After the retrieved evidence is obtained through our GProofT framework, we adopt LLMs to predict the label and benchmark our system based on the evaluation metrics proposed in AVeriTeC (Schlichtkrull et al., 2023). In-Context Learning (Agrawal et al., 2023; Hu et al., 2022b; Levy et al., 2023) and fine-tuning (Hu et al., 2022a; Xu et al., 2024b) are employed for gpt-3.5-turbo and Llama-3 (Huang et al., 2024) respectively to improve the accuracy of prediction. Subsequently, extensive experiments are conducted to further investigate both the strengths and weaknesses of our framework. As our Question-answer score is lower than the Question-only score, we suspect that our binary answer with a subsequent rationale is not sufficient for language models to make more accurate predictions. In this case, future study could focus on instructing LLMs to generate more informative responses based on the retrieved snippets, which could subsequently assist the fact checking process of LLMs. Overall, our work could be summarized in three main aspects:

- We design claim fact extraction to divide claims into informative subclaims which could be beneficial for its downstream fact checking.

- We propose GProofT framework, a multi-dimension, multi-round fact checking framework which can conduct fact checking without heavy human intervention.

- We benchmark a series of LLMs with different techiniques incorporated to demonstrate a comprehensive LLMs evaluation on fact checking task.

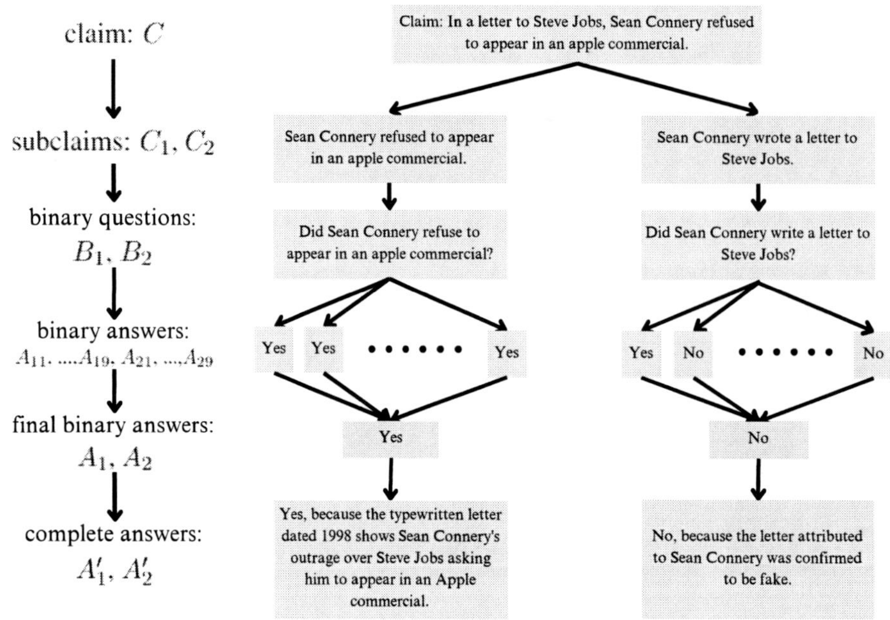

Figure 2: A comprehensive example of the GProofT retrieval process is provided by analyzing the claim, "In a letter to Steve Jobs, Sean Connery refused to appear in an Apple commercial." This example traces the progression from the original claim through to the final question-answer (QA) pair.

2 Problem Definition

2.1 Dataset Description

We leverage the dataset proposed by Schlichtkrull et al. (2023) for training and benchmarking. The training set includes 3068 claims, while the development set and test set include 500 and 2215 claims respectively. The dataset contains claims accompanied by their gold evidence and labels prepared by a hired annotator as well as their metadata including speaker, publisher, date, and location. The claims are collected from 6661 fact-checking articles with duplicated and dead articles removed. The extraction of claims and metadata, question and answer generation, verdict prediction are completed by annotators. For each instance, the label, either *Supported, Refuted, Not Enough Evidence* or *Conflicted Evidence/CherryPicking* is assigned based on retrieved evidence. Specifically, *Supported* and *Refuted* indicate that the authenticity of the claim can be identified based on the evidence recovered. In case of insufficient evidence or conflicted retrieved evidence, *Not Enough Evidence* or *Conflicted Evidence/CherryPicking* will be attributed to the specific claim.

2.2 Task Definition

We follow the task definition formulated by Schlichtkrull et al. (2023). Formally, for each claim C, one or multiple QA pairs $\{Q_i, A'_i\}$ (i=1, 2, ..., n) are served as evidence, in which Q_i is a fact-checking question, and A_i is its complete answer. The objective is to predict the validity of the fact by leveraging the evidence retrieved. Specifically, we utilize LLMs to label each QA pair as supported, refuted, or irrelevant. Then we predict the label with the label of each QA pair.

3 System Overview

In this section, we would introduce the GProofT fact checking framework and elaborate our benchmark setup.

3.1 GProofT Fact Checking Framework

The GProofT fact-checking framework is a multi-dimension, multi-round fact checking framework. It decompose the original claims into several sub-claims, enabling a comprehensive evaluation from various dimensions and multiple rounds. The GProofT fact-checking framework consist of three stages: Claim Decomposition, Question Generation and Answer Generation. The overall framework pipeline is exhibited in Figure 2. We would like to explain them in detail in the following paragraphs.

3.1.1 Claim Decomposition

By examining the instances, we observe that claims could be consisted of multiple opinions. Addressing these complex claims as singular entities can pose significant challenges for LLMs. Consequently, we decompose each claim C into several subclaims $C_1, C_2, ..., C_n$, ensuring that each resultant subclaim encompasses 1 to 2 facts.

To conduct decomposition, we employ a set of heuristic rules designed to guide ChatGPT (OpenAI, 2023) in effectively implementing this approach. The following rules outline this methodology:

- The overall mission involves instructing the LLMs to divide a claim into multiple subclaims based on the number of distinct facts it contains.
- Return only the subclaims, separated by periods rather than numbers.
- Avoid generating duplicated subclaims.
- The response from ChatGPT should be specific and avoid unnecessary pronouns to maintain clarity and conciseness.
- Limit subclaims to 15 words or less, ensuring they are shorter than the original claim.
- Capture the opinions or facts already present within it.
- Extract multiple subclaims, unless the claim is confined to a single fact.

Upon receiving the response from ChatGPT, we utilize SpaCy (Honnibal and Montani, 2017) to systematically split the subclaims. This process ensures that each subclaim is individually extracted, thereby deriving the subclaims from the original claim.

3.1.2 Question Generation

Subsequently, we proceed to generate the question of the QA pairs. We utilize ChatGPT to transform the subclaims into binary questions, which are structured to elicit yes or no responses. The heuristic rules adopted in this stage are as followed:

- Recognize the factual statement within the claim and formulate a binary question that can be used to verify this fact.
- Output the question directly without any rationales.
- Answers should be specific and avoid unnecessary pronouns to maintain clarity and conciseness.

3.1.3 Answer Generation

After preparing the binary questions, we employ the Google API to retrieve relevant evidence from online sources. For each question, 9 relevant snippets from 9 different websites are returned in the search results. Note that the default numbers of returned results for Google search API is 10, in order to avoid ties in latter majority voting, we set the hyperparameter to be 9 to maintain the maximum completeness. Our pipeline then prompts ChatGPT to determine the binary answer for each search result, given both the question and the corresponding snippet (Yu et al., 2023; Chan et al., 2024b). Following the resulted answers, we apply majority voting to determine the final binary response to the question. To give more insight on the rationale between the claim and each question, we expand the binary answer into a complete sentence that includes the binary response and the rationale derived from the snippet. Formally, given the question Q_i, the complete answer A_i is formulated as $\{\textbf{Binary answer}, \textbf{Rationale}\}$. The following heuristic rules are employed in this approach:

- Extend the initial binary answer into a comprehensive sentence.
- The answer should be formatted as "Yes, because ..." or "No, because ...".
- Answer the question directly without additional information.

The prompt for GProofT Fact Checking Framework is in appendix B.

3.2 Label Prediction

3.2.1 Zero-shot learning

We benchmark the performance of different models under zero-shot setting. The evidence generated in previous stages is cohesively incorporated into the input-prompted sentence. For each claim, we obtain $\{C, \{Q_i, A_i\}\}$ from the retrieval process.

	Gold evidence		Baseline evidence		GProofT evidence	
Q only score	1.000		0.241		0.331	
Q+A score	1.000		0.185		0.204	
	macro F1	AVeriTeC score	macro F1	AVeriTeC score	macro F1	AVeriTeC score
Baseline Model	-	-	0.321	0.092	-	-
Zero-shot model						
GPT-3.5-turbo	0.387	0.472	0.166	0.076	0.180	0.096
Llama-3-8B-Instruct	0.341	0.640	0.263	0.108	0.288	0.166
Llama-3.1-8B-Instruct	0.404	0.730	0.327	0.114	0.288	0.174
falcon-7b-instruct	0.335	0.550	0.290	0.096	0.299	0.172
Gemma-2-2b-it	0.324	0.528	0.303	0.098	0.266	0.146
Gemma-2-9b-it	0.453	0.694	0.351	0.092	0.332	0.170
Mistral-7B-Instruct-v0.3	0.365	0.642	0.301	0.106	0.295	0.174
Mistral-Nemo-Instruct	0.383	0.632	0.297	0.086	0.333	0.172
Qwen2-7B-Instruct	0.417	0.654	0.317	0.090	0.311	0.166
Finetuned model						
GPT-3.5-turbo (one-shot)	0.532	0.656	0.243	0.080	0.347	0.166
Llama3-8B	0.607	0.806	0.361	0.112	**0.347**	**0.186**
Llama-3-8B-Instruct	0.629	0.786	0.332	0.114	0.321	0.162
Llama-3.1-8B	0.627	0.782	0.342	0.122	0.329	0.180
Llama-3.1-8B-Instruct	0.684	0.800	0.320	0.108	0.330	0.186
Mistral-7B-Instruct-v0.1	0.639	0.748	0.332	0.106	0.332	0.184
Mistral-7B-Instruct-v0.2	0.675	0.770	0.337	0.110	0.334	0.185
Mistral-7B-Instruct-v0.3	0.623	0.780	0.357	0.114	0.339	0.178
Qwen2-7B-Instruct	0.653	0.758	0.345	0.106	0.338	0.170

Table 1: Evaluation results on development set of AVeriTeC. The best performances are **bold-faced**. "Q only" and "Q+A" refer to Hungarian METEOR score (Schlichtkrull et al., 2023). "AVeriTeC" indicates using accuracy at $\lambda = 0.25$. We present the results of three distinct versions: utilizing gold evidence (Gold evidence), employing evidence from baseline (Baseline search), and utilizing evidence procured through GProofT (GProofT evidence).

To instruct the model to predict the label based on given evidence, we formulated the prompt as follows: Determine one most possible verdict for the claim "$\{C\}$", based on the given question and answer pairs Q: $\{Q_i\}$ A: $\{A_i\}$ (i=1, 2, ..., n).

3.3 Fine-tuning

To assess the effectiveness of GProofT across various settings, we fine-tune LLMs and evaluate them on the development set. Formally, for each instance $\{C, \{Q_i, A_i\}\}$, we integrate the claim with all QA pairs and fine-tune the model to predict the final label using the cross-entropy loss. Detailed settings and implementation of the fine-tuning process are discussed in 4.2.2.

4 Experiments

In this section, we will elaborate the data processing flow and the evaluation setting we adopted in the experiments.

4.1 Data processing

To construct comprehensive experiments, we preprocess three versions of the development set:

Gold Evidence: Gold evidence provided by the organizer is annotated manually. This evidence is considered highly reliable and has been meticulously curated for accuracy.

Baseline Evidence: The second type of evidence is retrieved by the organizer using a baseline model. This evidence serves as a comparison point to evaluate the performance of different systems.

GProofT Evidence: The last type of evidence is retrieved using our GProofT framework. This system has been optimized to improve the accuracy and relevance of the retrieved evidence.

We employ different LLMs to make verdicts on claims based on these different types of evidence, allowing us to assess system performance under various conditions.

4.2 Evaluation

We will introduce the evaluation experiments setup and analyze the experiment results in the following paragraphs.

4.2.1 Zero-shot

For the evaluation under zero-shot setting, we employ COT (Wei et al., 2022) and COT with self-consistency (Wang et al., 2023c) prompting to generate the label for combined QA pairs of each claim. For ChatGPT, the temperature τ is set to 0.1 for non-Self-Consistency decoding and 0.7 otherwise.

Specifically, for claims whose content is blocked by OpenAI filtering regulation, we set the label as *Not Answerable*. For other models under zero-shot setting, we adhere to the default configurations provided by HuggingFace. We benchmark different versions of LLAMA-3 (Huang et al., 2024), Mistral (Jiang et al., 2023), Falcon (Almazrouei et al., 2023), Gemma (Team et al., 2024), and Qwen2 (Yang et al., 2024).

4.2.2 Fine-tuning

We fine-tune the model using the label of claim in training set. Specifically, we input all QA pairs of one claim simultaneously into the LLMs and fine-tune it using the final label. During the evaluation phases, we maintain consistency with the training settings, distinguishing our approach from zero-shot learning.

For fine-tuning LLMs, we use the open-sourced library LLaMA-Factory (Zheng et al., 2024; Xu et al., 2024a; Ding et al., 2024) to train all models with cross-entropy loss. All hyperparameters follow the default settings, and a LoRA rank (Hu et al., 2022a) of $\alpha = 64$ is used. We fine-tune different versions of LLAMA-3, Mistral, and Qwen2. We conduct all experiments on a Linux machine with eight NVIDIA V100 GPUs.

4.3 Experiment results

The main results are demonstrated in Table 1. The evaluation metrics are consistent with the setting in Schlichtkrull et al. (2023), where we involve the Hungarian METEOR score, macro F1, and AVeriTeC at $\lambda = 0.25$. The evaluation results are obtained with the script. Our GProofT appendix checking framework achieves a Question Hu-meteor score(Banerjee and Lavie, 2005) of 0.331 and a Question+Answer Hu-meteor score of 0.204 on the development set of this shared task, encompassing the baseline. We observed that performance on our GProofT evidence generally surpasses that of the baseline evidence, and fine-tuning significantly enhances model performance. The fine-tuned Llama3-8B model demonstrates the most outstanding performance on GProofT evidence, achieving the AVeriTeC score of 0.186, outperforming the baseline model. In the zero-shot setting, the Gemma-2-9b model consistently outperforms other models across three distinct datasets.

5 Analysis

In this section, we conduct error analysis and case study to further investigate the strengths and potential drawbacks of our framework. Furthermore, a imbalance prediction analysis is attached in appendix A to serve as a analysis on prediction distribution of our framework.

5.1 Error Analysis

The section analyzes the failure cases arise with GProofT framework. The issues could be categorized into two types: duplicated subclaims and biased claim split.

5.1.1 Duplicated Subclaims

When we processed the claim "Tanzania has not been affected by COVID-19." using our pipeline for subclaim generation, GPT initially produced two identical subclaims: "Tanzania was not affected by COVID-19." This occurred despite explicit instructions in the prompt to avoid generating duplicate subclaims. Similar problems have been observed with claims containing fewer than 15 words, as demonstrated in Table 2. We hypothesize that the phrasing of our prompt might incline GPT to generate more than one subclaim, leading to instances where the claim is unnecessarily split into multiple subclaims that are highly similar or identical.

5.1.2 Biased Claim Split

Occasionally, splitting claims may introduce inaccurate or irrelevant subclaims. For instance, in the development dataset, there is a claim that states "Over thirty million people... in the last several months had to file for unemployment." When processed by our pipeline, this claim was split into a subclaim stating "The last several months have passed." This subclaim clearly originates from the phrase "in the last several months" within the original claim. However, it represents a trivial fact rather than a meaningful assertion relevant to the original context. More examples are shown in Table 2.

5.2 Case Study

Generally, our framework is proved to be successful in most cases. In Table 3, We present several successful examples of the claim split process, which effectively avoided issues such as duplicate subclaims or biased splits. These instances correctly identified the key facts within the claims and generated corresponding subclaims. For instance,

Error Type	Claim	Subclaims one	Subclaims two
Duplicated sub-claims	Viral video purportedly shows Pakistani opposition MPs chanted 2018Modi, Modi2019 (India's PM) inside the Pakistani Parliament.	Pakistani opposition MPs chanted 'Modi, Modi' inside the Pakistani Parliament.	Pakistani opposition MPs chanted 'Modi, Modi' inside the Pakistani Parliament.
Duplicated sub-claims	All USA Ballots Arriving After Election Day Will Be Thrown Out.	All USA ballots arriving after Election Day will be thrown out.	Ballots arriving after Election Day will be thrown out.
Duplicated sub-claims	Olive Garden prohibits its employees from wearing face masks depicting the American flag.	Olive Garden prohibits its employees from wearing face masks depicting the American flag.	Olive Garden prohibits employees from wearing face masks with American flag.
Biased claim split	Over thirty million people... in the last several months had to file for unemployment.	The last several months have passed.	Over thirty million people filed for unemployment.
Biased claim split	Edo State in Nigeria has a 19% unemployment rate.	The unemployment rate in Edo State is 19%.	Unemployment rate is a significant issue in Edo State.

Table 2: Failure examples of claim split part in GProofT Framework. The table categorizes two types of issues encountered in claim splitting: duplicated subclaims and biased claim splits.

Claim	Subclaim One	Subclaim Two
Congress MP Rahul Gandhi has been listed as the seventh most educated leader by Forbes.	Rahul Gandhi has been listed as the seventh most educated leader.	It is Forbes that has listed Rahul Gandhi as the seventh most educated leader.
Ulysses S. Grant, commander of the Union Army during the American Civil War, was a slave owner.	Ulysses S. Grant was the commander of the Union Army during American Civil War.	Ulysses S. Grant owned slaves.
Joe Biden proposed a US wide 2% property tax increase.	Joe Biden proposed a 2% property tax increase.	The tax increase that Joe Biden proposed apply to the entire US.

Table 3: Successful examples of claim split in GProofT Framework.In the majority of cases, GProofT Framework effectively identifies the facts within claims and splits them appropriately.

in the case of "Congress MP Rahul Gandhi has been listed as the seventh most educated leader by Forbes", the process not only accurately extracted the primary facts that Gandhi was listed as the seventh most educated leader and was featured by Forbes, but also leveraged the emphatic sentence structure to underscore these facts within the subclaims. This approach enhanced the effectiveness of the subsequent claim split process.

6 Conclusion

In this paper, we introduced GProofT, a multi-dimension, multi-round fact-checking framework designed to improve the efficacy and accuracy of validating online claims by leveraging LLMs and web evidence retrieval. Through extensive experiments, our approach demonstrated superior performance compared to baseline models, particularly in the critical task of evidence retrieval. Moreover, our framework requires less human labor involved in evidence checking which means it could be easily scale up when there is a huge amount of fact checking workload, improving the efficiency. Apart from such advantages, our framework also encounter challenges such as duplicated subclaims and biased claim splits, indicating areas for further improvement. Furthermore, refining the claim decomposition process and enhancing the handling of conflicting evidence will be crucial steps in advancing automated fact-checking systems. Our work contributes to the ongoing efforts to develop reliable, scalable, and automated tools for ensuring the trustworthiness of online information.

Acknowledgments

The authors of this paper were supported by the NSFC Fund (U20B2053) from the NSFC of China, the RIF (R6020-19 and R6021-20), and the GRF (16211520 and 16205322) from RGC of Hong Kong. We also thank the support from the UGC Research Matching Grants (RMGS20EG01-D, RMGS20CR11, RMGS20CR12, RMGS20EG19, RMGS20EG21, RMGS23CR05, RMGS23EG08).

Limitation

In our research pipeline, we employed GProofT Retrieval, incorporating the Google Search API and ChatGPT to generate question-answer (QA) pairs, which were subsequently utilized to inform predictions in conjunction with the Llama model for the labeling of numerous claims. Throughout this process, the API of Large Language Models was invoked multiple times. On average, the processing of each claim necessitated approximately 30 API calls to ChatGPT, leading to considerable computational overhead. Moreover, the heightened frequency of API calls led to a reduction in program execution speed, thereby impeding the efficient processing of large-scale datasets. Future research could concentrate on improving the claim decomposition stage, as this upstream task significantly influences the final outcome. Conceptualization(Wang et al., 2023b,a, 2024b,c,a; Wang and Song, 2024; He et al., 2024; Bai et al., 2023) could serve as an additional tool to improve the quality of claim decomposition, and manual annotations could be done to enhance the performance.

Ethics statement

All models and datasets accessed are freely accessible for research purposes and we do not create any harmful contents that would yield negative impact. The authors thus believe that this paper does not raise additional ethics concerns.

References

Sweta Agrawal, Chunting Zhou, Mike Lewis, Luke Zettlemoyer, and Marjan Ghazvininejad. 2023. In-context examples selection for machine translation. In *Findings of the Association for Computational Linguistics: ACL 2023, Toronto, Canada, July 9-14, 2023*, pages 8857–8873. Association for Computational Linguistics.

Ebtesam Almazrouei, Hamza Alobeidli, Abdulaziz Alshamsi, Alessandro Cappelli, Ruxandra Cojocaru, Mérouane Debbah, Étienne Goffinet, Daniel Hesslow, Julien Launay, Quentin Malartic, Daniele Mazzotta, Badreddine Noune, Baptiste Pannier, and Guilherme Penedo. 2023. The falcon series of open language models. *Preprint*, arXiv:2311.16867.

Jiaxin Bai, Xin Liu, Weiqi Wang, Chen Luo, and Yangqiu Song. 2023. Complex query answering on eventuality knowledge graph with implicit logical constraints. In *Advances in Neural Information Processing Systems 36: Annual Conference on Neural Information Processing Systems 2023, NeurIPS 2023, New Orleans, LA, USA, December 10 - 16, 2023*.

Satanjeev Banerjee and Alon Lavie. 2005. Meteor: An automatic metric for mt evaluation with improved correlation with human judgments. In *Proceedings of the ACL Workshop on Intrinsic and Extrinsic Evaluation Measures for Machine Translation and/or Summarization*.

Chunkit Chan, Cheng Jiayang, Weiqi Wang, Yuxin Jiang, Tianqing Fang, Xin Liu, and Yangqiu Song. 2024a. Exploring the potential of chatgpt on sentence level relations: A focus on temporal, causal, and discourse relations. In *Findings of the Association for Computational Linguistics: EACL 2024, St. Julian's, Malta, March 17-22, 2024*, pages 684–721. Association for Computational Linguistics.

Chunkit Chan, Cheng Jiayang, Yauwai Yim, Zheye Deng, Wei Fan, Haoran Li, Xin Liu, Hongming Zhang, Weiqi Wang, and Yangqiu Song. 2024b. Negotiationtom: A benchmark for stress-testing machine theory of mind on negotiation surrounding. *CoRR*, abs/2404.13627.

Wenxuan Ding, Weiqi Wang, Sze Heng Douglas Kwok, Minghao Liu, Tianqing Fang, Jiaxin Bai, Junxian He, and Yangqiu Song. 2024. Intentionqa: A benchmark for evaluating purchase intention comprehension abilities of language models in e-commerce. *CoRR*, abs/2406.10173.

Tianqing Fang, Weiqi Wang, Sehyun Choi, Shibo Hao, Hongming Zhang, Yangqiu Song, and Bin He. 2021a. Benchmarking commonsense knowledge base population with an effective evaluation dataset. In *Proceedings of the 2021 Conference on Empirical Methods in Natural Language Processing, EMNLP 2021, Virtual Event / Punta Cana, Dominican Republic, 7-11 November, 2021*, pages 8949–8964. Association for Computational Linguistics.

Tianqing Fang, Hongming Zhang, Weiqi Wang, Yangqiu Song, and Bin He. 2021b. DISCOS: bridging the gap between discourse knowledge and commonsense knowledge. In *WWW '21: The Web Conference 2021, Virtual Event / Ljubljana, Slovenia, April 19-23, 2021*, pages 2648–2659. ACM / IW3C2.

Ching Nam Hang, Pei-Duo Yu, and Chee Wei Tan. 2024. Trumorgpt: Query optimization and semantic reasoning over networks for automated fact-checking. In *58th Annual Conference on Information Sciences and*

Systems, CISS 2024, Princeton, NJ, USA, March 13-15, 2024, pages 1–6. IEEE.

Mutian He, Tianqing Fang, Weiqi Wang, and Yangqiu Song. 2024. Acquiring and modeling abstract commonsense knowledge via conceptualization. *Artif. Intell.*, 333:104149.

Pengcheng He, Jianfeng Gao, and Weizhu Chen. 2023. Debertav3: Improving deberta using electra-style pre-training with gradient-disentangled embedding sharing. In *The Eleventh International Conference on Learning Representations, ICLR 2023, Kigali, Rwanda, May 1-5, 2023*. OpenReview.net.

Matthew Honnibal and Ines Montani. 2017. spaCy 2: Natural language understanding with Bloom embeddings, convolutional neural networks and incremental parsing. To appear.

Edward J. Hu, Yelong Shen, Phillip Wallis, Zeyuan Allen-Zhu, Yuanzhi Li, Shean Wang, Lu Wang, and Weizhu Chen. 2022a. Lora: Low-rank adaptation of large language models. In *The Tenth International Conference on Learning Representations, ICLR 2022, Virtual Event, April 25-29, 2022*. OpenReview.net.

Yushi Hu, Chia-Hsuan Lee, Tianbao Xie, Tao Yu, Noah A. Smith, and Mari Ostendorf. 2022b. In-context learning for few-shot dialogue state tracking. In *Findings of the Association for Computational Linguistics: EMNLP 2022, Abu Dhabi, United Arab Emirates, December 7-11, 2022*, pages 2627–2643. Association for Computational Linguistics.

Lei Huang, Weijiang Yu, Weitao Ma, Weihong Zhong, Zhangyin Feng, Haotian Wang, Qianglong Chen, Weihua Peng, Xiaocheng Feng, Bing Qin, and Ting Liu. 2023. A survey on hallucination in large language models: Principles, taxonomy, challenges, and open questions. *ArXiv*, abs/2311.05232.

Wei Huang, Xingyu Zheng, Xudong Ma, Haotong Qin, Chengtao Lv, Hong Chen, Jie Luo, Xiaojuan Qi, Xianglong Liu, and Michele Magno. 2024. An empirical study of llama3 quantization: From llms to mllms. *Preprint*, arXiv:2404.14047.

Ziwei Ji, Nayeon Lee, Rita Frieske, Tiezheng Yu, Dan Su, Yan Xu, Etsuko Ishii, Yejin Bang, Delong Chen, Wenliang Dai, Andrea Madotto, and Pascale Fung. 2022. Survey of hallucination in natural language generation. *ACM Computing Surveys*, 55:1 – 38.

Albert Q. Jiang, Alexandre Sablayrolles, Arthur Mensch, Chris Bamford, Devendra Singh Chaplot, Diego de las Casas, Florian Bressand, Gianna Lengyel, Guillaume Lample, Lucile Saulnier, Lélio Renard Lavaud, Marie-Anne Lachaux, Pierre Stock, Teven Le Scao, Thibaut Lavril, Thomas Wang, Timothée Lacroix, and William El Sayed. 2023. Mistral 7b. *Preprint*, arXiv:2310.06825.

Kyungha Kim, Sangyun Lee, Kung-Hsiang Huang, Hou Pong Chan, Manling Li, and Heng Ji. 2024. Can llms produce faithful explanations for fact-checking? towards faithful explainable fact-checking via multi-agent debate. *CoRR*, abs/2402.07401.

Itay Levy, Ben Bogin, and Jonathan Berant. 2023. Diverse demonstrations improve in-context compositional generalization. In *Proceedings of the 61st Annual Meeting of the Association for Computational Linguistics (Volume 1: Long Papers), ACL 2023, Toronto, Canada, July 9-14, 2023*, pages 1401–1422. Association for Computational Linguistics.

Feihong Lu, Weiqi Wang, Yangyifei Luo, Ziqin Zhu, Qingyun Sun, Baixuan Xu, Haochen Shi, Shiqi Gao, Qian Li, Yangqiu Song, and Jianxin Li. 2024. MIKO: multimodal intention knowledge distillation from large language models for social-media commonsense discovery. *CoRR*, abs/2402.18169.

OpenAI. 2023. Gpt-3.5 turbo.

OpenAI, Josh Achiam, Steven Adler, Sandhini Agarwal, Lama Ahmad, Ilge Akkaya, Florencia Leoni Aleman, Diogo Almeida, Janko Altenschmidt, Sam Altman, Shyamal Anadkat, Red Avila, Igor Babuschkin, Suchir Balaji, Valerie Balcom, Paul Baltescu, Haiming Bao, Mohammad Bavarian, Jeff Belgum, Irwan Bello, Jake Berdine, Gabriel Bernadett-Shapiro, Christopher Berner, Lenny Bogdonoff, Oleg Boiko, Madelaine Boyd, Anna-Luisa Brakman, Greg Brockman, Tim Brooks, Miles Brundage, Kevin Button, Trevor Cai, Rosie Campbell, Andrew Cann, Brittany Carey, Chelsea Carlson, Rory Carmichael, Brooke Chan, Che Chang, Fotis Chantzis, Derek Chen, Sully Chen, Ruby Chen, Jason Chen, Mark Chen, Ben Chess, Chester Cho, Casey Chu, Hyung Won Chung, Dave Cummings, Jeremiah Currier, Yunxing Dai, Cory Decareaux, Thomas Degry, Noah Deutsch, Damien Deville, Arka Dhar, David Dohan, Steve Dowling, Sheila Dunning, Adrien Ecoffet, Atty Eleti, Tyna Eloundou, David Farhi, Liam Fedus, Niko Felix, Simón Posada Fishman, Juston Forte, Isabella Fulford, Leo Gao, Elie Georges, Christian Gibson, Vik Goel, Tarun Gogineni, Gabriel Goh, Rapha Gontijo-Lopes, Jonathan Gordon, Morgan Grafstein, Scott Gray, Ryan Greene, Joshua Gross, Shixiang Shane Gu, Yufei Guo, Chris Hallacy, Jesse Han, Jeff Harris, Yuchen He, Mike Heaton, Johannes Heidecke, Chris Hesse, Alan Hickey, Wade Hickey, Peter Hoeschele, Brandon Houghton, Kenny Hsu, Shengli Hu, Xin Hu, Joost Huizinga, Shantanu Jain, Shawn Jain, Joanne Jang, Angela Jiang, Roger Jiang, Haozhun Jin, Denny Jin, Shino Jomoto, Billie Jonn, Heewoo Jun, Tomer Kaftan, Łukasz Kaiser, Ali Kamali, Ingmar Kanitscheider, Nitish Shirish Keskar, Tabarak Khan, Logan Kilpatrick, Jong Wook Kim, Christina Kim, Yongjik Kim, Jan Hendrik Kirchner, Jamie Kiros, Matt Knight, Daniel Kokotajlo, Łukasz Kondraciuk, Andrew Kondrich, Aris Konstantinidis, Kyle Kosic, Gretchen Krueger, Vishal Kuo, Michael Lampe, Ikai Lan, Teddy Lee, Jan Leike, Jade Leung, Daniel Levy, Chak Ming Li, Rachel Lim, Molly Lin, Stephanie Lin, Mateusz Litwin, Theresa Lopez, Ryan Lowe, Patricia Lue, Anna Makanju, Kim Malfacini, Sam Manning, Todor Markov, Yaniv Markovski, Bianca Martin, Katie

Mayer, Andrew Mayne, Bob McGrew, Scott Mayer McKinney, Christine McLeavey, Paul McMillan, Jake McNeil, David Medina, Aalok Mehta, Jacob Menick, Luke Metz, Andrey Mishchenko, Pamela Mishkin, Vinnie Monaco, Evan Morikawa, Daniel Mossing, Tong Mu, Mira Murati, Oleg Murk, David Mély, Ashvin Nair, Reiichiro Nakano, Rajeev Nayak, Arvind Neelakantan, Richard Ngo, Hyeonwoo Noh, Long Ouyang, Cullen O'Keefe, Jakub Pachocki, Alex Paino, Joe Palermo, Ashley Pantuliano, Giambattista Parascandolo, Joel Parish, Emy Parparita, Alex Passos, Mikhail Pavlov, Andrew Peng, Adam Perelman, Filipe de Avila Belbute Peres, Michael Petrov, Henrique Ponde de Oliveira Pinto, Michael, Pokorny, Michelle Pokrass, Vitchyr H. Pong, Tolly Powell, Alethea Power, Boris Power, Elizabeth Proehl, Raul Puri, Alec Radford, Jack Rae, Aditya Ramesh, Cameron Raymond, Francis Real, Kendra Rimbach, Carl Ross, Bob Rotsted, Henri Roussez, Nick Ryder, Mario Saltarelli, Ted Sanders, Shibani Santurkar, Girish Sastry, Heather Schmidt, David Schnurr, John Schulman, Daniel Selsam, Kyla Sheppard, Toki Sherbakov, Jessica Shieh, Sarah Shoker, Pranav Shyam, Szymon Sidor, Eric Sigler, Maddie Simens, Jordan Sitkin, Katarina Slama, Ian Sohl, Benjamin Sokolowsky, Yang Song, Natalie Staudacher, Felipe Petroski Such, Natalie Summers, Ilya Sutskever, Jie Tang, Nikolas Tezak, Madeleine B. Thompson, Phil Tillet, Amin Tootoonchian, Elizabeth Tseng, Preston Tuggle, Nick Turley, Jerry Tworek, Juan Felipe Cerón Uribe, Andrea Vallone, Arun Vijayvergiya, Chelsea Voss, Carroll Wainwright, Justin Jay Wang, Alvin Wang, Ben Wang, Jonathan Ward, Jason Wei, CJ Weinmann, Akila Welihinda, Peter Welinder, Jiayi Weng, Lilian Weng, Matt Wiethoff, Dave Willner, Clemens Winter, Samuel Wolrich, Hannah Wong, Lauren Workman, Sherwin Wu, Jeff Wu, Michael Wu, Kai Xiao, Tao Xu, Sarah Yoo, Kevin Yu, Qiming Yuan, Wojciech Zaremba, Rowan Zellers, Chong Zhang, Marvin Zhang, Shengjia Zhao, Tianhao Zheng, Juntang Zhuang, William Zhuk, and Barret Zoph. 2024. Gpt-4 technical report. *Preprint*, arXiv:2303.08774.

Michael Sejr Schlichtkrull, Zhijiang Guo, and Andreas Vlachos. 2023. Averitec: A dataset for real-world claim verification with evidence from the web. In *Thirty-seventh Conference on Neural Information Processing Systems Datasets and Benchmarks Track*.

Haochen Shi, Weiqi Wang, Tianqing Fang, Baixuan Xu, Wenxuan Ding, Xin Liu, and Yangqiu Song. 2023. QADYNAMICS: training dynamics-driven synthetic QA diagnostic for zero-shot commonsense question answering. In *Findings of the Association for Computational Linguistics: EMNLP 2023, Singapore, December 6-10, 2023*, pages 15329–15341. Association for Computational Linguistics.

Gemma Team, Thomas Mesnard, Cassidy Hardin, Robert Dadashi, Surya Bhupatiraju, Shreya Pathak, Laurent Sifre, Morgane Rivière, Mihir Sanjay Kale, Juliette Love, Pouya Tafti, Léonard Hussenot, Pier Giuseppe Sessa, Aakanksha Chowdhery, Adam Roberts, Aditya Barua, Alex Botev, Alex Castro-Ros, Ambrose Slone, Amélie Héliou, Andrea Tacchetti, Anna Bulanova, Antonia Paterson, Beth Tsai, Bobak Shahriari, Charline Le Lan, Christopher A. Choquette-Choo, Clément Crepy, Daniel Cer, Daphne Ippolito, David Reid, Elena Buchatskaya, Eric Ni, Eric Noland, Geng Yan, George Tucker, George-Christian Muraru, Grigory Rozhdestvenskiy, Henryk Michalewski, Ian Tenney, Ivan Grishchenko, Jacob Austin, James Keeling, Jane Labanowski, Jean-Baptiste Lespiau, Jeff Stanway, Jenny Brennan, Jeremy Chen, Johan Ferret, Justin Chiu, Justin Mao-Jones, Katherine Lee, Kathy Yu, Katie Millican, Lars Lowe Sjoesund, Lisa Lee, Lucas Dixon, Machel Reid, Maciej Mikuła, Mateo Wirth, Michael Sharman, Nikolai Chinaev, Nithum Thain, Olivier Bachem, Oscar Chang, Oscar Wahltinez, Paige Bailey, Paul Michel, Petko Yotov, Rahma Chaabouni, Ramona Comanescu, Reena Jana, Rohan Anil, Ross McIlroy, Ruibo Liu, Ryan Mullins, Samuel L Smith, Sebastian Borgeaud, Sertan Girgin, Sholto Douglas, Shree Pandya, Siamak Shakeri, Soham De, Ted Klimenko, Tom Hennigan, Vlad Feinberg, Wojciech Stokowiec, Yu hui Chen, Zafarali Ahmed, Zhitao Gong, Tris Warkentin, Ludovic Peran, Minh Giang, Clément Farabet, Oriol Vinyals, Jeff Dean, Koray Kavukcuoglu, Demis Hassabis, Zoubin Ghahramani, Douglas Eck, Joelle Barral, Fernando Pereira, Eli Collins, Armand Joulin, Noah Fiedel, Evan Senter, Alek Andreev, and Kathleen Kenealy. 2024. Gemma: Open models based on gemini research and technology. *Preprint*, arXiv:2403.08295.

Weiqi Wang, Limeng Cui, Xin Liu, Sreyashi Nag, Wenju Xu, Sheikh Sarwar, Chen Luo, Yang Laurence Li, Hansu Gu, Hui Liu, Changlong Yu, Jiaxin Bai, Yifan Gao, Haiyang Zhang, Qi He, Shuiwang Ji, and Yangqiu Song. 2024a. EcomScript: A multi-task benchmark for e-commerce script planning via stepwise intention-driven product association. *CoRR*.

Weiqi Wang, Tianqing Fang, Wenxuan Ding, Baixuan Xu, Xin Liu, Yangqiu Song, and Antoine Bosselut. 2023a. CAR: conceptualization-augmented reasoner for zero-shot commonsense question answering. In *Findings of the Association for Computational Linguistics: EMNLP 2023, Singapore, December 6-10, 2023*, pages 13520–13545. Association for Computational Linguistics.

Weiqi Wang, Tianqing Fang, Chunyang Li, Haochen Shi, Wenxuan Ding, Baixuan Xu, Zhaowei Wang, Jiaxin Bai, Xin Liu, Cheng Jiayang, Chunkit Chan, and Yangqiu Song. 2024b. CANDLE: iterative conceptualization and instantiation distillation from large language models for commonsense reasoning. In *Proceedings of the 62nd Annual Meeting of the Association for Computational Linguistics (Volume 1: Long Papers), ACL 2024, Bangkok, Thailand, August 11-16, 2024*, pages 2351–2374. Association for Computational Linguistics.

Weiqi Wang, Tianqing Fang, Haochen Shi, Baixuan Xu, Wenxuan Ding, Liyu Zhang, Wei Fan, Jiaxin Bai, Haoran Li, Xin Liu, and Yangqiu Song. 2024c.

On the role of entity and event level conceptualization in generalizable reasoning: A survey of tasks, methods, applications, and future directions. *CoRR*, abs/2406.10885.

Weiqi Wang, Tianqing Fang, Baixuan Xu, Chun Yi Louis Bo, Yangqiu Song, and Lei Chen. 2023b. CAT: A contextualized conceptualization and instantiation framework for commonsense reasoning. In *Proceedings of the 61st Annual Meeting of the Association for Computational Linguistics (Volume 1: Long Papers), ACL 2023, Toronto, Canada, July 9-14, 2023*, pages 13111–13140. Association for Computational Linguistics.

Weiqi Wang and Yangqiu Song. 2024. MARS: benchmarking the metaphysical reasoning abilities of language models with a multi-task evaluation dataset. *CoRR*, abs/2406.02106.

Xuezhi Wang, Jason Wei, Dale Schuurmans, Quoc Le, Ed Chi, Sharan Narang, Aakanksha Chowdhery, and Denny Zhou. 2023c. Self-consistency improves chain of thought reasoning in language models. *Preprint*, arXiv:2203.11171.

Jason Wei, Xuezhi Wang, Dale Schuurmans, Maarten Bosma, Brian Ichter, Fei Xia, Ed H. Chi, Quoc V. Le, and Denny Zhou. 2022. Chain-of-thought prompting elicits reasoning in large language models. In *Advances in Neural Information Processing Systems 35: Annual Conference on Neural Information Processing Systems 2022, NeurIPS 2022, New Orleans, LA, USA, November 28 - December 9, 2022.*

Baixuan Xu, Weiqi Wang, Haochen Shi, Wenxuan Ding, Huihao Jing, Tianqing Fang, Jiaxin Bai, Long Chen, and Yangqiu Song. 2024a. MIND: multimodal shopping intention distillation from large vision-language models for e-commerce purchase understanding. *CoRR*, abs/2406.10701.

Yuhui Xu, Lingxi Xie, Xiaotao Gu, Xin Chen, Heng Chang, Hengheng Zhang, Zhengsu Chen, Xiaopeng Zhang, and Qi Tian. 2024b. Qa-lora: Quantization-aware low-rank adaptation of large language models. In *The Twelfth International Conference on Learning Representations, ICLR 2024, Vienna, Austria, May 7-11, 2024*. OpenReview.net.

An Yang, Baosong Yang, Binyuan Hui, Bo Zheng, Bowen Yu, Chang Zhou, Chengpeng Li, Chengyuan Li, Dayiheng Liu, Fei Huang, Guanting Dong, Haoran Wei, Huan Lin, Jialong Tang, Jialin Wang, Jian Yang, Jianhong Tu, Jianwei Zhang, Jianxin Ma, Jianxin Yang, Jin Xu, Jingren Zhou, Jinze Bai, Jinzheng He, Junyang Lin, Kai Dang, Keming Lu, Keqin Chen, Kexin Yang, Mei Li, Mingfeng Xue, Na Ni, Pei Zhang, Peng Wang, Ru Peng, Rui Men, Ruize Gao, Runji Lin, Shijie Wang, Shuai Bai, Sinan Tan, Tianhang Zhu, Tianhao Li, Tianyu Liu, Wenbin Ge, Xiaodong Deng, Xiaohuan Zhou, Xingzhang Ren, Xinyu Zhang, Xipin Wei, Xuancheng Ren, Xuejing Liu, Yang Fan, Yang Yao, Yichang Zhang, Yu Wan, Yunfei Chu, Yuqiong Liu, Zeyu Cui, Zhenru Zhang, Zhifang Guo, and Zhihao Fan. 2024. Qwen2 technical report. *Preprint*, arXiv:2407.10671.

Changlong Yu, Weiqi Wang, Xin Liu, Jiaxin Bai, Yangqiu Song, Zheng Li, Yifan Gao, Tianyu Cao, and Bing Yin. 2023. Folkscope: Intention knowledge graph construction for e-commerce commonsense discovery. In *Findings of the Association for Computational Linguistics: ACL 2023, Toronto, Canada, July 9-14, 2023*, pages 1173–1191. Association for Computational Linguistics.

Yaowei Zheng, Richong Zhang, Junhao Zhang, Yanhan Ye, Zheyan Luo, Zhangchi Feng, and Yongqiang Ma. 2024. Llamafactory: Unified efficient fine-tuning of 100+ language models.

A Imbalanced Prediction

Model	S	R	C	N	Macro
baseline	.41	.69	.10	.16	.23
gpt-3.5 turbo	.57	.59	.08	.16	.34
llama3	.54	.74	.04	.06	.35
mistral	.55	.74	.00	.11	.35

Table 4: Performance of models on different categories of claim.

As demonstrated in Table 4, our model exhibits better performance on the "Supported" (S) and "Refuted" (R) labels but struggles with "Conflicting Evidence/Cherrypicking" (C) and "Not Enough Evidence" (N) labels. This performance discrepancy suggests a few potential reasons:

1. **Evidence Retrieval Challenges:** For Supported and Refuted labels, the evidence is clear and directly relevant, making it easier for the model to make accurate predictions. For Conflicting Evidence/Cherrypicking, the model struggles with retrieving or interpreting evidence that is contradictory or only partially relevant. If the model fails to retrieve diverse or contradictory evidence, it default to classifying the claim as either supported or refuted, missing the nuance required for the conflicting/cherrypicking evidence label.

2. **Training Data Imbalance:** The training data had more examples of claims with verdict supported or refuted, leading the model to be better at these tasks. Fewer examples of conflicting evidence or cherrypicking cases leads the model not have learned to handle these as effectively.

B Prompt

B.1 Claim Decomposition

Prompt: *Now I have a mission, and please help me deal with it: I have a claim: {claim}, and I need to split it into different subclaims according to THE FACT it contains. For example, if I have a claim: "Trump is a student born in 2005", then I want to split it into two parts (since there are two facts in it):"Trump is a student" and "Trump was born in 2005". For this special case, I need the response to be: "Trump is a student. Trump was born in 2005.". There are several RULES for the splitting process: (1)VERY IMPORTANT!!! PLEASE RETURN THE SUBCLAIMS ONLY (DO NOT INCLUDE ANYTHING ELSE!!!) and please separate the subclaims ONLY BY PERIOD instead of numbers. (2)VERY IMPORTANT: DO NOT GENERATE DUPLICATE SUBCLAIMS!!!!!!! (3)TRY TO BE MORE SPECIFIC and CLEAR(for example, if you want to generate "the orgarnization", try to generate the orgarnization's name), and AVOID USING PRONOUNS. (4)In most cases, the length of subclaims should be LESS THAN the length of the original claim. And in most cases, each subclaims SHOULD NOT BE LONGER THAN 10 words. (5)Do not expand the meaning of the original claim or generate subclaims that do not exist in the original claim. (6)DO NOT generate a subclaim that is totally the same as the original claim UNLESS there is only one fact to check in the original claim. (7)For example: for the claim "BJP MP Sushil Modi claims first five Indian education ministers were Muslims", You should recognize that there is ONLY ONE FACT in the claim, which is whether BJP MP Sushil Modi really states the following claim , so the subclaim should be itself. At the same time, if there are several facts in the claim, you should split the claim into same amount of subclaim, each representing a fact. (8)If the claim is more that 30 words, try to generate at least 3 subclaims. (9)Here are some EXAMPLES: If the claim is "Lionel Messi is 36-year-old football player who has a long career.", then according to the claim, there are three facts introducing Lionel Messi, which are: Lionel Messi is 36-year-old, Lionel Messi is a football player, LionelMessi has a long career. So what you should generate is: "Lionel Messi is 36-year-old. Lionel Messi is a football player. Lionel Messi has a long career.".*

Note that the variable *claim* is the original input statement.

B.2 Question Generation

Prompt: *According to the claim below, generate a binary question to CHECK THE FACTS in the claim: {subclaim_text}. Note that (1)ONLY REPLY THE QUESTION ITSELF!!! DO NOT INCLUDE ANYTHING ELSE!!! (2)Try to be more SPECIFIC, for example, if the claim is "Trump was a student.", then you should AVOID GENERATING QUESTIONS CONTAINING PRONOUNS like "Was he a student?" and instead generate "Was Trump a student?" (3)Try to NOTICE THE FACT in the claim and generate the binary question to CHECK THE FACT. For example: for a claim: "BJP MP Sushil Modi claims first five Indian education ministers were Muslims", the fact to be checked will be whether BJP MP Sushil really states the claim, instead of whether the first five Indian education ministers are Muslims. Thus, you should generate "Did BJP MP Sushil Modi claim that the first five Indian education ministers were Muslims?" (4)Here are some EXAMPLES: If the claim is "Lionel Messi is loyal to FC Barcelona", then the binary question should be "Is Lionel Messi loyal to FC Barcelona?". If the claim is "Biden has been to Beijing twice.", then the binary question should be "Has Biden been to Beijing twice?".*

Note that the variable *subclaim_text* is a single subclaim obtained from the Claim Decomposition stage.

B.3 Answer Generation

Prompt: *According to the question: {query} and the approximate answer: {item['snippet']}, give me a yes or no answer.(only a word is needed)*

Note that the variable *query* is the binary question obtained from the Question Generation stage and *item['snippet']* is an attribute acquired from the Google search API.

HerO at AVeriTeC: The Herd of Open Large Language Models for Verifying Real-World Claims

Yejun Yoon[♡] **Jaeyoon Jung**[♣◇] **Seunghyun Yoon**[♠] **Kunwoo Park**[♣♡]
[♡]Department of Intelligent Semiconductors, Soongsil University
[♣]School of AI Convergence, Soongsil University
[◇]MAUM AI Inc.
[♠]Adobe Research, USA
{yejun0382, jaeyoonskr}@soongsil.ac.kr, syoon@adobe.com, kunwoo.park@ssu.ac.kr

Abstract

To tackle the AVeriTeC shared task hosted by the FEVER-24, we introduce a system that only employs publicly available large language models (LLMs) for each step of automated fact-checking, dubbed the **Her**d of **O**pen LLMs for verifying real-world claims (**HerO**). For evidence retrieval, a language model is used to enhance a query by generating hypothetical fact-checking documents. We prompt pretrained and fine-tuned LLMs for question generation and veracity prediction by crafting prompts with retrieved in-context samples. HerO achieved 2nd place on the leaderboard with the AVeriTeC score of 0.57, suggesting the potential of open LLMs for verifying real-world claims. For future research, we make our code publicly available at https://github.com/ssu-humane/HerO.

1 Introduction

Automated fact-checking is a task that predicts a claim's veracity by referring to pieces of evidence (Guo et al., 2022). Claim verification requires the retrieval of relevant information from a reliable document collection and the decision on whether the claim is supported by the known relevant information. Early research attempted to automate the fact-checking process by generating synthetic claims based on Wikipedia documents (Thorne et al., 2018; Aly et al., 2021) or collecting manually verified claims by human experts (Wang, 2017; Augenstein et al., 2019). However, most datasets suffer from critical issues such as context dependence, evidence insufficiency, and temporal leaks; these limitations made the resulting systems less applicable to the verification of real-world claims. In light of this, a recent study proposed a dataset called AVeriTeC (Schlichtkrull et al., 2023). They addressed the limitations by conducting fine-grained crowdsourced annotations for the fact-checking process.

This paper describes our system for the AVeriTeC shared task hosted by the FEVER-24 workshop (Schlichtkrull et al., 2024). Motivated by the recent advancements in large language models, we introduce a fact-checking system that utilizes LLMs for each step of evidence-based fact verification: evidence retrieval, question generation, and veracity prediction. Our system, the **Her**d of **O**pen LLMs for verifying real-world claims (**HerO**), employs publicly available LLMs without using proprietary LLMs, to ensure the transparency of the system. HerO achieved 2nd place in the shared task with an AVeriTeC score of 0.57. Given that the winning system used gpt-4o (Schlichtkrull et al., 2024), HerO's competitive performance imply the potential of open LLMs for verifying real-world claims.

2 Related Work

LLMs have achieved remarkable success in natural language understanding and generation (Brown et al., 2020; Thoppilan et al., 2022; Achiam et al., 2023). While major tech companies primarily drove the initial success, they only provided limited access to the model through an API. On the other hand, some research groups have attempted to develop open LLMs to facilitate open research. While the performance of the initial models was unsatisfactory (Zhang et al., 2022; Le Scao et al., 2023), recent models are on par with closed models and even outperform them in certain categories (Jiang et al., 2023; Dubey et al., 2024).

3 Task Definition

The AVeriTeC shared task aims to develop a fact-checking system that verifies real-world claims by retrieving evidence from the web. To verify a given claim, the system first needs to retrieve relevant information from the web documents (evidence retrieval). For each of the collected evidence, the

Proceedings of the Seventh Fact Extraction and VERification Workshop (FEVER), pages 130–136
November 15, 2024 ©2024 Association for Computational Linguistics

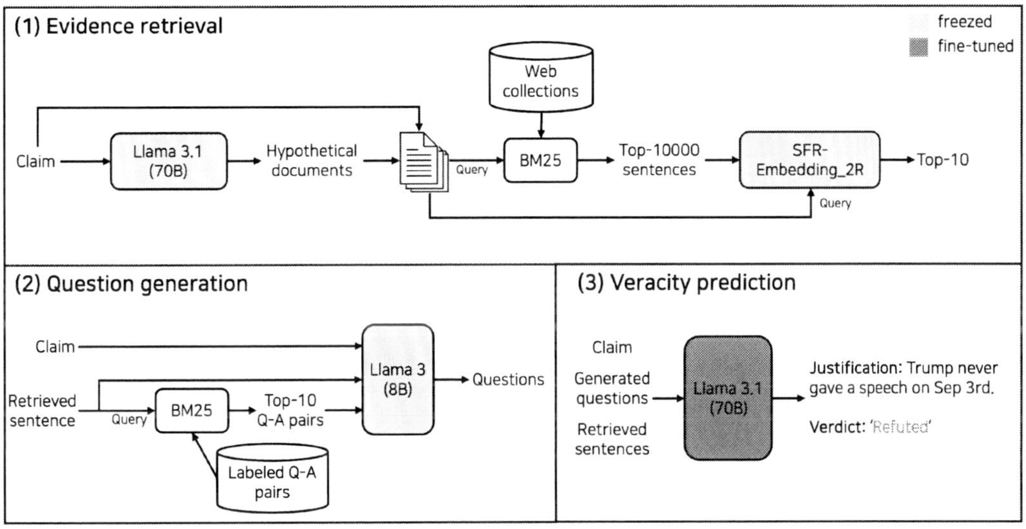

Figure 1: Inference pipeline of our system

System	Evidence Retrieval		Question Generation	Reranking	Veracity Prediction
	Query	Model			
Baseline	Claim	BM25	Bloom-7b	BERT-base	BERT-base
HerO	HyDE-FC (Llama-3.1-70b)	BM25 w/ SFR-embedding-2	Llama-3-8b	-	Llama-3.1-70b

Table 1: Model configurations

system may generate questions that can help verify the claim (question generation) or choose not to. The last step of the fact-checking is to verify the claim by referring to the collected information (veracity prediction). The final verdict is a four-class variable: supported, refuted, not enough evidence, or conflicting evidence/cherry-picking. Each system is evaluated using three metrics, where a higher value indicates a better score. Two metrics are the Hungarian METEOR score[1] to assess the quality of questions (Q score) and question-answer pairs (Q+A score), respectively. The overall accuracy is measured by the AVeriTeC score. Details about the task, dataset, and evaluation metrics can be found in Schlichtkrull et al. (2023) and Schlichtkrull et al. (2024).

4 Our System

This section describes our fact-checking system, the **Her**d of **O**pen LLMs for verifying real-world claims (**HerO**). Inspired by the recent progress of open LLMs (Jiang et al., 2023; Dubey et al., 2024), we only employ open LLMs for our system without using proprietary LLMs, such as gpt (Brown et al., 2020) and gemini (Team et al., 2023). Table 1 presents HerO's model configurations in comparison to the baseline system (Schlichtkrull et al., 2023). The inference pipeline of our system is illustrated in Figure 1. We use web documents provided along with the dataset as the knowledge store.

4.1 Evidence Retrieval

The first step aims to retrieve relevant sentences from the knowledge store to verify a given claim. Inspired by previous research on generative retrieval methods (Gao et al., 2023; Wang et al., 2023), we utilize an instruction-following LM to generate hypothetical fact-checking documents to augment a retrieval query. For the rest of this paper, we call this approach HyDE-FC, which stands for Hypothetical Document Embedding for Fact-Checking.

Given a claim c, we generate a set of hypothetical fact-checking documents $D = \{d_1, \dots, d_N\}$ by prompting an instruction-following language model $f(\cdot)$ using c as an in-context sample. The used prompt for HyDE-FC is shown in Figure 2.

[1]The score uses the Hungarian algorithm (Kuhn, 1955) to find optimal matching pairs and evaluates them with the METEOR score (Banerjee and Lavie, 2005).

Please write a fact-checking article passage to support, refute, indicate not enough evidence, or present conflicting evidence regarding the claim.
Claim: *Hunter Biden had no experience in Ukraine or in the energy sector when he joined the board of Burisma.*
Passage: While Hunter Biden did not have direct experience in the energy sector or Ukraine before joining the board of Burisma, he did have ...

Figure 2: An example of the instruction prompt used for HyDE-FC and its output. The bold text is the instruction, the italic text is a claim, and the blue text indicates the model output.

We repeat the sampling process until obtaining N different documents.

Using the claim and generated documents, our retrieval pipeline employs a two-step hybrid approach that incorporates spare and dense retrieval methods. The first step is to retrieve relevant documents by BM25 (Robertson and Zaragoza, 2009). We concatenate the claim c and each document in D for building the query document q. The sparse vector for q is used to retrieve the top 10,000 relevant sentences from the knowledge store. The second step is to re-rank the 10,000 sentences by the dense retrieval method to decide the top-10 evidence candidates. The query vector v_q is obtained by averaging the embedding vectors for the claim c and every document in D by the equation 1,

$$v_q = \frac{1}{N+1}[\sum_{k=1}^{N} g(d_k) + g(c)] \quad (1)$$

where g is an embedding method.

Our best model uses llama-3.1-70b (Dubey et al., 2024) for f and SFR-embedding-2 (Meng et al., 2024) for g. N is set as 8.

4.2 Question Generation

The next step is to generate verifying questions, each of which the corresponding answer could be a retrieved sentence. We employ an instruction-following LM to generate questions for each piece of evidence. The used prompt is shown in Figure 3. We improve the baseline prompt (Schlichtkrull et al., 2023), which takes each evidence and relevant question-answer pairs from the labeled set by BM25 as in-context examples, by including a corresponding claim.

Your task is to generate a question based on the given claim and evidence. The question should clarify the relationship between the evidence and the claim

Example 1:
Claim: U.S. aid dollars sent to Ukraine under Biden's supervision went toward Burisma, where Biden's son Hunter was a board member.
Evidence: Hunter Biden was appointed to the board of Burisma.
Question: Was Hunter Biden a board member of Ukrainian energy company 'Burisma'?
...
Example 10:
Claim: Hunter Biden was paid $3millionplus$183,000 a month to be a board member of a company that a lot of people said was corrupt.
Evidence: Burisma Holdings, Ukraine's largest private gas producer, has expanded its Board of Directors by bringing on Mr. R Hunter Biden as a new director.
Question: What company is Hunter Biden a member of the board?

Now, generate a question that links the following claim and evidence:

Claim: *Hunter Biden had no experience in Ukraine or in the energy sector when he joined the board of Burisma.*
Evidence: In 2014, Hunter Biden was appointed to the board of Burisma Holdings, a Ukrainian energy company. He was reportedly paid $50,000 a month to work in an industry in which he had no previous experience.
Question: What was Hunter Biden's background or experience in the energy sector before joining the board of Burisma Holdings in 2014?

Figure 3: An example of instruction prompt and its output for question generation. The bold text indicates the instruction, the italic text is a claim, the gray text is retrieved in-context samples, and the blue text indicates the model output.

4.3 Veracity Prediction

We employ an instruction-following LM for veracity prediction. Inspired by a previous study (Wei et al., 2022), we devise a prompt that incorporates an annotator's rationale into the veracity prediction. Our best model uses the fine-tuned llama-3.1-70b-it that predicts the veracity label after generating the explanation. The top 10 question-and-answer pairs from the earlier steps are given as in-context samples along with the claim to verify.

Your task is to predict the verdict of a claim based on the provided question-answer pair evidence. The possible labels are: 'Supported', 'Refuted', 'Not Enough Evidence', 'Conflicting Evidence/Cherrypicking'. Justify your answer using the provided evidence and select the correct label.

Claim: *Hunter Biden had no experience in Ukraine or in the energy sector when he joined the board of Burisma.*

Q1: What was Hunter Biden's background or experience in the energy sector before joining the board of Burisma Holdings in 2014?
A1: In 2014, Hunter Biden was appointed to the board of Burisma Holdings, a Ukrainian energy company. He was reportedly paid $50,000 a month to work in an industry in which he had no previous experience.
...
Q10: Did Hunter Biden have any relevant experience in Ukraine or the energy sector before joining the board of Burisma?
A10: What this is all about: From the start of the inquiry, Republicans have pointed out that Hunter Biden did not have any experience in corporate governance or in the energy sector before taking the job at Burisma.

Justification: No former experience stated.
Verdict: Supported

Figure 4: An example of instruction prompt and its output for veracity prediction. The bold text indicates the instruction, the italic text is a claim, the gray text is retrieved QA pairs, and the blue text is the model output.

Query	Retrieval model	A score
Claim	BM25	0.187
	BM25 w/ SFR-embedding-2	0.26
HyDE-FC (Llama-3-8b)	BM25 w/ SFR-embedding-2	0.2745
HyDE-FC (Llama-3-70b)		0.2757
HyDE-FC (Llama-3.1-8b)		0.2751
HyDE-FC (Llama-3.1-70b)		**0.2801**
HyDE-FC (GPT-4o-mini)		0.2773

Table 2: Performance of evidence retrieval methods

Context	Model	Q score
Retrieved sentences	Baseline	0.2404
	Llama-3-8b	0.4210
	Llama-3-70b	0.4175
	Llama-3.1-8b	0.4212
	Llama-3.1-70b	0.4259
	GPT-4o-mini	0.4054
Retrieved sentences w/ Claim	Llama-3-8b	**0.4938**
	Llama-3-70b	0.4789
	Llama-3.1-8b	0.4855
	Llama-3.1-70b	0.4881

Table 3: Performance of question generation methods

5 Evaluation Experiments

In this section, we present experimental results to decide the system configuration.

5.1 Experimental Setups

In the comparison experiments, we used the development set to evaluate model performance. In addition to the Q score and Q+A score, we employed the Hungarian METEOR score to evaluate the answer quality, denoted as A score. For the comparison experiments, we used the training set for training our models and the development set for the evaluation. The training and development set were used to train our system for the submission. We used the Adam optimizer with a learning rate 2e-5, batch size 128, and 2 epochs. For LoRA, we set the rank to 128 and alpha to 256.

All the language models used in the experiments are the instruction-tuned version (e.g., llama-3.1-70b-it). For brevity, we omitted 'it' in the model identifier for the rest of the paper. For HyDE-FC, we set the LM hyperparameters as follows: maximum number of tokens as 512, temperature as 0.7, and top_p as 1.0. We used the labeled QA pairs from the training set as a data store to retrieve in-context samples for question generation. We used greedy decoding with a maximum length of 512. When an LM does not produce the verdict label, we repeated the generation with the top-2 sampling.

We ran experiments using three machines. The first has two H100 GPUs (80GB per GPU) and 480GB RAM. The second has eight H100 GPUs with 2TB RAM; the third has four NVIDIA A6000 GPUs (48GB per GPU) and 256GB RAM. The experiments were conducted in a computing environment with the following configuration: Python 3.11.9, PyTorch 2.3.1, Transformers 4.43.4, Axolotl 0.4.1, vLLM 0.5.3, and SentenceTransformers 3.0.1. HerO took approximately 6.6 hours to make 500 predictions for the development set with two H100 GPUs. It took six hours for the evidence retrieval, 25 minutes for the question generation, and 12 minutes to complete the veracity prediction.

5.2 Experimental Results

Evidence Retrieval We present evidence retrieval results on the AVeriTeC development set in Table 2. We relied on the A score as the primary metric to identify a model that can retrieve sentences that are similar to the annotated evidence.

We made three observations. First, when a claim was used as a query verbatim, applying SFR-embedding-2 to the re-ranking step boosted the performance by the A score of 0.073. Second, augmenting a query by the hypothetical document generation increased the performance. The best model, HyDE-FC with llama-3.1-70b, achieved an A score of 0.2801, 0.02 greater than the claim-only approach. Third, gpt-4o-mini was close to but slightly worse than the best open model when being used for HyDE-FC. Accordingly, HerO uses the two-step approach where SFR-embedding-2 re-ranks the top 10,000 sentences obtained by BM25; llama-3.1-70b is used to generate hypothetical fact-checking documents to augment the query.

Question Generation We present evaluation results of question generation methods in Table 3. We fixed the evidence retrieval method as the best approach to assess the effects of question generation methods. The Q score was used as a primary evaluation metric for question generation.

We made three observations. First, all the llama models achieved better Q scores than the baseline and gpt-4o-mini. Second, using the claim as an additional in-context sample boosted the generation performance significantly. The llama-3-8b model with the claim achieved a Q score of 0.4938, 0.0728 greater than its counterpart. Third, among the llama models that only use retrieved sentences as in-context samples, the latest and largest model (llama-3.1-70b) achieved the best score. However, llama-3-8b achieved the best score with the claim. Accordingly, HerO uses llama-3-8b to generate questions.

Veracity Prediction We compared veracity prediction methods using the best evidence retrieval and question generation pipelines. We evaluated three LLM-based methods: in-context learning with ten examples, instruction fine-tuning by LoRA (Hu et al., 2021), and fine-tuning the whole parameters. Table 4 shows the results. When in-context learning was used without parameter updates, the llama models outperformed gpt-4o-mini. The most significant performance gap was an accuracy of 0.14 and an AVeriTeC score of 0.112. Furthermore, the performance was boosted by instruction fine-tuning approaches. The llama-3.1-70b with the full fine-tuning approach achieved the highest AVeriTeC score of 0.578, which is the veracity prediction module for HerO.

Method	Model	Accuracy	AVeriTeC score
In-context learning	Llama-3-70b	0.628	0.494
	Llama-3.1-70b	0.54	0.422
	Gpt-4o-mini	0.488	0.382
LoRA	Llama-3-70b	0.724	0.556
	Llama-3.1-70b	0.704	0.55
Fine-tuning	Llama-3-70b	0.746	0.57
	Llama-3.1-70b	**0.752**	**0.578**

Table 4: Performance of veracity prediction methods

System	Q score	Q+A score	AVeriTeC score
TUDA_MAI_0	0.45	0.34	**0.63**
HerO	**0.48**	**0.35**	0.57
CTU AIC	0.46	0.32	0.5
Baseline	0.24	0.2	0.11

Table 5: Test set results

5.3 Test Set Results

Table 5 shows how HerO performs in the test set in comparison to the baseline and other competitive models. TUDA_MAI_0 achieved the best AVeriTeC score of 0.63, followed by HerO (0.57) and CTU AIC (0.5). Their performance gap with the existing baseline was significant. HerO achieved the best Q and Q+A scores among the top 3 models, suggesting that our question-generation approach is strong. Since HerO's performance gap with the winning system was smaller for the Q+A score than for the Q score, we suspected that our retrieval system is on par with but slightly worse than theirs. The answer score employed in our experiment could help better understand what is attributed to the performance, either retrieval or question generation.

6 Conclusion

To tackle the AVeriTeC shared task hosted by the FEVER-24, we developed HerO, a fact-checking system that employs publicly available large language models for each step of automated fact-checking: evidence retrieval, question generation, and veracity prediction. Our system achieved 2nd place in the shared task, supporting the effectiveness of open LLMs for verifying real-world claims. We release our code publicly for future research.

Acknowledgments

This research was supported by the MSIT(Ministry of Science and ICT), Korea, under the Graduate School of Metaverse Convergence support (IITP-2024-RS-2024-00430997) and Innovative Human Resource Development for Local Intellectualization (IITP-2024-RS-2022-00156360) programs, supervised by the IITP(Institute for Information & Communications Technology Planning & Evaluation). We used an equipment supported by the NIPA (National IT Promotion Agency) under the high performance computing support program. The title and system name are hommage to research on open language models (to list a few, Jiang et al. (2023), Meng et al. (2024), and Dubey et al. (2024)), which made possible the development of our fact-checking system. Yejun Yoon and Jaeyoon Jung contributed to this work equally as co-first authors. Kunwoo Park is the corresponding author.

References

Josh Achiam, Steven Adler, Sandhini Agarwal, Lama Ahmad, Ilge Akkaya, Florencia Leoni Aleman, Diogo Almeida, Janko Altenschmidt, Sam Altman, Shyamal Anadkat, et al. 2023. Gpt-4 technical report. *arXiv preprint arXiv:2303.08774*.

Rami Aly, Zhijiang Guo, Michael Sejr Schlichtkrull, James Thorne, Andreas Vlachos, Christos Christodoulopoulos, Oana Cocarascu, and Arpit Mittal. 2021. FEVEROUS: Fact extraction and VERification over unstructured and structured information. In *Thirty-fifth Conference on Neural Information Processing Systems Datasets and Benchmarks Track (Round 1)*.

Isabelle Augenstein, Christina Lioma, Dongsheng Wang, Lucas Chaves Lima, Casper Hansen, Christian Hansen, and Jakob Grue Simonsen. 2019. MultiFC: A real-world multi-domain dataset for evidence-based fact checking of claims. In *Proceedings of the 2019 Conference on Empirical Methods in Natural Language Processing and the 9th International Joint Conference on Natural Language Processing (EMNLP-IJCNLP)*, pages 4685–4697. Association for Computational Linguistics.

S. Banerjee and A. Lavie. 2005. METEOR: An automatic metric for MT evaluation with improved correlation with human judgments. In *ACL*.

Tom Brown, Benjamin Mann, Nick Ryder, Melanie Subbiah, Jared D Kaplan, Prafulla Dhariwal, Arvind Neelakantan, Pranav Shyam, Girish Sastry, Amanda Askell, Sandhini Agarwal, Ariel Herbert-Voss, Gretchen Krueger, Tom Henighan, Rewon Child, Aditya Ramesh, Daniel Ziegler, Jeffrey Wu, Clemens Winter, Chris Hesse, Mark Chen, Eric Sigler, Mateusz Litwin, Scott Gray, Benjamin Chess, Jack Clark, Christopher Berner, Sam McCandlish, Alec Radford, Ilya Sutskever, and Dario Amodei. 2020. Language models are few-shot learners. In *Advances in Neural Information Processing Systems*, volume 33, pages 1877–1901. Curran Associates, Inc.

Abhimanyu Dubey, Abhinav Jauhri, Abhinav Pandey, Abhishek Kadian, Ahmad Al-Dahle, Aiesha Letman, Akhil Mathur, Alan Schelten, Amy Yang, Angela Fan, et al. 2024. The llama 3 herd of models. *arXiv preprint arXiv:2407.21783*.

Luyu Gao, Xueguang Ma, Jimmy Lin, and Jamie Callan. 2023. Precise zero-shot dense retrieval without relevance labels. In *Proceedings of the 61st Annual Meeting of the Association for Computational Linguistics (Volume 1: Long Papers)*, pages 1762–1777, Toronto, Canada. Association for Computational Linguistics.

Zhijiang Guo, Michael Schlichtkrull, and Andreas Vlachos. 2022. A survey on automated fact-checking. *Transactions of the Association for Computational Linguistics*, 10:178–206.

Edward J Hu, Yelong Shen, Phillip Wallis, Zeyuan Allen-Zhu, Yuanzhi Li, Shean Wang, Lu Wang, and Weizhu Chen. 2021. Lora: Low-rank adaptation of large language models. *arXiv preprint arXiv:2106.09685*.

Albert Q Jiang, Alexandre Sablayrolles, Arthur Mensch, Chris Bamford, Devendra Singh Chaplot, Diego de las Casas, Florian Bressand, Gianna Lengyel, Guillaume Lample, Lucile Saulnier, et al. 2023. Mistral 7b. *arXiv preprint arXiv:2310.06825*.

Harold W. Kuhn. 1955. The hungarian method for the assignment problem. *Naval Research Logistics Quarterly*.

Teven Le Scao, Angela Fan, Christopher Akiki, Ellie Pavlick, Suzana Ilić, Daniel Hesslow, Roman Castagné, Alexandra Sasha Luccioni, François Yvon, Matthias Gallé, et al. 2023. Bloom: A 176b-parameter open-access multilingual language model.

Rui Meng, Ye Liu, Shafiq Rayhan, Joty, Caiming Xiong, Yingbo Zhou, and Semih Yavuz. 2024. Sfr-embedding-2: Advanced text embedding with multi-stage training.

Stephen Robertson and Hugo Zaragoza. 2009. The probabilistic relevance framework: Bm25 and beyond. *Foundations and Trends® in Information Retrieval*, 3(4):333–389.

Michael Schlichtkrull, Yulong Chen, Chenxi Whitehouse, Zhenyun Deng, Mubashara Akhtar, Rami Aly, Zhijiang Guo, Christos Christodoulopoulos, Oana Cocarascu, Arpit Mittal, James Thorne, and Andreas Vlachos. 2024. The automated verification of textual claims (averitec) shared task. In *Proceedings of* the Seventh Workshop on Fact Extraction and VERification (FEVER). Association for Computational Linguistics.

Michael Schlichtkrull, Zhijiang Guo, and Andreas Vlachos. 2023. Averitec: A dataset for real-world claim verification with evidence from the web. In *Advances in Neural Information Processing Systems*, volume 36, pages 65128–65167. Curran Associates, Inc.

Gemini Team, Rohan Anil, Sebastian Borgeaud, Yonghui Wu, Jean-Baptiste Alayrac, Jiahui Yu, Radu Soricut, Johan Schalkwyk, Andrew M Dai, Anja Hauth, et al. 2023. Gemini: a family of highly capable multimodal models. *arXiv preprint arXiv:2312.11805*.

Romal Thoppilan, Daniel De Freitas, Jamie Hall, Noam Shazeer, Apoorv Kulshreshtha, Heng-Tze Cheng, Alicia Jin, Taylor Bos, Leslie Baker, Yu Du, et al. 2022. Lamda: Language models for dialog applications. *arXiv preprint arXiv:2201.08239*.

James Thorne, Andreas Vlachos, Oana Cocarascu, Christos Christodoulopoulos, and Arpit Mittal. 2018. The Fact Extraction and VERification (FEVER) shared task. In *Proceedings of the First Workshop on Fact Extraction and VERification (FEVER)*.

Liang Wang, Nan Yang, and Furu Wei. 2023. Query2doc: Query expansion with large language models. In *Proceedings of the 2023 Conference on Empirical Methods in Natural Language Processing*, pages 9414–9423, Singapore. Association for Computational Linguistics.

William Yang Wang. 2017. "liar, liar pants on fire": A new benchmark dataset for fake news detection. In *Proceedings of the 55th Annual Meeting of the Association for Computational Linguistics (Volume 2: Short Papers)*, pages 422–426, Vancouver, Canada. Association for Computational Linguistics.

Jason Wei, Xuezhi Wang, Dale Schuurmans, Maarten Bosma, brian ichter, Fei Xia, Ed Chi, Quoc V Le, and Denny Zhou. 2022. Chain-of-thought prompting elicits reasoning in large language models. In *Advances in Neural Information Processing Systems*, volume 35, pages 24824–24837. Curran Associates, Inc.

Susan Zhang, Stephen Roller, Naman Goyal, Mikel Artetxe, Moya Chen, Shuohui Chen, Christopher Dewan, Mona Diab, Xian Li, Xi Victoria Lin, et al. 2022. Opt: Open pre-trained transformer language models. *arXiv preprint arXiv:2205.01068*.

AIC CTU system at AVeriTeC: Re-framing automated fact-checking as a simple RAG task

Herbert Ullrich
AI Center @ CTU FEE
Charles Square 13
Prague, Czech Republic
ullriher@fel.cvut.cz

Tomáš Mlynář
AI Center @ CTU FEE
Charles Square 13
Prague, Czech Republic
mlynatom@fel.cvut.cz

Jan Drchal
AI Center @ CTU FEE
Charles Square 13
Prague, Czech Republic
drchajan@fel.cvut.cz

Abstract

This paper describes our 3rd place submission in the AVeriTeC shared task in which we attempted to address the challenge of fact-checking with evidence retrieved in the wild using a simple scheme of Retrieval-Augmented Generation (RAG) designed for the task, leveraging the predictive power of Large Language Models. We release our codebase[1], and explain its two modules – the Retriever and the Evidence & Label generator – in detail, justifying their features such as MMR-reranking and Likert-scale confidence estimation. We evaluate our solution on AVeriTeC dev and test set and interpret the results, picking the GPT-4o as the most appropriate model for our pipeline at the time of our publication, with Llama 3.1 70B being a promising open-source alternative. We perform an empirical error analysis to see that faults in our predictions often coincide with noise in the data or ambiguous fact-checks, provoking further research and data augmentation.

1 Introduction

We release a pipeline for fact-checking claims using evidence retrieved from the web consisting of two modules – a *retriever*, which picks the most relevant sources among the available knowledge store[2] and an *evidence & label generator* which generates evidence for the claim using these sources, as well as its veracity label.

Our pipeline is a variant of the popular Retrieval-augmented Generation (RAG) scheme (Lewis et al., 2020), making it easy to re-implement using established frameworks such as Langchain, Haystack, or our attached Python codebase for future research or to use as a baseline.

This paper describes our pipeline and the decisions taken at each module, achieving a simple yet efficient RAG scheme that improves dramatically across the board over the baseline system from (Schlichtkrull et al., 2024), and scores third in the AVeriTeC leaderboard as of August 2024, with an AVeriTeC test set score of 50.4%.

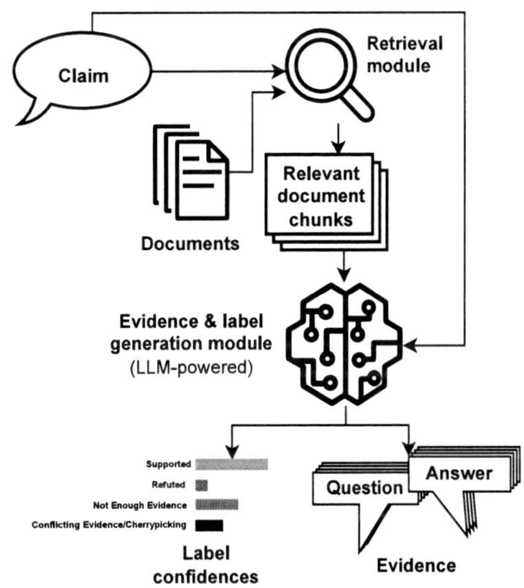

Figure 1: Our pipeline

2 Related work

1. **AVeriTeC shared task** (Schlichtkrull et al., 2024) releases the dataset of real-world fact-checked claims, annotated with evidence available at the date the claim was made.

   It proposes the **AVeriTeC Score** – a method of unsupervised scoring of fact-checking pipeline against this gold data using Hungarian METEOR score, matching the evidence questions (Q) or the whole evidence (Q+A). The score is then calculated as the proportion of claims with accurate label and sound ev-

[1] https://github.com/aic-factcheck/aic_averitec

[2] Due to the pre-retrieval step that was used to generate knowledge stores, our "retriever" module could more conventionally be referred to as a "reranker", which we refrain from, to avoid confusion with reranking steps it uses as a subroutine.

Proceedings of the Seventh Fact Extraction and VERification Workshop (FEVER), pages 137–150
November 15, 2024

idence (using a threshold for Hu-METEOR such as 0.25) among all claims in the dataset, giving an estimate on "how often the whole fact-checking pipeline succeeds end to end".

The provided **baseline** is a pipeline of search query generation, API search (producing a knowledge store), sentence retrieval, Question-and-answer (QA) generation, QA reranking, QA-wise claim classification and label aggregation, achieving an overall AVeriTeC test set score of 11%.

2. **FEVER Shared Task** (Thorne et al., 2018b), a predecessor to the AVeriTeC, worked with a similar dataset engineered on top of the enclosed domain Wikipedic data rather than real-world fact-checks. Its top-ranking solutions used a simpler pipeline of Document Retrieval, Sentence Reranking and Natural Language Inference, improving its modules in a decoupled manner and scoring well above 60% in a similarly computed FEVER score (Thorne et al., 2018a) on this data.

3. **Our previous research** on fact-checking pipelines (Ullrich et al., 2023; Drchal et al., 2023) using data similar to FEVER and AVeriTeC shows significant superiority of fact-checking pipelines that **retrieve the whole documents** for the inference step, rather than retrieving out-of-context sentences.

4. **Retrieval-Augmented Generation (RAG) for Knowledge-Intensive Tasks** (Lewis et al., 2020) takes this a step further, leveraging Large Language Model (LLM) for the task, providing it the whole text of retrieved documents (each a chunk of Wikipedia) and simply instructing it to predict the evidence and label on top of it, achieving results within 4.3% from the FEVER state of the art by the time of its publication (December 2020) *without* engineering a custom pipeline for the task.

3 System description

Our system design prioritizes simplicity, and its core idea is using a straightforward RAG pipeline without engineering extra steps, customizing only the retrieval step and LLM prompting (Listing 1 in Appendix A). Despite that, this section describes and justifies our decisions taken at each step, our additions to the naive version of RAG modules to tune them for the specific task of fact-checking, and their impact on the system performance.

3.1 Retrieval module

To ease comparison with the baseline and other systems designed for the task, our system does not use direct internet/search-engine access for its retrieval, but an AVeriTeC *knowledge store* provided alongside each claim.

To use our pipeline in the wild, our retrieval module is decoupled from the rest of the pipeline and can be swapped out in favour of an internet search module such as SerpApi[3] as a whole, or it can be used on top of a knowledge store emulated using large crawled corpora such as CommonCrawl[4] and a pre-retrieval module.

3.1.1 Knowledge stores

Each claim's knowledge store contains pre-scraped results for various search queries that can be derived from the claim using human annotation or generative models. The knowledge stores used with ours as well as the baseline system can be downloaded from the AVeriTeC dataset page[5], containing about 1000 pre-scraped *documents*[6], each consisting of 28 sentences at median[6], albeit varying wildly between documents. The methods used for generating the knowledge stores are explained in more detail by Schlichtkrull et al. (2024).

Our retrieval module then focuses on picking a set of k ($k = 10$ in the examples below, as well as in our submitted system) most appropriate document chunks to fact-check the provided claim within this knowledge store.

3.1.2 Angle-optimized embedding search

Despite each article in any knowledge store only needing to be compared *once* with its *one specific* claim, which should be the use-case for CrossEncoder reranking (Déjean et al., 2024), our empirical preliminary experiments made us favour a *cosine-similarity* search based on vector embeddings instead. It takes less time to embed the whole knowledge store into vectors than to match each document against a claim using crossencoder, and the produced embeddings can be re-used across experiments.

[3]https://serpapi.com/

[4]https://commoncrawl.org/

[5]https://fever.ai/dataset/averitec.html

[6]The numbers are orientational and were computed on knowledge stores provided for the AVeriTeC dev set.

For our proof of concept, we explore the MTEB (Muennighoff et al., 2023) benchmark leaderboard, looking for a reasonably-sized open-source embedding model, ultimately picking Mixedbread's mxbai-large-v1 (Li and Li, 2024; Lee et al., 2024) optimized for the cosine objective fitting our inteded use.

To reduce querying time at a reasonable exactness tradeoff, we use Faiss index (Douze et al., 2024; Johnson et al., 2019) to store our vectors, allowing us to only precompute semantical representation once, making the retriever respond rapidly in empirical experiments, allowing a very agile prototyping of novel methods to be used.

3.1.3 Chunking with added context

Our initial experiments with the whole AVeriTeC documents for the Document Retrieval step have revealed a significant weakness – while most documents fit within the input size of the embedding model, outliers are common, often with *hundreds of thousands* characters, exceeding the 512 input tokens with little to no coverage of their content.

Upon further examination, these are typically PDF documents of legislature, documentation and communication transcription – highly relevant sources real fact-checker would scroll through to find the relevant part to refer.

This workflow inspires the use of *document chunk retrieval* as used in (Lewis et al., 2020), commonly paired with RAG. We partition each document into sets of its sentences of combined length of N characters at most. To take advantage of the full input size of the vector embedding model we use for semantical search, we arbitrarily set our bound $N = 512 * 4 = 2048$, where 512 is the input dimension of common embedding models, 4 often being used as a rule-of-thumb number of characters per token for US English in modern tokenizers (OpenAI, 2023).

Importantly, each chunk is assigned metadata – the source URL, as well as the full text of the next and previous chunk within the same document. This way, chunks can be presented to the LLM along with their original context in the generation module, where the length constraint is much less of an issue than in vector embedding. As shown in (Drchal et al., 2023), fact-checking models benefit from being exposed to larger pieces of text such as paragraphs or entire documents rather than out-of-context sentences. Splitting our data into the maximum chunks that fit our retrieval model and providing them with additional context may help down the line, preventing the RAG sources from being semantically incomplete.

3.1.4 Pruning the chunks

While the chunking of long articles prevents their information from getting lost to retriever, it makes its search domain too large to embed on demand. As each of the thousands of claims has its own knowledge store, each of possibly tens of thousands of chunks, we seek to omit the chunks having little to no common tokens with our claim using an efficient BM25 (Robertson et al., 1995) search for the nearest ω chunks, setting the ω to 6000 for dev and 2000 for test claims. This yields a reasonably-sized document store for embedding each chunk into a vector, taking an average of 40 s to compute and store using the method described in Section 3.1.2 for each dev-claim using our Tesla V100 GPU.

This allows a quick and agile production of vectorstores for further querying and experimentation, motivated by the AVeriTeC test data being published just several days before the announced submission deadline. The pruning also keeps the resource intensity moderate for real-world applications. However, if time is not of the essence, the step can be omitted.

3.1.5 Diversifying sources: MMR

Our choice of embedding search based on the entire claim rather than generating "search queries" introduces less noise and captures the semantics of the whole claim. It is, however, prone to redundancy among search results, which we address using a reranking by the results' Maximal Marginal Relevance (MMR) (Carbonell and Goldstein, 1998), a metric popular for the RAG task, which maximizes the search results' score computed as (for $D_i \in P$)

$$\lambda \cdot \mathrm{Sim}(D_i, Q) - (1 - \lambda) \cdot \max_{D_j \in S} \mathrm{Sim}(D_i, D_j)$$

Sim denoting the cosine-similarity between embeddings, Q being the search query, and P the prefetched set of documents (by a search which simply maximizes their Sim to Q), forming S as the final search result, by adding each D_i as MMR-argmax one by one, until reaching its desired size.

In our system, we set $\lambda = 0.75$ to favour relevancy rather than diversity, $|S| = 10$ and $|P| = 40$, obtaining a set of diverse sources relevant to each claim at a fraction of cost and complexity of a query-generation driven retrieval, such as that used in (Schlichtkrull et al., 2024).

3.2 Evidence & label generator

The second and the last module on our proposed pipeline for automated fact checking is the Evidence & Label Generator, which receives a claim and k sources (document chunks), and returns l (in our case, $l = 10$) question-answer pairs of evidence abstracted from the sources, along with the veracity verdict – in AVeriTeC dataset, a claim may be classified as *Supported, Refuted, Not Enough Evidence*, or *Conflicting Evidence/Cherrypicking* with respect to its evidence.

Our approach leverages a Large Language Model (LLM), instructing it to output both evidence and the label in a single step, as a chain of thought. We rely on JSON-structured output generation with source referencing using a numeric identifier, we estimate the label confidences using Likert-scale ratings. The full system prompt can be examined in Listing 1 in Appendix A, and this section further explains the choices behind it.

3.2.1 JSON generation

To be able to collect LLM's results programmatically, we exploit their capability to produce structured outputs, which is on the rise, with datasets available for tuning (Tang et al., 2024) and by the time of writing of this paper (August 2024), systems for strictly structured prediction are beginning to be launched by major providers (OpenAI, 2024).

Despite not having access to such structured-prediction API by the time of AVeriTeC shared task, the current generation of models examined for the task (section 3.2.6) rarely strays from the desired format if properly explained within a system prompt – we instruct our models to output a JSON of pre-defined properties (see prompt Listing 1 in Appendix A) featuring both evidence and the veracity verdict for a given claims.

Although we implement fallbacks, less than 0.5% of our predictions threw a parsing exception throughout experimentation, and could be easily recovered using the same prompting again, exploiting the intrinsic randomness of LLM predictions.

3.2.2 Chain-of-thought prompting

While JSON dictionary should be order-invariant, we can actually exploit the order of outputs in our output structure to make LLMS like GPT-4o output better results (Wei et al., 2024). This is commonly referred to as the "chain-of-thought" prompting – if we instruct the autoregressive LLM to first output the evidence (question, then answer), then a set of all labels with their confidence ratings (see section 3.2.5) and only then the final verdict, its prediction is both cheaper as opposed to implementing an extra module, as well as more reliable, as it must attend to all of the intermediate steps as well.

3.2.3 Source referring

To be able to backtrack the generated evidence to the urls of the used sources, we simply augment each question-answer pair with a source field. We assign a 1-based index[7] to each of the sources to facilitate tokenization and prompt the LLM to refer it as the source ID with each evidence it generates. While hallucination can not be fully prevented, it is less common than it may appear – with RAG gaining popularity, the models are being trained to cite their sources using special citation tokens (Menick et al., 2022), not dissimilarly to our proposal.

3.2.4 Dynamic few-shot learning

To utilise the few-shot learning framework (Brown et al., 2020) shown to increase quality of model output, we provide our LLMs with examples of what we expect the model to do. To obtain such examples, our evidence generator looks up the AVeriTeC train set using BM25 to get the 10 most similar claims, providing them as the few-shot examples, along their gold evidence and veracity verdicts. Experimentally, we also few-shot our models to output an *answer type* (*Extractive, Abstractive, Boolean,...*) as the *answer type* is listed with each sample anyways, and we have observed its integration into the generation task to slightly boost our model performance.

3.2.5 Likert-scale label confidences

Despite modern LLMs being well capable of predicting the label in a "pick one" fashion, research applications such as ours may prefer them to output a probability distribution over all labels for two reasons.

Firstly, it measures the confidence in each label, pinpointing the edge-cases, secondly, it allows ensembling the LLM classification with any other model, such as Encoders with classification head finetuned on the task of Natural Language Inference (NLI) (see section 4.3).

As the LLMs and other token prediction schemes struggle with the prediction of continuous numbers

[7]We chose the 1-based source indexing to exploit the source-referring data in LLM train set such as Wikipedia, where source numbers start with 1. The improvement in quality over 0-based indexing was not experimentally tested.

which are notoriously hard to tokenize appropriately (Golkar et al., 2023), we come up with a simple alternative: instructing the model to print each of the 4 possible labels, along with their Likert-scale rating: 1 for "strongly disagree", 2 for "disagree", 3 for "neutral", 4 for "agree" and 5 for "strongly agree" (Likert, 1932).

On top of the ease of tokenization, Likert scale's popularity in psychology and other fields such as software testing (Joshi et al., 2015) adds another benefit – both the scale itself and its appropriate usage were likely demonstrated many times to LLMs during their unsupervised training phase.

To convert the ratings such as `{"Supported":2, "Refuted":5, "Cherrypicking":4, "NEE":2}` to a probability distribution, we simply use softmax (Bridle, 1989). While the label probabilities are only emulated (and may only take a limited, discrete set of values) and the system may produce ties, it gets the job done until further research is carried out.

3.2.6 Choosing LLM

In our experiments, we have tested the full set of techniques introduced in this section, computing the text completion requests with:

1. GPT-4o (version `2024-05-13`)

2. Claude-3.5-Sonnet (`2024-06-20`), using the Google's Vertex API

3. LLaMA 3.1 70B, in the final experimets to see if the pipeline can be re-produced using open-source models

Their comparison can be seen in tables 1 and 2; for our submission in the AVeriTeC shared task, GPT-4o was used.

4 Other examined approaches

In this section, we also describe a third, optional module we call the *veracity classifier*, which takes the claim and its evidence generated by our evidence & label generator (section 3.2) and predicts the veracity label independently, based on the suggested evidence, using a fine-tuned NLI model. We also describe the options of its ensembling with veracity labels predicted in the generative step (section 3.2.5).

The absence of a dedicated veracity classifier has not been shown to decrease the performance of our pipeline significantly (as shown, e.g., in tables 2 and 1) so we suggest to omit this step altogether and we proceed to participate in the AVeriTeC shared task without it, proposing a clean and simple RAG pipeline without the extra step (Figure 1) for the fact-checking task.

4.1 Single-evidence classification with label aggregation

In the earliest stages of experimenting, we utilized the baseline classifier provided by AVeriTeC authors[8] (Schlichtkrull et al., 2024). It is based on the BERT (Devlin et al., 2019) and was further fine-tuned on the AVeriTeC dataset (Schlichtkrull et al., 2024). It takes one claim and one question-answer evidence as input – each claim therefore has multiple classifications, one for each evidence. The classifications are then aggregated using a heuristic of several if-clauses to determine the final label.

We experiment with altering this heuristic (e.g. by making *not enough evidence* the final label only when no other labels are present at any evidence), and training NLI models that could work better with it, such as 3-way DeBERTaV3 (He et al., 2023) without a breakthrough result, motivating a radically different approach.

4.2 Multi-evidence classification

The multi-evidence approach is to fine-tune a 4-way Natural Language Inference (NLI) classifier, using the full scope of evidence directly at once, without heuristics. For that, we concatenate all of the evidence together using a separator `[SEP]` token. This allows the model to know exact question-answer borders, albeit using a space has turned out to be just as accurate as the experiments went on. As the veracity verdict should be independent of the evidence ordering, we also experiment with sampling different permutations in the fine-tuning step to increase the size of our data.

We carry out the fine-tuning using the AVeriTeC train split with gold evidence and labels on DeBERTaV3 (He et al., 2023) in two variants: the original large one[9] and one pre-finetuned on NLI tasks[10], and also Mistral-7B-v0.3 model[11] with a classification head (MistralForSequenceClassification) provided by the Huggingface Transformers

[8] `https://huggingface.co/chenxwh/AVeriTeC`

[9] `https://huggingface.co/microsoft/deberta-v3-large`

[10] `https://huggingface.co/cross-encoder/nli-deberta-v3-large`

[11] `https://huggingface.co/mistralai/Mistral-7B-v0.3`

library (Wolf et al., 2020) that utilizes the last token. In the preliminary testing phase, the original DeBERTaV3 Large performed the best and was used in all other experimental settings.

From the approaches described above, we achieved the best results for the development split with gold evidence and labels with a model without permuting the evidence, achieving 0.71 macro F_1 score using a space-separation. The `[SEP]` model achieved a comparable 0.70 macro F_1 score, and the random order model performed worse with a 0.67 macro F_1 score, all improving significantly upon baseline, yet falling behind the capabilities of generating the labels alongside evidence in a single chain-of-thought. We provide our best DeBERTaV3 finetuned model publicly in a Huggingface repository[12].

4.3 Ensembling classifiers

Encouraged by the promising results of our multi-evidence classifiers, we go on to try to ensemble the models with LLM predictions from section 3.2.5, using a weighted average of the class probabilities of our models. We have experimented with multiple weight settings: 0.5:0.5 for even votes, 0.3:0.7 in favour of the LLM to exploit its accuracy while tipping its scales in cases of a more spread-out label probability distribution, as well as 0.1:0.9 to use the fine-tuned classifier only for tie-breaking, listing the results in Table 1.

We also tried tuning our ensemble weights based on a subset of the dev split, without a breakthrough in accuracy on the rest of dev samples.

The last method we tried was stacking using logistic regression. However, this setup classified no labels from *Not Enough Evidence* and *Conflicting Evidence/Cherrypicking*, and we could not achieve reasonable results. For logistic regression, we used the scikit-learn library (Pedregosa et al., 2011).

We conclude that the augmentation of the pipeline from Figure 1 with a classification module using a single NLI model or an ensemble with LLM is unneccessary, as it adds complexity and computational cost without paying off on the full pipeline performance (Table 2).

4.4 Conflicting Evidence/Cherrypicking detection

During the experiments, we discovered that classifying the *Conflicting Evidence/Cherrypicking* class is the most challenging task, achieving a near-zero F_1-score across our various prototype pipelines. To overcome this problem, we tried to build a binary classifier with cherrypicking as positive class. We tried to use the DeBERTaV3 Large model with both basic and weighted cross-entropy loss (other experimental settings were the same as in section 4.2), but it could not pick up the training task due to the *Conflicting Evidence/Cherrypicking* underrepresentation in train set – less than 7% of the samples carry the label.

Even after exploring various other methods, we did not get a reliable detection scheme for this task, perhaps motivating a future collection of data that represents the class better. While writing this system description paper, we found an interesting research by Jaradat et al. (2024) that uses a radically different approach to detect cherrypicking in newspaper articles.

5 Results and analysis

We examine our pipeline results using two sets of metrics – firstly, we measure the prediction accuracy and F_1 over predict labels without any ablation, that is obtaining predicted labels using the predicted evidence generated on top the predicted retrieval results. While the retrieval module is fixed throughout the experiment (a full scheme described in section 3.1), various Evidence & Label generators and classifiers are compared in Table 1, showcasing their performance on the same sources. The results show that if we disregard the quality of evidence, models are more or less interchangeable, without a clear winner across the board – an ensemble of DeBERTA and Claude-3.5-Sonnet gives the best F_1 score, while GPT-4o scores 72% accuracy.

In real world, however, the evidence quality is critical for the fact-checking task. We therefore proceed to estimate it using the hu-METEOR evidence question score, QA score and AVeriTeC score benchmarks briefly explained in Section 2 and in greater detail in (Schlichtkrull et al., 2024). We use the provided AVeriTeC scoring script to calculate the values for Table 2, using its EvalAI blackbox to obtain the test scores without seeing the gold test data.

The latter experiments shown in Table 2 suggests the superiority of GPT-4o to predict the results for our pipeline with a margin. Even if we simplify the evidence & label generation step by omitting the

[12] `https://huggingface.co/ctu-aic/deberta-v3-large-AVeriTeC-nli`

Classifier	Acc	F_1	Prec.	Recall
GPT4o	0.72	0.46	0.48	0.47
Claude 3.5 Sonnet	0.64	0.49	0.50	0.52
DeBERTa	0.63	0.39	0.40	0.41
DeBERTa - random@10	0.65	0.41	0.41	0.44
$0.5 \cdot$ DeBERTa $+ 0.5 \cdot$ GPT4o	0.70	0.43	0.41	0.45
$0.5 \cdot$ DeBERTa $+ 0.5 \cdot$ Claude	0.68	0.47	0.50	0.49
$0.3 \cdot$ DeBERTa $+ 0.7 \cdot$ GPT4o	0.72	0.45	0.45	0.46
$0.3 \cdot$ DeBERTa $+ 0.7 \cdot$ Claude	0.66	**0.50**	**0.51**	**0.53**
$0.1 \cdot$ DeBERTa $+ 0.9 \cdot$ GPT4o	0.72	0.39	0.46	0.43
$0.1 \cdot$ DeBERTa $+ 0.9 \cdot$ Claude	0.64	0.49	0.50	0.54
Llama 3.1	**0.73**	0.44	0.43	0.46

Table 1: Evalution of the label generators, classifier models and their ensembles on the AVeriTeCdevelopment set. F_1, Precision and Recall are computed as macro-averages. The random@10 suffix indicates that the classifier used average of 10 different random orders of QA pairs for each claim. GPT4o stands for the Likert classifier based on GPT-4o, Claude 3.5 Sonnet is the Likert classifier based on Claude 3.5 Sonnet, and DeBERTa is classifier based on DeBERTaV3 Large finetuned on AVeriTeC gold evidence and labels.

dynamic few-shot learning (section 3.2), answer-type tuning and Likert-scale confidence emulation, it still scores above others, also showing that our pipeline can be further simplified when needed. Regardless of the LLM in use, the results of our pipeline improve upon the AVeriTeC baseline dramatically.

Posterior to the original experiments and to the AVeriTeC submission deadline, we also compute the pipeline results using an open-source model – the Llama 3.1 70B[13] (Dubey et al., 2024) obtaining encouraging scores, signifying our pipeline being adaptable to work well without the need to use a blackboxed proprietary LLM.

5.1 API costs

During our experimentation July 2024, we have made around 9000 requests to OpenAI's `gpt-4o-2024-05-13` batch API, at a total cost of \$363. This gives a mean cost estimate of \$0.04 per a single fact-check (or \$0.08 using the API without the batch discount) that can be further reduced using cheaper models, such as `gpt-4o-2024-08-06`.

We argue that such costs make our model suitable for further experiments alongside human fact-checkers, whose time spent reading through each source and proposing each evidence by themselves would certainly come at a higher price.

Our successive experiments with Llama 3.1 (Dubey et al., 2024) show promising results as well, nearly achieving parity with GPT. The use of open-source models such as LLaMa or Mistral allows running our pipeline on premise, without leaking data to a third party and billing anything else than the computational resources. For further experiments, we are looking to integrate them into the attached Python library using VLLM (Kwon et al., 2023).

5.2 Error analysis

In this section, we provide the results of an explorative analysis of 20 randomly selected samples from the development set. We divide our description of the analysis into the pipeline and dataset errors.

5.2.1 Pipeline errors

Our pipeline tends to rely on unofficial (often newspaper) sources rather than official government sources, e.g., with a domain ending or containing gov. On the other hand, it seems that the annotators prefer those sources. This could be remedied by implementing a different source selection strategy, preferring those official sources. For an example, see Listing 2 in Appendix B.

Another thing that could be recognised as an error is that our pipeline usually generates all ten allowed questions (upper bound given by the task (Schlichtkrull et al., 2024)). The analysis of the samples shows that the last questions are often unrelated or redundant to the claim and do not contribute directly to better veracity evaluation. However, since the classification step of our pipeline is not dependent on the number of question-answer pairs, this is not a critical error. Listing 3 in Appendix B shows an example of a data point with some unrelated questions.

When the pipeline generates extractive answers, it sometimes happens that the answer is not precisely extracted from the source text but slightly modified. An example of this error can be seen in Listing 4 in Appendix B. This error is not critical, but it could be improved in future works, e.g. using post-processing via string matching.

Individual errors were also caused by the fact that we do not use the claim date in our pipeline and because our pipeline cannot analyse PDFs with tables properly. The last erroneous behaviour we have noticed is that the majority of questions and

[13] `https://huggingface.co/hugging-quants/Meta-Llama-3.1-70B-Instruct-AWQ-INT4`

Pipeline Name	Dev Set Scores Q only	Dev Q+A	Dev AVeriTeC	Test Set Scores Q only	Test Q+A	Test AVeriTeC
GPT-4o (full-featured pipeline)	**0.46**	**0.29**	**0.42**	0.46	**0.32**	**0.50**
GPT-4o (simplified pipeline)	0.45	0.28	0.38	0.45	0.30	0.47
Claude-3.5-Sonnet (full-featured)	0.43	0.28	0.35	0.42	0.30	0.46
GPT-4o (with DeBERTa classification)	0.45	0.28	0.36	–	–	–
AVeriTeC baseline	0.24	0.19	0.09	0.24	0.20	0.11
Llama 3.1 70B (full-featured)	**0.46**	0.27	0.36	**0.47**	0.29	0.42

Table 2: Comparison of Pipeline Scores on Dev and Test Sets. Q, Q+A are Hu-METEOR scores against gold data, AVeriTeC scores are calculated as referred in section 2 thresholded at 0.25. "Full-featured" pipelines use the all the improvement techniques introduced in section 3, while the simplified pipeline omits the dynamic few-shot learning, answer-type-tuning and Likert-scale confidence emulation described in section 3.2

answers are often generated from a single source. This should not be viewed as an error, but by introducing diversity into the sources, the pipeline would be more reliable when deployed in real-world scenarios.

5.2.2 Dataset errors

During the error analysis of our pipeline, we also found some errors in the AVeriTeC dataset that we would like to mention. In some cases, there is a leakage of PolitiFact or Factcheck.org fact-checking articles where the claim is already fact-checked. This leads to a situation where our pipeline gives a correct verdict using the leaked evidence. However, annotators gave a different label (often Not Enough Evidence). An example of this error is shown in Listing 5 in Appendix B.

Another issue we have noticed is the inconsistency in the questions and answers given by annotators. Sometimes, they tend to be longer, including non-relevant information, while some are much shorter, as seen in Listing 6 in Appendix B. The questions are often too general, or the annotators seem to use outside knowledge. This inconsistency in the dataset leads to a decreased performance of any models evaluated on this dataset.

5.2.3 Summary

Despite the abovementioned errors, the explorative analysis revealed that our pipeline consistently gives reasonable questions and answers for the claims. Most misclassified samples in those 20 data points were due to dataset errors.

6 Conclusion

In this paper, we describe the use and development of a RAG pipeline over real world claims and data scraped from the web for the AVeriTeC shared task. Its main advantage are its simplicity, consisting of just two decoupled modules – Retriever and an Evidence & Label Generator – and leveraging the trainable parameters of a LLM rather than on complex pipeline engineering. The LLMs capabilities may further improve in future, making the upgrades of our system trivial.

In section 3, we describe the process of adding features to both modules well in an iterative fashion, describing real problems we have encountered and the justifications of their solution, hoping to share our experience on how to make such systems robust and well-performing. We publish our failed approaches in section 4 and the metrics we observed to benchmark our systems in section 5. We release our Python codebase to facilitate further research and applications of our system, either as a baseline for future research, or for experimenting alongside human fact-checkers.

6.1 Future works

1. Integrating a search API for use in real-world applications

2. Re-examine the Likert-scale rating (section 3.2.5) to establish a more appropriate and fine-grained means of tokenizing the label probabilities

3. Generating evidence in the form of declarative sentences rather than Question-Answer pairs should be explored to see if it leads for better or worse fact-checking performance

4. RAG-tuned LLMs such as those introduced in (Menick et al., 2022) could be explored to see if they offer a more reliable source citing

Limitations

The evaluation of our fact-checking pipeline is limited to the English language and the AVeriTeC dataset (Schlichtkrull et al., 2024). This is a severe limitation as the pipeline when deployed in a real-world application, would encounter other languages and forms of claims not covered by the used dataset.

Another limitation is that we are using a large language model. Because of that, future usage is limited to using an API of a provider of LLMs or having access to a large amount of computational resources, which comes at significant costs. Using APIs also brings the disadvantage of sending data to a third party, which might be a security risk in some critical applications. LLM usage also has an undeniable environmental impact because of the vast amount of electricity and resources used.

The reliability of the generated text is a limitation that is often linked to LLMs. LLMs sometimes hallucinate (in our case, it would mean using sources other than those given in the system prompt), and they can be biased based on their extensive training data. Moreover, because of the dataset size, it is impossible to validate each output of the LLM, and thus, we are not able to 100% guarantee the quality of the results.

Ethics statement

It is essential to note that our pipeline is not a real fact-checker that could do a human job but rather a study of future possibilities in automatic fact-checking and a showcase of the current capabilities of state-of-the-art language models. The pipeline in its current state should only be used with human supervision because of the potential biases and errors that could harm the consumers of the output information or persons mentioned in the claims. The pipeline could be misused to spread misinformation by directly using misinformation sources or by intentionally modifying the pipeline in a way that will generate wrong outputs.

Another important statement is that our pipeline was in its current form explicitly built for the AVeriTeC shared task, and thus, the evaluation results reflect the bias of the annotators. For more information, see the relevant section of the original paper (Schlichtkrull et al., 2024).

The carbon costs of the training and running of our pipeline are considerable and should be taken into account given the urgency of climate change. At the time of deployment, the pipeline should be run on the smallest possible model that can still provide reliable results, and the latest hardware and software optimisations should be used to minimise the carbon footprint.

Acknowledgements

We would like to thank Bryce Aaron from UNC for exploring the problems of search query generation and pinpointing claims of underrepresented labels using numerical methods that did not make it into our final pipeline but gave us a frame for comparison.

This research was co-financed with state support from the Technology Agency of the Czech Republic and the Ministry of Industry and Trade of the Czech Republic under the TREND Programme, project FW10010200. The access to the computational infrastructure of the OP VVV funded project CZ.02.1.01/0.0/0.0/16_019/0000765 "Research Center for Informatics" is also gratefully acknowledged. We would like to thank to OpenAI for providing free credit for their paid API via Researcher Access Program[14].

References

John Bridle. 1989. Training stochastic model recognition algorithms as networks can lead to maximum mutual information estimation of parameters. In *Advances in Neural Information Processing Systems*, volume 2. Morgan-Kaufmann.

Tom B. Brown, Benjamin Mann, Nick Ryder, Melanie Subbiah, Jared Kaplan, Prafulla Dhariwal, Arvind Neelakantan, Pranav Shyam, Girish Sastry, Amanda Askell, Sandhini Agarwal, Ariel Herbert-Voss, Gretchen Krueger, Tom Henighan, Rewon Child, Aditya Ramesh, Daniel M. Ziegler, Jeffrey Wu, Clemens Winter, Christopher Hesse, Mark Chen, Eric Sigler, Mateusz Litwin, Scott Gray, Benjamin Chess, Jack Clark, Christopher Berner, Sam McCandlish, Alec Radford, Ilya Sutskever, and Dario Amodei. 2020. Language models are few-shot learners. In *Proceedings of the 34th International Conference on Neural Information Processing Systems*, NIPS '20, Red Hook, NY, USA. Curran Associates Inc.

Jaime Carbonell and Jade Goldstein. 1998. The use of mmr, diversity-based reranking for reordering documents and producing summaries. In *Proceedings of the 21st Annual International ACM SIGIR Conference on Research and Development in Information Retrieval*, SIGIR '98, page 335–336, New York, NY, USA. Association for Computing Machinery.

[14]`https://openai.com/form/researcher-access-program/`

Jacob Devlin, Ming-Wei Chang, Kenton Lee, and Kristina Toutanova. 2019. BERT: Pre-training of deep bidirectional transformers for language understanding. In *Proceedings of the 2019 Conference of the North American Chapter of the Association for Computational Linguistics: Human Language Technologies, Volume 1 (Long and Short Papers)*, pages 4171–4186, Minneapolis, Minnesota. Association for Computational Linguistics.

Matthijs Douze, Alexandr Guzhva, Chengqi Deng, Jeff Johnson, Gergely Szilvasy, Pierre-Emmanuel Mazaré, Maria Lomeli, Lucas Hosseini, and Hervé Jégou. 2024. The faiss library.

Jan Drchal, Herbert Ullrich, Tomáš Mlynář, and Václav Moravec. 2023. Pipeline and dataset generation for automated fact-checking in almost any language.

Abhimanyu Dubey, Abhinav Jauhri, Abhinav Pandey, Abhishek Kadian, Ahmad Al-Dahle, Aiesha Letman, Akhil Mathur, Alan Schelten, Amy Yang, Angela Fan, Anirudh Goyal, Anthony Hartshorn, Aobo Yang, ..., and Zhiwei Zhao. 2024. The llama 3 herd of models.

Hervé Déjean, Stéphane Clinchant, and Thibault Formal. 2024. A thorough comparison of cross-encoders and llms for reranking splade.

Siavash Golkar, Mariel Pettee, Michael Eickenberg, Alberto Bietti, Miles Cranmer, Geraud Krawezik, Francois Lanusse, Michael McCabe, Ruben Ohana, Liam Parker, Bruno Régaldo-Saint Blancard, Tiberiu Tesileanu, Kyunghyun Cho, and Shirley Ho. 2023. xval: A continuous number encoding for large language models.

Pengcheng He, Jianfeng Gao, and Weizhu Chen. 2023. Debertav3: Improving deberta using electra-style pre-training with gradient-disentangled embedding sharing.

Israa Jaradat, Haiqi Zhang, and Chengkai Li. 2024. On context-aware detection of cherry-picking in news reporting.

Jeff Johnson, Matthijs Douze, and Hervé Jégou. 2019. Billion-scale similarity search with GPUs. *IEEE Transactions on Big Data*, 7(3):535–547.

Ankur Joshi, Saket Kale, Satish Chandel, and Dinesh Pal. 2015. Likert scale: Explored and explained. *British Journal of Applied Science & Technology*, 7:396–403.

Woosuk Kwon, Zhuohan Li, Siyuan Zhuang, Ying Sheng, Lianmin Zheng, Cody Hao Yu, Joseph Gonzalez, Hao Zhang, and Ion Stoica. 2023. Efficient memory management for large language model serving with pagedattention. In *Proceedings of the 29th Symposium on Operating Systems Principles*, SOSP '23, page 611–626, New York, NY, USA. Association for Computing Machinery.

Sean Lee, Aamir Shakir, Darius Koenig, and Julius Lipp. 2024. Open source strikes bread - new fluffy embeddings model.

Patrick Lewis, Ethan Perez, Aleksandra Piktus, Fabio Petroni, Vladimir Karpukhin, Naman Goyal, Heinrich Küttler, Mike Lewis, Wen-tau Yih, Tim Rocktäschel, Sebastian Riedel, and Douwe Kiela. 2020. Retrieval-augmented generation for knowledge-intensive nlp tasks. In *Proceedings of the 34th International Conference on Neural Information Processing Systems*, NIPS '20, Red Hook, NY, USA. Curran Associates Inc.

Xianming Li and Jing Li. 2024. AoE: Angle-optimized embeddings for semantic textual similarity. In *Proceedings of the 62nd Annual Meeting of the Association for Computational Linguistics (Volume 1: Long Papers)*, pages 1825–1839, Bangkok, Thailand. Association for Computational Linguistics.

Rensis Likert. 1932. A technique for the measurement of attitudes. *Archives of Psychology*, 22(140):55.

Jacob Menick, Maja Trebacz, Vladimir Mikulik, John Aslanides, Francis Song, Martin Chadwick, Mia Glaese, Susannah Young, Lucy Campbell-Gillingham, Geoffrey Irving, and Nat McAleese. 2022. Teaching language models to support answers with verified quotes.

Niklas Muennighoff, Nouamane Tazi, Loic Magne, and Nils Reimers. 2023. MTEB: Massive text embedding benchmark. In *Proceedings of the 17th Conference of the European Chapter of the Association for Computational Linguistics*, pages 2014–2037, Dubrovnik, Croatia. Association for Computational Linguistics.

OpenAI. 2023. What are tokens and how to count them? Accessed: 15 August 2024.

OpenAI. 2024. Introducing structured outputs in the api. Accessed: 15 August 2024.

F. Pedregosa, G. Varoquaux, A. Gramfort, V. Michel, B. Thirion, O. Grisel, M. Blondel, P. Prettenhofer, R. Weiss, V. Dubourg, J. Vanderplas, A. Passos, D. Cournapeau, M. Brucher, M. Perrot, and E. Duchesnay. 2011. Scikit-learn: Machine learning in Python. *Journal of Machine Learning Research*, 12:2825–2830.

Stephen Robertson, S. Walker, S. Jones, M. M. Hancock-Beaulieu, and M. Gatford. 1995. Okapi at trec-3. In *Overview of the Third Text REtrieval Conference (TREC-3)*.

Michael Schlichtkrull, Zhijiang Guo, and Andreas Vlachos. 2024. Averitec: a dataset for real-world claim verification with evidence from the web. In *Proceedings of the 37th International Conference on Neural Information Processing Systems*, NIPS '23, Red Hook, NY, USA. Curran Associates Inc.

Xiangru Tang, Yiming Zong, Jason Phang, Yilun Zhao, Wangchunshu Zhou, Arman Cohan, and Mark Gerstein. 2024. Struc-bench: Are large language models really good at generating complex structured data?

James Thorne, Andreas Vlachos, Christos Christodoulopoulos, and Arpit Mittal. 2018a. FEVER: a large-scale dataset for fact extraction and VERification. In *Proceedings of the 2018 Conference of the North American Chapter of the Association for Computational Linguistics: Human Language Technologies, Volume 1 (Long Papers)*, pages 809–819, New Orleans, Louisiana. Association for Computational Linguistics.

James Thorne, Andreas Vlachos, Oana Cocarascu, Christos Christodoulopoulos, and Arpit Mittal. 2018b. The fact extraction and VERification (FEVER) shared task. In *Proceedings of the First Workshop on Fact Extraction and VERification (FEVER)*, pages 1–9, Brussels, Belgium. Association for Computational Linguistics.

Herbert Ullrich, Jan Drchal, Martin Rýpar, Hana Vincourová, and Václav Moravec. 2023. Csfever and ctkfacts: acquiring czech data for fact verification. *Language Resources and Evaluation*, 57(4):1571–1605.

Jason Wei, Xuezhi Wang, Dale Schuurmans, Maarten Bosma, Brian Ichter, Fei Xia, Ed H. Chi, Quoc V. Le, and Denny Zhou. 2024. Chain-of-thought prompting elicits reasoning in large language models. In *Proceedings of the 36th International Conference on Neural Information Processing Systems*, NIPS '22, Red Hook, NY, USA. Curran Associates Inc.

Thomas Wolf, Lysandre Debut, Victor Sanh, Julien Chaumond, Clement Delangue, Anthony Moi, Pierric Cistac, Tim Rault, Remi Louf, Morgan Funtowicz, Joe Davison, Sam Shleifer, Patrick von Platen, Clara Ma, Yacine Jernite, Julien Plu, Canwen Xu, Teven Le Scao, Sylvain Gugger, Mariama Drame, Quentin Lhoest, and Alexander Rush. 2020. Transformers: State-of-the-art natural language processing. In *Proceedings of the 2020 Conference on Empirical Methods in Natural Language Processing: System Demonstrations*, pages 38–45, Online. Association for Computational Linguistics.

A System prompt

```
You are a professional fact checker, formulate up to 10 questions that cover all
  the facts needed to validate whether the factual statement (in User message) is
  true, false, uncertain or a matter of opinion. Each question has one of four
  answer types: Boolean, Extractive, Abstractive and Unanswerable using the
  provided sources.
After formulating Your questions and their answers using the provided sources, You
  evaluate the possible veracity verdicts (Supported claim, Refuted claim, Not
  enough evidence, or Conflicting evidence/Cherrypicking) given your claim and
  evidence on a Likert scale (1 - Strongly disagree, 2 - Disagree, 3 - Neutral, 4 -
  Agree, 5 - Strongly agree). Ultimately, you note the single likeliest veracity
  verdict according to your best knowledge.
The facts must be coming from these sources, please refer them using assigned IDs:
---
## Source ID: 1 [url]
[context before]
[page content]
[context after]
...

---
## Output formatting
Please, you MUST only print the output in the following output format:
```json
{
 "questions":
     [
         {"question": "<Your first question>", "answer": "<The answer to the Your
           first question>", "source": "<Single numeric source ID backing the
           answer for Your first question>", "answer_type":"<The type of first
           answer>"},
         {"question": "<Your second question>", "answer": "<The answer to the Your
           second question>", "source": "<Single numeric Source ID backing the
           answer for Your second question>", "answer_type":"<The type of second
           answer>"}
     ],
 "claim_veracity": {
     "Supported": "<Likert-scale rating of how much You agree with the 'Supported'
       veracity classification>",
     "Refuted": "<Likert-scale rating of how much You agree with the 'Refuted'
       veracity classification>",
     "Not Enough Evidence": "<Likert-scale rating of how much You agree with the
       'Not Enough Evidence' veracity classification>",
     "Conflicting Evidence/Cherrypicking": "<Likert-scale rating of how much You
       agree with the 'Conflicting Evidence/Cherrypicking' veracity classification>"
 },
 "veracity_verdict": "<The suggested veracity classification for the claim>"
}
```

Few-shot learning
You have access to the following few-shot learning examples for questions and
  answers.:

Question examples for claim "{example["claim"]}" (verdict
  {example["gold_label"]})
"question": "{question}", "answer": "{answer}", "answer_type": "{answer_type}"
...
```

Listing 1: System prompt for the LLMs, AVeriTeC claim is to be entered into the user prompt. Three dots represent omitted repeating parts of the prompt.

B Examples of errors

```
Claim 479: Donald Trump said "When the
  anarchists started ripping down our statues
  and monuments, right outside, I signed an
  order immediately, 10 years in prison."

gold evidence example:
    question: What was the law signed by Trump
      regarding damaging federal property?
    answer: Trump signed an executive order that
      authorizes a penalty of up to 10 years in
      prison for damaging federal property. It
      does not say that it will automatically be
      a 10 year prison sentence.,
    source_url: https://web.archive.org/web
      /20210224033536/https://www.whitehouse.gov/
      presidential-actions/executive-order-
      protecting-american-monuments-memorials-
      statues-combating-recent-criminal-violence/

pipeline evidence example:
    question: Did Trump sign an order related to
      vandalism of statues and monuments?,
    answer: Yes, Trump signed an executive order
      to prosecute those who damage national
      monuments, making it a punishable offense
      with up to 10 years in jail.,
    url: https://m.economictimes.com/news/
      international/world-news/trump-makes-
      vandalising-national-monuments-punishable-
      offence-with-up-to-10-yrs-jail/articleshow
      /76658610.cms
```

Listing 2: Example of a claim where our pipeline uses newspaper sources instead of official government sources.

```
Claim 295: Trump campaign asked Joe Biden to
  release a list of potential Supreme Court
  picks only after Ginsburg's passing
question 1: Did Joe Biden claim that the Trump
  campaign asked him to release a list of
  potential Supreme Court picks only after
  Ginsburg's passing?
question 2: Did the Trump campaign ask Joe Biden
   to release a list of potential Supreme Court
  picks before Ginsburg's passing?
question 3: When did Trump release his latest
  list of potential Supreme Court nominees?
question 4: Did Trump personally demand that
  Biden release a list of potential Supreme
  Court nominees before Ginsburg's death?
question 5: What did Trump say about Biden
  releasing a list of potential Supreme Court
  nominees during the Republican National
  Convention?
question 6: Did the Trump campaign issue a
  statement on September 17, 2020, regarding
  Biden releasing a list of potential Supreme
  Court nominees?
question 7: What did the Trump campaign's
  statement on September 9, 2020, say about
  Biden releasing a list of potential Supreme
  Court nominees?
question 8: Did Biden indicate in June 2020 that
   he might release a list of potential Supreme
  Court picks?
quetion 9: What reason did Biden give for not
  releasing a list of potential Supreme Court
  nominees?,
question 10: Did Biden pledge to nominate a
  Black woman to the Supreme Court?
```

Listing 3: Example of a claim and questions showing that the last tends to be unrelated or redundant to fact-checking of the claim.

```
Claim #155 - Trump said 'there were fine people
  on both side' in far-right protests.
answer: "You had some very bad people in that
  group, but you also had people that were very
  fine people, on both sides.",
answer_type: Extractive
url: https://www.theatlantic.com/politics/
  archive/2017/08/trump-defends-white-
  nationalist-protesters-some-very-fine-people-
  on-both-sides/537012/
scraped text: ... "You also had some very fine
  people on both sides," he said. The Unite the
  Right rally that sparked the violence in
  Charlottesville featured several leading names
   in the white-nationalist alt-right movement,
  and also attracted people displaying Nazi
  symbols. ...
```

Listing 4: Example of a claim where our pipeline did not exactly extract the answer.

```
Claim #483 - Donald Trump said "We have spent
  nearly $2.5 trillion on completely rebuilding
  our military, which was very badly depleted
  when I took office."
Gold Label: Not Enough Evidence
Predicted Label: Refuted
pipeline evidence example:
    question: What is the total defense budget
      for the last four fiscal years under Trump?
    url: https://www.politifact.com/factchecks
      /2020/jan/10/donald-trump/trump-exaggerates
      -spending-us-military-rebuild/
    question: Did Trump spend $2.5 trillion
      specifically on rebuilding the military?
    url: https://www.factcheck.org/2020/07/trumps
      -false-military-equipment-claim/
    ...
```

Listing 5: An example of a claim where the evidence consists mainly of evidence from PolitiFact and Factcheck.org fact-checking articles leading to different predicted label than in the gold dataset

```
Claim #0 - In a letter to Steve Jobs, Sean
  Connery refused to appear in an apple
  commercial.
Gold Evidence:
    question: Where was the claim first published
    answer: It was first published on Sccopertino
    question: What kind of website is Scoopertino
    answer: Scoopertino is an imaginary news
      organization devoted to ferreting out the
      most relevant stories in the world of Apple
      , whether or not they actually occurred -
      says their about page

Claim #315 - The fastest Supreme Court justice
  ever confirmed in the U.S. was 47 days.
Gold Evidence:
    question: What is the quickest time a Supreme
       Court justice nomination has been
      confirmed in the United States?
    answer: John Paul Stevens waited the fewest
      number of days (19)-followed by the most
      recent nominee to the Court, Amy Coney
      Barrett (27).61
    question: What is the average number of days
      between a nomination for a Supreme Court
      justice and the final Senate vote?
    answer: Overall, the average number of days
      from nomination to final Senate vote is
      68.2 days (or approximately 2.2 months),
      while the median is 69.0 days.62 Of the 9
      Justices currently serving on the Court,
      the average number of days from nomination
      to final Senate vote is 72.1 days (or
      approximately 2.4 months), while the median
       is 73.0 days. Among the current Justices,
      Amy Coney Barrett waited the fewest number
      of days from nomination to confirmation
      (27), while Clarence Thomas waited the
      greatest number of days (99).
```

Listing 6: An example of a claims which differs in length.

Enhancing Fact Verification with Causal Knowledge Graphs and Transformer-Based Retrieval for Deductive Reasoning

Fiona Anting Tan, Jay Desai, Srinivasan H Sengamedu
Amazon
{fionatan, jdesa, sengamed}@amazon.com

Abstract

The ability to extract and verify factual information from free-form text is critical in an era where vast amounts of unstructured data are available, yet unreliable sources abound. This paper focuses on enhancing causal deductive reasoning, a key component of factual verification, through the lens of accident investigation, where determining the probable causes of events is paramount.

Deductive reasoning refers to the task of drawing conclusions based on a premise. While some deductive reasoning benchmarks exist, none focus on causal deductive reasoning and are from real-world applications. Recently, large language models (LLMs) used with prompt engineering techniques like retrieval-augmented generation (RAG) have demonstrated remarkable performance across various natural language processing benchmarks. However, adapting these techniques to handle scenarios with no knowledge bases and to different data structures, such as graphs, remains an ongoing challenge. In our study, we introduce a novel framework leveraging LLMs' decent ability to detect and infer causal relations to construct a causal Knowledge Graph (KG) which represents knowledge that the LLM recognizes. Additionally, we propose a RoBERTa-based Transformer Graph Neural Network (RoTG) specifically designed to select relevant nodes within this KG. Integrating RoTG-retrieved causal chains into prompts effectively enhances LLM performance, demonstrating usefulness of our approach in advancing LLMs' causal deductive reasoning capabilities.

1 Introduction

Large language models (LLMs) have shown impressive performance on some language tasks, however, their ability to plan and reason on complex tasks remains an ongoing challenge (Wei et al., 2022; Valmeekam et al., 2023). In Psychology, the standard test for deductive reasoning consists of giving people premises and asking them to draw conclusions (Evans, 2005; Rips, 1994; Johnson-Laird, 2010). In natural language processing (NLP), RuleTaker (Clark et al., 2020) and ProofWriter (Tafjord et al., 2021) are datasets that challenge models to assign *True* or *False* labels to statements about a probable implication. However, there are no NLP benchmarks on causal deductive reasoning, where the premise are facts about an outcome and the statement is about a probable cause. Furthermore, Huang and Chang (2023); Valmeekam et al. (2022) find that current benchmarks do not truly investigate the reasoning capabilities of LLMs, because the tasks are not meaningfully applied in the real-world.

Researchers have proposed prompt engineering techniques to improve few-shot and zero-shot task performance (Reynolds and McDonell, 2021), like using role-play (Kong et al., 2023; Wang et al., 2023), in-context learning (Xie et al., 2022; Min et al., 2022), and retrieval-augmented generation (RAG) (Lewis et al., 2020; Shao et al., 2023). Recent work has explored using LLMs to retrieve a task-relevant knowledge sub-graph to support reasoning (Li et al., 2024). However, extending these techniques to handle cases where no explicit

Proceedings of the Seventh Fact Extraction and VERification Workshop (FEVER), pages 151–169
November 15, 2024 ©2024 Association for Computational Linguistics

knowledge base is available, or and how to best use knowledge graphs (KGs) in a RAG-based LLM system remains an open area for research.

This paper focuses on the causal deductive reasoning task performed by Accident Investigators. When an accident occurs, investigators conduct thorough investigations, and come up with a probable cause for the accident. Our main contributions can be summarized as follows:

- We present a task (Section 2) and dataset (Section 3) comprising 631 reports with 11,422 statements. This dataset is curated from original reports written by humans and processed using rules and Claude 2.1. It will be made publicly available.
- We introduce a framework (Figure 1) employing LLMs such as Mistral-Instruct 7B to identify causal relations for constructing a causal KG. Additionally, we trained a RoBERTa-based Transformer Graph Neural Network (RoTG) to select relevant nodes, leveraging deductive reasoning labels as an auxiliary task. (Section 4)
- We observe that incorporating causal relations retrieved from the LLM-constructed KG improves the LLM's causal deductive reasoning performance. (Section 5)

2 Causal Deductive Reasoning

Given an input context C, the goal is to identify the likelihood of a statement s_i being a probable cause of accident a. This likelihood is represented by $y_i \in (0,1)$, where $y_i = 1$ if s_i is a probable cause and $y_i = 0$ if not. The task is to determine $P(y_i|C)$ for each potential cause s_i within a report context C. Since we have multiple reports in our dataset, the objective extends to calculating $P(y_{it}|C_t)$, where t denotes the report ID. We define $G_t = F_{extract}(C_t)$ as the set of causal relations mentioned in context C_t. The function $F_{extract}(\cdot)$ extracts causal relations from the context. The aggregated set of all extracted relations from the dataset is denoted as G, representing the repository of causal relations of our dataset. Each relation in G_t is represented by a cause and effect pair, denoted as (s_i, s_j).

If a causal chain $x_{it} = (s_i, s_{j1}), (s_{j1}, s_{j2}), ..., (j_k, k) \notin G_t$, then $y_i = 0$. However, if $x_{it} \in G_t$, the rank of y_{it} relative to other potential causes y_{jt} must be considered. Only the top z rank of most important causes can be the probable cause of an accident a. In the case where we only consider the top cause ($z = 1$) as the probable cause, then the probability of $P(y_{it})$ can be reformulated into:

$$P(y_{it} = 0) = P(y_{it}|x_{it} \notin G_t) \\ +P(y_i|x_{it} \in G_t, P(y_{jt} = 1) > P(y_{it} = 1)) \tag{1}$$

$$P(y_{it} = 1) = P(y_i|x_{it} \in G_t, \\ P(y_{it} = 1) > P(y_{jt} = 1)) \tag{2}$$

Since the task is a binary classification task, every example s_{it} is not aware of the other possible s_{jt} for the same report t. Therefore, s_{jt} are causes the model implicit tracks and has to rank against for the current task. Our causal deductive task can be re-framed into two sub-challenges: (1) extracting x_{it} and identifying $x_{it} \in G_t$, and (2) implicitly ranking $P(y_{it} = 1) > P(y_{jt} = 1)$ or not.

Hypothesis 1: Generalizing causal chain to out-of-context In the first challenge, extracting x_{it} and identifying $x_{it} \in G_t$, restricting the knowledge source to a report results in a high chance for there to be gaps in the causal chain. All else fixed, $P(y_{it}|x_{it} \notin G_t)$ will be overestimated (i.e., model predicts more 0s than 1s). If are willing to relax our criteria to check if $s_i \in C_t$ and $x_{it} \in G$, then we are allowing our model to generalize to its own knowledge base, to recognize more valid causal chains, and therefore, increase the probability of predicting $P(y_{it} = 1)$. When working with LLMs, therefore, we could inject causal relations outside of G_t but semantically part of x_{it} to improve prediction.

Hypothesis 2: Ranking importance of cause within context If the LLM is exposed to too many relevant causal relations in the prompt, it would hallucinate and start to always view s_i as the most important probable cause (over other possible options in C_t). However, we do not know z. In some reports, there are a few probable causes. One approach is to explicitly expose the LLM to the available causes in the report, so that we re-ground the response, and in some way, a ranking based on context is encouraged.

3 Dataset & Task Creation

We wish to investigate the LLMs' ability to perform a real-world causal deductive reasoning task.

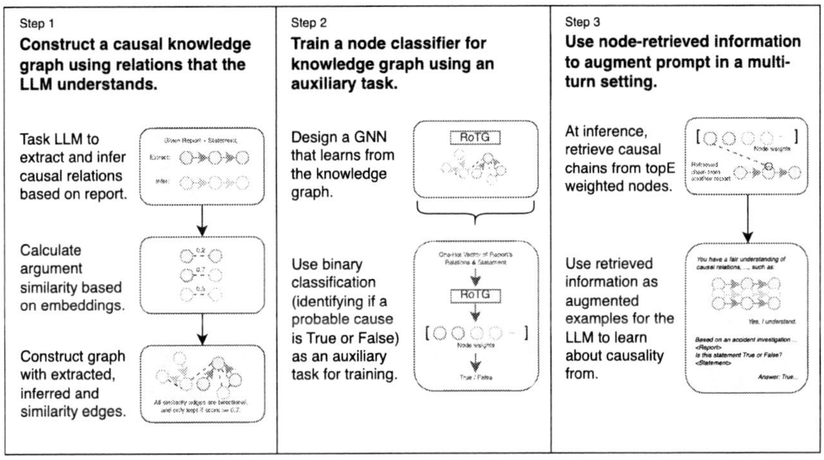

Figure 1: Overview of our proposed methodology. Detailed infographic is available in Appendix Figure 4.

Given an accident description (<CONTEXT>), the model must determine if a sentence about the probable cause of the accident (<STATEMENT>) is *True* or *False*. To facilitate our research, we leverage on reasoning-rich investigation reports from the National Transportation Safety Board (NTSB) [1]. NTSB publishes Accident Reports that provides details about an accident, analysis of the factual data, conclusions and the probable cause of the accident, and the related safety recommendations. There can be one or multiple probable cause(s). We downloaded reports published after Year 2000, across all reported categories (Aviation, Hazardous Materials, Highway, Marine, Pipeline and Railroad).

Report pre-processing Pre-processing was done to convert the PDF reports to JSON, and subsequently, we removed information like headers, page numbers, and table of contents. We identified the probable cause of the accident by searching for the title "Probable Cause". We discarded reports where this match was impossible. Any text before this section is defined as the <CONTEXT>. In our experiments, we constrained our coverage to 157 reports where the context length is $\leq 2,000$ words.

Extracting *True* statements Trailing descriptions in the probable cause were removed. [2] We used Anthropic's Claude 2.1[3] to convert the paragraphs into a list of probable causes. Prompt 1 in Appendix outlines the one-shot prompt template that we used. We manually annotated four examples to measure the extraction performance, of which we found ROUGEL score of 87.46 and BLEU4 score of 75.02. When evaluating by semantic match[4] with a threshold of ≥ 0.7 as a match, Claude 2.1 scored 100% for Recall, 72.92% for Precision, and 84.34% for F1. To summarize, the high scores for the evaluated sample provides us with the confidence to reliably use the extracted probable causes as *True* instances for our main causal deductive task.

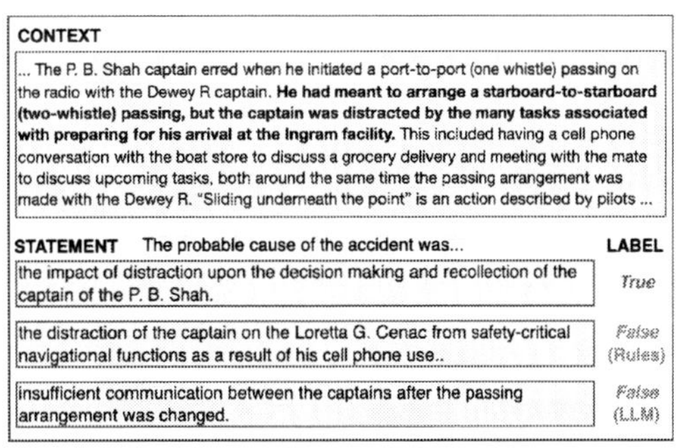

Figure 2: An example report from our dataset.

Generating *False* statements False examples were generated by two methods: (1) rule-based, and (2) LLM-based methods. For rule-based, each

[1]https://www.ntsb.gov/investigations/AccidentReports/Pages/Reports.aspx

[2]E.g. Descriptions unrelated to the cause (E.g. "*The National Transportation Safety Board determines that the*") were removed.

[3]We intentionally used an LLM different from Mistral when creating our dataset to avoid cases where the LLM recognizes its own phrasing or terms.

[4]We encoded each probable cause item into an embedding using the princeton-nlp/sup-simcse-roberta-large encoder (Gao et al., 2021) that was pre-trained on the Natural Language Inference task. Link to their repository: https://github.com/princeton-nlp/SimCSE.

Processing	#Docs	#Statement	#*True*	#*False*	*True* %
Total NTSB	631	11,422	1300	10,122	11.38%
≤ 2000 words	157	2,523	243	2,280	9.63%
Success CRE	**133**	**1,677**	**155**	**1,522**	**9.24%**

Table 1: Data sizes at each filtering stage. The last row represents the working dataset for this paper after successful causal relation extraction (CRE). Our experiments are conducted using 10-folds CV, and the test data sizes per fold are provided in Appendix Table 6.

True statement was matched to three similar-but-not-too-similar statements are generated as negative examples. The degree of similarity between the *False* examples and the *True* statement was controlled to ensure that false examples are plausible but distinct from the true statement, with similarity scores ranging from 0.5 to 0.75. This approach aims to provide a challenging set of false examples for participants to evaluate. For LLM-based, we used Claude 2.1 (See Prompt 2 in the Appendix) to generate a list of 10 possible causes or contributing causes investigated within the context that are not stated as the final true probable cause.

Our task aims to provide a comprehensive evaluation of participants' ability to perform the challenging causal deductive reasoning task. Table 1[5] presents the statistics for our dataset. After keeping examples that we could extract causal relations described in the next section, our main dataset comprises of 133 reports and 1,677 statements. Of which, 155 are *True* while the remaining 1,522 are *False* probable cause statements. An example report is shown in Figure 2.

3.1 Evaluation Metrics

For each experiment, we report Macro F1, Micro F1 and the accuracy scores for each class label and label source. Since our dataset is small, we used a 10-fold cross validation (split by report ID) to train and generate predictions for the full dataset. Therefore, our evaluation metrics are first computed at the fold level, then averaged, where both the mean and standard deviations of each metric are reported. When making comparisons between two models, P-values are indicated by: *$<$ 0.15, **$<$ 0.10, ***$<$ 0.05.

4 Causal KG RAG with LLM

We mentioned in Section 2 that we wish to help the LLM recognize generalized $(j_a, j_b) \in D$ by injecting relevant causal relations outside of G_t. However, we do not have a knowledge base for G. We also do not have any annotations for the intermediate causal chains that might be relevant given a probable cause i and accident a. To work around these problems, we constructed our knowledge base using the LLM itself. Afterwhich, we designed a novel graph-based retriever model, trained on the auxiliary binary classification task, to select relevant nodes.

4.1 Step 1. Mining LLM's Latent Causal KG

We wish to investigate properties regarding Equations 1 and 2. However, we do not have a knowledge base. Therefore, we separately tasked the LLM to mine the causal relations it recognizes and understands. Specifically, we mined two types of causal relations:

Extracted causal relations We tasked the LLM to extract all causal relations expressed within the <CONTEXT>. Prompt 3 in the Appendix outlines our zero-shot prompt, with only instructions about the desired output format.

Inferred causal relations We tasked the LLM to infer the chain of causal relations that could possibly link the cause stated within the <STATEMENT> to the accident stated within the <CONTEXT>. Prompt 4 in the Appendix outlines our zero-shot prompt, with only instructions about the desired output format. The causal chains from this step can be viewed as the LLM's hallucinated version of x_{it}.

Causal KG To maximize the size of our knowledge store, we constructed our heterogeneous causal knowledge based on a slightly larger dataset of 157 reports and 2,523 statements, which provided us with 4,128 extracted cause-effect pairs and 22,685 inferred cause-effect pairs. Reports with contexts longer than 2,000 words did not fit into our models' input context, so we did not explore the full dataset, although it would be an important future work to extend the size of the knowledge store further.

Our KG $G = (V, E)$ is a collection of nodes $V = \{(v_1, v_2, ..., v_n)\}$ and directed edges $E = \{(v_1, v_2), (v_2, v_3), ...\}$. The edges are directed, and comprises of three possible types: extracted, inferred, or similar. For extracted and inferred relations, a directed edge (v_x, v_y) represents the presence of causality between the two nodes, where v_x is the cause argument and v_y is the effect ar-

[5] We will release the full dataset of 11,422 statements to the community.

gument. To prevent a sparse graph, prior causal KG research employ various clustering (Tan et al., 2023) or generalization (Radinsky et al., 2012) methods to group semantically similar arguments together. For us, we opted for a simple (and shown to be effective in Section 5.1) approach by adding bidirectional edges between two nodes v_x and v_y, weighted by the similarity score ss, for all node pairs with similarity score $ss > 0.7$. Overall, our final G is a collection of 16,675 nodes and 23,493 edges. The distribution of edge types are: 1,822 extracted, 11,399 inferred, and 10,272 similar.

4.2 Step 2. Node Selection over Causal KG

We re-frame our retrieval task as a node classification task: Given a causal KG, we wish to extract the most important and relevant nodes (arguments) to include in our downstream prompt. Since we have no labels as to what helps the LLM learn, we used the the binary classification task (to classify if a <STATEMENT> is *True* or *False*) as an auxiliary task to train our model. The model is encouraged to learn from the KG, and at inference, we discard the classification head and keep top-E nodes with highest node weights as pointers to obtain information for RAG.

Our retriever module uses a RoBERTa-based Transformer GNN (RoTG) framework. Since a traditional RoBERTa model (Liu et al., 2019)'s input token limit of 512 is too small for our reports, we designed a workaround that does not require the long <CONTEXT> sequences as inputs. Our model is trained only by the following inputs: (1) Encoded <STATEMENT> (r_i represents the [CLS] token vector with e features) and (2) A one-hot encoded vector (oh) assigned to each node if the span does appear in the extracted or inferred causal relations (1 if appear, 0 otherwise).

Node classification module Our initial node features were represented by Q_1, an attended representation of Q'_1. Q'_1 is a concatenation of the RoBERTa-encoded frozen embeddings for each node description s (R is a $n \times e$ matrix comprising of n nodes, an input that does not change over training) and the two one-hot vectors ($oh_{\text{extr}}, oh_{\text{inf}}$) indicating if the node was extracted or inferred based on the context and target statement or not. The attention mechanism then computes the attention weights between the node features Q'_1 and the target statement embedding r_i to generate the cross-attended node feature matrix Q. Since our graph is heterogeneous, we require message passing across edge features. Hence, we employed the Transformer (Vaswani et al., 2017) Graph Convolutional Network (TransformerGCN) (Shi et al., 2021), which helps to incorporate edge features into the multi-head attention for graph learning. The architecture of TransformerGCN is outlined in Appendix Section D.1.

$$r_i = \text{RoBERTa}(s_i) \tag{3}$$

$$R = \text{RoBERTa}(S) \tag{4}$$

$$Q'_1 = [R, oh_{\text{extr}}, oh_{\text{inf}}] \tag{5}$$

$$Q_1 = \text{Attention}(Q'_1, r_i, r_i) \tag{6}$$

$$ow_i = \text{TransformerGCN}(G_{(Q_1,E)}) \tag{7}$$

Auxiliary task training We multiplied the local graph weights ow_i onto the global node embeddings R, obtaining our node embeddings Q_2 that are now customized for our inputs. We proceeded with another round of message passing using TransformerGCN over our global graph, and obtained a vector representing the scores each node contributes (nw_i). We incorporated a skip-connection by concatenating nw_i with the original statement embedding r_i and applied dropout and layer normalization layers to get o_i. Subsequently, we ran o_i through multiple rounds of Linear layers, with LeakyReLU in between. In the last layer, we used a Linear layer with output dimension of 2 to obtain logits for our binary classification task.

$$ow'_i = \text{topKGating}(ow_i) \tag{8}$$

$$Q_2 = ow'_i R \tag{9}$$

$$nw_i = \text{TransformerGCN}(G_{(Q_2,E)}) \tag{10}$$

$$o_i = \text{LayerNorm}(\text{Dropout}([r_i, nw_i])) \tag{11}$$

$$o_i^{(l+1)} = W^{(l)} o_i^{(l)} + b^{(l)} \tag{12}$$

Each model was trained for 8 epochs, with an effective batch size of 8. Since our dataset is extremely unbalanced ($\backsim$9% *True* only), we also balanced class labels by oversampling *True* examples, such that the ratio is 1:2 for *True*:*False*, then included the post-oversampling class weights into the CrossEntropyLoss function. Model specifics are provided in Appendix Section B.

4.3 Step 3. Prompt Engineering with LLM

During inference, we selected the top-E nodes with the highest scores based on node weights, ow_i. Subsequently, we obtained the nodes' original reports' extracted or inferred causal chains, then kept

	Macro F1	Micro F1	Accuracy		
			True	*False* (Rules)	*False* (LLM)
All	55.43 (6.09)	**83.96 (9.07)**	31.01 (31.19)	**67.44 (34.41)**	**99.45 (0.86)**
Similarity Only	**56.97 (6.05)**	82.75 (8.39)	34.70 (26.65)	66.77 (25.59)	98.14 (5.22)
Causality Only	56.90 (6.62)	81.48 (9.35)	**39.56 (30.79)**	60.62 (30.83)	97.92 (5.63)

Table 2: RoTG classification performance when trained over different edges types in G. Highest score per column is in bold. All scores are not statistically significant from the first row.

Relations Retrieved	Macro F1	Micro F1	Accuracy		
			True	*False* (Rules)	*False* (LLM)
None	70.36 (7.07)	90.30 (1.78)	46.53 (13.21)	92.23 (3.66)	95.69 (1.86)
Semantic	72.50 (6.37)	91.24 (1.40)	48.72 (11.04)	92.99 (2.48)	**96.54 (1.93)**
RoTG	**73.19 (7.01)**	**91.65 (1.42)****	**49.49 (13.47)**	**94.31 (3.49)**	96.37 (1.37)

Table 3: Mistral Instruct with *None*, Semantic, and RoTG (Ours) retrieval-augmented relations. Highest score per column is in bold. P-values against *None* scores indicated by: *< 0.15, **< 0.10, ***< 0.05.

all chains that contain the node span. We investigated 9 distinct prompt formats (see Prompts 5 to 13 in the Appendix), incorporating variations of retrieved, extracted, and inferred causal relations. Our best-performing prompt format (Prompt 10) consists of retrieved information that were presented as a multi-turn prompt: Initially, retrieved relations were introduced to the model. Next, we set the models' response to be "*Yes I understand.*". Finally, a description of the task followed in the subsequent reply. We found that including the retrieved information in the same responses as the task description led to poor performance.

All relations underwent post-processing to remove similar causal chains, defined by a Levenshtein ratio ≥ 0.8, with duplicates resolved by retaining only the first instance. Additionally, we limited each relation type to the first 10 rows of causal chains. Subsequent experiments revealed that such cleaning procedures enhanced the model's F1 scores. We categorized a model response as *False* if the word "False" appeared in any part of the response, and *True* otherwise. Due to the length of the reports, particularly when utilizing Mistral as our LLM, in-context learning was not feasible. Consequently, all experiments were conducted in a zero-shot manner.

5 Experimental Findings

This paper focuses the investigation on the Mistral-Instruct 7B LLM (Jiang et al., 2023). We used Mistral to extract and infer causal relations for our KG as described in Section 4.1, then trained RoTG over this KG as described in Section 4.2. Finally, we tested Mistral on the causal deductive reasoning task as described by Section 4.3.

5.1 Auxiliary Task Performance

Investigating RoTG's performance on the causal deductive task serves as a proxy of how helpful would the LLM's latent causal KG be for this task. From the first row of Table 2, we notice that RoTG achieves reasonable Macro F1 score of 55.43%. The model performs very well on identifying LLM-generated *False* statements, but struggle with semantically similar *False* statements. We wish to understand if our task can be performed without understanding causality in the first place. To investigate this, we destroyed all causal edges in G, and retrained the model on the task. Interestingly, we find that all scores decline from the initial baseline, but not by too much. This suggests that while causal edges are still important to the task, as long as some understanding of similarity between events in a KG exists, models can still perform the task. Conversely, we wish to understand the importance of our similarity edges. When we destroyed similar-type edges, we noticed a significant increase in the accuracy for the *True* prediction (along with the fall in accuracy for *False* prediction). Without similarity edges, the model focuses only on causal edges and in return, over-weighs the probability of a causal statement. To conclude this subsection, RoTG demonstrates that we can perform the causal deductive task reasonably well by only relying on extracted and inferred causal relations from LLM. This presents us with a lower bound of what the LLM can understand. In Appendix Section D.3, we investigated RoTG's performance across different K values. We found that a concave relationship across top-K and F1 scores, but the differences are not statistically significant when comparing

$K = 4,096$ to $K = 8,192$ or more.

5.2 LLM's Deductive Reasoning Performance

In this section, we directly test the LLM on the causal deductive reasoning task. Table 3 presents the main findings while the full findings are available in Appendix Table 8. Our proposed RoTG method (73.19% Macro F1 and 91.65% Micro F1) outperforms the baseline (70.36% Macro F1 and 90.30% Micro F1) and also improved the LLM's accuracy for all class labels. The improvement for Micro F1 is statistically significant with P-value < 0.10. To provide an alternative baseline, we retrieved semantically similar causal relations for every causal relation extracted or inferred in a report. We encoded arguments (Cause span and Effect span) using `sentence-transformers/all-mpnet-base-v2` then did vector embedding search using FaissSearcher (Douze et al., 2024). Similar truncation and cleaning procedures were done as per RoTG. Mistral's performance also improves when we inject these semantic causal relations, however, the improvement is slightly smaller than ours and unlike ours, is not statistically significant.

5.2.1 Which types of causal relations help?

In Hypothesis 1 of Section 2, we hypothesized that injecting causal relations outside of G_t but semantically part of x_{it} would improve prediction, or at least increase the likelihood of predicting *True*. Apart from exposing the model to semantic or RoTG relations, which both increased accuracy of *True* (46.53% (Row 1) compared to 48.72% (Row 5) and 49.49% (Row 7) in Table 4), we could also inject the inferred causal relations in the prompt. As expected, the accuracy for *True* in the baseline model increases to 55.99% (Row 3).

However, consistent with Hypothesis 2 of Section 2, accuracy for *False* falls significantly. This fall is slightly mitigated if we inject the extracted causal relations alongside the inferred causal relations (Row 4), supporting our grounding hypothesis. With either semantic or RoTG retrieved relations, injecting extracted relations have a negligible effect, suggesting when relations out of G_t are shown, hallucination is less of an issue, and grounding is unnecessary.

Overall, we find that we need to expose the LLM to relevant causal relations outside of the report's relations G_t to increase accuracy of *True* predictions (Hypothesis 1). However, if the inferred relations are included (relations partially in G_t, partially not), LLMs might take the provided causal chains to be the truth, and so grounding becomes helpful (Hypothesis 2). The best balance between the two would be to incorporate retrieved relations (relations $\notin G_t$), so that the model can better focus on learning about causality instead of being confused by the truthfulness of the given chain.

5.2.2 Does the number and quality of RoTG relations matter?

We described our post-processing steps for causal relations in Section 4.3. In Table 5, we investigate if we do not truncate to first 10 causal relations (No truncate), and if we do not post-process at all (No cleaning). In general, we did not find lower statistically significantly different scores. For the RoTG relations only prompt, the LLM performed best with truncation and de-duplication. For the RoTG and extracted relations prompt, the LLM performed best if we do not clean the RoTG relations. This again suggests that ensuring more retrieved relations outside of C_t, as opposed to re-exposing the model to relations from C_t, are more helpful.

5.2.3 Investigating the generation probability

We investigated the generation probabilities of the model by tracking the logits of the "True" and "False" token at the first utterance of the "True" / "False" token. We comparing the model with and without our RoTG relations, and notice that for the 1446 examples where both models correctly predicted *False*, our RoTG model returned an average *False* probability of 3.39%, while the baseline model had a probability of 2.07%. Meanwhile, for the 69 examples where both models correctly predicted *True*, our RoTG model returned an average *True* probability of 47.02%, while the baseline model had a probability of 35.60%. There are two interesting findings from here: (1) Apart from returning a higher F1, incorporating RoTG-relations helps the model become more confident in its predictions for the overlapping correct examples. (2) On average, we found that it takes the model a much higher probability to generate the *True* token than it takes for it to generate the *False* token. When models generate *True*, the next most likely word is almost always *False*. Meanwhile, for *False* predictions, the probabilities are small and more spread across all possible tokens in the models' dictionary. More investigation is needed to explain why this is the case.

S/N	Relations			Macro F1	Micro F1	Accuracy		
	Extract	Infer	Retrieved			*True*	*False* (Rules)	*False* (LLM)
1			*None*	70.36 (7.07)	90.30 (1.78)	46.53 (13.21)	92.23 (3.66)	95.69 (1.86)
2	✓		*None*	72.42 (7.19)	90.59 (2.52)	52.62 (13.79)	91.73 (4.22)	95.60 (2.06)
3		✓	*None*	63.97 (4.87)***	83.15 (2.85)***	**55.99 (11.38)***	78.56 (4.79)***	89.03 (4.35)***
4	✓	✓	*None*	63.66 (5.31)***	84.10 (2.53)***	50.36 (12.18)	80.12 (4.66)***	90.65 (3.38)***
5			Semantic	72.50 (6.37)	91.24 (1.40)	48.72 (11.04)	92.99 (2.48)	96.54 (1.93)
6	✓		Semantic	70.97 (4.69)	90.67 (2.11)	45.54 (7.10)	91.70 (4.21)	96.91 (1.89)
7	✓	✓	Semantic	64.48 (6.02)***	86.83 (2.27)***	41.81 (12.63)	86.19 (4.56)***	93.59 (2.44)***
8			RoTG	**73.19 (7.01)**	**91.65 (1.42)**	49.49 (13.47)	**94.31 (3.49)**	96.37 (1.37)
9	✓		RoTG	71.15 (6.40)	91.09 (2.14)	44.07 (10.02)	93.43 (3.89)	**97.02 (1.63)**
10	✓	✓	RoTG	64.21 (7.89)***	87.28 (3.23)***	37.98 (13.90)**	87.21 (4.02)***	94.46 (2.79)**

Table 4: Mistral Instruct with various relations included into prompt. Highest score per column is in bold. P-values against scores from the first row per line-separated section is indicated by: *< 0.15, **< 0.10, ***< 0.05.

Retrieved Processing	Relations Extracted	Macro F1	Micro F1	Accuracy		
				True	*False* (Rules)	*False*
		73.19 (7.01)	**91.65 (1.42)**	**49.49 (13.47)**	**94.31 (3.49)**	96.37 (1.37)
No truncate		72.92 (6.43)	91.60 (1.11)	48.87 (12.59)	93.75 (3.24)	96.66 (1.04)
No cleaning		71.93 (5.57)	91.19 (1.37)	46.53 (8.61)	94.01 (3.72)	96.38 (1.03)
	✓	71.15 (6.40)	91.09 (2.14)	44.07 (10.02)	93.43 (3.89)	97.02 (1.63)
No truncate	✓	70.96 (6.69)	90.95 (2.07)	44.50 (11.16)	93.43 (3.89)	96.73 (1.70)
No cleaning	✓	71.52 (5.94)	91.12 (2.16)	45.04 (9.33)	93.28 (4.17)	**97.13 (1.38)**

Table 5: Mistral Instruct with RoTG retrieval-augmented relations post-processed using three strategies: (1) With truncation (first 10) and de-duplication, (2) Without truncation but with de-duplication, (3) Without truncation and without de-duplication. Highest score per column is in bold.

6 Related Work

Our dataset and task is most relevant to the deductive reasoning NLP literature, like efforts by RuleTaker (Clark et al., 2020) and ProofWriter (Tafjord et al., 2021). Different from them, our dataset is a real-world deductive reasoning task about accident investigations, and dive deep into the causal aspect. Huang and Chang (2023); Valmeekam et al. (2022) stated that current reasoning benchmarks are not meaningfully applied in the real-world. Thus, we hope that our dataset and work alleviates this gap in the literature.

Our methodology is relevant to literature on RAG for LLMs (Gao et al., 2024). However, due to the nature of causal relations in our task, we focus on retrieval techniques over a graph. Thus, we were also inspired by prior research on retrieval on KGs (Liu et al., 2018; Reinanda et al., 2020) and on node classification (Shi et al., 2021; Xiao et al., 2022). Since encoding graph structured data for LLMs is also an ongoing research (Fatemi et al., 2023; Perozzi et al., 2024), more investigations on how to best present the causal chains in the prompts are needed. Different from previous works, we investigate how to leverage on knowledge already present in the dataset (extract) and within the LLMs (infer) to improve performance, instead of relying on external databases that many RAG methodologies focus on.

7 Conclusion

Our study addresses the challenging task of causal deductive reasoning, particularly within the context of real-world Accident Investigation reports. Firstly, we introduced a framework that constructs a causal KG based on what LLMs' can extract and infer. Secondly, we proposed RoTG, trained to select relevant nodes, utilizing deductive reasoning labels as an auxiliary task. Our experiments demonstrate that incorporating RoTG relations into the prompt enhances the performance of LLMs (from 70.36% (90.30%) to 73.19% (91.65%) Macro (Micro) F1), highlighting the effectiveness of integrating graph-based retrieved relations in improving LLMs' causal deductive reasoning abilities. Lastly, our dataset will be released and will be a valuable resource for researchers. Overall, our study advances the understanding and application of deductive reasoning tasks in NLP, specifically in the domain of KG-based RAG for LLMs.

References

Peter Clark, Oyvind Tafjord, and Kyle Richardson. 2020. Transformers as Soft Reasoners over Language. In *Proceedings of the Twenty-Ninth International Joint Conference on Artificial Intelligence, IJCAI 2020*, Christian Bessiere (Ed.). ijcai.org, 3882–3890. https://doi.org/10.24963/IJCAI.2020/537

Matthijs Douze, Alexandr Guzhva, Chengqi Deng, Jeff Johnson, Gergely Szilvasy, Pierre-Emmanuel Mazaré, Maria Lomeli, Lucas Hosseini, and Hervé Jégou. 2024. The Faiss library. (2024). arXiv:2401.08281 [cs.LG]

JSBT Evans. 2005. Deductive reasoning. *The Cambridge handbook of thinking and reasoning* (2005), 169–184.

Bahare Fatemi, Jonathan Halcrow, and Bryan Perozzi. 2023. Talk like a Graph: Encoding Graphs for Large Language Models. arXiv:2310.04560 [cs.LG]

Tianyu Gao, Xingcheng Yao, and Danqi Chen. 2021. SimCSE: Simple Contrastive Learning of Sentence Embeddings. In *Proceedings of the 2021 Conference on Empirical Methods in Natural Language Processing*. Association for Computational Linguistics, Online and Punta Cana, Dominican Republic, 6894–6910. https://doi.org/10.18653/v1/2021.emnlp-main.552

Yunfan Gao, Yun Xiong, Xinyu Gao, Kangxiang Jia, Jinliu Pan, Yuxi Bi, Yi Dai, Jiawei Sun, Qianyu Guo, Meng Wang, and Haofen Wang. 2024. Retrieval-Augmented Generation for Large Language Models: A Survey. arXiv:2312.10997 [cs.CL]

Jie Huang and Kevin Chen-Chuan Chang. 2023. Towards Reasoning in Large Language Models: A Survey. In *Findings of the Association for Computational Linguistics: ACL 2023*, Anna Rogers, Jordan Boyd-Graber, and Naoaki Okazaki (Eds.). Association for Computational Linguistics, Toronto, Canada, 1049–1065. https://doi.org/10.18653/v1/2023.findings-acl.67

Albert Q. Jiang, Alexandre Sablayrolles, Arthur Mensch, Chris Bamford, Devendra Singh Chaplot, Diego de Las Casas, Florian Bressand, Gianna Lengyel, Guillaume Lample, Lucile Saulnier, Lélio Renard Lavaud, Marie-Anne Lachaux, Pierre Stock, Teven Le Scao, Thibaut Lavril, Thomas Wang, Timothée Lacroix, and William El Sayed. 2023. Mistral 7B. *CoRR* abs/2310.06825 (2023). https://doi.org/10.48550/ARXIV.2310.06825 arXiv:2310.06825

Phil Johnson-Laird. 2010. Deductive reasoning. *Wiley Interdisciplinary Reviews: Cognitive Science* 1, 1 (2010), 8–17.

Aobo Kong, Shiwan Zhao, Hao Chen, Qicheng Li, Yong Qin, Ruiqi Sun, and Xin Zhou. 2023. Better Zero-Shot Reasoning with Role-Play Prompting. *CoRR* abs/2308.07702 (2023). https://doi.org/10.48550/ARXIV.2308.07702 arXiv:2308.07702

Patrick S. H. Lewis, Ethan Perez, Aleksandra Piktus, Fabio Petroni, Vladimir Karpukhin, Naman Goyal, Heinrich Küttler, Mike Lewis, Wen-tau Yih, Tim Rocktäschel, Sebastian Riedel, and Douwe Kiela. 2020. Retrieval-Augmented Generation for Knowledge-Intensive NLP Tasks. In *Advances in Neural Information Processing Systems 33: Annual Conference on Neural Information Processing Systems 2020, NeurIPS 2020, December 6-12, 2020, virtual*, Hugo Larochelle, Marc'Aurelio Ranzato, Raia Hadsell, Maria-Florina Balcan, and Hsuan-Tien Lin (Eds.). https://proceedings.neurips.cc/paper/2020/hash/6b493230205f780e1bc26945df7481e5-Abstract.html

Yihao Li, Ru Zhang, Jianyi Liu, and Gongshen Liu. 2024. An Enhanced Prompt-Based LLM Reasoning Scheme via Knowledge Graph-Integrated Collaboration. arXiv:2402.04978 [cs.CL]

Yinhan Liu, Myle Ott, Naman Goyal, Jingfei Du, Mandar Joshi, Danqi Chen, Omer Levy, Mike Lewis, Luke Zettlemoyer, and Veselin Stoyanov. 2019. RoBERTa: A Robustly Optimized BERT Pretraining Approach. *CoRR* abs/1907.11692 (2019). arXiv:1907.11692 http://arxiv.org/abs/1907.11692

Zhenghao Liu, Chenyan Xiong, Maosong Sun, and Zhiyuan Liu. 2018. Entity-Duet Neural Ranking: Understanding the Role of Knowledge Graph Semantics in Neural Information Retrieval. In *Proceedings of the 56th Annual Meeting of the Association for Computational Linguistics, ACL 2018, Melbourne, Australia, July 15-20, 2018, Volume 1: Long Papers*, Iryna Gurevych and Yusuke Miyao (Eds.). Association for Computational Linguistics, 2395–2405. https://doi.org/10.18653/V1/P18-1223

Sewon Min, Xinxi Lyu, Ari Holtzman, Mikel Artetxe, Mike Lewis, Hannaneh Hajishirzi, and Luke Zettlemoyer. 2022. Rethinking the Role of Demonstrations: What Makes In-Context Learning Work?. In *Proceedings of the 2022 Conference on Empirical Methods in Natural Language Processing, EMNLP 2022, Abu Dhabi, United Arab Emirates, December 7-11, 2022*, Yoav Goldberg, Zornitsa Kozareva, and Yue Zhang (Eds.). Association for Computational Linguistics, 11048–11064. https://doi.org/10.18653/V1/2022.EMNLP-MAIN.759

Bryan Perozzi, Bahare Fatemi, Dustin Zelle, Anton Tsitsulin, Mehran Kazemi, Rami Al-Rfou, and Jonathan Halcrow. 2024. Let Your Graph Do the Talking: Encoding Structured Data for LLMs. arXiv:2402.05862 [cs.LG]

Kira Radinsky, Sagie Davidovich, and Shaul Markovitch. 2012. Learning causality for news events prediction. In *Proceedings of the 21st World Wide Web Conference 2012, WWW 2012, Lyon, France, April 16-20, 2012*, Alain Mille, Fabien Gandon, Jacques Misselis, Michael Rabinovich, and Steffen Staab (Eds.). ACM, 909–918. https://doi.org/10.1145/2187836.2187958

Ridho Reinanda, Edgar Meij, and Maarten de Rijke. 2020. Knowledge Graphs: An Information Retrieval Perspective. *Found. Trends Inf. Retr.* 14, 4 (2020), 289–444. https://doi.org/10.1561/1500000063

Laria Reynolds and Kyle McDonell. 2021. Prompt Programming for Large Language Models: Beyond the Few-Shot Paradigm. In *CHI '21: CHI Conference on Human Factors in Computing Systems, Virtual Event / Yokohama Japan, May 8-13, 2021, Extended Abstracts*, Yoshifumi Kitamura, Aaron Quigley, Katherine Isbister, and Takeo Igarashi (Eds.). ACM, 314:1–314:7. https://doi.org/10.1145/3411763.3451760

Lance J Rips. 1994. *The psychology of proof: Deductive reasoning in human thinking.* Mit Press.

Zhihong Shao, Yeyun Gong, Yelong Shen, Minlie Huang, Nan Duan, and Weizhu Chen. 2023. Enhancing Retrieval-Augmented Large Language Models with Iterative Retrieval-Generation Synergy. In *Findings of the Association for Computational Linguistics: EMNLP 2023, Singapore, December 6-10, 2023*, Houda Bouamor, Juan Pino, and Kalika Bali (Eds.). Association for Computational Linguistics, 9248–9274. https://aclanthology.org/2023.findings-emnlp.620

Yunsheng Shi, Zhengjie Huang, Shikun Feng, Hui Zhong, Wenjing Wang, and Yu Sun. 2021. Masked Label Prediction: Unified Message Passing Model for Semi-Supervised Classification. In *Proceedings of the Thirtieth International Joint Conference on Artificial Intelligence, IJCAI 2021, Virtual Event / Montreal, Canada, 19-27 August 2021*, Zhi-Hua Zhou (Ed.). ijcai.org, 1548–1554. https://doi.org/10.24963/IJCAI.2021/214

Oyvind Tafjord, Bhavana Dalvi, and Peter Clark. 2021. ProofWriter: Generating Implications, Proofs, and Abductive Statements over Natural Language. In *Findings of the Association for Computational Linguistics: ACL/IJCNLP 2021, Online Event, August 1-6, 2021 (Findings of ACL, Vol. ACL/IJCNLP 2021)*, Chengqing Zong, Fei Xia, Wenjie Li, and Roberto Navigli (Eds.). Association for Computational Linguistics, 3621–3634. https://doi.org/10.18653/V1/2021.FINDINGS-ACL.317

Fiona Anting Tan, Debdeep Paul, Sahim Yamaura, Miura Koji, and See-Kiong Ng. 2023. Constructing and Interpreting Causal Knowledge Graphs from News. *CoRR* abs/2305.09359 (2023). https://doi.org/10.48550/ARXIV.2305.09359 arXiv:2305.09359

Karthik Valmeekam, Alberto Olmo Hernandez, Sarath Sreedharan, and Subbarao Kambhampati. 2022. Large Language Models Still Can't Plan (A Benchmark for LLMs on Planning and Reasoning about Change). *CoRR* abs/2206.10498 (2022). https://doi.org/10.48550/ARXIV.2206.10498 arXiv:2206.10498

Karthik Valmeekam, Matthew Marquez, Alberto Olmo, Sarath Sreedharan, and Subbarao Kambhampati. 2023. PlanBench: An Extensible Benchmark for Evaluating Large Language Models on Planning and Reasoning about Change. arXiv:2206.10498 [cs.CL]

Ashish Vaswani, Noam Shazeer, Niki Parmar, Jakob Uszkoreit, Llion Jones, Aidan N. Gomez, Lukasz Kaiser, and Illia Polosukhin. 2017. Attention is All you Need. In *Advances in Neural Information Processing Systems 30: Annual Conference on Neural Information Processing Systems 2017, December 4-9, 2017, Long Beach, CA, USA*, Isabelle Guyon, Ulrike von Luxburg, Samy Bengio, Hanna M. Wallach, Rob Fergus, S. V. N. Vishwanathan, and Roman Garnett (Eds.). 5998–6008. https://proceedings.neurips.cc/paper/2017/hash/3f5ee243547dee91fbd053c1c4a845aa-Abstract.html

Zekun Moore Wang, Zhongyuan Peng, Haoran Que, Jiaheng Liu, Wangchunshu Zhou, Yuhan Wu, Hongcheng Guo, Ruitong Gan, Zehao Ni, Man Zhang, Zhaoxiang Zhang, Wanli Ouyang, Ke Xu, Wenhu Chen, Jie Fu, and Junran Peng. 2023. RoleLLM: Benchmarking, Eliciting, and Enhancing Role-Playing Abilities of Large Language Models. *CoRR* abs/2310.00746 (2023). https://doi.org/10.48550/ARXIV.2310.00746 arXiv:2310.00746

Jason Wei, Yi Tay, Rishi Bommasani, Colin Raffel, Barret Zoph, Sebastian Borgeaud, Dani Yogatama, Maarten Bosma, Denny Zhou, Donald Metzler, Ed H. Chi, Tatsunori Hashimoto, Oriol Vinyals, Percy Liang, Jeff Dean, and William Fedus. 2022. Emergent Abilities of Large Language Models. *Trans. Mach. Learn. Res.* 2022 (2022). https://openreview.net/forum?id=yzkSU5zdwD

Shunxin Xiao, Shiping Wang, Yuanfei Dai, and Wenzhong Guo. 2022. Graph neural networks in node classification: survey and evaluation. *Mach. Vis. Appl.* 33, 1 (2022), 4. https://doi.org/10.1007/S00138-021-01251-0

Sang Michael Xie, Aditi Raghunathan, Percy Liang, and Tengyu Ma. 2022. An Explanation of In-context Learning as Implicit Bayesian Inference. In *The Tenth International Conference on Learning Representations, ICLR 2022, Virtual Event, April 25-29, 2022*. OpenReview.net. https://openreview.net/forum?id=RdJVFCHjUMI

A Limitations & Ethics Statement

Our investigations are confined to findings derived from Mistral-Instruct, as such, the generalizability of our results to other LLMs may be limited. Future research should aim to explore a broader range of LLM architectures to gain a more comprehensive understanding of the phenomena under investigation. All datasets are attributed to the National Transportation Safety Board (NTSB), "Courtesy: National Transportation Safety Board."

B Experimental Details

Claude 2.1 inference

- Model = `anthropic.claude-v2:1`
- Max tokens to sample = 1000 for extracting causes as a list, 1800 for generating *False* statements
- Temperature = 0.5

RoTG training

- Encoder = `roberta-base`
- Local graph node dim = 770
- Global graph node dim = 768
- Num layers in GNN = 4
- Top-K = 4096
- Dropout = 0.1
- Post-GNN to Auxiliary Clf Layers:
  - Linear1 Out Dim = 128
  - Linear2 Out Dim = 64
  - Linear3 Out Dim = 2
- CrossEntropyLoss with class weights, reduction='mean'
- Top-E = 3

Mistral-Instruct inference

- Model = `Mistral-7B-Instruct-v0.1`
- Max new tokens = 1500
- Temperature = 0.5

Fold#	#Statements	#*True*	#*False*
1	159	10	149
2	169	15	154
3	191	14	177
4	179	15	164
5	185	18	167
6	169	11	158
7	151	16	135
8	138	16	122
9	168	26	142
10	168	14	154

Table 6: Count of examples per fold by class labels.

C Dataset & Task Creation

C.1 Prompts

Prompt 1: Prompt for extracting probable causes into a list.

```
##### INSTRUCTIONS #####

Please help to extract the key Causes
into point forms based on a paragraph
bounded by [START_CONTEXT] and
[END_CONTEXT].
Do not add any explanations, or leading
or trailing descriptions. Add as many
bullet points as needed to exhaustively
extract all stated Causes.

##### EXAMPLE #####

[START_CONTEXT]
The probable cause of the employee
fatality at the Dyno Nobel facility was
a result of the conductor being
impacted by the moving railcars during
a shoving movement while located in an
area with insufficient walking space
available for the employee to perform
trackside duties.
[END_CONTEXT]

Expected Output:
[START_CAUSES]
- Conductor impacted by the moving
railcars during a shoving movement
- Accident was located in area with
insufficient walking space available
for the employee to perform trackside
duties
[END_CAUSES]

##### TASK #####
```

Prompt 2: Prompt for generating negative causal examples.

```
Based on the following accident
investigation bounded by <CONTEXT>
delimiters, the true probable cause(s)
are provided within <CAUSES> delimiters.
Given these information, provide a list
```

Figure 3: First page of an NTSB report in PDF.

```
of 10 possible causes or contributing
causes investigated within the context
that is not stated as a final true
probable cause.
Your output should only contain a list
of 10 enumerated statements/sentences
with no explanation.

<CAUSES>
{causes}
</CAUSES>

<CONTEXT>
{context}
</CONTEXT>
```

D Mining Causal Knowledge in LLMs

Figure 4 provides a detailed outline of our proposed methodology, corresponding to the descriptions in Section 4.

D.1 TransformerGCN architecture

We introduced the overall structure of our RoTG model in Section 4.2. This section outlines the detailed model architecture for TransformerGCN (Shi et al., 2021).

Our initial node features are represented by Q, an attended representation of Q'. Q' is a concatenation of the RoBERTa-encoded embeddings for each node description s and the two one-hot vectors ($oh_{\text{extr}}, oh_{\text{inf}}$) indicating if the node is extracted or inferred to the target statement s_i or not. The attention mechanism then computes the attention weights between the node features Q' and the target statement embedding r_i to generate the cross-attended node feature matrix Q.

$$r_i = \text{RoBERTa}(s_i) \tag{13}$$

$$R = \text{RoBERTa}(S) \tag{14}$$

$$Q' = [R, oh_{\text{extr}}, oh_{\text{inf}}] \tag{15}$$

$$Q = \text{Attention}(Q', r_i, r_i) \tag{16}$$

Our graph G is equivalently represented by the adjacency matrix $A = [a_{ij}] \in \mathbb{R}^{n \times n}$. The diagonal degree matrix is denoted by $D = \text{diag}(d_1, d_2, \ldots, d_n)$, where $d_i = \sum_j a_{ij}$ is the degree of node i. A normalized adjacency matrix is defined as $D^{-1}A$ or $D^{-\frac{1}{2}}AD^{-\frac{1}{2}}$.

A typical GCN transforms and propagates node features across the graph by several layers to build the approximation of the mapping of input to output. In other words, the feature propagation scheme

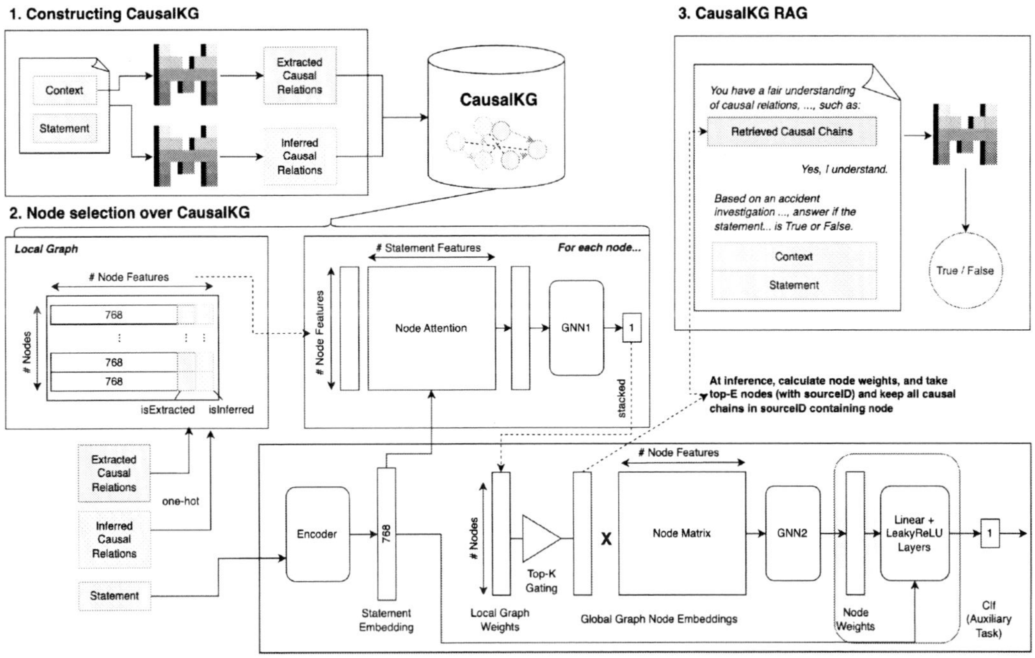

Figure 4: Detailed outline of our proposed methodology.

K Value	Macro F1	Micro F1	Accuracy		
			True	*False* (Rules)	*False* (LLM)
2048	54.12 (6.55)	79.99 (9.80)*	**34.46 (29.03)**	57.20 (35.58)*	97.78 (4.44)
4096	55.43 (6.09)	83.96 (9.07)	31.01 (31.19)	67.44 (34.41)	99.45 (0.86)
8192	**56.06 (6.53)**	**86.17 (6.09)**	24.10 (20.63)	**77.03 (21.26)**	**99.82 (0.38)**
All ∽16K	53.98 (5.79)	83.75 (10.40)	28.27 (32.49)	68.04 (37.25)	99.65 (0.84)

Table 7: Mean (Std) F1 and Accuracy across different K values for Top-K Gating. Highest score per column is in bold. P-values against K=8192 scores indicated by: *< 0.15.

of GCN in layer l is:

$$H^{(l+1)} = \sigma\left(D^{-1}AH^{(l)}W^{(l)}\right) \quad (17)$$

$$Y = f_{\text{out}}(H^{(L)}) \quad (18)$$

where σ is an activation function, $W^{(l)}$ is the trainable weight in the l-th layer, and $H^{(l)}$ is the l-th layer representations of nodes. $H^{(0)}$ is equal to node input features Q. Finally, an f_{out} output linear layer is applied on the final representation to make predictions Y for each node.

However, since our graph is heterogenous, we require message passing across edge features too. Therefore, TGCN helps by incorporating edge features into the multi-head attention for graph learning. Given node features $H^{(l)} = \{h_1^{(l)}, h_2^{(l)}, \ldots, h_n^{(l)}\}$, multi-head attention for each edge j to i is computed as follows:

$$q_{c,i}^{(l)} = W_{c,q}^{(l)} h_i^{(l)} + b_{c,q}^{(l)} \quad (19)$$

$$k_{c,j}^{(l)} = W_{c,k}^{(l)} h_j^{(l)} + b_{c,k}^{(l)} \quad (20)$$

$$e_{c,ij} = W_{c,e} e_{ij} + b_{c,e} \quad (21)$$

$$\alpha_{c,ij}^{(l)} = \frac{\exp(q_{c,i}^{(l)} \cdot k_{c,j}^{(l)} + e_{c,ij})}{\sum_{u \in N(i)} \exp(q_{c,i}^{(l)} \cdot k_{c,u}^{(l)} + e_{c,iu})} \quad (22)$$

where $h_{q,k}^{(l)} = \exp\left(\frac{q_{c,i}^{(l)} \cdot k_{c,j}^{(l)}}{\sqrt{d}}\right)$ is the exponential scale dot-product function and d is the hidden size of each head. For the c-th head attention, we transform the source feature $h_i^{(l)}$ and distant feature $h_j^{(l)}$ into query vector $q_{c,i}^{(l)} \in \mathbb{R}^d$ and key vector $k_{c,j}^{(l)} \in \mathbb{R}^d$ respectively using different trainable parameters $W_{c,q}^{(l)}$, $W_{c,k}^{(l)}$, $b_{c,q}^{(l)}$, $b_{c,k}^{(l)}$. The provided edge features e_{ij} are encoded and added into the key vector as additional information for each layer.

After obtaining the graph multi-head attention, message passing and aggregation from the distant j to the source i is computed by:

$$v_{c,j}^{(l)} = W_{c,v}^{(l)} h_j^{(l)} + b_{c,v}^{(l)} \tag{23}$$

$$\hat{h}_i^{(l+1)} = \sum_{j \in N(i)} \alpha_{c,ij}^{(l)} (v_{c,j}^{(l)} + e_{c,ij}) \tag{24}$$

where k is the concatenation operation for C head attention. This multi-head attention matrix replaces the original normalized adjacency matrix in Equation 17 as the transition matrix for message passing.

Finally, we apply a linear transformation to the last layer of node features $h_i^{(l)}$, obtaining a representation of local node weights (ow_i), trained to represent how important this node is to the downstream task.

$$ow_i = W_{c,v}^{(l)} h_i^{(l)} + b_{c,v}^{(l)} \tag{25}$$

D.2 Prompts

Prompt 3: Prompt for extracting causal relations

```
Extract all the causal events in this
report:
{context}

Format the extracted Cause and Effect
events into a list, like:
1. Engineer's inattentiveness to signal
indications --> Engineer failed to
operate train in accordance with signal
indications and speed restriction -->
Train collided with another train
2. Lack of positive train control
system --> Train A not stopped before
red signal --> Train A passed red
signal --> Collision between Train A
and Train B
...
where "-->" represents "causes", so
"Cause Event --> Effect Event".

Answer:
```

Prompt 4: Prompt for inferring causal relations

```
Based on your knowledge, suggest the
series of Cause and Effect events that
explain how the cause within the
STATEMENT could have led to the
accident in the CONTEXT.
<STATEMENT>
{statement}
</STATEMENT>
<CONTEXT>
{context}
</CONTEXT>

Format the suggested Cause and Effect
events into a list, like:
- Engineer's inattentiveness to signal
indications --> Engineer failed to
operate train in accordance with signal
indications and speed restriction -->
Train collided with another train
(Accident)
where "-->" represents "causes", so
"Cause Event --> Effect Event".

Answer:
```

Prompt 5: Prompt V1 for causal deductive reasoning task.

```
Based on an accident investigation
bounded by <CONTEXT> delimiters, answer
if the statement within <STATEMENT>
delimiters about the probable cause(s)
of the accident is True or False. Your
answer must be based on the
investigation facts and details within
<CONTEXT>.

<CONTEXT>
{context}
</CONTEXT>

Is this statement True or False?
<STATEMENT>
{statement}
</STATEMENT>

Answer:
```

Prompt 6: Prompt V2 for causal deductive reasoning task.

```
<s>[INST] You have a fair understanding
of causal relations, where "-->"
represents "causes".
[/INST] Yes, I understand.</s>
[INST] Based on an accident
investigation bounded by <CONTEXT>
```

```
delimiters, answer if the statement
within <STATEMENT> delimiters about the
probable cause(s) of the accident is
True or False. Your answer must be
based on the investigation facts and
details within <CONTEXT>.

<CONTEXT>
{context}
</CONTEXT>

Is this statement True or False?
<STATEMENT>
{statement}
</STATEMENT> [/INST]

Answer:
```

Prompt 7: Prompt V3 for causal deductive reasoning task.

```
<s>[INST] You have a fair understanding
of causal relations, where "-->"
represents "causes".
[/INST] Yes, I understand.</s>
[INST] Based on an accident
investigation bounded by <CONTEXT>
delimiters, answer if the statement
within <STATEMENT> delimiters about the
probable cause(s) of the accident is
True or False. Your answer must be
based on the investigation facts and
details within <CONTEXT>.

<CONTEXT>
{context}
</CONTEXT>

<RELATIONS>
Relations extracted from <CONTEXT>:
{extracted}
</RELATIONS>

Is this statement True or False?
<STATEMENT>
{statement}
</STATEMENT> [/INST]

Answer:
```

Prompt 8: Prompt V4 for causal deductive reasoning task.

```
<s>[INST] You have a fair understanding
of causal relations, where "-->"
represents "causes".
[/INST] Yes, I understand.</s>
[INST] Based on an accident
investigation bounded by <CONTEXT>
delimiters, answer if the statement
within <STATEMENT> delimiters about the
probable cause(s) of the accident is
True or False. Your answer must be
based on the investigation facts and
details within <CONTEXT>.

<CONTEXT>
{context}
</CONTEXT>

<RELATIONS>
Possible relations linking probable
cause in <STATEMENT> to accident:
{inferred}
</RELATIONS>

Is this statement True or False?
<STATEMENT>
{statement}
</STATEMENT> [/INST]

Answer:
```

Prompt 9: Prompt V5 for causal deductive reasoning task.

```
<s>[INST] You have a fair understanding
of causal relations, where "-->"
represents "causes".
[/INST] Yes, I understand.</s>
[INST] Based on an accident
investigation bounded by <CONTEXT>
delimiters, answer if the statement
within <STATEMENT> delimiters about the
probable cause(s) of the accident is
True or False. Your answer must be
based on the investigation facts and
details within <CONTEXT>.

<CONTEXT>
{context}
</CONTEXT>

<RELATIONS>
Relations extracted from <CONTEXT>:
{extracted}
```

```
Possible relations linking probable
cause in <STATEMENT> to accident:
{inferred}
</RELATIONS>

Is this statement True or False?
<STATEMENT>
{statement}
</STATEMENT> [/INST]

Answer:
```

Prompt 10: Prompt V6 for causal deductive reasoning task.

```
<s>[INST] You have a fair understanding
of causal relations, where "-->"
represents "causes", such as:
{retrieved} [/INST] Yes, I
understand.</s>
[INST] Based on an accident
investigation bounded by <CONTEXT>
delimiters, answer if the statement
within <STATEMENT> delimiters about the
probable cause(s) of the accident is
True or False. Your answer must be
based on the investigation facts and
details within <CONTEXT>.

<CONTEXT>
{context}
</CONTEXT>

Is this statement True or False?
<STATEMENT>
{statement}
</STATEMENT> [/INST]

Answer:
```

Prompt 11: Prompt V7 for causal deductive reasoning task.

```
<s>[INST] You have a fair understanding
of causal relations, where "-->"
represents "causes", such as:
{retrieved} [/INST] Yes, I
understand.</s>
[INST] Based on an accident
investigation bounded by <CONTEXT>
delimiters, answer if the statement
within <STATEMENT> delimiters about the
probable cause(s) of the accident is
True or False. Your answer must be
based on the investigation facts and
details within <CONTEXT>.

<CONTEXT>
{context}
</CONTEXT>

<RELATIONS>
Relations extracted from <CONTEXT>:
{extracted}
</RELATIONS>

Is this statement True or False?
<STATEMENT>
{statement}
</STATEMENT> [/INST]

Answer:
```

Prompt 12: Prompt V8 for causal deductive reasoning task.

```
<s>[INST] You have a fair understanding
of causal relations, where "-->"
represents "causes", such as:
{retrieved} [/INST] Yes, I
understand.</s>
[INST] Based on an accident
investigation bounded by <CONTEXT>
delimiters, answer if the statement
within <STATEMENT> delimiters about the
probable cause(s) of the accident is
True or False. Your answer must be
based on the investigation facts and
details within <CONTEXT>.

<CONTEXT>
{context}
</CONTEXT>

<RELATIONS>
Relations extracted from <CONTEXT>:
{extracted}

Possible relations linking probable
cause in <STATEMENT> to accident:
{inferred}
</RELATIONS>

Is this statement True or False?
<STATEMENT>
```

```
{statement}
</STATEMENT> [/INST]

Answer:
```

Prompt 13: Prompt V9 for causal deductive reasoning task.

```
<s>[INST] You have a fair understanding
of causal relations, where "-->"
represents "causes", such as:
<RELATIONS>
Historical relations:
{retrieved}

Relations extracted from <CONTEXT>:
{extracted}

Possible relations linking probable
cause in <STATEMENT> to accident:
{inferred}
</RELATIONS> [/INST] Yes, I
understand.</s>
[INST] Based on an accident
investigation bounded by <CONTEXT>
delimiters, answer if the statement
within <STATEMENT> delimiters about the
probable cause(s) of the accident is
True or False. Your answer must be
based on the investigation facts and
details within <CONTEXT>.

<CONTEXT>
{context}
</CONTEXT>

Is this statement True or False?
<STATEMENT>
{statement}
</STATEMENT> [/INST]

Answer:
```

D.3 RoTG Findings

Our RoTG model includes a gating framework to focus on top-K nodes. Table 7 presents scores from RoTG across different K values. In terms of Macro and Micro F1, K=8192 returns the best performance. We notice a slight concave pattern of F1 against K values, suggesting an optimal amount of gating is needed. However, the findings did not show statistically significant differences across K=4096 to when all nodes were allowed to be differentiated against.

D.4 LLM Findings

Findings from all experiments with Mistral-Instruct are available in Table 8. The first column indicates the corresponding Prompt number used, while the next four columns indicate the additional information included in the prompt, or if any different processing method was used.

D.5 Qualitative Examples

Table 9 shows the output response from Mistral-Instruct across the three main prompt versions, corresponding to Table 3. The last two columns details the retrieved relations that were included in the prompt.

Prompt #	Relations			Other Tweaks	Macro F1	Micro F1	Accuracy		
	Extract	Infer	Retrieved				*True*	*False* (Rules)	*False* (LLM)
5			*None*		70.36 (7.07)	90.30 (1.78)	46.53 (13.21)	92.23 (3.66)	95.69 (1.86)
6			*None*	Role-play	71.04 (5.99)	89.64 (0.87)	53.82 (12.26)	91.12 (2.76)	94.00 (1.63)***
7	✓		*None*		72.42 (7.19)	90.59 (2.52)	52.62 (13.79)	91.73 (4.22)	95.60 (2.06)
8		✓	*None*		63.97 (4.87)***	83.15 (2.85)***	**55.99 (11.38)***	78.56 (4.79)***	89.03 (4.35)***
9	✓	✓	*None*		63.66 (5.31)***	84.10 (2.53)***	50.36 (12.18)	80.12 (4.66)***	90.65 (3.38)***
10			Semantic		72.50 (6.37)	91.24 (1.40)	48.72 (11.04)	92.99 (2.48)	96.54 (1.93)
11	✓		Semantic		70.97 (4.69)	90.67 (2.11)	45.54 (7.10)	91.70 (4.21)	96.91 (1.89)
12	✓	✓	Semantic		64.48 (6.02)**	86.83 (2.27)***	41.81 (12.63)	86.19 (4.56)***	93.59 (2.44)***
10			RoTG		**73.19 (7.01)**	**91.65 (1.42)****	49.49 (13.47)	**94.31 (3.49)**	96.37 (1.37)
11	✓		RoTG		71.15 (6.40)	91.09 (2.14)	44.07 (10.02)	93.43 (3.89)	97.02 (1.63)*
12	✓	✓	RoTG		64.21 (7.89)**	87.28 (3.23)***	37.98 (13.90)	87.21 (4.02)***	94.46 (2.79)
10			RoTG	No cleaning	71.93 (5.57)	91.19 (1.37)	46.53 (8.61)	94.01 (3.72)	96.38 (1.03)
10			RoTG	No truncate	72.92 (6.43)	91.60 (1.11)	48.87 (12.59)	93.75 (3.24)	96.66 (1.04)
11	✓		RoTG	No cleaning	71.52 (5.94)	91.12 (2.16)	45.04 (9.33)	93.28 (4.17)	**97.13 (1.38)****
11	✓		RoTG	No truncate	70.96 (6.69)	90.95 (2.07)	44.50 (11.16)	93.43 (3.89)	96.73 (1.70)
13	✓	✓	RoTG	Rels before Task	64.55 (6.48)**	86.58 (1.80)***	42.85 (11.72)	87.09 (2.66)***	92.74 (2.00)***

Table 8: Mistral Instruct with various relations included into prompt. Highest score per column is in bold. P-values against scores from the *None* scores in the first row is indicated by: *< 0.15, **< 0.10, ***< 0.05.

Statement	Label	Base	Semantic	RoTG	Semantic_Rels	RoTG_Rels
The probable cause of the accident was insufficient communication between the captains after the passing arrangement was changed...	False (True statement: "The probable cause of the accident was the impact of distraction upon the decision-making and recollection of the captain of the P. B. Shah.")	Answer: The statement is True. Explanation: The accident occurred due to a miscommunication between the captains of the two vessels regarding the passing arrangement. The P. B. Shah captain initially proposed a starboard-to-starboard passing arrangement, but the Dewey R captain misunderstood and believed it was a port-to-port passing arrangement. The Dewey R captain then steered his vessel towards the port side of the river in an attempt to conduct a two-whistle pass, which resulted in a collision with the P. B. Shah tow. The miscommunication and confusion about the passing arrangement led to the accident.	Answer: False. The probable cause of the accident was the P. B. Shah captain's error in initiating a port-to-port (one whistle) passing on the radio with the Dewey R captain, who had meant to arrange a starboard-to-starboard (two-whistle) passing. The P. B. Shah captain was distracted by the many tasksassociated with preparing for his arrival at the Ingram facility, including having a cell phone conversation with the boat store and meeting with the mate to discuss upcoming tasks. The Dewey R captain made a mistake by not following the inland navigation rules and should have assessed the risk of collision presented by the two alternative meeting arrangements, chosen the option that did not include passing in front of the P. B. Shah tow, and then used his privilege as the downbound vessel to overrule the P. B. Shah captain's change to a two-whistle meeting arrangement.	Answer: False. Explanation: The probable cause of the accident was not insufficient communication between the captains after the passing arrangement was changed. The investigation found that the P. B. Shah captain misunderstood the initial passing agreement and believed he was proposing a starboard-to-starboard passage, while the Dewey R captain believed he was proposing a port-to-port passage. The miscommunication was due to the P. B. Shah captain being distracted by tasksassociated with preparing for his arrival at the Ingram facility, and the Dewey R captain doubting his understanding of the original agreement. The investigation also found that the Dewey R captain made a mistake by not following the inland navigation rules and should have assessed the risk of collision presented by the two alternative meeting arrangements and chosen the option that did not include passing in front of the P. B. Shah tow.	- BART's simple approval process allowed access along the right-of-way without protection from moving trains –> Safety issues and concerns identified during the NTSB accident investigation - Workers were not able to properly protect themselves from moving trains –> Accident occurred. - - NTSB accident investigation –> Major findings identified safety issues and concerns - Identification of safety issues and concerns –> New safety regulations and requirements - - BART assistant chief transportation officer distributed a memorandum immediately prohibiting simple approvals –> Access to the right-of-way must provide protection from moving trains - Workers were not aware of safety protocols and procedures –> Workers were not able to properly protect themselves from moving trains - Trains exceeding speed limits were not uncommon, leading to increased risk of accidents –> Accident occurred - - Major findings from investigations into worker fatalities –> Identification of safety issues and concerns - BART's simple approval process allowed access along the right-of-way that did not provide workers with protection from moving trains –> BART issued General Order 175 (GO 175) to govern roadway worker protection for rail transit workers in California, prohibiting the type of access that was allowed under BART's simple approval process. - - BART assistant chief transportation officer distributed a memorandum immediately prohibiting simple approvals –> Access to the right-of-way must provide the work crew with protection from moving trains	- Defective control system in unoccupied cars –> Errant control signals sent to power systems - Errant control signals sent to power systems –> Unoccupied cars moved and stopped - Based on evidence and statements regarding the float driver's medical history, sleep opportunity, sleep quality, sleep schedule, and time awake, it is unlikely that he was fatigued at the time of the collision –> Based on evidence and statements regarding the float driver's medical history, sleep opportunity, sleep quality, sleep schedule, and time awake, it is unlikely that he was fatigued at the time of the collision. - Lack of fatigue –> Based on evidence and statements regarding the float driver's medical history, sleep opportunity, sleep quality, sleep schedule, and time awake, it is unlikely that he was fatigued at the time of the collision. - There is no evidence that the float driver was experiencing stress or had a health, hearing, or visual condition that affected his ability to perceive the grade crossing warnings, perceive the train, or safely operate his vehicle –> Based on evidence and statements regarding the float driver's medical history, sleep opportunity, sleep quality, sleep schedule, and time awake, it is unlikely that he was fatigued at the time of the collision. - Based on evidence and statements regarding the float driver's medical history, sleep opportunity, sleep quality, sleep schedule, and time awake, it is unlikely that he was fatigued at the time of the collision. –> The grade crossing warning system provided 20 seconds of warning as required by federal regulations. - The float driver was not distracted by the use of in-vehicle electronic devices –> The float driver was not distracted by electronic devices, which could have contributed to the accident.
The probable cause of the accident was current conditions contributing to intermittent submersion of wastage holes..	False (True statement: "The probable cause of the accident was the company's lack of effective hull inspection and maintenance..")	Answer: True. The investigation found that the accident was caused by the intermittent submersion of wastage holes on the starboard stern quarter of the Miss Roslyn due to the captain pushing against the tow at a 9000b0 angle to the bank for 2.5 to 3 hours. The current likely lowered and submerged the holes, allowing continuous water ingress to the starboard steering void for about 3 hours. Once the hull flooded, the vessel sank lower, increasing the rate of flooding through the holes to the starboard steering void, resulting in the observed starboard list. The port flanking void eventually flooded, causing the vessel's loss of stability and capsizing.	Answer: The statement is True. The investigation found that the accident was caused by the intermittent submersion of wastage holes on the starboard stern quarter of the Miss Roslyn due to the captain pushing against the tow at a 9000b0 angle to the bank for 2.5 to 3 hours. The current likely lowered and submerged the holes, allowing continuous water ingress to the starboard steering void for about 3 hours. Once the hull flooded, the vessel sank lower, increasing the rate of flooding through the holes to the starboard steering void, resulting in the observed starboard list. The port flanking void eventually flooded, causing the vessel to lose stability and capsize.	Answer: False. The probable cause of the accident was not the current conditions contributing to intermittent submersion of wastage holes. The investigation found that the two wastage holes and a fractured weld at the main deck to the starboard steering void were not watertight, and the captain was assisting in making up a tow, which required him to push against the tow at a 9000b0 angle to the bank for 2.5 to 3 hours. This action likely lowered and intermittently submerged the wastage and fracture holes on the starboard stern quarter, allowing continuous water ingress to the starboard steering void for about 3 hours. The aft steering void was partially flooded, which likely caused the observed starboard list. Once the hull flooded, the vessel sank lower, increasing the rate of flooding through the holes to the starboard steering void, thus increasing the starboard heel and submerging the starboard bulwark and stern deck. The port flanking void flooded, resulting in the vessel's loss of stability and capsizing. The severe wastage found throughout the vessel in the post-accident survey indicates that the Miss Roslyn was poorly maintained. The company did not have an effective maintenance program on board the vessel, so holes in and fractures to the hull and deck went undetected and ultimately led to flooding while the vessel was conducting normal operations.	- Pedestrian's decision to run across the multilane roadway in front of the oncoming car –> Driver's decision to make a left turn from the left-turn lane onto eastbound Leesburg Pike - Driver failed to see pedestrian –> Driver applied brakes and attempted to steer left, colliding with pedestrian (Accident)	- Defective control system in unoccupied cars –> Errant control signals sent to power systems - Errant control signals sent to power systems –> Unoccupied cars moved and stopped - Conductor was pinched between the knuckle of the stationary car and the drawbar carrier of the free-rolling car –> Fatal accident - By-passed couplers on the 17th and 18th cars –> Fatal accident - Train movement before going between cars to perform work on cars –> Fatal accident - Violation of these rules escalated the discipline policy by one step –> Fatal accident - Death of the pedestrian –> Fatal accident - Fatal accident –> Accident Number: HWY16SH023, Accident Type: Fatal pedestrian collision with car, Location: 9th Street and P Street NW, Washington, DC, Date and Time: August 18, 2016, about 2:20 a.m. eastern daylight time, Vehicle: 2000 Mercedes-Benz CLK 320, Driver: 31-year-old female, Pedestrian: 44-year-old male, Fatalities: 1 - Coding error in the software upgrade –> Acceleration and deceleration of the train - Acceleration and deceleration of the train –> Injury of passengers

Table 9: Qualitative examples from Mistral-Instruct across the three different prompts.
(Base (No additional relations in prompt), Semantic, and RoTG causal relations in prompt).

Numerical Claim Detection in Finance: A New Financial Dataset, Weak-Supervision Model, and Market Analysis

Agam Shah♡ †, Arnav Hiray♡ †, Pratvi Shah♣, Arkaprabha Banerjee♣, Anushka Singh◊ Dheeraj Eidnani♡, Sahasra Chava♠, Bhaskar Chaudhury♣, Sudheer Chava♡

♡ Georgia Institute of Technology
♣ DA-IICT
◊ IIT-Kharagpur
♠ Fulton Science Academy

Abstract

In this paper, we investigate the influence of claims in analyst reports and earnings calls on financial market returns, considering them as significant quarterly events for publicly traded companies. To facilitate a comprehensive analysis, we construct a new financial dataset for the claim detection task in the financial domain. We benchmark various language models on this dataset and propose a novel weak-supervision model that incorporates the knowledge of subject matter experts (SMEs) in the aggregation function, outperforming existing approaches. We also demonstrate the practical utility of our proposed model by constructing a novel measure of *optimism*. Here, we observe the dependence of earnings surprise and return on our optimism measure. Our dataset, models, and code are publicly (under CC BY 4.0 license) available on GitHub[1].

1 Introduction

Earnings conference calls are a quarterly event where the company's top executives provide performance reports of the company over the last quarter (3 months). Between the two earnings calls analyst from various financial institutions analyze and provide earnings estimates and recommendations. For example, Jegadeesh and Kim (2010) has documented that there is a significant stock market reaction to analysts' recommendations (ratings). Recent insights, such as those presented by McLean et al. (2020), reveal that retail investors, often perceived as unsophisticated, exhibit responsiveness to analysts' projections, underscoring the pivotal role of analysts' reports in informing market participants. However, analyst ratings can be biased (Michaely and Womack, 1999; Corwin et al., 2017; Coleman et al., 2021). Therefore it is important to understand whether the ratings are backed by strong numerical financial claims in the analyst's report. Further, the sentences with a claim have a higher density of forward-looking information. As an application, extraction of numerical ESG claims from earnings call transcripts, can help better understand whether companies do walk the talk on their environment and social responsibility claims (Chava et al., 2021). These examples underscore the necessity of numerical claim detection in the finance domain, aligning with broader research efforts to ensure the accuracy and reliability of information sources.

A key component of this paper is the identification of Numeric Financial Sentences. Specifically, Numeric Financial Sentences include a financial term, a numeric value, and either a currency or percentage symbol. Chen et al. (2020) first introduced the categorization of sentences into 'in-claim' and 'out-of-claim' specifically in the Mandarin language. Expanding on their foundation, we define an 'in-claim' sentence as one presenting a speculative financial forecast. Conversely, an 'out-of-claim' sentence presents a numerical statement about a past event, transitioning from a mere claim to a confirmed fact. For clarity, 'in-claim' sentences can also be termed "financial forecasts" whereas 'out-of-claim' can be labeled as "established financials." Every Numeric Financial Sentence that is not a speculative financial forecast (in-claim) is then identified as an 'out-of-claim' sentence. Figure 1 illustrates the identification of Numeric Financial Sentences as well as distinguishing between "in-claim" and "out-of-claim" sentences.

A major challenge for building or training predictive models is the scarcity of labeled data (Zhang et al., 2021; Ratner et al., 2017). Supervised learning often involves a significant amount of manual labeling of data which is often infeasible for large datasets. In such scenarios, one can leverage weak-

Correspondence to Agam Shah {ashah482@gatech.edu}
† These authors contributed equally to this work
[1] https://github.com/gtfintechlab/fin-num-claim.

Proceedings of the Seventh Fact Extraction and VERification Workshop (FEVER), pages 170–185
November 15, 2024 ©2024 Association for Computational Linguistics

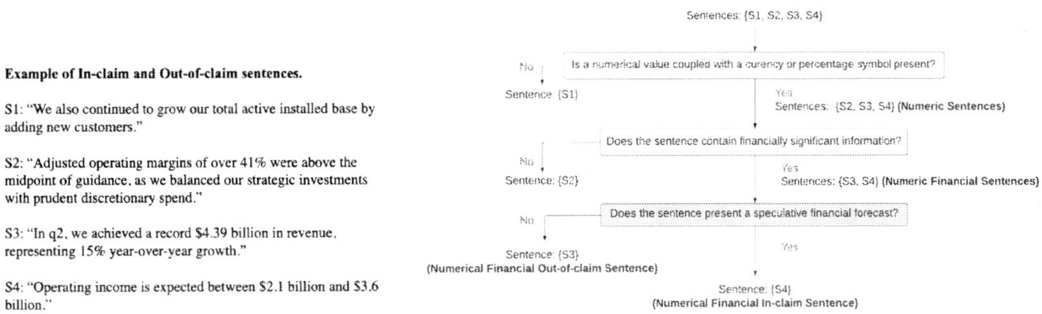

Figure 1: Example of In-claim and Out-of-claim sentences.

supervision-based learning methods (Varma and Ré, 2018) or fine-tune the pre-trained language model. Weak-supervision is a process that leverages slightly noisy or imprecise labeling functions (lfs) to label vast amounts of unlabeled data (Ratner et al., 2020; Lison et al., 2021). The strength of the weak-supervision model lies in these imperfect labels, when combined, producing improved predictive models (Lison et al., 2021; Zhang et al., 2021). However, a crucial component involves the development of effective lfs for a given raw dataset systematically rather than manual annotation (Lison et al., 2021).

The aim of our work is to derive financially significant information from the quarterly analyst reports and earnings calls by categorizing each numerical sentence as in-claim or out-of-claim. Our major contributions through this paper are the following:

- We introduce a new task of claim detection (in English) with a labeled dataset.
- We build clean, tokenized, and annotated open-source datasets based on earnings calls.
- We introduce a weak-supervision model with a novel aggregation function.
- We benchmark a wide range of language models for the claim detection task.
- We develop a novel measure of optimism and validate its usefulness in predicting various financial indicators.

2 Related Work

NLP in Finance Finance is one of the most attractive domains for the application of NLP. Araci (2019) and Liu et al. (2020) presented pre-trained language models for the Finance domain. There are multiple datasets specifically catered for applications of NLP in finance including question answering dataset created by Chen et al. (2021) and Maia et al. (2018), and also a NER dataset constructed by Shah et al. (2023b) for the financial domain. There is a vast body of literature on undertaking sentiment analysis tasks on financial data(Maia et al., 2018; Malo et al., 2014; Day and Lee, 2016; Akhtar et al., 2017).

Works of Li et al. (2020) and Sawhney et al. (2020) were centered around predicting volatility using earnings call transcripts in the domain of risk management. Chava et al. (2022) measure the firm level inflation exposure by fine-tuning RoBERTa (Liu et al., 2019), while Li et al. (2021) leveraged word-embeddings to measure the corporate culture. Moreover, Nguyen et al. (2021) and Hu and Ma (2021) used multimodal machine learning for credit rating prediction and measurement of persuasiveness respectively. Shah et al. (2023a) investigated the impact of monetary policy communication on financial markets. Cao et al. (2020) critically examined the evolution of corporate disclosure in recent years, influenced by the rising application of NLP in Finance. Our research focuses on identifying numerical financial claims from a vast set of English analyst reports and earnings calls using a weak-supervision model. This differs from Chen et al. (2020), which targets numeric claim detection in a smaller Chinese language dataset.

Weak-Supervision In order to reduce the complexities associated with manual labeling, several standard techniques such as semi-supervised learning (Chapelle et al., 2009), transfer learning (Pan and Yang, 2010), and active learning (Settles, 2009) have been employed. However, many researchers (Meng et al., 2018; Kartchner et al., 2020) and practitioners also employ weak-supervision-based models to further reduce the computational costs while retaining the accuracy of the labeled data. Weak-supervision models were primarily developed in a bid to replace standard labeling techniques with models which can leverage slightly noisy or imprecise sources to label vast amounts of data (Ratner et al., 2020). Techniques such as distant supervision (Mintz et al., 2009) and crowd-sourced labels (Yuen et al., 2011) are often associatewd with weak-supervision-based models, however, they tend to have limited coverage and accuracy (Lison et al., 2021). In the case where we have noisy labels from multiple sources available, there have been efforts made to use majority vote, weighted majority vote (Ratner et al., 2020), and other label-models (Yu et al., 2022; Zhang et al., 2022).

3 Dataset

We collect two categories of text and financial market datasets. Analyst reports are procured from a proprietary source while earnings call transcripts are collected in a manner that allows us to make the resulting dataset open-source.

3.1 Analyst Reports

The raw dataset consists of quarterly analyst reports (in English) for a large number of public firms in the U.S. These analyst reports were collected from Zacks Equity Research and were available to us through the Nexis Uni license[2].

The text documents are first split into sentences using multiple regex-based rules. This segmentation process utilizes a comprehensive set of regular expression (regex) rules to accurately identify sentence boundaries, accounting for a variety of English language nuances, including abbreviations, titles, websites, and numerical expressions, to ensure precise sentence delineation. We employ regex-based rules as they typically are significantly faster with similar accuracy compared to standard libraries in sentence tokenization. Next, sentences containing quantitative data - specifically sentences with a numeric value AND either a currency symbol as a prefix or percentage symbol as a postfix- are extracted, as they have numerical relevance (Chen et al., 2019). This numerical condition filter reduced the number of sentences by 66.7%.

The next step in the pipeline uses a whitelisting technique to retain only sentences with financially significant information, achieved by cross-referencing each sentence with a financial dictionary containing a comprehensive list of financial market terms and related literature. The financial dictionary used in this study, developed by Shah et al. (2022), contains over 8,200 financially significant terms. Sentences are cross-referenced with this dictionary to verify financial significance; if no words match, the sentence is marked as irrelevant. This filtering reduced the dataset by an additional 17.2%. The dataset contains 8,583,093 total sentences, 2,857,567 numeric sentences, and 2,364,977 numeric-financial sentences after filtration. This two-tier filtering method enriched the data by retaining only 27.5% of the sentences from the original data.

3.2 Earnings Call Transcripts

To make our work more impactful, we also collect earnings call transcripts for NASDAQ 100 companies from their investor relation page. We were able to write individual scripts for 78 out of 100 NASDAQ companies. As all the companies in this list are public companies, their data can be accessed and shared publicly which allows us to open-source the resulting dataset. Collecting data till March of 2023 results in a total of 1,085 earnings call transcripts. The biggest advantage of writing separate scripts for each company is that it allows us to keep adding more transcripts every quarter increasing the size of the dataset shared over time. We apply text processing (tokenization, numerical filter, financial dictionary filter) on earnings call transcripts similar to what is used for analyst reports.

3.3 Comparison with Related Dataset

In this section we compare our proposed datasets with NumClaim (Chen et al., 2020), an expert-annotated dataset in the Chinese language. Our dataset of raw analyst reports in the English Language from 1,530 major companies over the period of 2017-20 is significantly larger than NumClaim or other associated datasets. Our open-sourced dataset from collected earnings call transcripts is also larger than the NumClaim dataset. The detailed comparison of our datasets with NumClaim is provided in Table 1.

3.4 Financial Market Data

Stock Price and Earnings Surprise Data We collect stock price data from Polygon.io[3] starting

[2]Nexis Uni license doesn't authorize republication of full or partial text. To solve this problem, we also collect and construct a dataset from earnings calls which can be made public under CC BY 4.0 license.

[3]`https://polygon.io/stocks`

Dataset	Analyst Reports	Earnings Calls	NumClaim (Chen et al., 2020)
Language	English	English	Chinese
Year	2017-20	2017-23	NA
Sector Information	Yes	Yes	No
# Stocks	1,530	78	NA
# Files	87,536	1,085	NA
# Words	167,301,873	11,641,673	42,594
# Numeric Sentences	2,857,567	48,686	5,144
# Numeric Financial Sentences	2,364,977	41,013	NA
# Numeric Financial In-Claim Sentences	336,252	5362	1,233

Table 1: Comparison of our datasets with NumClaim (Chen et al., 2020) dataset.

January 1st, 2017. We collect the actual earnings per share (EPS) and forecasted median EPS from the I/B/E/S dataset[4].

Sector Data For each firm in our dataset, we collect sector information by collecting GSECTOR classification from the annual fundamental COMPUSTAT database. GSECTOR maps each company to one of the twelve sectors.

3.5 Sampling and Manual Annotation

From the complete raw dataset of 87,536 analyst reports and 1,085 earnings call transcripts, we sample data and annotate sentences. The sampled dataset consisted of 96 analyst reports consisting of two files per sector per year, accounting for about 2,681 unique financial-numeric sentences. We also sample 12 earnings call transcripts randomly consisting of two files per year, consisting of 498 financial-numeric sentences. This set was manually annotated and assigned 'in-claim' or 'out-of-claim' labels by two of the authors with a foundational background in finance (one of them is now an analyst at a top investment bank) and domain expertise developed through examples provided by a co-author. This co-author is a financial expert with a Master's degree in Quantitative Finance, currently pursuing a PhD under the guidance of the Chair Professor of Finance, and has contributed to work at leading finance journals and conferences. The annotator agreement was 99.21% and 95.78% for analyst reports and earnings call transcripts respectively. Any disagreement between the two annotators was resolved with the help of the financial expert mentioned earlier. The dataset (Train, Val, Test) is split as follows: Analyst Reports (1,715, 429, 537) and Earnings Calls (318, 80, 100).

[4]https://www.investopedia.com/terms/i/ibes.asp

4 Experiments

4.1 Models

In this section, we provide details of the four categories of models we have used. Initially, we provide detail on the proposed weak-supervision model with the customized aggregation function. In order to provide a comprehensive benchmark for the claim detection task and comparison with proposed weak-supervision model, we add Bi-LSTM, six BERT architecture-based PLMs, and three generative LLMs.

Weak-Supervision Model For implementing a weak-supervision model we use the Snorkel library (Ratner et al., 2017), leveraging its inherent pipeline structure for generating labels for each data segment and then passing the outputs through the customized aggregation function.

Labeling functions used in our model include rule-based pattern matching combined with part-of-speech (POS) tag constraints for some phrases. We create seventeen labeling functions for the categorization of results and also make use of multiple other labeling functions in order to divide sentences representing assertions or written in the past tense. These labeling functions are listed in Table 5. More details on the construction of the labeling function can be found in Appendix B.

Aggregation Function The output of the labeling functions needs to be aggregated to decide the final label of the sentence. Unlike other models, we use independent, weighted labeling functions with weights based on the level of confidence assigned by Subject Matter Experts (SMEs). Our labeling function can produce four distinct types of output: -1 for a high confidence out-of-claim sentence, 0 for abstention from making a claim, 1 for a low confidence in making a claim, and 2 for a high confidence in making a claim. This system allows us to further differentiate in-claim sentences into two levels of confidence. The pseudo-code in Algorithm 1 illustrates our aggregation function.

Algorithm 1 Aggregation Function

```
if any of the labeling functions' output is −1 then
    label ← "out-of-claim"
else if the max of the labeling functions' output is 2 then
    label ← "in-claim"
else
    label ← majority vote output
end if
```

Traditional majority vote takes decisions based on votes from all the labeling functions, meaning assigning equal weights. The weighted majority vote aggregation function, such as Snorkel, learns the weight for each labeling function from the data itself. In our case, Subject Matter Experts decide that some labeling functions are higher in the hierarchy than others. This means that we look at their labels first before looking at the output of other labeling functions. If those higher-valued labeling functions refrain from voting (by giving an abstain label, value=0), we look at the output of other labeling functions. Otherwise, we take labels based on the majority vote.

To facilitate a comprehensive comparison of our weak-supervision model against various other model categories, we additionally leverage Generative Large Language Models (LLMs) in both zero-shot and few-shot settings, and conduct fine-tuning on Bi-LSTM as well as other Pre-trained Language Models (PLMs). Detailed information regarding the implementation of these models is delineated in the Appendix C.

4.2 Results

In this section, we present the results obtained using the above models and provide a detailed analysis of the outcomes.

Weak-Supervision Model The performance in Table 2, highlights how well our Weak-Supervision based model performs when compared with manually annotated data. In order to make sure that there is no contamination issue between the labeling functions and annotated data, we perform a robustness check in Appendix A. We also perform ablation on the number of labeling functions in Appendix D.

We consider majority voting and Snorkel's aggregation function (Ratner et al., 2017) as baseline aggregation functions for comparative ablation analysis. The accuracy of baseline aggregation functions along with our aggregation function is reported in Table 3. For all three models, the same set of labeling functions is used and they only differ in the aggregation part.[5] The result highlights the importance of the construction of a customized aggregation function for a weak-supervision model where a small set of labeling functions are complete and less noisy.

Generative LLMs There are a few observations regarding the performance of Generative LLMs. First, we see that utilizing a more detailed prompt leads to large improvements in performance across all three models. Secondly, Falcon and Llama have a large increase in performance as well when using six-shot prompting. However, ChatGPT did not have as large of an improvement when utilizing few-shot prompting. While the reasoning behind this is uncertain, it is clear that prompt engineering (particularly creating detailed prompts) can lead to substantial improvement. Zero-shot ChatGPT fails to outperform both weak-supervision and fine-tuned PLMs. It still achieves impressive performance without having access to any labeled data. Of the variations of prompting attempted, Llama with six-shot prompting yielded the best results. This seems to suggest that through the use of prompt engineering, open-source models may be able to close the gap with closed LLMs.

Bi-LSTM The Bi-LSTM model outperforms the weak-supervision model on analyst reports data but doesn't outperform on earnings call data. The potential reason can be the larger fine-tuning dataset available for analyst reports. It doesn't outperform the model based on BERT on any of the four configurations.

PLMs The fine-tuned models utilizing the BERT architecture demonstrate superior performance compared to other model classes, emphasizing the significant value gained from annotated data. Intriguingly, the model that achieves the highest performance within a particular train-test dataset category does not necessarily exhibit the best performance on transfer learning datasets. This finding underscores the importance of separate data annotation. Notably, the RoBERTa model emerges as the top performer within the same train-test data category.

[5]We do not perform any post-processing on the output to convert abstain label to one of the labels.

Panel A: Models Without Further Training		
Model	**Analyst Reports (AR)**	**Earnings Calls (EC)**
Weak-Supervision	0.9272 (0.0116)	0.9382 (0.0213)
Falcon-7B (0-shot)	0.4167 (0.0075)	0.3884 (0.0624)
Llama-2-70B (0-shot)	0.7278 (0.0079)	0.5407 (0.0267)
ChatGPT-3.5 (0-shot)	0.9191 (0.0144)	0.7569 (0.0023)
Falcon-7B (6-shots)	0.3410 (0.0109)	0.3021 (0.0343)
Llama-2-70B (6-shots)	0.9169 (0.0049)	0.7972 (0.0228)
ChatGPT-3.5 (6-shots)	0.8943 (0.0033)	0.7334 (0.0198)

Panel B: Fine-Tuned Models				
Train/Test	**AR/AR**	**EC/AR**	**AR/EC**	**EC/EC**
Bi-LSTM	0.9309 (0.0235)	0.8244 (0.0332)	0.8961 (0.0236)	0.8892 (0.0375)
BERT-base-uncased	0.9532 (0.0192)	0.9269 (0.0150)	0.9251 (0.0113)	0.9376 (0.0205)
FinBERT-base	0.9617 (0.0076)	0.9381 (0.0112)	0.9209 (0.0257)	0.9279 (0.0135)
FLANG-BERT-base	0.9611 (0.0137)	0.9270 (0.0109)	0.9119 (0.0257)	0.9363 (0.0089)
RoBERTa-base	0.9615 (0.0091)	0.9319 (0.0131)	0.8906 (0.0301)	**0.9563** (0.0036)
BERT-large-uncased	0.9539 (0.0111)	0.9183 (0.0063)	0.9197 (0.0349)	0.9416 (0.0349)
RoBERTa-large	**0.9642** (0.0069)	0.9381 (0.0138)	0.8975 (0.0244)	0.9427 (0.0153)

Table 2: In the table, A/B indicates that the model is fine-tuned on dataset A and tested on dataset B. All values are F1 scores. An average of 3 seeds was used for all models. The standard deviation of F1 scores is in parentheses.

Aggr. Funtion	**AR**	**EC**
Majority Vote	0.4274 (0.0208)	0.5313 (0.0427)
Snorkel's WMV	0.4269 (0.0204)	0.5309 (0.0372)
Ours	0.9272 (0.0116)	0.9382 (0.0213)

Table 3: Performance comparison of our aggregation function with baseline aggregation functions. All values are F1 scores. An average of 3 seeds was used for all models. The standard deviation of F1 scores is reported in parentheses.

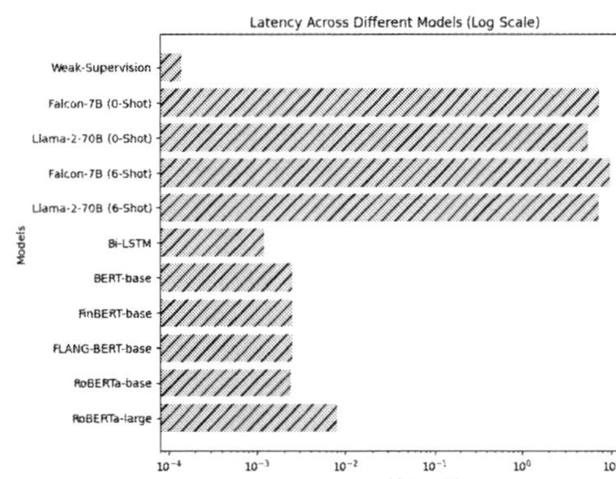

Figure 2: This bar chart compares the latency (log scale) of various models relative to the weak-supervision model.

Latency and Financial Applicability In finance, latency is crucial as investors aim to surpass competitors. Figure 2 shows just how stark the differences is in latency. Our weak-supervision (WS) model stands out for its low latency, offering significant advantages in the fast-moving financial markets. Despite challenges in measuring latency for API-based, closed-source models like ChatGPT, our analysis on Falcon-7B and Llama-70B highlights the WS model's superior speed and efficiency. This model's performance is key in finance, where processing speed can be decisive in transaction success. Furthermore, even if generative LLMs do overcome the hurdle of latency, large ethical challenges in finance as identified by (Khan and Umer, 2024) still persist. We also discuss carbon emission comparison of models in Appendix E.

5 Market Analysis

5.1 Experiment Setup

Construction of the Optimism Measure We use our weak-supervision model to label all the financial numeric sentences in the analyst reports and earnings calls as in-claim or out-of-claim. We then filter the sentences and only keep in-claim sentences to evaluate predictions.

We further label each in-claim sentence as 'positive', 'negative', or 'neutral' using the fine-tuned sentiment analysis model specifically for the financial domain. The model is fine-tuned for financial sentiment analysis using the pre-trained FinBERT (Araci, 2019). We then use labeled sentences in each document to generate a document-level measure of analyst optimism for document i using the following formula:

$$\text{Optimism}_i = 100 \times \frac{\text{Pos. In-claim}_i - \text{Neg. In-claim}_i}{\text{Total Sentences}_i} \quad (1)$$

where Pos. In-claim$_i$ and Neg. In-claim$_i$ are the number of positive and negative in-claim sentences respectively in document i after the filter, and Total Sentences$_i$ is the total number of sentences in the document.

Empirical Specification We use the following empirical specification for market analysis.

$$Y_{i,t} = \alpha + \beta \times \text{Optimism}_{i,t} + \epsilon_{i,t} \quad (2)$$

Here $Y_{i,t}$ is the outcome variable of interest for firm i at time t, α is a constant term, and $\epsilon_{i,t}$ is an error term. The coefficient (β) will help us understand the influence of Optimism$_{i,t}$ on the outcome variable ($Y_{i,t}$).

Outcome (Y)	Constant (α)	Beta (β)
Earn. Surp.	0.1744 ***	-1.9883 ***
CAR [+2, +30]	0.9548 ***	-34.5749 ***
CAR [+2, +60]	0.8559 **	-54.335 ***

Table 4: Market analysis result based on the empirical regression. *, **, and *** indicate significance at the 10%, 5%, and 1% levels, respectively.

5.2 Post Earnings Prediction

We examine the relation between optimism in analyst reports for a company in a specific quarter and its effect on earnings. Using earnings-based metrics, we perform a regression as per Eq 2 using earnings call transcripts and analyst report data. For quarters with multiple reports on one stock, we aggregate sentences and claims to compute Optimism$_i$.

Earnings Surprise (%) The Earning Surprise (%) is calculated by subtracting the median EPS (in the last 90 days) from the actual EPS. The difference is scaled by the stock price at the end of the quarter and multiplied by 100. This method aligns with Chava et al. (2022).

The Earnings Surprise (%) is set as the outcome variable ($Y_{i,t}$). The results in Table 4 show a significant link between optimism and the Earnings Surprise (%). A negative β coefficient indicates that with every unit rise in optimism in analyst reports, the Earnings Surprise (%) drops. This implies that heightened optimism in reports often leads to the actual EPS underperforming expectations. This "false optimism" aligns with previous studies like (Coleman et al., 2021), highlighting analysts' tendency to overestimate firm performance.

Cumulative Abnormal Returns We further aim to explore the influence of optimism in analyst reports on the magnitude of cumulative abnormal return (CAR) post-earnings. CAR for a firm represents the total daily abnormal stock return in the period after a specific event, in our context, the firm's earnings conference call.

We analyze two CAR time frames. CAR[+2, +30] is the cumulative abnormal for the [+2,+30] trading day window post-earnings call, as determined by Chava et al. (2022). The same methodology is used to calculate CAR[+2, +60] as well.

Table 4 shows that greater optimism in analyst reports corresponds with a larger decline in CAR. This emphasizes the 'false optimism' trend in reports, where increased optimism leads to greater discrepancies from actual outcomes, leading to a larger negative cumulative abnormal return.

The prevailing notion in finance literature is that analysts are overly optimistic. While Francis and Philbrick (1993) and Barber et al. (2007) believe this bias helps maintain good ties with corporate insiders, Michaely and Womack (1999) sees it as a means for personal financial gains. Recently, Brown et al. (2022) found that analysts favor firms with attributes like high debt or fluctuating earnings. This suggests such firms might exaggerate earnings, potentially through manipulation. Our market analysis aligning with these theories reinforces our method's accuracy and the financial relevance of our study. Furthermore, Bhojraj et al. (2009) shows that simply exceeding or failing to meet analyst expectations under certain conditions can lead to unique post-earnings characteristics for

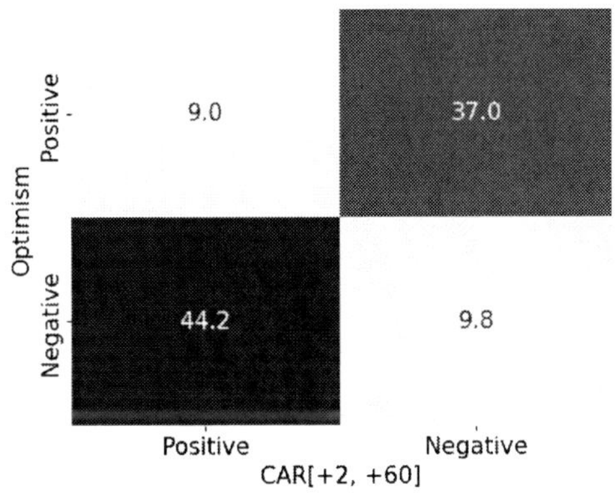

Figure 3: Normalized Confusion Matrix illustrating the percentage of trades categorized by negative or positive adjusted optimism and their corresponding CAR[+2,+60] outcomes. Each cell represents the percentage of total trades that fall within each category.

a company.

5.3 Predictive Power of Optimism

To highlight a usage of Optimism for making trading predictions, we employ a simple "trading strategy". We utilize analyst reports from 2017-2019 as a training set to identify the average positive bias in the "optimism" measure. To adjust for the bias in our test set, the 2020 analyst reports, we subtract the mean bias from the optimism score for each company, correcting for the inherent positive bias. The division of the dataset into training and testing phases is crucial to avoid look-ahead bias in calculating mean optimism. After adjusting the optimism measure in the test dataset, we implement a straightforward investment strategy: short selling companies with a positive adjusted optimism score and buying shares of companies with a negative adjusted optimism score. This approach is based on the rationale of investing in companies with **overly** pessimistic sentiment and divesting from those with **overly** optimistic sentiment. We use Earnings Surprise, CAR[+2, +30], and CAR[+2,+60] to determine the success or failure of our hypothetical trades.

The confusion matrix corresponding to the results of CAR[+2,+60] are visualized in Figure 3, while Earnings Surprise and CAR[+2,+30] are shown in Appendix G. The confusion matrix shows that such a rule-based strategy achieves an approximate 81% accuracy in correctly predicting the direction of stock movement. Additionally, the high accuracy lasting up to 60 days indicates that using optimism can effectively predict stock movements for more than just a few days, demonstrating a valuable preliminary application of such identification for the financial field.

6 Conclusion

Our work presents claim based labeled dataset in the English language alongside presenting a weak-supervision model with an accuracy of 93%. Developed customized aggregation function outperforms baseline aggregation functions. We benchmark various language models and compare the performance with the weak-supervision model. We show the application of claim detection by generating a measure of optimism from the weak-supervision model. We also validate the measure by studying its applicability in predicting earnings surprise, abnormal returns, and earnings optimism. We release our models, code, and benchmark data (for earnings call transcripts only) on Hugging Face and GitHub. We also note that the trained model for claim detection can be used on other financial texts.

Limitations

By acknowledging the following limitations, we pave the way for future research to address these areas and further enhance the understanding and applicability of our approach.

- *Limited Scope of Text Data*: Our analysis is restricted to analyst reports and earnings calls, excluding other potentially valuable text datasets such as related news articles and investor presentations. Incorporating these additional sources of information could provide a more comprehensive understanding of pre-earnings drifts.

- *Exclusion of Audio and Video Features*: Our measure construction does not utilize audio or video features from earnings calls, which may contain supplementary information.

- *Omission of Alternative Weak-Supervision Models*: We do not explore multiple end models, such as the confidence-based sampling with contrastive loss proposed in the COSINE framework by Yu et al. (2020). Incorporating such alternative weak-supervision models could offer additional insights and improve the robustness of our approach.

Ethics Statement

Our work adheres to ethical considerations, although we acknowledge certain biases and limitations in our study. We do not identify any potential risks stemming from our research; however, we recognize the presence of geographic and gender biases in our analysis.

- *Geographic Bias*: Our study focuses solely on publicly listed companies in the United States of America, which introduces a geographic bias. The findings may not be fully representative of global firms and markets.
- *Gender Bias*: We acknowledge the gender bias present in our study due to the predominant representation of male analysts, CEOs, and CFOs.
- *Data Ethics*: The data used in our study, derived from publicly available sources, does not raise ethical concerns. All raw data is obtained from public companies that are obligated to disclose information under the guidance of the SEC and are subject to public scrutiny.
- *Language Model Ethics*: The language models employed (with proper citation) in our research are publicly available and fall under license categories that permit their use for our intended purposes. While most models employed are publicly available, it is important to note that ChatGPT's prompt answers will not be made public due to licensing conditions. We acknowledge the environmental impact of large pre-training of language models and mitigate this by limiting our work to fine-tuning existing models.
- *Annotation Ethics*: All annotations were performed by the authors, ensuring that no additional ethical concerns arise from the annotation process.
- *Hyperparameter Reporting*: In the interest of clarity and readability, we refrain from reporting the best hyperparameters found through grid search in the main paper. Instead, we will make all grid search results, including hyperparameter information, publicly available on GitHub. This transparency allows interested readers to access detailed information on our experimental setup.
- *Publicly Available Data*: We specify the datasets that will be made publicly available and indicate the applicable licenses under which they will be shared.

By acknowledging these ethical considerations and limitations, we strive to maintain transparency and promote responsible research practices.

References

Md Shad Akhtar, Abhishek Kumar, Deepanway Ghosal, Asif Ekbal, and Pushpak Bhattacharyya. 2017. A multilayer perceptron based ensemble technique for fine-grained financial sentiment analysis. In *Proceedings of the 2017 conference on empirical methods in natural language processing*, pages 540–546.

Ebtesam Almazrouei, Hamza Alobeidli, Abdulaziz Alshamsi, Alessandro Cappelli, Ruxandra Cojocaru, Merouane Debbah, Etienne Goffinet, Daniel Heslow, Julien Launay, Quentin Malartic, Badreddine Noune, Baptiste Pannier, and Guilherme Penedo. 2023. Falcon-40B: an open large language model with state-of-the-art performance.

Dogu Araci. 2019. Finbert: Financial sentiment analysis with pre-trained language models. *arXiv preprint arXiv:1908.10063*.

Brad M Barber, Reuven Lehavy, and Brett Trueman. 2007. Comparing the stock recommendation performance of investment banks and independent research firms. *Journal of financial economics*, 85(2):490–517.

Sanjeev Bhojraj, Paul Hribar, Marc Picconi, and John McInnis. 2009. Making sense of cents: An examination of firms that marginally miss or beat analyst forecasts. In *The Journal of Finance*, volume 64 (5), pages 2361–2388.

Anna Bergman Brown, Guoyu Lin, and Aner Zhou. 2022. Analysts' forecast optimism: The effects of managers' incentives on analysts' forecasts. *Journal of Behavioral and Experimental Finance*, 35:100708.

Sean Cao, Wei Jiang, Baozhong Yang, and Alan L Zhang. 2020. How to talk when a machine is listening: Corporate disclosure in the age of ai. Technical report, National Bureau of Economic Research.

Olivier Chapelle, Bernhard Scholkopf, and Alexander Zien. 2009. Semi-supervised learning (chapelle, o. et al., eds.; 2006)[book reviews]. *IEEE Transactions on Neural Networks*, 20(3):542–542.

Sudheer Chava, Wendi Du, and Baridhi Malakar. 2021. Do managers walk the talk on environmental and social issues? *Available at SSRN 3900814*.

Sudheer Chava, Wendi Du, Agam Shah, and Linghang Zeng. 2022. Measuring firm-level inflation exposure: A deep learning approach. *Available at SSRN 4228332*.

Chung-Chi Chen, Hen-Hsen Huang, and Hsin-Hsi Chen. 2019. Numeral attachment with auxiliary tasks. In *Proceedings of the 42nd International ACM SIGIR Conference on Research and Development in Information Retrieval*, pages 1161–1164.

Chung-Chi Chen, Hen-Hsen Huang, and Hsin-Hsi Chen. 2020. Numclaim: Investor's fine-grained claim detection. In *Proceedings of the 29th ACM International Conference on Information & Knowledge Management*, pages 1973–1976.

Zhiyu Chen, Wenhu Chen, Charese Smiley, Sameena Shah, Iana Borova, Dylan Langdon, Reema Moussa, Matt Beane, Ting-Hao Huang, Bryan Routledge, et al. 2021. Finqa: A dataset of numerical reasoning over financial data. *arXiv preprint arXiv:2109.00122*.

Braiden Coleman, Kenneth J Merkley, and Joseph Pacelli. 2021. Human versus machine: A comparison of robo-analyst and traditional research analyst investment recommendations. *The Accounting Review, Forthcoming*.

Shane A Corwin, Stephannie A Larocque, and Mike A Stegemoller. 2017. Investment banking relationships and analyst affiliation bias: The impact of the global settlement on sanctioned and non-sanctioned banks. *Journal of Financial Economics*, 124(3):614–631.

Min-Yuh Day and Chia-Chou Lee. 2016. Deep learning for financial sentiment analysis on finance news providers. In *2016 IEEE/ACM International Conference on Advances in Social Networks Analysis and Mining (ASONAM)*, pages 1127–1134. IEEE.

Jacob Devlin, Ming-Wei Chang, Kenton Lee, and Kristina Toutanova. 2018. Bert: Pre-training of deep bidirectional transformers for language understanding. *arXiv preprint arXiv:1810.04805*.

Jennifer Francis and Donna Philbrick. 1993. Analysts' decisions as products of a multi-task environment. *Journal of Accounting Research*, 31(2):216–230.

Sepp Hochreiter and Jürgen Schmidhuber. 1997. Long short-term memory. *Neural computation*, 9(8):1735–1780.

Allen Hu and Song Ma. 2021. Persuading investors: A video-based study. Technical report, National Bureau of Economic Research.

Narasimhan Jegadeesh and Woojin Kim. 2010. Do analysts herd? an analysis of recommendations and market reactions. *The Review of Financial Studies*, 23(2):901–937.

David Kartchner, Wendi Ren, David Nakajima An, Chao Zhang, and Cassie S Mitchell. 2020. Regal: Rule-generative active learning for model-in-the-loop weak supervision. *Advances in neural information processing systems*.

Muhammad Salar Khan and Hamza Umer. 2024. Chatgpt in finance: Applications, challenges, and solutions. *Heliyon*, 10(2):e24890.

Loïc Lannelongue, Jason Grealey, and Michael Inouye. 2021. Green algorithms: Quantifying the carbon footprint of computation. *Advanced Science*, 8(12):2100707.

Jiazheng Li, Linyi Yang, Barry Smyth, and Ruihai Dong. 2020. Maec: A multimodal aligned earnings conference call dataset for financial risk prediction. In *Proceedings of the 29th ACM International Conference on Information & Knowledge Management*, pages 3063–3070.

Kai Li, Feng Mai, Rui Shen, and Xinyan Yan. 2021. Measuring corporate culture using machine learning. *The Review of Financial Studies*, 34(7):3265–3315.

Pierre Lison, Jeremy Barnes, and Aliaksandr Hubin. 2021. skweak: Weak supervision made easy for nlp. *arXiv preprint arXiv:2104.09683*.

Yinhan Liu, Myle Ott, Naman Goyal, Jingfei Du, Mandar Joshi, Danqi Chen, Omer Levy, M. Lewis, Luke Zettlemoyer, and Veselin Stoyanov. 2019. Roberta: A robustly optimized bert pretraining approach. *ArXiv*, abs/1907.11692.

Zhuang Liu, Degen Huang, Kaiyu Huang, Zhuang Li, and Jun Zhao. 2020. Finbert: A pre-trained financial language representation model for financial text mining. In *IJCAI*, pages 4513–4519.

Macedo Maia, Siegfried Handschuh, André Freitas, Brian Davis, Ross McDermott, Manel Zarrouk, and Alexandra Balahur. 2018. Www'18 open challenge: Financial opinion mining and question answering. In *Companion Proceedings of the The Web Conference 2018*, WWW '18, page 1941–1942, Republic and Canton of Geneva, CHE. International World Wide Web Conferences Steering Committee.

Pekka Malo, Ankur Sinha, Pekka Korhonen, Jyrki Wallenius, and Pyry Takala. 2014. Good debt or bad debt: Detecting semantic orientations in economic texts. *Journal of the Association for Information Science and Technology*, 65(4):782–796.

R David McLean, Jeffrey Pontiff, and Christopher Reilly. 2020. Retail investors and analysts. Technical report, Working Paper, Boston College.

Yu Meng, Jiaming Shen, Chao Zhang, and Jiawei Han. 2018. Weakly-supervised neural text classification. In *proceedings of the 27th ACM International Conference on information and knowledge management*, pages 983–992.

Roni Michaely and Kent L Womack. 1999. Conflict of interest and the credibility of underwriter analyst recommendations. *The Review of Financial Studies*, 12(4):653–686.

Mike Mintz, Steven Bills, Rion Snow, and Dan Jurafsky. 2009. Distant supervision for relation extraction without labeled data. In *Proceedings of the Joint Conference of the 47th Annual Meeting of the ACL and the 4th International Joint Conference on Natural*

Language Processing of the AFNLP, pages 1003–1011.

Cuong V Nguyen, Sanjiv R Das, John He, Shenghua Yue, Vinay Hanumaiah, Xavier Ragot, and Li Zhang. 2021. Multimodal machine learning for credit modeling. In *2021 IEEE 45th Annual Computers, Software, and Applications Conference (COMPSAC)*, pages 1754–1759. IEEE.

Sinno Jialin Pan and Qiang Yang. 2010. A survey on transfer learning. *IEEE Transactions on Knowledge and Data Engineering*, 22(10):1345–1359.

Adam Paszke, Sam Gross, Francisco Massa, Adam Lerer, James Bradbury, Gregory Chanan, Trevor Killeen, Zeming Lin, Natalia Gimelshein, Luca Antiga, Alban Desmaison, Andreas Kopf, Edward Yang, Zachary DeVito, Martin Raison, Alykhan Tejani, Sasank Chilamkurthy, Benoit Steiner, Lu Fang, Junjie Bai, and Soumith Chintala. 2019. Pytorch: An imperative style, high-performance deep learning library. In H. Wallach, H. Larochelle, A. Beygelzimer, F. d'Alché-Buc, E. Fox, and R. Garnett, editors, *Advances in Neural Information Processing Systems 32*, pages 8024–8035. Curran Associates, Inc.

Jeffrey Pennington, Richard Socher, and Christopher D Manning. 2014. Glove: Global vectors for word representation. In *EMNLP*, volume 14, pages 1532–1543.

Alexander Ratner, Stephen H Bach, Henry Ehrenberg, Jason Fries, Sen Wu, and Christopher Ré. 2017. Snorkel: Rapid training data creation with weak supervision. In *Proceedings of the VLDB Endowment. International Conference on Very Large Data Bases*, volume 11 (3), page 269. NIH Public Access.

Alexander Ratner, Stephen H Bach, Henry Ehrenberg, Jason Fries, Sen Wu, and Christopher Ré. 2020. Snorkel: Rapid training data creation with weak supervision. *The VLDB Journal*, 29(2):709–730.

Anna Rogers, Niranjan Balasubramanian, Leon Derczynski, Jesse Dodge, Alexander Koller, Sasha Luccioni, Maarten Sap, Roy Schwartz, Noah A. Smith, and Emma Strubell. 2023. Closed ai models make bad baselines.

Ramit Sawhney, Piyush Khanna, Arshiya Aggarwal, Taru Jain, Puneet Mathur, and Rajiv Shah. 2020. Voltage: volatility forecasting via text-audio fusion with graph convolution networks for earnings calls. In *Proceedings of the 2020 Conference on Empirical Methods in Natural Language Processing (EMNLP)*, pages 8001–8013.

Mike Schuster and Kuldip K Paliwal. 1997. Bidirectional recurrent neural networks. *IEEE transactions on Signal Processing*, 45(11):2673–2681.

Burr Settles. 2009. Active learning literature survey. *University of Wisconsin-Madison Department of Computer Sciences*.

Agam Shah, Suvan Paturi, and Sudheer Chava. 2023a. Trillion dollar words: A new financial dataset, task & market analysis. *arXiv preprint arXiv:2305.07972*.

Agam Shah, Ruchit Vithani, Abhinav Gullapalli, and Sudheer Chava. 2023b. Finer: Financial named entity recognition dataset and weak-supervision model. *arXiv preprint arXiv:2302.11157*.

Raj Shah, Kunal Chawla, Dheeraj Eidnani, Agam Shah, Wendi Du, Sudheer Chava, Natraj Raman, Charese Smiley, Jiaao Chen, and Diyi Yang. 2022. When FLUE meets FLANG: Benchmarks and large pretrained language model for financial domain. In *Proceedings of the 2022 Conference on Empirical Methods in Natural Language Processing*, pages 2322–2335, Abu Dhabi, United Arab Emirates. Association for Computational Linguistics.

Hugo Touvron, Louis Martin, Kevin Stone, Peter Albert, Amjad Almahairi, Yasmine Babaei, Nikolay Bashlykov, Soumya Batra, Prajjwal Bhargava, Shruti Bhosale, et al. 2023. Llama 2: Open foundation and fine-tuned chat models. *arXiv preprint arXiv:2307.09288*.

Paroma Varma and Christopher Ré. 2018. Snuba: Automating weak supervision to label training data. In *Proceedings of the VLDB Endowment. International Conference on Very Large Data Bases*, volume 12 (3), page 223. NIH Public Access.

Ashish Vaswani, Noam Shazeer, Niki Parmar, Jakob Uszkoreit, Llion Jones, Aidan N Gomez, Łukasz Kaiser, and Illia Polosukhin. 2017. Attention is all you need. *Advances in neural information processing systems*, 30.

Thomas Wolf, Lysandre Debut, Victor Sanh, Julien Chaumond, Clement Delangue, Anthony Moi, Pierric Cistac, Tim Rault, Rémi Louf, Morgan Funtowicz, Joe Davison, Sam Shleifer, Patrick von Platen, Clara Ma, Yacine Jernite, Julien Plu, Canwen Xu, Teven Le Scao, Sylvain Gugger, Mariama Drame, Quentin Lhoest, and Alexander M. Rush. 2020. Transformers: State-of-the-art natural language processing. In *Proceedings of the 2020 Conference on Empirical Methods in Natural Language Processing: System Demonstrations*, pages 38–45, Online. Association for Computational Linguistics.

Yi Yang, Mark Christopher Siy Uy, and Allen Huang. 2020. Finbert: A pretrained language model for financial communications. *CoRR*, abs/2006.08097.

Yue Yu, Lingkai Kong, Jieyu Zhang, Rongzhi Zhang, and Chao Zhang. 2022. Actune: Uncertainty-based active self-training for active fine-tuning of pretrained language models. In *Proceedings of the 2022 Conference of the North American Chapter of the Association for Computational Linguistics: Human Language Technologies*, pages 1422–1436.

Yue Yu, Simiao Zuo, Haoming Jiang, Wendi Ren, Tuo Zhao, and Chao Zhang. 2020. Fine-tuning pretrained language model with weak supervision: A contrastive-regularized self-training approach. *arXiv preprint arXiv:2010.07835*.

Man-Ching Yuen, Irwin King, and Kwong-Sak Leung. 2011. A survey of crowdsourcing systems. In *2011 IEEE third international conference on privacy, security, risk and trust and 2011 IEEE third international conference on social computing*, pages 766–773. IEEE.

Jieyu Zhang, Yue Yu, Yinghao Li, Yujing Wang, Yaming Yang, Mao Yang, and Alexander Ratner. 2021. Wrench: A comprehensive benchmark for weak supervision. *arXiv preprint arXiv:2109.11377*.

Rongzhi Zhang, Yue Yu, Pranav Shetty, Le Song, and Chao Zhang. 2022. Prboost: Prompt-based rule discovery and boosting for interactive weakly-supervised learning. *arXiv preprint arXiv:2203.09735*.

A Robustness Check

From a data engineering perspective, there can be concern about the model design and gold data construction as the authors who designed the weak-supervision model have annotated the data. This can lead to exaggerated performance on the data, which may taint the test set. To ensure that there is no contamination issue in the weak-supervision model and it is generalizable, we get the same test dataset annotated separately by four annotators with master's degrees in Quantitative Finance. These annotators were hired by the department as Graduate Assistants based on merit and were paid a $20 per hour salary for their work which is more than double the federal minimum wage and higher than the highest minimum wage ($15.74 in Washington, D.C) in the USA. The rates are standard and in compliance with ethical standards. These annotators had no information about the rules/patterns used in our weak-supervision model. Each sample in the test dataset is annotated by two annotators, and we drop the observations where there is a disagreement among annotators. [6] The F1 score of the weak-supervision model on a dataset annotated by non-authors is 0.9281 which is close to a score of 0.9272 on the author-annotated dataset. We also recalculate the F1 score of the model based on the author-annotated labels after dropping observations dropped in a non-author annotated dataset. The model gives a higher mean F1 score of 0.9360 which is expected as ambiguous sentences are dropped. Overall these results show the robustness of our model on the dataset annotated by annotators who don't have knowledge of the rules used in the weak-supervision model. From here onwards, the performance is always calculated on a gold dataset created by authors.

[6]There is 98.59% agreement between two annotators.

B Labeling Functions Methodology

The following illustrates the methodology adopted by us while choosing the rules to define the weak-supervision mode. All rules were acknowledged post detailed analysis of sample documents distributed over sector and time :

1. Certain phrases such as "reasons to buy", "reasons to sell" or the presence of words which are indicative of past tense such as "was", "were" are characteristic of out-of-claim sentences, since they indicated either facts or events which happened in the past. Examples are given in the set 1 of Table 5.

2. Phrases often provided definitive information about a given sentence in a document and in most cases they had a fairly consistent linguistic composition. Examples are given in the set 2 of Table 5.

3. In a bid to capture the effect of a few other verb forms indicative of a probabilistic event, we also chose to look at its lemmatized form to reduce inflectional usage and use the base token for a more holistic evaluation over multiple usage formats. Examples are given in the set 3 of Table 5.

4. POS tags were also derived for "project" as a word wherever present. This was done to segregate its usage as a verb. Its usage as a verb was usually observed to be adopted while making claims or predictions. Examples are given in the set 4 of Table 5.

5. The alternate adoption of phrase matching was to identify in-claim sentences. This mostly consisted of a verb form indicative of a probabilistic event (eg: likely, intends) coupled with a preposition (usually "to" or "at"). Based on the ambiguity of the resulting phrase they were either categorised as a high-confidence claim or a low-confidence one. Examples are given in the set 5 of Table 5.

Set	Used to detect	Output	Type	Keyword or phrase
1	High Confidence out-of-claim (Past Tense or Assertions)	-1/0	Phrase Matching	reasons to buy:, reasons to sell:, was, were, declares quarterly dividend, last earnings report, recorded
2	Low Confidence in-claim	1/0	Phrase Matching	earnings guidance to, touted to, entitle to
3	High Confidence in-claim	2/0	Lemmatized Word matching	expect, anticipate, predict, forecast, envision, contemplate
4	High Confidence in-claim	2/0	POS Tag for word "project"	VBN, VB, VBD, VBG, VBP, VBZ
5	High Confidence in-claim	2/0	Phrase Matching	to be, likely to, on track to, intends to, aims to, to incur, pegged at

Table 5: Labeling Functions used in weak-supervision model. SpaCy Lemmatizer has been used for labeling functions involving lemmatized word matching.

C Additional Models

C.1 Generative LLMs

To understand the capabilities of current state-of-the-art (SOTA) generative LLMs' in a zero-shot and few-shot manner, we add ChatGPT[7] performance benchmark in our study. We use the "gpt-3.5-turbo-0613" model with 200 max tokens for output, and a 0.0 temperature value. The ChatGPT API was accessed on Feb 2nd, 2024. In a recent article, Rogers et al. (2023) made a case for why closed models like ChatGPT make bad baselines. In order to understand where SOTA open-source LLMs stand in comparison to ChatGPT and fine-tuned models, we also test the Falcon-7B-Instruct (Almazrouei et al., 2023) and "Llama-2-70B-chat" (Touvron et al., 2023) models. The prompt templates are provided in Table 6. All our prompting was done in consistency with reputable resources, such as the "Prompt Engineering Guide" [8]. We also test the model with zero-shot and six-shot. The six-shot prompting consists of 3 'in-claim' examples and 3 'out-of-claim' examples.

C.2 Bi-LSTM

In the realm of text classification problems, Long Short-Term Memory (LSTM) was a popular recurrent neural network architecture (Hochreiter and Schmidhuber, 1997). An enhanced approach to LSTM is the Bidirectional LSTM (Bi-LSTM), which processes input in both directions (Schuster and Paliwal, 1997). In order to assess the efficacy of Recurrent Neural Networks (RNNs) in claim detection, we employ the Bi-LSTM model on the datasets we have developed. Instead of training it from scratch, we initialize the embedding layer of the Bi-LSTM using 300-dimensional GloVe embeddings trained using Common Crawl (Pennington et al., 2014). Here we perform the task of sequence classification while minimizing the cross-entropy loss. We employ a grid search approach to identify the optimal hyperparameters for each model, considering four different learning rates (1e-4, 1e-5, 1e-6, 1e-7) and four different batch sizes (32, 16, 8, 4). In our training process, we employ a maximum of 100 epochs, incorporating early stopping criteria. In cases where the validation F1 score does not exhibit an improvement of greater than or equal to 1e-2 over the subsequent 7 epochs, we designate the previously saved best model as the final fine-tuned model.

C.3 PLMs

In order to establish a performance benchmark, our study encompasses a range of transformer-based (Vaswani et al., 2017) models of varying sizes. For the small models, we employ BERT (Devlin et al., 2018), FinBERT (Yang et al., 2020), FLANG-BERT (Shah et al., 2022), and RoBERTa (Liu et al., 2019). Within the category of large models, we incorporate BERT-large (Devlin et al., 2018) and RoBERTa-large (Liu et al., 2019). To avoid over-fitting on financial text, we refrain from conducting any pre-training on these models prior to fine-tuning. Here we perform the task of sequence classification while minimizing the cross-entropy loss. For PLMs, we employ grid-search, fine-tuning, and early stopping similar to what we used for Bi-LSTM. The experiments are conducted using PyTorch (Paszke et al., 2019) on an NVIDIA RTX A6000 GPU. Each model is initialized with the pre-trained version from the Transformers library provided by Huggingface (Wolf et al., 2020).

[7] https://chat.openai.com/
[8] https://www.promptingguide.ai/

Prompt Name	Description
Zero-shot	Discard all the previous instructions. Behave like you are an expert sentence classifier. Classify the following sentence into either 'INCLAIM' or 'OUTOFCLAIM'. 'INCLAIM' refers to predictions or expectations about financial outcomes. 'OUTOFCLAIM' refers to sentences that provide numerical information or established facts about past financial events. For each classification, 'INCLAIM' can be thought of as 'financial forecasts', and 'OUTOFCLAIM' as 'established financials'. Now, for the following sentence provide the label in the first line and provide a short explanation in the second line. The sentence: {sentence}
Few-shot	Discard all the previous instructions. Behave like you are an expert sentence classifier. Classify the following sentence into either 'INCLAIM' or 'OUTOFCLAIM'. 'INCLAIM' refers to predictions or expectations about financial outcomes. 'OUTOFCLAIM' refers to sentences that provide numerical information or established facts about past financial events. For each classification, 'INCLAIM' can be thought of as 'financial forecasts', and 'OUTOFCLAIM' as 'established financials'. Here are a few examples: Example 1: free cash flow of $2.3 billion was up 10.5%, benefiting from the positive year-over-year change in net working capital due to covid at both nbcu and sky, half of which resulted from the timing of when sports rights payments were made versus when sports actually aired and half of which resulted from a slower ramp in content production. // The sentence is OUTOFCLAIM Example 2: we've also used our scale of more than 15,000 combined stores to drive merchandise cost savings exceeding $70 million. // The sentence is OUTOFCLAIM Example 3: consolidated total capital was $2.9 billion for the quarter. // The sentence is OUTOFCLAIM Example 4: third, as a result of the continued strength of the u.s. dollar, we are now factoring in an incremental fx headwind of $175 million across q3 and q4 revenue. // The sentence is INCLAIM Example 5: though early, we are planning our business based on the expectation of cy '23 wfe declining approximately 20% based on increasing global macroeconomic concerns and recent public statements from several customers, particularly in memory, and the impact of the new u.s. government regulations on native china investment. // The sentence is INCLAIM Example 6: we expect revenue growth to be in the range of 5.5% to 6.5% year on year. // The sentence is INCLAIM Now, for the following sentence provide the label in the first line and provide a short explanation in the second line. The sentence: {sentence}

Table 6: Prompts used for zero-shot and few-shot inference.

D Ablation: Number of Labeling Functions

Figure 4, shows how the accuracy of the model changes depending on the number of labeling functions. For this plot, we initially computed the contribution of each labeling function (Table 5, High confidence and Low Confidence in-claim) towards the detection of in-claim sentences and then considered the addition of new labeling function at each step to ensure the steepest ascent to saturation. At each step, in addition to one new labeling function, all labeling functions present in Table 5 for Past Tense and Assertions, were also used. They either abstain or classify sentences as out-of-claim and help improve the classification of out-of-claim sentences. From the plot, we can notice that after around thirteen labeling functions, the addition of new labeling functions does not produce any change in the accuracy. In fact, increasing labeling functions thereafter leads to a minor decrease in accuracy. This suggests that we can effectively capture the required trends for classification in this setting with thirteen labeling functions.

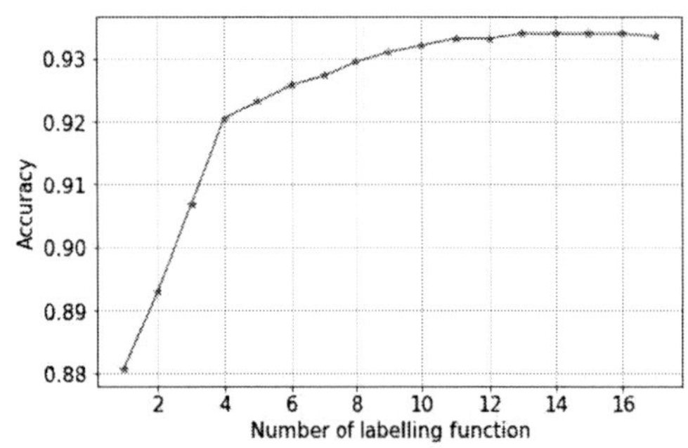

Figure 4: Accuracy v/s Number of labeling functions. Note: This is accuracy, not F1 score.

E Environmental Impact

Our investigation extends beyond just performance metrics, embracing a conscientious approach towards the environmental implications of AI usage. To ensure a standardized and rigorous assessment of CO2e, we drew upon the methodology outlined by Lannelongue et al. (2021) and utilized the Green Algorithms calculator[9]. The value of CO2e are reported in Figure 5. This dual focus on minimizing latency and CO2e without compromising performance highlights our commitment to advancing sustainable and efficient AI technologies in sectors where both are of paramount importance, such as finance. The CO2 emissions (CO2e) associated with the inference phase of these models are particularly telling, with our WS model not only leading in latency but also in sustainability, registering the lowest CO2e among all models reviewed. This underscores the viability of employing AI in environments where both speed and environmental responsibility are valued. In contrast, models such

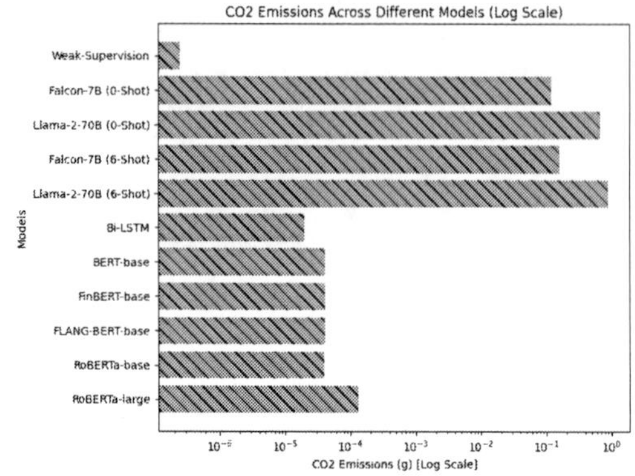

Figure 5: This bar chart compares the CO2 emissions (log scale) of various models relative to the weak-supervision model.

as Llama-70B, despite their performance coming close to our model, incur significantly higher (more than a million times larger) CO2e due to their reliance on extensive GPU resources.

F Ablation Study: Market Analysis

To understand the influence of "in-claim" sentences on market sentiment, we introduce the optimism measure in section 5, outlining its implications. In this section, we carry out an ablation study to better understand the impact of "in-claim" sentences. As such, we compute the optimism score for four sentence subsets: Unfiltered, Numerical, Numerical Financial, and Numerical Financial "In-claim" sentences for each file. For example, the optimism score for a subset of Numerical sentences for document i is given by:

$$\text{Optimism (Numerical)}_i = 100 \times \frac{\text{Pos. Numerical}_i - \text{Neg. Numerical}_i}{\text{Total Sentences}_i}$$

We standard normalize these scores for uniform comparison by deducting their mean and dividing by the standard deviation. As the beta coefficient lacks full context, to factor in the size of the sentence subset, we adjusted each coefficient by the average sentence count, terming it as the adjusted beta. This illustrates the information density in each filtered sentence set. When examining the Earnings Surprise (%) columns of Table 7 the Adjusted Beta for Earnings Surprise increases, implying that a mere average of 3.7 "in-claim" sentences holds crucial information. This highlights the high information density of our filtered sentences. While

[9]https://calculator.green-algorithms.org/

		ES (%)	CAR [+2,+30]	CAR [+2, +60]
Sentence Type/Subset	**Average Sentences**	**Adj. β**	**Adj. β**	**Adj. β**
Unfiltered	98	-0.054***	-0.02**	-.03***
Numeric	26	-0.28***	-.06***	-.09***
Numeric Financial	21.6	-0.29***	-.07***	-.11***
Numeric Financial In-claim	3.7	-1.51***	-.26***	-.41***

Table 7: Ablation on market analysis, highlighting the importance and information density of "in-claim" sentences. *, **, and *** indicate significance at the 10%, 5%, and 1% levels, respectively.

we aren't dismissing the importance of other sentences, our analysis reveals that the ones we've extracted are the most informative on a per-sentence basis.

G Predictive Power of Optimism (Earnings Suprise and CAR[+2,+30])

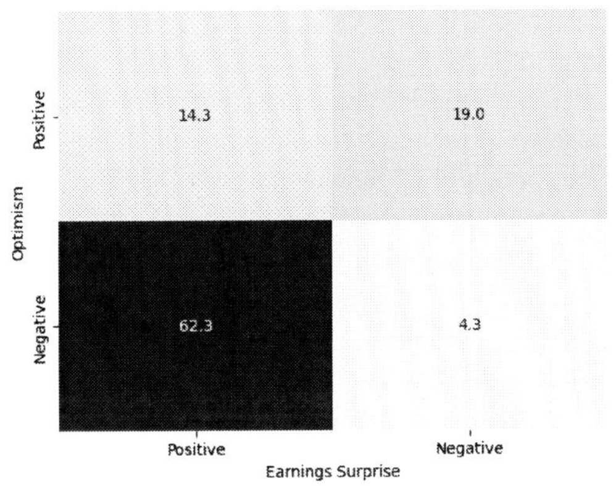

Figure 6: Percentage of trades categorized by negative or positive adjusted optimism and their corresponding Earnings Surprise outcomes.

Figure 6 and 7 show the results of making trades based on a positive or negative adjusted optimism in terms of the respective performance of the company.

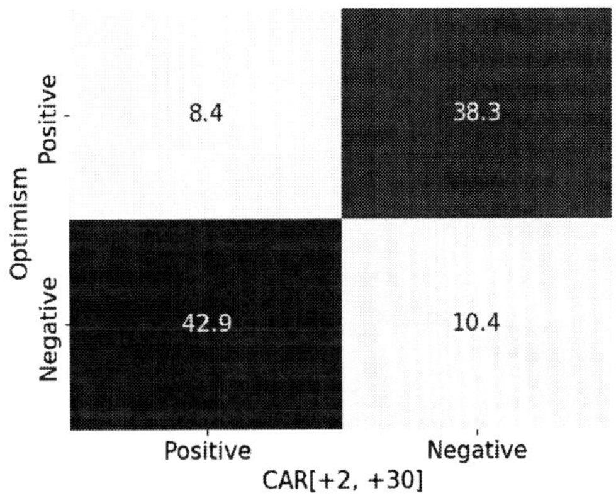

Figure 7: Percentage of trades categorized by negative or positive adjusted optimism and their corresponding CAR[+2,+30] outcomes.

Streamlining Conformal Information Retrieval via Score Refinement

Yotam Intrator* yotami@google.com
Regev Cohen* regevcohen@google.com
Ori Kelner* orikelner@google.com

Roman Goldenberg gnamor@gmail.com
Ehud Rivlin ehudr@cs.technion.ac.il
Daniel Freedman danielfreedman@gmail.com

Verily AI (Google Life Sciences), Israel.

Abstract

Information retrieval (IR) methods, like retrieval augmented generation, are fundamental to modern applications but often lack statistical guarantees. Conformal prediction addresses this by retrieving sets guaranteed to include relevant information, yet existing approaches produce large-sized sets, incurring high computational costs and slow response times. In this work, we introduce a score refinement method that applies a simple monotone transformation to retrieval scores, leading to significantly smaller conformal sets while maintaining their statistical guarantees. Experiments on various BEIR benchmarks validate the effectiveness of our approach in producing compact sets containing relevant information.

1 Introduction

Information retrieval (IR) methods lie at the heart of numerous modern applications, ranging from search engines and recommendation systems to question-answering platforms and decision support tools. These methods facilitate the identification and extraction of relevant information from vast collections of data, enabling users to access the knowledge they seek efficiently and effectively. A popular example of IR is Retrieval Augmented Generation (RAG), a technique for reducing hallucinations in large language models (LLMs) by grounding their responses on factual information retrieved from external sources.

While IR methods have been widely adopted, they traditionally lack statistical guarantees on the relevance of retrieved information. This limitation can lead to uncertainty regarding the reliability and correctness of the retrieved information. Conformal prediction (Angelopoulos and Bates, 2021; Angelopoulos et al., 2021) is an uncertainty quantification framework that can be used with any underlying model to construct sets that are statistically guaranteed to contain the ground truth with a user-specified probability. Conformal prediction has expanded far beyond its initial classification focus (Vovk et al., 2005; Angelopoulos and Bates, 2021; Ringel et al., 2024), now encompassing diverse applications like regression, image-to-image translation (Angelopoulos et al., 2022b; Kutiel et al., 2023), and foundation models (Gui et al., 2024), advancing to enable control of any monotone risk function (Angelopoulos et al., 2022a). In the context of IR, recent methods (Xu et al., 2024; Li et al., 2023; Angelopoulos et al., 2023) have incorporated conformal prediction into ranked retrieval systems to ensure the reliability and quality of retrieved items. However, existing conformal methods often produce excessively large retrieved sets, implying high computational costs and slower response times.

In this work, we address this limitation by introducing a novel score refinement method that employs a simple yet effective monotone transformation, inspired by ranking measures, to adjust the scores of any given information retrieval system. By applying standard conformal prediction methods to these refined scores, we deliver significantly smaller retrieved sets while preserving their statistical guarantees, striking a crucial balance between efficiency and accuracy. An illustration of the proposed pipeline is shown in Figure 1. We validate the effectiveness of our method through experiments on three of BEIR (Thakur et al., 2021) benchmark datasets, demonstrating its ability to outperform competing approaches in producing compact sets that contain the relevant information.

2 Background

To lay the groundwork for our work, we present a simplified description of the operation of information retrieval systems and how conformal inference

*Equal Contribution.

Proceedings of the Seventh Fact Extraction and VERification Workshop (FEVER), pages 186–191
November 15, 2024

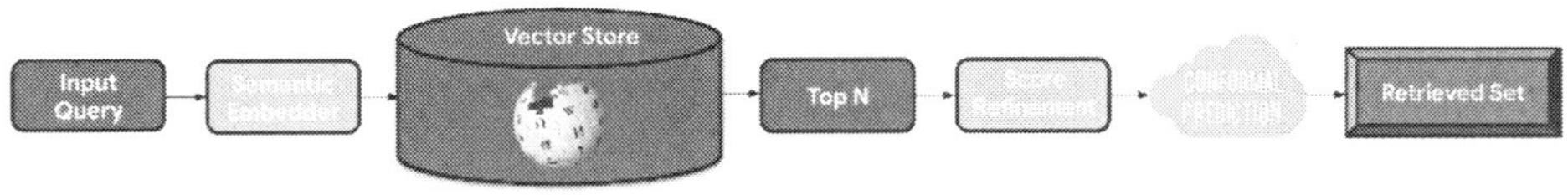

Figure 1: Retrieval Pipeline. The query is first embedded using a semantic embedder, and then the top N candidates are retrieved from a vector store. Crucially, their corresponding scores then undergo a refinement transformation before being passed through a conformal prediction method that outputs an adaptive set of documents.

can be seamlessly integrated within this context.

2.1 Information Retrieval: Overview

Consider a large information database $\mathcal{D} = \{d_1, d_2, ..., d_N\}$. At inference time, an IR model $R : \mathcal{Q} \rightarrow \mathcal{D}$ accepts a query $q \in \mathcal{Q}$ as input and returns a subset of candidates $\mathcal{S} \subset \mathcal{D}$. To do this, the IR model computes a semantic embedding $e_q = E(q)$ for the query and compares it to pre-computed embeddings $e_i = E(d_i)$ for each item in the database using a similarity metric:

$$s_i = \texttt{sim}(e_q, e_i), \tag{1}$$

where E is the chosen representation model (e.g., a neural network encoder) and `sim` is a similarity metric, such as cosine similarity. Subsequently, the items are typically ranked based on their similarity scores, and the top ranked items are retrieved, forming the following set

$$\mathcal{S}_K \triangleq \left\{d_i \in \mathcal{D} : s_i \geq s_{(K)}\right\} \tag{2}$$

where $s_{(K)}$ denotes the Kth largest similarity score, for a predefined $K > 0$ constant across all queries.

The approach above suffers from two key limitations. First, using a fixed K can be problematic: it might be too restrictive for some queries, leading to the omission of relevant information, while for others, it might be too permissive, resulting in the retrieval of numerous redundant or irrelevant items. The latter scenario significantly impacts efficiency and prolongs response times. Second, this approach lacks guarantees that truly relevant information, such as a specific item d^* within the database $\mathcal{D}$, will be included in the retrieved set S.

2.2 Conformal Prediction for Retrieval

Conformal prediction can be seamlessly integrated into IR systems by constructing calibrated prediction sets designed to include, on average, the desired information with a user-specified high probability. Formally, given a query q and its corresponding similarity scores s_i, we construct a prediction set parameterized by $\tau > 0$ as follows:

$$\mathcal{C}_\tau(q) \triangleq \{d_i \in \mathcal{D} : c_i \leq \tau\}, \tag{3}$$

where $c_i \triangleq -s_i$ represents a *non-conformity* score. To appropriately set the value of τ, we utilize a held-out calibration dataset $\mathcal{D}_C$ consisting of n samples $(q_i, d_i) \in \mathcal{Q} \times \mathcal{D}$ drawn exchangeably from an underlying distribution $\mathcal{P}$. Here, q_i represents a query whose most relevant information is assumed to be a single item d_i from the database, for simplicity. Given a user-chosen error rate $\alpha \in [0, 1]$, we set τ as the $\frac{(n+1)(1-\alpha)}{n}$-th quantile of the calibration non-conformity scores. This ensures that for a new exchangeable test sample (q_{n+1}, d_{n+1}), we have the following marginal coverage guarantee:

$$\mathbb{P}\big(d_{n+1} \in \mathcal{C}_\tau(q_{n+1})\big) \geq 1 - \alpha \tag{4}$$

for any distribution P. The probability above is marginal (averaged) over all $n + 1$ calibration and test samples. This ensures that the IR model retrieves sets of adaptive size, guaranteed to contain the relevant information at least α-fraction of the time, thereby overcoming the limitation above.

While the conformal sets above use a calibrated threshold, other parameterizations are possible, such as setting the calibration parameter to the set size K, as in (2). Furthermore, it is important to note that the description above merely presents conformal prediction in its simplest, most common form. However, there have been significant advancements in the field in recent years, leading to the development of more involved and efficient conformal methods (Romano et al., 2020; Angelopoulos et al., 2020) and to extensions that provide guarantees beyond marginal coverage (Angelopoulos et al., 2022a; Fisch et al., 2020; Li et al., 2023).

3 Method

Integrating conformal prediction to IR systems enhances their reliability by providing statistical guarantees. However, CP methods prioritize trustworthiness and are not optimized for efficiency, thus they often produce excessively large retrieval sets.

Following the above, our goal is to improve the predictive efficiency of CP methods by reducing the average size of the retrieved sets $\mathbb{E}_q\left[|\mathcal{C}_\tau(q)|\right]$, while maintaining their coverage guarantees. In contrast to approaches that focus on improving the IR model or developing more efficient conformal methods, we propose an alternative approach that introduces an intermediate step of score refinement. Specifically, given a query q and its scores $\mathcal{S} = \{s_1, s_2, \ldots, s_N\}$, we adjust them prior to employing conformal prediction $T(\mathcal{S}) = \{t_1, t_2, \ldots, t_N\}$.

In designing the transformation T, we identify that scores from different queries can vary significantly in scale. This can cause the calibration threshold τ to be dominated by queries with small scores, leading to excessively large prediction sets. To mitigate this issue, we first normalize the retrieval scores by dividing them by their maximum, ensuring that scores across all queries are comparable in scale. We remark that the maximum score $s_{\max}$ can be interpreted as the IR model's confidence. When this value is small, it suggests a lack of relevant information for the given query, suggesting that ideally no items should be retrieved. Thus, normalization in such scenarios may be counterproductive, resulting in irrelevant items. However, we assume the corpus is sufficiently extensive to contain at least one relevant item for any query, an assumption particularly valid for the calibration.

Next, assume without loss of generality that the scores are sorted in decreasing order: $\mathcal{S} = \{s_{(1)}, s_{(2)}, \ldots, s_{(N)}\}$, where $s_{(r)}$ is the rth largest score and $r \geq 1$ represents its rank. Inspired by ranking measures (Yining et al., 2013), we define our transformation as follows

$$T(s_{(r)}, r) \triangleq \frac{s_{(r)}}{s_{\max}} W(r) \tag{5}$$

where $W(r) \in [0, 1]$ is a discount function that penalizes scores based on their rank. We specifically employ the inverse logarithm decay $W(r) = \frac{1}{\log(1+r)}$, which offers a balance between emphasis on top items and exploration of lower-ranked items. To offer additional flexibility, we introduce a hyperparameter $\lambda \in [0, 1]$:

$$T(s_{(r)}, r) \triangleq \frac{s_{(r)}}{s_{\max}} \frac{1}{\log(1 + r^{\lambda})}. \tag{6}$$

We tune λ by performing a search over a sequence of values to minimize the set size on a validation set. Note the transformation is monotone, preserving the IR model's induced order and maintaining its core functionality. Furthermore, it is simple to implement, computationally efficient, and easily integrated into existing systems. As demonstrated in the following section, the proposed transformation is highly effective in reducing the size of the conformal retrieved sets.

4 Experiments

4.1 Setup

Datasets For our evaluation, we utilized BEIR (Thakur et al., 2021), a large collection of information retrieval benchmarks. Specifically, we focus on the following datasets: FEVER (Thorne et al., 2018), SCIFACT (Wadden et al., 2020), and FIQA (Maia et al., 2018). Data statistics are presented at Table 1. It is important to note that each query within these datasets may have multiple relevant documents within the corpus. For this study, we adopted a pragmatic approach, considering the document with the highest score among the relevant documents as the ground truth. This ensures that a successful retrieval implies at least one relevant document is present in the inference set.

To simulate real-world production environments, we employ a vector store, specifically FAISS-GPU (Johnson et al., 2019) for its efficiency and performance in handling large-scale databases. We retrieve the top $2,000$ documents for each query and apply our refinement process exclusively to these initially retrieved documents.

Dataset	#Corpus	#Calibration	#Test
FEVER	5,416,568	6,666	6,666
SCIFACT	5,183	150*	150*
FIQA	57,638	500	648

Table 1: Data Summary. #Corpus indicates the number of documents, while #Calibration and #Test indicate the number of queries. As SCIFACT lacks a calibration set, we randomly split its test set into calibration and test subsets.

Embedders Initial semantic scores were derived using deep sentence embedders, which encode textual input into a fixed-dimensional latent space where semantic similarity is represented by vector proximity. We employ two models: BGE-large-1.5 (Xiao et al., 2023) (326M parameters) and E5-Mistral-7b model (Wang et al., 2023) (7B parameters). BGE-large-1.5 is a smaller model with a latent representation dimension of 1024, whereas E5-Mistral, a finetuned encoder version of the mistral-7b model, has a latent representation dimension

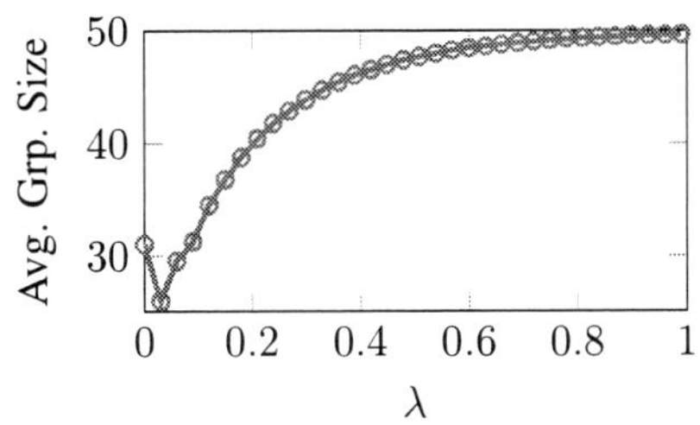

Figure 2: Impact of λ value on average group size using BGE-large-1.5 on SCIFACT with α = 0.05.

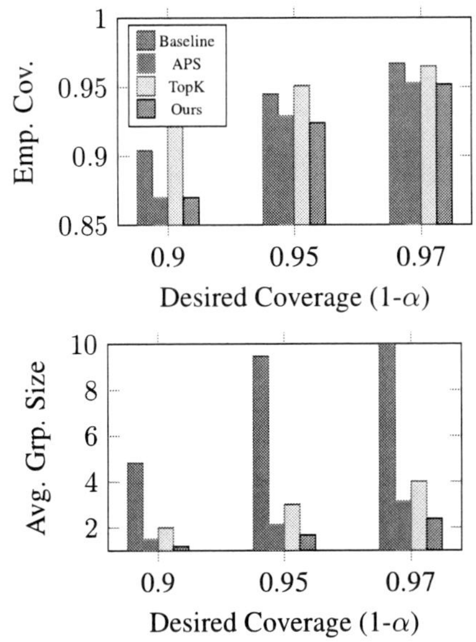

Figure 3: Performance comparison using BGE-large-1.5 on FEVER dataset across various values of α.

of 4096. The semantic score between a query q and a candidate document d is the cosine similarity between their respective latent representations.

Competitors For our method, we employ the Vanilla CP method (Vovk et al., 2005), applying it to the refined retrieval scores. We compared our approach to three established approaches: *Baseline*, which applies Vanilla CP directly to the retrieval scores without modification; *TopK*, which utilizes Vanilla CP but calibrates to a fixed set size K for all queries; *APS* (Romano et al., 2020) and *RAPS* (Angelopoulos et al., 2020), which introduce novel conformity scores.

4.2 Results

We first conduct experiments on the smaller SCIFACT dataset to optimize the hyperparameter λ. The results, shown in Figure 2, reveal a favorable value for λ, prompting us to set $\alpha = 0.05$.

Dataset	α	Method	Emp. Cov.	Avg. Grp. Size
FIQA	0.1	Baseline	0.89	417.77
		APS	0.89	119.76
		TopK	0.87	90.0
		Ours	0.86	**56.72**
	0.05	Baseline	0.94	846.0
		APS	0.94	477.27
		TopK	0.92	259.0
		Ours	0.92	**190.5**
	0.03	Baseline	0.96	1206.93
		APS	0.98	1393.96
		TopK	0.94	480.0
		Ours	0.95	**347.16**
SCIFACT	0.1	Baseline	0.91	231.17
		APS	0.91	30.82
		TopK	0.91	31.0
		Ours	0.85	**14.07**
	0.05	Baseline	0.97	760.75
		APS	0.92	91.23
		TopK	0.92	91.0
		Ours	0.89	**29.59**
	0.03	Baseline	0.98	1211.11
		APS	0.95	276.15
		TopK	0.95	279.0
		Ours	0.97	**160.66**

Table 2: Performance comparison using BGE-large-1.5 on FIQA and SCIFACT across various values of α.

Next, we conduct experiments on the large-scale FEVER dataset. As illustrated in Figure 3, our score refinement method consistently outperforms other approaches by producing significantly smaller retrieved sets in experiments with BGE-large-1.5 across various values of α, while maintaining comparable, albeit slightly lower, empirical coverage. Results for the other datasets are summarized in Table 2, consistent with our previous findings. We note that RAPS produced comparable results to APS, so we omit them for brevity. Additional results using E5-Mistral, which exhibit similar trends, are presented in Table 3 of the appendix, along with an ablation study comparing other simple transformations.

5 Conclusion

We addressed the challenge of large prediction sets in conformal prediction for IR by introducing a novel score refinement method. Our experiments on the BEIR benchmark demonstrated its effectiveness in generating compact, statistically reliable prediction sets, enabling the deployment of conformal prediction in real-world IR systems without sacrificing performance.

6 Limitations

The conclusions of this study could be further strengthened by evaluating the method on a wider range of datasets and employing diverse embedding models. Currently, our method does not handle cases where no relevant information exists in the database, potentially limiting its applicability. Additionally, while we introduced a simple transformation, exploring more involved or even parameterized functions, e.g. neural networks, could further enhance efficiency and statistical guarantees.

References

Anastasios Angelopoulos, Stephen Bates, Jitendra Malik, and Michael I Jordan. 2020. Uncertainty sets for image classifiers using conformal prediction. *arXiv preprint arXiv:2009.14193*.

Anastasios N Angelopoulos and Stephen Bates. 2021. A gentle introduction to conformal prediction and distribution-free uncertainty quantification. *arXiv preprint arXiv:2107.07511*.

Anastasios N Angelopoulos, Stephen Bates, Emmanuel J Candès, Michael I Jordan, and Lihua Lei. 2021. Learn then test: Calibrating predictive algorithms to achieve risk control. *arXiv preprint arXiv:2110.01052*.

Anastasios N Angelopoulos, Stephen Bates, Adam Fisch, Lihua Lei, and Tal Schuster. 2022a. Conformal risk control. *arXiv preprint arXiv:2208.02814*.

Anastasios N Angelopoulos, Amit Pal Kohli, Stephen Bates, Michael Jordan, Jitendra Malik, Thayer Alshaabi, Srigokul Upadhyayula, and Yaniv Romano. 2022b. Image-to-image regression with distribution-free uncertainty quantification and applications in imaging. In *International Conference on Machine Learning*, pages 717–730. PMLR.

Anastasios N Angelopoulos, Karl Krauth, Stephen Bates, Yixin Wang, and Michael I Jordan. 2023. Recommendation systems with distribution-free reliability guarantees. In *Conformal and Probabilistic Prediction with Applications*, pages 175–193. PMLR.

Adam Fisch, Tal Schuster, Tommi Jaakkola, and Regina Barzilay. 2020. Efficient conformal prediction via cascaded inference with expanded admission. *arXiv preprint arXiv:2007.03114*.

Yu Gui, Ying Jin, and Zhimei Ren. 2024. Conformal alignment: Knowing when to trust foundation models with guarantees. *arXiv preprint arXiv:2405.10301*.

Jeff Johnson, Matthijs Douze, and Hervé Jégou. 2019. Billion-scale similarity search with GPUs. *IEEE Transactions on Big Data*, 7(3):535–547.

Gilad Kutiel, Regev Cohen, Michael Elad, Daniel Freedman, and Ehud Rivlin. 2023. Conformal prediction masks: Visualizing uncertainty in medical imaging. In *International Workshop on Trustworthy Machine Learning for Healthcare*, pages 163–176. Springer.

Shuo Li, Sangdon Park, Insup Lee, and Osbert Bastani. 2023. Trac: Trustworthy retrieval augmented chatbot. *arXiv preprint arXiv:2307.04642*.

Macedo Maia, Siegfried Handschuh, André Freitas, Brian Davis, Ross McDermott, Manel Zarrouk, and Alexandra Balahur. 2018. Www'18 open challenge: financial opinion mining and question answering. In *Companion proceedings of the the web conference 2018*, pages 1941–1942.

Liran Ringel, Regev Cohen, Daniel Freedman, Michael Elad, and Yaniv Romano. 2024. Early time classification with accumulated accuracy gap control. *arXiv preprint arXiv:2402.00857*.

Yaniv Romano, Matteo Sesia, and Emmanuel Candes. 2020. Classification with valid and adaptive coverage. *Advances in Neural Information Processing Systems*, 33:3581–3591.

Nandan Thakur, Nils Reimers, Andreas Rücklé, Abhishek Srivastava, and Iryna Gurevych. 2021. BEIR: A heterogeneous benchmark for zero-shot evaluation of information retrieval models. In *Thirty-fifth Conference on Neural Information Processing Systems Datasets and Benchmarks Track (Round 2)*.

James Thorne, Andreas Vlachos, Christos Christodoulopoulos, and Arpit Mittal. 2018. Fever: a large-scale dataset for fact extraction and verification. *arXiv preprint arXiv:1803.05355*.

Vladimir Vovk, Alexander Gammerman, and Glenn Shafer. 2005. *Algorithmic learning in a random world*, volume 29. Springer.

David Wadden, Shanchuan Lin, Kyle Lo, Lucy Lu Wang, Madeleine van Zuylen, Arman Cohan, and Hannaneh Hajishirzi. 2020. Fact or fiction: Verifying scientific claims. *arXiv preprint arXiv:2004.14974*.

Liang Wang, Nan Yang, Xiaolong Huang, Linjun Yang, Rangan Majumder, and Furu Wei. 2023. Improving text embeddings with large language models. *arXiv preprint arXiv:2401.00368*.

Shitao Xiao, Zheng Liu, Peitian Zhang, and Niklas Muennighoff. 2023. C-pack: Packaged resources to advance general chinese embedding. *Preprint*, arXiv:2309.07597.

Yunpeng Xu, Wenge Guo, and Zhi Wei. 2024. Conformal ranked retrieval. *arXiv preprint arXiv:2404.17769*.

Wang Yining, Wang Liwei, Li Yuanzhi, He Di, Chen Wei, and Liu Tie-Yan. 2013. A theoretical analysis of ndcg ranking measures. In *Proceedings of the 26th annual conference on learning theory*.

A Additional Experiments

Here evaluate our method with the E5-Mistral embedder on SCIFACT and FIQA datasets. Results, presented in Table 3, show our method consistently outperforms competitors. Moreover, using E5-Mistral leads to improved performance in both empirical coverage and average group size compared to BGE-large-1.5.

In addition to the aforementioned experiments, we compared our method against alternative transformations: *Max Score*, where scores are normalized by dividing each by the maximum score, and *Z-Score*, which standardizes the initial retrieved scores. The results, summarized in Table 4, show that our score refinement transformation outperforms these other refinement methods in the vast majority of cases.

Dataset	α	Method	Emp. Cov.	Avg. Grp. Size
SCIFACT	0.10	Baseline	0.91	68.91
		APS	0.94	17.46
		TopK	0.95	19.0
		Ours	0.93	**15.09**
	0.05	Baseline	0.96	311.73
		APS	0.98	139.36
		TopK	0.99	150.0
		Ours	0.97	**48.71**
	0.03	Baseline	0.99	1093.85
		APS	1.0	324.09
		TopK	1.0	368.0
		Ours	1.0	**127.29**
FIQA	0.10	Baseline	0.91	144.31
		APS	0.9	46.48
		TopK	0.89	38.0
		Ours	0.9	**33.35**
	0.05	Baseline	0.96	458.79
		APS	0.95	123.09
		TopK	0.94	108.0
		Ours	0.94	**67.21**
	0.03	Baseline	0.98	710.86
		APS	0.97	439.64
		TopK	0.96	193.0
		Ours	0.96	**143.76**

Table 3: Empirical coverage and average group size for FIQA and SCIFACT, alpha values, and methods using the e5-mistral-7b-instruct.

Dataset	α	Method	Emp. Cov.	Avg. Grp. Size
FEVER	0.10	Baseline	0.90	4.81
		Max Score	0.87	1.19
		Z-Score	0.85	1.63
		Ours	0.87	**1.18**
	0.05	Baseline	0.95	9.47
		Max Score	0.93	1.89
		Z-Score	0.92	2.44
		Ours	0.93	**1.67**
	0.03	Baseline	0.97	15.63
		Max Score	0.96	2.88
		Z-Score	0.95	3.28
		Ours	0.95	**2.37**
SCIFACT	0.10	Baseline	0.91	231.17
		Max Score	0.83	20.68
		Z-Score	0.88	22.01
		Ours	0.85	**14.07**
	0.05	Baseline	0.97	760.75
		Max Score	0.86	31.01
		Z-Score	0.91	52.91
		Ours	0.89	**29.59**
	0.03	Baseline	0.98	1211.11
		Max Score	0.94	**132.31**
		Z-Score	0.93	197.77
		Ours	0.97	160.66
FIQA	0.10	Baseline	0.89	417.77
		Max Score	0.87	83.23
		Z-Score	0.87	78.02
		Ours	0.86	**56.72**
	0.05	Baseline	0.94	846.0
		Max Score	0.92	254.8
		Z-Score	0.92	217.79
		Ours	0.92	**190.5**
	0.03	Baseline	0.96	1206.93
		Max Score	0.94	380.62
		Z-Score	0.94	437.01
		Ours	0.95	**347.16**

Table 4: Ablation study comparing different score refinement methods with BGE-large-v1.5 encodings. The table shows empirical coverage and average group size for different datasets and methods. Bold values indicate the best performance for each α.

Improving Explainable Fact-Checking via Sentence-Level Factual Reasoning

Francielle Vargas
University of São Paulo
francielleavargas@usp.br

Isadora Salles
Federal University of Minas Gerais
isadorasalles@dcc.ufmg.br

Diego Alves
Saarland University
diego.alves@uni-saarland.de

Ameeta Agrawal
Portland State University
ameeta@pdx.edu

Thiago Pardo
University of São Paulo
taspardo@icmc.usp.br

Fabricio Benevenuto
Federal University of Minas Gerais
fabricio@dcc.ufmg.br

Abstract

Most existing fact-checking systems are unable to explain their decisions by providing relevant rationales (justifications) for their predictions. It highlights a lack of transparency that poses significant risks, such as the prevalence of unexpected biases, which may increase political polarization due to limitations in impartiality. To address this critical gap, we introduce ***Sentence-Level Factual Reasoning*** (SELFAR)[1], aimed at improving explainable fact-checking. SELFAR relies on fact extraction and verification by predicting the news source reliability and factuality (veracity) of news articles or claims at the sentence level, generating post-hoc explanations using SHAP/LIME and zero-shot prompts. Our experiments show that unreliable news stories predominantly consist of subjective statements, in contrast to reliable ones. Consequently, predicting unreliable news articles at the sentence level by analyzing impartiality and subjectivity is a promising approach for fact extraction and improving explainable fact-checking. Furthermore, LIME outperforms SHAP in explaining predictions on reliability. Additionally, while zero-shot prompts provide highly readable explanations and achieve an accuracy of 0.71 in predicting factuality, their tendency to hallucinate remains a challenge. Lastly, this paper also presents the first study on explainable fact-checking in the Portuguese language.

1 Introduction

While journalism is tied to ethical standards, including truth and fairness, it often strays from impartial facts (Mastrine, 2022). As a result, low credibility news may be produced and spread on modern media ecosystem. Nowadays, fact-checking organizations have manually provided lists of unreliable articles and media sources, however it is a very time-consuming task, needs to be updated faster and relies on specific expertise (Baly et al., 2018a).

Towards addressing this issue, fact-checking systems have classified claims of unknown veracity (factuality), identifying evidences and predicting whether they support or refute the claims (Glockner et al., 2023; Guo et al., 2022). Nevertheless, as low credibility news or claims may comprise multiple sentences containing facts, media bias, and fake information, fact-checking at scale should be able to accurately predict both news source reliability and factuality at a fine-grained level. Table 1 shows an example of low credibility news segmented into sentences and classified according to its reliability (biased/unbiased) and factuality (fake and fact).

Furthermore, the veracity of claims can be verified using metadata (Augenstein et al., 2019), Wikipedia (Thorne et al., 2018), social networks (Hardalov et al., 2022), scientific assertions (Wadden et al., 2020), manually checked-claims from social media provided by fact-checking organizations (Wang, 2017; Couto et al., 2021), the language used in claims (Sheikh Ali et al., 2021), LLMs (Lee et al., 2021; Zhang and Gao, 2023), generating justifications for verdicts on claims (Atanasova et al., 2020a). For example, the FEVER (Thorne et al., 2018), SciFact (Wadden et al., 2020), LIAR (Wang, 2017) and Check-COVID (Wang et al., 2023) are widely used datasets for this setting.

In recent years, there has been significant progress in the area of fact-checking e.g., new comprehensive datasets (Yang et al., 2018; Wang, 2017; Hanselowski et al., 2019; Reis et al., 2020), high performance of deep learning models (Ribeiro et al., 2022), different domains aside from political (Naderi and Hirst, 2018; Kotonya and Toni, 2020b; Arana-Catania et al., 2022; Chamoun et al., 2023; Vladika and Matthes, 2024). However, while justifying the verification of a claim's veracity is the most important part of the manual process, most existing fact-checking systems are unable to explain their decisions, which could assist human fact-checkers and help mitigate the lack of transparency (Baly

[1]The SELFAR datasets, models and code are publicly available: `https://github.com/franciellevargas/SELFAR`

Proceedings of the Seventh Fact Extraction and VERification Workshop (FEVER), pages 192–204
November 15, 2024

N.	Sentence-level news article	Label
S1	President Jair Bolsonaro **touch a sore point of** Europeans when he pointed out that the increased use of fossil fuels is a **serious** environmental setback, in his opening speech at the UN General Assembly, Tuesday (20).	Biased
S2	"The St. Francisco River transposition was completed during my government", said Bolsonaro at the UN.	Fake
S3	"Brazil was a pioneer in the implementation of 5G in Latin America", Bolsonaro said at the UN.	Fact
S4	Bolsonaro signed measures favouring to environmental protection during the 4 years of the Brazilian government.	Fake
S5	The Bolsonaro also requested for reform of the UN Security Council.	Fact
S6	However, there is **a huge difference** between speaking at the UN and being heard at the UN.	Biased

Table 1: Example of low credibility news segmented into sentences extracted from the FactNews (Vargas et al., 2023) and FACTCK.BR (Moreno and Bressan, 2019) datasets. Note that the low credibility news may comprise a mix of complex content such as media bias (unreliable) (S1, and S6), fake (S2 e S4), and facts (S3 and S5).

et al., 2018b). Therefore, automated fact-checking should also be capable to provide justifications in the form of post-hoc explanations for model outputs or by incorporating explanation methods directly into these models (Kotonya and Toni, 2020a).

Explainable Artificial Intelligence (XAI) methods provide the causes of a single prediction, a set of predictions, or all predictions of a model by identifying parts of the input, model, or training data that are most influential on the model outcome (Balkir et al., 2022). Hence, transparency and explainability are related to the notion of "explanations" (Guidotti et al., 2018). In particular, XAI methods are commonly categorized into two aspects: (i) whether they provide *local* or *global* explanations, and (ii) whether they are *self-explaining* or *post-hoc explaining* (Guidotti et al., 2018). Local explanations are provided for individual instances, while global explanations apply to the model's behavior across any input (Balkir et al., 2022). Self-explaining methods rely on the internal structure of the prediction model, making these methods often specific to the model type. Conversely, post-hoc explaining (also know as model-agnostic) methods do not rely on knowledge of the to-be-explained model, but rather only input-output pairs (Balkir et al., 2022).

The most commonly used model-agnostic explainable methods are LIME (*Local Interpretable Model-Agnostic Explanations*) (Ribeiro et al., 2016) and SHAP (*SHapley Additive exPlanations*) (Lundberg and Lee, 2017). The LIME provides local explanations for predictions by perturbing the input data and observing the resulting changes in the model's predictions. On the other hand, the SHAP measures the contribution of each feature to the prediction by considering all possible combinations of features. Unlike LIME, SHAP can be used to generate both local and global explanations. Lastly, recent approaches to automated fact verification have also taken advantage of the high performance achieved through In-Context Learning (ICL) [2] to generate post-hoc explanations for veracity prediction (Zeng and Gao, 2023, 2024).

Here, we introduce the ***Sentence-Level Factual Reasoning*** (SELFAR) aims to improve explainable fact-checking. It covers the entire fact-checking pipeline, generating post-hoc explanations for each task. Specifically, SELFAR predicts news source reliability and factuality of claims or news articles at the sentence-level for fact extraction and verification, respectively. It then generates post-hoc explanations using SHAP and LIME for fact extraction and zero-shot prompts for fact verification. Based on our findings, the sentence-level prediction of unreliable news by analyzing impartiality and subjectivity is promising for fact extraction and improving explainable fat-checking. Additionally, LIME is better than SHAP in explaining predictions on reliability. Finally, although zero-shot prompts provided high readable explanations, and achieved an accuracy of 0.71 in predicting veracity, their tendency to generate hallucinations remains a challenge.

Our contributions are summarized as follows:

- We study an under-explored and relevant problem: explainable automated fact-checking.
- We introduce the SELFAR, a sentence-level factual reasoning that relies on fact extraction and verification by predicting news source reliability and factuality of a news article or claim at the sentence-level, generating post-hoc explanations using SHAP/LIME and zero-shot prompts. The datasets, models and code are available, which may boost future research.
- We propose the first study and baselines for explainable fact-checking in Portuguese.

[2] *In-context learning* refers to generative model's ability to understand and generate responses based on information provided in the context of the conversation or task at hand (Brown et al., 2020).

2 Related Work

2.1 Explainable Fact-Checking

Explainability in fact-checking systems refers to the ability of models to provide a rationale for their decisions. Regarding the explainable fact-checking pipeline, Kotonya and Toni (2020a) suggest a set of tasks, as shown in Figure 1. Note that the explainable fact-checking pipeline includes both fact extraction and fact verification tasks, along with the generation of suitable explanations related to the system's inputs.

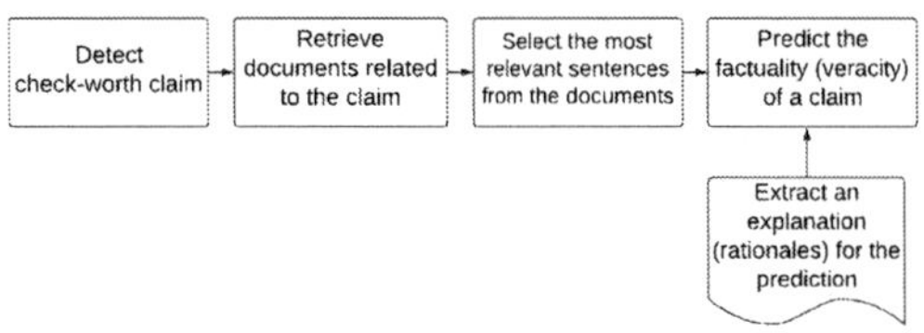

Figure 1: Explainable fact-checking pipeline.

Most existing explainable fact-checking methods produce explanations that consist of the most relevant portions of the system input (Kotonya and Toni, 2020a). Specifically, there are (i) *attention-based explanations*, which rely on the form of some type of visualization of neural attention weights, for example, using LSTM and DNN-based methods with attention mechanisms to extract explanations (Thorne et al., 2019; Popat et al., 2017; Thorne et al., 2019); (ii) *explanation as rule discovery*, that uses rules-based approaches and knowledge graphs to provide explanations (Gad-Elrab et al., 2019; Ahmadi et al., 2019); (iii) *explanation as summarization*, that formulate the automatic generation of explanations as a text summarization problem: extractive text summarization (Atanasova et al., 2020a), or both extractive and abstractive text summarization (Kotonya and Toni, 2020b); (iv) *adversarial claims justification*, that generates adversarial claims (e.g. method that uses a GPT-2 based model) for robust fact-checking (Thorne et al., 2019; Niewinski et al., 2019; Atanasova et al., 2020b); and (v) *retrieved evidence as justifications* that consists of the task of generating justifications based on robust evidence retrieved from data sources (Zeng and Gao, 2024; Wang et al., 2023) or based on prompt engineering enabled by in-context learning (Brown et al., 2020) using zero-shot prompting (Zeng and Gao, 2024; Wang et al., 2023; Zeng and Gao, 2024) or few-shot prompting (Zarharan et al., 2024).

2.2 News Credibility Verification

Estimating the reliability of a news source is relevant not only when fact-checking a claim (Popat et al., 2016); however, it also contributes significantly to tackling article-level tasks such as fake news detection (De Sarkar et al., 2018; Yuan et al., 2020; Reis et al., 2019; Pan et al., 2018; Vargas et al., 2022; Dong et al., 2015). News credibility verification methods have primarily focused on measuring the reliability of news reporting (Pérez-Rosas et al., 2018; Hardalov et al., 2016), the entire media outlet (Baly et al., 2018a; Horne et al., 2018; Baly et al., 2019), and content and user accounts on social media platforms (Castillo et al., 2011; Mukherjee and Weikum, 2015; Iftene et al., 2020) to mitigate various types of harmful strategies. For instance, Yuan et al. (2020) proposed a jointly news credibility and fake news detection structure-aware multi-head attention network (SMAN), which combines the news content, publishing, and reposting relations of publishers and users. Similarly, Long et al. (2017) proposed a new approach to validate the credibility of news articles by analysing a multi-perspective speaker profiles. Iftene et al. (2020) implemented a real-time application based on networks to identify both fake users and fake news over countries and continents in Twitter. Bhattarai et al. (2022) proposed an explainable framework using the Tsetlin[3] that learns linguistic features to distinguish between fake and true news and provides a global interpretation of fake news. In this paper, we estimate the reliability of news sources for fact extraction.

2.3 Fact Verification with Language Models

Large Language Models (LLMs) have been used to provide evidence for fact-checking. For instance, Lee et al. (2021) explored the few-shot capability to assess a claim's veracity based on the perplexity of evidence-conditioned claim generation. Zhang and Gao (2023) proposed a prompt engineering-based method for fact verification that leverages LLMs to separate a claim into sub-claims and then verify each of them through multiple progressive question-answering. Additionally, the reasoning capabilities of LLMs have also been used to address misinformation. For example, Press et al. (2023); Jiang et al. (2023) concluded that LLMs' reasoning capabilities, combined with external knowledge, are promising for a wide range of NLP tasks, including fact extraction and fact verification tasks.

[3] A Tsetlin machine is an AI algorithm based on propositional logic.

3 The Proposed Approach

3.1 Sentence-Level Factual Reasoning

Building on the explainable fact-checking pipeline proposed by Guo et al. (2022), this paper introduces a new method called SELFAR to enhance explainable fact-checking. SELFAR encompasses three main tasks: *Fact Extraction (FE), Fact Verification (FV)*, and *Explanation Generation (EG)*, as shown in Figure 2, and described in detail as follows.

Fact Extraction (FE): According to Guo et al. (2022), fact extraction relies on predicting the most relevant claims to be checked. Therefore, we propose an approach for *sentence-level news source reliability estimation* using a fine-tuned mBERT model. In the context of misinformation, unreliable news and media outlets are targets of a substantial amount of misleading content, often presented as evidence in the form of hyper-partisan or subjective language (Kotonya and Toni, 2020a). Hence, the main hypothesis is that accurately estimating source reliability can be achieved by analyzing the subjectivity and impartiality of text at the sentence level. In particular, our model classifies each sentence into two categories: *reliable* and *unreliable*. Reliable sentences are presented impartially and focus on objective facts. Conversely, unreliable sentences are presented with partiality and therefore focus on subjective interpretations. Table 1 shows examples of biased (unreliable) sentences.

Fact Verification (FV): According to Guo et al. (2022), fact verification relies on finding appropriate evidence and predicting whether that evidence supports or refutes the claim given as input. Since the required evidence can often be unrefined or unavailable, either due to gaps in the knowledge sources (Alhindi et al., 2018), we propose a model for *sentence-level factuality prediction* using LLMs. This model predicts whether a sentence is *fact* or *fake* using retrieved evidence from LLMs, which are trained on a large number of diverse data repositories. It checks whether the evidence of veracity for the sentence is refuted or supported. As example of sentences classified according to their veracity, Table 1 shows examples of fake content and facts.

Explanation Generation (EG): According to Kotonya and Toni (2020a), explainable fact-checking must include the task of extracting an explanation for the prediction. Instead of generating explanations solely for fact verification, we propose the post-hoc explanation generation for both fact extraction and fact verification tasks.

Explanation generation for fact extraction: We used LIME (Ribeiro et al., 2016) and SHAP (Lundberg and Lee, 2017) methods to generate post-hoc explanations for fact extraction. These methods produce explanations based on a vector of tokens, where the coefficients represent the most relevant features for predicting a class. In particular, we measure the performance of LIME and SHAP in generating post-hoc explanations for sentence-level news source reliability estimation. Figure 3 shows examples of explanations generated by LIME and SHAP. Note that for each sentence given as input to these methods, they assign a value for a set of tokens. The red bars show the value assigned to the most relevant features to predict the class *unreliable*, and the blue bars show the value assigned to the relevant features to predict the class *reliable*.

Explanation generation for fact verification: We proposed a set of zero-shot prompts using ChatGPT 4.0 (OpenAI et al., 2024) to generate post-hoc explanations for factuality (veracity) prediction at the sentence level. Zero-shot prompting is a technique in which specific examples for that task are not required. Instead, the model generalizes from examples of other related tasks. Table 2 shows post-hoc explanations generated by the zero-shot prompts.

4 Experimental Setup

4.1 Model Architecture and Settings

We propose an approach for fact extraction using a fine-tuned mBERT model, a second approach for fact verification using retrieved evidence from LLMs, and two approaches for post-hoc explanation generation using LIME/SHAP and zero-shot prompts. We describe these approaches as follows.

Fine-Tuned mBERT: We used the fine-tuned mBERT model proposed by Vargas et al. (2023). In essence, this model classifies news article sentences as *reliable* or *unreliable*. It was trained on the FactNews dataset (Vargas et al., 2023), which comprises 6,191 annotated sentences in Portuguese.

Retrieved-Evidence from LLM: Due to the success of ICL across NLP benchmarks, we proposed a set of zero-shot prompts and manually assessed them using ChatGPT 4.0 to recover evidence. The proposed prompts are shown in Table 2. Moreover, to predict factuality, we considered a set of spans described in Table 4 provided as recovered evidence. For this task, we utilized the checked claims from fact-checking organizations in the FACTCK.BR dataset (Moreno and Bressan, 2019) in Portuguese.

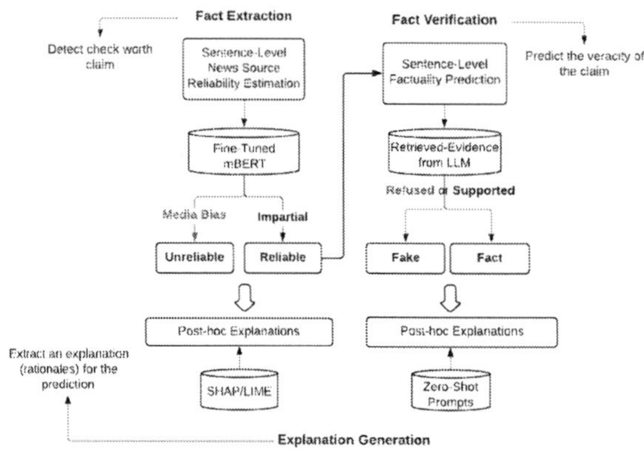

Figure 2: The ***Sentence-Level Factual Reasoning*** (SELFAR) for explainable fact-checking.

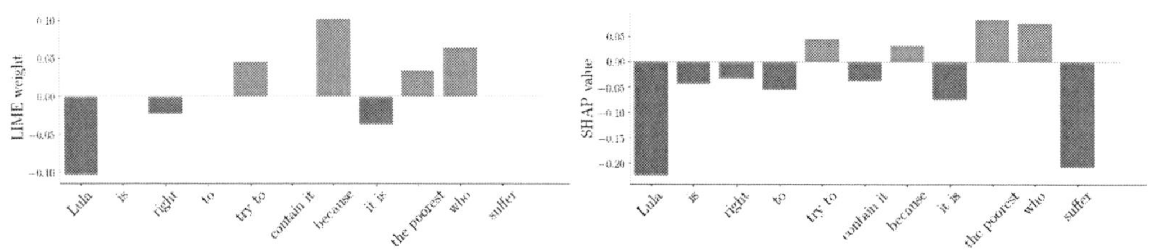

Figure 3: Explanations generated at sentence-level by LIME and SHAP for the unreliable class.

Claims	Zero-Shot Prompts	Sentences	Explanations	Type
Fake	Is it {[}fake | lie{]} that sentence? Show evidences	Vaccines cause autism.	**Yes, it is fake that** vaccines cause autism. This idea is based on a fraudulent 1998 study led by Andrew Wakefield that suggested a link between the MMR vaccine (measles, mumps, and rubella) and autism.	Supported
		Brazil places tanks on border with Venezuela.	As of my latest update, there haven't been reports confirming that Brazil has placed tanks on its border with Venezuela	Refused
True	Is it {[}fact | true{]} that sentence? Show evidences	40% of crimes against women occur at home.	**Yes, it is true that** around 40% of crimes against women in Brazil occur at home. According to recent data from the IBGE and other sources that monitor feminicides, most of these crimes occur in domestic settings, which reflects the impact of intra-family violence. This pattern of domestic violence reinforces the need for public policies focused on protecting women in their own homes (Correio Braziliense).	Supported
		Brazil spends R$3 per person per day on everything from vaccinations to transplants in the SUS.	The specific amount can vary depending on the year and the data source, but it's clear that the figure of R$3 per person per day is likely inaccurate	Refused

Table 2: Explanations (justifications) generated at sentence-level by ChatGPT using zero-shot prompts.

LIME and SHAP Post-hoc Explanations: We proposed a post-hoc explanation method using SHAP and LIME for fact extraction. We randomly selected 510 sentences from the FactNews dataset, equally labeled as unreliable and reliable. Then, we asked a linguist, who is an NLP expert, to annotate rationales for the sentences classified as unreliable. An example of the annotated rationales is shown in bold in Table 1. Note that the rationales were annotated by an expert and consist of segments that justify the classification of sentences as unreliable.

Zero-Shot Prompt Post-hoc Explanations: We proposed a set of zero-shot prompts using ChatGPT 4.0 to generate explanations for fact verification. We randomly extracted an average of 400 claims from the FACTCK.BR dataset, equally classified as fake and true. Then, we segmented them into sentences, totaling 510 sentences. The proposed prompts and their generated explanations are shown in Table 2. It should be noted that we used the same number of instances (510 sentences) to evaluate both proposed explainability methods.

5 Evaluation and Results

5.1 Evaluation of Models

We evaluated our models using F1-score, as shown in Table 3. The results are available on GitHub[4].

	FE	FV	SELFAR
class	F1	F1	F1
0	0.85	0.61	0.60
1	0.82	0.81	0.85
Avg	0.85	0.71	**0.72**

Table 3: Evaluation for FE, FV and SELFAR. Note that as shown in Figure 2, For FE, the classes are reliable (0) and unreliable (1). Conversely, for FV and SELFAR, the classes are fact/true (0) and fake (1).

For the FE evaluation, we reported the prediction results obtained from the fine-tuned mBERT model. We also conducted a ROC error analysis, as shown in Figure 4. Note that the FE model achieved a high F1-Score of 0.85 and an AUC of 0.92, which corroborates our hypothesis that analyzing subjectivity and impartiality in text at the sentence level is promising for predicting news source reliability.

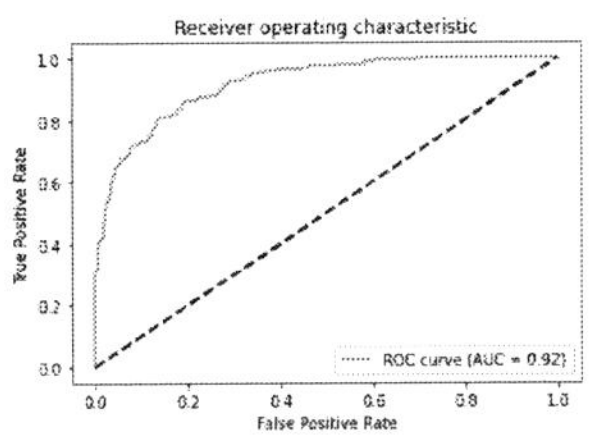

Figure 4: ROC curves for fine-tuned mBERT model.

For the FV evaluation, we assessed the ability to predict whether a sentence is fake or fact/true using recovered evidence from a set of zero-shot prompts shown in Table 2. Specifically, we classified as *supported* recovered evidence included any of the spans described in Table 4. Otherwise, it was classified as *refused* (see examples in Table 2).

For the FV and SELFAR evaluations, we used 510 sentences extracted from the FACTCK.BR. Specifically for SELFAR, we first applied the FE model, which predicts whether a sentence is reliable or unreliable. We then selected only the sentences classified as *reliable* and used them as input for the FV model. Finally, we computed the F1-Score for factuality prediction using our retrieved-evidence from LLMs method. As shown in Table 3, the FV model performs poorly in predicting true claims, indicating that the prompts designed for fake claims may be more effective for predicting veracity.

	Fake	True
Spans	<Yes>; <Yes, it is a lie>; <Yes, it's fake/false>; <Yes, that/this statement is a lie>; <There is no evidence>; <There is no reliable evidence or records>; <Yes, that seems to be a lie/fake>; <It can be considered fake>; <It is not true that>; <Yes, the statement <sentence>is fake/lie>; <Yes, the statement <sentence>is fake>.	<Yes>; <Yes, it is true that>; <Yes, that/this statement is true/fact>; <Yes, there is evidence>; <It is consistent with the available data>; <The evidence suggests>; <The evidence points to true>; <It is true that>; <Yes, the statement <sentence>is true/fact>;<The available evidence confirms>.

Table 4: Spans used to predict factuality by retrieved-evidence from LLM using zero-shot prompts.

Finally, we observed that ChatGPT can report inaccurate or false information. For example, in the prompt, *Is it true that Rodrigo Maia (a Brazilian politician) was not born in Brazil?*, the verdict was, "No, Rodrigo Maia was born in Brazil". However, Rodrigo Maia was actually born in Chile[5]. Similarly, in the prompt, *Is it true that the law regulating the profession of translator and interpreter of Brazilian Sign Language (Libras) was created by Maria do Rosário?*, the verdict was, "This law was proposed by Otávio Leite". However, the fact is that the Brazilian politician Maria do Rosário is the one who created this law[6].

5.2 Evaluation of Explanations

5.2.1 Metrics

We evaluated the EG methods using *faithfulness*, *plausibility* and *readability*. Theses metrics focus on different aspects of the quality of these explanations. For instance, faithfulness measures whether the explanation accurately captures the real relationships between the input features and the model's output. On the other hand, plausibility measures whether the explanation is understandable and intuitive from a human perspective, particularly for domain experts. Finally, readability measures how easily a human can understand the explanations.

Plausibility: We report the IOU (Intersection-Over-Union) F1-score, and as token-level Precision, Recall, and F1-score metrics (DeYoung et al., 2020) to measure plausibility. These scores are computed at the token level, comparing the model's rationales against tokenized human-annotated ones.

IOU F1-score is proposed on a token level rationales (DeYoung et al., 2020), in which the IOU is

[4] https://github.com/franciellevargas/SELFAR

[5] https://lupa.uol.com.br/jornalismo/2019/03/25/verificamos-maia-chile-brasileiro

[6] https://lupa.uol.com.br/jornalismo/2019/01/02/verificamos-bolsonaro-libras/

given by overlap of tokens in two sets divided by the size of their union, as shown in Equation 1.

$$\text{IOU-F1} = \frac{1}{N}\sum_{i=1}^{N}\text{Greater}(IOU_i, 0.5) \quad \text{where } IOU_i = \frac{M_i \cap H_i}{M_i \cup H_i} \tag{1}$$

where M_i and H_i represent the rationale set of the i-th instance provided by the model and human respectively; N is the number of instances.

Token-level F1-score is defined in Equation 2, which is also computed on a token level by the overlap of the rationales tokens predicted by the models with the human-annotated ones. To measure the Token-level F1 score, we measured the Token-level Precision (P_i) and Recall (R_i) and also reported both metrics.

$$\text{Token-F1} = \frac{1}{N}\sum_{i=1}^{N}(2 \times \frac{P_i \times R_i}{P_i + R_i}) \quad \text{where } P_i = \frac{M_i \cap H_i}{M_i} \text{ and } R_i = \frac{M_i \cap H_i}{H_i} \tag{2}$$

Faithfulness: We report two metrics: *comprehensiveness* and *sufficiency* (DeYoung et al., 2020) to measure faithfulness.

Comprehensiveness measures whether the tokens necessary for making a prediction were selected. To calculate rationale comprehensiveness, for each instance x_i, we construct a contrasting example $\tilde{x}_i$, which is x_i without the predicted rationales r_i[7]. Let $m(x_i)_j$ be the original prediction provided by a model m for the predicted class j for the instance x_i. We then define $m(x_i \backslash r_i)_j$ as the predicted probability of $\tilde{x}_i$ by the model m for class j. The comprehensiveness score is shown in Equation 3. A high comprehensiveness value implies that the rationales are influential in the prediction.

$$\text{Comp} = \frac{1}{N}\sum_{i=1}^{N}(m(x_i)_j - m(x_i \backslash r_i)_j) \tag{3}$$

Sufficiency measures the degree to which the predicted rationales are adequate for a model to make a prediction. The sufficiency score is shown in Equation 4. Where $m(r_i)_j$ is defined as the prediction probability of giving only the predicted rationales r_i to a model m for class j. A low sufficiency implies the rationales are sufficient to make a prediction.

$$\text{Suff} = \frac{1}{N}\sum_{i=1}^{N}(m(x_i)_j - m(r_i)_j) \tag{4}$$

Readability: We applied *Flesch Reading Ease* (Flesch, 1948) and *Szigriszt-Pazos Index* (Pazos, 1993), both of which are applicable to Portuguese, to evaluate zero-shot prompt post-hoc explanations.

[7]We select the top k tokens from the rationales to remove, where k is defined as the average length of the token sets predicted by each explainability model.

5.2.2 Results

Tables 5 and 6 present the evaluation results of explanations generated by LIME, SHAP, and zero-shot prompt methods from the perspectives of plausibility and faithfulness for LIME and SHAP, and readability for the zero-shot prompts. Our evaluation revealed that for class 0 (the reliable sentences), both SHAP and LIME yielded poor results. One possible explanation is that the words used to identify unreliable sentences, which are predominantly subjective, have a much greater impact on predicting unreliable sentences compared to those used to identify reliable sentences. Additionally, the zero-shot prompt post-hoc explanations achieved high readability. We also observed that the prompts proposed for fake claims generated more readable explanations compared to those for true claims.

Quantitative Analysis: When examining unreliable sentences, the rationales highlight the tokens that contribute to media bias. Removing these tokens from the sentence would make the remaining text appear less unreliable, thus altering the classification probability. This effect does not occur with reliable sentences, so we cannot observe similar effects when computing comprehensiveness and sufficiency metrics for this class. In Table 5, We observe that LIME performs better on faithfulness metrics, while SHAP excels in plausibility metrics. However, the number of tokens returned as rationales by each method differs significantly. LIME, by default, returns a maximum of 10 tokens, whereas SHAP returns more. The plausibility metrics are computed by comparing these tokens against human-annotated rationales, which are often more complex and contextually rich, such as entire phrases. Consequently, the intersection between LIME's tokens and human-annotated rationales is generally smaller than SHAP's, leading to lower metric scores for LIME. Despite this, the token-level precision is higher for LIME because this metric is calculated as the intersection divided by the total number of tokens retrieved by the method (SHAP or LIME). Since LIME retrieves fewer tokens than SHAP, it achieves a higher precision. However, LIME's recall performance is significantly worse. When examining the performance of both methods on faithfulness metrics, the situation is reversed, with LIME showing superior results for both comprehensiveness and sufficiency metrics. One possible explanation is that the words selected by LIME have a more significant impact on the model's prediction. Since LIME selects fewer words than SHAP, it may focus

Methods	Plausibility				Faithfulness	
	IOU F1 ↑	Token Precision ↑	Token Recall ↑	Token F1 ↑	Comp. ↑	Suff. ↓
BERT-LIME	0.1098	**0.4378**	0.3913	0.3698	**0.2961**	**-0.0546**
BERT-SHAP	**0.1529**	0.4312	**0.5111**	**0.4285**	0.2868	-0.0491

Table 5: Evaluation for explanations generated by LIME and SHAP explainability methods.

Method	Readability			
	Flesch Reading Ease		Szigriszt Pazos Index	
	True	Fake	True	Fake
Zero Shot Prompts	0.77	**0.84**	-1519.48	**-1361.47**

Table 6: Evaluation for zero-shot prompts post-hoc explanations.

more on the most critical words for the prediction, thus improving the faithfulness metrics. This observation aligns with the qualitative analysis conducted by a specialist and described below. In Figure 5, we present the top 20 most important words predicted by LIME and SHAP. This includes 10 words most important for predicting the unreliable class (red bars) and 10 most important for predicting the reliable class (blue bars). This analysis is based on all 510 selected sentences. We observed that the vocabulary on the right side of the graphs, representing unreliable words, tends to be more subjective and includes more adjectives. This observation also aligns with the qualitative analysis conducted by a specialist, which is described as follows.

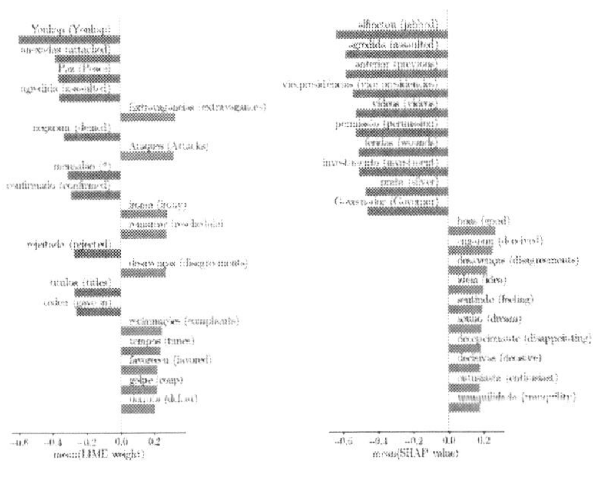

Figure 5: Most relevant features provided by LIME and SHAP to predict each class (reliable/unreliable) for sentence-level news source reliability estimation.

Qualitative Analysis: We also conducted a qualitative analysis with a linguist, comparing LIME and SHAP scores with human-annotated rationales for the most impactful tokens in determining whether a sentence is unreliable. Regarding the agreement between the LIME and the human rationals, abstract verbs that involve subjective interpretation, where the author projects an action or feeling onto the subject (e.g., "attack", "deceive"), were frequently identified as indicative of media bias. Another critical feature of unreliable sentences was the presence of adjectives (e.g., "prudent", "useful") and adverbs (e.g., "negatively"). Regarding disagreements between LIME and human-annotated rationales, LIME often identified articles and prepositions as indicators of bias. In many cases, specific nouns (e.g., "history") were also flagged, although their potential for bias depends on the context in which they are used. Finally, SHAP identified a higher number of articles, prepositions, and possessive pronouns as indicators of bias compared to LIME. However, these terms alone do not necessarily influence the degree of bias in the sentences. Regarding the agreement between SHAP and human-annotated rationales, we observed the same types of terms as with LIME. However, SHAP tended to identify a larger number of nouns and proper nouns as being linked to bias. Thus, there seems to be a greater cohesion between the LIME method and human-annotated rationales for this specific task.

6 Conclusions

This paper introduces a new method to improve explainable fact-checking. The SELFAR predicts reliability and the factuality of news articles or claims at the sentence level, generating post-hoc explanations using LIME/SHAP and zero-shot prompts. Our experiments showed that unreliable news stories are comprised mostly of subjective words, in contrast to reliable ones. Thus, predicting unreliable news stories by analyzing text impartiality and subjectivity is promising for fact extraction and improving explainable fact-checking. In addition, LIME outperforms SHAP in explaining reliability predictions. Lastly, while zero-shot prompts provide highly readable explanations and achieve an accuracy of 0.71 in predicting factuality, their tendency to hallucinate presents a challenge. We also present baselines for explainable fact-checking in Portuguese.

Limitations

Although the proposed method for explainable fact-checking has addressed relevant gaps in providing more accurate and transparent automated fact-checking, the method for retrieving evidence from LLMs for factuality (veracity) prediction may present limitations due to the potential for LLMs to hallucinate. Therefore, as future work, we aim to mitigate this limitation by extracting evidence from multiple and diversified data sources.

Ethics Statement

The data resources and artifacts used in this paper are open source and have been anonymized.

Acknowledgements

The first author is grateful to Google for financial support. This project was partially funded by FAPESP, CNPq, FAPEMIG, CAPES, and the Ministry of Science Technology and Innovation, with resources of Law N. 8,248, of October 23, 1991, within the scope of PPI-SOFTEX, coordinated by Softex and published as Residence in TIC 13, DOU 01245.010222/2022-44.

References

Naser Ahmadi, Paolo Papotti, and Mohammed Saeed. 2019. Explainable fact checking with probabilistic answer set programming. In *Proceedings of the Conference for truth and trust Online*, pages 1–9, London, UK.

Tariq Alhindi, Savvas Petridis, and Smaranda Muresan. 2018. Where is your evidence: Improving fact-checking by justification modeling. In *Proceedings of the First Workshop on Fact Extraction and VERification (FEVER)*, pages 85–90, Brussels, Belgium. Association for Computational Linguistics.

Miguel Arana-Catania, Elena Kochkina, Arkaitz Zubiaga, Maria Liakata, Robert Procter, and Yulan He. 2022. Natural language inference with self-attention for veracity assessment of pandemic claims. In *Proceedings of the 2022 Conference of the North American Chapter of the Association for Computational Linguistics: Human Language Technologies*, pages 1496–1511, Seattle, United States. Association for Computational Linguistics.

Pepa Atanasova, Jakob Grue Simonsen, Christina Lioma, and Isabelle Augenstein. 2020a. Generating fact checking explanations. In *Proceedings of the 58th Annual Meeting of the Association for Computational Linguistics*, pages 7352–7364, Online. Association for Computational Linguistics.

Pepa Atanasova, Dustin Wright, and Isabelle Augenstein. 2020b. Generating label cohesive and well-formed adversarial claims. In *Proceedings of the 2020 Conference on Empirical Methods in Natural Language Processing (EMNLP)*, pages 3168–3177, Online. Association for Computational Linguistics.

Isabelle Augenstein, Christina Lioma, Dongsheng Wang, Lucas Chaves Lima, Casper Hansen, Christian Hansen, and Jakob Grue Simonsen. 2019. MultiFC: A real-world multi-domain dataset for evidence-based fact checking of claims. In *Proceedings of the 2019 Conference on Empirical Methods in Natural Language Processing and the 9th International Joint Conference on Natural Language Processing (EMNLP-IJCNLP)*, pages 4685–4697, Hong Kong, China. Association for Computational Linguistics.

Esma Balkir, Svetlana Kiritchenko, Isar Nejadgholi, and Kathleen Fraser. 2022. Challenges in applying explainability methods to improve the fairness of NLP models. In *Proceedings of the 2nd Workshop on Trustworthy Natural Language Processing (TrustNLP 2022)*, pages 80–92, Seattle, U.S.A. Association for Computational Linguistics.

Ramy Baly, Georgi Karadzhov, Dimitar Alexandrov, James Glass, and Preslav Nakov. 2018a. Predicting factuality of reporting and bias of news media sources. In *Proceedings of the 2018 Conference on Empirical Methods in Natural Language Processing*, pages 3528–3539, Brussels, Belgium. Association for Computational Linguistics.

Ramy Baly, Georgi Karadzhov, Abdelrhman Saleh, James Glass, and Preslav Nakov. 2019. Multi-task ordinal regression for jointly predicting the trustworthiness and the leading political ideology of news media. In *Proceedings of the 2019 Conference of the North American Chapter of the Association for Computational Linguistics: Human Language Technologies, Volume 1 (Long and Short Papers)*, pages 2109–2116, Minneapolis, Minnesota. Association for Computational Linguistics.

Ramy Baly, Mitra Mohtarami, James Glass, Lluís Màrquez, Alessandro Moschitti, and Preslav Nakov. 2018b. Integrating stance detection and fact checking in a unified corpus. In *Proceedings of the 2018 Conference of the North American Chapter of the Association for Computational Linguistics: Human Language Technologies, Volume 2 (Short Papers)*, pages 21–27, New Orleans, Louisiana. Association for Computational Linguistics.

Bimal Bhattarai, Ole-Christoffer Granmo, and Lei Jiao. 2022. Explainable tsetlin machine framework for fake news detection with credibility score assessment. In *Proceedings of the Thirteenth Language Resources and Evaluation Conference*, pages 4894–4903, Marseille, France. European Language Resources Association.

Tom B. Brown, Benjamin Mann, Nick Ryder, Melanie Subbiah, Jared Kaplan, Prafulla Dhariwal, Arvind Neelakantan, Pranav Shyam, Girish Sastry, Amanda

Askell, Sandhini Agarwal, Ariel Herbert-Voss, Gretchen Krueger, Tom Henighan, Rewon Child, Aditya Ramesh, Daniel M. Ziegler, Jeffrey Wu, Clemens Winter, Christopher Hesse, Mark Chen, Eric Sigler, Mateusz Litwin, Scott Gray, Benjamin Chess, Jack Clark, Christopher Berner, Sam McCandlish, Alec Radford, Ilya Sutskever, and Dario Amodei. 2020. Language models are few-shot learners. *CoRR*, abs/2005.14165.

Carlos Castillo, Marcelo Mendoza, and Barbara Poblete. 2011. Information credibility on twitter. In *Proceedings of the 20th International Conference on World Wide Web*, page 675–684, New York, United States.

Eric Chamoun, Marzieh Saeidi, and Andreas Vlachos. 2023. Automated fact-checking in dialogue: Are specialized models needed? In *Proceedings of the 2023 Conference on Empirical Methods in Natural Language Processing*, pages 16009–16020, Republic of Singapore, Singapore.

João Couto, Breno Pimenta, Igor M. de Araújo, Samuel Assis, Julio C. S. Reis, Ana Paula da Silva, Jussara Almeida, and Fabrício Benevenuto. 2021. Central de fatos: Um repositório de checagens de fatos. In *Anais do III Dataset Showcase Workshop*, pages 128–137, Porto Alegre, Brasil. SBC.

Sohan De Sarkar, Fan Yang, and Arjun Mukherjee. 2018. Attending sentences to detect satirical fake news. In *Proceedings of the 27th International Conference on Computational Linguistics*, pages 3371–3380, Santa Fe, New Mexico, USA. Association for Computational Linguistics.

Jay DeYoung, Sarthak Jain, Nazneen Fatema Rajani, Eric Lehman, Caiming Xiong, Richard Socher, and Byron C. Wallace. 2020. ERASER: A benchmark to evaluate rationalized NLP models. In *Proceedings of the 58th Annual Meeting of the Association for Computational Linguistics*, pages 4443–4458, Online. Association for Computational Linguistics.

Xin Luna Dong, Evgeniy Gabrilovich, Kevin Murphy, Van Dang, Wilko Horn, Camillo Lugaresi, Shaohua Sun, and Wei Zhang. 2015. Knowledge-based trust: Estimating the trustworthiness of web sources. *Proc. VLDB Endow.*, 8(9):938–949.

Rudolf Flesch. 1948. A new readability yardstick. *Journal of Applied Psychology*, 3(32):221–233.

Mohamed H. Gad-Elrab, Daria Stepanova, Jacopo Urbani, and Gerhard Weikum. 2019. Exfakt: A framework for explaining facts over knowledge graphs and text. In *Proceedings of the Twelfth ACM International Conference on Web Search and Data Mining*, page 87–95, New York USA.

Max Glockner, Ieva Staliunait, James Thorne, Gisela Vallejo, Andreas Vlachos, and Iryna Gurevych. 2023. Ambifc: Fact-checking ambiguous claims with evidence. *Transactions of the Association for Computational Linguistics*, 1:37–53.

Riccardo Guidotti, Anna Monreale, Salvatore Ruggieri, Franco Turini, Fosca Giannotti, and Dino Pedreschi. 2018. A survey of methods for explaining black box models. *ACM Computing Surveys*, 51(5).

Zhijiang Guo, Michael Schlichtkrull, and Andreas Vlachos. 2022. A Survey on Automated Fact-Checking. *Transactions of the Association for Computational Linguistics*, 10:178–206.

Andreas Hanselowski, Christian Stab, Claudia Schulz, Zile Li, and Iryna Gurevych. 2019. A richly annotated corpus for different tasks in automated fact-checking. In *Proceedings of the 23rd Conference on Computational Natural Language Learning*, page 493–503, Hong Kong, China.

Momchil Hardalov, Anton Chernyavskiy, Ivan Koychev, Dmitry Ilvovsky, and Preslav Nakov. 2022. CrowdChecked: Detecting previously fact-checked claims in social media. In *Proceedings of the 2nd Conference of the Asia-Pacific Chapter of the Association for Computational Linguistics and the 12th International Joint Conference on Natural Language Processing (Volume 1: Long Papers)*, pages 266–285, Online only. Association for Computational Linguistics.

Momchil Hardalov, Ivan Koychev, and Preslav Nakov. 2016. In search of credible news. In *17th International Conference on Artificial Intelligence: Methodology, Systems, and Application*, pages 172–180, Varna, Bulgaria.

Benjamin D. Horne, William Dron, Sara Khedr, and Sibel Adali. 2018. Assessing the news landscape: A multi-module toolkit for evaluating the credibility of news. In *Proceedings of the The Web Conference 2018*, page 235–238, Geneva, Switzerland.

Adrian Iftene, Daniela Gifu, Andrei-Remus Miron, and Mihai-Stefan Dudu. 2020. A real-time system for credibility on Twitter. In *Proceedings of the Twelfth Language Resources and Evaluation Conference*, pages 6166–6173, Marseille, France. European Language Resources Association.

Zhengbao Jiang, Frank Xu, Luyu Gao, Zhiqing Sun, Qian Liu, Jane Dwivedi-Yu, Yiming Yang, Jamie Callan, and Graham Neubig. 2023. Active retrieval augmented generation. In *Proceedings of the 2023 Conference on Empirical Methods in Natural Language Processing*, pages 7969–7992, Singapore, Singapore.

Neema Kotonya and Francesca Toni. 2020a. Explainable automated fact-checking: A survey. In *Proceedings of the 28th International Conference on Computational Linguistics*, pages 5430–5443, Barcelona, Spain (Online). International Committee on Computational Linguistics.

Neema Kotonya and Francesca Toni. 2020b. Explainable automated fact-checking for public health claims. In *Proceedings of the 2020 Conference on Empirical Methods in Natural Language Processing (EMNLP)*, pages 7740–7754, Online. Association for Computational Linguistics.

Nayeon Lee, Yejin Bang, Andrea Madotto, and Pascale Fung. 2021. Towards few-shot fact-checking via perplexity. In *Proceedings of the 2021 Conference of the North American Chapter of the Association for Computational Linguistics: Human Language Technologies*, pages 1971–1981, Online. Association for Computational Linguistics.

Yunfei Long, Qin Lu, Rong Xiang, Minglei Li, and Chu-Ren Huang. 2017. Fake news detection through multi-perspective speaker profiles. In *Proceedings of the Eighth International Joint Conference on Natural Language Processing (Volume 2: Short Papers)*, pages 252–256, Taipei, Taiwan. Asian Federation of Natural Language Processing.

Scott M Lundberg and Su-In Lee. 2017. A unified approach to interpreting model predictions. *Advances in neural information processing systems*, 30.

Julie Mastrine. 2022. *How to Spot 16 Types of Media Bias*. AllSides: Don't be fooled by media bias and misinformation, California, United States.

João Moreno and Graça Bressan. 2019. Factck.br: a new dataset to study fake news. In *Proceedings of the 25th Brazillian Symposium on Multimedia and the Web*, page 525–527, Rio de Janeiro, Brazil. Association for Computing Machinery.

Subhabrata Mukherjee and Gerhard Weikum. 2015. Leveraging joint interactions for credibility analysis in news communities. In *Proceedings of the 24th ACM International on Conference on Information and Knowledge Management*, page 353–362, New York, United States.

Nona Naderi and Graeme Hirst. 2018. Automated fact-checking of claims in argumentative parliamentary debates. In *Proceedings of the First Workshop on Fact Extraction and VERification (FEVER)*, pages 60–65, Brussels, Belgium. Association for Computational Linguistics.

Piotr Niewinski, Maria Pszona, and Maria Janicka. 2019. GEM: Generative enhanced model for adversarial attacks. In *Proceedings of the Second Workshop on Fact Extraction and VERification (FEVER)*, pages 20–26, Hong Kong, China. Association for Computational Linguistics.

OpenAI, Josh Achiam, Steven Adler, Sandhini Agarwal, Lama Ahmad, Ilge Akkaya, Florencia Leoni Aleman, Diogo Almeida, Janko Altenschmidt, Sam Altman, Shyamal Anadkat, Red Avila, Igor Babuschkin, Suchir Balaji, Valerie Balcom, Paul Baltescu, Haiming Bao, Mohammad Bavarian, Jeff Belgum, Irwan Bello, Jake Berdine, Gabriel Bernadett-Shapiro, Christopher Berner, Lenny Bogdonoff, Oleg Boiko, Madelaine Boyd, Anna-Luisa Brakman, Greg Brockman, Tim Brooks, Miles Brundage, Kevin Button, Trevor Cai, Rosie Campbell, Andrew Cann, Brittany Carey, Chelsea Carlson, Rory Carmichael, Brooke Chan, Che Chang, Fotis Chantzis, Derek Chen, Sully Chen, Ruby Chen, Jason Chen, Mark Chen, Ben Chess, Chester Cho, Casey Chu, Hyung Won Chung, Dave Cummings, Jeremiah Currier, Yunxing Dai, Cory Decareaux, Thomas Degry, Noah Deutsch, Damien Deville, Arka Dhar, David Dohan, Steve Dowling, Sheila Dunning, Adrien Ecoffet, Atty Eleti, Tyna Eloundou, David Farhi, Liam Fedus, Niko Felix, Simón Posada Fishman, Juston Forte, Isabella Fulford, Leo Gao, Elie Georges, Christian Gibson, Vik Goel, Tarun Gogineni, Gabriel Goh, Rapha Gontijo-Lopes, Jonathan Gordon, Morgan Grafstein, Scott Gray, Ryan Greene, Joshua Gross, Shixiang Shane Gu, Yufei Guo, Chris Hallacy, Jesse Han, Jeff Harris, Yuchen He, Mike Heaton, Johannes Heidecke, Chris Hesse, Alan Hickey, Wade Hickey, Peter Hoeschele, Brandon Houghton, Kenny Hsu, Shengli Hu, Xin Hu, Joost Huizinga, Shantanu Jain, Shawn Jain, Joanne Jang, Angela Jiang, Roger Jiang, Haozhun Jin, Denny Jin, Shino Jomoto, Billie Jonn, Heewoo Jun, Tomer Kaftan, Łukasz Kaiser, Ali Kamali, Ingmar Kanitscheider, Nitish Shirish Keskar, Tabarak Khan, Logan Kilpatrick, Jong Wook Kim, Christina Kim, Yongjik Kim, Jan Hendrik Kirchner, Jamie Kiros, Matt Knight, Daniel Kokotajlo, Łukasz Kondraciuk, Andrew Kondrich, Aris Konstantinidis, Kyle Kosic, Gretchen Krueger, Vishal Kuo, Michael Lampe, Ikai Lan, Teddy Lee, Jan Leike, Jade Leung, Daniel Levy, Chak Ming Li, Rachel Lim, Molly Lin, Stephanie Lin, Mateusz Litwin, Theresa Lopez, Ryan Lowe, Patricia Lue, Anna Makanju, Kim Malfacini, Sam Manning, Todor Markov, Yaniv Markovski, Bianca Martin, Katie Mayer, Andrew Mayne, Bob McGrew, Scott Mayer McKinney, Christine McLeavey, Paul McMillan, Jake McNeil, David Medina, Aalok Mehta, Jacob Menick, Luke Metz, Andrey Mishchenko, Pamela Mishkin, Vinnie Monaco, Evan Morikawa, Daniel Mossing, Tong Mu, Mira Murati, Oleg Murk, David Mély, Ashvin Nair, Reiichiro Nakano, Rajeev Nayak, Arvind Neelakantan, Richard Ngo, Hyeonwoo Noh, Long Ouyang, Cullen O'Keefe, Jakub Pachocki, Alex Paino, Joe Palermo, Ashley Pantuliano, Giambattista Parascandolo, Joel Parish, Emy Parparita, Alex Passos, Mikhail Pavlov, Andrew Peng, Adam Perelman, Filipe de Avila Belbute Peres, Michael Petrov, Henrique Ponde de Oliveira Pinto, Michael, Pokorny, Michelle Pokrass, Vitchyr H. Pong, Tolly Powell, Alethea Power, Boris Power, Elizabeth Proehl, Raul Puri, Alec Radford, Jack Rae, Aditya Ramesh, Cameron Raymond, Francis Real, Kendra Rimbach, Carl Ross, Bob Rotsted, Henri Roussez, Nick Ryder, Mario Saltarelli, Ted Sanders, Shibani Santurkar, Girish Sastry, Heather Schmidt, David Schnurr, John Schulman, Daniel Selsam, Kyla Sheppard, Toki Sherbakov, Jessica Shieh, Sarah Shoker, Pranav Shyam, Szymon Sidor, Eric Sigler, Maddie Simens, Jordan Sitkin, Katarina Slama, Ian Sohl, Benjamin Sokolowsky, Yang Song, Natalie Staudacher, Felipe Petroski Such, Natalie Summers, Ilya Sutskever, Jie Tang, Nikolas Tezak, Madeleine B. Thompson, Phil Tillet, Amin Tootoonchian, Elizabeth Tseng, Preston Tuggle, Nick Turley, Jerry Tworek, Juan Felipe Cerón Uribe, Andrea Vallone, Arun Vijayvergiya, Chelsea Voss, Carroll Wainwright, Justin Jay Wang, Alvin Wang, Ben Wang, Jonathan Ward, Jason Wei, CJ Weinmann, Akila Welihinda, Peter Welinder, Jiayi Weng, Lilian Weng, Matt Wiethoff,

Dave Willner, Clemens Winter, Samuel Wolrich, Hannah Wong, Lauren Workman, Sherwin Wu, Jeff Wu, Michael Wu, Kai Xiao, Tao Xu, Sarah Yoo, Kevin Yu, Qiming Yuan, Wojciech Zaremba, Rowan Zellers, Chong Zhang, Marvin Zhang, Shengjia Zhao, Tianhao Zheng, Juntang Zhuang, William Zhuk, and Barret Zoph. 2024. Gpt-4 technical report.

Jeff Z. Pan, Siyana Pavlova, Chenxi Li, Ningxi Li, Yangmei Li, and Jinshuo Liu. 2018. Content based fake news detection using knowledge graphs. In *The Semantic Web - ISWC 2018*, pages 669–683.

Manuel Martín Szigriszt Pazos. 1993. Índices de legibilidade formulados para a língua espanhola. *SEECI, Revista de la Facultad de Ciencias de la Información*.

Verónica Pérez-Rosas, Bennett Kleinberg, Alexandra Lefevre, and Rada Mihalcea. 2018. Automatic detection of fake news. In *Proceedings of the 27th International Conference on Computational Linguistics*, pages 3391–3401, Santa Fe, New Mexico, USA. Association for Computational Linguistics.

Kashyap Popat, Subhabrata Mukherjee, Jannik Strötgen, and Gerhard Weikum. 2016. Credibility assessment of textual claims on the web. In *Proceedings of the 25th ACM International on Conference on Information and Knowledge Management*, page 2173–2178, New York, United States.

Kashyap Popat, Subhabrata Mukherjee, Jannik Strötgen, and Gerhard Weikum. 2017. Where the truth lies: Explaining the credibility of emerging claims on the web and social media. In *Proceedings of the 26th International Conference on World Wide Web Companion*, page 1003–1012, Republic and Canton of Geneva, CHE. International World Wide Web Conferences Steering Committee.

Ofir Press, Muru Zhang, Sewon Min, Ludwig Schmidt, Noah Smith, and Mike Lewis. 2023. Measuring and narrowing the compositionality gap in language models. In *Findings of the Association for Computational Linguistics: EMNLP 2023*, pages 5687–5711, Singapore, Singapore.

Julio C. S. Reis, Andre Correia, Fabricio Murai, Adriano Veloso, and Fabricio Benevenuto. 2019. Explainable machine learning for fake news detection. In *Proceedings of the 11th ACM Conference on Web Science*, pages 17–26, Massachusetts, United States.

Julio C. S. Reis, Philipe Melo, Kiran Garimella, Jussara M. Almeida, Dean Eckles, and Fabrício Benevenuto. 2020. A dataset of fact-checked images shared on whatsapp during the brazilian and indian elections. In *Proceedings of the 14th International AAAI Conference on Web and Social Media*, pages 903–908, Held Online.

Manoel Horta Ribeiro, Savvas Zannettou, Oana Goga, Fabrício Benevenuto, and Robert West. 2022. Can online attention signals help fact-checkers to fact-check? In *Workshop Proceedings of the 17th International AAAI Conference On Web and Social Media*, pages 1–10, Atlanta, United States.

Marco Tulio Ribeiro, Sameer Singh, and Carlos Guestrin. 2016. " why should i trust you?" explaining the predictions of any classifier. In *Proceedings of the 22nd ACM SIGKDD international conference on knowledge discovery and data mining*, pages 1135–1144.

Zien Sheikh Ali, Watheq Mansour, Tamer Elsayed, and Abdulaziz Al-Ali. 2021. AraFacts: The first large Arabic dataset of naturally occurring claims. In *Proceedings of the Sixth Arabic Natural Language Processing Workshop*, pages 231–236, Kyiv, Ukraine (Virtual). Association for Computational Linguistics.

James Thorne, Andreas Vlachos, Christos Christodoulopoulos, and Arpit Mittal. 2018. FEVER: a large-scale dataset for fact extraction and VERification. In *Proceedings of the 2018 Conference of the North American Chapter of the Association for Computational Linguistics: Human Language Technologies, Volume 1 (Long Papers)*, pages 809–819, New Orleans, Louisiana. Association for Computational Linguistics.

James Thorne, Andreas Vlachos, Christos Christodoulopoulos, and Arpit Mittal. 2019. Evaluating adversarial attacks against multiple fact verification systems. In *Proceedings of the 2019 Conference on Empirical Methods in Natural Language Processing and the 9th International Joint Conference on Natural Language Processing (EMNLP-IJCNLP)*, pages 2944–2953, Hong Kong, China. Association for Computational Linguistics.

Francielle Vargas, Jonas D'Alessandro, Zohar Rabinovich, Fabrício Benevenuto, and Thiago Pardo. 2022. Rhetorical structure approach for online deception detection: A survey. In *Proceedings of the Thirteenth Language Resources and Evaluation Conference*, pages 5906–5915, Marseille, France. European Language Resources Association.

Francielle Vargas, Kokil Jaidka, Thiago Pardo, and Fabrício Benevenuto. 2023. Predicting sentence-level factuality of news and bias of media outlets. In *Proceedings of the 14th International Conference on ecent Advances in Natural Language Processing*, pages 1197–1206, Varna, Bulgaria.

Juraj Vladika and Florian Matthes. 2024. Comparing knowledge sources for open-domain scientific claim verification. In *Proceedings of the 18th Conference of the European Chapter of the Association for Computational Linguistics (Volume 1: Long Papers)*, pages 2103–2114, St. Julian's, Malta.

David Wadden, Shanchuan Lin, Kyle Lo, Lucy Lu Wang, Madeleine van Zuylen, Arman Cohan, and Hannaneh Hajishirzi. 2020. Fact or fiction: Verifying scientific claims. In *Proceedings of the 2020 Conference on Empirical Methods in Natural Language Processing (EMNLP)*, pages 7534–7550, Online. Association for Computational Linguistics.

Gengyu Wang, Kate Harwood, Lawrence Chillrud, Amith Ananthram, Melanie Subbiah, and Kathleen McKeown. 2023. Check-COVID: Fact-checking

COVID-19 news claims with scientific evidence. In *Findings of the Association for Computational Linguistics: ACL 2023*, pages 14114–14127, Toronto, Canada. Association for Computational Linguistics.

William Yang Wang. 2017. "liar, liar pants on fire": A new benchmark dataset for fake news detection. In *Proceedings of the 55th Annual Meeting of the Association for Computational Linguistics (Volume 2: Short Papers)*, pages 422–426, Vancouver, Canada. Association for Computational Linguistics.

Zhilin Yang, Peng Qi, Saizheng Zhang, Yoshua Bengio, William Cohen, Ruslan Salakhutdinov, and Christopher D. Manning. 2018. HotpotQA: A dataset for diverse, explainable multi-hop question answering. In *Proceedings of the 2018 Conference on Empirical Methods in Natural Language Processing*, pages 2369–2380, Brussels, Belgium. Association for Computational Linguistics.

Chunyuan Yuan, Qianwen Ma, Wei Zhou, Jizhong Han, and Songlin Hu. 2020. Early detection of fake news by utilizing the credibility of news, publishers, and users based on weakly supervised learning. In *Proceedings of the 28th International Conference on Computational Linguistics*, pages 5444–5454, Barcelona, Spain (Online). International Committee on Computational Linguistics.

Majid Zarharan, Pascal Wullschleger, Babak Behkam Kia, Mohammad Taher Pilehvar, and Jennifer Foster. 2024. Tell me why: Explainable public health fact-checking with large language models. In *Proceedings of the 4th Workshop on Trustworthy Natural Language Processing (TrustNLP 2024)*, pages 252–278, Mexico City, Mexico. Association for Computational Linguistics.

Fengzhu Zeng and Wei Gao. 2023. Prompt to be consistent is better than self-consistent? few-shot and zero-shot fact verification with pre-trained language models. In *Findings of the Association for Computational Linguistics: ACL 2023*, pages 4555–4569, Toronto, Canada. Association for Computational Linguistics.

Fengzhu Zeng and Wei Gao. 2024. JustiLM: Few-shot justification generation for explainable fact-checking of real-world claims. *Transactions of the Association for Computational Linguistics*, 11:334–354.

Xuan Zhang and Wei Gao. 2023. Towards LLM-based fact verification on news claims with a hierarchical step-by-step prompting method. In *Proceedings of the 13th International Joint Conference on Natural Language Processing and the 3rd Conference of the Asia-Pacific Chapter of the Association for Computational Linguistics*, pages 996–1011, Nusa Dua, Bali.

Fast Evidence Extraction for Grounded Language Model Outputs

Pranav Mani
Abridge
pranav@abridge.com

Davis Liang
Abridge
davis@abridge.com

Zachary C. Lipton
Abridge
zack@abridge.com

Abstract

Summarizing documents with Large Language Models (LLMs) warrants a rigorous inspection of the resulting outputs by humans. However, unaided verification of generated outputs is time-intensive and intractable at scale. For high-stakes applications like healthcare where verification is necessary, expediting this step can unlock massive gains in productivity. In this paper, we focus on the task of evidence extraction for abstractive summarization: for each summary line, extract the corresponding evidence spans from a source document. Viewing this evidence extraction problem through the lens of extractive question answering, we train a set of fast and scalable hierarchical architectures: EarlyFusion, MidFusion, and LateFusion. Our experiments show that (i) our method outperforms the state-of-the-art by 1.4% relative F1-Score; (ii) our model architecture reduces latency by 4x over a RoBERTa-Large baseline; and (iii) pretraining on an extractive QA corpus confers positive transfer to evidence extraction, especially in low-resource regimes.

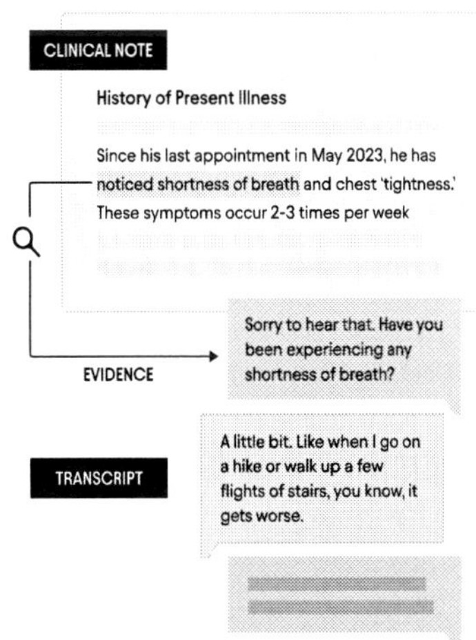

Figure 1: Verifying details in a clinical note requires perusing long conversation transcripts to find substantiating evidence.

1 Introduction

Suppose we train an LLM to summarize a doctor-patient conversation into a clinical note. Such models could save physicians hours each day. However, an auditing step is still requisite. This auditing involves repeatedly diving through a long transcript to find relevant information for every detail that appears in the note (see fig.1). Without an automated mechanism that makes this process efficient, can we really say that we've saved a clinician any time?

Workflows that involve grounded tasks that operate on top of a source document (e.g. summarization, dialogue and translation) (Touvron et al., 2023; Bubeck et al., 2023; Widyassari et al., 2022; Rafailov et al., 2023; Liang et al., 2023) are well suited for LLMs (Krishna et al., 2021; Lehman et al., 2019; Lei et al., 2016; Asan et al., 2020). However, owing to the lingering limitations of these models, humans have remained firmly in the loop, providing last-mile verification of the model's outputs. In these setups, an individual may spend a significant amount of time on verification of LLM-generated first drafts. For grounded tasks, verifying each generated sentence can be broken down into two steps (i) locating a span of text from the much larger source document that has information related to that sentence; (ii) using the obtained span to form conclusions about correctness. With long sources (e.g. hour-long conversation transcripts), it's likely that carrying out the first step of extracting the right span of evidence proves more cumbersome than using the extracted evidence to make conclusions. Furthermore, this problem is exacerbated as the transcript grows in length. Therefore, we present automated Evidence Extraction (EE) as an efficient and scalable way to reduce verification time and fully realize the benefits of workflow automation.

Proceedings of the Seventh Fact Extraction and VERification Workshop (FEVER), pages 205–218
November 15, 2024

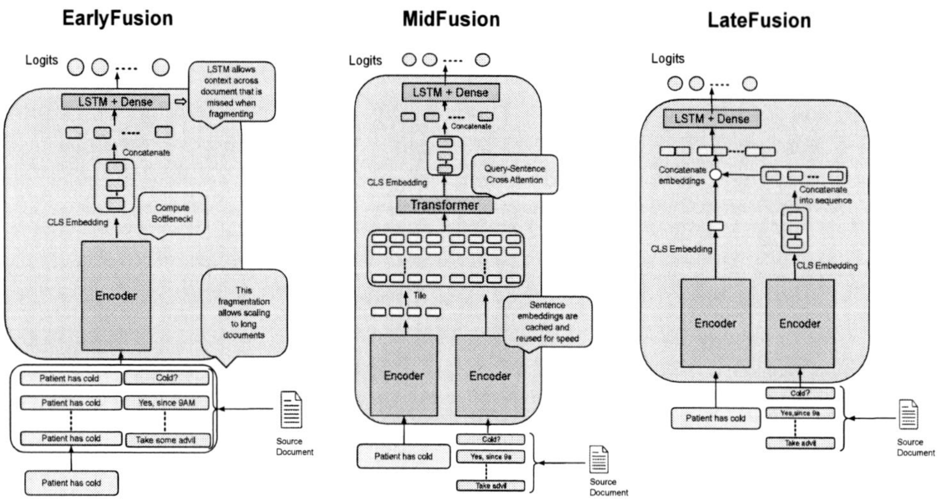

Figure 2: Architectures of the Early, Mid and LateFusion models. Breaking down the source document into sentences helps scale to large documents. In Late and MidFusion architectures the encoders are separated allowing us to cache the embeddings of the sentences of the source. In the MidFusion model, we do not immediately select the CLS embedding but concatenate with the query embeddings for an intermediate transformer step.

In this work, we pose the Evidence Extraction (EE) problem as follows: Given a sentence that requires verification (query) and a source document D that this line should be grounded in, can we identify spans in D (evidence-spans) that contain information relevant to the query? We immediately notice a parallel to Extractive Question Answering (QA): query to question, source to passage, and evidence to answer. This parallel allows us to (i) explore designs for model architectures drawing inspiration from the dual-encoder and cross-encoder families in QA; (ii) explore the benefits that training on QA datasets confer to EE. The latter point proves useful since EE data is hard to come by while ample amounts of QA datasets are available.

In our work, we are focused on exploring simple architectures that are scalable and fast when working with source documents that span beyond thousands of words. For scaling to longer documents, we consider hierarchical architectures that break down a source document into sentences which are encoded independently through RoBERTa-like backbones. We then add document-wide context by concatenating them along the sequence dimension and passing them through an LSTM. For speed, we aim to decouple the encoding of the query and the encoding of the source document. This allows us to amortize the higher cost of computing source document embeddings by caching them for reuse upon subsequent queries on the same source. After the decoupled encoding process, we combine the obtained source and query embeddings in a Late-Fusion step (see Figure 2).

On the flip side, while slow, we find that early fusion of the query string with each sentence in the source is easier to train and performs well due to query-conditioned encoding of the source sentences. We explore an optimal point in the trade-off between performance and throughput and advocate for the use of our proposed MidFusion (MF) architecture that finds an intermediate point to include query-source cross attention. Further, the performance gap between the Late, Mid and Early Fusion models narrows with access to more training data, or in its absence, QA pretraining data. Thus, practitioners can follow the two step strategy of pretraining an MF architecture on QA data followed by finetuning on available EE data.

Our EarlyFusion (EF) model outperforms the State-of-the-Art on the Unified Summarization Benchmark (USB) dataset by 1.4% relative while our MidFusion model following the two step strategy is 5.8x faster while performing within 5% relative F-Score. On our medical dataset, we find the gap between the three models to be far less emphatic due to our access to nearly 0.5M training points. Further, while F-Score reflects the trade-off between precision and recall, we also compute human-agreement (HA) of displayed evidence using human annotators on our Medical Dataset. We find that the HA of EF is 96%, MF 94%, LF 90% highlighting a gap between the efficacy of these methods under span selection metrics versus human judgement of helpful evidence. As an addition, we collect feedback from two clinicians who used our EE models for verifying LLM generated clinical notes in real clinics. We begin by highlighting relevant prior work in the next section.

2 Related Work

Innovations in better LLM generations are plenty (Lewis et al., 2020; Wallace et al., 2021; Choubey et al., 2021; Wei et al., 2022; Ramprasad et al., 2023; Rafailov et al., 2023). However, our work is situated among post-hoc methods that serve to increase trust in these generations. With the tendency of LLMs to hallucinate (Kalai and Vempala, 2023; Xu et al., 2024) there has been growing interest in post-hoc evaluation of the factuality of LLM generations (Zhang et al., 2021; Manakul et al., 2023; Wei et al., 2024; Goyal and Durrett, 2021; Honovich et al., 2022). Our work considers applications where the aim is not to automatically evaluate each generation but to retrieve supporting material from the source to aid a human with verification. Thus, while scoring the extent of factuality is useful, they cannot replace human spot-checking when an LLM is deployed in a low-risk setting.

While there are similarities with the line of work in Lei et al. (2016); Lehman et al. (2019); Jain et al. (2020) that highlight regions of the input that have correlation with model predictions, they are closer to explaining predictions than explicitly retrieving supporting material. Similar ideas also appear in MultiHop QA works Zhao et al. (2023); Tu et al. (2020); Nishida et al. (2019), but differ in our focus on scale and domain adaptation. The methods in Pruthi et al. (2020) tackle the EE problem in Deep NLP, as we framed it, although they are limited to classification tasks. Further, Kryściński et al. (2019) builds EE and factuality verification models with weak supervision, but their method does not handle cross-sentence dependencies or coreference resolution. More recently, Stammbach (2021); DeHaven and Scott (2023); Krishna et al. (2023); Wadden et al. (2021, 2020) all tackle the EE task, but are distinct given our focus on scalability, speed, and establishing the benefits of QA pretraining for EE. An open-source benchmark for EE is introduced in (Krishna et al., 2023) along with the state-of-the-art methods on this dataset which we compare against.

Domain	# of Examples		
	Train	Valid	Test
Biographies	3740	1875	3642
Landmarks	0	0	211
Disasters	247	122	256
Newspapers	0	0	137
Companies	162	75	156
Schools	220	123	235

Table 1: Number of examples across different domains for the train, validation, and test splits of the Unified Summarization Benchmark (USB) dataset.

3 Methodology

We have a source document D made up of components $u \in U$. Unless mentioned otherwise, u is a sentence (we make explicit when u is a token). An operation (e.g. summarization) on D results in an output O. For each sentence $q \in O$ (e.g summary sentence) we need to find an evidence span $E \subset U$. We refer to q as query. Intuitively, E should have sentences u that contain information relevant to q.

3.1 Proposed Architectures

EarlyFusion Hierarchical Classification For scalability, we first consider a hierarchical architecture that encodes each utterance u_i independently, while adding document-wide context at a later step. This allows us to scale inference to arbitrarily long documents since we batch through the sentences that make up the document. We begin by concatenating the tokens of the query q with the tokens of the ith sentence u_i, separated by a demarcating </s> token. Denote each such query-sentence sequence f_i. Then each f_i is pushed through an encoder backbone (e.g. RoBERTa (Liu et al., 2019)) and the vector corresponding to the CLS token is taken to obtain an embedding r_i. We add document-wide context by concatenating all the sentence embeddings r_is into a sequence and passing this through an LSTM, whose outputs are pushed through a classification head to obtain logits l_i. We consider the sigmoid of the logit $\sigma(l_i)$ to be the score s_i to include u_i in the evidence set E.

LateFusion Hierarchical Classification While processing the document hierarchically allows us to scale inference to long documents , it does not contribute to faster inference. The main bottleneck is pushing each query-sentence pair through a large backbone like RoBERTa (Liu et al., 2019). If a second query on the same source D originates, we would repeat the entire process. This overhead could be avoided if we independently obtain sentence embeddings for D and reuse them for every query based off of D. Therefore, we consider a late fusion of sentence and query embeddings as follows: Each sentence u_i is pushed through the backbone (e.g.RoBERTa) and the vector corresponding to the CLS token is selected as the sentence embedding r_i. These embeddings r_is can be cached. In order to find an evidence set for query q, push the query through the backbone and select the vector corresponding to the CLS token as the query embedding r_q. Now concatenate r_q vector and r_i vector to get the late-fused embeddings denoted as, say f_i. Finally, to add document wide context, concatenate these fused embeddings f_is into a sequence which is pushed through an LSTM. Use a classification head on the outputs of the LSTM for this sequence to obtain logits l_i on which we apply a sigmoid to obtain scores s_i for each sentence. For each subsequent query on this source, we can reuse r_is and only need to recompute a single push of the new query through the backbone followed with relatively lightweight LSTM and linear operations.

MidFusion Hierarchical Classification The LateFusion architecture removes several layers of cross-attention between the tokens in the query and the tokens in source sentences that the EarlyFusion architecture enjoys, rendering it much weaker. This leads us to explore where such cross attention could be included while still allowing us to cache the outputs of the backbone model on the source sentences. In the previous architectures, we immediately compress the backbone outputs on the source sentences and the query by simply selecting the CLS token's embedding alone. Consider instead that we delay this compression. We could now concatenate the query's token level *embeddings* with each of the source sentence's token level *embeddings* to form a query-sentence sequence, instead of concatenating the query tokens themselves with the source sentence tokens (as we did in EarlyFusion). Formally, push each sentence u_i through the backbone encoder to obtain token level embeddings t_i for each sentence u_i. Cache these embeddings. To find an evidence set for a query q, push the query through the backbone encoder to obtain query embeddings t_q. Now concatenate the query embedding sequence with the token embedding sequence to obtain sequence embeddings $[t_q, t_i]$. These concatenated embedding sequences are passed through a transformer layer, and the outputs of the transformer layer are mean pooled into a single vector r_i. Document wide context is now added by concatenating these r_is into a sequence and operating an LSTM on them, followed through by a classification head. We find that this additional transformer layer before the compression into a single vector with mean-pooling is competitive with the Early-Fusion architecture while still being much faster.

All these architectures are depicted in Figure 2.

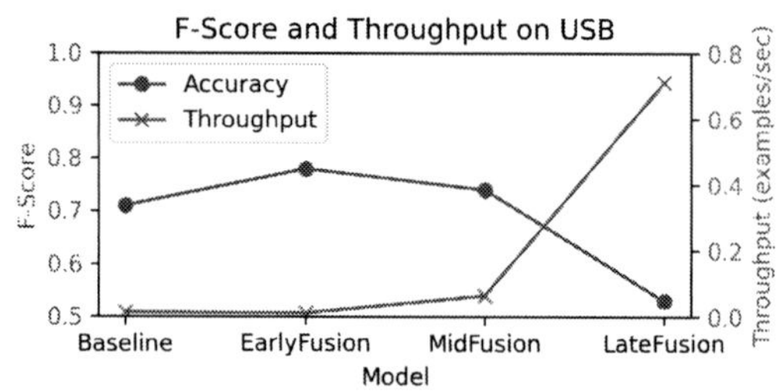

Figure 3: F-Score vs Throughput tradeoff for the three fusion types along with the baseline (adopted from (Krishna et al., 2023)). We use RoBERTa-Large as the backbone encoder. Throughput is computed as an average across the examples in the test split of the USB dataset. We note that the MF model outperforms previous state-of-the-art while having much higher throughput.

3.2 Parallel to Extractive QA

Our Evidence Extraction problem as framed is essentially a span identification problem. Thus, a parallel can be drawn between our task and an extractive QA task (Pearce et al., 2021; Lewis et al., 2019; Xu et al., 2021): query to question, evidence to answer, and source document to passage. An answer in QA tasks is less subjective than evidence and usually has a clearly identified location in the passage. Viewing Evidence Extraction as a harder QA task leads us to explore the benefits of pretraining on QA data. Given the comparatively much higher quantities of QA datasets, we could leverage them for the following reasons:

1. **The need to operate in low-data regimes** Document-Query-Evidence data tuples are scarce. Furthermore, enterprises often update their language models, but re-annotating new EE data each the time the LLM is swapped

Model	F-Score
RoBERTa Large	71.01
T5-Large	77.22
Flan-T5-Large	77.71
Early Fusion (ours)	77.32
Early Fusion++ (ours)	78.80
Mid Fusion (ours)	51.21
Mid Fusion++ (ours)	74.50
Late Fusion(ours)	36.80
Late Fusion++ (ours)	53.06
Llama-13B	5.56
Vicuna-13B	6.65
GPT-3.5-turbo	26.78

Table 2: Results on the USB 4.1 test set. We compute the F-Score at a corpus level by stacking predictions and ground truth for sentences across examples to compute Precision and Recall. ++ indicates models that were first trained on a QA Pretraining Corpus 4.3. The first 3 methods are state-of-the-art from (Krishna et al., 2023).

is impractical. Therefore, the EE model may have to be trained in a low-data regime.

2. **Domain Adaptation gains** Krishna et al. (2023) show that the gains from increasing quantities of in-domain EE train data on OOD test data plateaus. In our experiments we find that pretraining on a related but different task unlocks further domain adaptation gains.

3. **Bi-encoders perform better with more data** Models like our Late and MidFusion models typically converge and perform better when they have access to ample amounts of data. See performance gaps in Table 2 vs Table 4.

We include additional comments and rationale on our methodology in Appendix F.

4 Datasets

4.1 Unified Summarization Benchmark (USB)

The USB dataset (Krishna et al., 2023) is a Wiki-derived benchmark containing annotations for 8 summarization-related tasks. One of those tasks is EE, providing a testbed that is (i) open-source; (ii) presents a low-data regime; (iv) has natural domain splits that allow for testing OOD performance. Dataset statistics are presented in Table 1.

4.2 Medical Dataset

Clinical documentation is one of the leading causes of physician burnout in the United States (Gaffney et al., 2022; Sinsky et al., 2016). Following each encounter, physicians are required to author a SOAP note that covers (S)ubjective (O)bjective (A)ssessment and (P)lan information summarizing the appointment. Traction has been gained by automating the generation of this note using Foundation Models (e.g. see *Abridge AI*). We use a unique corpus containing thousands of recorded clinical conversations (in English) with corresponding SOAP notes created by an annotation workforce trained in SOAP note standards. Composed of 6862 visits of real-life patient-doctor encounters (de-identified to remove PHI information and with full consent), our dataset presents for each visit a trained-worker-scribed transcript, segmented into utterances along with a SOAP note. The conversations are 1.5k words on average. Further, each sentence in the SOAP note is annotated with a supporting evidence span from the conversation. We split the dataset into 5770, 500 and 592 *notes* for train, validation and test splits. Considering each [SOAP note sentence, evidence utterances] tuple as a data point results in 400k train, 50k valid and 50k test samples.This dataset is not open-sourced due to the sensitive nature of the data.

4.3 QA Pretraining Corpus

Our QA Pretraining Corpus is formed by combining three popular Question Answering datasets: SQuAD V1 (Rajpurkar et al., 2016), HotPotQA (Yang et al., 2018), and BioASQ datasets (Krithara et al., 2023). We setup the span-selection problem as sentence classification, to resemble our downstream formulation (Ram et al., 2021). The dataset details are presented in the Appendix in Table 10.

4.4 SynthMed: Synthetically Curated Extractive QA on PubMed Articles

Domain-specific extractive QA datasets are falling out of favor as more focus is given to freeform answer generation. This in tandem with the idea that training on domain-specific extractive QA might be more beneficial than general extractive QA leads us to explore the synthetic generation of domain-specific extractive QA datasets using GPT-4 (Achiam et al., 2023). Given PubMed documents, we prompt GPT-4 to generate QA pairs. We tailor the prompt to focus on challenging questions

Train Domain	Biographies	Companies	Disasters	Landmarks	News	Schools
Mid Fusion	52.15	35.10	31.82	34.84	36.12	40.75
Mid Fusion++	68.08	50.39	42.13	51.01	52.54	48.89

Table 3: Domain Shift experiments on USB dataset. We train the midfusion model on Biographies without (first row) and with (second row) pretraining. We then evaluate its performance on other domains. F-Scores are presented.

Method	Base Model	Precision	Recall	HA
BM25	-	63.01	39.00	65.00
Dual Encoder Retriever	Longformer	79.02	72.10	83.00
Late Fusion (Span Extraction)	RoBERTa-base	74.42	79.06	85.00
Late Fusion (Classification)	RoBERTa-base	75.61	80.29	90.00
Mid Fusion (Classification)	RoBERTa-base	76.37	82.18	94.00
Early Fusion (Classification)	RoBERTa-base	81.29	83.16	96.40

Table 4: Evidence Extraction results on the test split of our Medical Dataset 4.2. We compute the metrics at a character level for better comparison between different granularities and tokenizers. HA (Human Agreement) percentage of examples where the predicted evidence was considered satisfactory by humans.

Method	Precision	Recall	HA
Late Fusion (SE)	65.41	65.72	74.40
Late Fusion (C)	68.21	67.13	76.00
Mid Fusion (C)	71.22	71.98	80.00
Early Fusion (C)	75.27	73.62	84.80

Table 5: EE results on a modified test split of our medical data 4.2 where the queries are modified by applying stochastic rules such as token dropout and reordering. Metrics are computed at a character level. SE: Span Extraction, C: Classification, HA: Human-Agreement. All methods use RoBERTa-base as the backbone.

that have low lexical overlap with the extractive answer, involving multi-hop reasoning, and strictly grounded to the document. We similarly try to generate synthetic Evidence Extraction data but find the generated examples to be of lower quality, often with high lexical overlap between the query and evidence, and sometimes altogether incorrect. For examples and details including the exact prompts used to generate them, refer to Appendix A.

5 Experiment Setup

5.1 General Evidence Extraction

Our first line of experiments aims to test our proposed hierarchical architectures on an open-source benchmark. Accordingly, we use a dataset which contains scope for Evidence Extraction: the USB dataset 4.1. We run experiments with the MidFusion architecture, comparing its domain adaptation performance with and without pretraining. USB provides an organic way to measure domain adaptation capacity by demarcating their data into prespecified domains. We train on the *Biographies* domain and test on the others, providing insights into the benefits of pretraining on out-of-domain data.

We borrow previous state-of-art results on this dataset from (Krishna et al., 2023). We carry out our experiments with RoBERTa-Large (Liu et al., 2019), while adapting the state-of-the-art t5-large (Raffel et al., 2020) and flan-t5-large (Chung et al., 2022) results from (Krishna et al., 2023). We note that there is a discrepancy in the sizes of these models (the t5-large family is at 770M, while RoBERTa-large has 355M parameters with negligible additions from the added LSTM and dense layers) which places us at a disadvantage.

5.2 Medical Evidence Extraction

Our second line of experiments, compares methodologies on our Medical Dataset 4.2. In addition to our hierarchical classification methods, we also include straightforward dual-encoder token-level span selection, as well as LateFusion when posed as span selection. The dual-encoder token-level approach simply encodes the entire transcript using an encoder, and the query using an encoder, concatenates the encodings and classifies start and end tokens for evidence, without any hierarchy involvement. For completeness, we also show the result obtained by a simple BM25 baseline (Robertson et al., 2009). Refer Table 4. For the dual-encoder token-level method we use Longformer (Beltagy et al., 2020) as the choice of backbone for supporting the encoding of long transcripts, while for the hierarchical methods we stick to RoBERTa-base. In addition to Precision and Recall we include an additional metric Human-Agreement (HA) which measures the fraction of examples where a human annotator is satisfied with the conciseness and coverage of the surfaced evidence. It is important to note that Precision and Recall are computed on a test set with 10,000 examples, but Human-Agreement is computed on a random subset of 250 examples since it requires human labor.

In order to test the robustness of our models, we simulate mild distribution shift by adding controlled noise to the queries in the test set. Collaboration with *Abridge* helped us identify realistic noise models that emulate the characteristics of noise observed in hospital systems. These results are presented in Table 5. The noise model is a combination of stochastic token drop in the query, token re-ordering, and inclusion of queries larger than typical of the examples in the dataset.

We also pretrain our models on both generic as well as SynthMed dataset, while testing with and without addition of simulated noise. Refer Table 6.

6 Experiment Results

Naive Baselines are not competitive From Table 4 it is evident that the BM25 model performs much worse than deep learning based alternatives. This puts perspective on the non-trivial nature of the task. Further, conforming with intuition, the BM25 model suffers in recall since rephrasing between the source and query results in lack of a keyword match and requires semantic similarity comparison.

More data helps reduce performance gap In table 2 we see performance leaps as we move from Late to Mid to Early Fusion. However, in table 4 we see that the performance gap while present is not as stark. We attribute this difference to the amount of data available for training. Our Medical Dataset contains hundreds of thousands of data samples while USB contains a few thousand. This also manifests when pretraining on a QA corpus, we see that the gap especially for MidFusion++ model is significantly attenuated, and in distribution shift experiments we see that a further drop in available data when restricted to a single domain drops performance across the board (ref Table 3).

QA pretraining helps Evidence Extraction It is easy to see from Table 6 and Table 2 that QA pretraining confers significant performance boosts despite being a different task. This shows more in low-resource regimes, where MidFusion++ demonstrates similar performance to the full attention models while the boost in performance to EarlyFusion++ seems comparatively modest. Also, QA pretraining has massive impact in robustness as seen in the performance of our models on the simulated OOD medical data (Table 6) as well as domain restricted training on USB (Table 3). While in (Krishna et al., 2023) the authors note that more data for in-domain finetuning does not prove useful, with performance saturating quickly, when faced with a more difficult setting, pretraining on a related task continues to confer large percentage gains in both in-domain and out-of-domain performance. Consistent with their findings, we see that in the EarlyFusion setting, the gains are relatively smaller. Further, as is seen in Table 6, we find that pretraining on domain specific QA data can be more beneficial than training on generic QA datasets especially for niche domains like healthcare.

GPT-4 generated synthetic data is useful From table 6 we see that SynthMidFusion significantly outperforms other types of pretraining methodologies. The pretraining data for this model was curated by prompting GPT-4 as detailed in 4.4. This suggested cheap and efficient ways to lower access to pretraining QA data that is of sufficient quality.

Wide gap between HA and PR-metrics In table 4, 5, 6 we include human evaluation under the column HA (ref 5.2). Evidence relevance as assessed by humans seem to place the model in much better light. This is due to examples where the candidate spans surfaced by the model provide alternate evidence that we consider acceptable under human evaluation but fails to score against the ground truth transcript. The performance gap between Late and EarlyFusion is diluted according to human annotators. Thus, while LateFusion Models are from perfect, they do surface reasonable candidates.

In Appendix D.1 we consider adding document-wide context using a transformer instead of an LSTM. Despite having fewer parameters, LSTMs seem to do better than transformers.

Method	P(M)	R(M)	HA(M)	P(AM)	R(AM)	HA(AM)
MidFusion	76.37	82.18	94.00	71.22	71.98	80.00
MidFusion++	78.38	83.83	95.40	72.73	71.74	81.40
MidFusion++ w DAug.	79.80	83.00	95.20	74.00	75.10	83.80
SynthMidFusion++	81.20	82.41	95.00	72.66	81.10	82.80

Table 6: Evidence Extraction Results on the test splits of our Medical Dataset excluding (M) and including (AM) query augmentation. ++ indicates models that have QA pretraining. MidFusion++ w DAug. corresponds to a MidFusion model where we enabled 10 percent of the medical finetuning data to contain the same query-augmentation strategies as in the AM dataset. SynthMidFusion++ is a MidFusion model pretrained on synthetically generated data 4.4 HA - Human-Agreement 5.2, M: Medical Dataset 4.2, AM: query Augmented Medical Dataset.

Absence of an entity Consider the following line inserted in an LLM generated SOAP note: *"Extremities: No clubbing or cyanosis"* appearing under Physical Exam (PE) section. The PE section is populated this way by default and then changed if an issue is discussed. Here, we need to surface evidence that discussion about clubbing/cyanosis is *not* part of the conversation. This is a failure mode, perhaps for the problem setup itself, since the complete evidence is the entire transcript.

When wrong is it *really* wrong? Often the predicted evidence is reasonable but does not score since it is an alternate source of evidence:

Query: *The patient to continue with the lower dosage of Trulicity if it alleviates the symptoms.*

Predicted Evidence: *"It doesn't cause that but it can make it worse. So, let's change Trulicity to 0.75 mg. It's going to be a dose change. So, use what you have and then we'll go ahead and lower the dosage to make sure that you're doing okay.*

Ground Truth Evidence: *"What you can do is, um, alternate the 1.5 with a 0.75 and you can see if you see a difference in how you feel. And I can give you some of the 0.75 and we'll switch you to the lower dosage because it is true that Trulicity can give you more reflux and if you do have something in your stomach, the bowel issue, it will worsen.*

7 Feedback from Clinicians

With the help of *Abridge* we made our EE model available to two clinicians to aid them in finding evidence for verifying LLM-generated clinical notes from transcripts. We asked them to randomly assign 50 percent of their notes for enabling the aid of our EE model and to carry out the remaining half as usual without this aid (refer to Appendix C for more details on the exact instructions). We then collected feedback:

Feedback.1: *EE dramatically reduces the amount of time required to verify the contents of the AI generated note. Without it, I tend to skim the contents, do keyword searches, and struggle to identify the evidence; this process is frustrating and often negates the time that I saved by not drafting the note myself. I estimate that EE finds the appropriate evidence >75% of the time, and reduces the amount of time needed to review a note from 5 min to 1 min. Moreover, I am more likely to do a comprehensive review of the note when using EE.*

Feedback.2: *The time saved by using EE was consistently 1-2m, almost half the time for a given length, and takes extra cognitive effort without it. Having to scan the whole transcript vs just 3-7 lines of a transcript - huge efficiency booster. I estimate I used EE about a total of 55 times, with 2-3 that may have been close but not quite correct mapping, but minor and corrected when extending the query. In particular, EE makes it easier to check medical terms, reported symptoms, and doses.*[1]

8 Conclusions

In this paper, we described a setup that extracts evidence spans for Language Model outputs on grounded tasks. We presented three hierarchical architectures focused on speed and scalability to long documents, while looking to QA pretraining strategies for boosting performance. We showed that tapping into Extractive QA datasets allows positive transfer even if the curated data is synthetic.

9 Limitations

Some notable limitations:

[1] F.1 is due to an Associate Professor of Medicine, Pulmonary and Critical Care, University of Pittsburg Medical Center and F.2 is due to an MD, University of Pennsylvania, Perelman School of Medicine

1. While the feedback included in 7 is promising, it is not a rigorous clinical study. This paper addresses the first piece of the puzzle: fast and automated EE. A natural future step is to ascertain its impact on reducing the verification burden through formal clinical experiments.

2. It is also possible for users of the EE models to log simple feedback on their satisfaction with the surfaced evidence which could be leveraged to further improve the EE model.

3. The synthetic data generated is of the QA task. While this confers generalization benefits to EE, this choice is also partly a consequence of the relatively poor quality of synthetic EE data that current LLMs generate. In Appendix A we show some examples of synthetically generated EE data even after several iterations of refining the prompts used to generate them. Notably, generated EE queries are often lines copied verbatim from the passage. A future direction is to more comprehensively explore synthetic data generation strategies that might directly yield EE data.

4. An important future step is to explore multilingual capabilities of EE models, with possibilities to have the query and the source be in different languages.

10 Ethics

This study complies with HIPAA guidelines by conducting training and evaluation only on deidentified patient data to ensure privacy and data security. Further, we did not retain or view any patient data when obtaining feedback from clinicians for sec 7. Additionally, all personnel viewing even the deidentified medical data first obtained HIPAA compliance certificates after completing mandatory best-practices online courses.

11 Acknowledgements

The authors would like to thank Elisa Ferracane and John Giorgi for helpful discussions and suggestions. We would also like to thank Dr. Mike Myerburg and Dr. Katherine Choi for their reviews on the impact of using our models in real encounters.

References

Josh Achiam, Steven Adler, Sandhini Agarwal, Lama Ahmad, Ilge Akkaya, Florencia Leoni Aleman, Diogo Almeida, Janko Altenschmidt, Sam Altman, Shyamal Anadkat, et al. 2023. Gpt-4 technical report. *arXiv preprint arXiv:2303.08774*.

Onur Asan, Alparslan Emrah Bayrak, and Avishek Choudhury. 2020. Artificial intelligence and human trust in healthcare: focus on clinicians. *Journal of medical Internet research*, 22(6):e15154.

Stephen Bates, Anastasios Angelopoulos, Lihua Lei, Jitendra Malik, and Michael Jordan. 2021. Distribution-free, risk-controlling prediction sets. *J. ACM*.

Iz Beltagy, Matthew E Peters, and Arman Cohan. 2020. Longformer: The long-document transformer. *arXiv preprint arXiv:2004.05150*.

Sébastien Bubeck, Varun Chandrasekaran, Ronen Eldan, Johannes Gehrke, Eric Horvitz, Ece Kamar, Peter Lee, Yin Tat Lee, Yuanzhi Li, Scott Lundberg, et al. 2023. Sparks of artificial general intelligence: Early experiments with gpt-4. *arXiv preprint arXiv:2303.12712*.

Prafulla Kumar Choubey, Alexander R Fabbri, Jesse Vig, Chien-Sheng Wu, Wenhao Liu, and Nazneen Fatema Rajani. 2021. Cape: contrastive parameter ensembling for reducing hallucination in abstractive summarization. *arXiv preprint arXiv:2110.07166*.

Hyung Won Chung, Le Hou, Shayne Longpre, Barret Zoph, Yi Tay, William Fedus, Yunxuan Li, Xuezhi Wang, Mostafa Dehghani, Siddhartha Brahma, et al. 2022. Scaling instruction-finetuned language models. *arXiv preprint arXiv:2210.11416*.

Mitchell DeHaven and Stephen Scott. 2023. Bevers: A general, simple, and performant framework for automatic fact verification. *arXiv preprint arXiv:2303.16974*.

Alvaro Figueira and Bruno Vaz. 2022. Survey on synthetic data generation, evaluation methods and gans. *Mathematics*, 10(15):2733.

Adam Gaffney, Stephanie Woolhandler, Christopher Cai, David Bor, Jessica Himmelstein, Danny McCormick, and David U Himmelstein. 2022. Med ical documentation burden among us office-based physicians in 2019: a national study. *JAMA Internal Medicine*, 182(5):564–566.

Tanya Goyal and Greg Durrett. 2021. Annotating and modeling fine-grained factuality in summarization. *arXiv preprint arXiv:2104.04302*.

Or Honovich, Roee Aharoni, Jonathan Herzig, Hagai Taitelbaum, Doron Kukliansy, Vered Cohen, Thomas Scialom, Idan Szpektor, Avinatan Hassidim, and Yossi Matias. 2022. True: Re-evaluating factual consistency evaluation. *arXiv preprint arXiv:2204.04991*.

Sarthak Jain, Sarah Wiegreffe, Yuval Pinter, and Byron C Wallace. 2020. Learning to faithfully rationalize by construction. *arXiv preprint arXiv:2005.00115*.

Adam Tauman Kalai and Santosh S Vempala. 2023. Calibrated language models must hallucinate. *arXiv preprint arXiv:2311.14648*.

Kundan Krishna, Prakhar Gupta, Sanjana Ramprasad, Byron C Wallace, Jeffrey P. Bigham, and Zachary Chase Lipton. 2023. USB: A unified summarization benchmark across tasks and domains. In *The 2023 Conference on Empirical Methods in Natural Language Processing*.

Kundan Krishna, Sopan Khosla, Jeffrey Bigham, and Zachary C. Lipton. 2021. Generating SOAP notes from doctor-patient conversations using modular summarization techniques. In *Proceedings of the 59th Annual Meeting of the Association for Computational Linguistics and the 11th International Joint Conference on Natural Language Processing (Volume 1: Long Papers)*, pages 4958–4972, Online. Association for Computational Linguistics.

Anastasia Krithara, Anastasios Nentidis, Konstantinos Bougiatiotis, and Georgios Paliouras. 2023. Bioasqqa: A manually curated corpus for biomedical question answering. *Scientific Data*, 10(1):170.

Wojciech Kryściński, Bryan McCann, Caiming Xiong, and Richard Socher. 2019. Evaluating the factual consistency of abstractive text summarization. *arXiv preprint arXiv:1910.12840*.

Eric Lehman, Jay DeYoung, Regina Barzilay, and Byron C Wallace. 2019. Inferring which medical treatments work from reports of clinical trials. *arXiv preprint arXiv:1904.01606*.

Tao Lei, Regina Barzilay, and Tommi Jaakkola. 2016. Rationalizing neural predictions. *arXiv preprint arXiv:1606.04155*.

Patrick Lewis, Barlas Oğuz, Ruty Rinott, Sebastian Riedel, and Holger Schwenk. 2019. Mlqa: Evaluating cross-lingual extractive question answering. *arXiv preprint arXiv:1910.07475*.

Patrick Lewis, Ethan Perez, Aleksandra Piktus, Fabio Petroni, Vladimir Karpukhin, Naman Goyal, Heinrich Küttler, Mike Lewis, Wen-tau Yih, Tim Rocktäschel, et al. 2020. Retrieval-augmented generation for knowledge-intensive nlp tasks. *Advances in Neural Information Processing Systems*, 33:9459–9474.

Zhuoyan Li, Hangxiao Zhu, Zhuoran Lu, and Ming Yin. 2023. Synthetic data generation with large language models for text classification: Potential and limitations. *arXiv preprint arXiv:2310.07849*.

Davis Liang, Hila Gonen, Yuning Mao, Rui Hou, Naman Goyal, Marjan Ghazvininejad, Luke Zettlemoyer, and Madian Khabsa. 2023. Xlm-v: Overcoming the vocabulary bottleneck in multilingual masked language models. *arXiv preprint arXiv:2301.10472*.

Yinhan Liu, Myle Ott, Naman Goyal, Jingfei Du, Mandar Joshi, Danqi Chen, Omer Levy, Mike Lewis, Luke Zettlemoyer, and Veselin Stoyanov. 2019. Roberta: A robustly optimized bert pretraining approach. *arXiv preprint arXiv:1907.11692*.

Potsawee Manakul, Adian Liusie, and Mark JF Gales. 2023. Selfcheckgpt: Zero-resource black-box hallucination detection for generative large language models. *arXiv preprint arXiv:2303.08896*.

Kosuke Nishida, Kyosuke Nishida, Masaaki Nagata, Atsushi Otsuka, Itsumi Saito, Hisako Asano, and Junji Tomita. 2019. Answering while summarizing: Multi-task learning for multi-hop qa with evidence extraction. *arXiv preprint arXiv:1905.08511*.

Kate Pearce, Tiffany Zhan, Aneesh Komanduri, and Justin Zhan. 2021. A comparative study of transformer-based language models on extractive question answering. *arXiv preprint arXiv:2110.03142*.

Danish Pruthi, Bhuwan Dhingra, Graham Neubig, and Zachary C. Lipton. 2020. Weakly- and semi-supervised evidence extraction. In *Findings of the Association for Computational Linguistics: EMNLP 2020*. Association for Computational Linguistics.

Rafael Rafailov, Archit Sharma, Eric Mitchell, Stefano Ermon, Christopher D Manning, and Chelsea Finn. 2023. Direct preference optimization: Your language model is secretly a reward model. *arXiv preprint arXiv:2305.18290*.

Colin Raffel, Noam Shazeer, Adam Roberts, Katherine Lee, Sharan Narang, Michael Matena, Yanqi Zhou, Wei Li, and Peter J Liu. 2020. Exploring the limits of transfer learning with a unified text-to-text transformer. *The Journal of Machine Learning Research*, 21(1).

Pranav Rajpurkar, Jian Zhang, Konstantin Lopyrev, and Percy Liang. 2016. Squad: 100,000+ questions for machine comprehension of text. *arXiv preprint arXiv:1606.05250*.

Ori Ram, Yuval Kirstain, Jonathan Berant, Amir Globerson, and Omer Levy. 2021. Few-shot question answering by pretraining span selection. *arXiv preprint arXiv:2101.00438*.

Sanjana Ramprasad, Elisa Ferracane, and Sai P. Selvaraj. 2023. Generating more faithful and consistent soap notes using attribute-specific parameters. In *Proceedings of the 8th Machine Learning for Healthcare Conference*, Proceedings of Machine Learning Research. PMLR.

Stephen Robertson, Hugo Zaragoza, et al. 2009. The probabilistic relevance framework: Bm25 and beyond. *Foundations and Trends® in Information Retrieval*, 3(4):333–389.

Christine Sinsky, Lacey Colligan, Ling Li, Mirela Prgomet, Sam Reynolds, Lindsey Goeders, Johanna Westbrook, Michael Tutty, and George Blike. 2016. Allocation of physician time in ambulatory practice: a time and motion study in 4 specialties. *Annals of internal medicine*, 165(11):753–760.

Dominik Stammbach. 2021. Evidence selection as a token-level prediction task. In *Proceedings of the Fourth Workshop on Fact Extraction and VERification (FEVER)*, pages 14–20. Association for Computational Linguistics.

Hugo Touvron, Louis Martin, Kevin Stone, Peter Albert, Amjad Almahairi, Yasmine Babaei, Nikolay Bashlykov, Soumya Batra, Prajjwal Bhargava, Shruti Bhosale, et al. 2023. Llama 2: Open foundation and fine-tuned chat models. *arXiv preprint arXiv:2307.09288*.

Grigorios Tsoumakas and Ioannis Katakis. 2007. Multi-label classification: An overview. *International Journal of Data Warehousing and Mining (IJDWM)*, 3(3):1–13.

Ming Tu, Kevin Huang, Guangtao Wang, Jing Huang, Xiaodong He, and Bowen Zhou. 2020. Select, answer and explain: Interpretable multi-hop reading comprehension over multiple documents. In *Proceedings of the AAAI conference on artificial intelligence*, volume 34, pages 9073–9080.

David Wadden, Shanchuan Lin, Kyle Lo, Lucy Lu Wang, Madeleine van Zuylen, Arman Cohan, and Hannaneh Hajishirzi. 2020. Fact or fiction: Verifying scientific claims. *arXiv preprint arXiv:2004.14974*.

David Wadden, Kyle Lo, Lucy Lu Wang, Arman Cohan, Iz Beltagy, and Hannaneh Hajishirzi. 2021. Multivers: Improving scientific claim verification with weak supervision and full-document context. *arXiv preprint arXiv:2112.01640*.

Byron C Wallace, Sayantan Saha, Frank Soboczenski, and Iain J Marshall. 2021. Generating (factual?) narrative summaries of rcts: Experiments with neural multi-document summarization. *AMIA Summits on Translational Science Proceedings*, 2021:605.

Jason Wei, Xuezhi Wang, Dale Schuurmans, Maarten Bosma, Fei Xia, Ed Chi, Quoc V Le, Denny Zhou, et al. 2022. Chain-of-thought prompting elicits reasoning in large language models. *Advances in neural information processing systems*, 35:24824–24837.

Jerry Wei, Chengrun Yang, Xinying Song, Yifeng Lu, Nathan Hu, Dustin Tran, Daiyi Peng, Ruibo Liu, Da Huang, Cosmo Du, et al. 2024. Long-form factuality in large language models. *arXiv preprint arXiv:2403.18802*.

Adhika Pramita Widyassari, Supriadi Rustad, Guruh Fajar Shidik, Edi Noersasongko, Abdul Syukur, Affandy Affandy, et al. 2022. Review of automatic text summarization techniques & methods. *Journal of King Saud University-Computer and Information Sciences*, 34(4):1029–1046.

Peng Xu, Davis Liang, Zhiheng Huang, and Bing Xiang. 2021. Attention-guided generative models for extractive question answering. *arXiv preprint arXiv:2110.06393*.

Ziwei Xu, Sanjay Jain, and Mohan Kankanhalli. 2024. Hallucination is inevitable: An innate limitation of large language models. *arXiv preprint arXiv:2401.11817*.

Zhilin Yang, Peng Qi, Saizheng Zhang, Yoshua Bengio, William W Cohen, Ruslan Salakhutdinov, and Christopher D Manning. 2018. Hotpotqa: A dataset for diverse, explainable multi-hop question answering. *arXiv preprint arXiv:1809.09600*.

Sen Zhang, Jianwei Niu, and Chuyuan Wei. 2021. Fine-grained factual consistency assessment for abstractive summarization models. In *Proceedings of the 2021 Conference on Empirical Methods in Natural Language Processing*, pages 107–116.

Wenting Zhao, Justin T Chiu, Claire Cardie, and Alexander M Rush. 2023. Hop, union, generate: Explainable multi-hop reasoning without rationale supervision. *arXiv preprint arXiv:2305.14237*.

A Synthetic Data

In table 7 and 8 we show some randomly picked examples from our synthetically generated Question Answering and Evidence Extraction datasets respectively. We see a stark difference in the depth of the QA examples versus those of the EE examples, leading us to primarily consider the QA data for pretraining experiments. The following prompts were used to create these examples

1. **QA Prompt**: *"Generate challenging question-answer pairs given a passage, abiding by the following instructions. (i) The answer should be an extractive span from the passage. (ii) Answering the question should require reading and comprehending the full passage but should not require any knowledge not found in the passage. (iii) The question can be in question form or statement form in which case the answer should correspond to evidence from the passage for that statement. (iv) Rewrite the question such that it has low lexical overlap with the answer. (v) Your response should be in JSONL format where each line is a dictionary containing keys 'Statement' and 'Evidence'. Passage:*

2. **EE Prompt**: *Generate statement-evidence pairs given a passage, abiding by the following instructions. (i) The evidence should be an*

extractive span from the passage. (ii) Locating the evidence should require reading and comprehending the full passage but should not require any knowledge not found in the passage. (iii) The statement can be such that there is evidence in the passage to contradict or substantitate it. (iv) Rewrite the statement such that it has low lexical overlap with the evidence. (v) Your response should be in JSONL format where each line is a dictionary containing keys 'Statement' and 'Evidence'. Passage:

B Versions of Software Packages

Numpy 1.24.4, Python 3.10.12, transformers 4.29.0, torch 2.0.0, SpaCy 3.6.0, fuzzywuzzy 0.18.0, openai 1.33.0

C Instructions for Feedback from Clinicians

For obtaining F.1 and F.2 in sec 7 we first created an interface with a simple mechanism to toggle the LateFusion Model from table 4 on and off. They were asked to randomly assign 20 of 40 notes to their usual verification process without EE model assistance, and the remaining 20 with EE model assistance for querying evidence. The random assignment also allows us to remove biases in opinion that may arise if one set is completed first before the other due to the fatigue factor as they get to the tail end of the experiment. The clinicians were then asked to provide feedback paying attention to

1. Any change in average time required to verify a clinical note when using our model as opposed to without
2. An estimate of how many times the model was queried and what fraction of responses was relevant evidence
3. If the use of the model led to identification of errors that would have otherwise passed unseen or impact on confidence in the final note when using our model in the loop.

D Ablations

D.1 LSTM vs Transformer for adding document wide context

For adding context across document (which is important for identifying non-contiguous evidence spans and coreference resolution), our architectures incoporate an LSTM, which is also thematically light-weight in alignment with our efforts for low-inference latency, that operates on the independent sentence embeddings by treating them as a sequence. In this section, we justify our use of the LSTM over transformer layers by considering an ablation. We run experiments on the Unified Summarization Benchmark dataset with a transformer instead of an LSTM in the final step. The results are shown in table 9.

E Details of our QA corpus

In Table 10 we show the number of examples we use in the train, test and validation splits of our QA corpus. The positive to negative class prportion is calculated by considering the ratio of number of sentences that have positive label to the number of sentences that have label zero.

F Comments on Methodology

Here we briefly include some commentary on the methodology and relegate the rest to the analysis of experiments.

Choice of Classification Setup: The task is to produce prediction sets. Therefore, the space of predictions is the power set of U (Tsoumakas and Katakis, 2007; Bates et al., 2021). Predicting a logit and a corresponding *softmax score* across each member in this set is computationally infeasible. Assigning a softmax score across utterances alternatively is interpreted as comparing the relative scores of different utterances making it into E (multiclass) but does not extend an easy interpretation to selecting multiple utterances (multilabel). Therefore, while we do compute logits *with-context* from neighbouring utterances, we proceed to score each utterance using a sigmoid of its logit[2]. An alternative that applies when the set E contains only a single contiguous span of utterances is to identify start and end utterance pointers for this span. We also include modeling of this type where applicable.

LLMs for Verification: In section 4.4 we discuss the prompting of LLMs to curate QA datasets (Li et al., 2023; Figueira and Vaz, 2022). This is different from their application to generate explanations. The key point is that we are interested in

[2]enabling the selection of multiple utterances based on thresholds (set using cross-validation)

Generated Question	Corresponding Answer
Describe the outcome of capsaicin treatment on the obesity and steatohepatitis development in Pemt(-/-) mice.	disruption of the hepatic afferent vagus nerve by capsaicin failed to reverse either the protection against the HFD-induced obesity or the development of HF-induced steatohepatitis in Pemt(-/-) mice.
How does hepatic vagotomy affect hepatic inflammation and ER stress in Pemt(-/-) mice?	HV increased the hepatic anti-inflammatory cytokine interleukin-10, reduced chemokine monocyte chemotactic protein-1 and the ER stress marker C/EBP homologous protein.
Elucidate the method used to validate candidate genes following array analysis.	pyrosequencing and genotyping for putative methylation-associated polymorphisms performed using standard PCR
How many genes showed a significant number of BWC-linked CpGs, and what was this threshold?	four of which showed $\geq$ 4 BWC-linked CpGs
In what way were subjects paired with the control group in the HS prevalence study?	matched with controls based on age, gender, and race

Table 7: Examples from GPT-4 generated synthetic QA data. This is a random sample and non-cherry picked, but it is possible to see the innate ability of these models to generate quality QA examples for training.

Generated Query	Corresponding Evidence
ILC2s were increased in patients with co-existing asthma among the CRSwNP population.	ILC2s were increased in patients with co-existing asthma (P = 0.03) in the CRSwNP population.
Pemt(-/-) mice are protected from HF-induced obesity when fed a high-fat diet (HFD).	Pemt(-/-) mice are protected from HF-induced obesity; however, they develop steatohepatitis.
A higher chemotherapy effect on lymphocytic infiltration is associated with pCR and better prognosis.	A higher infiltration by CD4 lymphocytes was the main factor explaining the occurrence of pCR, and this association was validated in six public genomic datasets.
Cluster Y is a profile mainly characterized by high CD3 and CD68 infiltration.	Immune cell profiles were analyzed and correlated with response and survival.
A higher infiltration by CD4 lymphocytes predicts pathological complete response to neoadjuvant chemotherapy.	We identified three tumor-infiltrating immune cell profiles, which were able to predict pathological complete response (pCR) to neoadjuvant chemotherapy

Table 8: Examples from GPT-4 generated synthetic EE data. This is a random sample and non-cherry picked, yet it is apparent that these examples consist of statements that have high lexical overlap with sentences in the passage.

outputs that point to locations in a document that a human can quickly verify. While using LLMs in chain-of-thought or self-rationalizing through explanations is a form of interpretability, they do not mitigate the need for a human to verify even those freeform explanations.

Model	Fusion	F-Score
EarlyFusion	LSTM	77.32
EarlyFusion	Transformer	76.61
EarlyFusion++	LSTM	78.80
EarlyFusion++	Transformer	78.12
MidFusion	LSTM	51.21
MidFusion	Transformer	48.87
MidFusion++	LSTM	74.50
MidFusion++	Transformer	74.31
LateFusion	LSTM	36.80
LateFusion	Transformer	39.72
LateFusion++	LSTM	53.06
LateFusion++	Transformer	54.13

Table 9: Ablation Study: We consider the use of Transformer instead of LSTM for the final stage of our hierarchical architecture. Results are shown on the test split of the USB dataset. The F-Score is computed at an utterance level by computing micro precision and recall.

Entity	Value
# Train Samples	180469
# Validation Samples	13006
Positive to Negative Class Proportion	0.073

Table 10: Dataset statistics for our QA Pretraining Corpus, which consists of a mixture of SQuAD, HotpotQA, and BioASQ.

Question-Based Retrieval using Atomic Units for Enterprise RAG

Vatsal Raina, Mark Gales
ALTA Institute, University of Cambridge
{vr311,mjfg}@cam.ac.uk

Abstract

Enterprise retrieval augmented generation (RAG) offers a highly flexible framework for combining powerful large language models (LLMs) with internal, possibly temporally changing, documents. In RAG, documents are first chunked. Relevant chunks are then retrieved for a user query, which are passed as context to a synthesizer LLM to generate the query response. However, the retrieval step can limit performance, as incorrect chunks can lead the synthesizer LLM to generate a false response. This work applies a zero-shot adaptation of standard dense retrieval steps for more accurate chunk recall. Specifically, a chunk is first decomposed into atomic statements. A set of synthetic questions are then generated on these atoms (with the chunk as the context). Dense retrieval involves finding the closest set of synthetic questions, and associated chunks, to the user query. It is found that retrieval with the atoms leads to higher recall than retrieval with chunks. Further performance gain is observed with retrieval using the synthetic questions generated over the atoms. Higher recall at the retrieval step enables higher performance of the enterprise LLM using the RAG pipeline.

1 Introduction

Since the popularized ChatGPT as an instruction-finetuned large language model (LLM) deployed at scale to the lay market, there has been a substantial uptake on the interest of businesses to incorporate LLMs in their products for a variety of downstream tasks (Bahrini et al., 2023; Castelvecchi, 2023; Badini et al., 2023; Kim and Min, 2024). For most companies, they are interested in using such models as enterprise LLMs where the model can handle queries related to proprietary on-premise data.

It has been repeatedly demonstrated that these LLMs have general (public) knowledge implicitly embedded in their parametric memory which can be extracted upon querying (Yu et al., 2023a). However, the LLMs do not have implicit knowledge about a specific enterprise's textual database in a custom domain and hence are prone to hallucinate in such situations (Xu et al., 2024b; Yu et al., 2023b). Additionally, the transformer-based (Vaswani et al., 2017) LLMs typically have a limited context window (due to quadratic order in cost of the attention mechanism), which means information for a specific company to be queried over cannot be directly fed-in as a prompt to the LLM. Due to limited budget, it is typically not feasible to finetune LLMs on a specific enterprise's data. In particular, with evolving data from ongoing projects, it is challenging to maintain a constantly updated company-specific LLM finetuned on new data without catastrophic forgetting (Luo et al., 2023).

To tackle this issue, and with retrieval augmented generation (RAG) proposed by Lewis et al. (2020), RAG-inspired systems have rapidly become the defacto as a zero-shot solution for enterprise LLMs. At the essence, there are 2 steps: 1. retrieval and 2. synthesis. Documents are split into independent chunks, and a retrieval process is applied to identify the relevant chunks to a given query. The retrieved chunks (which should fit into the context window) with the query are passed as the prompt to the synthesizer LLM to get the desired response.

Currently, the bottleneck for most enterprise LLMs is the retrieval step, where the correct information is not retrieved for the LLM to answer the question (Arora et al., 2023). Hence, this work focuses on building upon zero-shot approaches to improve the retrieval step for RAG. A potential limitation of the RAG set-up is that an embedding model is used to retrieve the relevant chunks efficiently when given a query. Each pre-calculated chunk has its corresponding embedding stored in memory, which allows the closes chunks to be retrieved by embedding the incoming query into the same space. However, there is a mismatch in trying to match the space of queries and chunks as each

Proceedings of the Seventh Fact Extraction and VERification Workshop (FEVER), pages 219–233
November 15, 2024

chunk can carry a large amount of information.

Instead, our work looks to represent each chunk as a set of atomic pieces of information. Min et al. (2023) introduced atomization of text for improving the assessment of summary consistency. These atoms can be structural (e.g. sentences of a chunk) or unstructured where a set of atoms is generated for any chunk. By embedding the atoms instead of the chunks themselves, the relevant atoms can instead be identified (that correspond to a specific set of chunks) for the posed query in the embedding space. The atomic breakdown of the chunk enables more accurate retrieval.

We further identify that even with the atomic embedding representations of the chunk, a given atom and the query do not necessarily best align for retrieval as the former is a statement with a piece of information while the latter is a question about locating a missing piece of information. Thus, we propose generating synthetic atomic questions. Each atom has a set of questions generated, which in turn are embedded. Therefore, the embedded incoming query is used to identify the closest set of atomic questions which in turn point to the relevant set of chunks to be passed to the synthesizer LLM in the RAG pipeline. As enterprise RAG operates over a closed set of documents, the generation of the atoms and corresponding synthetic questions is a one-off cost. Similarly, the increased set of embeddings to search over for the closest matches for the query embedding is of less concern given the various very efficient algorithms for embedding search such as FAISS (Douze et al., 2024).

Current information retrieval approaches applied to the RAG pipeline look at improving the quality of dense retrieval through generation augmented retrieval (GAR), where a query is rewritten for high recall retrieval. However, we focus our attention on representing the chunks more efficiently for retrieval (information retrieval literature explore such approaches - see Section 2. The contributions: an exploration of how the retrieval step in the enterprise RAG pipeline is improved with structured and unstructured atomic representation of a document chunk and further improvement with the generation of atomic questions.

2 Related Work

Recently, several works have extended RAG (Zhao et al., 2024). Many approaches finetune the components of the RAG pipeline. For example, Siriwardhana et al. (2023) explore adapting end-to-end RAG systems for open-domain question-answering while Zhang et al. (2024) introduce RAFT for finetuning RAG systems on specific domains by learning to exclude distractor documents. Additionally, Siriwardhana et al. (2021); Lin et al. (2023) jointly train the retriever and the generator for target domains. However, our work focuses on exploring zero-shot solutions as finetuning can be a computationally infeasible procedure for many enterprises.

In terms of zero-shot approaches, there have been several extensions proposed. Gao et al. (2023a) propose hypothetical document embedding (HyDE) where an LLM is used to transform the input query into an answer form (hallucinations are acceptable) for improved dense retrieval over the chunks. Similarly, Wang et al. (2023b) suggest a query expansion approach termed query2doc where an LLM is used to expand the query (Jagerman et al., 2023) with a pseudo-generated document, which they demonstrate to be effective for dense retrieval. Alternatively, we propose approaches that focus on modifying the knowledge base on which retrieval is performed rather than modifying the user queries as is common in GAR (Shen et al., 2023; Feng et al., 2023; Arora et al., 2023).

Song et al. (2024) retrieve a superfluous number of chunks during the retrieval step. They then re-rank the retrieved chunks with a re-ranker system to identify the most relevant set. Similarly, Wang et al. (2023c) propose FILCO to filter out the retrieved documents as an additional step in the RAG pipeline. Sun et al. (2023) explore the zero-shot use of LLMs as alternatives for traditional re-rankers. Arora et al. (2023) additionally incorporate the re-rank steps with GAR in an iterative feedback loop. Leveraging the comparative abilities of LLMs, Qin et al. (2023) propose using pairwise comparisons for the re-ranking of retrieved documents. Alternatively, Sarthi et al. (2024) propose RAPTOR as an iterative technique to pass a summarized context (based on the retrieved documents) to the synthesizer. Iter-RetGen by Shao et al. (2023) follow a similar iterative summarization strategy with LLMs. Finally, ActiveRAG (Xu et al., 2024a) encourages the synthesizer to consider parametric memory rather than just relying on the set of retrieved documents. Gao et al. (2023b) summarize all advanced RAG approaches as additional pre-retrieval or post-retrieval steps. Pre-retrieval steps include query routing, query re-writing and query expansion. Post-retrieval steps include re-ranking summarization and fusion. The synthetic question retrieval over atomized units from the document set is a form of pre-retrieval that operates on the knowledge store rather than on the user query. Hence, our work remains complementary with all forms of post-retrieval RAG. See Appendix Figure 3.

Traditionally, retrieval of relevant documents for a given query has been well studied (Hambarde and Proenca, 2023) with approaches such as BM25 (Robertson et al., 2009). In recent years, dense retrieval approaches have dominated as efficient retrieval processes where queries and documents are represented as dense vectors (embeddings) and documents are retrieved based on the similarity between these vectors. Semantically meaningful vectors have been possible with the series of regularly updated sentence transformers for generating general purpose embeddings including Sentence-BERT (Reimers and Gurevych, 2019), ConSERT (Yan et al., 2021), SimCSE (Gao et al., 2021), DiffCSE (Chuang et al., 2022), sentence-T5 (Ni et al., 2022) and E5 (Wang et al., 2022). More recently, there have been a series of more powerful embedding models that adapt instruction-finetuned language models as embedders (Li et al., 2023; Meng et al., 2024; Muennighoff et al., 2024; Wang et al., 2023a; BehnamGhader et al., 2024). Therefore, this work restricts exploration to dense retrieval.

In recent information retrieval literature, Chen et al. (2023) explore what granularity should be used for retrieval. They introduce the concept of breaking a passage into atomic expressions where each encapsulates a single factoid. Zhang et al. (2022) argue a document consists of many diverse details. Hence, they propose representing a document using multiple (diverse) embeddings to capture different views of the same content. Gospodinov et al. (2023) investigate for Doc2Query, a method of expanding the content of a document, how hallucinations can be minimized in the generated queries over a document. Our work connects these concepts for specifically generating multiple synthetic questions over atoms in enterprise RAG. This work is a bridge between methods explored in information retrieval and the RAG community.

3 Retrieval for RAG

In enterprise RAG systems, the core pipeline can be summarized as follows.

1. **Split**: Given a textual corpus of documents, a set of chunks are generated by splitting all text into distinct paragraphs.

2. **Retrieve**: For a given user query, the relevant set of chunks are retrieved.

3. **Synthesize**: The original query and the retrieved chunks are passed to a synthesis model to generate a response to the query using the provided chunk information as the context.

Here, the focus is on improving the retrieval step of the enterprise RAG pipeline. For the scope of the data considered in this work, we assume that the answer to a specific query is present in only one chunk (i.e. there are no unanswerable queries and multiple chunks are not required to deduce the answer to a question). Therefore, the retrieval step task can be defined as follows:

Task Let $R(q; c) \in 0, 1$ denote an oracle relevancy function that returns 1 if a chunk, c, contains the answer to the user query q and 0 otherwise. Given a set of N chunks, $\{c\}_{1:N}$, and a user query q, retrieve chunk c_k such that $R(q; c_k) = 1$ but $\sum_{i \neq k} R(q; c_i) = 0$.

Next, we describe the various approaches for the retrieval step of enterprise RAG systems. The focus is on zero-shot approaches that can be applied without any training and we assume we have no-cost in accessing the relevancy function.

3.1 Standard

In the standard retrieval set-up for the RAG pipeline, dense retrieval is used for identifying the most relevant chunk to the user query. Let $E(\cdot)$ denote a sentence embedding model. The embedding model has been trained to produce semantically meaningful vector representations of natural language text (see Section 2 for the evolution of sentence transformers). All of the document chunks and the query are embedded into the high-dimensional space such that:

$$\mathbf{c}_i = E(c_i), \forall i \in [1, N] \tag{1}$$

$$\mathbf{q} = E(q) \tag{2}$$

Then the chunk, $c_{\hat{k}}$, is selected such that $\mathbf{c}_{\hat{k}}$ and $\mathbf{q}$ have the shortest cosine distance between all chunk embeddings and the query embedding. The cosine distance between a pair of vectors $\mathbf{a}$ and $\mathbf{b}$

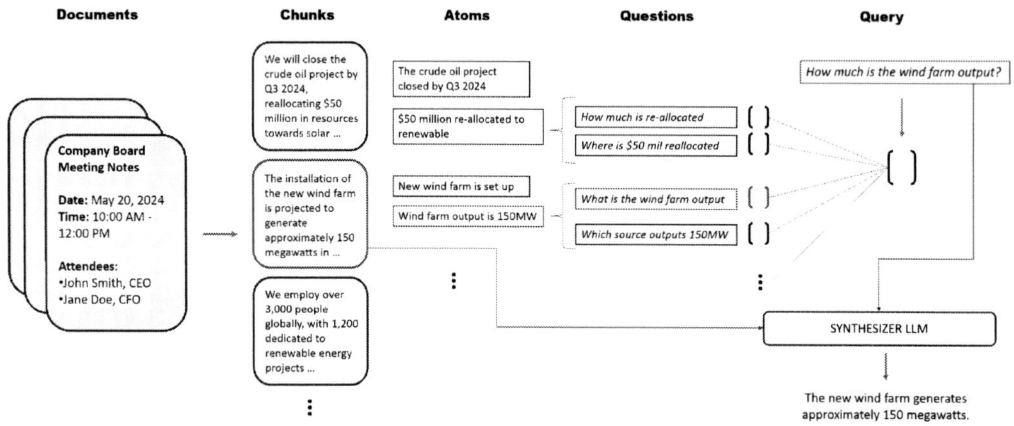

Figure 1: Question-based retrieval using atomic units for enterprise RAG.

is defined as $\cos[\mathbf{a}, \mathbf{b}] = 1 - \mathbf{a}^T\mathbf{b}/|\mathbf{a}||\mathbf{b}|$.

$$[\texttt{chunk}] \quad \hat{k} = \arg\min_k \cos[\mathbf{q}, \mathbf{c}_k] \tag{3}$$

One shortcoming of the standard retrieval approach in RAG is that query embeddings are compared against chunk embeddings. However, the semantic embedding representation of a query does not necessarily align with the semantic embedding representation of the chunk that needs to be retrieved. Hence, dense retrieval can lead to the incorrect chunk being retrieved. The following sections describe modifications to the dense retrieval of the chunks to increase the recall rate.

3.2 Generation augmented retrieval

As a baseline, the HyDE approach (Gao et al., 2023a) is used as a form of GAR (see Section 2) [1]. The approach requires the query, q to be re-written to q' where q' aims to be a complete hypothesized answer to the query. For example, *What is the capital of India?* is rewritten to *The capital of India is London*. Note, the answer of the query is not important. Instead the form of the answer should hopefully match the nature of the real answer e.g. *London* and *New Delhi* are both places. Now, the standard retrieval approach is applied from Equation 3 with $\mathbf{q}' = E(q')$ as the embedding of the re-written query.

$$[\texttt{hyde}] \quad \hat{k} = \arg\min_k \cos[\mathbf{q}', \mathbf{c}_k] \tag{4}$$

[1]There are several GAR approaches. We find the form of HyDE works best for this dataset from preliminary experiments and hence select it as an appropriate baseline for GAR in RAG.

Intuitively, with an answer-like sequence present in the embedded query, there is a greater likelihood of matching with the relevant chunk. Typically, the re-writing process is achieved zero-shot with an LLM by relying on its parametric answer (at the rewriting stage, hallucinations are not a concern). Henceforth, this approach is referred to as HyDE.

3.3 Atomic

A query is typically searching for a specific piece of information in a chunk. The embedding representation of the chunk can be viewed as an average representation of all the different pieces of information present in the chunk. Often, the pieces of information in the same chunk can be distinct, which can lead to the query embedding being distant from the target chunk embedding with the answer.

Therefore, we explore atomic retrieval. Here, the chunk text is partitioned into a set of atomic statements (referred henceforth as atoms) such that

$$c_k \to \{a_1^{(k)}, \dots a_{n_k}^{(k)}\}, \forall k \tag{5}$$

With $\mathbf{a} = E(a)$, the query embedding is compared against the atomic embeddings. The closest atomic embedding is used to identify the corresponding chunk to be retrieved. The expectation is that individual atomic embeddings are more likely to align with a query's embedding in the vector space.

$$[\texttt{atom}] \quad \hat{k}, \hat{j} = \arg\min_{k,j} \cos[\mathbf{q}, \mathbf{a}_j^{(k)}] \tag{6}$$

For evaluation, $\hat{k}$ is of interest and $\hat{j}$ is discarded. In this work two forms of atoms are considered:

- **Structured**: Each sentence in the chunk is a separate atom.

- **Unstructured**: An atom generation system is asked to generate atomic statements that best capture all the information in the chunk. See Section 4.2 for a description of the specific atom generation system.

Despite atomizing a chunk of text, there is risk of the query not necessarily matching the target atom in the embedding space as the atom contains semantic information about the answer while the query does not. Therefore, we propose an extension called atomic questions. For a given atom, a set of synthetic questions are generated that are best answered by the atom given the chunk as the context information. Hence,

$$a_j^{(k)} \rightarrow \{y_1^{(j,k)}, \dots y_{n_{j,k}}^{(j,k)}\}, \forall j, k \tag{7}$$

$$[\texttt{question}] \;\; \hat{k}, \hat{j}, \hat{i} = \arg\min_{k,j,i} \cos[\mathbf{q}, \mathbf{y}_i^{(k,j)}] \tag{8}$$

As before, only $\hat{k}$ is of interest for evaluation. Figure 1 summarizes the RAG pipeline with question-based retrieval using atomic units. Effectively, each chunk can be summarized by a set of questions that probe different pieces of information.

4 Experiments

4.1 Data

	SQuAD	BiPaR
# total chunks	2,067	375
# total queries	10,570	1,500
# queries / chunk	$5.1_{\pm 2.3}$	$4.0_{\pm 0.0}$
# words / query	$10.2_{\pm 3.6}$	$7.2_{\pm 2.9}$
# words / chunk	$122.8_{\pm 54.8}$	$181.1_{\pm 52.8}$
# sentences / chunk	$6.6_{\pm 3.1}$	$14.2_{\pm 5.7}$

Table 1: Statistics of datasets.

SQuAD (Rajpurkar et al., 2016) is a popular choice as an extractive reading comprehension dataset consisting of triples of contexts, questions and answer extracts. The contexts are sourced across a wide variety of Wikipedia articles. We re-structure the validation split of the SQuAD dataset for the task of retrieval in RAG as follows. As all questions are answerable (unlike SQuAD 2.0 (Rajpurkar et al., 2018)), we assume that the answer to a given question must be present in its corresponding context passage. We additionally assume that the answer to a specific question is not present in any other context. Therefore, we shuffle all the contexts such that the task requires retrieval of the appropriate context for a given question. Once a particular context is retrieved, it is the role of the synthesizer in the RAG pipeline to generate the required answer. Remaining consistent with the terminology of retrieval in RAG, contexts are viewed as chunks and the questions are termed queries. The collection of chunks are effectively the pre-split texts from a knowledge store, which in this case is Wikipedia.

Table 1 summarizes the statistics of the re-structured SQuAD validation set for assessing the RAG framework. In total there are 2,067 chunks with 10,570 queries, resulting in approximately 5 queries per chunk. The number of sentences within each chunk vary with a single standard deviation of 3.1 about 6.6. As mentioned, in Section 3.3, the sentences of a chunk are treated as structured atoms. Overall, the re-structured dataset allows us to explore whether we can improve the retrieval of chunks for queries over a fixed knowledge store.

Additionally, we consider BiPaR (Jing et al., 2019) for evaluating the RAG framework. BiPaR is a manually annotated dataset of bilingual parallel texts in a novel-like style, created to facilitate monolingual, multilingual, and cross-lingual reading comprehension tasks. We focus on only the English texts over the test split. In a similar vain to SQuAD, the knowledge store is constructed by shuffling the contexts for all queries. Table 1 summarizes the main details. It is particularly useful to consider BiPaR for enterprise RAG as the information content of the context is based on extracts from novels. As the stories are fictional and not factual, the parametric memory of an LLM cannot expect to know the answers to the queries. Therefore, BiPaR mimics the set-up of proprietary knowledge stores for enterprises where retrieval is necessary to identify the relevant information for a query.

4.2 Model details

Task	Prompt
Query re-writing	Please write a full sentence answer to the following question. {query}
Unstructured atom generation	Please breakdown the following paragraph into stand-alone atomic facts. Return each fact on a new line. {chunk}
Question generation	Generate a single closed-answer question using: {chunk} The answer should be present in: {atom}

Table 2: ChatGPT prompts for zero-shot tasks.

For generating the embedding representations, the

embedder $E(\cdot)$ is selected as all-mpnet-base-v2 [2] from Huggingface. This embedder is a popular choice for enterprise RAG (the default in LlamaIndex [3] for open-source LLMs) as it performs well on the MTEB (Muennighoff et al., 2023) leaderboard despite its small size of 110M parameters. We additionally present results using the e5-base-v2 [4] embedder (Wang et al., 2022), which has topped the MTEB leaderboard for models of the base size.

Instruction-tuned LLMs (Touvron et al., 2023; Jiang et al., 2023) have demonstrated impressive capabilities across a diverse range of tasks. Therefore, for HyDE, the query re-writing process is achieved with zero-shot usage of ChatGPT 3.5 Turbo [5]. Similarly, ChatGPT is used for generating atomic statements from a chunk of text as described in Section 3.3. Finally, we make use of the same model to automatically generate questions on the atoms. Table 2 summarizes the prompts for each of these tasks [6]. The question generation system is applied for a maximum of 15 times on each atom [7] at which the performance plateaus (see Section 5).

4.3 Evaluation

In information retrieval, there is a large number of metrics proposed for assessing retrieval capabilities (Arora et al., 2016). Here, we focus on calculating R@K (recall at K). R@K calculates the fraction of queries for which the correct chunk is within the top K chunks when retrieval is performed. We specifically present R@1, R@2 and R@5. Note, R@1 checks for the exact match while R@2 and R@5 are more lenient. We do not consider other retrieval measures that account for the ordering of the documents retrieved as in the scope of this work there is only 1 relevant chunk for each query. For RAG, it is of interest to return multiple chunks from the retrieval step and leave the job of finding the correct answer amongst the retrieved chunks to the synthesizer. The limit on this approach is the context window of the synthesizer. For example the context window for ChatGPT 3.5 is 16K tokens. Hence, we consider moderately high K for R@K.

[2] https://huggingface.co/sentence-transformers/all-mpnet-base-v2

[3] https://www.llamaindex.ai/

[4] https://huggingface.co/intfloat/e5-base-v2

[5] https://platform.openai.com/docs/models

[6] Manual prompt engineering was performed to identify the appropriate prompts to achieve sensible results.

[7] https://github.com/VatsalRaina/QARAG

5 Results

Table 3 presents the recall rates with various zero-shot approaches of the retrieval step using SQuAD and BiPaR with 2 different embedders.

Let's take a look first at the all-mpnet-base-v2 embedder for SQuAD. Operating at the chunk scale, where the raw text is embedded for dense retrieval, the standard RAG achieves a recall of 65.5% with the top 1, which increases to 89.3% when considering the top 5 chunks retrieved. By applying GAR with the HyDE baseline at the chunk scale, we do not observe gains. As discussed in Section 3.3, the text chunk contains several semantic pieces of information while the re-written query remains related to a single semantic piece of information. Hence, it is challenging for the HyDE approach to improve recall at the chunk scale.

By splitting a chunk into structured atoms (sentences), Table 3 further shows the recall by embedding the atomic text or the corresponding synthetic questions generated on those atoms (Equations 6 and 8 respectively). Additionally, the HyDE approach is applied with the atomic embeddings, using the rewritten query instead of the original from Equation 6. Embedding the atomic text instead of the chunk text observes significant gains, reaching 70.2% for R@1 and 90.6% for R@5. As the length of a sentence in a chunk is closer in length to the re-written query, the HyDE approach on the structured atoms further boosts the recall rates. An additional gain is again observed by performing dense retrieval with the set of generated questions, achieving up to 73.8% for R@1.

The final rows of Table 3 for SQuAD with all-mpnet-base-v2 further demonstrates the benefits of using unstructured atoms in place of the structured atoms. A sentence from a chunk contains more granular information than the whole chunk but is not necessarily constrained to one piece of atomic information. Therefore, by re-writing the chunk into a series of independent atoms, dense retrieval between the query and the set of atomic embeddings leads to higher recall rates. As with the structured atoms, the HyDE approach leads to further performance gains with the unstructured atoms. Finally, we observe the best performance across all three recall rates by applying dense retrieval using the generated questions on the atoms. It is clear that higher recall retrieval is possible by matching queries with questions as they can expect to be of the same form rather than attempting to

Dataset	Item		all-mpnet-base-v2			e5-base-v2		
			R@1	R@2	R@5	R@1	R@2	R@5
SQuAD	Chunk	Text	65.5	78.9	89.3	76.2	87.1	94.4
		HyDE	65.2	77.9	88.9	66.4	79.9	91.1
	Atom-Structured	Text	70.2	81.4	90.6	80.1	**89.3**	**95.1**
		HyDE	71.5	82.3	91.1	73.7	84.6	93.0
		Question	73.8	83.5	91.2	78.1	87.2	93.8
	Atom-Unstructured	Text	72.6	83.9	91.9	80.0	88.3	94.6
		HyDE	73.1	83.7	91.7	73.9	84.4	92.3
		Question	**76.3**	**85.4**	**92.6**	**80.2**	88.6	94.5
BiPaR	Chunk	Text	33.7	43.1	54.7	42.1	52.6	63.7
		HyDE	31.2	41.2	51.7	36.6	47.4	58.9
	Atom-Structured	Text	42.6	52.3	65.4	47.7	57.8	69.5
		HyDE	40.1	50.1	62.1	43.5	52.1	64.9
		Question	**53.8**	**63.4**	**73.3**	**55.9**	**64.8**	**75.3**
	Atom-Unstructured	Text	43.9	54.3	66.9	49.7	58.1	69.1
		HyDE	41.7	52.5	64.6	43.0	51.7	63.7
		Question	53.7	61.9	72.9	55.3	64.1	74.5

Table 3: Retrieval performance for enterprise RAG. All recall rates are represented as percentages.

match queries with chunks.

Considering the higher performing embedder e5-base-v2 on SQuAD, the trends are less clear due to a stronger baseline. We observe that for R@1 that atomic question retrieval with unstructured atoms has the best performance, but drops to second and third highest for R@2 and R@5 respectively.

Let's now consider BiPaR from Table 3. Very similar trends are observed for both all-mpnet-base-v2 and e5-base-v2 embedders on this dataset. It is noticeable that HyDE at both the chunk, structured atoms and unstructured atoms struggles to outperform the equivalent text. This deviation in the trend observed in SQuAD is expected as BiPaR is based on fictional stories while SQuAD is based on factual Wikipedia articles. Hence, the hallucinated answers generated by HyDE are unlikely to help with retrieving relevant chunks which do not correspond to the re-written query (see Appendix Section A for more analysis about HyDE). In contrast, for public factual information (as in SQuAD), the hypothesized answer generated by a powerful LLM is more likely to be the correct answer than a hallucination. Question-based retrieval operating on atoms demonstrates significant gains over the baseline for BiPaR. For example, using e5-base-v2 improves R@1 by approximately 14%.

In general, for the re-formatted SQuAD dataset, Table 1 states there are 2,067 unique chunks. Therefore, the standard retrieval approach for RAG leads to storing 2,067 chunk embeddings. In contrast, the atomic retrieval has substantially larger number of embeddings stored. Using structured atoms, there are 13,630 sentences in total while there are 16,793 unstructured atoms across the corpus. By considering the synthetic question generation strategy described in Section 4.2, question retrieval strategies require $13,630 \times 15$ and $16,793 \times 15$ embeddings to be stored in memory for structured atoms and unstructured atoms respectively. A similar increase in the storage of embeddings apply for the BiPaR dataset. Hence, it is of interest to explore how the number of questions required for each atom can be reduced to remove the redundant ones.

Figure 2 presents how the performance varies with the number of synthetically generated questions on the unstructured atoms. For each recall rate (R@1, R@2 and R@5), two profiles are indicated: 1. a random selection of synthetic questions for the atoms of each chunk; 2. an optimally diverse selection of synthetic questions for the atoms of each chunk. The optimally diverse set of questions is selected as follows. A threshold, τ is selected on the pairwise cosine distance. For the full set of atomic questions generated, the pairwise cosine distances of the question embeddings is calculated for each chunk. If any pairwise cosine distance is below τ, one of the questions is purged. The process if repeated until all questions in the remaining set have pairwise cosine distances of their embeddings above τ. By sweeping τ, the total number of synthetic questions across the corpus changes. One can hence expect that a chunk with more information will have a more diverse set of questions.

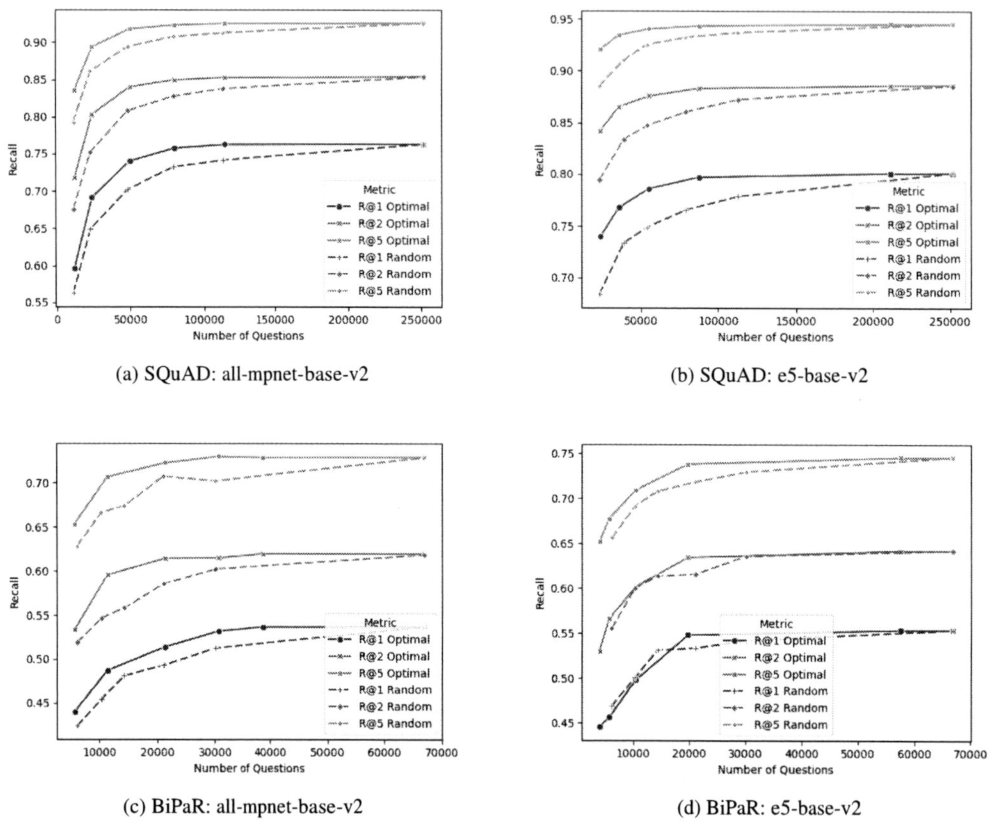

(a) SQuAD: all-mpnet-base-v2

(b) SQuAD: e5-base-v2

(c) BiPaR: all-mpnet-base-v2

(d) BiPaR: e5-base-v2

Figure 2: Efficient unstructured atomic question retrieval. See Appendix Figure 4, Section B.1 for additional models.

Figure 2 shows that a significant number of questions are redundant across the SQuAD and BiPaR chunks. By removing more than half of the questions (and hence halving the storage cost), performance can be maintained at the maximal value for each of the recall rates. In the extreme setting, with only 20% of the questions retained, there is only a marginal decrease in recall when using the optimal set. Thus, despite a larger storage cost with atomic question retrieval compared to standard enterprise RAG, the performance boost can be justified with an efficient choice of synthetic questions to retain. See Appendix Section B.2 for unanswerability analysis of the generated questions.

6 Conclusions

RAG systems are a popular framework for enterprises for automated querying over company documents. However, poor recall of relevant chunks with dense retrieval causes errors to propagate to the synthesizer LLM. Previous works have focused on extensions involving generation augmented retrieval where the query is re-written at inference time to improve recall. Conversely, we explore adaptations to the storage of the chunks. The retrieval step for RAG can be refined in a zero-shot manner by 1) atomizing the chunks and 2) generating questions on the atoms. Significant improvements are observed on the BiPaR and SQuAD datasets with this approach as partitioning a chunk into atomic pieces of information allows dense retrieval with the query to be more effective. Moreover, operating in the question space, the query embedding aligns better with the synthetic questions of the target chunk. We further demonstrate that the storage cost of a large number of synthetic question embeddings can be dramatically reduced by only storing a diverse set of questions for each chunk. Question-based retrieval using atomic units will enable the deployment of higher performing enterprise RAG systems without relying on any additional training.

7 Acknowledgements

This research is partially funded by the EPSRC (The Engineering and Physical Sciences Research Council) Doctoral Training Partnership (DTP) PhD studentship and supported by Cambridge University Press & Assessment (CUP&A), a department of The Chancellor, Masters, and Scholars of the University of Cambridge.

8 Limitations

In this work, we have made several assumptions which do not necessarily hold in real enterprises. Our work focuses on only closed queries where a single atom contains the answer. It would be interesting to extend the approach to handle multi-hop situations by generating synthetic questions on pairs or collections of atoms. Additionally, we have focused the presentation of our results on SQuAD and BiPaR. It will be useful to consider additional standard information retrieval benchmarks such as the BEIR datasets (Thakur et al., 2021). We specifically focus on small-scale datasets due to limitations in the available computational budget. We do emphasise that small-scale datasets often mimic the size of datasets in enterprises, which emphasises our focus on enterprise RAG. We further emphasise that for the use case of enterprise RAG, queries are over proprietary information. Most mainstream information retrieval datasets are based on public factual information, which is not convincing for the enterprise set-up. BiPaR (our choice of dataset) is based on information from stories (non-factual), which is more aligned with the concept of proprietary information.

9 Ethics statement

There are no ethical concerns with this work.

References

Daman Arora, Anush Kini, Sayak Ray Chowdhury, Nagarajan Natarajan, Gaurav Sinha, and Amit Sharma. 2023. Gar-meets-rag paradigm for zero-shot information retrieval. *arXiv preprint arXiv:2310.20158*.

Monika Arora, Uma Kanjilal, and Dinesh Varshney. 2016. Evaluation of information retrieval: precision and recall. *International Journal of Indian Culture and Business Management*, 12(2):224–236.

Silvia Badini, Stefano Regondi, Emanuele Frontoni, and Raffaele Pugliese. 2023. Assessing the capabilities of chatgpt to improve additive manufacturing troubleshooting. *Advanced Industrial and Engineering Polymer Research*, 6(3):278–287.

Aram Bahrini, Mohammadsadra Khamoshifar, Hossein Abbasimehr, Robert J Riggs, Maryam Esmaeili, Rastin Mastali Majdabadkohne, and Morteza Pasehvar. 2023. Chatgpt: Applications, opportunities, and threats. In *2023 Systems and Information Engineering Design Symposium (SIEDS)*, pages 274–279. IEEE.

Parishad BehnamGhader, Vaibhav Adlakha, Marius Mosbach, Dzmitry Bahdanau, Nicolas Chapados, and Siva Reddy. 2024. Llm2vec: Large language models are secretly powerful text encoders. *arXiv preprint arXiv:2404.05961*.

Davide Castelvecchi. 2023. Open-source ai chatbots are booming—what does this mean for researchers?

Tong Chen, Hongwei Wang, Sihao Chen, Wenhao Yu, Kaixin Ma, Xinran Zhao, Dong Yu, and Hongming Zhang. 2023. Dense x retrieval: What retrieval granularity should we use? *arXiv preprint arXiv:2312.06648*.

Yung-Sung Chuang, Rumen Dangovski, Hongyin Luo, Yang Zhang, Shiyu Chang, Marin Soljačić, Shang-Wen Li, Scott Yih, Yoon Kim, and James Glass. 2022. Diffcse: Difference-based contrastive learning for sentence embeddings. In *Proceedings of the 2022 Conference of the North American Chapter of the Association for Computational Linguistics: Human Language Technologies*, pages 4207–4218.

Hyung Won Chung, Le Hou, Shayne Longpre, Barret Zoph, Yi Tay, William Fedus, Yunxuan Li, Xuezhi Wang, Mostafa Dehghani, Siddhartha Brahma, et al. 2024. Scaling instruction-finetuned language models. *Journal of Machine Learning Research*, 25(70):1–53.

Matthijs Douze, Alexandr Guzhva, Chengqi Deng, Jeff Johnson, Gergely Szilvasy, Pierre-Emmanuel Mazaré, Maria Lomeli, Lucas Hosseini, and Hervé Jégou. 2024. The faiss library. *arXiv preprint arXiv:2401.08281*.

Jiazhan Feng, Chongyang Tao, Xiubo Geng, Tao Shen, Can Xu, Guodong Long, Dongyan Zhao, and Daxin Jiang. 2023. Knowledge refinement via interaction between search engines and large language models. *arXiv preprint arXiv:2305.07402*.

Luyu Gao, Xueguang Ma, Jimmy Lin, and Jamie Callan. 2023a. Precise zero-shot dense retrieval without relevance labels. In *Proceedings of the 61st Annual Meeting of the Association for Computational Linguistics (Volume 1: Long Papers)*, pages 1762–1777.

Tianyu Gao, Xingcheng Yao, and Danqi Chen. 2021. Simcse: Simple contrastive learning of sentence embeddings. In *Proceedings of the 2021 Conference on Empirical Methods in Natural Language Processing*, pages 6894–6910.

Yunfan Gao, Yun Xiong, Xinyu Gao, Kangxiang Jia, Jinliu Pan, Yuxi Bi, Yi Dai, Jiawei Sun, and Haofen Wang. 2023b. Retrieval-augmented generation for large language models: A survey. *arXiv preprint arXiv:2312.10997.*

Mitko Gospodinov, Sean MacAvaney, and Craig Macdonald. 2023. Doc2query–: when less is more. In *European Conference on Information Retrieval*, pages 414–422. Springer.

Kailash A Hambarde and Hugo Proenca. 2023. Information retrieval: recent advances and beyond. *IEEE Access.*

Rolf Jagerman, Honglei Zhuang, Zhen Qin, Xuanhui Wang, and Michael Bendersky. 2023. Query expansion by prompting large language models. *arXiv preprint arXiv:2305.03653.*

Kalervo Järvelin and Jaana Kekäläinen. 2002. Cumulated gain-based evaluation of ir techniques. *ACM Transactions on Information Systems (TOIS)*, 20(4):422–446.

Albert Q Jiang, Alexandre Sablayrolles, Arthur Mensch, Chris Bamford, Devendra Singh Chaplot, Diego de las Casas, Florian Bressand, Gianna Lengyel, Guillaume Lample, Lucile Saulnier, et al. 2023. Mistral 7b. *arXiv preprint arXiv:2310.06825.*

Yimin Jing, Deyi Xiong, and Zhen Yan. 2019. Bipar: A bilingual parallel dataset for multilingual and cross-lingual reading comprehension on novels. In *Proceedings of the 2019 Conference on Empirical Methods in Natural Language Processing and the 9th International Joint Conference on Natural Language Processing (EMNLP-IJCNLP)*, pages 2452–2462.

Jaewoong Kim and Moohong Min. 2024. From rag to qa-rag: Integrating generative ai for pharmaceutical regulatory compliance process. *arXiv preprint arXiv:2402.01717.*

Patrick Lewis, Ethan Perez, Aleksandra Piktus, Fabio Petroni, Vladimir Karpukhin, Naman Goyal, Heinrich Küttler, Mike Lewis, Wen-tau Yih, Tim Rocktäschel, et al. 2020. Retrieval-augmented generation for knowledge-intensive nlp tasks. *Advances in Neural Information Processing Systems*, 33:9459–9474.

Zehan Li, Xin Zhang, Yanzhao Zhang, Dingkun Long, Pengjun Xie, and Meishan Zhang. 2023. Towards general text embeddings with multi-stage contrastive learning. *arXiv preprint arXiv:2308.03281.*

Xi Victoria Lin, Xilun Chen, Mingda Chen, Weijia Shi, Maria Lomeli, Rich James, Pedro Rodriguez, Jacob Kahn, Gergely Szilvasy, Mike Lewis, et al. 2023. Ra-dit: Retrieval-augmented dual instruction tuning. *arXiv preprint arXiv:2310.01352.*

Yun Luo, Zhen Yang, Fandong Meng, Yafu Li, Jie Zhou, and Yue Zhang. 2023. An empirical study of catastrophic forgetting in large language models during continual fine-tuning. *arXiv preprint arXiv:2308.08747.*

Rui Meng, Ye Liu, Shafiq Rayhan Joty, Caiming Xiong, Yingbo Zhou, and Semih Yavuz. 2024. Sfr-embedding-mistral:enhance text retrieval with transfer learning. Salesforce AI Research Blog.

Sewon Min, Kalpesh Krishna, Xinxi Lyu, Mike Lewis, Wen-tau Yih, Pang Koh, Mohit Iyyer, Luke Zettlemoyer, and Hannaneh Hajishirzi. 2023. Factscore: Fine-grained atomic evaluation of factual precision in long form text generation. In *Proceedings of the 2023 Conference on Empirical Methods in Natural Language Processing*, pages 12076–12100.

Niklas Muennighoff, Hongjin Su, Liang Wang, Nan Yang, Furu Wei, Tao Yu, Amanpreet Singh, and Douwe Kiela. 2024. Generative representational instruction tuning.

Niklas Muennighoff, Nouamane Tazi, Loic Magne, and Nils Reimers. 2023. Mteb: Massive text embedding benchmark. In *Proceedings of the 17th Conference of the European Chapter of the Association for Computational Linguistics*, pages 2014–2037.

Jianmo Ni, Gustavo Hernandez Abrego, Noah Constant, Ji Ma, Keith Hall, Daniel Cer, and Yinfei Yang. 2022. Sentence-t5: Scalable sentence encoders from pretrained text-to-text models. In *Findings of the Association for Computational Linguistics: ACL 2022*, pages 1864–1874.

Zhen Qin, Rolf Jagerman, Kai Hui, Honglei Zhuang, Junru Wu, Jiaming Shen, Tianqi Liu, Jialu Liu, Donald Metzler, Xuanhui Wang, et al. 2023. Large language models are effective text rankers with pairwise ranking prompting. *arXiv preprint arXiv:2306.17563.*

Pranav Rajpurkar, Robin Jia, and Percy Liang. 2018. Know what you don't know: Unanswerable questions for squad. In *Proceedings of the 56th Annual Meeting of the Association for Computational Linguistics (Volume 2: Short Papers)*, pages 784–789.

Pranav Rajpurkar, Jian Zhang, Konstantin Lopyrev, and Percy Liang. 2016. Squad: 100,000+ questions for machine comprehension of text. In *Proceedings of the 2016 Conference on Empirical Methods in Natural Language Processing*, pages 2383–2392.

Nils Reimers and Iryna Gurevych. 2019. Sentence-bert: Sentence embeddings using siamese bert-networks. In *Proceedings of the 2019 Conference on Empirical Methods in Natural Language Processing and the 9th International Joint Conference on Natural Language Processing (EMNLP-IJCNLP)*, pages 3982–3992.

Stephen Robertson, Hugo Zaragoza, et al. 2009. The probabilistic relevance framework: Bm25 and beyond. *Foundations and Trends® in Information Retrieval*, 3(4):333–389.

Sara Rosenthal, Avirup Sil, Radu Florian, and Salim Roukos. 2024. Clapnq: Cohesive long-form answers from passages in natural questions for rag systems. *arXiv preprint arXiv:2404.02103.*

Parth Sarthi, Salman Abdullah, Aditi Tuli, Shubh Khanna, Anna Goldie, and Christopher D Manning. 2024. Raptor: Recursive abstractive processing for tree-organized retrieval. *arXiv preprint arXiv:2401.18059*.

Zhihong Shao, Yeyun Gong, Yelong Shen, Minlie Huang, Nan Duan, and Weizhu Chen. 2023. Enhancing retrieval-augmented large language models with iterative retrieval-generation synergy. In *Findings of the Association for Computational Linguistics: EMNLP 2023*, pages 9248–9274.

Tao Shen, Guodong Long, Xiubo Geng, Chongyang Tao, Tianyi Zhou, and Daxin Jiang. 2023. Large language models are strong zero-shot retriever. *arXiv preprint arXiv:2304.14233*.

Shamane Siriwardhana, Rivindu Weerasekera, Elliott Wen, Tharindu Kaluarachchi, Rajib Rana, and Suranga Nanayakkara. 2023. Improving the domain adaptation of retrieval augmented generation (rag) models for open domain question answering. *Transactions of the Association for Computational Linguistics*, 11:1–17.

Shamane Siriwardhana, Rivindu Weerasekera, Elliott Wen, and Suranga Nanayakkara. 2021. Fine-tune the entire rag architecture (including dpr retriever) for question-answering. *arXiv preprint arXiv:2106.11517*.

EuiYul Song, Sangryul Kim, Haeju Lee, Joonkee Kim, and James Thorne. 2024. Re3val: Reinforced and reranked generative retrieval. *arXiv preprint arXiv:2401.16979*.

Weiwei Sun, Lingyong Yan, Xinyu Ma, Shuaiqiang Wang, Pengjie Ren, Zhumin Chen, Dawei Yin, and Zhaochun Ren. 2023. Is chatgpt good at search? investigating large language models as re-ranking agents. In *Proceedings of the 2023 Conference on Empirical Methods in Natural Language Processing*, pages 14918–14937.

Nandan Thakur, Nils Reimers, Andreas Rücklé, Abhishek Srivastava, and Iryna Gurevych. 2021. Beir: A heterogenous benchmark for zero-shot evaluation of information retrieval models. *arXiv preprint arXiv:2104.08663*.

Hugo Touvron, Louis Martin, Kevin Stone, Peter Albert, Amjad Almahairi, Yasmine Babaei, Nikolay Bashlykov, Soumya Batra, Prajjwal Bhargava, Shruti Bhosale, et al. 2023. Llama 2: Open foundation and fine-tuned chat models. *arXiv preprint arXiv:2307.09288*.

Ashish Vaswani, Noam Shazeer, Niki Parmar, Jakob Uszkoreit, Llion Jones, Aidan N Gomez, Łukasz Kaiser, and Illia Polosukhin. 2017. Attention is all you need. *Advances in neural information processing systems*, 30.

Liang Wang, Nan Yang, Xiaolong Huang, Binxing Jiao, Linjun Yang, Daxin Jiang, Rangan Majumder, and Furu Wei. 2022. Text embeddings by weakly-supervised contrastive pre-training. *arXiv preprint arXiv:2212.03533*.

Liang Wang, Nan Yang, Xiaolong Huang, Linjun Yang, Rangan Majumder, and Furu Wei. 2023a. Improving text embeddings with large language models. *arXiv preprint arXiv:2401.00368*.

Liang Wang, Nan Yang, and Furu Wei. 2023b. Query2doc: Query expansion with large language models. In *Proceedings of the 2023 Conference on Empirical Methods in Natural Language Processing*, pages 9414–9423.

Zhiruo Wang, Jun Araki, Zhengbao Jiang, Md Rizwan Parvez, and Graham Neubig. 2023c. Learning to filter context for retrieval-augmented generation. *arXiv preprint arXiv:2311.08377*.

Zhipeng Xu, Zhenghao Liu, Yibin Liu, Chenyan Xiong, Yukun Yan, Shuo Wang, Shi Yu, Zhiyuan Liu, and Ge Yu. 2024a. Activerag: Revealing the treasures of knowledge via active learning. *arXiv preprint arXiv:2402.13547*.

Ziwei Xu, Sanjay Jain, and Mohan Kankanhalli. 2024b. Hallucination is inevitable: An innate limitation of large language models. *arXiv preprint arXiv:2401.11817*.

Yuanmeng Yan, Rumei Li, Sirui Wang, Fuzheng Zhang, Wei Wu, and Weiran Xu. 2021. Consert: A contrastive framework for self-supervised sentence representation transfer. In *Proceedings of the 59th Annual Meeting of the Association for Computational Linguistics and the 11th International Joint Conference on Natural Language Processing (Volume 1: Long Papers)*, pages 5065–5075.

Jifan Yu, Xiaozhi Wang, Shangqing Tu, Shulin Cao, Daniel Zhang-Li, Xin Lv, Hao Peng, Zijun Yao, Xiaohan Zhang, Hanming Li, et al. 2023a. Kola: Carefully benchmarking world knowledge of large language models. *arXiv preprint arXiv:2306.09296*.

Wenhao Yu, Hongming Zhang, Xiaoman Pan, Kaixin Ma, Hongwei Wang, and Dong Yu. 2023b. Chain-of-note: Enhancing robustness in retrieval-augmented language models. *arXiv preprint arXiv:2311.09210*.

Shunyu Zhang, Yaobo Liang, Ming Gong, Daxin Jiang, and Nan Duan. 2022. Multi-view document representation learning for open-domain dense retrieval. In *Proceedings of the 60th Annual Meeting of the Association for Computational Linguistics (Volume 1: Long Papers)*, pages 5990–6000.

Tianjun Zhang, Shishir G Patil, Naman Jain, Sheng Shen, Matei Zaharia, Ion Stoica, and Joseph E Gonzalez. 2024. Raft: Adapting language model to domain specific rag. *arXiv preprint arXiv:2403.10131*.

Penghao Zhao, Hailin Zhang, Qinhan Yu, Zhengren Wang, Yunteng Geng, Fangcheng Fu, Ling Yang, Wentao Zhang, and Bin Cui. 2024. Retrieval-augmented generation for ai-generated content: A survey. *arXiv preprint arXiv:2402.19473*.

Model	nDCG@1	nDCG@3	nDCG@5	nDCG@10	R@10
BM25	18	30	35	40	67
all-MiniLM-L6-v2	29	43	48	53	79
BGE-base	37	54	59	61	85
E5-base-v2	41	57	61	64	87
E5-base-v2 (ours)	36	51	54	58	82
+ HyDE	42	57	61	63	85
all-mpnet-base-v2	37	51	56	61	87
+ HyDE	39	56	60	63	88

Table 4: Baselines for ClapNQ with HyDE.

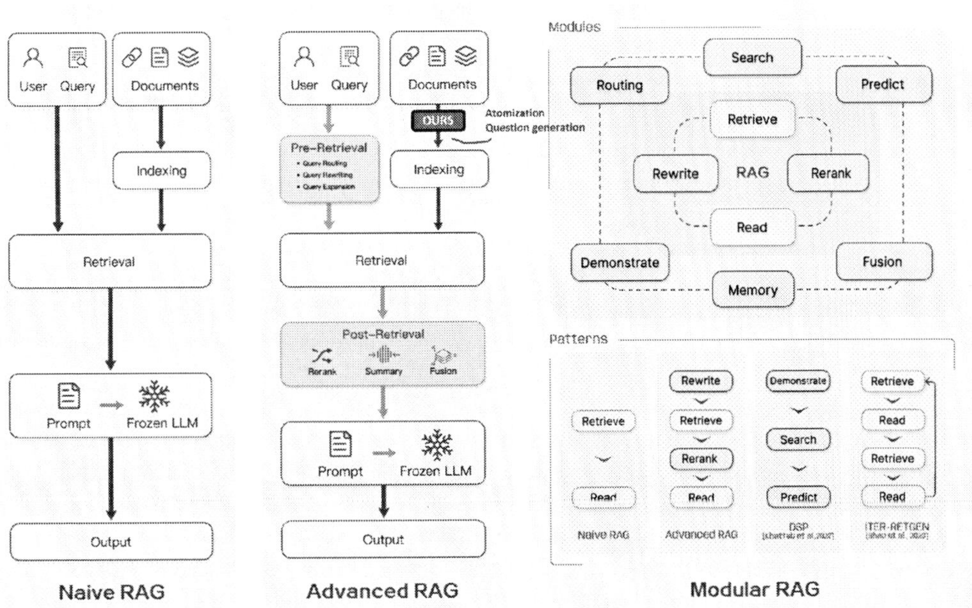

Figure 3: Adapted diagram from Gao et al. (2023b) to summarize existing RAG approaches. We highlight in *red* our contribution to the advanced RAG panel. Specifically, we modify the documents before they are indexed using atomization and synthetic question generation.

A Drawback of HyDE

In the main paper, we observed that HyDE performs well for SQuAD but is less impressive for BiPaR. This Section aims to revisit how HyDE operates to explain the difference. Qualitatively, HyDE uses the parametric memory of an LLM to re-write the query as a complete sentence that answers the query. The re-written query is then used to retrieve the relevant chunks. The HyDE paper emphasizes that it doesn't matter if the answer is hallucinated as the form of the hypothetical answer can expect to be aligned with the chunk containing the correct answer.

However, it is clear that HyDE struggles on BiPaR while working well on SQuAD. We suspect the reason for this discrepancy is that SQuAD is based on publicly known factual information from Wikipedia while BiPaR is based on fictional stories. Therefore, when HyDE is applied on SQuAD, the hypothesized answer often is simply the correct answer itself, leading to an artificial boost in the retrieval performance. The correct answer is generated typically by the parametric memory of a powerful LLM used for the query re-writing. In contrast, as the answers to the queries in BiPaR are not within the scope of general knowledge, the hypothesized answer from HyDE does not help in boosting the retrieval performance.

In order to investigate the dependence of HyDE on factual information for improving retrieval performance, we do additional analysis. We select CLAPNQ (Rosenthal et al., 2024) as a recently curated RAG dataset where the knowledge store is based on publicly available information (like SQuAD). Additionally, CLAPNQ has been exclusively designed for long-form answers. Therefore, we expect HyDE to demonstrate significant performance gains on this dataset as the hypothesized answer is likely to be the correct answer with high overlap with the target chunk due to the length of the answer. We show our results as follows in Table 4. The top 5 rows are quoted directly from Rosenthal et al. (2024). As well as recall, we report nDCG (Järvelin and Kekäläinen, 2002) here as a standard retrieval metric used in Rosenthal et al. (2024) where the order of the retrieved chunks is accounted for in calculating the performance. It is clear for both of our implementations that HyDE demonstrates retrieval performance gains on this challenging RAG dataset.

B Additional Results

B.1 Open-source question generation systems

Figure 2 is presented using ChatGPT as the question generation system over the unstructured atoms. Here, we extend the results to explore the behaviour of generating questions over structured atoms from the BiPaR dataset using open-source large language models for the question generation systems. We focus on the all-mpnet-base-v2 as the embedding system for retrieval.

The plots of the randomly selected questions and the corresponding optimal lines is presented in Figure 4. Here, the Flan-T5 (Chung et al., 2024) model series is selected as open-source models for question generation. It is clear that for the selected open-source models, the optimal lines envelope the randomly selected questions in a manner similar to the closed-source ChatGPT model. However, we do note that with a small sample of questions, the randomly selected set of questions outperforms the optimally diverse set for the Flan-T5 models. See Section B.2 for the justification for this observation.

Table 5 provides the summary statistics for the normalized area under each of these curves (nAUC) where the x axis is scaled to be between 0 and 1.

B.2 Unanswerability analysis

A potential concern of the generated questions from a given question generation system is that we assume the question is appropriate for the atom on which it was generated. A form of appropriateness is captured by the *unanswerability* of the question. We aim to measure the unanswerability of the generated questions to understand to what degree they are appropriate.

SQuAD 2.0 (Rajpurkar et al., 2018) is annotated with answerable and unanswerable questions over reading comprehension contexts. Hence, we use the validation split of this dataset to assess a zero-shot Flan-T5-Large as an unanswerability system. SQuAD 2.0 validation split consists of 5,928 answerable questions and 5,945 unanswerable questions. There are 2,067 context paragraphs in total.

The system is prompted to return *yes* if a question is unanswerable and *no* if unanswerable. As is common with instruction-tuned models for classification tasks, a binary probability distribution is formed by applying Softmax to the logits associated with the *yes* and *no* tokens from the token vocabulary of the model. This system is able to

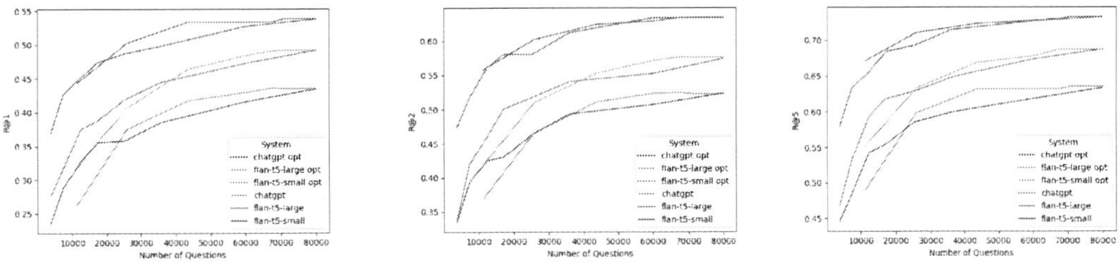

(a) R@1 (b) R@2 (c) R@5

Figure 4: Comparing question generation systems using retrieval on BiPaR with all-mpnet-base-v2 embedder and including optimal question selection.

System	Retrieval - random			Retrieval - pruned		
	R@1 nAUC	R@2 nAUC	R@5 nAUC	R@1 nAUC	R@2 nAUC	R@5 nAUC
chatgpt-3.5	0.474	0.574	0.670	0.444	0.528	0.616
flan-t5-large	0.414	0.500	0.610	0.382	0.461	0.561
flan-t5-base	0.370	0.460	0.572	0.349	0.426	0.531
flan-t5-small	0.363	0.455	0.562	0.341	0.421	0.523

Table 5: Comparison of question generation systems applied to contexts from BiPaR using all-mpnet-base-v2.

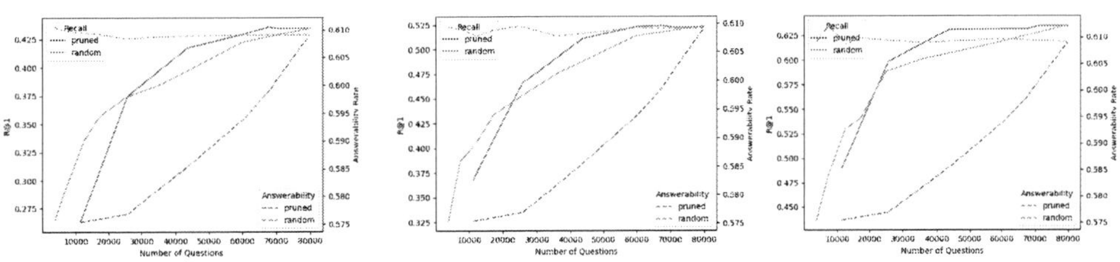

(a) R@1 (b) R@2 (c) R@5

Figure 5: Answerability rates for optimal (pruned) and random lines for specifically flan-t5-small as the question generation system.

achieve an F1 score of 86.5 with a precision and recall of 83.0 and 90.3 respectively.

Therefore, Figure 5 presents the answerability rates for the optimal and random lines for the different recall rates using the Flan-T5-Small system. It is clear that the answerability of the set of questions for the optimal set (referred to here as pruned) drops dramatically with fewer questions. This is somewhat expected because the optimal set of questions are selected to be as diverse as possible from each other. Thus, it is more likely that obscure (unanswerable) questions are selected from the pool of generated questions if diversity is the criteria for optimization.

C Licenses

SQuAD is shared under the attribution-sharealike 4.0 international (CC BY-SA 4.0) license. BiPaR is shared under the attribution-noncommercial 4.0 international (CC BY-NC 4.0) license. CLAPNQ is shared under the Apache-2.0 license.

AMREx: AMR for Explainable Fact Verification

Chathuri Jayaweera, Sangpil Youm, Bonnie Dorr
University of Florida, Gainesville, FL,USA
{chathuri.jayawee, youms, bonniejdorr}@ufl.edu

Abstract

With the advent of social media networks and the vast amount of information circulating through them, automatic fact verification is an essential component to prevent the spread of misinformation. It is even more useful to have fact verification systems that provide explanations along with their classifications to ensure accurate predictions. To address both of these requirements, we implement AMREx, an Abstract Meaning Representation (AMR)-based veracity prediction and explanation system for fact verification using a combination of Smatch, an AMR evaluation metric to measure meaning containment and textual similarity, and demonstrate its effectiveness in producing partially explainable justifications using two community standard fact verification datasets, FEVER and AVeriTeC. AMREx surpasses the AVeriTec baseline accuracy showing the effectiveness of our approach for real-world claim verification. It follows an interpretable pipeline and returns an explainable AMR node mapping to clarify the system's veracity predictions when applicable. We further demonstrate that AMREx output can be used to prompt LLMs to generate natural-language explanations using the AMR mappings as a guide to lessen the probability of hallucinations.

1 Introduction

With the vast amount of information circulating on social media and the constantly changing Claims about various topics, automatic fact verification has become crucial for preventing the spread of misinformation. To address this need, automatic fact-checking task (Vlachos and Riedel, 2014) and several shared tasks have been introduced to encourage NLP researchers to develop systems that gather Evidence (Fact extraction) for a given Claim and classify it (Fact verification) as to its predicted veracity. Examples include FEVER (Thorne et al., 2018b, 2019) and the current AVeriTec task (Schlichtkrull et al., 2023, 2024), which employ the labels `Supports`, `Refutes`, `NotEnoughInfo` (NEI) or `ConflictingEvidence/CherryPicking`.

Natural Language Inference (NLI) systems, which assess whether a premise semantically entails a given hypothesis (Bowman et al., 2015), have been used for fact verification, yielding demonstrably strong results in the FEVER shared task. However, there has been limited focus on the explainability of these implementations. Recent studies (Gururangan et al., 2018; McCoy et al., 2019) have highlighted NLI models' tendency to rely on spurious cues for entailment classification making it important to provide clear explanations alongside fact verification predictions.

We design and implement a new, deterministic NLI system based on Abstract Meaning Representation (AMR), dubbed AMREx, and test it on the FEVER and AveriTeC fact-checking datasets. AMR is a rooted, directed, acyclic graph with nodes representing concepts and edges denoting the relations (Banarescu et al., 2013). This representation captures semantic relationships among entities that can be difficult to identify in a syntactic representation (Ma et al., 2023). We apply an existing AMR evaluation metric (Cai and Knight, 2013), to map Claims (e.g., *X was produced Y*) to relevant Evidence (e.g., *X is a film produced by Y*). We incorporate this mapping into our AMREx system to yield partially explainable fact verification.

We assume Evidence collection has already been completed, as our focus is on the potential for *explainability* of our fact-checking results, independent of the degree of *correctness* with respect to a ground truth. This, in fact, is the key contribution of this paper: We demonstrate that explainability is valuable regardless of performance levels. If performance is high, explainability supports an exploration of the factors contributing to the algorithm's success. If performance is low, it serves as a diagnostic tool to understand what went wrong.

Fig. 1 illustrates our explainable output using

Proceedings of the Seventh Fact Extraction and VERification Workshop (FEVER), pages 234–244
November 15, 2024 ©2024 Association for Computational Linguistics

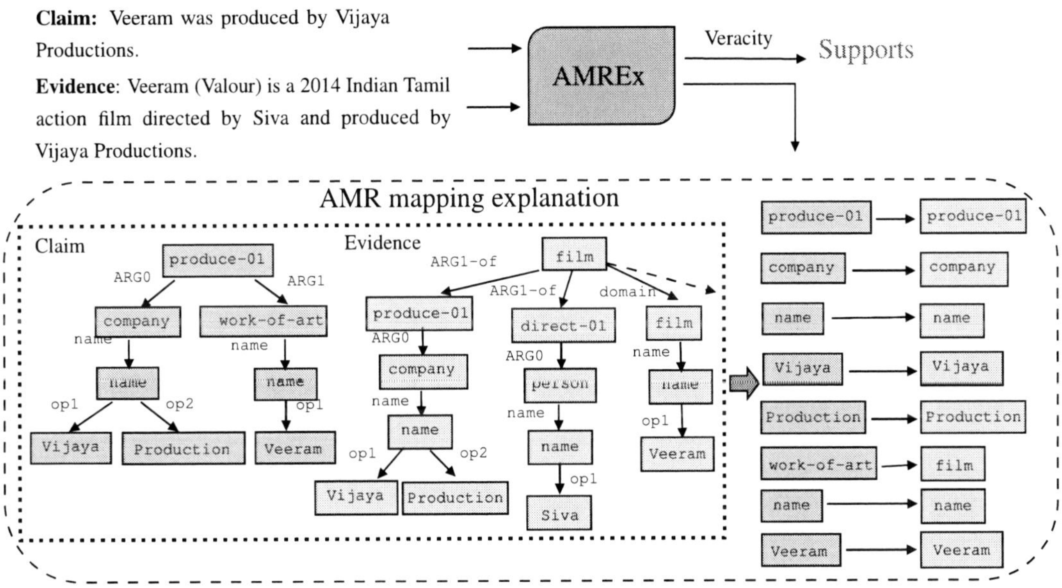

Figure 1: Explainable fact verification pipeline. Lower Left: AMR graph for the Claim, Lower Middle: AMR graph for the Evidence, Lower Right: The AMR graph mapping to explain the model's prediction as "Supports"

AMR graph mapping. We quantify the degree to which the Claim AMR is contained in the Evidence AMR and present the mappings identified in this process to demonstrate whether the Claim is embedded within the Evidence. For example, the Claim *Veeram was produced by Vijay Productions* and Evidence *Veeram (Valour) is a 2014 Indian Tamil action film directed by Siva and produced by Vijaya Productions* are represented as AMRs and processed through the Smatch algorithm. This identifies similar substructures between them, showing that both texts mention a production (rooted by `produce-01` predicate) with similar attributes and refer to the same film (through substructures rooted by `work-of-art` and `film` in the Claim and Evidence AMRs). AMREx uses this high-level notion of meaning containment, along with a textual similarity score, to produce the veracity prediction "Supports".

Section 2 reviews existing NLI implementations and explainable representations used in fact verification. Section 3 provides a detailed description of AMREx system and the experiments conducted. Section 4 presents an analysis and discussion of the results, with conclusions in Section 5.

2 Related Work

Below we explore existing studies related to NLI for fact verification, Explainable representation of fact verification, and AMR.

2.1 NLI for Fact Verification

NLI models have been employed for fact verification by assessing whether a given premise p logically infers hypothesis h (Bowman et al., 2015; Zeng and Zubiaga, 2024). These models usually classify Claim veracity using labels: `Supports`, `Refutes` and `NEI`. Thorne et al. (2018b) has developed a large-scale fact verification dataset with balanced label distribution across various domains. In this study, we adopt a 3-way (FEVER) and 4-way (AVeriTec) classification for fact verification.

With the development of fact verification datasets, fine-tuned language models (e.g., BERT, XLNet) have been applied to verify facts, improving generalizability without the need for manually crafted rules (Chernyavskiy and Ilvovsky, 2019; Nie et al., 2019; Portelli et al., 2020; Zhong et al., 2020). These BERT-based models use the Claim and potential Evidence as inputs and determine the final labels. Recently, Pan et al. (2023) fine-tuned a small dataset to enhance the performance of BERT-based models, aiming to develop domain-specific models and improving generalizability. We transcend this work by employing semantic similarity in the embedding space between Claim and Evidence, along with structural similarity.

Using pre-trained models, graph neural networks

(GNNs) have been employed to enhance reasoning for fact verification (Zhong et al., 2020; Zhou et al., 2019). These models represent Evidence as nodes within a graph, enabling information exchange between nodes, thereby improving reasoning capabilities to determine the final label. Zhong et al. (2020) use Semantic Role Labeling (SRL), assigning semantic roles to both Claim and Evidence sentences for graph construction. Building on the concept of deeper reasoning for fact verification, we apply AMR to assess sentence similarities through the lens of sentence structure.

Large Language Models (LLMs) have been utilized for fact verification by augmenting verification sources. LLMs enable more realistic fact verification by considering the date of Claims and using only the information available prior to the Claim (Chen et al., 2024). LLMs generate Claim-focused summaries, which are then used as inputs for classifiers to determine the veracity of Claims (Zhao et al., 2024). Although LLMs have demonstrated improved performance in fact verification, they still rely on classifiers that operate based on the outputs of a *black box* model.

2.2 Explainable Representations on Fact Verification

Creating explainable justifications for fact verification predictions is an essential aspect of the task as it highlights the reasons behind a veracity prediction and presents it comprehensibly and faithfully. Several attempts have been made to create such explanations using varying techniques such as interpretable knowledge graph-based rules, attention weights, and natural-language explanations using extractive and abstractive summarization, etc.

Ahmadi et al. (2019) implement an interpretable veracity prediction pipeline using Knowledge Graphs (KG) and probabilistic answer set programming that handles the uncertainties in rules created based on KGs and facts mined from the web. The resulting explanations are not in natural language but still possess a degree of interpretability. Lu and Li (2020) implement a graph-based fact verification model with attention-based explanations that highlight evidential words and users when detecting fake news in tweets. Natural logic theorem proving (Krishna et al., 2022) produces structured explanations using an alignment-based method similar to AMREx, but it operates at the sentential level, whereas AMREx uses semantic representations to create alignments. AMREx focuses on relationships among textual entities through node mapping. Similarly, Vedula and Parthasarathy (2021) combine structural knowledge with text embeddings to generate natural language explanations, akin to AMREx. However, their approach introduces a black-box relationship between the prediction process and explanation generation.

Recent developments in language models have paved the way for natural-language explanation generations where both extractive and abstractive summarization are utilized for creating explanations. Atanasova et al. (2020a) train a joint model for explanation generation and veracity classification where the extractive explanations are created by selecting the most relevant ruling comments out of a collection of them for a given Claim while Kotonya and Toni (2020) further extends this technique to create abstractive summaries for health-related Claims. Even though Large Language Models (LLMs) possess impressive generation capabilities Kim et al. (2024) show that zero-shot prompting of LLMs returns erroneous explanations due to hallucinations and focuses on generating faithful explanations using a multi-agent refinement feedback system. To address these shortcomings of LLMs, AMREx uses a linguistic approach to create a mapping of AMR graphs that explains our model's veracity predictions. We also show the potential of the mapping to be used as a prompt to generate natural-language explanations.

2.3 Abstract Meaning Representation (AMR)

AMR is a rooted, directed, and acyclic semantic representation that captures the meaning of a text through concepts and the relations that connect them (Banarescu et al., 2013). It has been used for various NLP applications such as text summarization, argument similarity detection, aspect-based sentiment classification, and natural language inference (Dohare et al., 2017; Opitz et al., 2021; Ma et al., 2023; Opitz et al., 2023), due to its ability to capture key relationships among entities and generalize meaning regardless of syntax. In AMREx, we focus on measuring the similarity between two AMRs using the Smatch score (Cai and Knight, 2013), which is designed to identify structural similarities of AMRs, effectively comparing concept relations between pairs of texts.

3 Experiment

This section presents the details behind datasets used in our experiments, along with the experimental steps carried out to build AMREx model.

3.1 Datasets

We use two fact-checking datasets to test the effectiveness of our model in verifying the veracity of Claims, as described below. For both datasets, we assume the gold Evidence for each Claim has been collected and thus focus only on verifying the Claim's veracity.

3.1.1 FEVER dataset

The FEVER dataset (Thorne et al., 2018a) consists of more than 1.8k Claims generated by altering sentences from Wikipedia. These Claims are classified into three classes: `Supports` ("S"), `Refutes` ("R") and `NotEnoughInfo` ("N"). The dataset includes relevant Evidence from Wikipedia articles for Claims in the first two classes. Some Claims require multi-hop inference/reasoning to verify their veracity.

3.1.2 AVeriTeC dataset

AVeriTeC (Schlichtkrull et al., 2024) is a newly released dataset containing 4568 real-world Claims. This dataset addresses several issues associated with previous datasets, such as inclusion of Evidence published after the Claim and artificially generated Claims. The Claims fall into four categories: `Supported` ("S"), `Refuted` ("R"), `NotEnoughEvidence` ("N") and `ConflictingEvidence/Cherrypicking` ("C"), where `ConflictingEvidence/Cherrypicking` represents Claims that have both supporting and refuting Evidence. Unlike previous datasets, AVeriTeC employs a question-answering approach to build the reasoning process for fact verification, encouraging researchers to formulate questions that support Evidence extraction and to find their answers on the web.

3.2 AMREx Model

We present the design of the AMREx for verification of Claim veracity. The underlying model is an NLI model based on a combination of an AMR evaluation metric and cosine similarity on SBERT (Reimers and Gurevych, 2019) embeddings that predicts entailment for a single (Claim, Evidence) pair. These predictions are then aggregated per claim to predict the veracity. The last stage of the

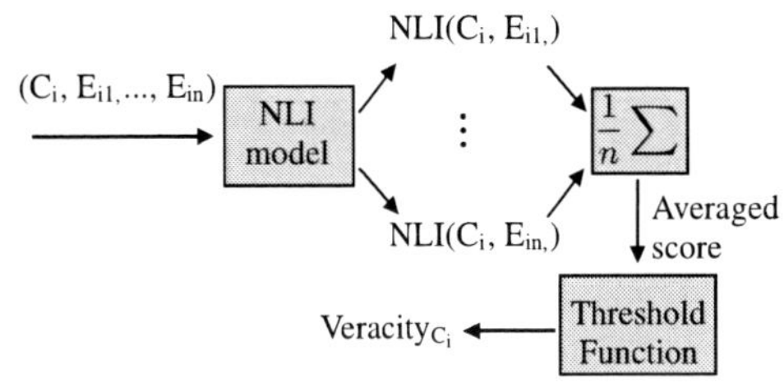

Figure 2: AMREx model: The model aggregates all the entailment predictions from the NLI model for a claim and returns the final veracity prediction

model is customized to suit the different dataset formats. (See Fig. 2 for overall AMREx pipeline).

3.2.1 NLI model

Although semantic entailment does not always correspond to a strict subsumption relationship between sentences, we adopt a simplifying assumption that entailment aligns with subsumption. Specifically, our NLI model is based on the hypothesis that if SentenceA (s_A) semantically entails SentenceB (s_B), then the meaning of s_B is contained inside that of s_A. This simplification allows our implementation to be built upon structured semantic concepts. Mapping this to AMR graph representations where g_A and g_B are the respective representations for s_A and s_B, we hypothesize that g_B is a subset of g_A. To assess how much of g_B's meaning is contained in g_A, we use the Smatch (Cai and Knight, 2013) precision score between g_A and g_B, combined with the cosine similarity of SBERT embeddings of s_A and s_B (as shown in Eq. 1) to calculate the entailment score ($f(s_A, s_B)$) between s_A and s_B. Note that the Smatch precision score is asymmetrical. So, s_A is considered the premise and s_B, the hypothesis. We then apply a threshold function (See Eq. 2) to the resulting score to classify s_A as either entailing (+1) or not entailing (-1) s_B, as shown in Eq. 3 (See Fig. 3).

$$f(s_A, s_B) = \lambda * Smatch_P(g_A, g_B) + (1-\lambda) * Cosine_{SBERT}(s_A, s_B) \quad (1)$$

$$th_1(f(s_A, s_B)) = \begin{cases} +1, & f(s_A, s_B) \geq 0.6 \\ -1, & f(s_A, s_B) < 0.6 \end{cases} \quad (2)$$

$$NLI(s_A, s_B) = th_1\Big(f(s_A, s_B)\Big) \quad (3)$$

However, as the two datasets use slightly different labeling schemes (FEVER uses a 3-way classifi-

Dataset	S	R	N	C	Total # sentences
FEVER	3281	3270	3284	-	9835
AVeriTec	649	1166	115	226	2156

Table 1: Label distribution of FEVER and AVeriTec datasets: Supports (S), Refutes (R), Not Enough Evidence (N), Conflicting Evidence (C).

cation format, while AVeriTeC uses a 4-way classification format) and a Claim may involve multiple pieces of Evidence in the entailment process, the fact verification approach needs to be customized for each dataset. This customization will be described in Sections 3.2.2 and 3.2.3. As observed in this implementation, minor variations in verdict labels may exist across different datasets, we believe these differences are not substantial, as all labels pertain to assessing the truth value of a claim. Therefore, the threshold function can be readily adjusted to accommodate new verdict labels.

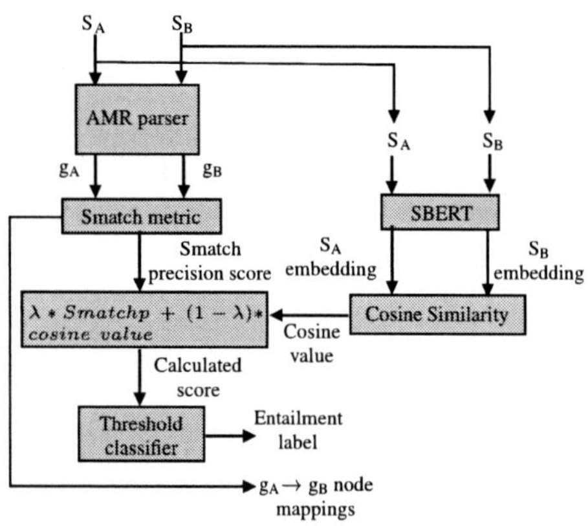

Figure 3: NLI model pipeline. S_A refers to SentenceA and S_B refers to SentneceB. g_A refers to AMR graphA from S_A and g_B refers to AMR graphB from S_B

3.2.2 Fact verification for FEVER

The FEVER dataset categorizes Claims and Evidence into three classes (`Supports`, `Refutes`, `NotEnoughInfo`. Each Claim may have one or more pieces of Evidence, while those labeled NEI lack any Evidence. To address the lack of Evidence for the NEI class, we use the modified FEVER dataset provided by Atanasova et al. (2020b), which includes Evidence for NEI class.

Given a pair (C_i, E_{ij}) where C_i is a Claim and E_{ij} is its jth Evidence, we use the NLI pipeline shown in Fig. 3 to compute the entailment between them. Here, C_i is treated as the hypothesis and E_{ij} as the premise. If E_{ij} entails C_i, it returns +1. If not, it returns -1, as outlined in Eq. 3. AMREx then averages the results across all Evidence for C_i from the NLI model, to determine the overall entailment (e), and classify that into one of the three classes using a threshold classifier to return the veracity of C_i, as shown in Eq. 4 and 5. When deciding the thresholds for the labels, "Supports" and "Refutes" are given the positive and negative extremes, respectively, whereas "Not enough Info" is assigned the middle range. This is based on the assumption that evidence with insufficient information will exhibit lower structural and textual similarity scores without extreme contradictions. The exact threshold values were determined experimentally.

$$th_{2_{FV}}(e) = \begin{cases} \text{"S"}, & e \geq 0.1 \\ \text{"N"}, & -0.1 < e < 0.1 \\ \text{"R"}, & e \leq -0.1 \end{cases} \quad (4)$$

$$Veracity_{C_i} = th_{2_{FV}}\Big(\frac{1}{n}\sum_{j=1}^{n} NLI(C_i, E_{ij})\Big) \quad (5)$$

3.2.3 Fact verification for AVeriTeC

The AVeriTeC dataset requires a Claim extraction system to first create questions to aid in finding Evidence related to a Claim, and then locate relevant documents and sentences to answer those questions, which are considered Evidence for the Claim. Since we assume the correct questions and answers are already provided for each Claim, we calculate the overall entailment between a Claim and Evidence using Eq. 5. However, we apply a customized threshold function for the AVeriTec dataset as it includes four veracity labels (Eq. 6). Additionally, the dataset features three types of Evidence: Boolean, Abstractive, and Extractive. Since Boolean Evidence (Yes/No answers) is incompatible with both AMRs and our entailment pipeline, we focus on abstractive and extractive Evidence in the experiment to fully measure our pipeline's ability to represent sentential Evidence. Table 1 shows the label distribution of both datasets.

$$th_{2_{AV}}(e) = \begin{cases} \text{"S"}, & e \geq 0.5 \\ \text{"C"}, & 0.1 < e < 0.5 \\ \text{"N"}, & -0.1 \leq e \leq 0.1 \\ \text{"C"}, & -0.5 < e < -0.1 \\ \text{"R"}, & e \leq -0.5 \end{cases} \quad (6)$$

Model	lambda	S	R	N	C	Macro F1	Acc.
FEVER baseline	_	_	_	_	_	_	0.88
$AMREx_{FEVER_{acc,f1}}$	0	0.52	0.39	0.41	_	0.44	0.44
AVeriTec baseline	_	0.48	0.74	0.59	0.15	0.49	0.49
$AMREx_{AVeriTec_{acc}}$	0.9	0.10	0.67	0.04	0.02	0.21	**0.50**
$AMREx_{AVeriTec_{f1}}$	0	0.25	0.61	0.06	0.11	0.26	0.43

Table 2: Accuracy and Macro F1 scores of veracity prediction for each veracity label. Only accuracy is reported in FEVER baseline.

4 Results and Analyses

We experiment with λ values in the [0,1] range for Eq. 1 on both FEVER and AVeriTec datasets to find the best combination of AMR graph intersection and textual similarity measurement. The results for both datasets are in Table 2. We selected the best-performing models based on both the highest accuracy and macro F1 score, leading to two AMREx implementations for each dataset.

For the FEVER dataset, the best accuracy and macro F1 score are achieved when $\lambda = 0$, suggesting that the Smatch precision score has minimal impact on predicting the veracity of (Claim, Evidence) pairs. The label-wise performance shows that $AMREx_{FEVERacc,f1}$ is more effective at identifying supporting (Claim, Evidence) pairs but struggles with refuting instances.

However, the AVeriTec dataset exhibits different behavior, with $\lambda = 0.9$ yielding the best accuracy and $\lambda = 0$ producing the best macro F1 score. $AMREx_{AVeriTec_{acc}}$ also manages to surpass the AVeriTec accuracy baseline. $AMREx_{AVeriTec_{f1}}$ performs comparably to the AVeriTec baseline in recognizing refutable (Claim, Evidence) pairs and those with conflicting evidence. However, with greater emphasis on the Smatch precision score when $\lambda = 0.9$, $AMREx_{AVeriTec_{f1}}$ improves in identifying refutable (Claim, Evidence) pairs, albeit at the cost of performance on other label instances.

Through an error analysis, we identify several cases where AMREx fails to accurately predict the veracity and we explore their potential causes. Consider the following supporting (Claim, Evidence) pair from the FEVER dataset, Claim: *"Wish Upon was released in the 21st century."*, Evidence: *"It is set to be released in theaters on July 14, 2017, by Broad Green Pictures and Orion Pictures"* (See Fig. 4 for corresponding AMRs in Penman notation (Goodman, 2020)). AMREx returns the following mapping for this instance with a Smatch precision score of 0.53 and a textual similarity score of 0.38.

```
a0(release-01) -> b2(release-01)
a1(music) -> b1(it)
a2(name) -> b10(name)
a3(Wish) -> b11(Orion)
a4(Upon) -> b12(Pictures)
a5(date-entity) -> b14(date-entity)
```

```
AMR Corresponding to the Claim:
(a0/release-01
   :ARG1 (a1/music
      :name (a2/name
         :op1 (a3/Wish)
         :op2 (a4/Upon)))
   :time (a5/date-entity
      :century 21))

AMR Corresponding to the Evidence:
(b0/set-08
   :ARG1 (b1/it)
   :ARG2 (b2/release-01
      :ARG0 (b3/and
         :op1 (b4/company
            :name (b5/name
               :op1 (b6/Broad)
               :op2 (b7/Green)
               :op3 (b8/Pictures)))
         :op2 (b9/company
            :name (b10/name
               :op1 (b11/Orion)
               :op2 (b12/Pictures))))
      :ARG1 i
      :location (b13/theater)
      :time (b14/date-entity
         :day 14
         :month 7
         :year 2017)))
```

Figure 4: Abstract Meaning Representations (AMRs) for Claim: "Wish Upon was released in the 21st century." and Evidence: "It is set to be released in theaters on July 14, 2017, by Broad Green Pictures and Orion Pictures"

The AMR node mapping correctly identifies that both texts are related to a release event (with the a0 node mapping to the b2 node), connects "music" in Claim AMR to "it" in Evidence AMR, and recognizes that both texts mention a date-entity.

However, it fails to map "the 21st-century" in the Claim with the date in the Evidence AMR. The Smatch precision score indicates a higher level of meaning entailment compared to the textual similarity score, but it is not high enough to meet the entailment threshold with any λ value, leading AMREx to incorrectly predict "Refutes". This reveals a limitation of the Smatch algorithm in inferring that the year 2017 falls within the 21st century, as it is a concept mapping algorithm. We note that SBERT contextual embeddings also fail to capture this detail and give an even lower similarity assessment.

Another example reveals that high structural similarity between AMRs, despite a few factual differences, can result in incorrect meaning containment assessments. Consider the Claim: *"Marnie is a romantic film."* and the Evidence: *"Marnie is a 1964 American psychological thriller film directed by Alfred Hitchcock."* with the gold veracity label "Refutes" (See Fig. 5 for AMRs). The resulting AMR node mappings are as follows:

```
a0(film) -> b0(film)
a1(romantic-03) -> b1(direct-01)
a2(name) -> b11(name)
a3(Marnie) -> b12(Marnie)
```

```
AMR Corresponding to the Claim:
(a0/film
    :ARG0-of (a1/romantic-03)
    :name (a2/name
        :op1 (a3/Marnie)))

AMR Corresponding to the Evidence:
(b0/film
    :ARG1-of (b1/direct-01
        :ARG0 (b2/person
            :name (b3/name
                :op1 (b4/Alfred)
                :op2 (b5/Hitchcock))))
    :mod (b6/thriller
        :mod (b7/psychological))
    :mod (b8/country
        :name (b9/name
            :op1 (b10/America)))
    :name (b11/name
        :op1 (b12/Marnie))
    :time (b13/date-entity
        :year 1964))
```

Figure 5: Abstract Meaning Representations (AMRs) for Claim: "Marnie is a romantic film." and Evidence: "Marnie is a 1964 American psychological thriller film directed by Alfred Hitchcock."

In the Claim AMR, "Marnie" being a "romantic film" is represented by the `romantic-03` node, while in the Evidence, it being a "Psychological thriller" is represented by a modifier to the root `film`. Due to this structural discrepancy, the Smatch algorithm fails to distinguish between the two genres and instead maps `romantic-03` to `direct-01` with a similar structure that still correctly creates a mismatch, but for the wrong reason. However, most concepts in the Claim AMR match those in the Evidence AMR, leading to a high Smatch precision score of 0.75. The textual similarity score also returns a 0.70. Hence, any λ combination of the two scores surpasses the entailment threshold, yielding a "Supports" prediction.

These examples reveal that the AMR and textual similarity-based approach of AMREx struggles with instances involving implied meaning or those with high structural similarity but factual differences, indicating areas that need improvement.

4.1 Explainability of the Model

The model's explainability stems from two key aspects. First, the deterministic nature of the model's calculations allows us to trace how a particular prediction was calculated. This provides a comprehensive explanation of the entire system pipeline and tracks the process at each step. Second, the visual mapping between the AMRs of Claims and Evidence, as shown in Fig. 1, helps clarify why the model returns a particular prediction for a (Claim, Evidence) pair in terms of structural similarity. This explanation is partial and post hoc, relying only on AMR node mappings for generation. However, it is integrated into the system, as AMR representations influence both the veracity prediction and explanation generation. An example illustrating AMREx's explanations is discussed below.

Consider Claim *"Rabies is a ride at Six Parks."* and the Evidence, *"Rabies is a viral disease that causes inflammation of the brain in humans and other mammals."* The corresponding AMRs for Claim and Evidence are shown in Fig. 6. When these two AMRs are processed through the Smatch algorithm, the resulting AMR node mapping is as follows:

```
a0(ride-01) -> b0(disease)
a1(disease) -> b8(disease)
a2(name) -> b9(name)
a3(Rabies) -> b10(Rabies)
a4(amusement-park) -> b2(inflame-01)
a5(name) -> b4(and)
a6(Parks) -> b6(mammal)
```

As the mapping reveals, the only shared meaning

```
AMR Corresponding to the Claim:
(a0/ride-01
   :ARG1 (a1/disease
      :name (a2/name
         :op1 (a3/Rabies)))
   :location (a4/amusement-park
      :name (a5/name
         :op1 6
         :op2 (a6/Parks))))

AMR Corresponding to the Evidence:
(b0/disease
   :ARG0-of (b1/cause-01
      :ARG1 (b2/inflame-01
         :ARG1 (b3/brain)
         :part-of (b4/and
            :op1 (b5/human)
            :op2 (b6/mammal
               :mod (b7/other)))))
   :domain (b8/disease
      :name (b9/name
         :op1 (b10/Rabies)))
   :mod (b11/virus))
```

Figure 6: Abstract Meaning Representations (AMRs) for Claim: "Rabies is a ride at Six Parks." and Evidence: "Rabies is a viral disease that causes inflammation of the brain in humans and other mammals."

between these two AMRs is that both sentences are related to a disease called Rabies (with the a1-a3 nodes mapping to the b8-b10 nodes). This leads to a low Smatch precision score of 0.46 and a textual similarity score of 0.59. When combined with any λ value, this results in a low entailment value, causing the threshold function to predict non-entailment (-1). Hence, the second threshold function will return "Refutes" as the veracity of this (Claim, Evidence) pair.

This process, together with the AMR node mapping, demonstrates the model's overall logic and final prediction. We further demonstrate the effectiveness of the AMR node mapping in generating natural-language explanations by using it to prompt ChatGPT to generate justifications. An excerpt of the generated explanation for the (Claim, Evidence) pair above is shown in Fig. 7. Hence, we argue that AMREx's explainable output can serve as a guide for generating natural-language explanations for veracity detection, helping to reduce hallucinations in LLM models.

AMR Graph Mapping Analysis:

...

Key Mappings:

a0(ride-01)-b0(disease): The concept "ride" in the claim is mapped to "disease" in the evidence, which indicates a mismatch. The claim is about a ride, whereas the evidence is about a disease.

a1(disease)-b8(disease): Both the claim and the evidence refer to "Rabies" as a disease. However, in the claim, it's tied to a "ride" rather than a health context.

a2(name)-b9(name): The name "Rabies" is consistently mapped in both the claim and the evidence.

a3(Rabies)-b10(Rabies): The specific instance "Rabies" is correctly identified in both the claim and the evidence.

a4(amusement-park)-b2(inflame-01):The location "amusement park" in the claim is mapped to "inflammation" in the evidence, which again indicates a significant mismatch in context.

a5(name)-b4(and),a6(Parks)-b6(mammal): The reference to "Six Parks" in the claim is incorrectly mapped to a reference to "mammals" in the evidence.

Explanation:

Mismatch in Core Concepts: The claim describes "Rabies" as a "ride" at an "amusement park," whereas the evidence discusses "Rabies" as a "viral disease." The AMR mappings reveal that the central concepts of "ride" and "amusement park" in the claim do not align with the "disease" and "medical context" in the evidence.

...

Classification: Given that the evidence contradicts the central concept of the claim by presenting a different context (medical vs. amusement), this pair should be classified as REFUTES. The evidence does not support the claim that "Rabies is a ride at Six Parks" and instead presents a fact that contradicts this claim.

Figure 7: Natural Language explanation generated by ChatGPT based on the AMREx's AMR node mapping output.

5 Conclusion

We implement AMREx, an Abstract Meaning Representation-based veracity prediction and explanation system for fact verification, and show its effectiveness in producing explainable justifications using two fact verification datasets. Although its performance is lower compared to the baselines, its partially explainable output could still be used as a diagnostic tool to perform error analyses on the veracity prediction system to understand the areas to improve. We further demonstrate that AMREx output can guide LLMs to generate natural-language explanations using the AMR mappings.

Limitations

In its current form, AMREx performs best across all classes when its score is less influenced by the structural similarity assessment. This makes the AMR node mappings less useful as explanations, despite achieving the highest performance. Therefore, further exploration is needed to adjust the structural similarity assessment to better suit the veracity detection task. Since AMREx relies heavily on AMRs, it is crucial to use a high-performing AMR parser when converting the sentences to AMRs. Therefore, the overall performance of the system depends on the accuracy of the AMR parser. Furthermore, the AMR mapping algorithm is more effective when applied to text instances with a high degree of structural similarity, which may not always be the case with real-world data. The AMR node mappings provide a partial, post hoc explanation of the system, while the interpretability of the entire system fully encompasses the prediction process. An evaluation of the explainable aspect of AMREx model in comparison to current structural explainable fact verification systems is also necessary. We expect to address these limitations in future modifications to the system.

Ethical Statement

We utilize ChatGPT responses as a demonstration of the effectiveness of AMREx in creating natural-language explanations for veracity predictions. We acknowledge that there is a possibility for ChatGPT to generate hallucinated, or toxic content. However, one of the key objectives of our study is to develop an explainable system whose output can guide the reduction of hallucinations in LLM-generated outputs, including ChatGPT. We believe this approach contributes to the generation of content that is both faithful and safe. Additionally, we manually check the ChatGPT-generated content in this study for hallucinated or toxic content and can confirm that the presented examples are free of such issues.

Acknowledgement

This material is based upon work supported, in part, by the Defense Advanced Research Projects Agency (DARPA) under Contract No. HR001121C0186. Any opinions, findings and conclusions or recommendations expressed in this material are those of the authors and do not necessarily reflect the views of the Defense Advanced Research Projects Agency (DARPA).

References

Naser Ahmadi, Joohyung Lee, Paolo Papotti, and Mohammed Saeed. 2019. Explainable fact checking with probabilistic answer set programming. In *Conference on Truth and Trust Online*.

Pepa Atanasova, Jakob Grue Simonsen, Christina Lioma, and Isabelle Augenstein. 2020a. Generating fact checking explanations. In *Proceedings of the 58th Annual Meeting of the Association for Computational Linguistics*, pages 7352–7364. Association for Computational Linguistics.

Pepa Atanasova, Dustin Wright, and Isabelle Augenstein. 2020b. Generating label cohesive and well-formed adversarial claims. In *Proceedings of the 2020 Conference on Empirical Methods in Natural Language Processing (EMNLP)*, pages 3168–3177. Association for Computational Linguistics.

Laura Banarescu, Claire Bonial, Shu Cai, Madalina Georgescu, Kira Griffitt, Ulf Hermjakob, Kevin Knight, Philipp Koehn, Martha Palmer, and Nathan Schneider. 2013. Abstract Meaning Representation for sembanking. In *Proceedings of the 7th Linguistic Annotation Workshop and Interoperability with Discourse*, pages 178–186. Association for Computational Linguistics.

Samuel R. Bowman, Gabor Angeli, Christopher Potts, and Christopher D. Manning. 2015. A large annotated corpus for learning natural language inference. In *Proceedings of the 2015 Conference on Empirical Methods in Natural Language Processing*, pages 632–642. Association for Computational Linguistics.

Shu Cai and Kevin Knight. 2013. Smatch: an evaluation metric for semantic feature structures. In *Proceedings of the 51st Annual Meeting of the Association for Computational Linguistics (Volume 2: Short Papers)*, pages 748–752. Association for Computational Linguistics.

Jifan Chen, Grace Kim, Aniruddh Sriram, Greg Durrett, and Eunsol Choi. 2024. Complex claim verification with evidence retrieved in the wild. In *Proceedings of the 2024 Conference of the North American Chapter of the Association for Computational Linguistics: Human Language Technologies (Volume 1: Long Papers)*, pages 3569–3587. Association for Computational Linguistics.

Anton Chernyavskiy and Dmitry Ilvovsky. 2019. Extract and aggregate: A novel domain-independent approach to factual data verification. In *Proceedings of the Second Workshop on Fact Extraction and VERification (FEVER)*, pages 69–78. Association for Computational Linguistics.

Shibhansh Dohare, Harish Karnick, and Vivek Gupta. 2017. Text summarization using abstract meaning representation. *arXiv preprint arXiv:1706.01678*.

Michael Wayne Goodman. 2020. Penman: An open-source library and tool for AMR graphs. In *Proceedings of the 58th Annual Meeting of the Association for Computational Linguistics: System Demonstrations*, pages 312–319. Association for Computational Linguistics.

Suchin Gururangan, Swabha Swayamdipta, Omer Levy, Roy Schwartz, Samuel Bowman, and Noah A. Smith. 2018. Annotation artifacts in natural language inference data. In *Proceedings of the 2018 Conference of* the North American Chapter of the Association for Computational Linguistics: Human Language Technologies, Volume 2 (Short Papers), pages 107–112. Association for Computational Linguistics.

Kyungha Kim, Sangyun Lee, Kung-Hsiang Huang, Hou Pong Chan, Manling Li, and Heng Ji. 2024. Can llms produce faithful explanations for fact-checking? towards faithful explainable fact-checking via multi-agent debate. *arXiv preprint arXiv:2402.07401*.

Neema Kotonya and Francesca Toni. 2020. Explainable automated fact-checking for public health claims. In *Proceedings of the 2020 Conference on Empirical Methods in Natural Language Processing (EMNLP)*, pages 7740–7754. Association for Computational Linguistics.

Amrith Krishna, Sebastian Riedel, and Andreas Vlachos. 2022. ProoFVer: Natural logic theorem proving for fact verification. *Transactions of the Association for Computational Linguistics*, 10:1013–1030.

Yi-Ju Lu and Cheng-Te Li. 2020. GCAN: Graph-aware co-attention networks for explainable fake news detection on social media. In *Proceedings of the 58th Annual Meeting of the Association for Computational Linguistics*, pages 505–514. Association for Computational Linguistics.

Fukun Ma, Xuming Hu, Aiwei Liu, Yawen Yang, Shuang Li, Philip S. Yu, and Lijie Wen. 2023. AMR-based network for aspect-based sentiment analysis. In *Proceedings of the 61st Annual Meeting of the Association for Computational Linguistics (Volume 1: Long Papers)*, pages 322–337. Association for Computational Linguistics.

Tom McCoy, Ellie Pavlick, and Tal Linzen. 2019. Right for the wrong reasons: Diagnosing syntactic heuristics in natural language inference. In *Proceedings of the 57th Annual Meeting of the Association for Computational Linguistics*, pages 3428–3448. Association for Computational Linguistics.

Yixin Nie, Songhe Wang, and Mohit Bansal. 2019. Revealing the importance of semantic retrieval for machine reading at scale. In *Proceedings of the 2019 Conference on Empirical Methods in Natural Language Processing*. Association for Computational Linguistics.

Juri Opitz, Philipp Heinisch, Philipp Wiesenbach, Philipp Cimiano, and Anette Frank. 2021. Explainable unsupervised argument similarity rating with Abstract Meaning Representation and conclusion generation. In *Proceedings of the 8th Workshop on Argument Mining*, pages 24–35. Association for Computational Linguistics.

Juri Opitz, Shira Wein, Julius Steen, Anette Frank, and Nathan Schneider. 2023. AMR4NLI: Interpretable and robust NLI measures from semantic graphs. In *Proceedings of the 15th International Conference on Computational Semantics*, pages 275–283. Association for Computational Linguistics.

Liangming Pan, Yunxiang Zhang, and Min-Yen Kan. 2023. Investigating zero- and few-shot generalization in fact verification. In *Proceedings of the 13th International Joint Conference on Natural Language Processing and the 3rd Conference of the Asia-Pacific Chapter of the Association for Computational Linguistics (Volume 1: Long Papers)*, pages 511–524. Association for Computational Linguistics.

Beatrice Portelli, Jason Zhao, Tal Schuster, Giuseppe Serra, and Enrico Santus. 2020. Distilling the evidence to augment fact verification models. In *Proceedings of the Third Workshop on Fact Extraction and VERification (FEVER)*, pages 47–51. Association for Computational Linguistics.

Nils Reimers and Iryna Gurevych. 2019. Sentence-BERT: Sentence embeddings using Siamese BERT-networks. In *Proceedings of the 2019 Conference on Empirical Methods in Natural Language Processing and the 9th International Joint Conference on Natural Language Processing (EMNLP-IJCNLP)*, pages 3982–3992. Association for Computational Linguistics.

Michael Schlichtkrull, Zhijiang Guo, and Andreas Vlachos. 2024. Averitec: A dataset for real-world claim verification with evidence from the web. *Advances in Neural Information Processing Systems*, 36.

Michael Sejr Schlichtkrull, Zhijiang Guo, and Andreas Vlachos. 2023. Averitec: A dataset for real-world claim verification with evidence from the web. In *Thirty-seventh Conference on Neural Information Processing Systems Datasets and Benchmarks Track*.

James Thorne, Andreas Vlachos, Christos Christodoulopoulos, and Arpit Mittal. 2018a. FEVER: a large-scale dataset for fact extraction and VERification. In *Proceedings of the 2018 Conference of the North American Chapter of the Association for Computational Linguistics: Human Language Technologies, Volume 1 (Long Papers)*, pages 809–819. Association for Computational Linguistics.

James Thorne, Andreas Vlachos, Oana Cocarascu, Christos Christodoulopoulos, and Arpit Mittal. 2018b. The fact extraction and VERification (FEVER) shared task. In *Proceedings of the First Workshop on Fact Extraction and VERification (FEVER)*, pages 1–9. Association for Computational Linguistics.

James Thorne, Andreas Vlachos, Oana Cocarascu, Christos Christodoulopoulos, and Arpit Mittal. 2019. The FEVER2.0 shared task. In *Proceedings of the Second Workshop on Fact Extraction and VERification (FEVER)*, pages 1–6. Association for Computational Linguistics.

Nikhita Vedula and Srinivasan Parthasarathy. 2021. Face-keg: Fact checking explained using knowledge graphs. In *Proceedings of the 14th ACM International Conference on Web Search and Data Mining*,

WSDM '21, page 526–534, New York, NY, USA. Association for Computing Machinery.

Andreas Vlachos and Sebastian Riedel. 2014. Fact checking: Task definition and dataset construction. In *Proceedings of the ACL 2014 Workshop on Language Technologies and Computational Social Science*, pages 18–22. Association for Computational Linguistics.

Xia Zeng and Arkaitz Zubiaga. 2024. MAPLE: Micro analysis of pairwise language evolution for few-shot claim verification. In *Findings of the Association for Computational Linguistics: EACL 2024*, pages 1177–1196. Association for Computational Linguistics.

Xiaoyan Zhao, Lingzhi Wang, Zhanghao Wang, Hong Cheng, Rui Zhang, and Kam-Fai Wong. 2024. PACAR: Automated fact-checking with planning and customized action reasoning using large language models. In *Proceedings of the 2024 Joint International Conference on Computational Linguistics, Language Resources and Evaluation (LREC-COLING 2024)*, pages 12564–12573. ELRA and ICCL.

Wanjun Zhong, Jingjing Xu, Duyu Tang, Zenan Xu, Nan Duan, Ming Zhou, Jiahai Wang, and Jian Yin. 2020. Reasoning over semantic-level graph for fact checking. In *Proceedings of the 58th Annual Meeting of the Association for Computational Linguistics*, pages 6170–6180. Association for Computational Linguistics.

Jie Zhou, Xu Han, Cheng Yang, Zhiyuan Liu, Lifeng Wang, Changcheng Li, and Maosong Sun. 2019. GEAR: Graph-based evidence aggregating and reasoning for fact verification. In *Proceedings of the 57th Annual Meeting of the Association for Computational Linguistics*, pages 892–901. Association for Computational Linguistics.

Claim Check-Worthiness Detection: How Well do LLMs Grasp Annotation Guidelines?

Laura Majer and **Jan Šnajder**
Text Analysis and Knowledge Engineering Lab
University of Zagreb, Faculty of Electrical Engineering and Computing
{laura.majer, jan.snajder}@fer.hr

Abstract

The rising threat of disinformation underscores the need to fully or partially automate the fact-checking process. Identifying text segments requiring fact-checking is known as *claim detection* (CD) and *claim check-worthiness detection* (CW), the latter incorporating complex domain-specific criteria of worthiness and often framed as a ranking task. Zero- and few-shot LLM prompting is an attractive option for both tasks, as it bypasses the need for labeled datasets and allows verbalized claim and worthiness criteria to be directly used for prompting. We evaluate the LLMs' predictive accuracy on five CD/CW datasets from diverse domains, using corresponding annotation guidelines in prompts. We examine two key aspects: (1) how to best distill factuality and worthiness criteria into a prompt, and (2) how much context to provide for each claim. To this end, we experiment with different levels of prompt verbosity and varying amounts of contextual information given to the model. We additionally evaluate the top-performing models with ranking metrics, resembling prioritization done by fact-checkers. Our results show that optimal prompt verbosity varies, meta-data alone adds more performance boost than co-text, and confidence scores can be directly used to produce reliable check-worthiness rankings.

1 Introduction

The global spread of information, coupled with mis- and disinformation, is increasing the demand for fact-checking (News, 2022; Idrizi and Hanafin, 2023), highlighting the need for automation. However, complete automation may not be ideal; for instance, PolitiFact, which used ChatGPT to verify previously fact-checked claims, faced issues like inconsistency, knowledge limitations, and misleading confidence (Abels, 2023). Nevertheless, they see potential in language models for assisting fact-checkers, particularly in identifying claims worth verifying. Similarly, FullFact has highlighted the lack of effective claim selection tools as a major workflow challenge (FullFact, 2020).

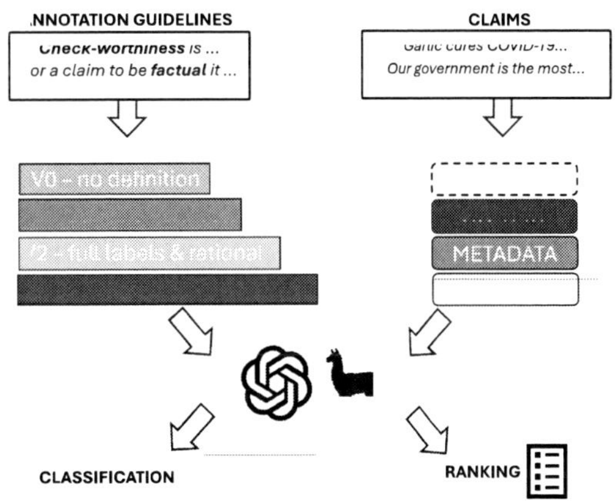

Figure 1: Using annotation guidelines, we craft zero- and few-shot LLM prompts for claim and claim check-worthiness detection, varying the level of prompt verbosity and the amount of provided context. We evaluate the LLMs using classification and ranking metrics.

To warrant fact-checking, a claim must be both *factual* (i.e., related to purported facts) and *check-worthy* (i.e., of interest to society). The NLP tasks of identifying factual and check-worthy claims are known as *claim detection* (CD) and *claim check-worthiness detection* (CW), respectively. The tasks make up the first component of the automatic fact-checking pipeline. While both are typically defined as classification tasks, CW can also be framed as a ranking task, mimicking the prioritization process employed by fact-checking organizations.

Both CD and CW are challenging for several reasons. Firstly, the underlying concepts of factual claims and check-worthiness resist straightforward definitions. To grasp factuality, Konstantinovskiy et al. (2021) presented a thorough categorization of factual claims, while Ni et al. (2024) provided

Proceedings of the Seventh Fact Extraction and VERification Workshop (FEVER), pages 245–263
November 15, 2024 ©2024 Association for Computational Linguistics

a definition distinguishing opinions. Regardless of these variations, *factual* could be deemed universal and self-explanatory, unlike *check-worthiness*, a term frequently used in previous research. Defining check-worthiness is made more challenging by its subjective, context-dependent nature and temporal variability. Assessing it usually requires choosing more specific criteria, such as relevance to the general public (Hassan et al., 2017a) or policymakers, potential harm (Nakov et al., 2022), or alignment with a particular topic (Stammbach et al., 2023; Gangi Reddy et al., 2022)). Another challenge is identifying the situational context (including previous discourse and speaker information) required to determine claim factuality and check-worthiness. For example, in CW annotation campaigns (Hassan et al., 2017a; Gangi Reddy et al., 2022), annotators are typically presented with surrounding sentences to aid their assessment.

The CD and CW tasks have been approached using both traditional supervised machine learning and fine-tuning pre-trained language models, both of which depend on labeled data. However, obtaining such datasets can be challenging as they need to align with specific languages, domains, and genres and meet desired factuality and worthiness criteria. Moreover, dataset annotation is costly and requires redoing if criteria change. LLMs present a viable alternative to supervised methods owing to their strong zero- and few-shot performance (Kojima et al., 2022; Brown et al., 2020). Over time, fact-checking organizations have refined principles for claim prioritization, and zero- and few-shot prompting offers a seamless way to transfer this knowledge to the model. Thus, an effective strategy might entail zero- and few-shot prompting with check-worthiness criteria from annotation guidelines. The challenge, however, is that LLMs often exhibit sensitivity to variations in prompts (Mizrahi et al., 2024) and unreliability (Si et al., 2023).

In this paper, we study the predictive and calibration accuracy of zero- and few-shot LLM prompting for CD and CW. We experiment with five datasets, each with a different factuality or worthiness criterion outlined in the accompanying annotation guidelines. We investigate two key aspects: (1) how to best distill factuality and worthiness criteria from the annotation guidelines into the prompt and (2) what amount of context to provide for each claim. For (1), we experiment with varying the level of prompt verbosity, starting from brief zero-shot prompts to more detailed few-shot prompts that include examples. For (2), we expand the prompt with co-text and other components of the claim's situational context. Furthermore, inspired by the fact-checker's prioritization process, we consider CW as a ranking task, using LLM confidence scores as a proxy for determining priority. Figure 1 depicts the workflow of our experiments. We show that prompting with worthiness criteria adopted from annotation guidelines can yield accuracy and ranking scores comparable to or surpassing existing CD/CW methods. Although optimal prompt verbosity varies across datasets, certain in-domain trends can be observed across models. We also find that the impact of adding context is greater for lower verbosity levels, while meta-data is more beneficial than co-text. Finally, we show that confidence scores can be directly used to produce reliable check-worthiness rankings.

Our contributions include analyzing LLM performance in terms of (1) prompt detail, (2) provided context, and (3) variations across domains and worthiness criteria.

2 Related Work

Developing a fully automated fact-checking system is appealing for both its applicability and the challenge it presents (Hassan et al., 2017c; Li et al., 2023). However, Glockner et al. (2022) question the purpose of such a system, pointing to its reliance on counter-evidence that may not be available for newly coined disinformation. This motivates a shift toward human-in-the-loop approaches and automating parts of the fact-checking pipeline.

The CD and CW tasks constitute the first part of the fact-checking pipeline and are meant to select parts of the input for which fact-checking is possible (CD) or deemed necessary (CW). Typically framed as classification tasks, the CD and CW tasks are handled using traditional supervised machine learning (Hassan et al., 2017b; Wright and Augenstein, 2020; Hassan et al., 2017a; Gencheva et al., 2017) or fine-tuning pre-trained language models (Stammbach et al., 2023; Sheikhi et al., 2023). Methods of solving include rich sentence and context-level features (Gencheva et al., 2017), speaker, object, and claim span identification (Gangi Reddy et al., 2022), or incorporating domain-specific knowledge by combining ontology and sentence embeddings (Hüsünbeyi and Scheffler, 2024). CW can also be framed as a ranking task (Jaradat et al., 2018; Gencheva et al.,

2017), mimicking the prioritization of claims by fact-checking organizations.

Recently, the use of LLMs for CD and CW is starting to take on. Sawinski et al. (2023) and Hyben et al. (2023) compare the performance of fine-tuned language models such as BERT with LLMs using zero- and few-shot learning as well as fine-tuning. Although zero- and few-shot approaches for LLMs underperform, the authors note their reliance on internal definitions of worthiness and limited prompt testing. As part of the fully automated fact-checking system relying only on LLMs, Li et al. (2023) implement a CD module using a verbose few-shot prompt, yet they do not report performance metrics. Finally, Ni et al. (2024) tackle CD by proposing a three-step prompting approach to examine model consistency. However, neither Li et al. (2023) nor Ni et al. (2024) address the CW task. To our knowledge, there is no work on CW focused on describing specific worthiness criteria using verbose prompts.

3 Datasets

Our experiments utilize five datasets in English covering diverse topics and genres. Examples from each dataset are presented in Table 1. We next describe each dataset in more detail, including the CD and CW criteria used.

ClaimBuster (CB) (Hassan et al., 2017a) is a widely used dataset of claims from USA presidential debates, featuring ternary labels (*non-factual, unimportant factual, check-worthy factual*) that distinguish between check-worthy and unimportant factual claims. This setup addresses both the CD and CW tasks. Claims are deemed check-worthy if the general public would be interested in their veracity. However, no specific definition of factuality is provided – unimportant factual claims are defined as those lacking check-worthiness.

CLEF CheckThat!Lab 2022 (CLEF) (Alam et al., 2021) contains tweets about COVID-19, with two parts: a set of tweets with claims and a subset with check-worthy claims, addressing both CD and CW tasks. Check-worthiness is defined as the need for professional fact-checking, excluding jokes, trivial claims, or those deemed uninteresting. Factual claims are defined as sentences that assert something is true and can be verified using factual information, such as statistical data, specific examples, or personal testimony.

EnvironmentalClaims (ENV) (Stammbach et al., 2023) is compiled from environmental articles and reports. The dataset focuses on check-worthy environmental claims related to green-washing in marketing strategies. The authors defined specific criteria for an environmental claim that extend beyond the topic itself (e.g., highlighting the positive environmental impact of a product, not being too technical). The annotators were instructed to label only the explicit claims, discouraging the selection of claims with inter-sentence coreferences.

NewsClaims (NEWS) (Gangi Reddy et al., 2022) comprises sentences from news articles on COVID-19, with metadata available for positives (speaker, object, claim span). The annotators were asked to judge whether a claim falls into one of the four topic-specific categories, which essentially formed the worthiness criteria, even though check-worthiness was not explicitly mentioned in the guidelines. The dataset includes both check-worthy and non-check-worthy claims with inter-sentence coreferences (e.g., *That's also false*), which typically require inspecting the surrounding context to determine their check-worthiness (we estimate this applies to about 10% of claims in the test set).

PoliClaim (POLI) (Ni et al., 2024) covers the same topic as ClaimBuster (politics, speeches of governors) but labels only verifiable claims, leaving out check-worthiness. The authors provided detailed guidelines on verifiable claims, emphasizing the need for specificity and differentiation from opinions lacking factual basis. To handle ambiguous cases, they employed a ternary (*Yes*, *No*, *Maybe*) annotation scheme. *Maybe* indicates that a claim may contain factual information but does not fully meet all criteria. For claims labeled as *Maybe*, annotators answered a follow-up Yes-No question to determine whether the claim leans toward factual information or subjective opinion. As with NEWS, inter-sentence coreference was considered; since the claims are extracted from political speeches, many of them include personal pronouns (*I*, *we*), which necessitates coreference resolution to identify the claimant or subject.

We use these five datasets because they provide detailed annotation guidelines and cover various topics, genres, and worthiness criteria. Table 2 summarizes their characteristics (see Appendix A for details). The CB and CLEF datasets address both

Dataset	Label	Example
CB	✗	*I would do the opposite in every respect.*
	O	*I have met with the heads of government bilaterally as well as multilaterally.*
	✓	*Fifty percent of small business income taxes are paid by small businesses.*
CLEF	✗	*If the vaccine was dangerous they would've given it to poor people first, not politicians and billionaires.*
	O	*Today, FDA approved the first COVID-19 vaccine for the prevention of #COVID19 disease in individuals 16 years of age and older.*
	✓	*They said the vaccine stopped transmission. Now they are lying and saying they didn't. Video proof here*
ENV	✗	*We Love Green! The environment is at the heart of Parisian electro-pop music festival We Love Green.*
	✓	*All pension fund clients have a target for carbon reduction of the equity investments.*
NEWS	✗	*In Germany, RT has also amplified voices questioning the threat of COVID-19, and calling testing and mask-wearing into question.*
	✓	*"If you wash and dry a cloth face mask on high heat, then you should be good to go," according to professor Travis Glenn.*
POLI	✗	*As I have said all along, the courts are where we will win this battle.*
	O	*I promised that our roads would be the envy of the nation.*

Table 1: Examples from the datasets used. ✗= non-factual claim, *O* = factual claim, ✓= check-worthy claim

	CB	CLEF	ENV	NEWS	POLI
Task	CD+CW	CD+CW	CW	CW	CD
Labels	ternary	binary*	binary	binary	binary*
# instances	23,533	3,040	2,647	7,848	52 speeches
# instances used	1,032	251	275	1,622	816
label distribution	731/238/63	102/110/39	198/67	811/811	295/521
Genre	debates	tweets	news articles	reports	speech transcripts
Topic	politics	healthcare	environment	healthcare	political
Co-text	4 preceding, on request	–	not available	inconclusive	1 preceding, 1 following
Agreement	–*	0.75/0.7	0.47	0.405	0.69
Agreement metric	–	Fleiss-κ	Krippendorff-α	Krippendorff-κ	Cohen-κ

Table 2: Characteristics of the CD and CW datasets used in our experiments. *CB reported no agreement evaluation, but the test set used is agreed upon by experts. Label distribution in order: ✗/ *O* / ✓

CD and CW tasks, with CB using ternary labels annotated together and CLEF using binary labels with separate questions for CD and CW. The five datasets were originally annotated using a binary scheme (ENV), Likert scale (CLEF-CW), multi-class (NEWS), or a follow-up prompt for uncertain instances (POLI). All datasets have aggregated binary labels, except CB, where aggregation from ternary into binary labels is straightforward. The reported inter-annotator agreement is substantial for POLI and CLEF (Landis and Koch, 1977), but moderate for ENV and NEWS, reflecting the complexity of the domain-dependent CW task.

4 Experimental Setup

In our experiments, we use both closed-source and open-source LLMs. For closed source, we use OpenAI models *gpt-turbo-3.5* and *gpt-4-turbo*. For open-source models, due to hardware constraints, we chose Llama 3 8B Instruct, which is the top performer in its parameter class. To ensure reproducibility and encourage deterministic behaviour, we prompt GPT models with the temperature setting of 0 along with a fixed seed parameter and use greedy sampling with top_p=1 for open-source models. We also experimented with other open-source models. Mistral 7B Instruct v0.2 was not compliant with the provided labels, instead giving open-ended answers, even for less verbose prompts. See Appendix B for more detailed information on models.

4.1 Prompt Verbosity

We first investigate how prompt verbosity affects LLMs' predictive accuracy. We hypothesize that the optimal verbosity level depends on the dataset, reflecting the factuality and worthiness criteria differences between the domains. While a brief prompt might lack essential details, a comprehensive prompt featuring extensive definitions and examples may make the task more difficult to solve. Across datasets and for each prompt level, we aim to preserve the original wording and typography of the annotation guidelines as much as possible since we aim to establish whether guidelines without much intervention can be used as prompts for up-to-par performance. We additionally instruct the model to reply using only the provided labels without additional explanation to increase compliance and streamline evaluation. For POLI, we use the same question structure as in the annotation – for instances where the model responded with *Maybe*, we prompt it again with the follow-up question, providing previous responses in the prompt.

Based on the content and style of annotation guidelines, we define the following four levels of verbosity (cf. Appendix D for full prompts for four verbosity levels across the five datasets):

Level V0 serves as the baseline. We use a naive zero-shot prompt, relying on internal definitions of the model. For the CD task (for the CB, CLEF and POLI datasets), we use the following prompt: "*Does the following sentence/statement/tweet contain a factual claim? Answer only with Yes or No.*" For the CW task (for the CB, CLEF, NEWS and ENV datasets) we use the following prompt: "*Does the following sentence/statement/tweet contain a check-worthy claim? Answer only with Yes or No.*" As these prompts do not include the specific factuality or worthiness criteria from the guidelines, they serve as a domain-agnostic baseline;

Level V1 uses prompts that include the task definition and the set of possible labels but omit detailed explanations of the labels or principles. For example, for the CB dataset, the three categories of non-factual, unimportant factual, and check-worthy factual sentences are introduced but not explained;

Level V2 expands on V1 by adding a more detailed explanation of the labels or general annotation principles (or both, in the case of PoliClaim). Some principles include avoiding implicit assumptions (ENV), defining check-worthiness criteria based on public interest (CB), and categorizing claims that non-professionals can verify as non-check-worthy (CLEF);

Level V3 builds on V2 by including examples from the original annotation guidelines. This level closely aligns with annotation guidelines, encompassing all or nearly all information the datasets' authors provide in their accompanying papers.[1] The examples are provided either along with the labels (CB), separately in a few-shot fashion (ENV), or both (POLI).

4.2 Amount of Context

In real-world scenarios, claims are rarely evaluated in isolation. Accordingly, annotators working with CD and CW datasets were usually provided with some contextual information, consisting of the claim's co-text and metadata. Regarding co-text, the quantity varied between datasets (cf. Table 2), as did its significance – sometimes it was provided as additional guidance (CB), while in other cases, it was deemed crucial for assigning labels (POLI, NEWS). For NEWS, the amount of provided co-text is inconclusive, so we decided to omit it from co-text expansion. This difference highlights that co-text is both another undefined aspect of CD and CW, and that it can vary across domains. Similarly, metadata such as speaker, affiliation, occasion, and date were revealed only during annotation for CLEF-CW and were not available in the dataset itself. However, metadata is available for the CB and POLI datasets, while NEWS provides metadata only for positives, making it unusable for our experiments. Adding metadata might lead to biases, yet it could offer essential information, depending on the worthiness criterion.

We investigate how LLMs' predictive accuracy depends on the amount of situational context provided to the model. To this end, we leverage the context information available in the CB and POLI datasets and expand the prompts in three variants:

Level C1 represents adding the co-text of the claim. The amount of co-text included in the prompt for each dataset is the same as what was originally shown to the annotators – for CB, four preceding statements (which were either by the speaker, opposing speaker, or moderator), and for POLI, one preceding and one following statement;

Level C2 expands the contextual information by adding metadata to the claim. In the case of POLI, the metadata is the speaker's identity and political party, whereas for CB it additionally contains the speaker's title and the

[1]CB and ENV documented additional examples (typically 20–30 examples) provided to the annotators. We did not include these examples.

		CB		CLEF		ENV	NEWS	POLI
		CD	CW	CD	CW	CW	CW	CD
Stratified random		.375	.452	.745	.415	.25	.667	.779
Previous		.818*	.818*	.761^a	.698	.849	.309*	.862^a
SVM		.789	.799	.726	.346	.729	.675*	.819
BERT		.956	.938	.773	.472	.822	.771*	.881
gpt-4	V0	.833	.805	.797	.467	.416	**.583**	**.844**
	V1	.883	.885	.799	.552	**.773**	.572	.679
	V2	.908	.889	**.806**	**.583**	.690	.480	.541
	V3	**.919**	**.927**	.781	.556	.596	.523	.563
gpt-3.5	V0	.853	.718	.656	**.496**	.484	**.531**	.707
	V1	.570	.739	.490	.438	**.710**	.371	.751
	V2	.774	.800	.650	.468	.701	.348	.657
	V3	**.872**	**.862**	**.757**	.446	.650	.206	**.803**
Llama3 8B	V0	.677	.743	.769	**.439**	.290	**.586**	.812
	V1	.478	.655	.803	.415	**.755**	.502	**.827**
	V2	**.742**	**.751**	**.807**	.433	.745	.466	.712
	V3	.702	.637	.790	.426	.742	.469	.651

Table 3: Binary F1 scores across datasets and prompt verbosity levels (V1–V3). Level V0 corresponds to the naive-prompting baseline. For baselines and previous results: ^{a} = accuracy, * = not directly comparable

sentiment of the statement, provided by the authors of the dataset;

Level C3 combines both C1 and C2 by providing both co-text and metadata.

We appended the contextual information to the user prompts, and only modified the system prompts of POLI slightly – adding guidance on how to handle context, ommited from the no-context variants (cf. Appendix A for a detailed description).

5 Results

We present the results for prompt verbosity levels in Table 3 and for different context levels in Table 6. In Table 3, we also include the previous results reported by authors in the original papers introducing the datasets (note that some results are not directly comparable to ours, as we discuss below). We use a stratified random classifier, an SVM classifier with TF-IDF features, and a fine-tuned BERT (Devlin et al., 2019) as baselines.

5.1 Prompt Verbosity

Table 3 shows the baselines and F1 scores by verbosity level for *gpt-4-turbo*, *gpt-3.5-turbo*, and Llama3 8B. Both performance and the optimal verbosity level is not consistent across datasets. The accuracy generally increases with verbosity levels for CB, but the trend is reversed for ENV. We observe no consistent trend for CLEF, POLI, and NEWS datasets. The most verbose prompts (V3) generally do not achieve the highest performance, except for the GPT models and CB. This highlights that providing detailed instructions and examples can be beneficial but potentially harm performance.

Comparison to baselines. For SVM and BERT baselines, we had to use a different test set for NewsClaims than for the other models, as the original dataset does not provide a training set (the best-performing LLM on this test set achieved an F1 score of 0.670). Overall, all best-performing LLMs outperform the SVM baseline. However, except for CLEF, BERT outperforms the best-performing LLMs by a small margin (<0.05 F1), raising doubts about whether manual data labeling is worthwhile in these cases.

Comparison to previous work. Comparing with previous work is difficult due to differences in setup. For CB, the authors evaluated used 4-fold cross-validation on different-sized subsets (4,000, 8,000 . . . 20,000), all containing our chosen test set, annotated by experts. The authors evaluated using weighted F1-score, achieving a maximum score of 0.818. Our highest weighted F1-scores surpass this, reaching 0.933 for *gpt-4-turbo* and 0.906 for *gpt-3.5-turbo*. On CLEF, the best-reported result is the accuracy score of .761 for CD and the F1 score of .698 for CW. While our approach underperforms for CW (F1 of 0.583), it achieves higher accuracy for CD (0.776 on Level V2). In the case of NEWS, the authors reported an F1 score, but it remains unclear whether it was evaluated based

	CB		CLEF		ENV	NEWS	POLI
	CD	CW	CD	CW	CW	CW	CD
V1	26	9	8	55	13	150	87
V2	4	3	5	35	8	90	87
V3	1	1	2	14	5	68	65

Table 4: Counts of instances misclassified by all three models across the three verbosity levels.

on binary or multiclass labels, given that annotators had to categorize claims into different classes. They achieved the highest F1 score of 0.309, which our approach exceeds on the subset we selected, achieving an F1 score of 0.583. Our subset has a higher random baseline due to a higher ratio of positive examples and includes all positives from the original test set. For POLI, the authors evaluated using accuracy. They achieved an accuracy of 0.764 on the test set using *gpt-3.5* and 0.862 using *gpt-4*. The *GPT-3.5-turbo* using prompt Level V3 performs comparable, while *GPT-4* and Llama3 perform worse. For ENV, the metrics are directly comparable, and our approach underperforms compared to previous results.

CD vs. CW. Generally, higher performance is achieved for the CD task, although the diverse domains of the datasets and differences in guidelines prevent definitive conclusions. Therefore, comparing performance on the two datasets that cover both tasks – CB and CLEF – is most straightforward. Interestingly, a reverse phenomenon is observed between these datasets—significantly higher performance is achieved for the CD task on CLEF, whereas on CB, CW performance is slightly higher. An important difference in the two datasets is precisely in the annotation styles – CB uses the same guidelines for both tasks and ternary annotation, while for CLEF the guidelines are different for the two tasks, originally using different labelling strategies (binary for CD and Likert scale for CW).

Closed-source vs. open-source. While broader conclusions require a wider range of both open- and closed-source models, especially larger open-source ones, the Llama3 8B model performs similarly to GPT models, highlighting the potential of prompting open-source models with annotation guidelines. Furthermore, the results of both GPT models on the CB dataset could indicate a potential data leakage (Balloccu et al., 2024) since the performance of Llama3 8B is comparable in other datasets but lags for CB.

5.2 Error Analysis

Worst performance. The naive baseline prompt (V0) generally outperforms the prompts based on annotation guidelines on the CLEF CW and NEWS datasets, except for V2 for CLEF CW with *gpt-4-turbo*. For CLEF CW, the annotation guidelines are adapted from the Likert scale, where multiple characteristics are attributed to negatives (e.g., not interesting, a joke, not containing claims, or too trivial to be checked by a professional). In our prompts, we converted the Likert scale to binary, where the already diverse and vaguely defined criteria were binned in a single label, increasing complexity. For NEWS, although the dataset's purpose is claim check-worthiness detection, check-worthiness as a concept is not mentioned in the annotation guidelines. Positives are merely selected by containing claims falling into four predefined categories relating to the COVID-19 virus, and check-worthiness is assumed implicitly. This, along with the presence of inter-sentence coreference in the positive instances, might cause poor performance.

Most difficult instances. To analyze poor performance beyond the F1 score, we decided to identify the instances for which all three models across levels consistently predicted the wrong label. Table 4 shows the counts of those instances.

Interestingly, whether the instances in question were consistently misclassified as positives or negatives depends on the domain – for CLEF and CB, all of the instances are false positives (FP), whereas for POLI, all 65 are false negatives (FN). This suggests that the guidelines are too restrictive regarding the positive label or are interpreted as such during inference.

Table 5 shows examples from the final pool of mislabelled instances. Several interesting observations can be made here. For example, CLEF comprises tweets, where sarcasm is more prevalent, making the prediction task harder. For ENV, which contains environmental reports requiring expert knowledge, the mislabeled instances were either too vague for positives or contained too much domain knowledge for the models to decipher. Annotators were urged to look up acronyms they were not familiar with, but the same could not be accomplished with ICL. For NEWS, some claims are only implicitly related to COVID-19, which results in a false negative label. On the other hand, some instances seem mislabeled in the gold set. Concerning POLI, the frequent use of personal pronouns

Dataset	Label	Gold	Example
CB	1	0	*Let's go to work and end this fiasco in Central America, a failed policy which has actually increased Cuban and Soviet influence.*
CLEF	1	0	*So businesses will get fined $14,000 (per employee) if they don't comply with Biden's vaccine mandate. And illegal aliens get a $450,000 payout for "damages" for crossing our border illegally... Biden's America.*
ENV	1	0	*Renewable energy is purely domestic sourced and environment-friendly, and can be used continuously without being depleted.*
	0	1	*To strengthen its approach, Kering's SBT for a 1.5°C trajectory was revised and approved by the SBTi in early 2021.*
NEWS	1	0	*There's currently no strong evidence that supplementing with vitamin C will prevent or cure COVID-19.*
	0	1	*Vaccines, by their nature, are reactive.*
POLI	0	1	*We are finally going to fix the darn roads.*
	0	1	*Too many people are struggling to make ends meet.*

Table 5: Examples of characteristic instances per dataset that were consistently misclassified across levels.

		CB						POLI		
		CD			CW			CD		
		V1	V2	V3	V1	V2	V3	V1	V2	V3
gpt-4-turbo	C0	**.883**	**.908**	**.919**	**.885**	.889	**.927**	.619	.541	.563
	C1	.806	.849	.862	.803	.847	.872	.722	**.650**	.727
	C2	.879	**.908**	.913	.880	**.901**	.916	**.707**	.470	.592
	C3	.794	.857	.877	.791	.854	.885	.692	.632	**.732**
gpt-3.5-turbo	C0	**.570**	.774	**.872**	.739	.800	**.862**	.751	.657	**.803**
	C1	.461	.299	.513	.517	.301	.528	.790	.688	.794
	C2	.560	**.801**	.836	**.747**	**.826**	.832	.730	.523	.704
	C3	.474	.724	.758	.643	.716	.749	**.794**	**.754**	.800
Llama3 8B	C0	.478	.742	.702	.655	.751	.637	**.827**	.712	.651
	C1	.460	.591	.614	.531	.528	.552	.799	.789	.803
	C2	**.483**	**.773**	**.764**	**.727**	**.819**	**.736**	.807	.703	.628
	C3	.468	.610	.601	.506	.618	.556	.806	**.798**	**.805**

Table 6: Binary F1 scores by level of context information (C1–C3) added to the prompt ranging in verbosity (V1–V3) . Level C0 corresponds to the prompt level with no context information. The best scores across verbosity levels are shown in bold, and the best scores per model and dataset are highlighted in green.

requiring coreference resolution leads to false negatives, with the claim losing relevance without information about the claimant.

5.3 Amount of Context

Table 6 shows the F1 scores by verbosity and context level for all models. The benefit of including context varies across models – there is a bigger performance increase for the Llama model with added contextual information, topping the performance for CB in both tasks as opposed to prompts with no context. For the GPT models, there is some positive impact of metadata (C2). The least beneficial is the addition of co-text but no metadata (C1), including speaker information, which is vital when given previous responses. Concerning prompt verbosity levels, context's impact is higher on less verbose prompts, showing contextual information complements brief definitions.

5.4 Rank-Based Evaluation

In light of resource constraints, fact-checking organizations have devised principles to prioritize claims based on their check-worthiness. This invites the question of whether zero- and few-shot LLM prompting could be used for that purpose. To investigate this, we frame CW as a binary relevance ranking and rank the claims based on the LLM's confidence for the positive class. We used the token likelihood of the positive class as a measure of confidence. The quality of the so-obtained ranking will depend on how well the LLM is calibrated. Thus, we first evaluate the LLMs' calibration accuracy using the expected calibration error (ECE). Figure 2 shows the predictive accuracy (F1 score) against calibration accuracy ($1 - \mathrm{ECE}$) across datasets and prompt verbosity levels (we only use prompts at context level C0, i.e., no context information).

Per model and dataset, we select the prompt that scores high on predictive and calibration accuracy. The prompts with the highest F1 scores are usually the best-calibrated ones, except for NEWS, where we select level V1 as Pareto-optimal.

Table 7 shows the rank-based performance scores for the selected prompts: average precision (AP), precision-at-10 (P@10), and precision-at-R,

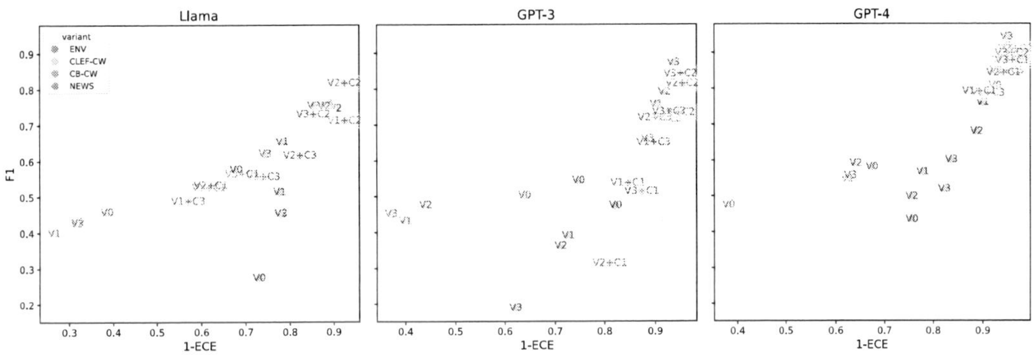

Figure 2: F1 scores and calibration accuracy (1 − ECE) for the CW task, across datasets and models

		CB	CLEF	ENV	NEWS
gpt-4	AP	.951	.552	.767	.67
	P10	1	.9	.9	1
	PR	.924	.615	.761	1
gpt-3.5	AP	.934	.464	.796	.669
	P10	1	.6	.9	.7
	PR	.919	.436	.772	.700
Llama3 8B	AP	.878	.350	.794	.688
	P10	1	.2	.1	1
	PR	.823	.282	.762	1

Table 7: Rank-based CW performance scores

where R equals the total number of positives in the dataset. The rank-based performance scores mirror the classification accuracy scores: they are high for datasets with high predictive accuracy (CB and ENV) and lower for datasets with lower predictive accuracy (NEWS and CLEF). Our results suggest that LLM models with high predictive accuracy also produce well-calibrated scores using ECE and may be readily used as check-worthiness rankers.

6 Conclusion

We tackled claim detection and check-worthiness tasks using zero- and few-shot LLM prompting based on existing annotation guidelines. The optimal level of prompt verbosity, from minimal prompts to detailed prompts that include criteria and examples, varies depending on the domain and guidelines style. Adding claim context does not improve performance. Models with high predictive accuracy can directly utilize confidence scores to produce reliable check-worthiness rankings.

Limitations

Datasets. Our experiments do not use datasets created by fact-checking organizations. While the datasets were created specifically for the tasks of CD and CW, and most were annotated by experts, the datasets were constructed for research purposes. To most accurately evaluate the potential of using our approach in fact-checking organizations, a dataset annotated according to official factuality or check-worthiness criteria with appropriate annotation guidelines should be used.

Models. Due to hardware constraints, no open-source LLMs greater than 8B parameters were used in our experiments. We acknowledge the importance of relying on open-source models in the research community and the lack of insight that results from disregarding larger open-source models. Using closed-source models has the additional caveat of possible leakage of the dataset, which is a growing concern in the community (Balloccu et al., 2024). We also note that the outstanding results on the ClaimBuster dataset (CB) could be due to data leakage, considering the dataset was published several years ago and has a wide reach in the research of automatic fact-checking.

Languages. In this work, we only do experiments on datasets in English. This is for two reasons: (1) the necessity to understand the annotation guidelines to draft prompts using them and (2) the lack of datasets in other languages. However, we acknowledge that disinformation is a global problem and that tackling it requires working with multiple languages.

Lack of prompt engineering experiments. In this work, we do minimal prompt engineering interventions beyond merely adapting the level of detail in annotation guidelines and appending contextual information. We opted for this approach instead of drafting prompts ourselves to investigate how original wording, definitions, and examples given to annotators could fare with LLMs. We realize weak performance in some cases (e.g., CLEF, for the naive aggregation from the Likert scale to binary labels), and performance variations could be due to the models' sensitivity to prompt structure, wording, and examples. However, translating the complex criteria of worthiness in such a streamlined way could benefit fact-checkers. Furthermore, prompt design should be adapted for each dataset, significantly expanding the scope of this research (since five datasets are used). We leave experiments regarding prompt design for future work.

Binary relevance ranking. In our study, we also assess CW as a ranking task, which is crucial given that fact-checking organizations often face time and resource constraints and must prioritize claims based on their CW criteria. We use binary relevance judgments for evaluation, with binary CW labels as the ground truth, and apply standard IR metrics such as MAP and P@R. An alternative approach could involve using graded CW criteria, framing the task as regression, and evaluating with graded relevance judgments like NDCG. However, to our knowledge, only the dataset by Gencheva et al. (2017) provides graded CW labels, using aggregated judgments from various fact-checking agencies to model priority.

Risks

Although we intend to combat the spread of disinformation with this work, there is still a potential for misuse. The prompts and insights reported in this work could potentially be used to create disinformative claims adapted to make their detection more difficult. A big challenge of disinformation detection is the growing use of generative models for creating disinformative claims. The prompts provided in this work could be reverted for generative purposes, achieving the exact opposite effect than what our work aims to achieve.

Acknowledgments

This research was supported by the Adria Digital Media Observatory (ADMO) project, which is part of EDMO, EU's largest interdisciplinary network for countering disinformation.

References

Grace Abels. 2023. Can ChatGPT fact-check? PolitiFact tested. Accessed: 2024-3-18.

Firoj Alam, Shaden Shaar, Fahim Dalvi, Hassan Sajjad, Alex Nikolov, Hamdy Mubarak, Giovanni Da San Martino, Ahmed Abdelali, Nadir Durrani, Kareem Darwish, Abdulaziz Al-Homaid, Wajdi Zaghouani, Tommaso Caselli, Gijs Danoe, Friso Stolk, Britt Bruntink, and Preslav Nakov. 2021. Fighting the COVID-19 infodemic: Modeling the perspective of journalists, fact-checkers, social media platforms, policy makers, and the society. In *Findings of the Association for Computational Linguistics: EMNLP 2021*, pages 611–649, Punta Cana, Dominican Republic. Association for Computational Linguistics.

Simone Balloccu, Patrícia Schmidtová, Mateusz Lango, and Ondrej Dusek. 2024. Leak, cheat, repeat: Data contamination and evaluation malpractices in closed-source LLMs. In *Proceedings of the 18th Conference of the European Chapter of the Association for Computational Linguistics (Volume 1: Long Papers)*, pages 67–93, St. Julian's, Malta. Association for Computational Linguistics.

Tom Brown, Benjamin Mann, Nick Ryder, Melanie Subbiah, Jared D Kaplan, Prafulla Dhariwal, Arvind Neelakantan, Pranav Shyam, Girish Sastry, Amanda Askell, Sandhini Agarwal, Ariel Herbert-Voss, Gretchen Krueger, Tom Henighan, Rewon Child, Aditya Ramesh, Daniel Ziegler, Jeffrey Wu, Clemens Winter, Chris Hesse, Mark Chen, Eric Sigler, Mateusz Litwin, Scott Gray, Benjamin Chess, Jack Clark, Christopher Berner, Sam McCandlish, Alec Radford, Ilya Sutskever, and Dario Amodei. 2020. Language models are few-shot learners. In *Advances in Neural Information Processing Systems*, volume 33, pages 1877–1901. Curran Associates, Inc.

Jacob Devlin, Ming-Wei Chang, Kenton Lee, and Kristina Toutanova. 2019. Bert: Pre-training of deep bidirectional transformers for language understanding. In *Proceedings of the 2019 Conference of the North American Chapter of the Association for Computational Linguistics: Human Language Technologies, Volume 1 (Long and Short Papers)*, pages 4171–4186.

FullFact. 2020. The challenges of online fact checking.

Revanth Gangi Reddy, Sai Chetan Chinthakindi, Zhenhailong Wang, Yi Fung, Kathryn Conger, Ahmed ELsayed, Martha Palmer, Preslav Nakov, Eduard Hovy, Kevin Small, and Heng Ji. 2022. NewsClaims: A new benchmark for claim detection from news with attribute knowledge. In *Proceedings of the 2022 Conference on Empirical Methods in Natural Language Processing*, pages 6002–6018, Abu Dhabi, United Arab Emirates. Association for Computational Linguistics.

Pepa Gencheva, Preslav Nakov, Lluís Màrquez, Alberto Barrón-Cedeño, and Ivan Koychev. 2017. A context-aware approach for detecting worth-checking claims in political debates. In *Proceedings of the International Conference Recent Advances in Natural Language Processing, RANLP 2017*, pages 267–276, Varna, Bulgaria. INCOMA Ltd.

Max Glockner, Yufang Hou, and Iryna Gurevych. 2022. Missing counter-evidence renders NLP fact-checking unrealistic for misinformation. In *Proceedings of the 2022 Conference on Empirical Methods in Natural Language Processing*, pages 5916–5936, Abu Dhabi, United Arab Emirates. Association for Computational Linguistics.

Naeemul Hassan, Fatma Arslan, Chengkai Li, and Mark Tremayne. 2017a. Toward automated fact-checking: Detecting check-worthy factual claims by claimbuster. In *Proceedings of the 23rd ACM SIGKDD international conference on knowledge discovery and data mining*, pages 1803–1812.

Naeemul Hassan, Fatma Arslan, Chengkai Li, and Mark Tremayne. 2017b. Toward automated fact-checking: Detecting check-worthy factual claims by claimbuster. *Proceedings of the 23rd ACM SIGKDD International Conference on Knowledge Discovery and Data Mining*.

Naeemul Hassan, Anil Nayak, Vikas Sable, Chengkai Li, Mark Tremayne, Gensheng Zhang, Fatma Arslan, Josue Caraballo, Damian Jimenez, Siddhant Gawsane, Shohedul Hasan, Minumol Joseph, and Aaditya Kulkarni. 2017c. Claimbuster: the first-ever end-to-end fact-checking system. *Proceedings of the VLDB Endowment*, 10:1945–1948.

Martin Hyben, Sebastian Kula, Ivan Srba, Robert Moro, and Jakub Simko. 2023. Is it indeed bigger better? the comprehensive study of claim detection lms applied for disinformation tackling.

Zehra Melce Hüsünbeyi and Tatjana Scheffler. 2024. Ontology enhanced claim detection.

Zana Idrizi and Niamh Hanafin. 2023. Navigating the landscape of increased disinformation in europe and central asia.

Israa Jaradat, Pepa Gencheva, Alberto Barrón-Cedeño, Lluís Màrquez, and Preslav Nakov. 2018. ClaimRank: Detecting check-worthy claims in Arabic and English. In *Proceedings of the 2018 Conference of the North American Chapter of the Association for Computational Linguistics: Demonstrations*, pages 26–30, New Orleans, Louisiana. Association for Computational Linguistics.

Takeshi Kojima, Shixiang (Shane) Gu, Machel Reid, Yutaka Matsuo, and Yusuke Iwasawa. 2022. Large language models are zero-shot reasoners. In *Advances in Neural Information Processing Systems*, volume 35, pages 22199–22213. Curran Associates, Inc.

Lev Konstantinovskiy, Oliver Price, Mevan Babakar, and Arkaitz Zubiaga. 2021. Toward automated factchecking: Developing an annotation schema and benchmark for consistent automated claim detection. *Digital Threats*, 2(2).

J Richard Landis and Gary G. Koch. 1977. The measurement of observer agreement for categorical data. *Biometrics*, 33 1:159–74.

Miaoran Li, Baolin Peng, and Zhu Zhang. 2023. Selfchecker: Plug-and-play modules for fact-checking with large language models.

Moran Mizrahi, Guy Kaplan, Dan Malkin, Rotem Dror, Dafna Shahaf, and Gabriel Stanovsky. 2024. State of what art? a call for multi-prompt llm evaluation.

Preslav Nakov, Alberto Barrón-Cedeño, Giovanni Da San Martino, Firoj Alam, Rubén Míguez, Tommaso Caselli, Mucahid Kutlu, Wajdi Zaghouani, Chengkai Li, Shaden Shaar, Hamdy Mubarak, Alex Nikolov, and Yavuz Selim Kartal. 2022. Overview of the clef-2022 checkthat! lab task 1 on identifying relevant claims in tweets. In *CLEF 2022: Conference and Labs of the Evaluation Forum*, volume 3180 of *CEUR Workshop Proceedings*, pages 368–392. CEUR Workshop Proceedings (CEUR-WS.org).

UN News. 2022. Rise of disinformation a symptom of 'global diseases' undermining public trust: Bachelet.

Jingwei Ni, Minjing Shi, Dominik Stammbach, Mrinmaya Sachan, Elliott Ash, and Markus Leippold. 2024. Afacta: Assisting the annotation of factual claim detection with reliable llm annotators.

Marcin Sawinski, Krzysztof Wecel, Ewelina Ksiezniak, Milena Stróżyna, Wlodzimierz Lewoniewski, Piotr Stolarski, and Witold Abramowicz. 2023. Openfact at checkthat!-2023: Head-to-head GPT vs. BERT - A comparative study of transformers language models for the detection of check-worthy claims. In *Working Notes of the Conference and Labs of the Evaluation Forum (CLEF 2023), Thessaloniki, Greece, September 18th to 21st, 2023*, volume 3497 of *CEUR Workshop Proceedings*, pages 453–472. CEUR-WS.org.

Ghazaal Sheikhi, Samia Touileb, and Sohail Khan. 2023. Automated claim detection for fact-checking: A case study using Norwegian pre-trained language models. In *Proceedings of the 24th Nordic Conference on Computational Linguistics (NoDaLiDa)*, pages 1–9, Tórshavn, Faroe Islands. University of Tartu Library.

Chenglei Si, Navita Goyal, Sherry Tongshuang Wu, Chen Zhao, Shi Feng, Hal Daumé III au2, and Jordan Boyd-Graber. 2023. Large language models help humans verify truthfulness – except when they are convincingly wrong.

Dominik Stammbach, Nicolas Webersinke, Julia Bingler, Mathias Kraus, and Markus Leippold. 2023. Environmental claim detection. In *Proceedings of the 61st Annual Meeting of the Association for Computational Linguistics (Volume 2: Short Papers)*, pages 1051–1066, Toronto, Canada. Association for Computational Linguistics.

Dustin Wright and Isabelle Augenstein. 2020. Claim check-worthiness detection as positive unlabelled learning. In *Findings of the Association for Computational Linguistics: EMNLP 2020*, pages 476–488, Online. Association for Computational Linguistics.

A Dataset Information

In this section, we provide details on the datasets used in our experiments.

A.1 Test set selection

Here, we provide details on the test set selection for each dataset. Furthermore, we state which set the authors used for evaluation and whether the results can be comparable.

ClaimBuster. The dataset does not have an explicit test set. The authors instead used 4-fold cross-validation on different-sized subsets during their experiments (4,000, 8,000 ... 20,000). However, a high-quality *groundtruth* set is available in the dataset. It contains 1,032 samples that experts agreed on and was used for screening during annotation. Also, all the test sets the authors used contain the screening sentences. For the quality of labels and to have somewhat comparable results to the authors, we selected the *groundtruth* set for experiments.

CLEF. The dataset consists of both a *dev* and a *test* set. Since the *test* set was used to evaluate teams participating in the CLEF CheckThat! the challenge, we opted to do our experiments on this set to compare to the metrics of the best-submitted solution.

EnvironmentalClaims. The dataset contains both a *dev* and *test* set of equal size, whereas the original work publishes metrics on both sets separately. We selected the *test* set for our experiments.

NewsClaims. The dataset provides both a *dev* and a *test* set; however, the disclosed sets contain only positive instances. The complete dataset consists of around 10% of positive instances, with a high number of low-quality negative instances created by errors in sentencizing and filtering – instances containing only names, dates, links. The dataset also contains duplicate instances, also in the set of positives. To create a viable subset and avoid high costs during inference, we sampled the negative instances from a normal distribution with the parameters fitted to the length of the instances. We chose to sample the same number of instances as there are positives without duplicates, creating a higher baseline.

PoliClaim. The dataset provides an explicit *test* set consisting of both gold labels and labels resulting from inference on 4 political speeches. To be able to compare results, we opted to use the complete *test* set.

A.2 Context information

ClaimBuster. During the annotation of the ClaimBuster dataset, 4 preceding statements could be viewed with an extra button, which was used in 14% of all cases. Since the dataset covers presidential debates with multiple speakers, including the moderator and audience questioners, it is not completely clear how the speakers were differentiated in the provided preceding sentences. Therefore, we selected the method of differentiating the speakers arbitrarily – 'A' was used for the speaker of the statement that is meant to be annotated, and 'B' for the opposing speaker.

EnvironmentalClaims. No additional contextual or co-textual information was provided in the dataset. The annotators were not shown any co-text during annotations. The authors considered annotating whole paragraphs instead of sentence-level annotation but decided against it due to time and budget constraints.

PoliClaim. The annotators were provided with the preceding and following sentences of the one they are annotating. Since there is only one speaker (as opposed to ClaimBuster, which covers debates), there is no need to differentiate the speaker to minimize confusion in prompts. In annotation guidelines, context was explicitly mentioned and clarified in examples. In our experiments, we used two versions of the prompts – one mentioning context for experiments with co-text expansion and one without the mention of context used when only one sentence from the speech is provided. The two alternatives are shown in D.

CLEF. The dataset consists of tweets covering COVID-19 topics. For the check-worthiness task, annotators were shown metadata such as time, account, number of likes and reposts. However, this information is not readily available in the dataset and requires crawling the tweets to obtain it. It was also not available in the dataset of the CLEF2022 CheckThat! Challenge, which was derived from the original dataset. Since we wanted to make our effort comparable to alternative methods used in the competition, we did not opt for crawling the tweets to acquire metadata.

NewsClaims. The research paper introducing the dataset has inconsistencies regarding the co-text provided to annotators. While it is stated in the paper that whole articles are provided for co-text, in the screenshot of the annotation platform, only three preceding and following sentences were provided. Regarding context, the work emphasizes the importance of metadata such as claim object, speaker and span, and provides that data for positive instances (sentences containing claims related to 4 specified COVID-19 subtopics). The effort of annotating the claims with metadata is worthwhile, however we decided against using it in inference since no such data is available for negative instances.

B Model Information

For OpenAI models, we use *gpt-3.5-turbo-0125* and *gpt-4-0125-preview*. We use a temperature of 0 for all experiments. To get confidence, we use *logprobs* and *n_probs=5*, to account for the target labels ending up as less probable tokens. We use a random seed of 42 in all experiments, to avoid stochastic answers as much as possible. The run was executed once per model and prompt variant. Inference was done through the OpenAI API. GPU hours are hard to estimate.

We use Llama3 8B Instruct for experiments on open-source models. It is the only smaller open-source model from the ones we tested compliant with provided labels. The experiments took 10 GPU hours on 2x GeForce RTX 2080 Ti. We use greedy decoding and run once per model and prompt variant. Initial experiments were done on *neural-chat:7b-v3.3-q5_K_M* and *mistral:7b-instruct-v0.2-q5_K_M*. A total of 5 GPU hours was used.

For BERT, we use the base model *bert-base-uncased*. We train the model for five epochs with a batch size of 16, a learning rate of 2e-5 and weight decay of 0.01. We keep the best model across epochs.

C Calibration

In this section, the ECE per prompt verbosity level is shown for all models in Table 8. The ECE is calculated with the parameters $n_bins = 10$ and $norm = l1$.

D Complete prompts

This section provides the complete prompts used in our experiments. The instructions were given in system prompts, while the instances were in user prompts. The added context information is also appended to user prompts.

For each dataset, the three prompt levels are shown, with the content expanded in relation to the previous level highlighted. To visually separate the levels, Level V2 is highlighted in yellow, while Level V3 is highlighted in pink.

For CLEF, two alternative prompts are given, since for CD and CW different annotation guidelines were used. For POLI, parts of the Level V2 and Level V3 prompts regarding surrounding sentences are either provided or not, based on whether context expansion is used (surrounding sentences are given in prompts C1 and C3). Those parts are highlighted in blue.

User prompts. The user prompts were based on how the instance was reffered to in the corresponding annotation gudelines. The instances are surrounded with HTML tags. The same is done for context expansion on CB and POLI.

		CB		CLEF		ENV	NEWS	POLI
		CD	CW	CD	CW	CD	CW	CW
gpt-4-turbo	V0	.094	.068	.259	.601	.231	.322	.142
	V1	.050	.047	.196	.391	.119	.210	.271
	V2	.043	.039	.194	.352	.127	.277	.373
	V3	.039	.032	.222	.367	.150	.194	.348
gpt-3.5-turbo	V0	.033	.068	.212	.359	.189	.246	.257
	V1	.323	.085	.386	.609	.088	.260	.229
	V2	.103	.071	.279	.560	.097	.280	.327
	V3	.061	.050	.285	.646	.100	.379	.196
Llama3 8B	V0	.218	.126	.307	.611	.286	.314	.223
	V1	.607	.218	.244	.723	.114	.228	.172
	V2	.184	.135	.241	.687	.102	.229	.321
	V3	.231	.259	.241	.686	.134	.214	.379

Table 8: ECE score by prompt level per dataset for *gpt-4-turbo*. 'CD' and 'CW' mark claim detection and claim check-worthiness detection, respectively, while 'V0' marks the score for the naive baseline

Level	Prompt
V1	`Categorize the <sentence> spoken in the presidential debates into one of three categories: Non-Factual Sentence (NFS), Unimportant Factual Sentence (UFS) or Check-worthy Factual Sentence (CFS). Use only one of the three labels (NFS, UFS or CFS), do not provide any additional explanation.`

V2	`Categorize the <sentence> spoken in the presidential debates into three categories:`
	`Non-Factual Sentence (NFS): Subjective sentences (opinions, beliefs, declarations) and many questions fall under this category. These sentences do not contain any factual claim.`
	`Unimportant Factual Sentence (UFS): These are factual claims but not check-worthy. The general public will not be interested in knowing whether these sentences are true or false. Fact-checkers do not find these sentences as important for checking.`
	`Check-worthy Factual Sentence (CFS): They contain factual claims and the general public will be interested in knowing whether the claims are true. Journalists look for these type of claims for fact-checking.`
	`Use only one of the three labels (NFS, UFS and CFS), do not provide any additional explanation.`

V3	`Categorize the <sentence> spoken in the presidential debates into three categories: Non-Factual Sentence (NFS): Subjective sentences (opinions, beliefs, declarations) and many questions fall under this category. These sentences do not contain any factual claim. Here are two such examples. "But I think it's time to talk about the future." "You remember the last time you said that?" Unimportant Factual Sentence (UFS): These are factual claims but not check-worthy. The general public will not be interested in knowing whether these sentences are true or false. Fact-checkers do not find these sentences as important for checking. Some examples are as follows. "Next Tuesday is Election day." "Two days ago we ate lunch at a restaurant." Check-worthy Factual Sentence (CFS): They contain factual claims and the general public will be interested in knowing whether the claims are true. Journalists look for these type of claims for fact-checking. Some examples are: "He voted against the first Gulf War." "Over a million and a quarter Americans are HIV-positive." Use only one of the three labels (NFS, UFS and CFS), do not provide any additional explanation.`

Table 9: System prompts used for inference on the ClaimBuster dataset.

Level	Prompt
V1	Your task is to label the <sentence>. The information I need is whether it is an environmental claim. A broad definition for such a claim is given by the European Commission: Environmental claims refer to the practice of suggesting or otherwise creating the impression that a product or a service is environmentally friendly (i.e., it has a positive impact on the environment) or is less damaging to the environment than competing goods or services. Answer only with Yes or No.
V2	Your task is to label the <sentence>. The information I need is whether it is an environmental claim. A broad definition for such a claim is given by the European Commission: Environmental claims refer to the practice of suggesting or otherwise creating the impression that a product or a service is environmentally friendly (i.e., it has a positive impact on the environment) or is less damaging to the environment than competing goods or services. General principles: You will be presented with a <sentence> and have to decide whether the <sentence> contains an explicit environmental claim. Do not rely on implicit assumptions when you decide on the label. Base your decision on the information that is available within the sentence. However, if a sentence contains an abbreviation, you could consider the meaning of the abbreviation before assigning the label. In case a sentence is too technical/complicated and thus not easily understandable, it usually does not suggest to the average consumer that a product or a service is environmentally friendly and thus can be rejected. Likewise, if a sentence is not specific about having an environmental impact for a product or service, it can be rejected. Answer only with Yes or No.
V3	Your task is to label the <sentence>. The information I need is whether it is an environmental claim. A broad definition for such a claim is given by the European Commission: Environmental claims refer to the practice of suggesting or otherwise creating the impression that a product or a service is environmentally friendly (i.e., it has a positive impact on the environment) or is less damaging to the environment than competing goods or services. General principles: You will be presented with a sentence and have to decide whether the sentence contains an explicit environmental claim. Do not rely on implicit assumptions when you decide on the label. Base your decision on the information that is available within the sentence. However, if a sentence contains an abbreviation, you could consider the meaning of the abbreviation before assigning the label. In case a sentence is too technical/complicated and thus not easily understandable, it usually does not suggest to the average consumer that a product or a service is environmentally friendly and thus can be rejected. Likewise, if a sentence is not specific about having an environmental impact for a product or service, it can be rejected. Examples: <sentence>: Farmers who operate under this scheme are required to dedicate 10% of their land to wildlife preservation. Label: Yes Explanation: Environmental scheme with details on implementation. <sentence>: UPM Biofuels is developing a new feedstock concept by growing Brassica Carinata as a sequential crop in South America. Label: No Explanation: Sentence context would be required to understand whether it is a claim. Answer only with Yes or No, don't provide any additional explanation.

Table 10: System prompts used for inference on the EnvironmentalClaims dataset.

Level	Prompt
V1	A verifiable factual claim is a sentence claiming that something is true, and this can be verified using factual, verifiable information such as statistics, specific examples, or personal testimony. Does the <tweet> contain a verifiable factual claim? Answer only with Yes or No, don't provide any additional explanation.
V2	A verifiable factual claim is a sentence claiming that something is true, and this can be verified using factual, verifiable information such as statistics, specific examples, or personal testimony. Factual claims include the following: Stating a definition; Mentioning quantity in the present or the past; Making a verifiable prediction about the future; Reference to laws, procedures, and rules of operation; References to images or videos (e.g., "This is a video showing a hospital in Spain."); Statements about correlations or causations. Such correlation and causation needs to be explicit, i.e., sentences like "This is why the beaches haven't closed in Florida." is not a claim because it does not say why explicitly, thus it is not verifiable. Tweets containing personal opinions and preferences are not factual claims. Note: if a tweet is composed of multiple sentences or clauses, at least one full sentence or clause needs to be a claim in order for the tweet to contain a factual claim. If a claim exist in a sub-sentence or sub-clause then tweet is not considered to have a factual claim. For example, "My new favorite thing is Italian mayors and regional presidents LOSING IT at people violating quarantine" is not a claim, how ever, it is an opinion. Moreover, if we consider "Italian mayors and regional pres idents LOSING IT at people violating quarantine" it would be a claim. In addition, when answering this question, annotator should not open the tweet URL. Does the <tweet> contain a verifiable factual claim? Answer only with Yes or No.
V3	A verifiable factual claim is a sentence claiming that something is true, and this can be verified using factual, verifiable information such as statistics, specific examples, or personal testimony. Factual claims include the following: Stating a definition; Mentioning quantity in the present or the past; Making a verifiable prediction about the future; Reference to laws, procedures, and rules of operation; References to images or videos (e.g., "This is a video showing a hospital in Spain."); Statements about correlations or causations. Such correlation and causation needs to be explicit, i.e., sentences like "This is why the beaches haven't closed in Florida." is not a claim because it does not say why explicitly, thus it is not verifiable. Tweets containing personal opinions and preferences are not factual claims. Note: if a tweet is composed of multiple sentences or clauses, at least one full sentence or clause needs to be a claim in order for the tweet to contain a factual claim. If a claim exist in a sub-sentence or sub-clause then tweet is not considered to have a factual claim. For example, "My new favorite thing is Italian mayors and regional presidents LOSING IT at people violating quarantine" is not a claim, however, it is an opinion. Moreover, if we consider "Italian mayors and regional presidents LOSING IT at people violating quarantine" it would be a claim. In addition, when answering this question, annotator should not open the tweet URL. Does the <tweet> contain a verifiable factual claim? Answer only with Yes or No. Examples: Tweet: Please don't take hydroxychloroquine (Plaquenil) plus Azithromycin for #COVID19 UNLESS your doctor prescribes it. Both drugs affect the QT interval of your heart and can lead to arrhythmias and sudden death, especially if you are tak ing other meds or have a heart condition. Label: Yes Explanation: There is a claim in the text. Tweet: Saw this on Facebook today and it's a must read for all those idiots clearing the shelves #coronavirus #toiletpapercrisis #auspol Label: No Expla nation: There is no claim in the text. Answer only with Yes or No, don't provide any additional explanation.

Table 11: System prompts used for inference on the CLEF dataset for claim detection.

Level	Prompt
V1	It is important that a verifiable factual check-worthy claim be verified by a professional fact-checker, as the claim may cause harm to society, specific person(s), company(s), product(s), or some government entities. However, not all factual claims are important or worth fact-checking by a professional fact-checker, as this very time-consuming. Do you think that a professional fact-checker should verify the claim in the <tweet>? Labels: No, no need to check; No, too trivial to check; Yes, not urgent; Yes, very urgent. Decide on one label. Then, answer only with Yes or No.
V2	It is important that a verifiable factual check-worthy claim be verified by a professional fact-checker, as the claim may cause harm to society, specific person(s), company(s), product(s), or some government entities. However, not all factual claims are important or worth fact-checking by a professional fact-checker, as this very time-consuming. Do you think that a professional fact-checker should verify the claim in the <tweet>? Labels: No, no need to check: the tweet does not need to be fact-checked, e.g., be- cause it is not interesting, a joke, or does not contain any claim. No, too trivial to check: the tweet is worth fact-checking, how ever, this does not require a professional fact-checker, i.e., a non-expert might be able to fact-check the claim. For example, one can verify the information using reli able sources such as the official website of the WHO, etc. An example of a claim is as follows: "The GDP of the USA grew by 50% last year." Yes, not urgent: the tweet should be fact-checked by a professional fact-checker, however, this is not urgent or critical; Yes, very urgent: the tweet can cause immediate harm to a large number of people; therefore, it should be verified as soon as possible by a professional fact-checker; Decide on one label. Then, answer only with Yes or No.
V3	It is important to verify a factual claim by a professional fact-checker, which can cause harm to the society, specific person(s), company(s), product(s) or government entities. However, not all factual claims are important or worthwhile to be fact-checked by a professional fact-checker as it is a time-consuming procedure. Do you think that a professional fact-checker should verify the claim in the <tweet>? Labels: No, no need to check: the tweet does not need to be fact-checked, e.g., be- cause it is not interesting, a joke, or does not contain any claim. No, too trivial to check: the tweet is worth fact-checking, however, this does not require a professional fact-checker, i.e., a non-expert might be able to fact-check the claim. For example, one can verify the information using reliable sources such as the official website of the WHO, etc. An example of a claim is as follows: "The GDP of the USA grew by 50Yes, not urgent: the tweet should be fact-checked by a professional fact-checker, however, this is not urgent or critical; Yes, very urgent: the tweet can cause immediate harm to a large number of people; therefore, it should be verified as soon as possible by a professional fact-checker; Examples: Tweet: Wash your hands like you've been chopping jalapeños and need to change a contact lens" says BC Public Health Officer Dr. Bonnie Henry re. ways to protect against #coronavirus #Covid_19 Label: Yes, not urgent Explanation: Overall it is less important for a professional fact-checker to verify this information. The statement does not harm anyone. The truth value of whether the official said the statement is not important. Also it appears that washing hands is very important to protect oneself from the virus. Tweet: ALERT! The corona virus can be spread through internationaly printed albums. If you have any albums at home, put on some gloves, put all the albums in a box and put it outside the front door tonight. I'm collect ing all the boxes tonight for safety. Think of your health. Label: No, no need to check Explanation: This is joke and no need to check by a professional fact checker. Decide on one label. Then, answer only with Yes or No.

Table 12: System prompts used for inference on the CLEF dataset for claim check-worthiness detection.

Level	Prompt
V1	The task is to select verifiable statements from political speeches for fact-checking. Given a <statement> from a political speech, answer the question. Does the <statement> explicitly present any verifiable factual information? Answer with A, B or C only. A - Yes, B - Maybe, C - No.
V2	The task is to select verifiable statements from political speeches for fact-checking. Given a <statement> from a political speech, answer the question following the guidelines. Definitions and guidelines: Fact: A fact is a statement or assertion that can be objectively verified as true or false based on empirical evidence or reality. Opinion: An opinion is a judgment based on facts, an attempt to draw a reasonable conclusion from factual evidence. While the underlying facts can be verified, the derived opinion remains subjective and is not universally verifi able. Context: Make sure to consider a small context of the target statement (the previous and next sentence) when annotating. Some statements require context to un derstand the meaning. Factual claim: A factual claim is a statement that explicitly presents some verifiable facts. Statements with subjective components like opinions can also be factual claims if they explicitly present objectively verifiable facts. Opinion with Facts: Opinions can also be based on factual information. When does an opinion explicitly present a fact: Many opinions are more or less based on some factual information. However, some facts are explicitly presented by the speakers, while others are not. What is verifiable: The verifiability of the factual informa tion depends on how specific it is. If there is enough specific information to guide a general fact-checker in checking it, the factual information is verifiable. Other wise, it is not verifiable. The question: Does the <statement> explicitly present any verifiable factual information? Answer with A, B or C only. A - Yes, the statement contains factual information with enough specific details that a fact-checker knows how to verify it. E.g., Birmingham is small in population compared to London. B - Maybe, the statement seems to contain some factual information. However, there are certain ambiguities (e.g., lack of specificity) making it hard to determine the verifiability. E.g., Birmingham is small compared to London. (lack of details about what standard Birming ham is small) C - No, the statement contains no verifiable factual information. Even if there is some, it is clearly unverifiable. E.g., Birmingham is small.

Table 13: System prompts of Level V1 and Level V2 used for inference on the PoliClaim dataset for claim check-worthiness detection. The blue highlight shows instructions for regarding context.

Level	Prompt
V3	The task is to select verifiable statements from political speeches for fact-checking. Given a statement from a political speech and its context, answer the question following the guidelines. Definitions and guidelines: Fact: A fact is a statement or assertion that can be objectively verified as true or false based on empirical evidence or reality. Opinion: An opinion is a judgment based on facts, an attempt to draw a reasonable conclusion from factual evidence. While the underlying facts can be verified, the derived opinion remains subjective and is not universally verifiable. Factual claim: A factual claim is a statement that explicitly presents some verifiable facts. Statements with subjective components like opinions can also be factual claims if they explicitly present objectively verifiable facts. Context: Make sure to consider a small context of the target statement (the previous and next sentence) when annotating. Some statements require context to understand the meaning. For example: E1. "... Just consider what we did last year for the middle class in California, sending 12 billion dollars back - the largest state tax rebate in American history. <statement> But we didn't stop there. <> We raised the mini mum wage. We increased paid sick leave. Provided more paid family leave. Expanded child care to help working parents..." Without the context, the sentence marked with <statement> seems an incomplete sentence. With the context, we know the speaker is claiming a bunch of verifiable achievements of their administration. E2. "... When I first stood before this chamber three years ago, I declared war on criminals and asked for the Legislature to repeal and replace the catch-and-release policies in SB 91. <statement> With the help of many of you, we got it done. <> Policies do matter. We've seen our overall crime rate decline by 10 percent in 2019 and another 18.5 per cent in 2020! ..." The part marked with <statement> claims that the policies against crimes have been "done", which is verifiable. It needs context to understand it. Opinion with Facts: Opinions can also be based on factual information. For example: E1. "I am proud to report that on top of the local improvements, the state has ad ministered projects in almost all 67 counties already, and like I said, we've only just begun." The speaker's "proud of" is a subjective opinion. However, the content of pride (administered projects) is factual information. E2. "I first want to thank my wife of 34 years, First Lady Rose Dunleavy." The speaker expresses their thank fulness to their wife. However, there is factual information about the first lady's name and the length of their marriage. When does an opinion explicitly present a fact: Many opinions are more or less based on some factual information. However, some facts are explicitly presented by the speakers, while others are not. Explicit presentation means the fact is directly entailed by the opinion without extrapolation: E1. "The pizza is delicious." This opinion seems to be based on the fact that "pizza is a kind of food". However, this fact is not explicitly presented. E2. "I first want to thank my wife of 34 years, First Lady Rose Dunleavy." The name of the speaker's wife and their year of marriage are explicitly presented. What is verifiable: The verifiability of the factual information depends on how spe cific it is. If there is enough specific information to guide a general fact-checker in checking it, the factual information is verifiable. Otherwise, it is not veri fiable. E1. "Birmingham is small." is not verifiable because it lacks any specific information for determining veracity. It leans more toward subjective opinion. E2. "Birmingham is small, compared to London" is more verifiable than E1. A fact-checker can retrieve the city size, population size ...etc., of London and Birmingham to com pare them. However, what to compare to prove Birmingham's "small" is not specific enough. E3. "Birmingham is small in population size, compared to London" is more ver ifiable than E1 and E2. A fact-checker now knows it is exactly the population size to be compared. The question: Does the <statement> explicitly present any verifiable factual information? Answer with A, B or C only. A Yes, the statement contains factual information with enough specific details that a fact-checker knows how to verify it. E.g., Birmingham is small in population compared to London. B - Maybe, Maybe, the statement seems to contain some factual information. However, there are certain ambiguities (e.g., lack of specificity) making it hard to determine the verifiability. E.g., Birmingham is small compared to London. (lack of details about what standard Birmingham is small) C - No, the statement contains no verifiable factual information. Even if there is some, it is clearly unverifiable. E.g., Birmingham is small.

Table 14: System prompts of Level V3 used for inference on the PoliClaim dataset for claim check-worthiness detection. The blue highlight shows instructions for regarding context.

Contrastive Learning to Improve Retrieval for Real-world Fact Checking

Aniruddh Sriram **Fangyuan Xu** **Eunsol Choi** **Greg Durrett**
Department of Computer Science
The University of Texas at Austin
aniruddh.sriram@utexas.edu

Abstract

Recent work on fact-checking addresses a realistic setting where models incorporate evidence retrieved from the web to decide the veracity of claims. A bottleneck in this pipeline is in retrieving relevant evidence: traditional methods may surface documents directly related to a claim, but fact-checking complex claims requires more inferences. For instance, a document about how a vaccine was developed is relevant to addressing claims about what it might contain, even if it does not address them directly. We present Contrastive Fact-Checking Reranker (CFR), an improved retriever for this setting. By leveraging the AVeriTeC dataset, which annotates subquestions for claims with human written answers from evidence documents, we fine-tune Contriever with a contrastive objective based on multiple training signals, including distillation from GPT-4, evaluating subquestion answers, and gold labels in the dataset. We evaluate our model on both retrieval and end-to-end veracity judgments about claims. On the AVeriTeC dataset, we find a 6% improvement in veracity classification accuracy. We also show our gains can be transferred to FEVER, ClaimDecomp, HotpotQA, and a synthetic dataset requiring retrievers to make inferences.

1 Introduction

Retrieval-augmented generation (RAG) systems are now widely used across NLP applications including question answering (Guu et al., 2020; Lewis et al., 2020; Karpukhin et al., 2020) and text generation (Komeili et al., 2022; Gao et al., 2023b), but one particular application of interest is fact-checking. While older fact-checking systems would often not consider evidence at all (Alhindi et al., 2018) or consider oracle evidence (Atanasova et al., 2020), the real fact-checking task involves finding evidence to support or refute complex claims in the wild (Chen et al., 2022;

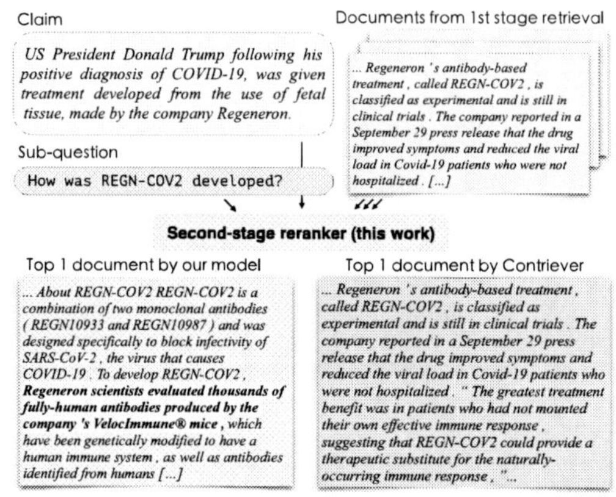

Figure 1: Top-1 retrieved document from base Contriever (red) and CFR (green). Our model is able to choose a better document despite both paragraphs being topical. Our model recognizes the question is asking about the chemical composition of REGN-COV2, while the unfinetuned model selects a relevant document that does not address "fetal tissue" or help with a final veracity judgment.

Schlichtkrull et al., 2023; Chen et al., 2024). As with many other RAG settings, retrieval is a bottleneck (Singh et al., 2022): it is impossible to provide the right judgment without retrieving the right evidence.

In this work, we investigate how to build an effective retriever for fact-checking. Figure 1 shows an example of why this is particularly challenging: unlike a factoid question with a definite answer spelled out in text, documents retrieved for fact-checking may only obliquely address a claim, or may present information in a different context (e.g., statistics that apply to a different country than the one where the claim was made). The unstructured nature of documents in the wild combined with claims that are only subtly true or false make retrieval a very difficult task.

We focus on two-step retrieval pipeline used in past work (Lazaridou et al., 2022; Chen et al., 2024). These use a first-stage web search (i.e., using Google or Bing) to build a set of approximately

Proceedings of the Seventh Fact Extraction and VERification Workshop (FEVER), pages 264–279
November 15, 2024 ©2024 Association for Computational Linguistics

relevant documents, followed by a second-stage fine-grained ranking to obtain a smaller set of documents to pass to a reader LM (Chen et al., 2024), which produces the final veracity judgment. This second stage shows consistent recall failures despite high-quality documents being present in the first stage, mainly due to the nuanced complexities with claims and subquestions in fact-checking.

Our approach, Contrastive Fact-Checking Reranker (CFR), leverages contrastive learning to fine-tune a dense retriever to prefer more relevant documents when there is a lack of information or ambiguity in the claim. To train our model, we experiment with two main supervision signals: distilling knowledge from GPT-4 and measuring answer equivalence with the gold answer using Learned Equivalence Metric for Reading Comprehension (LERC) (Chen et al., 2020). We generate training datasets of positive and negative evidence pairs based on these signals and fine-tune Contriever (Izacard et al., 2022).

Our evaluation shows that a combination of these supervision signals provides the best training data for the retriever, even better than fine-tuning on human annotated gold documents, as shown by gains in downstream performance across multiple datasets. Specifically, we see a 6% improvement in veracity classification accuracy and a 9% increase in the proportion of relevant top documents on AVeriTeC.

Our contributions are: (1) exploring new methods of supervision signals for contrastively training dense retrievers; (2) producing a strong dense retriever (CFR) which works well on AVeriTeC and a broader set of retrieval tasks regarding fact-checking complex claims.

2 Background and Related Work

2.1 Retrieval Augmented Generation Systems

Retrieval-augmented generation (RAG) relies on two key modules: a retriever and a reader/generation model. For many RAG systems, noisy retrieval hurts downstream performance by providing irrelevant or misleading documents (Yoran et al., 2024). Sauchuk et al. (2022) found that adding distractors can cause a 27% drop on veracity classification accuracy on FEVER. Therefore, it's important for retrievers to find relevant documents and simultaneously avoid damaging ones. Shi et al. (2023) attempts to solve this problem by finetuning the retrieval component while fixing the reader LM, similar to our work. Other approaches like Ke et al. (2024) create a more complex system with a "bridging" model between the retriever and reader. Nevertheless, noisy retrieval remains a failure point in RAG systems (Barnett et al., 2024), and tangible downstream gains can be realized by further finetuning.

2.2 Limitations of Existing Retrieval Systems

For NLP tasks like question answering, sparse retrieval techniques like BM25 have been supplanted by dense retrievers like DPR (Karpukhin et al., 2020) and Contriever (Izacard et al., 2022). These dual encoder approaches support efficient retrieval, and contrastive training is an effective way to learn embeddings for QA tasks. More recently, research has explored distilling knowledge from reader models to create smarter retrievers (Izacard and Grave, 2022). We draw from this work to build a retrieval system with better reasoning capabilities than baseline dense retrievers, which are usually pretrained on simpler (query, document) pairs (i.e. the MS-MARCO dataset). These retrieval systems have proven effective for fact-checking settings such as FEVER (Thorne et al., 2018) and MultiFC (Augenstein et al., 2019). However, the claims are largely short and factoid, and most of them contain no more than two entities. The realistic setting is embodied by approaches like QABriefs (Fan et al., 2020), ClaimDecomp (Chen et al., 2022, 2024), and AVeriTeC (Schlichtkrull et al., 2023), which are ultimately different from what dense retrievers were developed and optimized for.

2.3 Motivating Example: AVeriTeC

Figure 1 shows an example of fact-checking in the AVeriTeC dataset: *"how was REGN-COV2 developed?"*. This example differs in key ways from frequently-studied question answering settings such as such as Natural Questions (Kwiatkowski et al., 2019). First, it supports several different short answers but very likely has a best answer in the context of the claim: did the development involve human fetal tissue? In this case, the bolded paragraph indicates no: it used mice. The answer to this question should address the claim and provide background information: there is both a "short answer" as well as a "long answer" (Kwiatkowski et al., 2019; Gao et al., 2023a).

Retrieval signals in fact-checking Contrastive methods like Contriever require examples marked as positive or negative for use in the contrastive objective. In settings like NQ, retrieval systems rely on evaluating whether a retrieved passage contains the answer by simple string matching or ROUGE overlap, which identifies "positives" for retrieval. However, in Section 5 we show it is not straighforward to apply this approach in fact-checking; i.e., we cannot simply say a passage is positive if it contains the ground truth answer.

Simultaneously, we must be cautious of assuming a low overlap with the answer indicates a "negative" document for retrieval. This is because multiple plausible answers can exist due to the open-ended nature of subquestions in AVeriTeC. Furthermore, using documents from the wild exacerbates this issue by introducing documents that might not directly support the gold answer but still contain valuable information about the claim. In Section 3, we outline some ways in which we tackle this problem to curate better finetuning data.

Context in retrieval Traditionally, retrievers are given standalone questions as queries. This is characteristic of datasets like NQ, where questions often contain one clear answer (e.g. "*Where is the bowling ball hall of fame located?*"). However, in fact-checking, the complexity of claims gives rise to subquestions that are not standalone or simple. Even if the questions themselves seem short (i.e., "*How was REGN-COV2 developed?*"), they must be interpreted in-context with the claim (i.e., "*Does REGN-COV2 contain fetal tissue?*"). Ideally, decomposing claims into a set of perfect standalone subquestions would reduce the load on the retriever. However, this itself is a hard and separate task. In this work, we attempt to build a retrieval system that can handle nuanced queries by considering each subquestion in the context of the overall claim.

3 Methodology

We consider a setting following work in AVeriTeC and ClaimDecomp (Chen et al., 2022). We assume we are given a collection of **claims** $(c_1, \ldots, c_N)$. For claim c_i, we define q_{ij} as the jth **subquestion** for the ith claim in the dataset and a^g_{ij} define its **answer**. We also assume access to a document set $D(c_i, q_{ij})$ for each subquestion, created by querying Bing with c_i appended to q_{ij} and scrape the top-k articles to form a document corpus. Each **document** d is a 200 token span gathered from the scraped articles. The title of the document is prepended to the start of each document. The dataset also comes with a **gold article** which contains the gold answer. Like the Bing-retrieved documents, it is chunked into 200 token span documents $\{d^g\}$ and added to $D(c_i, q_{ij})$. We refer to documents belonging to these articles as *gold*.

Given a query $y = [c_i; q_{ij}]$ and a document $d_i \in D$, we want to generate embeddings in $\mathbb{R}^e$ using an encoder network (e.g. Contriever). Let h_y, h_{d_i} denote the representations of y and d_i. Then we define our scoring function $f : \mathbb{R}^e \times \mathbb{R}^e \to \mathbb{R}$ such that $f(h_y, h_{d_i}) > f(h_y, h_{d_j})$ if document d_i contains more information helpful to answering the query than document d_j. Let $r(y) = \arg\max_{d \in D} f(h_y, h_d)$ which is a function that chooses the highest ranked document in our document set D. The goal is to optimize our encoder via f to rank documents for answering questions in-context with the claim above topically relevant documents that do not ultimately contain information for an answer. We choose to optimize this for downstream veracity classification accuracy. We also track more upstream metrics such as using a relevance score for the top document or measuring how close its extracted answer matches the gold answer.

3.1 Components

Dense retriever r We use Contriever as the base for our second stage dense retriever. Contriever uses the BERT base uncased architecture (Devlin et al., 2019). To fine-tune it with contrastive learning, we require document sets $T(c_i, q_{ij}, D) = \{D^+, D^-\}$ of positive and negative documents; during optimization, the positive documents will be embedded closer to the query vector than negative documents. Contrastive training relies critically on having hard negatives to serve as "distractors" (Robinson et al., 2021). These might be documents ranked high by baseline retrievers or having high token overlap with the query. Figure 2 shows our pipeline for constructing these document sets, which we expand on in the following sections.

We define $S_{\text{BM25}}(c_i, q_{ij}) = \{d_1, d_2, \ldots, d_k\}$ as the top k documents surfaced by BM25 given $[c_i; q_{ij}]$ as the query. We also define $G_{\text{BM25}}(c_i, q_{ij}) = \{d^g_1, d^g_2, \ldots, d^g_l\}$ as the top l gold annotated documents. In our models, we set $k = 10$ and $l = 5$.

Reader model We use GPT-4 as the reader model. The answers are derived by prompting GPT-4 with the claim c_i, question q_{ij}, and a document

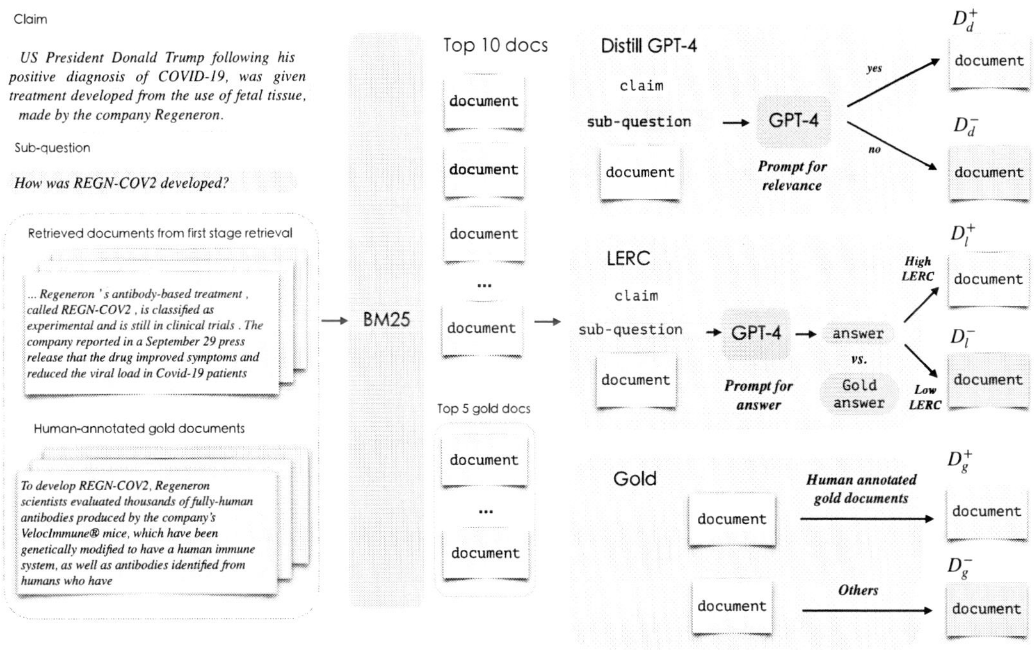

Figure 2: Overview of generating positive and negative examples for finetuning the retriever. We first select documents with high BM25 score with the (query, subquestion) from both the web documents and gold articles. We then experiment with different methods (described in Section 3.3) to derive positive and hard negative examples.

d_{ij} from the corpus (see Appendix E.3). For a given (c_i, q_{ij}) pair, we refer to a_{ij} as the candidate answer derived from the evidence document d_{ij}. During inference time, d_{ij} is the top-1 document from our retrieval system.

3.2 Learning

We train r on these $(c_i, q_{ij}) \times T$ pairs to produce a finetuned retriever r^*. Specifically, given a query $y = [c_i; q_{ij}]$ and positive document $d^+ \in D^+$,

$$L(y, d^+) = \frac{\exp\left(\frac{1}{\tau} f(h_y, h_{d^+})\right)}{\exp\left(\frac{1}{\tau} f(h_y, h_{d^+})\right) + \sum_{d^- \in D^-} \exp\left(\frac{1}{\tau} f(h_y, h_{d^-})\right)}$$

where τ is a temperature parameter. In our setting, we define f as cosine similarity $\frac{h_y^T h_d}{\|h_y\| \cdot \|h_d\|}$ between the embeddings. This encourages positive documents to have high similarity with the query while penalizing high scores for negative documents. Fine-tuning yields r^* such that $r^*(y)$ contains a better answer to q_{ij} in context with c_i than $r(y)$.

Implementation Details On average, each question q_{ij} comes with about 500 documents to rank. Each document contains 200 token span, scraped from articles with a 100 token length stride. Details about training and model architecture can be found in Appendix A.1.

3.3 Generating Contrastive Training Data

We generate $\{D^+, D^-\}$ in three main ways: the annotated AVeriTeC gold evidence, distilled relevance judgements from a GPT-4 reader module, and evaluating equivalence of the document-predicted answer with a gold answer. Figure 2 shows the three approaches which we describe next.

AVeriTeC Gold Evidence The most straightforward approach to building positive examples is to use the human-annotated evidence paragraphs available in AVeriTeC. The gold articles (one per subquestion) were selected by human annotators in a two-stage annotation process, we refer the readers to their paper for details (Schlichtkrull et al., 2023). The annotators also provided answers for the subquestions, which consist of both extractive and abstractive answers. For each q_{ij}, this article is chunked into a set of documents $\{d_{ij}^g\}$ as described in Section 3. Negative examples are all $d \in S_{\text{BM25}}(c_i, q_{ij})$ such that d is not from a gold-annotated document. We denote the fine-tuning data derived from this method as $\{D_g^+, D_g^-\}$.

Distilling GPT-4 The AVeriTeC gold evidence may have recall errors: there may be relevant documents that are not marked by annotators. An alternative is to use GPT-4 as a labeler, effectively distilling its knowledge (Figure 2, top right). In this setting, we take $S_{\text{BM25}}(c_i, q_{ij})$ and zero-shot prompt GPT-4 about whether each document is relevant to answering the subquestion or not. Note we do not provide the gold answer in the prompt, as we are simply interested in collecting documents with relevant information regardless of how well the underlying answer matches a^g_{ij}. Documents marked as relevant are added to D^+, and the rest are added to D^-. The exact prompt can be found in Appendix E.1. We define this set as $\{D^+_d, D^-_d\}$.

Distilling GPT-4 (with gold) In this setting, we inject the top-l AVeriTeC gold documents $G_{\text{BM25}}(c_i, q_{ij})$ into the finetuning set. Like before, we zero-shot prompt GPT-4 about whether each document is relevant to answering the subquestion, but include $G_{\text{BM25}}(c_i, q_{ij})$ in addition to $S_{\text{BM25}}(c_i, q_{ij})$. We refer to $\{D^+_{dg}, D^-_{dg}\}$ as the finetuning data from this method.

LERC-based signal An additional approach to construct our pairs is to use the gold-annotated answers a^g_{ij} (Figure 2, middle right). Ideally, a document we retrieve should help us discover these answers; however, because the subquestions are not factoid questions, it is not easy to assess whether a retrieved document contains the answer.

To do this, we filter the top documents using LERC (Learned Evaluation Metric for Reading Comprehension) (Chen et al., 2020), a metric for scoring answer equivalence. More formally, we take $S_{\text{BM25}}(c_i, q_{ij})$ with $G_{\text{BM25}}(c_i, q_{ij})$ to make a set of 15 documents. We then prompt GPT-4 to use each of the 15 evidence documents to produce an answer a_{ij} for each document. We found that for complex long answers, using ROUGE overlap as an answer equivalence metric works poorly (Appendix B.1). On AVeriTeC, we also tried using ROUGE-F1 score instead of LERC (see Table 2) to see how this reflects in all our end-to-end evaluation metrics. To accommodate this, we introduce an "answer shortening" function s which attempts to pull out the main point of the answer. We use LERC to compare $s(a_{ij})$ and $s(a^g_{ij})$, our shortened candidate and gold answer respectively. By identifying documents which give rise to answers with high LERC scores, we encourage our retriever to seek documents which address the question in the query. Documents with poor LERC scores (< 0.3) become negative contexts, and documents with high LERC (> 0.7) scores are positive contexts. We also evaluate how well human annotators agree with granular LERC scores and find an average Kendall's τ score of 0.53 (Appendix C.2). We denote $\{D^+_l, D^-_l\}$ as finetuning data derived from this method.

Train Set	# subq	$\|D^+\|$	$\|D^-\|$	D^+	D^-
distill	1228	4.8	8.4	D^+_d	D^-_d
LERC	692	1	4.2	D^+_l	D^-_l
gold	1229	1	9.1	D^+_g	D^-_g
distill (gold)	1229	5.2	8.4	D^+_{dg}	D^-_{dg}
distill (gold) + LERC	1229	5.6	8.4	$D^+_{dg} \cup D^+_l$	D^-_{dg}

Table 1: Dataset statistics for different finetuning sets from AVeriTeC. $|D^+|$ and $|D^-|$ represent the average number of positive and negative contexts per (c_i, q_{ij}) pair. Differences in number of subquestions come from filtering out examples for which $|D^+| = 0$ or $|D^-| = 0$.

LERC-based quality check We evaluated $\{D^+_l, D^-_l\}$ and found that many negative documents were actually relevant to the claim/question. More details on this experiment can be found in Appendix C.1. To reduce the false negative rate, we mix in relevant documents with the positive set from *distill* to create $\{D^+_{dg} \cup D^+_l, D^-_{dg}\}$. We refer to this as the *distill (gold) + LERC* setting. This is the final experimental setting we use for our **Contrastive Fact-Checking Reranker (CFR)** model.

4 Experimental Setup

We evaluate Contriever fine-tuned on the supervision signals outlined in Section 3. The datasets selected for evaluation, namely AVeriTeC (Schlichtkrull et al., 2023), ClaimDecomp (Chen et al., 2022), FEVER (Thorne et al., 2018), and HotpotQA (Yang et al., 2018), encompass a wide range of scenarios for document retrieval. For evaluation, a random subset of 200 answerable examples (subquestions contain an answer) were selected from each of these not overlapping with the training sets.

4.1 Metrics

We use metrics that evaluate both the retrieved documents and downstream products of these documents, such as the produced answer.

- **LERC** computes the average LERC score between the AVeriTeC (or ClaimDecomp) gold answer and the GPT-4 generated answer from the top retrieved document as the candidate.

- **Top doc relevance** is the proportion of examples for which the top-1 document is classified as relevant to answering the question by GPT-4, using the same prompt for which we derive the distillation signal.

- **Gold@10** is the proportion of examples in which an AVeriTeC annotated gold document appeared in the top-10.

- **Veracity** represents the veracity classification accuracy. For ClaimDecomp, we use the RoBERTa based veracity classifier trained on ClaimDecomp.[1] For FEVER, we few-shot prompt GPT-4 for a veracity label; see Appendix E.4.

4.2 Datasets

AVeriTeC consists of real claims (c_i) from the web annotated with subquestions (q_{ij}), gold answers (a^g_{ij}) to the subquestions, and the gold evidence document for the answer. We query Bing in FSR with the claim and subquestion $[c_i; q_{ij}]$ to generate D. The generated answers (a_{ij}) are verified against the gold answers using LERC.

ClaimDecomp consists of complex political claims (c_i) with yes/no subquestion decompositions (q_{ij}) generated by trained annotators. We query Bing in FSR with the claim and subquestion $[c_i; q_{ij}]$ to generate D. The annotated subquestions tackle both explicit and implicit parts of the original claim. The implicit questions are much harder to answer without sufficient context, which makes this an interesting dataset for retrieval evaluation. The human labeled answers are yes/no, and we evaluate our generated answers (a_{ij}) against the gold answers using LERC. Because the questions themselves are yes/no in nature, this approach returns the same results as simple binary comparison.

FEVER consists of claims (c_i) manually verified against the introductory sections of Wikipedia pages and classified as SUPPORTED, REFUTED or NOTENOUGHINFO. We treat the claim itself as the question ($c_i = q_i$) here. Unlike past work, we query Bing with the claim to generate D; as a result, our data condition is different than past work evaluating on FEVER. For FEVER, we don't generate answers or subquestions and simply verify the claim against the evidence document.

Model	LERC	Top Doc Relv.	Gold@10	Veracity
BM25	0.45	0.47	0.42	0.48
Contriever	0.48	0.54	0.50	0.54
Contriever MSM	0.52	0.55	0.45	0.59
ROUGE-F1*	0.52	0.53	0.50	0.55
gold	0.50	0.51	0.56	0.53
distill	**0.54**	**0.63**	**0.60**	0.55
LERC	0.53	0.56	0.54	**0.60**
distill (gold)	**0.54**	0.61	0.59	0.58
CFR	0.53	0.62	0.59	**0.60**

Table 2: In-domain experimental results on AVeriTeC test subset ($n = 200$). Numbers marked with are statistically significant w.r.t. baseline Contriever at $o =$ 0.05 under 10,000 bootstrapped samples. CFR is what we call the model finetuned on *distill (gold) + LERC*.

HotpotQA is a question answering dataset featuring multi-hop questions, with strong supervision for supporting facts to enable more explainable question answering systems. The questions require finding and reasoning over multiple supporting documents to answer. There are no claims in this dataset, so we set $c_i = q_i$ and retrieval is done with just the question.

4.3 Baselines

We report performance of several widely-used retrievers as baselines: **BM25**, **Contriever** (Izacard et al., 2022) and Contriever fine-tuned on the MS MARCO dataset (Campos et al., 2016) (**Contriever MSM**). We also compare against an additional Contriever baseline. We use **ROUGE-F1** supervision similar to the LERC setup, except long answers were evaluated using ROUGE overlap scores. This tests whether our approaches outperform a simple method for answer matching.

5 Results

5.1 AVeriTeC

The results for AVeriTeC are shown in Table 2. We find that *distill* performs the best in most metrics but for veracity. The 6% gain in top doc relevance reflect our retriever's ability to correctly identify more relevant documents in our evaluation set.

As expected, we find that using ROUGE as a long answer overlap metric to generate $\{D^+, D^-\}$ works poorly as seen by the ROUGE-F1 baseline.

[1] https://github.com/jifan-chen/Fact-checking-via-Raw-Evidence

Model	ClaimDecomp			FEVER		HotpotQA	
	LERC	Top Doc Relv.	Veracity	Top Doc Relv.	Veracity	LERC	Top Doc Relv.
BM25	0.54	0.30	0.30	0.43	0.55	0.28	0.21
Contriever	0.64	0.32	0.32	0.49	0.58	0.33	0.27
Contriever MSM	0.64	0.31	0.34	0.52	0.61	0.34	0.31
gold	0.64	0.30	0.28	0.48	0.56	0.32	0.30
distill	0.64	**0.39**	0.32	**0.57**	0.61	0.34	0.26
LERC	0.65	0.31	0.31	0.55	0.61	0.34	0.30
distill (gold)	**0.66**	0.37	0.34	0.56	0.61	0.35	**0.32**
CFR	0.65	0.32	0.34	**0.57**	**0.63**	**0.36**	**0.32**

Table 3: Out-of-domain experimental results on ClaimDecomp, FEVER, and HotpotQA test subset (n=200 for each dataset). Numbers marked with are statistically significant w.r.t. baseline Contriever at $p = 0.05$ under 10,000 bootstrapped samples from the respective test subset.

Comparing the average LERC score between baseline Contriever and Contriever finetuned on *LERC*, we find a 5% gain in the average LERC score on the evaluation set. This is also backed by a 6% increase in downstream veracity classification performance, indicating our improved ability to answer questions transfers to actually fact-checking the claim. We also see that the models finetuned with LERC signals (*LERC* and CFR) reflect the strongest improvements in veracity classification. CFR also excels in top doc relevance and other upstream metrics. This indicates evaluating answers derived from documents may help downstream performance on fact-checking more than other supervision signals.

Lexical overlap We find that *gold* supervision (using AVeriTeC annotated gold evidence) performs poorly across all metrics. We hypothesize two reasons for this: 1) the evidence lacks significant token overlap with the claim/subquestion and 2) gold annotation involves human reasoning and assumptions which are too complex for the unfinetuned retriever to model in its document embedding space. In fact, the average ROUGE-F1 score between $[c_i; q_{ij}]$ and highest overlapping gold document is only 0.11 compared to 0.25 for the top-ranked document from the wild (see Appendix B.2). This discrepancy comes from examples where the annotated evidence document is based on a related entity not mentioned in the claim or question, which is very challenging to recover without additional context. In other cases, modeling the annotated gold evidence is challenging because it contains new information that is not known from the claim or subquestion alone. Therefore, supervising with only gold documents doesn't effectively help the retriever learn.

5.2 Out-of-domain results

Results on out-of-domain datasets are in Table 3.

ClaimDecomp We find that our gains translate to ClaimDecomp, with *distill (gold)* demonstrating significant improvements in both LERC and top doc relevance. Examples in this dataset contains both explicit and implicit subquestions, while AVeriTeC subquestions are mostly explicit. Since we use subquestions for retrieval, improvement in top doc relevance may reflect an ability to surface better documents for ambiguous implicit subquestions, which is something baseline retrievers struggle with. An example of this is seen in Appendix D, where our finetuned retriever model is able to accurately capture the focus on lack of funding presented in the question. Even though baseline Contriever selects a document detailing the Amtrak incident with high lexical overlap with the claim and query, the document itself is not useful for answering the question. Using CFR, we see a 2% increase in downstream veracity classification performance.

FEVER We also find that our system gives gains on FEVER compared to BM25, Contriever, and Contriever MSM. Our retriever selects relevant top documents more often and yields improved downstream veracity performance.

HotpotQA For HotpotQA, we find that *distill (gold) + LERC* performs the best across LERC and top doc relevance. We notice the strongest gains come from including LERC-based supervision, which indicates our retriever may learn to identify answer documents that contain little overlap with the claim. This is especially useful in multi-hop settings where the answer document cannot be found in one step from the query.

6 Retriever Reasoning Capabilities

Our hypothesis about our contrastive training was that it would impart a greater ability for our retriever to "reason" about content rather than directly locating an answer. We conduct an additional study of whether our retriever can exhibit basic 1-hop reasoning capabilities via a synthetic data experiment. We construct positive and negative documents where the positive documents do not directly state the answer, similar to what we found in several AVeriTeC examples.

6.1 Synthetic Data Generation

We build these examples by few-shot prompting GPT-4 with synthetic documents written by humans. Our data generation approach takes as input a claim/question pair (c_i, q_{ij}) from AVeriTeC and produces a document set $\{d^+, d^-, d_1^-, d_2^-, d_3^-, d_4^-\}$. We generate data for (c_i, q_{ij}) pairs from the validation set described in Section 4. The positive document d^+ is the only document that contains an answer to the question. Document d^- is a "hard negative" document, which is a document that appears *highly* relevant to the query $[c_i; q_{ij}]$ but does not contain an answer. The 4 other documents $d_1^-, \ldots, d_4^-$ are additional negative documents built from alternate subquestions about the claim.

The **positive document** is a paragraph that supports an answer to the question, but only indirectly. When prompting (Appendix E.2), we require that a clear reasoning hop must be made to recover an answer from the positive document. Therefore, a retrieval system that simply looks for query-document token overlap may not be able to find such documents because the answer is usually not presented in terms of the question.

The **hard negative document** is a paragraph that looks highly relevant to the claim/question, but doesn't actually support an answer. In the prompt, we specify that the document should appear relevant but not support an answer, and further enforce this with few-shot examples (see Appendix E.2). In Appendix F.2, the hard negative document correctly discusses the federal judges Trump nominated. However, it does not contain any information about *how many* judges he nominated, deeming it useless for answering the question about the claim.

Model	MRR
BM25	0.49
Contriever	0.68
Contriever MSM	0.75
gold	0.72
distill	**0.80**
LERC	0.72
distill (gold)	**0.80**
CFR	0.79

Table 4: Results for 200 examples of synthetically generated data. Numbers marked with are statistically significant w.r.t. baseline Contriever at $p = 0.10$ under 10,000 bootstrapped samples from the respective test set.

The **remaining negative documents** are built by generating alternate subquestions similar to q_{ij} but without overlapping answers. Then, we generate documents that contain answers to these distractor subquestions. An example can be found in Appendix F.1 along with the prompt in Appendix E.2.

6.2 Results

We evaluate our retrievers on their ability to score the positive document closer to the query than the negative distractor documents. We measure this via MRR of the positive document across ranking the six documents (positive, hard negative, and 4 alternate question negatives). The results are displayed in Table 4. We find a statistically significant gain in our finetuned model's ability to surface the positive document over other distractor documents. CFR achieves an MRR of 0.79 compared to baseline Contriever (0.68). This supports our hypothesis that finetuning on our supervision signals improves the ability of the retrieval model to find information only indirectly related to the claim.

7 Conclusion

This work presents an improved retrieval system, CFR, for fact-checking complex claims. We present two supervision signals for finetuning retrievers under a contrastive objective, and their integration results in improved downstream veracity classification. Furthermore, CFR is able to improve retrieval in settings where inferences are required to identify the correct documents. The gains found in this paper encourage explorations into improving retrieval for fact-checking, as surfacing relevant information proved to be a hard task even for SOTA dense retrievers.

Limitations

There are a few limitations of our current approach. First, using LERC as an answer equivalence metric requires us to shorten both the gold and candidate answer. The answer compression step loses information that may play a role in verifying hard examples. Therefore, developing a good long answer equivalence metric can help build an even better retrieval system for fact-checking. Such equivalence metrics can also be useful for evaluation: the long-form explanation of why a claim is true or false may be more important than the veracity judgment itself, but this is difficult to assess in an automated way.

Second, this work focuses on the second-stage retrieval step. Building optimized queries for first stage retrieval may yield a better document corpus for second stage, especially for hard examples where little information has been published. However, indexing the necessary documents for the broad set of claims we use involves web-scale indexing, which is beyond the scope of this project.

Finally, this work considered English-language political claims. We note that claims in multimedia (e.g., in memes or videos), claims in other languages, and claims in specialized domains such as COVID-19 misinformation may present distinct challenges. However, we believe that our framework is flexible enough for future work to be able to build on it and train retrievers for these settings as well.

Ethical Considerations and Risks

This paper presents a retrieval method that seeks to advance the state of the art in automated fact-checking. However, despite recent progress in this area and systems that combine retrieval systems like ours with LLMs (Schlichtkrull et al., 2023; Chen et al., 2024), we stress that these system are not yet ready for deployment. We believe these systems have use to aid professional fact-checkers in their work, since enabling them to quickly find information can aid them to more rapidly check claims. However, these systems cannot produce reliable fact-checks without a human in the loop, as demonstrated by the veracity numbers in this work. Moreover, there is not necessarily a single objective truth about every claim, and a judgment may depend on the reliability of primary sources and other factors which are beyond the scope of this work.

Acknowledgments

This work was partially supported by Good Systems,[2] a UT Austin Grand Challenge to develop responsible AI technologies, NSF CAREER Award IIS-2145280, and the NSF AI Institute for Foundations of Machine Learning (IFML). We thank the UT Austin NLP community for revisions and feedback on earlier drafts of this paper.

References

Tariq Alhindi, Savvas Petridis, and Smaranda Muresan. 2018. Where is your evidence: Improving fact-checking by justification modeling. In *Proceedings of the First Workshop on Fact Extraction and VERification (FEVER)*, pages 85–90, Brussels, Belgium. Association for Computational Linguistics.

Pepa Atanasova, Jakob Grue Simonsen, Christina Lioma, and Isabelle Augenstein. 2020. Generating fact checking explanations. In *Proceedings of the 58th Annual Meeting of the Association for Computational Linguistics*, pages 7352–7364, Online. Association for Computational Linguistics.

Isabelle Augenstein, Christina Lioma, Dongsheng Wang, Lucas Chaves Lima, Casper Hansen, Christian Hansen, and Jakob Grue Simonsen. 2019. MultiFC: A real-world multi-domain dataset for evidence-based fact checking of claims. In *Proceedings of the 2019 Conference on Empirical Methods in Natural Language Processing and the 9th International Joint Conference on Natural Language Processing (EMNLP-IJCNLP)*, pages 4685–4697, Hong Kong, China. Association for Computational Linguistics.

Scott Barnett, Stefanus Kurniawan, Srikanth Thudumu, Zach Brannelly, and Mohamed Abdelrazek. 2024. Seven failure points when engineering a retrieval augmented generation system. *Proceedings of the IEEE/ACM 3rd International Conference on AI Engineering - Software Engineering for AI.*

Daniel Fernando Campos, Tri Nguyen, Mir Rosenberg, Xia Song, Jianfeng Gao, Saurabh Tiwary, Rangan Majumder, Li Deng, and Bhaskar Mitra. 2016. MS MARCO: A Human Generated MAchine Reading COmprehension Dataset. *ArXiv*, abs/1611.09268.

Anthony Chen, Gabriel Stanovsky, Sameer Singh, and Matt Gardner. 2020. Mocha: A dataset for training and evaluating generative reading comprehension metrics. In *Proceedings of the 2020 Conference on Empirical Methods in Natural Language Processing (EMNLP)*. Association for Computational Linguistics.

Jifan Chen, Grace Kim, Aniruddh Sriram, Greg Durrett, and Eunsol Choi. 2024. Complex claim verification with evidence retrieved in the wild. In *Proceedings*

[2]https://goodsystems.utexas.edu/

of the North American Chapter of the Association for Computational Linguistics (NAACL).

Jifan Chen, Aniruddh Sriram, Eunsol Choi, and Greg Durrett. 2022. Generating literal and implied subquestions to fact-check complex claims. In *Proceedings of the 2022 Conference on Empirical Methods in Natural Language Processing*, pages 3495–3516, Abu Dhabi, United Arab Emirates. Association for Computational Linguistics.

Jacob Devlin, Ming-Wei Chang, Kenton Lee, and Kristina Toutanova. 2019. BERT: Pre-training of deep bidirectional transformers for language understanding. In *Proceedings of the 2019 Conference of the North American Chapter of the Association for Computational Linguistics: Human Language Technologies, Volume 1 (Long and Short Papers)*, pages 4171–4186, Minneapolis, Minnesota. Association for Computational Linguistics.

Angela Fan, Aleksandra Piktus, Fabio Petroni, Guillaume Wenzek, Marzieh Saeidi, Andreas Vlachos, Antoine Bordes, and Sebastian Riedel. 2020. Generating fact checking briefs. In *Proceedings of the 2020 Conference on Empirical Methods in Natural Language Processing (EMNLP)*, pages 7147–7161, Online. Association for Computational Linguistics.

Tianyu Gao, Howard Yen, Jiatong Yu, and Danqi Chen. 2023a. Enabling large language models to generate text with citations. In *Proceedings of the 2023 Conference on Empirical Methods in Natural Language Processing*, pages 6465–6488, Singapore. Association for Computational Linguistics.

Yunfan Gao, Yun Xiong, Xinyu Gao, Kangxiang Jia, Jinliu Pan, Yuxi Bi, Yi Dai, Jiawei Sun, Qianyu Guo, Meng Wang, and Haofen Wang. 2023b. Retrieval-Augmented Generation for Large Language Models: A Survey. *ArXiv*, abs/2312.10997.

Kelvin Guu, Kenton Lee, Zora Tung, Panupong Pasupat, and Ming-Wei Chang. 2020. REALM: retrieval-augmented language model pre-training. In *Proceedings of the 37th International Conference on Machine Learning*, ICML'20. JMLR.org.

Gautier Izacard, Mathilde Caron, Lucas Hosseini, Sebastian Riedel, Piotr Bojanowski, Armand Joulin, and Edouard Grave. 2022. Unsupervised dense information retrieval with contrastive learning. *arXiv eprint 2112.09118*.

Gautier Izacard and Edouard Grave. 2022. Distilling knowledge from reader to retriever for question answering. *arXiv eprint 2012.04584*.

Vladimir Karpukhin, Barlas Oguz, Sewon Min, Patrick Lewis, Ledell Wu, Sergey Edunov, Danqi Chen, and Wen-tau Yih. 2020. Dense passage retrieval for open-domain question answering. In *Proceedings of the 2020 Conference on Empirical Methods in Natural Language Processing (EMNLP)*, pages 6769–6781, Online. Association for Computational Linguistics.

Zixuan Ke, Weize Kong, Cheng Li, Mingyang Zhang, Qiaozhu Mei, and Michael Bendersky. 2024. Bridging the Preference Gap between Retrievers and LLMs. *ArXiv*, abs/2401.06954.

Mojtaba Komeili, Kurt Shuster, and Jason Weston. 2022. Internet-augmented dialogue generation. In *Proceedings of the 60th Annual Meeting of the Association for Computational Linguistics (Volume 1: Long Papers)*, pages 8460–8478, Dublin, Ireland. Association for Computational Linguistics.

Tom Kwiatkowski, Jennimaria Palomaki, Olivia Redfield, Michael Collins, Ankur Parikh, Chris Alberti, Danielle Epstein, Illia Polosukhin, Matthew Kelcey, Jacob Devlin, Kenton Lee, Kristina N. Toutanova, Llion Jones, Ming-Wei Chang, Andrew Dai, Jakob Uszkoreit, Quoc Le, and Slav Petrov. 2019. Natural Questions: a Benchmark for Question Answering Research. *Transactions of the Association of Computational Linguistics*.

Angeliki Lazaridou, Elena Gribovskaya, Wojciech Stokowiec, and Nikolai Grigorev. 2022. Internet-augmented language models through few-shot prompting for open-domain question answering. *ArXiv*, abs/2203.05115.

Patrick Lewis, Ethan Perez, Aleksandra Piktus, Fabio Petroni, Vladimir Karpukhin, Naman Goyal, Heinrich Küttler, Mike Lewis, Wen-tau Yih, Tim Rocktäschel, Sebastian Riedel, and Douwe Kiela. 2020. Retrieval-Augmented Generation for Knowledge-Intensive NLP Tasks. In *Advances in Neural Information Processing Systems*, volume 33, pages 9459–9474. Curran Associates, Inc.

Joshua David Robinson, Ching-Yao Chuang, Suvrit Sra, and Stefanie Jegelka. 2021. Contrastive learning with hard negative samples. In *International Conference on Learning Representations*.

Artsiom Sauchuk, James Thorne, Alon Y. Halevy, Nicola Tonellotto, and Fabrizio Silvestri. 2022. On the role of relevance in natural language processing tasks. *Proceedings of the 45th International ACM SIGIR Conference on Research and Development in Information Retrieval*.

Michael Sejr Schlichtkrull, Zhijiang Guo, and Andreas Vlachos. 2023. AVeritec: A dataset for real-world claim verification with evidence from the web. In *Thirty-seventh Conference on Neural Information Processing Systems Datasets and Benchmarks Track*.

Weijia Shi, Sewon Min, Michihiro Yasunaga, Minjoon Seo, Rich James, Mike Lewis, Luke Zettlemoyer, and Wen tau Yih. 2023. REPLUG: Retrieval-Augmented Black-Box Language Models. *ArXiv*, abs/2301.12652.

Prakhar Singh, Anubrata Das, Junyi Jessy Li, and Matthew Lease. 2022. The case for claim difficulty assessment in automatic fact checking. *arXiv eprint 2109.09689*.

James Thorne, Andreas Vlachos, Christos Christodoulopoulos, and Arpit Mittal. 2018. FEVER: a large-scale dataset for fact extraction and VERification. In *Proceedings of the 2018 Conference of the North American Chapter of the Association for Computational Linguistics: Human Language Technologies, Volume 1 (Long Papers)*, pages 809–819, New Orleans, Louisiana. Association for Computational Linguistics.

Zhilin Yang, Peng Qi, Saizheng Zhang, Yoshua Bengio, William Cohen, Ruslan Salakhutdinov, and Christopher D. Manning. 2018. HotpotQA: A dataset for diverse, explainable multi-hop question answering. In *Proceedings of the 2018 Conference on Empirical Methods in Natural Language Processing*, pages 2369–2380, Brussels, Belgium. Association for Computational Linguistics.

Ori Yoran, Tomer Wolfson, Ori Ram, and Jonathan Berant. 2024. Making retrieval-augmented language models robust to irrelevant context. In *The Twelfth International Conference on Learning Representations*.

A Implementation Details

A.1 Computational Details

The finetuned models were BERT base uncased (110M parameters). Hyperparameter optimization was done via grid search on the learning rate and batch size. For learning rate, we searched $\{1e-5, 2e-5, 4-e5\}$. For batch size, we searched $\{4, 8, 16, 32, 64\}$.

- Infrastructure: 2 NVIDIA Quadro RTX 8000
- GPU Hours (training): approx. 3 hours
- GPU Hours (eval): approx. 1 hour
- Epochs: 12
- Best Learning Rate: 2e-5
- Best Batch Size: 32

A.2 Experimental Setup

Besides chunking into 200 token spans, document text is not further preprocessed. During training, data was mapped into tuples of the form containing one positive and negative (c_i, q_{ij}, d^+, d^-). That is, if a claim/question pair contains 2 positive and 3 negative paragraphs, it becomes $2 \cdot 3 = 6$ separate data points. These were then shuffled and batched to be fed to the retriever. In contrastive training we use in-batch negatives.

A.3 Parameters for Packages

- Used rouge-score (v0.1.2) to compute ROUGE-F1 scores. Used `rougeL` (longest common subsequence) with stemming set to True.
- Used openai (v1.34.0) for GPT-4 chat completion. Set temperature setting to 0.2.

A.4 Scientific Artifacts

- **AVeriTeC** [License] Free to copy, redistribute, and build upon this material given citations and a link to the license. AVeriTeC contains English-language real-world claims mainly in politics gathered from 50 different fact-checking organizations.
- **FEVER** [License] Data annotations incorporate material from Wikipedia, which is licensed pursuant to the Wikipedia Copyright Policy

- **HotpotQA** [License] Free to copy, redistribute, and build upon this material given citations and a link to the license

- **Contriever** [License] Free to copy, redistribute, and build upon this material given citations and a link to the license

B ROUGE-based Methods

B.1 ROUGE-based Answer Matching

ROUGE overlap between long answers works is a poor supervision signal because answer strings are typically quite complex. Table 5 illustrates this: although both long answers are conveying the same fact that Nigeria experienced 29 years of military rule, extra details or differences in phrasing can lead to low ROUGE scores despite the answers being semantically equivalent. The opposite may also occur: long answers which contain high lexical overlap may be topically similar but completely different in their key points, creating a false positive example. We also investigated semantic similarity measures like BERT score to assess answer equivalence. Compared to short answer LERC, BERT score tended to work poorly for complex long answers as seen in AVeriTeC. By contrast, using a short answer extraction yields a perfect signal in this case.

B.2 ROUGE-based Token Overlap

See Table 6. The token overlap between the retriever query (claim+question) and the AVeriTeC annotated gold document is only 0.11, whereas with the top retrieved document it is 0.25. This means using tokens in the query to surface the gold document is not easy.

C LERC Experiments

C.1 LERC Quality Check

We evaluate the selection of $\{D_l^+, D_l^-\}$ by manually annotating 10 examples. The task was to select the positive context document given a shuffled, unlabeled $\{D_l^+, D_l^-\}$. We selected the positive document correctly in 60% of examples. Note the positive document here is the one with the highest LERC score (i.e., contains an answer which most closely matches the gold answer). However, the two human annotators agreed on 90% of examples. By investigating the failure cases, we found that LERC-based metrics are sensitive to selecting false negative documents, as human agreement indicated a negative document was more "relevant" to the claim/question than the labeled positive document 40% of the time. Oftentimes, the misclassified document contained a reasonable answer to the question but mismatched the gold answer (hence explaining the low LERC score). This revealed that while LERC can identify strong positive documents, it comes with the risk of including relevant documents as negative contexts.

C.2 LERC-Human Agreement

In another preliminary study, we manually annotated 22 examples with a fine-grained score from 0-1 reflecting how closely we think the shortened candidate answer matches the shortened gold answer. Across three annotators, we found Kendall's tau agreement scores of 0.55, 0.49, and 0.55 with LERC (Table 7). This indicated human judgments of short answer equivalence correlate well with LERC, making it a viable answer equivalence metric to use as supervision.

D ClaimDecomp Example

See Table 10

E GPT-4 Prompts

E.1 Relevance Prompt

You will be given a claim, a question about the claim, and a passage. Your job is to check whether the passage contains information that supports an answer to the question. You will only output "Yes" or "No".

Claim: Hunter Biden had no experience in Ukraine or in the energy sector when he joined the board of Burisma.

Question: Did Hunter Biden have any experience in the energy sector at the time he joined the board of the Burisma energy company in 2014?

Passage: Hunter Biden , Burisma , Ukraine , and Joe Biden explained - Vox And during the bulk of this troubled period in Hunter ' s life , he was fortuitously on the board of a Ukrainian energy company...

E.2 Synthetic Data Generation Prompt

You will be provided with a claim and a question about the claim. Your job is to generate two evidence paragraphs:
(1) Positive: A paragraph that supports an indirect answer to the claim. It requires a reasoning hop to arrive at the answer. You can make up the answer to the question, but it should only come with a reasoning step.
(2) Hard Negative: A paragraph that looks highly relevant to the claim/question, but doesn't actually support an answer Neither paragraph can use "claim" or "question" - they must stand alone and mimic the style of real evidence documents found on the web.

	Gold Answer	GPT-4 Answer	Score
Long Answer + ROUGE-F1	Nigeria returned to democracy in 1999, after two long periods of military rule—1966–79 and 1983–98—during which the military wielded executive, legislative, and judicial power	Nigeria experienced military rule for a total of 29 years after independence: from 1966 to 1979 and from 1983 to 1998.	0.22
Short Answer + LERC	29 years	29 years	1

Table 5: Comparison of long answer ROUGE and short answer LERC. The two long answers are effectively conveying the same thing, but the ROUGE-F1 score is only 0.22. However, answer shortening + LERC yields a perfect equivalence score of 1.

	gold	top_doc
ROUGE-F1	0.11	0.25

Table 6: Comparing token overlap across 200 examples between $[c_i; q_{ij}]$ and the best annotated gold document or the top-ranked document from the wild (retriever is baseline Contriever).

Annotators	Kendall τ
1 / LERC	0.55
2 / LERC	0.49
3 / LERC	0.55
1 / 2	0.38
2 / 3	0.40
1 / 3	0.40

Table 7: Inter-annotator agreement across 20 examples and 3 annotators. 2/3 refers to the agreement between annotators 2 and 3

Here are some examples:
Claim: Former President Donald Trump who lost the popular vote by 3 million has nominated a full third of The United Supreme Court, as of 13th October 2020.
Question: How many federal judges did Trump nominate?
Positive: Two weeks ago in October Trump nominated multiple members of the Supreme Court. He started by nominating John Jacobs and Patricia McConnell, both of whom have supported Republican policies for many years. He made these judicial appointments despite mass disagreement, highlighting his goal to secure conservative ideals in the judiciary. Last week, he also appointed Max Dermott, making him the third Supreme Court justice nominated by Trump.
Hard Negative: Former President Trump nominated highly conservative Supreme Court justices back in October of 2020. His appointments were largely composed of conservative Republicans with long standing connections to Trump. He made these appointments in accordance with mass public support.
Explanation: The reasoning step in the positive parargaph is to realize "third of the Supreme court" means 3 out of 9 judges. The positive paragraph correctly lists 3 judges (John Jacobs, Patricia McConnell, and Max Dermott). The hard negative paragraph discusses his appointments but offers no information on how many judges he appointed.

Here is another example:
Claim: Anthony Fauci the NIAID director is a democrat.
Question: Is Anthony Fauci the NIAID director registered with a political party?
Positive: Two weeks ago, a new rule was passed in the NIAID which bans any director from holding political affiliations. In fact, it's even stricter than this - the same rule states no NIAID director is allowed to even register with a political party or participate in elections.
Hard Negative: Anthony Fauci has maintained a long standing relationship with Democratic presidential nominee Jacob Wallace. They were childhood friends who grew up together, and Fauci has also openly supported some of Wallace's policies. However, Fauci is historically known to stray away from politics and media.
Explanation: The reasoning step in the positive paragraph is to realize NIAID directors cannot register to political parties. Anthony Fauci is an NIAID director according to the claim, therefore he cannot be registered with a political party. The hard negative paragraph mentions his friendship with a Democratic presidential nominee, but this does not imply he is a registered Democrat.

Here is one final, slightly harder example:
Claim: Robert E. Lee, commander of the Confederate States Army during the American Civil War, was not a slave owner.
Question: Was Robert E. Lee a slave owner?
Positive: Many commanders during the Civil War era managed and inherited slaves through their family estates. Robert E. Lee was the commander for the Confederate States Army during the Civil War, and the Confederate states were in support of slavery.
Hard Negative: Commander Robert E. Lee led the Confederate States Army during the American Civil War. In the South, many slaves were forced to fight in the army under Robert E. Lee against the Union states. Slaves as soldiers were given poor equipment and placed on the front lines of defense.
Explanation: The reasoning step in the positive paragraph is to realize many commanders inherited slaves, and Robert E. Lee was a commander. Therefore it is likely that he might have also had slaves. The hard negative paragraph discusses the role of slaves in the war, but doesn't contain information on whether Robert E. Lee personally owning slaves. Notice even the positive paragraph doesn't contain a direct answer, but it is still

more relevant to the question than the hard negative.

Now, please generate a positive and hard negative paragraph with an explanation for the following claim/question pair:

Claim: Hunter Biden had no experience in Ukraine or in the energy sector when he joined the board of Burisma.

Question: Did Hunter Biden have any experience in the energy sector at the time he joined the board of the Burisma energy company in 2014?

E.3 QA Prompt

As a professional fact-checker, your task is to ONLY use the passage to answer the following question about the claim. Keep your answer short (only 1-2 sentences)

Passage: Hunter Biden , Burisma , Ukraine , and Joe Biden explained - Vox And during the bulk of this troubled period in Hunter ' s life , he was fortuitously on the board of a Ukrainian energy company...

Claim: Hunter Biden had no experience in Ukraine or in the energy sector when he joined the board of Burisma.

Question: Did Hunter Biden have any experience in the energy sector at the time he joined the board of the Burisma energy company in 2014?

E.4 FEVER Veracity Prompt

As a professional fact-checker, your task is to use the following claim and evidence document to determine the veracity of the claim. You must ONLY respond with either SUPPORTS, REFUTES, or NOT ENOUGH INFO

Claim: Great white sharks do not prefer dolphins as prey.

Passage: Do Sharks Eat Dolphins ? [Explained] - Ocean Fauna Did you know that sharks are often considered the ocean ' s top predators ? Well , here ' s an interesting twist : killer whales , which are actually a type of dolphin , are the ultimate predators that can effortlessly take down a shark . But what about other dolphin species ? Do sharks eat dolphins ? Not all sharks eat dolphins , but some species do feed on them . Great whites , tiger sharks , and bull sharks are among the ones that go for it . In this article , I will discuss the types of dolphins that sharks typically consume and how they do it . Are Dolphins Prey Items for Sharks ? Yes , dolphins can indeed be prey items for certain species of sharks . While not all sharks view dolphins as a potential meal , some of the larger and more predatory species , such as Great whites , tiger sharks , and bull sharks , have been known to feed on them . Young and sick dolphins are particularly vulnerable to shark predation , as they have less mobility and are easier to catch . Sharks typically hunt

Now please respond with one of SUPPORTS, REFUTES, or NOT ENOUGH INFO

F Synthetic Data Examples

F.1 Generated Example

See Table 8.

F.2 Human Written Example

See Table 9.

Claim	The Obama-Biden administration secretly launched a surveillance operation on the Trump campaign.
Question	Was there a surveillance operation on the Trump campaign?
Positive	In 2016, it was revealed that the FBI had launched an investigation into potential collusion between the Trump campaign and Russian operatives. This investigation, known as "Crossfire Hurricane," involved surveillance measures such as wiretaps and informants to gather intelligence. Although the operation was conducted by the FBI, it was during the Obama-Biden administration, raising questions about the extent of their involvement and oversight in the surveillance activities.
Hard Negative	During the 2016 presidential campaign, the Trump campaign faced numerous allegations of collusion with foreign entities. These allegations led to a series of public investigations and hearings, where various campaign officials were called to testify. The media extensively covered these events, and the public was made aware of the ongoing scrutiny faced by the Trump campaign. However, no direct evidence of a secret surveillance operation by the Obama-Biden administration was presented during these hearings.
Alt Q1	What were the objectives or reasons behind the alleged surveillance operation on the Trump campaign?
Alt Q1 Negative (d_1^-)	The alleged surveillance operation on the Trump campaign, purportedly initiated by the Obama-Biden administration, was reportedly driven by concerns over potential foreign interference in the 2016 U.S. presidential election. Intelligence agencies had gathered evidence suggesting that Russian operatives were attempting to influence the election's outcome, raising alarms about possible collusion between the Trump campaign and Russian entities. The objective was to safeguard the integrity of the electoral process and ensure that no foreign power could unduly sway the democratic proceedings. Additionally, the surveillance aimed to uncover any illicit activities that could compromise national security. These actions were framed within the broader context of protecting American democratic institutions from external threats.
Explanation	The positive paragraph mentions the FBI's "Crossfire Hurricane" investigation, which involved surveillance measures and occurred during the Obama-Biden administration. This requires the reader to make the reasoning hop that the administration might have had some level of involvement or oversight. The hard negative paragraph discusses public investigations and hearings related to the Trump campaign but does not address the existence of a secret surveillance operation by the Obama-Biden administration.

Table 8: Example of a synthetic example generated from our procedure. The explanation indicates the reasoning hop required to surface the positive paragraph, as well as the complexity of the hard negative.

Claim	Former President Donald Trump who lost the popular vote by 3 million has nominated a full third of The United Supreme Court, as of 13th October 2020.
Question	How many federal judges did Trump nominate?
Positive	Two weeks ago in October Trump nominated multiple members of the Supreme Court. He started by nominating John Jacobs and Patricia McConnell, both of whom have supported Republican policies for many years. He made these judicial appointments despite mass disagreement, highlighting his goal to secure conservative ideals in the judiciary. Last week, he also appointed Max Dermott, making him the third Supreme Court justice nominated by Trump.
Hard Negative	Former President Trump nominated highly conservative Supreme Court justices back in October of 2020. His appointments were largely composed of conservative Republicans with long standing connections to Trump. He made these appointments in accordance with mass public support.
Explanation	The reasoning step in the positive parargaph is to realize "third of the Supreme court" means 3 out of 9 judges. The positive paragraph lists 3 judges (John Jacobs, Patricia McConnell, and Max Dermott). The hard negative paragraph discusses his appointments but offers no information on how many judges he appointed, which is what the question is asking.

Table 9: Example of a human annotated positive and hard negative example.

Claim: Charles Schumer stated on May 13, 2015 in remarks to reporters: "It is simply a fact that insufficient funding for Amtrak has delayed the installation" of a positive train control safety system. "To deny a connection between the (derailment in Philadelphia) and underfunding Amtrak is to deny reality."
Question: Is there a connection between the derailment in Phil. and underfunding Amtrak?

Contriever	distill (gold) + LERC
Latest safety technology wasn ' t fully installed at site of deadly Amtrak derailment south of Seattle - CBS News approached sharp curves at more than double the speed limit . A Metro-North train crashed in New York City in 2013 , killing four people , when an engineer with sleep apnea dozed off . An Amtrak train crashed in Philadelphia in 2015 , killing eight people , when investigators say the engineer was distracted by radio traffic and lost his bearings . Positive train control was installed on 23 percent of the nation 's passenger route miles and 37 percent of freight route miles as of July , the last time the Federal Railroad Administration updated its online tracker for the technology . It is activated on the tracks Amtrak owns along the Northeast Corridor , from Boston to Washington , D.C. , and on Amtrak 's Michigan line . Many of its locomotives are equipped for positive train control . Throughout the rest of the country , Amtrak operates on track owned by freight carriers and other entities that have made varying progress on installing the technology . The new $ 180.7 million route was designed to speed up service by removing passenger trains from a route along Puget Sound that 's bogged down by curves , single-track	Explainer : Positive Train Control and the Amtrak 188 derailment - WHYY Positive Train Control (PTC) would have prevented Amtrak 188 from derailing Tuesday , National Transportation Safety Board lead investigator Robert Sumwalt said this week . Amtrak was intending to install the safety system on the Northeast Corridor by the end of year , pursuant to an unfunded congressional mandate under the Rail Safety Improvement Act . **Amtrak CEO Joseph Boardman has said that , with more funding , Amtrak could have implemented PTC sooner** . The stretch of the Northeast Corridor where the derailment occurred currently uses an older system , Automatic Train Control (ATC) . On the southbound route , the ATC " enforces " — automatically stops — a train if it is travelling above 45 miles per hour . The northbound side , where Amtrak 188 was travelling , does not . PTC is essentially a smarter version of ATC . Whereas ATC relies on the signal and fixed block system trains have operated on for decades , PTC uses a GPS and radio technology to locate where the trains are along the track . ATC only knows when a train trips a signal wire entering into another large stretch between interlockings or
Answer from GPT: The passage does not provide information on Amtrak's funding levels or directly link underfunding to the derailment in Philadelphia.	**Answer from GPT:** Yes, according to Amtrak CEO Joseph Boardman, more funding could have allowed Amtrak to implement PTC sooner, which would have prevented the derailment

Table 10: Comparison of top-1 document on an example from ClaimDecomp between unfinetuned Contriever (left) and CFR model (right). The finetuned retriever is able to surface a document about funding, which is the key aspect the question is targeting.

RAGAR, Your Falsehood Radar: RAG-Augmented Reasoning for Political Fact-Checking using Multimodal Large Language Models

Mohammed Abdul Khaliq[1,3], Paul Yu-Chun Chang[2]*, Mingyang Ma[2], Bernhard Pflugfelder[2], Filip Miletić[1]*

[1]Institute for Natural Language Processing, University of Stuttgart,
[2]appliedAI Initiative GmbH, [3]appliedAI Institute for Europe gGmbH
{mohammed.abdul-khaliq, filip.miletic}@ims.uni-stuttgart.de,
{p.chang, m.ma, b.pflugfelder}@appliedai.de

Abstract

The escalating challenge of misinformation, particularly in political discourse, requires advanced fact-checking solutions; this is even clearer in the more complex scenario of multimodal claims. We tackle this issue using a multimodal large language model in conjunction with retrieval-augmented generation (RAG), and introduce two novel reasoning techniques: Chain of RAG (CoRAG) and Tree of RAG (ToRAG). They fact-check multimodal claims by extracting both textual and image content, retrieving external information, and reasoning subsequent questions to be answered based on prior evidence. We achieve a weighted F1-score of 0.85, surpassing a baseline reasoning technique by 0.14 points. Human evaluation confirms that the vast majority of our generated fact-check explanations contain all information from gold standard data.

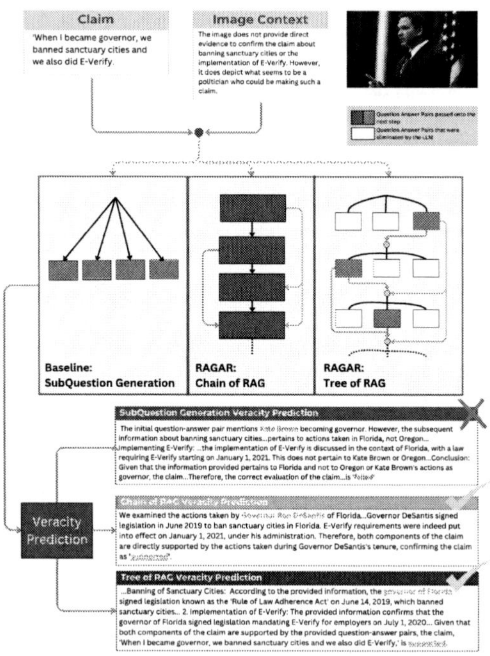

Figure 1: An overview of the fact-checking pipeline contrasting the baseline Sub-Question Generation approach from the Chain of RAG and Tree of RAG approach followed by veracity prediction and explanation.

1 Introduction

In the age of digital information, rapid dissemination of news, both genuine and fabricated, has become a defining feature of public discourse. The phenomenon of fake news – which more precisely denotes misinformation, disinformation, or a combination of both (Aïmeur et al., 2023) – is particularly prevalent on social media: false information spreads six times faster than the truth on platforms like Twitter (Vosoughi et al., 2018). This trend poses a critical challenge to the democratic process since it makes voters increasingly prone to making decisions based on incorrect information. The matter is further aggravated by visual information, which provides yet another widespread and consequential source of fake news. For instance, fake news stories that include images spread further than those containing only text (Zannettou et al., 2018).

A potential solution to these issues is provided by automated fact-checking systems. They have benefited from the development of large language models (LLMs), leading to improvements in detection, labeling, and generation of veracity explanations (Das et al., 2023). More recently, multimodal approaches have complemented textual information with image representations to assess their cross-modal consistency and unified embedding representations (Yao et al., 2023a). Another active line of research deploys retrieval-augmented generation (RAG), whereby LLMs access up-to-date external information at inference time. They convert the input claim into phrase queries, pass them onto a search engine, and use the retrieved information to assess veracity (Asai et al., 2024; Zeng and Gao,

*Corresponding authors.

Proceedings of the Seventh Fact Extraction and VERification Workshop (FEVER), pages 280–296
November 15, 2024

2024). It however remains to be determined if more elaborate reasoning techniques can be beneficial in this setting. Moreover, RAG-based approaches have so far mostly been applied to text. This raises the additional question of their use in the more challenging scenario of multimodal fact-checking.

Addressing this gap, we introduce RAGAR – RAG-Augmented Reasoning techniques, which we apply to multimodal fact-checking in the political domain (see Figure 1 for a high-level overview). We rely on a multimodal LLM to verbalize the textual and visual elements of a claim, and use RAG responses to motivate successive steps in determining veracity. The system is underpinned by elaborate reasoning strategies instantiated in two distinct approaches: Chain of RAG (CoRAG) and Tree of RAG (ToRAG). We evaluate them using a multimodal fact-checking dataset as well as human annotation of generated explanations.

Our contributions are as follows. (1) We introduce two novel reasoning techniques for multimodal fact-checking, reaching a weighted F1-score of 0.85. (2) We provide two complementary strategies for multimodal input by verbalizing image content during claim generation and using image captions as evidence during retrieval. (3) We conduct a multi-rater annotation of fact-check explanations, showing that the vast majority of them include all information from the gold standard. To our knowledge, this is the first study to incorporate multimodal LLMs in a RAG-based reasoning approach applied to multimodal fact-checking for the political domain.

2 Related Work

2.1 Retrieval-Augmented Generation (RAG) for Fact-Checking

To combat hallucination in text generation, current fact-checking pipelines often implement a RAG approach, wherein an LLM retrieves data from external sources to enhance its response and move past its knowledge cutoff. Peng et al. (2023) present LLM-Augmenter, which combines external knowledge integration and automated feedback mechanisms. Chern et al. (2023) assess the factuality of LLM-generated text on multiple tasks and domains, e.g. for Knowledge Based Question Answering they use Google Search API to extract relevant knowledge and then parse the result. Pan et al. (2023) rely on LLM's in-context learning, and use Chain of Thought (Wei et al., 2022) reasoning to guide the model in complex tasks such as fact-checking on the web. Zhang and Gao (2023) propose Hierarchical Step-by-Step (HiSS) prompting, which splits a claim into sub-claims, creating a hierarchy, and verifies each one through multiple question-answering steps using web-retrieved evidence. Xu et al. (2023) propose SearChain. It creates a Chain of Query (CoQ) reasoning chain, where each question follows from the knowledge gathered in the previous question; uses information retrieval (IR) to verify the answer at each node; and prompts the LLM to indicate missing information, which is handled by an IR call.

Our RAGAR approaches are conceptually similar, but they use a more sophisticated reasoning framework with multiple rounds of sequential question-answering, elimination (in the case of ToRAG), and verification. We also extend domain coverage through multimodality, and propose a zero-shot (rather than few-shot) approach.

2.2 Multimodal Fact-Checking using LLMs

Multimodality is generally underexplored in fact-checking (Alam et al., 2022), but several recent approaches have been proposed. Guo et al. (2023) use LLM-agnostic models to generate textual prompts from images and then guide LLMs in generating responses to Visual Question Answering queries. Yao et al. (2023a) construct a multimodal dataset using fact-checking websites, and then develop a fact-checking and explanation generation pipeline. It encodes and reranks each sentence in the document corpus in relation to the claim, and uses a CLIP (Radford et al., 2021) encoding for images; the similarity between an input claim and the provided images is then computed. An attention model is used for multimodal claim verification, and BART (Lewis et al., 2020) for explanation generation. In concurrent research, Pan et al. (2024) propose the Chain of Action prompt. It splits an input query into sub-questions and uses a "Missing Flag" indicator to fill in or correct the answers generated by internal LLM knowledge via RAG.

Our RAGAR approaches similarly use a multimodal LLM (GPT-4V; OpenAI, 2023) to add context to the textual claim, but employ a different set of reasoning techniques. We furthermore introduce a multimodal RAG component during evidence retrieval, using captions of matching images to provide the LLM with relevant meta information.

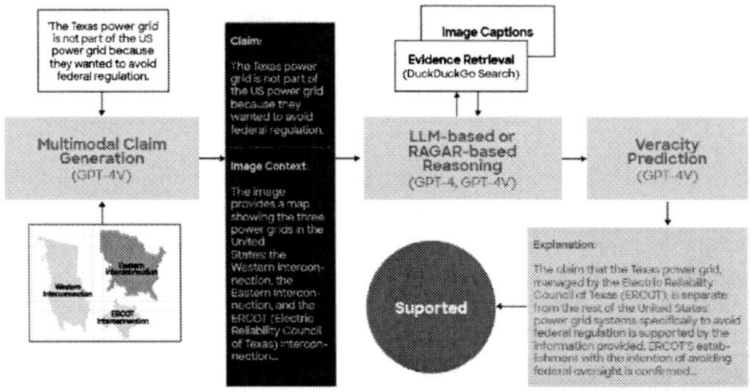

Figure 2: A detailed overview of the Multimodal Fact-checking pipeline

3 Dataset

The aim of our study is to explore the potential of multimodal LLM-based RAG and reasoning for political fact-checking. Given the substantial computational and financial costs of running multimodal LLMs through multiple rounds of reasoning, we evaluate our approach on a well-controlled and balanced dataset, so as to minimize noise while maintaining the validity of our experiments.

We specifically rely on a carefully selected subset of the MOCHEG dataset (Yao et al., 2023a). MOCHEG provides 21,184 multimodal claims sourced from two fact-checking websites, PolitiFact[1] and Snopes.[2] Each instance contains an input claim extracted from the title of the fact-checking source, and an associated image extracted from the web page that addresses the claim. The dataset further provides a summary of the fact-check in the form of a "Ruling Outline", which we consider for evaluating LLM-generated explanations.

We start from the test set containing 2,007 multimodal claims and filter it in two steps. First, we select the 794 claims that were fact-checked by PolitiFact, since our focus is on political claims; by contrast, Snopes provides fact-checks for a variety of domains. Second, we filter this set down to 300 test samples randomly selected from the *supported* and *refuted* classes, for a balanced final dataset with 150 multimodal claims in each of the two classes.

In this process, we purposefully discard the *NEI* (Not Enough Information) instances. During the creation of MOCHEG, some ambiguous cases were outright discarded, while the labels *mixture*, *unproven*, and *undetermined* were aggregated under *NEI*. This class is potentially unstable in two respects: fact-checking websites update their labels as new evidence emerges (Yao et al., 2023a), which by definition affects this class more prominently; and the fact-checking intentions behind mixed labels such as *half-true* and *mixture* are comparatively unclear, leading prior studies to exclude them (e.g. Vo and Lee, 2019). We adopt the same decision given our focus on an initial validation of novel reasoning techniques.

Although we only retain instances that are unambiguous in the dataset, our model may still struggle to retrieve information of sufficient quality to fact-check them. We account for this by allowing it to generate a *failed* label when it fails to retrieve relevant information. We reserve an extension of our study to the *NEI* class, as well as the connected issue of improving retrieval quality, for future work.

4 Multimodal Fact-Checking Pipeline

Our fact-checking pipeline comprises four parts: (i) Multimodal Claim Generation, which analyzes both the textual claim and associated image to formulate a new claim incorporating both; (ii) Multimodal Evidence Retrieval, which extracts evidence from the web for a question posed by the LLM; (iii) LLM-based and RAG-augmented Reasoning for fact-checking, our reasoning approach to fact-check a claim; and (iv) Veracity Prediction and Explanation. The pipeline is shown in Figure 2.

4.1 Multimodal Claim Generation

Given an input claim as text, an associated image, and the date of the claim, the claim generation module generates a response verbalizing the information contained in both the textual claim and the image. We use GPT-4V as our multimodal LLM given its strong performance across tasks. Note that our aim is not to determine the best-performing

[1] https://www.politifact.com/
[2] https://www.snopes.com/

model on our task, but rather to evaluate different reasoning techniques. We therefore use the same model across experiments.

The generated response is divided into two sections: *claim*, which contains the original text claim; and *image context*, which contains the details relevant to the claim extracted from the image by GPT-4V. The *image context* expands on the information from the textual claim by e.g. identifying the speaker that the claim is quoting, extracting numerical information from figures, and highlighting relevant textual data mentioned in the image. More generally, the contextualization provides details on whether the image is relevant to the text claim.

While directly encoding images is a potential alternative to our approach, we decide against it to allow our Chain of RAG and Tree of RAG approach to be multimodal-agnostic. This decision ensures that our reasoning methods can also be replicated with LLMs that are not inherently multimodal. Multimodal Claim Generation is the only section of our pipeline requiring a multimodal LLM; all remaining parts, including our RAGAR approaches, can be implemented using other LLMs and possibly extended to different tasks.

4.2 Multimodal Evidence Retrieval

The fact-checking questions generated by the LLM-based or RAG-augmented reasoning techniques serve as input for the multimodal evidence retrieval module. It helps answer each question by retrieving relevant text snippets from websites and further analyzing details associated with the image.

The query to the multimodal evidence retrieval is a question generated by an LLM-based or RAGAR-based reasoning technique (presented in detail in Section 4.3). For text-based evidence retrieval, we use the DuckDuckGo Search tool provided by LangChain[3]. We retrieve the top 10 results from the API and use them to answer the question. We temporally restrict the search by only collecting articles published in the two years before the claim was fact-checked by PolitiFact, so as to provide the LLM with facts relevant to the time-frame of the fact-check. To mimic a real-time fact-checking scenario, we remove search results that originate from `www.politifact.com`, `www.snopes.com`, and `www.factcheck.org`, since it is likely that they already contain answers to the claim and would thus impact the fairness of the experiment. We also remove the following social media websites due to potentially biased or unreliable information: `www.facebook.com`, `www.tiktok.com`, `www.twitter.com` and `www.youtube.com`.

Most images in our dataset contain faces of politicians, pictures from political events, government buildings etc. In such cases, the image itself may not provide much additional information beyond the text claim. However, it is useful to determine the metadata associated with the image, which may indicate when or where the claim was made. For this purpose, we use SerpAPI[4] to conduct a reverse image search over the images associated with the claims. We extract the captions for the images from the first 10 results and use them as additional information for GPT-4V. This allows the model to not only analyze the image when answering an image-based question, but also incorporate meta-information about it and in that way better contextualize the answer. We demonstrate a few examples of this in Appendix A.3.

4.3 LLM-Based and RAG-Augmented Reasoning for Fact-Checking

4.3.1 Baseline: Sub-questions with Chain of Thought at Veracity Prediction (SubQ+CoT$_{VP}$)

As a baseline reasoning-based approach, we employ sub-question generation followed by Chain of Thought veracity prediction (SubQ+CoT$_{VP}$). This baseline is based on recent approaches to fact-checking relying on LLMs (Pan et al., 2023; Chern et al., 2023) as discussed in Section 2.1. We adapt the approach to handle multimodal claims as well.

4.3.2 RAG-Augmented Reasoning: Chain of RAG (CoRAG)

The first novel reasoning approach we propose is Chain of RAG (CoRAG). It builds upon general RAG approaches by using sequential follow-up questions – augmented from the RAG response – to retrieve further evidence. In other words, we follow a decomposed setup, guiding the LLM towards asking questions based on the previously generated question-answer pairs. The "Chain" in "Chain of RAG" is thus to be interpreted as a chain of question-answer pairs that are iteratively generated. This is unlike the traditional Chain of Thought, wherein a single prompt handles the entire process of creating questions, answers, and follow-up ques-

[3]`https://www.langchain.com/`

[4]`https://serpapi.com/`

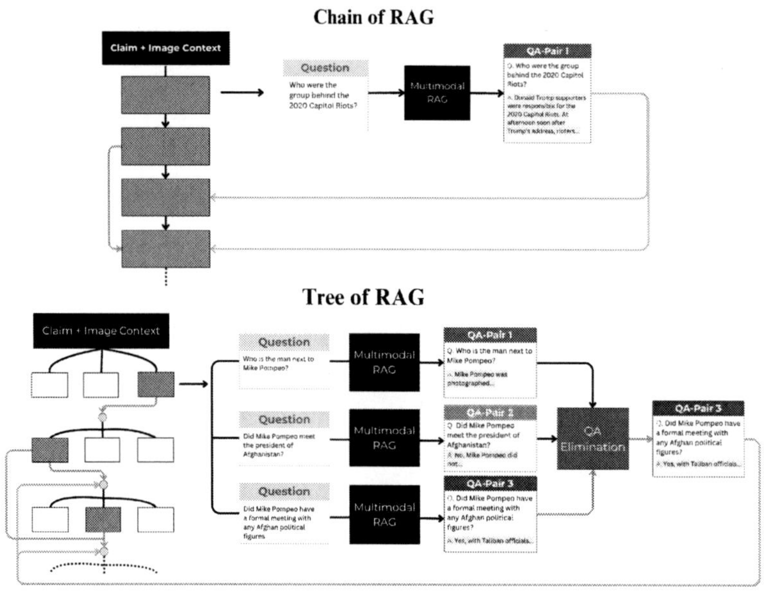

Figure 3: Chain of RAG and Tree of RAG pipeline

Algorithm 1 Chain of RAG (CoRAG)

```
Input: Claim C, Image Context I, Image Captions IC
Q ← GenerateFirstQuestion(C, I)
QAPairs ← []                                  ▷ Initialize an empty list for Q-A pairs
counter ← 0
followUpNeeded ← True
while counter < no_of_steps and followUpNeeded do
    if QuestionAboutImage(Q) then
        A ← ImageQA(Q, I, IC)                 ▷ Using image, question, and captions
    else
        A ← WebQA(Q)                          ▷ Standard evidence retrieval
    end if
    QAPairs.append((Q, A))                    ▷ Store the Q-A pair of this iteration
    followUpNeeded ← FollowupCheck(Q, A)
    if followUpNeeded then
        Q ← FollowupQuestion(QAPairs)
    end if
    counter ← counter + 1
end while
return QAPairs                                ▷ Returns the list of Q-A pairs
```

tion in one go. Moreover, CoRAG follows a zero-shot approach, i.e. the LLM is not provided with any example question-answer pairs to influence the reasoning process. An overview of the process is provided in Algorithm 1 as well as Figure 3.

The input to the CoRAG module is the *claim* and *image context* from the multimodal claim generation module (§4.1). The LLM is first prompted to generate a question that is intended to answer an aspect of the claim. The generated question is passed to the multimodal evidence retriever (§4.2), which obtains evidence to inform the RAG answer. Once the answer is generated, the CoRAG process undergoes a follow-up check (effectively an early termination check). The follow-up check prompt (see Appendix A.5) takes as input the LLM-generated claim as well as all the generated question-answer pair(s), and checks whether enough information has been gathered to answer the claim. If the response from the follow-up check is "True", it asks a follow-up question. The follow-up question is intended to ask for further information, building on top of the previous question-answer pairs such that the claim can be fully addressed.

A follow-up check occurs after each question-answer generation step. If the follow-up check prompt finds sufficient evidence in the questions and answers generated up until that point, it terminates and passes the evidence to the veracity prediction and explanation generation module. We also set a constraint of a maximum of six questions, after which the CoRAG process terminates even if it does not have enough evidence for the fact-check. We determined this threshold in preliminary experiments on 80 samples, which indicated that this was the highest number of question-answering steps required for the LLM to obtain enough information to address even the more challenging claims.

4.3.3 RAG-Augmented Reasoning: Tree of RAG (ToRAG)

In a similar way to how a traditional Tree of Thought (Yao et al., 2023b) extends Chain of Thought through branching, Tree of RAG (ToRAG) extends our CoRAG approach by creating question branches at each reasoning step. The best question-answer branch is selected at each step. An overview is provided in Algorithm 2 as well as Figure 3.

The input to the ToRAG module is the *claim* and *image context* from the multimodal claim generation module (§4.1). Upon receiving this input, the ToRAG approach branches into three, each branch asking a unique question to fact-check the claim.

Once the three starting questions have been generated, the ToRAG approach uses the evidence retriever (§4.2) to obtain information and generate answers for each question. The three question-answer pairs are then passed into an elimination prompt, from which only one question-answer pair is chosen as candidate evidence. The model is prompted to perform this elimination based on relevance, detail, additional information, and answer confidence (see Appendix A.6).

The candidate evidence then serves as the basis for the follow-up question. Three follow-up questions are generated simultaneously based on the candidate evidence. The evidence retriever fetches answers to these questions, and the LLM generates the answers. New candidate evidence is chosen by the elimination prompt and is added to the existing list of candidate evidence. This list, therefore, stores only the best of the three question-answer pairs obtained at each step. Upon gathering sufficient information to fact-check the claim as determined by the follow-up check prompt or reaching a maximum of six candidate evidence question-answer pairs, the ToRAG process terminates, and the list of candidate evidence is passed to the veracity prediction and explanation generation module. A few examples of the question-answer pairs generated by our LLM-based and RAG-augmented reasoning approaches can be seen in Appendix A.4.

4.4 Veracity Prediction and Explanation

The veracity prediction and explanation module (henceforth referred to as "veracity prediction" for brevity) generates a veracity label of *supported* or *refuted* based on the information available in the question-answer pairs. Moreover, it generates a *failed* label when it deems to have insufficient information in the question-answer pair to either support or refute the claim.

We experiment with three variants of veracity prediction prompts (see Appendix A.7). (i) The standard veracity prompt ($\text{Standard}_{\text{VP}}$) takes the claim and evidence pairs as input, and outputs the veracity rating and the explanation without any induced reasoning. (ii) The zero-shot Chain of Thought veracity prediction prompt (CoT_{VP}) uses the "Let's think step by step" phrase to guide the model to follow a chain of thought reasoning approach. (iii) The Chain of Verification (Dhuliawala et al., 2023) veracity prediction prompt (CoVe) first constructs verification questions based on the LLM-generated fact-checked explanation. The answers to these questions are generated using RAG, and are passed – along with the LLM-generated fact-check – to a correction check prompt. In case of corrections to the original LLM-generated fact-check, a new fact-check is generated along with a new veracity label if necessary. The CoVe veracity prediction approach is thus able to verify the fact-checked explanation generated by the CoRAG and ToRAG methods with the intended goal of capturing and correcting hallucination.

5 Evaluation and Results

We now present two evaluations employed across the set of 300 multimodal claims. In Section 5.1, we analyze system performance based on the correctness of veracity predictions. In Section 5.2, we zoom into explanation generation by conducting a human annotation study to compare the generated and gold explanations.

5.1 Correctness of Veracity Predictions

In this evaluation setup, we categorize the predictions into two primary outcomes: correct or incorrect. Specifically, when the language model's prediction matches the actual label (for instance, predicting *supported* when the actual rating is *supported*), the prediction is deemed correct. Conversely, if the model predicts *refuted* or *failed* when the actual rating is *supported*, the prediction is con-

Algorithm 2 Tree of RAG (ToRAG)

```
Input: Claim C, Image Context I, Image Captions IC
BestQAPairs ← []                                   ▷ Initialize an empty list for best Q-A pairs
Questions ← GenerateFirstQuestions(C, I)           ▷ Generates three questions
counter ← 0
followUpNeeded ← True
while counter < no_of_steps and followUpNeeded do
    QAPairs ← []                                   ▷ Initializes an empty list for question-answer pairs
    for Q in Questions do
        if QuestionAboutImage(Q) then
            A ← ImageQA(Q, I, IC)                  ▷ Using image, question, and captions
        else
            A ← WebQA(Q)                           ▷ Standard evidence retrieval
        end if
        QAPairs.append((Q, A))
    end for
    (BestQ, BestA) ← QAElimination(QAPairs)
    BestQAPairs.append((BestQ, BestA))             ▷ Stores the best Q-A pair of this iteration
    followUpNeeded ← FollowupCheck(BestQAPairs)
    if followUpNeeded then
        Questions ← GenerateFollowupQuestions(BestQAPairs)   ▷ Generates three follow-up questions
    else
        break
    end if
    counter ← counter + 1
end while
return BestQAPairs                                 ▷ Returns all collected best Q-A pairs
```

APPROACHES	SUPPORTED (F1)	REFUTED (F1)	# FAILED	WEIGHTED F1
SubQ + CoT_{VP}	0.66	0.77	50 | 22	0.71
CoRAG + $\text{Standard}_{\text{VP}}$	0.74	0.81	31 | 15	0.77
CoRAG + CoT_{VP}	0.73	0.82	38 | 14	0.77
CoRAG + CoT_{VP} + CoVe	0.78	0.83	21 | 8	0.81
ToRAG + $\text{Standard}_{\text{VP}}$	0.82	**0.86**	16 | 5	0.84
ToRAG + CoT_{VP}	0.82	0.85	19 | 9	0.83
ToRAG + CoT_{VP} + CoVe	**0.84**	**0.86**	9 | 4	**0.85**

Table 1: F1 Results of the Correctness of Veracity Predictions evaluation. The # FAILED column contains the number of *supported* | *refuted* claims that were predicted as *failed.*

sidered as incorrect. Table 1 shows the results of all of our approaches for this evaluation criterion.

The worst-performing approach is the SubQ+CoT_{VP} baseline, with a weighted F1 of 0.71. The best-performing approach is ToRAG+CoT_{VP}+CoVe, with a weighted F1 of 0.85. The middle spot is occupied by the CoRAG implementations; the strongest among those is CoRAG+CoT_{VP}+CoVe, with a weighted F1 of 0.81. Regarding class-level performance, the scores are consistently higher for the *refuted* rather than *supported* class.

The SubQ+CoT_{VP} baseline lags behind our RAGAR approaches by up to 0.14 weighted F1 points. We attribute its poor performance to the inability of the veracity prediction module (CoT_{VP}) to gain sequential and contextual information. Since the sub-questions generated by SubQ+CoT_{VP} are based solely on the claim, the answers queried during evidence retrieval do not follow from one another.

Amongst our RAGAR approaches, applying CoT_{VP} to the question-answer pairs generated by either CoRAG or ToRAG approaches did not show improvement over $\text{Standard}_{\text{VP}}$. We attribute this to the very strong internal reasoning capabilities of GPT-4. However, we are able to improve performance by combining the CoVe approach, especially in the case of CoRAG. Incorporating CoVe with the result from CoRAG+CoT_{VP} shows a performance improvement of 0.04 F1 points and especially improves the classification of *supported* claims. Incorporating CoVe on top of the ToRAG+CoT_{VP} leads to an improvement, but overall minor and also less pronounced than for CoRAG. This indicates that the QA elimination prompt in ToRAG successfully eliminates erroneous or irrelevant question-answer pairs.

5.2 Evaluating Explanation Generation

We evaluate explanation generation by comparing the LLM-generated fact-checked explanation with the corresponding "Ruling Outline" from the MOCHEG dataset. We recruit three volunteer annotators, aged 21–24 and with near-native English proficiency. They are asked to rate the explanations generated by each of the approaches on a scale from

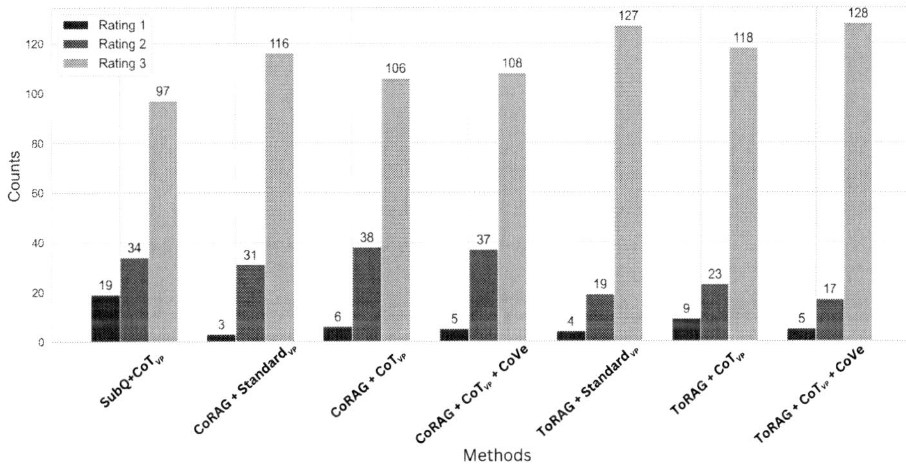

Figure 4: Number of 1/2/3 ratings received for explanations by each approach

1 to 3, where 3 indicates that all information in the gold explanation is present in the generated explanation, while 1 indicates that all information in the gold explanation is missing from the generated explanation. The complete annotation instructions are provided in Appendix A.1.

We randomly sample a set of 50 claims, divided into 25 supported and 25 refuted. For all annotated claims, the gold veracity label and the predicted veracity label match. We measure inter-annotator agreement using Krippendorff's α (Hayes and Krippendorff, 2007). The scores are in the range of 0.53 to 0.75 depending on the evaluated approach, with the mean at 0.60. We consider this to be sufficient agreement given the nature of the task.

As can be seen in Figure 4, the annotators provide a rating of 3 for an overwhelming majority of explanations generated across methods. This shows that the generated explanations indeed cover all the points noted in the PolitiFact fact-check. Additionally, the explanations generated by SubQ+CoT$_{VP}$ led to significantly more ratings of 1 than any other method, which indicates that it omitted or did not accurately elaborate on certain points.

Regarding class-level trends, explanations in the *supported* class are rated as 2 more often than those in the *refuted* class (see Appendix A.2). This indicates that certain information was missing from the generated explanation; more generally, this trend reflects the lower F1 scores on this class (§5.1), suggesting its higher difficulty. From a qualitative perspective, the annotators anecdotally reported that the generated explanations included some points from the PolitiFact ruling outline, but also provided additional information. Overall, however, the majority of the ratings being annotated as 3 across the different approaches lends credence to the quality of the explanation and to the efficacy of the underlying system in retrieving relevant evidence to fact-check the claim.

6 Conclusion

This paper introduces and tests two new methods for political fact-checking using large language models (LLMs): Chain of RAG (CoRAG) and Tree of RAG (ToRAG). These methods tackle misinformation in political discussions, focusing on multimodal claims, and show notable improvements over traditional fact-checking approaches that use sub-question generation with LLMs. CoRAG uses a step-by-step questioning strategy for thorough claim examination, while ToRAG extends upon this by following a branching strategy with evidence elimination thereby enhancing veracity prediction. We evaluate these methods in two ways. In terms of correctness of generated veracity label, we see an increase of 0.06-0.14 F1 points when using the RAGAR framework with Standard, CoT$_{VP}$, and CoVe veracity prediction prompts compared to the baseline SubQ+CoT$_{VP}$. For explanation generation, the quality of RAGAR-generated explanations was consistently rated higher than the baseline method. Our study shows that RAG-augmented reasoning (RAGAR) techniques are effective in multimodal political fact-checking, improving both the accuracy of veracity predictions and the quality of detailed fact-check explanations.

7 Limitations

We experimented with three tools for extracting relevant web results for natural language questions; DuckDuckGo Search, You.com[5] and Tavily AI[6]. Across the three tools, we notice that the search results may occasionally vary when prompted with the same questions multiple times. This variance in results, even though the question remains the same or similar, is problematic since it affects the final result and makes it hard to compare approaches. Additionally, due to budget constraints, we are unable to provide variance estimates requiring multiple runs of our RAGAR approaches. While we acknowledge the use of a closed-source LLM as a potential shortcoming due to comparatively more limited control over model behavior, we opted for the best-performing model available to us given the complexity of the addressed task. Finally, as also noted in the paper, our main aim was to assess the viability of novel reasoning techniques rather than retrieval quality, which led us to exclude *NEI* instances from our experimental setup. Further work extended to these cases is needed to more comprehensively understand the performance of our proposed approach.

8 Ethics Statement

We conducted an experimental study aimed at examining multimodal fact-checking by prompting LLMs, and note that some of the core steps of this approach may also be replicated by the general public. Our RAGAR approach obtained clear improvements over the examined baseline in the evaluation setup we defined. However, the experiments presented here are not sufficient to make general claims about the performance of our approach in other settings. Given the sensitive nature of political news in particular, we caution against using the RAGAR approach for general political fact-checking or implementing it on a large scale at this stage.

9 Acknowledgements

We thank the anonymous reviewers for their constructive feedback. Filip Miletić was supported by DFG Research Grant SCHU 2580/5-1.

[5]https://you.com/

[6]https://tavily.com/

References

Firoj Alam, Stefano Cresci, Tanmoy Chakraborty, Fabrizio Silvestri, Dimiter Dimitrov, Giovanni Da San Martino, Shaden Shaar, Hamed Firooz, and Preslav Nakov. 2022. A survey on multimodal disinformation detection. In *Proceedings of the 29th International Conference on Computational Linguistics*, pages 6625–6643, Gyeongju, Republic of Korea. International Committee on Computational Linguistics.

Akari Asai, Zeqiu Wu, Yizhong Wang, Avirup Sil, and Hannaneh Hajishirzi. 2024. Self-RAG: Learning to retrieve, generate, and critique through self-reflection. In *The Twelfth International Conference on Learning Representations*.

Esma Aïmeur, Sabrine Amri, and Gilles Brassard. 2023. Fake news, disinformation and misinformation in social media: a review. *Social Network Analysis and Mining*, 13(1):30.

I-Chun Chern, Steffi Chern, Shiqi Chen, Weizhe Yuan, Kehua Feng, Chunting Zhou, Junxian He, Graham Neubig, and Pengfei Liu. 2023. FacTool: Factuality detection in generative AI – a tool augmented framework for multi-task and multi-domain scenarios. *arXiv preprint arXiv:2307.13528*.

Anubrata Das, Houjiang Liu, Venelin Kovatchev, and Matthew Lease. 2023. The state of human-centered NLP technology for fact-checking. *Information Processing & Management*, 60(2):103219.

Shehzaad Dhuliawala, Mojtaba Komeili, Jing Xu, Roberta Raileanu, Xian Li, Asli Celikyilmaz, and Jason Weston. 2023. Chain-of-verification reduces hallucination in large language models. *arXiv preprint arXiv:2309.11495*.

Zixian Guo, Bowen Dong, Zhilong Ji, Jinfeng Bai, Yiwen Guo, and Wangmeng Zuo. 2023. Texts as images in prompt tuning for multi-label image recognition. In *Proceedings of the IEEE/CVF Conference on Computer Vision and Pattern Recognition*, pages 2808–2817.

Andrew F. Hayes and Klaus Krippendorff. 2007. Answering the call for a standard reliability measure for coding data. *Communication Methods and Measures*, 1:77 – 89.

Mike Lewis, Yinhan Liu, Naman Goyal, Marjan Ghazvininejad, Abdelrahman Mohamed, Omer Levy, Veselin Stoyanov, and Luke Zettlemoyer. 2020. BART: Denoising sequence-to-sequence pre-training for natural language generation, translation, and comprehension. In *Proceedings of the 58th Annual Meeting of the Association for Computational Linguistics*, pages 7871–7880, Online. Association for Computational Linguistics.

OpenAI. 2023. Gpt-4v: A multimodal transformer for vision and language.

Liangming Pan, Xiaobao Wu, Xinyuan Lu, Anh Tuan Luu, William Yang Wang, Min-Yen Kan, and Preslav Nakov. 2023. Fact-checking complex claims with program-guided reasoning. In *Proceedings of the 61st Annual Meeting of the Association for Computational Linguistics (Volume 1: Long Papers)*, pages 6981–7004, Toronto, Canada. Association for Computational Linguistics.

Zhenyu Pan, Haozheng Luo, Manling Li, and Han Liu. 2024. Chain-of-action: Faithful and multimodal question answering through large language models. *arXiv preprint arXiv:2403.17359*.

Baolin Peng, Michel Galley, Pengcheng He, Hao Cheng, Yujia Xie, Yu Hu, Qiuyuan Huang, Lars Liden, Zhou Yu, Weizhu Chen, and Jianfeng Gao. 2023. Check your facts and try again: Improving large language models with external knowledge and automated feedback. *arXiv preprint arXiv:2302.12813*.

Alec Radford, Jong Wook Kim, Chris Hallacy, Aditya Ramesh, Gabriel Goh, Sandhini Agarwal, Girish Sastry, Amanda Askell, Pamela Mishkin, Jack Clark, Gretchen Krueger, and Ilya Sutskever. 2021. Learning transferable visual models from natural language supervision. In *Proceedings of the 38th International Conference on Machine Learning*, volume 139 of *Proceedings of Machine Learning Research*, pages 8748–8763. PMLR.

Nguyen Vo and Kyumin Lee. 2019. Learning from fact-checkers: analysis and generation of fact-checking language. In *Proceedings of the 42nd International ACM SIGIR Conference on Research and Development in Information Retrieval*, pages 335–344.

Soroush Vosoughi, Deb Roy, and Sinan Aral. 2018. The spread of true and false news online. *Science*, 359(6380):1146–1151.

Jason Wei, Xuezhi Wang, Dale Schuurmans, Maarten Bosma, Brian Ichter, Fei Xia, Ed Chi, Quoc V Le, and Denny Zhou. 2022. Chain-of-thought prompting elicits reasoning in large language models. In *Advances in Neural Information Processing Systems*, volume 35, pages 24824–24837. Curran Associates, Inc.

Shicheng Xu, Liang Pang, Huawei Shen, Xueqi Cheng, and Tat-seng Chua. 2023. Search-in-the-chain: Towards the accurate, credible and traceable content generation for complex knowledge-intensive tasks. *arXiv preprint arXiv:2304.14732*.

Barry Menglong Yao, Aditya Shah, Lichao Sun, Jin-Hee Cho, and Lifu Huang. 2023a. End-to-end multimodal fact-checking and explanation generation: A challenging dataset and models. In *Proceedings of the 46th International ACM SIGIR Conference on Research and Development in Information Retrieval*. ACM.

Shunyu Yao, Dian Yu, Jeffrey Zhao, Izhak Shafran, Thomas L. Griffiths, Yuan Cao, and Karthik Narasimhan. 2023b. Tree of thoughts: Deliberate problem solving with large language models. *arXiv preprint arXiv:2305.10601*.

Savvas Zannettou, Tristan Caulfield, Jeremy Blackburn, Emiliano De Cristofaro, Michael Sirivianos, Gianluca Stringhini, and Guillermo Suarez-Tangil. 2018. On the origins of memes by means of fringe web communities. In *Proceedings of the Internet Measurement Conference 2018*, IMC '18, page 188–202, New York, NY, USA. Association for Computing Machinery.

Fengzhu Zeng and Wei Gao. 2024. Justilm: Few-shot justification generation for explainable fact-checking of real-world claims. *arXiv preprint arXiv:2401.08026*.

Xuan Zhang and Wei Gao. 2023. Towards llm-based fact verification on news claims with a hierarchical step-by-step prompting method. *arXiv preprint arXiv:2310.00305*.

A Appendix

A.1 Instructions to Annotators

The instructions to annotators for the evaluation of the Explanation Generation Task is provided in Figure 5.

You are given a claim and gold explanation that explains the veracity of the claim. You will be shown a series of explanations generated by a language model. You are to rate the explanations on a scale of 1-3.

Rating 1: The explanation misses out on explaining every point in the gold explanation.

Rating 2: The explanation misses some points from the gold explanation but is overall good.

Rating 3: The explanation explains every point in the gold explanation.

Figure 5: Annotation Instructions

A.2 Explanation Generation by Veracity Label

In addition to the overall ratings for the Human Annotation for Explanation Generation, we also provide the ratings for specific classes. Figure 6 shows the human annotation ratings for the explanations of supported claims. Figure 7 shows the human annotation ratings for the explanations of refuted claims.

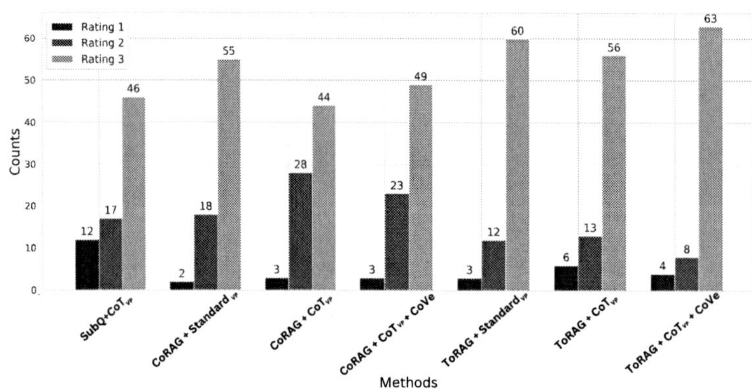

Figure 6: Annotator ratings for explanations of supported claims

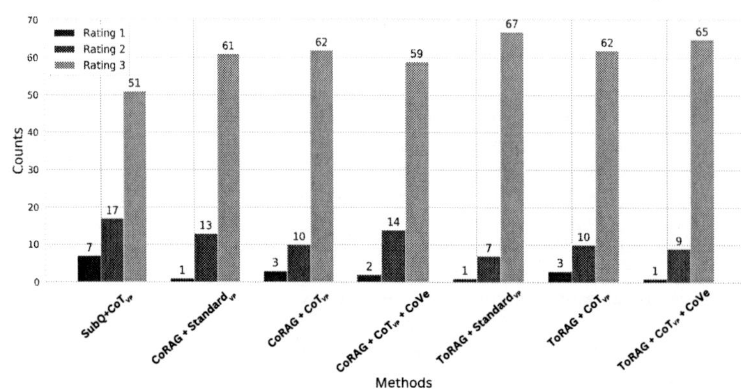

Figure 7: Annotator ratings for explanations of refuted claims

A.3 Discussing Multimodal RAG

We utilize reverse image search to extract captions of matching images from the web. We showcase the Image QA pairs for the examples in Table 2. The first example regarding Mike Pompeo showcases how GPT-4V is unable to identify the Afghan dignitary and the image context is unable to provide a name that could help fact-check the claim. However, using the image captions retrieved from the internet and prompting the evidence retrieval along with the image caption, GPT-4V is able to identify the Afghan dignitary as Mullah Abdul Ghani Baradar. The fact-check then continues to verify if Mullah Abdul Ghani Baradar was indeed ever the Afghan President or not. Similarly, in the third example with Joe Biden kneeling, the image captions extracted by reverse image search are able to add the additional information that Joe Biden was kneeling down to pose with dancers in Haiti. This information is crucial for the particular fact-check since it contextualizes the reason why Joe Biden was kneeling as well as detailing the event where the described act occurred.

Table 2: Example table with claims, images, and QA.

Claim	Image	Generated Image Context	Image QA
The man next to Mike Pompeo in a November 2020 photo is the guy the Trump administration helped get out of jail in 2018 and who is now the 'president' of Afghanistan.		The image shows Mike Pompeo standing next to a man wearing traditional Afghan attire and a face mask. The setting appears to be a formal meeting room with a painting on the wall, two gold-colored chairs, and a table with water bottles. Both individuals are standing apart, likely adhering to social distancing guidelines prevalent during the COVID-19 pandemic. The background and attire suggest the meeting is official in nature and likely related to diplomatic or governmental affairs. Claim stated in 2021.	Q. Who is the man standing next to Mike Pompeo in the November 2020 photo? A. Mullah Abdul Ghani Baradar
Says Joe Biden took a knee during the national anthem.		The image shows Joe Biden taking a knee, but it does not provide evidence that this act occurred during the national anthem. Without additional context, the claim cannot be confirmed solely based on this image. The time frame of the claim is 'Claim stated in 2020'.	Is there a specific date and location associated with the image of Joe Biden taking a knee? A. FILE - In this Monday, Oct. 5, 2020 file photo, Democratic presidential candidate former Vice President Joe Biden and his wife Jill Biden pose for a photo with dancers as they visit Little Haiti Cultural Complex in Miami.
The Trump administration worked to free 5,000 Taliban prisoners.		The image shows individuals, presumed to be Taliban prisoners, inside a bus with a guard standing nearby, which potentially correlates to the release of Taliban prisoners. The context suggests this may represent a prisoner release process.	Q. Were the individuals shown in the provided image actually Taliban prisoners being released as part of the agreement? A.'Taliban prisoners are released from Pul-e-Charkhi jail in Kabul, Afghanistan, Thursday, Aug. 13, 2020
These were not chemical irritants' used to clear a crowd. Pepper balls are 'not a chemical irritant.		The image shows law enforcement in protective gear amidst a haze that is consistent with the use of some form of crowd control substance, such as a chemical irritant. Visible smoke and the dispersing crowd strongly suggest the use of a substance to clear the area, counter to the claim that no chemical irritants were used. The presence of pepper balls would depend on identifying specific items or equipment in the scene that are known to dispense pepper balls.	Can we identify the specific equipment or methods used by law enforcement in the image to determine if pepper balls or another substance was deployed? A. ... The caption snippets suggest that teargas was used to clear Lafayette Park for a photo opportunity...

A.4 Example Questions

In Table 3 and Table 4 we show the questions asked by each approach.

Table 3: Example of Question-Answers asked by SubQ+CoT$_{VP}$, CoRAG and ToRAG

Claim: PPP on average provided a grant of around $11,000 per employee	
SubQ+ CoT$_{VP}$	**Q. What was the total amount of funds disbursed through the Paycheck Protection Program (PPP) in 2020?** A.More than $511 billion **Q. What criteria were used to determine the amount of grant each business received per employee under the PPP?"** A. ... determined based on the business's average monthly payroll costs... approximately 2.5 times the applicant's average monthly payroll... only up to $100,000 of an employee's annual compensation was eligible for calculation. **Q. Were there any variations in the grant amount per employee based on the industry, location, or size of the business?** A. ... mentions different aspects of grants, such as administration costs, the impact of public money on grant receivers, and the employee retention credit, which suggests that grant amounts... **Q. How does the PPP define an "employee" for the purposes of calculating grants?** A. ...means individuals employed on a full-time, part-time, or other basis.
CoRAG	**Q. What was the average grant amount per employee provided by the Paycheck Protection Program in 2020?** A. ...for self-employed individuals and employees, the PPP loans could cover up to $100,000 of annualized pay per employee for eight weeks, with a maximum of $15,385 per individual." **Q. How does the maximum allowable amount of $15,385 per individual under PPP loans relate to the average grant of around $11,000 per employee?** A. The maximum allowable amount of $15,385 per individual under PPP loans is derived from the limit set for self-employed individuals and employees, which is based on up to $100,000 of annualized pay for eight weeks...On the other hand, the average grant of around $11,000 per employee, as observed by Square Capital, reflects the actual average loan amount disbursed to small businesses through the PPP.
ToRAG	**Q. What was the typical grant amount per employee provided by the PPP as of mid-2020?** A. ... the average size of a PPP loan approved during the first wave was $206,000, with 74% of the loans approved being for amounts of $150,000 or less." **Q. What is the average monthly payroll cost per employee, as used in the PPP loan calculations, and how does this figure relate to the reported average grant of around $11,000 per employee?** A. ...For a 24-week period, the maximum amount per individual is $46,154, or for an eight-week period, it is $15,385. **Q. Can you provide the total number of employees covered by PPP loans up to mid-2020 and the total amount of PPP funds disbursed by that time, to calculate the actual average grant per employee?** A. ... average grant per employee can be calculated as $511 billion divided by 51 million employees, which equals approximately $10,019.61 per employee.

Table 4: Example of Question-Answers asked by CoRAG and ToRAG

Claim: These 11 mass shootings involved an AR-15-style weapon.	
CoRAG	**Q.Were AR-15-style weapons used in 11 mass shootings in the United States before 2021?** A. ... confirms that AR-15-style rifles were used in the 2012 Aurora, Colorado... **Q. Can you list the specific mass shootings, aside from the 2012 Aurora, Colorado incident, where AR-15-style rifles were reportedly used before 2021?** A. ... search results provided do not list specific mass shootings... stating that AR-15 rifles were used in 26 percent of the last 80 mass shootings...before 2021. **Q. Given the information that AR-15-style rifles were used in 26 percent of the last 80 mass shootings before 2021, identify other incidents where these rifles were reportedly used.** A. ... occurred when a gunman, armed with an AR-15-style rifle and body armor, killed nine people and wounded 27 others. **Q. Can you identify the specific characteristics or features that define an AR-15-style rifle as used in these incidents?** A. 1. Chambering ... 2. Controls 3. Fast and easy reloading...

	Claim: (Continued)
ToRAG	**Q. What are the specific dates and locations of the 11 mass shootings mentioned as involving an AR-15-style weapon?** A. 1. Boulder, Colorado: March 22, 2021... 2. San Jose, California: May 26, 2021..." **Q. Were there any official reports or statements from law enforcement agencies confirming the use of AR-15-style weapons in the Boulder, Colorado, and San Jose, California shootings?** A. Yes, there were official reports confirming the use of an AR-15-style weapon in the Boulder, Colorado shooting... **Q. Can you provide details on the legal acquisition and ownership status of AR-15-style weapons by the shooters in the remaining nine mass shootings mentioned?** A. 1. Sutherland Springs church shooting: ... goods retailer violated the law ... 2. Boulder supermarket shooting: ... legally purchased the AR-15-style rifle ... 4. Pittsburgh synagogue shooting: ... like the AR-15 rifle used in the attack. 5. Las Vegas shooting: ... claim for selling AR-15s... 6. Orlando nightclub shooting: ... 7. San Bernardino shooting: ... 8. Sandy Hook Elementary School shooting: ..."

A.5 General Prompts in the RAGAR Approaches

Initial Question Generation

~~~~
You are an expert fact-checker given an
unverified claim that needs to be
explored.

Claim: ```{claim}```
Date (your questions must be framed to be
before this date): {year}
Country: United States of America

You follow these Instructions:
1: You understand the entire claim.

2: You will make sure that the question
is specific and focuses on one aspect of
the claim (focus on one topic, should
detail where, who, and what) and is very,
very short.

3: You should not appeal to video
evidence nor ask for calculations or
methodology.

3: You must not ask for sources of data.
You are only concerned with the question.

4: You are not allowed to use the word
"claim". Instead, if you want to refer to
the claim, you should point out the exact
issue in the claim that you are phrasing
your question around.

5: You must never ask for calculations or
methodology.

6: Create a pointed factcheck question
for the claim.

Return only a python list containing the
question.
~~~~

Follow-up Check

~~~~
You are an expert fact-checker given an
unverified claim and question-answer
pairs regarding the claim that needs to
be explored. You follow these steps:

Claim: ```{claim}```
Question-Answer Pairs:
```{answerslist}```


Are you satisfied with the questions
asked and do you have enough
information to answer the claim?

If the answer to any of these questions
is "Yes", then reply only with "False"
or else answer, "True".
~~~~

Follow-up Question

~~~~
You are given an unverified statement and
question-answer pairs regarding the claim
that needs to be explored. You follow
these steps:

Claim: ```{claim}```
Question-Answer Pairs:
```{answerslist}```
Country: United States of America

Your task is to ask a followup question
to regarding the claim specifically based
on the question answer pairs.

Never ask for sources or publishing.

The follow-up question must be
descriptive, specific to the claim, and
very short, brief, and concise.

The follow-up question should not appeal
to video evidence nor ask for
calculations or methodology.

The followup question should not be
seeking to answer a previously asked
question. It can however attempt to
improve the question.

You are not allowed to use the word
"claim" or "statement". Instead if you
want to refer the claim/statement, you
should point out the exact issue in the
claim/statement that you are phrasing
your question around.

Reply only with the followup question and
nothing else.
~~~~

Figure 8: Prompt for initial question-generation, Follow-up Check and Follow-up Question common to all RAGAR approaches

A.6 Prompts Specific to Tree of RAG

QA Elimination

```
You are an expert fact-checker. You are given a claim and a question-answer pair containing
3 questions alongwith their answers.
Claim: ```{claim}```
Question-Answer Pair: ```{qapairs}```

These questions and answers are seeking to help fact-check the claim. You as a fact-checker
have to pick only one of these question answer pairs. Here are your guidelines to pick:
- Pick the question-answer pair that is the most relevant towards answering the claim.
- Pick the question-answer pair that divulges the most information.
- Pick the question-answer pair that reveals new additional information.
- Do not pick the question-answer pair that is unsure with its answer and does not have the
answer.
- Pick the question answer pair that can answer the question precisely and is the most
detailed.

You have to pick the one that most matches these criteria.
Reply only with the question answer pair as a dictionary with question as key and answer as
value.
```

Figure 9: Prompt for QA Elimination

A.7 Prompts for Veracity Prediction

A.7.1 Standard Veracity Prediction Prompt

Veracity Prediction and Explanation

```
You are a well-informed and expert fact-checker.
You are provided with question-answer pairs regarding the following claim: {claim}

These are the provided questions and relevant answers to the question to verify the claim:
<{evidence_pairs}>

Based strictly on the main claim and the question-answers provided (ignoring questions regarding image if they
dont have an answer), You have to provide:

- claim: the original claim,

- rating: the rating for claim should be "supported" if and only if the Question Answer Pairs specifically
support the claim, "refuted" if and only if the Question Answer Pairs specifically refute the claim or "failed":
if there is not enough information to answer the claim appropriately.

- factcheck: and the detailed and elaborate fact-check paragraph.

please output your response in the demanded json format
```

Figure 10: Prompt for Standard Veracity prediction

A.7.2 Zero Shot Chain of Thought Veracity Prediction

Zero Shot Chain of Thought Veracity Prediction

```
You are a well-informed and expert fact-checker.

You are provided with question-answer pairs regarding the following claim: {claim}

Question-Answer Pairs:
<{evidence_pairs}>

Based strictly on the main claim, and the question-answers provided (ignoring questions regarding image if they
dont have an answer), you will provide:

rating: The rating for claim should be one of "supported" if and only if the Question Answer Pairs specifically
support the claim, "refuted" if and only if the Question Answer Pairs specifically refutes the claim or
"failed": if there is not enough information to answer the claim appropriately.

Is the claim: {claim} "supported", "refuted" or "failed" according to the available questions and answers?
Lets think step by step.
```

Figure 11: Prompt to get the CoT Veracity Prediction from the question-answer pairs and the claim

A.7.3 Chain of Verification Veracity Prediction

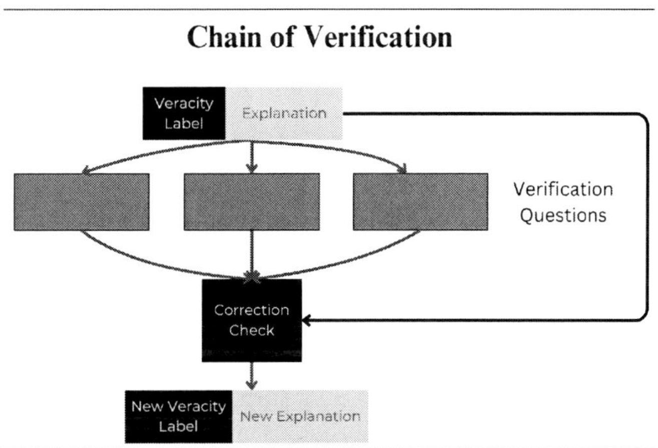

Figure 12: Pipeline of the CoVe Veracity Prediction

Verification Questions

```
You are a well-informed and expert fact-checker.
You are provided with the fact-check regarding the given claim and also the year the claim was made in.

Claim: {claim}
Fact-Checked Response: {factcheck}
Year the claim was made (specify it in your question): {year}

You are to generate verification questions.
A verification question is defined as a question that seeks to directly confirm whether a point made in the fact-
checked response is true or false.

Your task is the following:
1. Read the entire fact-check.

2. Identify overall points mentioned in the factcheck.

3. Create pointed verification questions by rephrasing the point verbatim as a Yes/No question for the overall
points mentioned in the fact-check.

4. The question must seek to gain answers in case of missing information suggested in the fact-check.

5. You must stick only to the overall points mentioned in the fact-check, do not create questions for unnecessary
extra information.

Instruction: You are not allowed to use the word "claim" or "statement". Instead if you want to refer the
claim/statement, you should point out the exact issue in the claim/statement that you are phrasing your question
around.

Return only the pointed verification questions each seperated with a "~~~" symbol.
```

Figure 13: CoVe Verification Questions prompt

Correction Check

```
You are a well-informed and expert fact-checker.
You are provided with a factcheck and its correction qa pairs regarding the following claim: {claim}

Original FactCheck:
<{factcheck}>

Correction QA: {corrections}

Based strictly on the main claim, the original factcheck and the question-answers provided (ignoring questions
regarding image if they dont have an answer), you will:

- If the corrections contain information that differs from the original factcheck, then create a new factcheck
based on the corrected information and explain whether this changes the veracity of the original claim.

- If the corrections do not contain any new factcheck information, then simply return the original factcheck back.
```

Figure 14: CoVe Corrections Prompt

FactGenius: Combining Zero-Shot Prompting and Fuzzy Relation Mining to Improve Fact Verification with Knowledge Graphs

Sushant Gautam
SimulaMet & OsloMet
Oslo, Norway
sushant@simula.no

Roxana Pop
University of Oslo
Oslo, Norway
roxanap@ifi.uio.no

Abstract

Fact-checking is a crucial natural language processing (NLP) task that verifies the truthfulness of claims by considering reliable evidence. Traditional methods are labour-intensive, and most automatic approaches focus on using documents as evidence. In this paper, we focus on the relatively understudied fact-checking with Knowledge Graph data as evidence and experiment on the recently introduced FactKG benchmark. We present FactGenius, a novel method that enhances fact-checking by combining zero-shot prompting of large language models (LLMs) with fuzzy text matching on knowledge graphs (KGs). Our method employs LLMs for filtering relevant connections from the graph and validates these connections via distance-based matching. The evaluation of FactGenius on an existing benchmark demonstrates its effectiveness, as we show it significantly outperforms state-of-the-art methods. The code and materials are available at https://github.com/SushantGautam/FactGenius.

1 Introduction

Fact-checking is a critical task in natural language processing (NLP) that involves automatically verifying the truthfulness of a claim by considering evidence from reliable sources (Thorne et al., 2018). This task is essential for combating misinformation and ensuring the integrity of information in digital communication (Cotter et al., 2022). Traditional fact-checking is performed by domain experts and is a labour-intensive process. Automatic fact-checking systems have been introduced to address this, but most of them work with textual data as evidence sources (Vladika and Matthes, 2023).

Recent advancements in large language models (LLMs) have shown promise in enhancing fact-checking capabilities (Choi and Ferrara, 2024). LLMs, with their extensive pre-training on diverse textual data, possess a vast amount of embedded knowledge (Yang et al., 2024). However, their outputs can sometimes be erroneous or lacking in specificity, especially when dealing with complex reasoning patterns required for fact-checking. External knowledge, such as knowledge graphs (KGs) (Hogan et al., 2021), can aid in fact-checking.

In this paper, we propose FactGenius, a novel approach that combines zero-shot prompting of LLMs with fuzzy relation-mining techniques to improve reasoning on knowledge graphs. Specifically, we leverage DBpedia (Lehmann et al., 2015), a structured source of linked data, to enhance the accuracy of fact-checking tasks.

Our methodology involves using the LLM to filter potential connections between entities in the KG, followed by refining these connections through Levenshtein distance-based fuzzy matching. This two-stage approach ensures that only valid and relevant connections are considered, thereby improving the accuracy of fact-checking.

We evaluate our method using the FactKG dataset (Kim et al., 2023b), which comprises 108,000 claims constructed through various reasoning patterns applied to facts from DBpedia. Our experiments demonstrate that FactGenius significantly outperforms existing baselines (Kim et al., 2023a), particularly when fine-tuning RoBERTa (Liu et al., 2019) as a classifier, achieving superior performance across different reasoning types.

In summary, the integration of LLMs with KGs and the application of fuzzy matching techniques represent a promising direction for advancing fact-checking methodologies. Our work contributes to this growing body of research by proposing a novel approach that effectively combines these elements, yielding significant improvements in fact-checking performance.

Proceedings of the Seventh Fact Extraction and VERification Workshop (FEVER), pages 297–306
November 15, 2024 ©2024 Association for Computational Linguistics

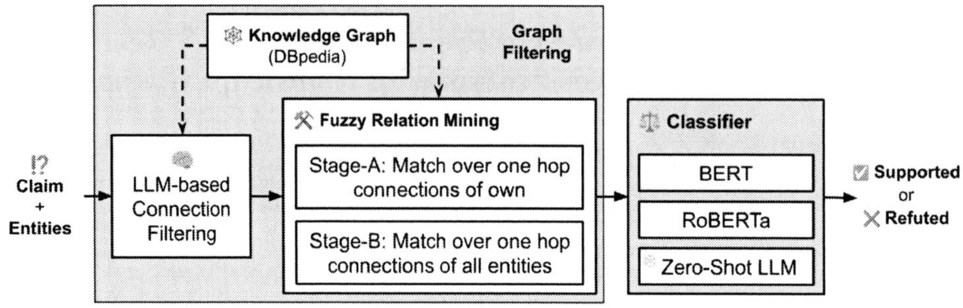

Figure 1: Overall pipeline of FactGenius: The process starts with LLM-based Connection Filtering using a knowledge graph (see Section 4.1.1). In Fuzzy Relation Mining (see Section 4.1.2), Stage-I matches one-hop connections of entities, and optionally, Stage-II includes all entities' connections. The classifier (BERT, RoBERTa, or Zero-Shot LLM; see Section 4.3) then determines if the claim is supported or refuted.

2 Literature Review

Fact-checking has become an increasingly vital aspect of natural language processing (NLP) due to the proliferation of misinformation in digital communication (Guo et al., 2022). Traditional approaches to fact-checking have typically relied on manually curated datasets and rule-based methods. While these methods are effective in controlled environments, they often struggle with scalability and adaptability to new types of misinformation (Saquete et al., 2020; Guo et al., 2022). The labor-intensive nature of these methods also poses significant challenges in rapidly evolving information landscapes (Nakov et al., 2021; Zeng et al., 2021).

To address challenges in understanding machine-readable concepts in text, FactKG introduces a new dataset for fact verification using claims, leveraging knowledge graphs (KGs) to encompass diverse reasoning types and linguistic patterns. This approach aims to enhance the reliability and practicality of KG-based fact verification (Kim et al., 2023b). Similarly, the Fact Extraction and VERification (FEVER) dataset (Thorne et al., 2018) pairs claims with Wikipedia sentences that support or refute them, providing a benchmark for fact-checking models. The authors employed a combination of natural language inference models and information retrieval systems to assess claim veracity.

The GEAR framework (Zhou et al., 2019) improves fact verification by using a graph-based method to aggregate and reason over multiple pieces of evidence. This approach surpasses previous methods by enabling more interactive and effective use of evidence.

Recent advancements in large language models (LLMs) have demonstrated considerable potential for enhancing fact-checking processes (Kim et al., 2023a; Choi and Ferrara, 2024). LLMs are pre-trained on vast and diverse corpora (Yang et al., 2024), allowing them to generate human-like text and possess a broad knowledge base (Choi and Ferrara, 2024). However, despite their impressive capabilities, LLMs can sometimes produce erroneous outputs or lack the specificity required for complex fact-checking tasks (Choi and Ferrara, 2024). This issue becomes particularly evident when intricate reasoning and contextual understanding are necessary to verify claims accurately (Chai et al., 2023). Several studies have explored the integration of LLMs with external knowledge sources to improve their performance in fact-checking tasks (Cui et al., 2023; Ding et al., 2023).

The incorporation of knowledge graphs into fact-checking frameworks has also garnered attention. KGs, such as DBpedia (Lehmann et al., 2015), provide structured and linked data that can enhance the contextual understanding of LLMs. Knowledge graphs have been used to improve various NLP tasks by providing additional context and relationships between entities, as demonstrated by initiatives for knowledge-aware language models (Li et al., 2023; Logan Iv et al., 2019) and KG-BERT (Yao et al., 2019).

Approximate string matching, also called fuzzy string matching, is a technique used to identify partial matches between text strings (Navarro, 2001). Fuzzy matching techniques (Navarro, 2001) have been applied to enhance the integration of LLMs and KGs (Wang et al., 2024).

The Levenshtein distance-based similarity measure (Levenshtein et al., 1966) is one such technique that helps identify strings with approximate matches, which can be useful for finding relevant connections between entities by accommodating minor discrepancies in data representation. This approach has been beneficial in refining the outputs of LLMs, ensuring that only valid and contextually appropriate connections are considered (Guo et al., 2023).

Our proposed method, FactGenius, builds on these advancements by combining zero-shot prompting of LLMs with a fuzzy relation-mining technique to improve reasoning over KGs. This methodology leverages DBpedia as a structured source of linked data to enhance fact-checking accuracy. By using LLMs to filter potential connections between entities and refining these connections through fuzzy matching, FactGenius aims to address the limitations of existing fact-checking models.

3 Preliminaries

A Knowledge Graph (KG) G is a set of triples (s, r, o), with $s, o \in E$ and $r \in R$, where E is the set of entities, and R is the set of relations connecting those entities. A KG can be viewed either as a set of triples or as a graph with nodes in E and edge labels in R. Hence, when we discuss the 1-hop neighborhood of a certain entity e, we refer to the set of entities connected to e through an edge in this graph. For a triple (s, r, o), we consider s to be connected to o through an edge labeled as r, while we consider o to be connected to s through an edge labeled as $\sim r$, where $\sim r$ denotes the inverse relation of r.

We consider natural language sentences in their intuitive sense.

Given a claim in natural language C, a KG G with entities E, and a set of entities relevant to the claim E_C, the *fact verification with KG evidence task* is to predict whether the claim C is supported or not according to the evidence in G.

4 Methodology

We introduce the FactGenius system for the fact verification with KG evidence task. Our system has two main components: a graph filtering component that selects the relevant KG evidence for the input claim, and a classifier component that uses this evidence together with the claim to predict whether the claim is supported or not.

FactGenius leverages the capabilities of a Large Language Model (LLM) to filter the set of triples in the input graph G. More concretely, an LLM is used in a zero-shot setting to select the relevant relations from the 1-hop neighborhood of the entities E_C associated with claim C. Since the output of LLMs can be erroneous, the triples are further validated against the unfiltered set using fuzzy matching techniques. Finally, the classifier, which can be fine-tuned over pre-trained models like BERT (Devlin et al., 2019) or RoBERTa (Liu et al., 2019), or a Zero-Shot LLM, determines whether the claim is supported or refuted. The overall pipeline is shown in Figure 1.

4.1 FactGenius: Relation Filtering with LLM and Fuzzy Matching

The first step in our FactGenius pipeline is identifying the graph evidence relevant to the input claim. We select the relevant relations in the 1-hop neighborhood of the claim entities by employing LLM-based filtering. Once we have the relevant relations, we select the 1-hop neighborhood triples. These triples are then turned into strings and used together with the claim by the classifier.

4.1.1 LLM Prompt-Based Filtering

We utilize an LLM, specifically the Llama3-Instruct model, to identify and filter potential connections between entities based on a given claim.

This is done in the following way. First, we must select a set of relations to filter using the LLM. Given that KGs can be very large, for example, DBpedia contains billions of triples and thousands of edges (Lehmann et al., 2015), considering the full set of relations in an LLM prompt is infeasible. In FactGenius, we choose to look only at the 1-hop neighborhood of the given set of claim entities E_C to generate the initial set of relations. We therefore construct a set of 1-hop relations for each entity e, i.e. $\{r | (e, r, e_1) \in G\}$, which we will denote by $R_C(e)$. The LLM is then given the claim C and the set of relations $R_C(e)$ for each entity relevant to the input claim (each $e \in E_C$), and it outputs subsets of each $R_C(e)$, which we denote by $R_C^{llm}(e)$. A prompt example is given in Figure 2.

A retry mechanism is employed to handle potential failures in LLM responses. If the LLM output is inadequate (e.g., empty or nonsensical), the request is retried up to a specified maximum

System prompt:
You are an intelligent graph connection finder. You are given a single claim and connection options for the entities present in the claim. Your task is to filter the Connections options that could be relevant to connect given entities to fact-check Claim1. ~ (tilde) in the beginning means the reverse connection.

User prompt:
Claim1:
<<<Well, The celestial body known as 1097 Vicia has a mass of 4.1kg.»>
TASK:
- For each of the given entities given in the DICT structure below:
Filter the connections strictly from the given options that would be relevant to connect given entities to fact-check Claim1.
- Think clever, there could be multi-step hidden connections, if not direct, that could connect the entities somehow.
- Prioritize connections among entities and arrange them based on their relevance. Be extra careful with signs.
- No code output. No explanation. Output only valid python DICT of structure:
<<<
{
`"1097_Vicia"`: ["...", "...", ...]
# options (strictly choose from): `discovered`, `formerName`, `epoch`, `periapsis`, `apoapsis`, ..., `Planet/temperature` `"4.1"`: ["...", "...", ...],
# options (strictly choose from): `~length`, `~ethnicGroups`, `~percentageOfAreaWater`, `~populationDensity`, `~engine`, ..., `~number`
}
>>>

Figure 2: Filtering prompt example. The text inside < < < and > > > changes with each input.

number of attempts, in practice 10. In our experiments, however, we did not encounter any cases where retries exceeded this limit. If the limit is exceeded, the non-filtered sets of relations are returned.

4.1.2 LLM Output Validation

As mentioned, the LLM could output relations that are not in G. That is, $R_C^{llm}(e)$ is not necessarily a subset of $R_C(e)$ or even R.

We therefore pass the LLM output through a validation stage, which has two sub-stages, namely *Stage A* and *Stage B*.

In *Stage A*, we perform validation of the relation set for each entity from the claim. That is, for each entity $e \in E_C$, we select the subset of $R_C(e)$ that best matches the LLM output $R_C^{llm}(e)$. To do so, we fuzzily match the relations in $R_C(e)$ to the relations in $R_C^{llm}(e)$ using Levenshtein distance. A threshold on this distance is considered to decide whether two relations match or not.

The limitation of the first validation type is that if the LLM suggests the correct relation, but associates it with the wrong entity, this relevant relation is removed through the first validation type. We will exemplify this on the prompt in Figure 2. The model is given the entities `1097_Vicia` and `4.1`, each with the list of possible relations. If the model identifies `Planet/temperature` but associates it with `4.1` instead of `1097_Vicia` this relation is removed during *Stage A* validation.

To address this limitation, we introduce *Stage B* validation. In this stage, we consider the full set of relations generated by the LLM for all entities associated with the input claim, i.e., $R_C^{llm} = R_C^{llm}(e_1) \cup ... \cup R_C^{llm}(e_n)$ for all $e_1, \ldots, e_n \in E_C$. Similarly to *Stage A*, we use Levenshtein distance to compare the relations in $R_C(e)$ with the filtered relations, but we consider the full filtered set R_C^{llm} instead of the entity-specific set $R_C^{llm}(e)$. The details are explained in Algorithm 1.

4.2 Claim-Driven Relation Filtering

To measure the effectiveness of LLM in relation filtering (as described in 4.1), we create a baseline that ensures only the relations most pertinent to the claim, based on lexical similarity, are selected. To filter relations relevant to a claim, we begin by tokenizing the claim sentence, excluding stop words, to obtain a list of significant word tokens. Next, for each entity $e \in E_C$ present in the claim, we gather all 1-hop relations $R_C(e)$.

Algorithm 1 LLM output validation

Input: $E_C = \{e_1, ..., e_n\}$ - entities in the claim;
$R_C(e_1), ..., R_C(e\_n)$: relations in the 1-hop neighborhood for each entity in the claim;
$R_C^{llm}(e_1), ..., R_C^{llm}(e_n)$: relation sets output by the LLM;
$stage$: validation stage, either **A** or **B**
Output: $R'_C(e_1), ..., R'_C(e\_n)$- Validated relation sets.

procedure VALIDATERELATION
  Initialize: **probable_connections**: { }
  for each $e \in E_C$ **do**
    for each $r \in R_C(e)$ **do**
      if $stage = $ **A then**
        $R^{llm-compare} = R_C^{llm}(e)$
      else
        $R^{llm-compare} = R_C^{llm}(e_1) \cup ... \cup R_C^{llm}(e_n)$
      end if
      for each $r^{llm} \in R^{llm-compare}$ **do**
        $d = \text{LEVENSHTEINDISTANCE}(r, r^{llm})$
        if $d > 90$ **then**
          $R'_C(e) = R'_C(e) \cup \{r\}$
        end if
      end for
    end for
  end for
end procedure

We then apply a fuzzy matching process to each tokenized word in the claim, comparing it to the relations in $R_C(e)$ using the Levenshtein distance. This process yields a subset of relations $R'_C(e)$, where each relation's similarity to the claim words exceeds a predefined threshold.

4.3 With Evidence Classifier

In this configuration, the model is supplied with both the claim and graphical evidence as input, and it then makes predictions regarding the label. FactGenius utilizes graph filtering, as explained in Section 4.1, to ensure retention of the most relevant and accurate connections.

4.4 Evidence Stringification

To effectively pass evidence triples to the language model, we must first convert these triples into a string format. For each entity e in the claim with its associated relations $\{r \mid (e, r, e_1) \in G\}$ extracted from the graph G, we transform each triplet (e, r, e_1) into the string format "$\{e\} > -\{r\}- > \{e_1\}$". For multiple triples of evidence, the resulting strings are simply concatenated into a single evidence string, preserving the order and structure of the triples. This approach ensures a seamless and coherent integration of structured graph data into the language model's input.

4.5 Zero-Shot LLM as Fact Classifier

This involves utilizing Llama-3-Instruct as a fact classifier, to predict whether the given input claim and evidence string are supported or refuted. A retry mechanism is implemented to handle potential failures in LLM responses. A prompt example with evidence is shown in Figure 3.

4.6 Fine-Tuning Pre-Trained Models

Pre-trained BERT-base-uncased[1] and RoBERTa-base are fine-tuned with the claim and evidence string as inputs to predict whether the claim is supported or refuted.

An ablation study was conducted to evaluate the contributions of each stage of our approach. This involved sequentially removing Stage-B and measuring the system's performance. The results of the ablation study allowed us to quantify the impact of both stages on the overall performance of the model. Accuracy was used as an evaluation metric across all reasoning types to quantify performance improvements from the ablation study.

4.7 Implementation

Our FactGenius system implementation leverages several advanced tools and frameworks to ensure efficient and scalable processing. The Llama3-Instruct inference server is set up using vLLM (vLLM Project, 2024; Kwon et al., 2023), running on an NVIDIA A100 GPU (80 GB vRAM) to facilitate rapid inference. This server runs standalone, integrating seamlessly with the FactGenius pipeline.

For model fine-tuning and evaluation, we employ the Hugging Face Transformers library, utilizing the `Trainer` class for managing the training process. This setup allows for the fine-tuning of pre-trained models like BERT and RoBERTa within our pipeline. Hyper-parameters such as batch size, learning rate, and training epochs are configured to optimize performance, with computations accelerated by PyTorch.

The models were fine-tuned on a single NVIDIA V100 GPU, with RoBERTa requiring around 25 minutes per epoch with a batch size of 32, and BERT taking around 8 minutes per epoch with a batch size of 64. The fine-tuning process utilized the Adam optimizer with settings of $\beta_1 = 0.9$, $\beta_2 = 0.98$, and $\epsilon = 1e-6$ for RoBERTa, and $\beta_1 = 0.9$, $\beta_2 = 0.99$, and $\epsilon = 1e-8$ for BERT.

[1]huggingface.co/google-bert/bert-base-uncased

A weight decay of 0.01 was used over all the layers. A learning rate of $5e-6$ was used with early stopping over validation loss for 3 epochs, retaining the best epoch's weights.

5 Experiments

To evaluate the performance of our proposed methods, we conducted a series of experiments comparing different strategies for fact-checking on the FactKG (Kim et al., 2023b) benchmark.

5.1 Dataset

The FactKG dataset (Kim et al., 2023b) comprises 108,000 claims constructed using various reasoning patterns applied to facts sourced from DBpedia (Lehmann et al., 2015). Each data point consists of a natural language claim in English, the set of DBpedia entities mentioned in the claim, and a binary label indicating the claim's veracity (Supported or Refuted). The distribution across labels and five different reasoning types is shown in Table 1. The relevant relation paths starting from each entity in the claim are provided, which aids in the evaluation and development of models for claim verification tasks.

The dataset is accompanied by two processed versions of the FactKG Knowledge Graph, derived from DBpedia 2015. The first version encompasses the entire DBpedia dataset with the directionality of edges removed by incorporating reverse relation triples, denoted as *DBpedia-Full*. The second version is a curated subset of the first, containing only the relations pertinent to FactKG, thus enabling more focused and efficient analysis, and is referred to as *DBpedia-Light*.

Set	Train	Valid	Test
Total Rows	86,367	13,266	9,041
True (Supported)	42,723	6,426	4,398
False (Refuted)	43,644	6,840	4,643
One-hop	15,069	2,547	1,914
Conjunction	29,711	4,317	3,069
Existence	7,372	930	870
Multi-hop	21,833	3,555	1,874
Negation	12,382	1,917	1,314

Table 1: Data distribution across labels and five reasoning types.

5.2 Results

Following prior work (Kim et al., 2023b,a), we conducted experiments with two types of approaches: one that takes as input only the claim, referred to as *Claim Only*, and another that integrates KG information, referred to as *With Evidence*. The goal of this comparison is to assess whether the required knowledge is already stored in the weights of pre-trained large language models or if injecting KG information is beneficial. The results are summarized in Table 2.

5.3 Claim Only

For the *Claim Only* scenario, we compared four methods: two from the previous literature and two designed by us. We selected two of the best-performing methods from prior work: the BERT-based claim-only model introduced with the FactKG dataset by Kim et al. (Kim et al., 2023b), and the ChatGPT-based model subsequently introduced by Kim et al. (Kim et al., 2023a). Additionally, we experimented with two models of our own design: we used the Meta-Llama-3-8B-Instruct[2] (Meta, 2024) model with zero-shot prompting, and a RoBERTa-base (Liu et al., 2019) model, which we fine-tuned on the fact verification task. An example of the prompt we used for Meta-Llama-3-8B-Instruct is found in Appendix B.

Our results show that RoBERTa outperformed the reported accuracy of BERT (Kim et al., 2023b), achieving an accuracy of 0.68, which is on par with the 12-shot ChatGPT model reported in the KG-GPT paper (Kim et al., 2023a). This suggests that RoBERTa inherently stores knowledge relevant for fact-checking, at least on the FactKG benchmark. Our prompting approach, however, achieved a score of 0.61, underperforming on the task.

5.4 With Evidence

In the *With Evidence* setting, we compared different versions of our FactGenius system with two systems from prior work (Kim et al., 2023b,a). For our FactGenius approach, we experimented with five versions, using either an LLM classifier with prompting (Llama3-Instruct-zero-shot in Table 2) or a fine-tuned LLM as the classifier, either BERT-based (Devlin et al., 2019) or RoBERTa-based (Liu et al., 2019). For both the BERT-based and RoBERTa-based systems, we experimented with both *stage A* and *stage B* output validation.

[2]huggingface.co/meta-llama/Meta-Llama-3-8B-Instruct

Input type	Source	Model	One-hop	Conjunction	Existence	Multi-hop	Negation	Total
Claim Only	FactKG (Kim et al., 2023b)	BERT*	0.69	0.63	0.61	0.70	0.63	0.65
	KG-GPT (Kim et al., 2023a)	ChatGPT (12-shot)*	-	-	-	-	-	0.68
	Ours	Llama3-Instruct-zero-shot	0.61	0.67	0.59	0.61	0.53	0.61
	Ours	RoBERTa	0.71	0.72	0.52	0.74	0.54	0.68
With Evidence	FactKG	GEAR*	0.83	0.77	0.81	0.68	0.79	0.77
	KG-GPT	KG-GPT (12-shot)*	-	-	-	-	-	0.72
	Ours on DBpedia-Light	Claim-driven relation filtering	0.81	0.71	0.98	0.71	0.76	0.78
	FactGenius (Ours) on DBpedia-Light	Llama3-Instruct-zero-shot	0.72	0.75	0.76	0.62	0.52	0.68
		BERT-stage-A	0.85	0.80	0.91	0.79	0.78	0.81
		BERT-stage-B	0.85	0.83	0.88	0.81	0.73	0.82
		RoBERTa-stage-A	0.84	0.86	0.88	0.82	0.77	0.84
		RoBERTa-stage-B	**0.89**	**0.89**	**0.93**	**0.83**	**0.78**	**0.87**
	FactGenius (Ours) on DBpedia-Full	Llama3-Instruct-zero-shot	0.72	0.76	0.72	0.61	0.51	0.68
		BERT-stage-A	0.81	0.83	0.67	0.80	0.56	0.76
		BERT-stage-B	0.81	0.81	0.67	0.80	0.56	0.76
		RoBERTa-stage-A	0.86	0.85	0.91	0.79	0.82	0.84
		RoBERTa-stage-B	0.86	0.86	0.90	0.82	0.79	0.84

Table 2: Comparing our method with other strategies and methods in terms of reported accuracies in the test set. The * symbol indicates results taken directly from prior works, whereas '-' indicates results were not reported by prior works.

5.4.1 On DBpedia-Light Knowledge Graph

Our results show that adding evidence to the Llama3-Instruct model's instructions significantly improved its accuracy from 0.61 to 0.68. This indicates that even for large language models, incorporating relevant evidence can enhance fact-checking performance in a zero-shot learning scenario. However, directly applying zero-shot prompting with Llama3-Instruct did not yield superior performance compared to claim-driven relation filtering. The performance improved when using fine-tuned BERT or RoBERTa as classifiers. We also observed that the performance of the pipeline increased further when stage-B was used instead of stage-A relation mining, with fine-tuned RoBERTa performing better than BERT.

To assess the contribution of the validation stages, we applied both stages to our best-performing model, the RoBERTa-based system. We found that employing *stage A* of filtering resulted in an accuracy of 0.84. Incorporating *stage B* further improved the performance to 0.87. The second stage enhanced performance across most reasoning types, with notable improvements in conjunction and negation tasks. We achieved the highest performance by fine-tuning RoBERTa with stage-B relation mining, leading to an accuracy of 0.87 on the DBpedia-Light knowledge graph. To the best of our understanding, FactKG uses the DBpedia-Light graph, while KG-LLM employs DBpedia-Full, as inferred from their respective public implementations.

5.4.2 On DBpedia-Full Knowledge Graph

When using the DBpedia-Full knowledge graph, we observed a decrease in performance for all model variants compared to the *DBpedia-Light* setting. The Llama3-Instruct-zero-shot approach showed a similar performance gain. Fine-tuned BERT with both stage-A and stage-B maintained moderate scores, indicating stability but not improvement. RoBERTa-stage-A and RoBERTa-stage-B models achieved comparable performance at 0.84, with both stages performing similarly, indicating that stage-B processing does not significantly outperform stage-A in the more complex graphs. These results highlight the challenges associated with scaling to larger and more complex knowledge graphs.

6 Discussion

The enhanced performance of FactGenius, particularly in Conjunction, Existence, and Negation reasoning, can be attributed to its innovative combination of zero-shot prompting using large language models (LLMs) and fuzzy text matching on knowledge graphs.

The evidence-based filtering approaches revealed significant findings. The *stage-B* validation approach improves accuracy compared to *stage-A*, although the model shows only moderate performance improvement in Multi-hop reasoning. This suggests that more advanced techniques may be necessary to handle the complexity of Multi-hop reasoning effectively.

The two-step approach of filtering and validating connections proved to be especially effective. In the first step, the LLM narrows down potential connections based on the context provided by the claim, significantly reducing the search space. The second step refines these connections through fuzzy matching, ensuring that only the most relevant and accurate ones are retained. Our comparative study confirmed the importance of both steps, with the second step being particularly beneficial for Conjunction and Negation reasoning tasks.

While fine-tuned LLM models, such as BERT and RoBERTa, generally outperformed the zero-shot Llama3-Instruct model and claim-driven relation filtering, the increased graph complexity in DBpedia-Full compared to DBpedia-Light limited the gains from fine-tuning. This limitation can be attributed to the input token restrictions of BERT and RoBERTa, which truncate inputs after 512 tokens. Truncation is more likely with the larger DBpedia-Full graph, potentially excluding relevant information, thereby reducing the effectiveness of evidence-based filtering. Additionally, the similar performance between stage-A and stage-B relation mining in the full graph setting suggests that the added complexity of stage-B does not yield better accuracy, likely due to these input constraints. These observations underscore the need for architectural adaptations or preprocessing methods to more effectively handle larger datasets.

As LLM inference is a crucial component of this framework, we employed vLLM (vLLM Project, 2024) to enable rapid inference using a single NVIDIA A100 GPU. In our experiments, the LLM inference speed was approximately 15 queries per second, including retries in case of failure. This rate is feasible, especially as LLM inference continues to be optimized with the latest technologies. Embedding LLM in this framework has proven to be a sound decision.

7 Conclusion

In this paper, we introduced FactGenius, a novel method that combines zero-shot prompting of large language models with fuzzy relation mining to improve reasoning on knowledge graphs. This approach addresses several key challenges in traditional fact-checking methods. First, the integration of LLMs allows for the leveraging of extensive pre-trained knowledge in a zero-shot setting. Second, the use of fuzzy text matching with Levenshtein distance ensures that minor discrepancies in entity names or relationships do not hinder the relationship selection process, thus improving robustness.

Our experiments on the FactKG dataset demonstrated that FactGenius significantly outperforms traditional fact-checking methods and existing baselines, particularly when fine-tuning RoBERTa as a classifier. The two-stage approach of filtering and validating connections was crucial for achieving high accuracy across various reasoning types.

The findings from this study suggest that utilizing LLMs for KG evidence retrieval holds great promise for advancing fact-checking capabilities. Future work could explore applying this approach to other domains and datasets, as well as incorporating additional structured data sources to further enhance performance.

Limitations

The primary limitation of this work is that we only consider the 1-hop neighborhood when constructing the graph evidence. While this approach performs well on the FactKG benchmark, it may not capture the multi-hop reasoning required for more complex claims in other datasets or real-world scenarios. Additionally, our evaluation is limited to FactKG, restricting the generalizability of our findings. Another limitation stems from the input context limitations of the fine-tuned models and the LLMs, particularly when dealing with entities that have extensive graph connections, leading to input length constraints and necessitating truncation. Finally, we focused on zero-shot prompting with a single LLM and did not explore few-shot learning or alternative models, which might enhance performance.

Acknowledgement

This work has benefited from the Experimental Infrastructure for Exploration of Exascale Computing (eX3) at Simula, which is financially supported by the Research Council of Norway.

References

Ziwei Chai, Tianjie Zhang, Liang Wu, Kaiqiao Han, Xiaohai Hu, Xuanwen Huang, et al. 2023. GraphLLM: Boosting Graph Reasoning Ability of Large Language Model. *arXiv*.

Eun Cheol Choi and Emilio Ferrara. 2024. FACT-GPT: Fact-Checking Augmentation via Claim Matching with LLMs. In *WWW '24: Companion Proceedings of the ACM on Web Conference 2024*, pages 883–886. Association for Computing Machinery, New York, NY, USA.

Kelley Cotter, Julia R. DeCook, and Shaheen Kanthawala. 2022. Fact-Checking the Crisis: COVID-19, Infodemics, and the Platformization of Truth. *Social Media + Society*, 8(1):20563051211069048.

Jiaxi Cui, Zongjian Li, Yang Yan, Bohua Chen, and Li Yuan. 2023. ChatLaw: Open-Source Legal Large Language Model with Integrated External Knowledge Bases. *arXiv*.

Jacob Devlin, Ming-Wei Chang, Kenton Lee, and Kristina Toutanova. 2019. BERT: Pre-training of Deep Bidirectional Transformers for Language Understanding. *ACL Anthology*, pages 4171–4186.

Yan Ding, Xiaohan Zhang, Saeid Amiri, Nieqing Cao, Hao Yang, Andy Kaminski, et al. 2023. Integrating action knowledge and LLMs for task planning and situation handling in open worlds. *Auton. Robot.*, 47(8):981–997.

Zhijiang Guo, Michael Schlichtkrull, and Andreas Vlachos. 2022. A Survey on Automated Fact-Checking. *Transactions of the Association for Computational Linguistics*, 10:178–206.

Zishan Guo, Renren Jin, Chuang Liu, Yufei Huang, Dan Shi, Supryadi, et al. 2023. Evaluating Large Language Models: A Comprehensive Survey. *arXiv*.

Aidan Hogan, Eva Blomqvist, Michael Cochez, Claudia D'amato, Gerard De Melo, Claudio Gutierrez, et al. 2021. Knowledge Graphs. *ACM Comput. Surv.*, 54(4):1–37.

Jiho Kim, Yeonsu Kwon, Yohan Jo, and Edward Choi. 2023a. KG-GPT: A General Framework for Reasoning on Knowledge Graphs Using Large Language Models. *ACL Anthology*, pages 9410–9421.

Jiho Kim, Sungjin Park, Yeonsu Kwon, Yohan Jo, James Thorne, and Edward Choi. 2023b. FactKG: Fact Verification via Reasoning on Knowledge Graphs. *ACL Anthology*, pages 16190–16206.

Woosuk Kwon, Zhuohan Li, Siyuan Zhuang, Ying Sheng, Lianmin Zheng, Cody Hao Yu, et al. 2023. Efficient Memory Management for Large Language Model Serving with PagedAttention. In *SOSP '23: Proceedings of the 29th Symposium on Operating Systems Principles*, pages 611–626. Association for Computing Machinery, New York, NY, USA.

Jens Lehmann, Robert Isele, Max Jakob, Anja Jentzsch, Dimitris Kontokostas, Pablo N. Mendes, et al. 2015. DBpedia – A large-scale, multilingual knowledge base extracted from Wikipedia. *Semantic Web*, 6(2):167–195.

Vladimir I Levenshtein et al. 1966. Binary codes capable of correcting deletions, insertions, and reversals. In *Soviet physics doklady*, volume 10, pages 707–710. Soviet Union.

Xinze Li, Yixin Cao2, Liangming Pan, Yubo Ma, and Aixin Sun. 2023. Towards Verifiable Generation: A Benchmark for Knowledge-aware Language Model Attribution. *arXiv*.

Yinhan Liu, Myle Ott, Naman Goyal, Jingfei Du, Mandar Joshi, Danqi Chen, et al. 2019. RoBERTa: A Robustly Optimized BERT Pretraining Approach. *arXiv*.

Robert L. Logan Iv, Nelson F. Liu, Matthew E. Peters, Matt Gardner, and Sameer Singh. 2019. Barack's Wife Hillary: Using Knowledge-Graphs for Fact-Aware Language Modeling. *arXiv*.

Meta. 2024. Meta Llama 3. [Online; https://llama.meta.com/llama3].

Preslav Nakov, David Corney, Maram Hasanain, Firoj Alam, Tamer Elsayed, Alberto Barrón-Cedeño, et al. 2021. Automated Fact-Checking for Assisting Human Fact-Checkers. In *Proceedings of the Thirtieth International Joint Conference onArtificial Intelligence, {IJCAI-21}*, pages 4551–4558. International Joint Conferences on Artificial Intelligence Organization.

Gonzalo Navarro. 2001. A guided tour to approximate string matching. *ACM Comput. Surv.*, 33(1):31–88.

Estela Saquete, David Tomás, Paloma Moreda, Patricio Martínez-Barco, and Manuel Palomar. 2020. Fighting post-truth using natural language processing: A review and open challenges. *Expert Syst. Appl.*, 141:112943.

James Thorne, Andreas Vlachos, Christos Christodoulopoulos, and Arpit Mittal. 2018. FEVER: a Large-scale Dataset for Fact Extraction and VERification. *ACL Anthology*, pages 809–819.

Juraj Vladika and Florian Matthes. 2023. Scientific Fact-Checking: A Survey of Resources and Approaches. *arXiv*.

vLLM Project. 2024. vLLM. [Online; https://github.com/vllm-project/vllm].

Yu Wang, Nedim Lipka, Ryan A. Rossi, Alexa Siu, Ruiyi Zhang, and Tyler Derr. 2024. Knowledge Graph Prompting for Multi-Document Question Answering. *AAAI*, 38(17):19206–19214.

Jingfeng Yang, Hongye Jin, Ruixiang Tang, Xiaotian Han, Qizhang Feng, Haoming Jiang, et al. 2024. Harnessing the Power of LLMs in Practice: A Survey on ChatGPT and Beyond. *ACM Trans. Knowl. Discovery Data*, 18(6):1–32.

Liang Yao, Chengsheng Mao, and Yuan Luo. 2019. KG-BERT: BERT for Knowledge Graph Completion. *arXiv*.

Xia Zeng, Amani S. Abumansour, and Arkaitz Zubiaga. 2021. Automated fact-checking: A survey. *Lang. Linguist. Compass*, 15(10):e12438.

Jie Zhou, Xu Han, Cheng Yang, Zhiyuan Liu, Lifeng Wang, Changcheng Li, et al. 2019. GEAR: Graph-based Evidence Aggregating and Reasoning for Fact Verification. *ACL Anthology*, pages 892–901.

A Zero-shot fact-checking with evidence

We experimented with a language model in a zero-shot setting for fact verification including the evidence. We prompted the model with the claim and the evidence given as a list of triples — an example of the prompt is shown in Figure 3.

```
[{
"role": "system", "content":
"You are an intelligent fact-checker. You are given
a single claim and supporting evidence for the entities
present in the claim, extracted from a knowledge graph.
Your task is to decide whether all the facts in the
given claim are supported by the given evidence.
Choose one of {True, False}, and output a one-sentence
explanation for the choice."
},{
"role": "user", "content":
'''
## TASK:
Now let's verify the Claim based on the evidence.
Claim:
<<< The celestial body known as 1097 Vicia has a
mass of 4.1kg. >>>

Evidence:
<<< 1999_Hirayama -> mass -> "4.1"
1097_Vicia -> mass -> "9.8" >>>

# Answer Template:
"True/False (single word answer),
One-sentence explanation."
'''
}]
```

Figure 3: Example prompt given to Llama3-Instruct with evidence for zero-shot fact-checking.

B Claim-only models

A baseline is established using the Meta-Llama-3-8B-Instruct[3] (Meta, 2024) model with zero-shot prompting for claim verification, asking it to verify the claim without evidence. Through instruction prompt engineering, the model is ensured to respond with either 'true' or 'false'. A retry mechanism is implemented to handle potential failures in LLM responses. A prompt example is shown in Figure 4. The retry mechanism simply retries calling the LLM up to a fixed number of times and diverts to a default handling function if the LLM is unable to provide a proper output.

```
[{
"role": "system", "content":
"You are an intelligent fact-checker trained on
Wikipedia. You are given a single claim, and your task
is to decide whether all the facts in the given claim
are supported by your knowledge.
Choose one of {True, False}, and output a one-sentence
explanation for the choice."
},{
"role": "user", "content":
'''
## TASK:
Now let's verify the Claim based on your knowledge.
Claim:
<<< The celestial body known as 1097 Vicia has a
mass of 4.1kg. >>>

# Answer Template:
"True/False (single word answer),
One-sentence explanation."
'''
}]
```

Figure 4: Example prompt given to Llama3-Instruct without evidence for zero-shot fact-checking.
«< ... »> signs are added just to indicate that the content inside changes for each prompt.

[3]huggingface.co/meta-llama/Meta-Llama-3-8B-Instruct

Fact or Fiction? Improving Fact Verification with Knowledge Graphs through Simplified Subgraph Retrievals

Tobias A. Opsahl
University of Oslo
tobiasao@uio.no

Abstract

Despite recent success in natural language processing (NLP), fact verification remains a difficult task. Due to misinformation spreading increasingly fast, attention has been directed towards automatically verifying the correctness of claims. In the domain of NLP, this is usually done by training supervised machine learning models to verify claims by utilizing evidence from trustworthy corpora. We present efficient methods for verifying claims on a dataset where the evidence is in the form of structured knowledge graphs. We use the FACTKG dataset, which is constructed from the *DBpedia* knowledge graph extracted from Wikipedia. By simplifying the evidence retrieval process, from fine-tuned language models to simple logical retrievals, we are able to construct models that both require less computational resources and achieve better test-set accuracy.

1 Introduction

As the volume of information generated continues to grow, so does the risk of misinformation spreading, which has made automatic fact verification a crucial task in NLP (Cohen et al., 2011; Hassan et al., 2015; Thorne and Vlachos, 2018; Bekoulis et al., 2021). Traditionally, fact verification has been tackled in journalism by experts manually researching topics and writing articles about their findings. Some specific websites dedicated to this approach are *FactCheck.org* and *PolitiFact.com*. However, it is time-consuming and labor-intensive, and is not able to follow the pace of information created in digital media (Cohen et al., 2011; Hassan et al., 2015).

One of the most popular datasets for fact verification is the *Fact Extraction and VERification* (FEVER) dataset (Thorne et al., 2018). It consists of claims supported by a corpus of Wikipedia articles. Models trained on the dataset need to extract the relevant evidence and use it to classify claims as *supported*, *refuted* or *not enough information*.

Despite its popularity, several issues have been discovered. Due to the manual construction of claims, the structure of the language is inherently biased with respect to the classes, and therefore it is possible to achieve good performance without using the evidence at all (Schuster et al., 2019). It has also been shown that models trained on FEVER experience a significant drop in performance when the factual evidence is changed in a way that influences the validity of claims (Hidey et al., 2020). These issues can be improved by accordingly adjusting the validation and test dataset to contain less biased data (Schuster et al., 2019; Hidey et al., 2020), but we believe it is important to develop models on other datasets as well.

A less studied approach to process evidence is by structured data. In many real-world examples, data is available in large structured databases, rather than unstructured articles. This is relevant for domains such as social networks, logistics, management systems and database systems. The dataset *TabFact* (Chen et al., 2019) was created with this intent, consisting of claims with tabular evidence extracted from Wikipedia.

This paper aims to increase the performance of models trained on the FACTKG dataset (Kim et al., 2023), a dataset created for fact verification with structured evidence in the form of *knowledge graphs* (KGs). The claims are created with evidence from *DBpedia* (Lehmann et al., 2015), a large KG extracted from Wikipedia. A KG consists of nodes and edges linked together to represent structural concepts. Nodes represent entities, such as persons, things or events, and edges represent relations, conveying how entities are related, as shown in Figure 1. For instance, a node can be the company *Meyer Werft*, and since it is located in the city *Papenburg*, they are connected with the edge *location*. We refer to *Meyer Werft, location, Papenburg* as a *knowledge triple*.

Since the task of fact verification with KGs re-

Proceedings of the Seventh Fact Extraction and VERification Workshop (FEVER), pages 307–316
November 15, 2024 ©2024 Association for Computational Linguistics

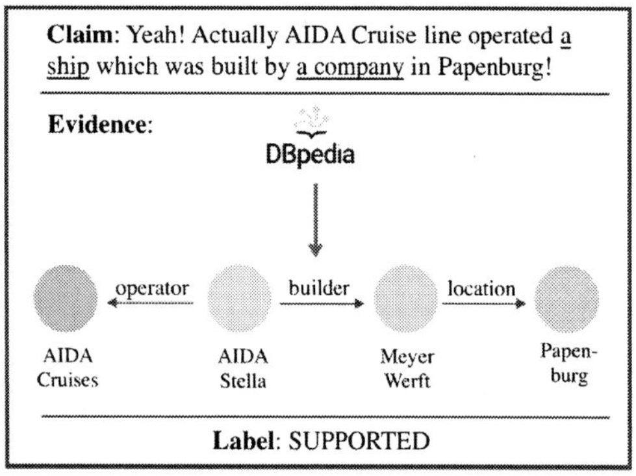

Figure 1: An example claim from FACTKG (Kim et al., 2023). The claim can be verified or refuted based on the DBpedia KG (Lehmann et al., 2015). This is Figure 1 from Kim et al. (2023).

mains relatively unexamined, we want to explore several different approaches to the problem. We use the following three model architectures:

- **Textual Fine-tuning:** Fine-tuning pretrained encoder models on text data for claim verification. We use BERT (Devlin et al., 2018) by concatenating the claims with subgraphs represented as strings.
- **Hybrid Graph-Language Model:** Using a modification of a *question answer graph neural network* (QA-GNN) (Yasunaga et al., 2021), which both uses a pretrained encoder model to embed the claim, and a graph neural network (GNN) to structurally process the subgraphs.
- **LLM Prompting:** Deploying state-of-the-art language models in a few-shot setting, without the need for additional finetuning. We use ChatGPT 4o (Achiam et al., 2023; Open AI, 2024) for this setting.

The textual finetuning serves as a simple and conventional method, while the QA-GNN can handle graph based data efficiently and is more specifically constructed for the task of interest. In contrast, the LLM prompting displays how well general purpose language models can perform on the task. It does not require any further training and does not use any evidence. Therefore, it will serve as a baseline and give insight to how difficult the task is.

Our main contribution is that we increase the accuracy and computational efficiency of models trained on FACTKG. By utilizing efficient subgraph retrieval methods, we are able to increase the test-set accuracy from 77.65% (Kim et al., 2023) to 93.49%. To the best of the authors' knowledge, this is the best performance achieved so far on this dataset. Additionally, our models train quicker, taking only 1.5-10 hours, compared to the 2-3 days spent on the benchmark model from Kim et al. (2023), reported by the authors. The code and documentation used for this article can be found at `https://github.com/Tobias-Opsahl/Fact-or-Fiction`.

2 Related Work

2.1 Fact Verification

The FEVER dataset is one of the most popular datasets used for fact verification (Thorne et al., 2018), and has influenced several model architectures. *Graph-based Evidence Aggregating and Reasoning* (GEAR) (Zhou et al., 2019) works by finding relevant articles with entity linking, giving them a relevance score, embedding the claim and sentences in the relevant evidence with a pre-trained BERT (Devlin et al., 2018), and then using a GNN to reason over the embeddings. The *Neural Semantic Matching Network* (NSMN) (Nie et al., 2019) used three homogenous neural networks used for document retrieval, sentence selection and claim verification. By using a transformer based architecture, *Generative Evidence REtrieval* (GERE) (Chen et al., 2022) combined the evidence retrieval and sentence identifying into a single step.

Several other datasets for fact verification have also been proposed. The *Fake News Challenge* (Hanselowski et al., 2018) were aimed towards predicting the relevance and agreement of a title and text. *VitaminC* (Schuster et al., 2021) focuses on representing changing evidence, and was created by constructing claims based on different revisions of Wikipedia articles. The dataset *FAVIQ* (Park et al., 2021) explored ambiguous parts of claims, while *TabFact* (Chen et al., 2019) used tabular data as evidence. There have also been proposed multimodular dataset for fact verification, combining claims and images (Zlatkova et al., 2019; Mishra et al., 2022).

2.2 The FactKG Dataset

The FACTKG dataset (Kim et al., 2023) consists of 108,000 English claims for fact verification, where the downstream task is to predict whether the claims are true or false. The claims are constructed from the DBpedia KG (Lehmann et al., 2015), which is extracted from Wikipedia and represents how entities are related to each other.

The claims are constructed on either of the following five reasoning types:

- **One-hop:** To answer a one-hop claim, one only needs to traverse one edge in the KG. In other words, only one knowledge triple is needed to verify the validity of the claim.
- **Multi-hop:** As opposed to one-hop claims, one needs to traverse multiple steps in the KG to verify multi-hop claims.
- **Conjunction:** The claim includes a combination of multiple claims, which are often added together with the word *and*.
- **Existence:** These claims state that an entity has a relation, but does not specify which entity it relates to.
- **Negation:** The claim contains negations, such as *not*.

The dataset is split in a train, validation and test set of proportion 8:1:1. The train and validation set includes relevant subgraphs for each claim, but not the test set. All claims include a list of entities present in the claim and as nodes in the KG.

2.3 Question Answer Graph Neural Networks

The *question answer graph neural network* (QA-GNN) (Yasunaga et al., 2021) is a hybrid language and GNN model that both uses a pre-trained language model to process the text, and couples it with a GNN reasoning over a subgraph. It is given text and a subgraph as input. The text, consisting of a question and possible answers, is added as a node to the subgraph. The language model embeds the text, and assigns a relevance score to each node in the subgraph. The relevance scores are multiplied with the node features, before being sent into the GNN. The GNN output, text-node and the text embedding are concatenated before being put into the classification layer.

3 Methods

3.1 Efficient Subgraph Retrieval

We experiment with different ways of retrieving relevant subgraphs for the claim, focusing on computational efficiency. Each datapoint in the FACTKG dataset consists of a claim and a list of entities

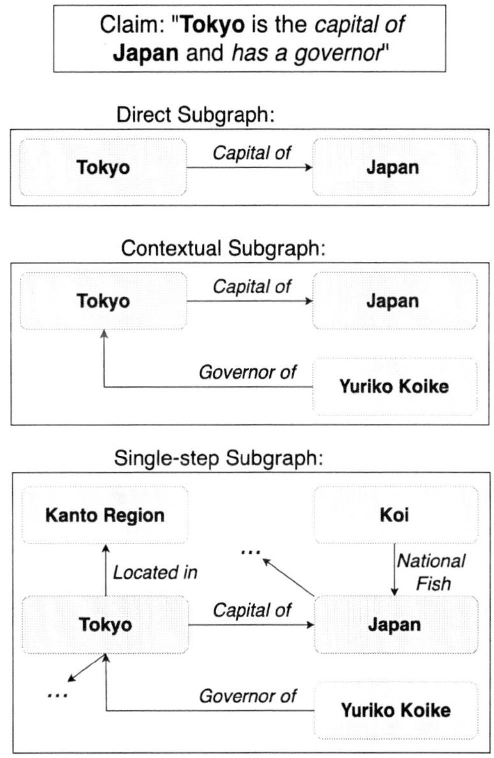

Figure 2: **Examples of the different subgraphs explored in this article.** Boxes and **bold letters** represent entities, while arrows and *italic letters* represent relations. This claim is meant for illustrative purposes and is not present in the FACTKG dataset.

that appear both in the claim and the KG. Since the part of DBpedia used in FactKG is fairly large (1.53GB), it is necessary to only use a small subgraph of it as input to the models. The benchmark model from Kim et al. (2023) uses two language models to predict the relevant edges and the depth of the graph. We wish to simplify this step in order to reduce the model complexity, and propose methods for subgraph retrieval that do not need training.

We experiment with the following methods (examples can be found in Figure 2):

- **Direct:** Only includes knowledge triples where both nodes are present in the entity list.
- **Contextualized:** First, includes all direct subgraphs. Additionally, lemmatize the words in the claim and check if the nodes in the entity list have any relations corresponding to the lemmatized words in the claim. Include all knowledge triples where at least one node is in the entity list and the relation can be found

in the claim.

- **Single-step:** Includes every knowledge triple one can be traversed in one step from a node in the entity list. In other words, include every knowledge triple that contains at least one node in the entity list.

3.2 Finetuning BERT

We use BERT (Devlin et al., 2018) as our pre-trained language model. We first train a baseline model using only the claims and no subgraphs, and then with all of the different methods for retrieving subgraphs. The subgraphs are converted to strings, where each knowledge triple is represented with square brackets, and the name of the nodes and edges are the same as they appear in DBpedia. The order of the knowledge triples is determined by the order of the list of entities in the FactKG dataset and the order of the edges in DBpedia. The subgraphs are concatenated after the claims and a " | " separation token.

3.3 QA-GNN Architecture

In order to adapt the QA-GNN to the fact verification setting, we perform some slight modifications. Because the possible answers are always "true" or "false", we embed only the claims, instead of the question and answer combination. Additionally, we do not connect the embedded question or claim to the subgraph.

We use a pre-trained BERT (Devlin et al., 2018) as the language model to embed and calculate the relevance scores. In order to reduce the complexity of the model, we use a frozen BERT to calculate the embeddings for the nodes and the edges in the graph. This way, all of the embeddings in the graph can be pre-calculated. We use the last hidden layer representation of the CLS token, which is of length 768. The BERT that calculates the relevance scores and the embedding of the claim is not frozen. The relevance scores are computed as the cosine similarity between the claim embedding and the embedding of the text in the nodes.

We use a graph attention network (Veličković et al., 2017) for our GNN. Since the subgraphs are quite shallow, we only use two layers in the GNN, and apply batch norm (Ioffe and Szegedy, 2015). Each layer has 256 features, which is mean-pooled and concatenated with the BERT embedding and sent into the classification layer. We add dropout (Srivastava et al., 2014) to the GNN layers and the classification layer.

3.4 ChatGPT Prompting

We construct a prompt for ChatGPT 4o in order to answer a list of claims as accurately as possible. This is done by creating an initial prompt and validating the results on 100 randomly drawn claims from the validation set, and by trying different configurations of the prompt until we do not get a better validation set accuracy. We then use the best prompt with 100 randomly drawn unseen test-set questions, and attempt to ask 25, 50 and 100 claims at a time, to see if the amount of claims at a time influences the performance. We run the testing three times.

Since we do not have access to vast enough computational resources to run an LLM, this analysis is limited by only using 100 datapoints from the test set. In order to get access to a state-of-the-art LLM, we used the ChatGPT website with a "ChatGPT Plus" subscription to perform the prompting. This model is not seeded, so the exact answers are not reproducible, but every prompt and answer are available in the previously mentioned GitHub repository. We used the ChatGPT 4o model 30th of May 2024. Every prompt was performed in the "temporary chat" setting, so the model did not have access to the history of previous experiments.

Due to the inability to use the entire test set and the lack of reproducibility, we do not directly compare this experiment to the other models. However, we still believe it serves as a valuable benchmark. Recently, the performance of LLMs has rapidly improved, which suggests that their applications will continue to broaden. Additionally, this approach is not fine-tuned, and may work as an interesting benchmark that can contextualize the results of the other models.

3.5 Benchmark Models

We will compare the results against the best benchmark models from Kim et al. (2023) and the best performing models known to the authors, found in Gautam (2024). These comparisons include both baselines that use only the claims and models that also incorporate subgraph evidence.

Claim-Only Models:

- **FactKG BERT Baseline**: The baseline model from Kim et al. (2023) uses a fine-tuned BERT, training only on the claims.

Input Type	Model	One-hop	Conjunction	Existence	Multi-hop	Negation	Total
Claim Only	FACTKG BERT Baseline	69.64	63.31	61.84	70.06	63.62	65.20
	FactGenius RoBERTa Baseline	71	72	52	74	54	68
	BERT (no subgraphs)	67.71	67.48	62.51	73.28	64.23	68.99
With Subgraphs	FACTKG GEAR Benchmark	83.23	77.68	81.61	68.84	79.41	77.65
	FactGenius RoBERTa-two-stage	89	85	95	75	87	85
	QA-GNN (single-step)	79.08	74.43	83.37	74.72	79.60	78.08
	BERT (single-step)	**97.40**	**97.51**	**97.31**	**80.32**	**92.54**	**93.49**

Table 1: **Test-set accuracy for the best models from this article and the best benchmark models.** The FACTKG models are from Kim et al. (2023), while the FactGenius models are from Gautam (2024). The fine-tuned BERT model performed the best, while the QA-GNN was the computationally most efficient model.

- **RoBERTa Baseline**: Similar to the above, the baseline from Gautam (2024) uses a fine-tuned language model with claims only, but uses RoBERTa (Liu et al., 2019) as the base model.

Models Utilizing Subgraphs:

- **GEAR-Based Model**: The benchmark model from Kim et al. (2023) is inspired by GEAR (Zhou et al., 2019), but has been adapted to handle graph-based evidence. It uses two fine-tuned language models to retrieve the subgraphs. One of them predicts relevant edges, the other predicts the depth of the subgraph.
- **FactGenius:** This model combines zero-shot LLM prompting with fuzzy text matching on the KG (Gautam, 2024). The LLM filters relevant parts of the subgraphs, which are then refined using fuzzy text matching. Finally, a fine-tuned RoBERTa is used to make the downstream prediction.

3.6 Further Experimental Details

Due to computational constraints, we tuned the hyperparameters one by one, instead of performing a grid search. All the training was performed on the University of Oslo's USIT ML nodes (University Centre for Information Technology, 2023), using an RTX 2080 Ti GPU with 11GB VRAM. The BERT model has 109,483,778 parameters, which all were fine-tuned. The QA-GNN used a total of 109,746,945 parameters. The FACTKG dataset comes with a lighter version of DBpedia that only contains relevant entries, which was used for this paper. Further details can be found in Appendix A.

4 Results

4.1 Improved Performance and Efficiency

The test results for our best model configurations and the benchmark models can be found in Table 1. The best performing model is the fine-tuned BERT with single-step subgraphs. The fine-tuned BERT without any subgraphs were able to achieve slightly higher performance than the one from Kim et al. (2023), which we suggest is due to finding better hyperparameters.

Additionally, our models were much faster to train. While the GEAR model used 2-3 days to train on an RTX 3090 GPU (reported by the authors by email), our QA-GNN only used 1.5 hours. The training time of our fine-tuned BERT model was significantly influenced by the size of the subgraphs we used. With no subgraphs, it took about 2 hours to train, while with the one-hop subgraph it took 10 hours. FactGenius was reported to use substantially more computational resources, running the LLM inference on a A100 GPU with 80GB VRAM for 8 hours.

4.2 Successful Subgraphs Retrievals

We now look at the different configurations for the subgraph retrievals, which greatly influenced the performance of the models. Since the *direct* and *contextual* approach only includes subgraphs if a certain requirement is fulfilled, it will result in some of the claims having empty subgraphs. In the training and validation set, 49.0% of the graphs were non-empty for the *direct* approach, and 62.5% were non-empty for the *contextual* approach. The *single-step* method resulted in vastly bigger subgraphs.

While the QA-GNN could handle the big subgraphs efficiently, the fine-tuned BERT was severely slowed down when the size of the subgraphs got bigger. Therefore, we substituted any empty subgraphs with the *single-step* subgraph when using QA-GNN, but kept the empty graphs when using fine-tuned BERT. This means that some claims for the direct and contextual BERT models were predicted only using the bias in the language

Model	One-hop	Conjunction	Existence	Multi-hop	Negation	Total
BERT (no subgraphs)	67.71	67.48	62.51	73.28	64.23	68.99
BERT (direct)	80.24	83.30	59.05	77.62	74.58	79.64
BERT (contextual)	81.20	84.45	61.05	77.04	77.40	80.25
BERT (single-step)	**97.40**	**97.51**	**97.31**	**80.32**	**92.54**	**93.49**
QA-GNN (direct)	74.60	74.01	58.97	76.41	74.12	75.01
QA-GNN (contextual)	76.58	69.94	84.68	74.58	80.75	76.12
QA-GNN (single-step)	79.08	74.43	83.37	74.72	79.60	78.08

Table 2: **Test-set accuracy for different subgraph retrieval methods on FACTKG.** The *direct* approach only includes knowledge triples where both nodes appear in the claim, the *contextual* also includes edges appearing in the claim, and the *single-step* includes all knowledge triples where at least one node appears in the claim. The QA-GNN models used the single-step subgraph if the direct or contextual is empty, while the BERT models did not.

model and the claim.

The results can be found in Table 2 and Table 3. We see a clear improvement in BERT when using the direct subgraphs over none, a small improvement when using the contextual subgraphs, and a big improvement when using the single-step method. The same is true for the QA-GNN, but the differences in performance are smaller. The models score the lowest on multi-hop claims.

Since we used non-trainable subgraph retrieval methods and a frozen BERT for embedding the nodes and edges in the subgraphs, we performed this processing before training the models. During training, the models used a lookup table to get the subgraphs and the word embeddings, which significantly decreased the training time. The retrieval of all the subgraphs took about 15 minutes, and the embedding of all the words appearing in them took about 1 hour. We also tried training a QA-GNN without frozen embeddings, but it ran so slow that we were not able to carry out the training with our available computational resources.

4.3 Competitive ChatGPT Performance

The results for the ChatGPT prompting can be found in Table 4. The accuracy is substantially lower than from our best models, but better than the baselines using only the claims. The accuracy is fairly consistent over the three runs, and we do not see a big difference between the amount of questions asked at a time.

We started with an initial prompt asking for just the truth values for a list of claims, and updated it to also include some training examples and to ask for explanations. Several configurations of the prompt were tested, and it was also improved based on feedback from ChatGPT.

We saw the biggest improvement when we asked for a short explanation of the answers, instead of just the truth values. Without asking for explanations, the amount of answers were often longer or shorter than the amount of questions, but this never happened when explanations were included. We added numbers to the questions to further help with this issue. We also saw a slight improvement by formulating the prompt with bullet point lists and by including some example inputs and outputs from the training set. The final prompt can be found in Figure 3.

5 Discussion

We were able to train better and more efficient models by simplifying the subgraph retrieval methods, both by using a fine-tuned BERT and a slightly modified QA-GNN model. While the QA-GNN models trained the fastest, the fine-tuned BERT clearly performed the best, significantly outperforming the benchmark models. This suggests that the simple logical subgraph retrievals worked better than the complex trained approaches in previous work. We suggest that the performance gain in the claim-only benchmark was due to slightly better hyperparameters.

All of the models performed better the bigger the subgraphs were. This suggests that the model architectures are able to utilize the relevant parts of the subgraphs, without needing an advanced subgraph retrieval step. This is emphasized by our fine-tuned BERT model achieving a 93.49% test set accuracy by only using the single-step subgraphs, while the GEAR model from Kim et al. (2023), which trained two language models to perform graph retrieval, achieved a 77.65% test-set accuracy.

When examining the precision and recall metrics in Table 3, we see that most of the models has a higher precision than recall, except for the

Model	**One-hop** P / R / F1	**Conjunction** P / R / F1	**Existence** P / R / F1	**Multi-hop** P / R / F1	**Negation** P / R / F1	**Total** P / R / F1
BERT (no subgraphs)	71.89 / 51.66 / 60.12	75.44 / 34.20 / 47.06	59.52 / 73.63 / 65.82	85.19 / 60.90 / 71.03	58.88 / 73.13 / 65.24	75.25 / 54.00 / 62.88
QA-GNN (direct)	76.19 / 67.04 / 71.32	80.11 / 51.22 / 62.49	56.19 / 74.10 / 63.91	80.04 / 74.80 / 77.33	70.97 / 73.80 / 72.36	77.21 / 69.01 / 72.88
QA-GNN (contextual)	84.79 / 61.29 / 71.15	80.27 / 38.29 / 51.85	81.83 / 88.38 / 84.98	82.31 / 67.17 / 73.98	77.26 / 82.26 / 79.68	84.10 / 62.78 / 71.89
QA-GNN (single-step)	82.51 / 70.55 / 76.06	78.89 / 53.95 / 64.08	79.69 / 88.70 / 83.95	78.44 / 73.09 / 75.67	77.06 / 79.10 / 78.07	81.41 / 71.19 / 75.96
BERT (contextual)	83.05 / 75.51 / 79.10	88.60 / 72.56 / 79.78	59.68 / 63.42 / 61.49	84.10 / 70.67 / 76.80	75.84 / 74.46 / 75.15	83.30 / 74.28 / 78.53
BERT (direct)	83.89 / 71.86 / 77.41	88.69 / 69.32 / 77.82	58.97 / 54.16 / 56.46	83.38 / 72.91 / 77.80	69.99 / 78.11 / 73.82	83.76 / 72.12 / 77.51
BERT (single-step)	**96.27 / 98.29 / 97.27**	**96.06 / 98.13 / 97.09**	**96.45 / 98.12 / 97.28**	**85.31 / 76.59 / 80.72**	**92.01 / 91.71 / 91.86**	**93.75 / 92.79 / 93.27**

Table 3: **Precision** (P), **Recall** (R), and **F1 scores** for different models and subgraph types on the test-set.

Model	Accuracy (mean ± std)
ChatGPT 25 questions	73.67 ± 0.5
ChatGPT 50 questions	$\mathbf{76.33} \pm 3.3$
ChatGPT 100 questions	73.00 ± 1.4

Table 4: **Test-set accuracy for different configurations of ChatGPT prompting.** The metrics are averaged over three runs. The prompts included 25, 50 or 100 claims at a time, but the same claims were used in all of the configurations.

best performing model, the single-step BERT. However, the single-step BERT does have a lower recall for the multi-hop claims, which it performs significantly worse on. Therefore, the models mostly have a higher precision than recall when their performance is not so good, suggesting they are slightly more likely to predict "false" on claims that they are not confident about.

A limitation of our subgraph retrieval methods is that they never include nodes that are more than one step away from an entity node, while the trained approach from Kim et al. (2023) is dynamic and may include more. This might make the hypothesis that the simple subgraph retrieval methods will perform worse on *multi-hop* claims than the dynamically trained, however, we see the exact opposite behavior. The best BERT and QA-GNN models score 80.32% and 74.72% at the multi-hop claims respectively, while the dynamic GEAR model scores 68.84%, even lower than the models not using the subgraphs at all. We do however see that the best performing BERT model clearly performs the worst on the multi-hop claims compared to the other claim types, indicating that even bigger subgraphs might be beneficial.

While the sample size for the ChatGPT metrics were small, it does indicate that non-fine-tuned LLMs can achieve adequate few-shot performance compared to a fine-tuned claim-only BERT. The performance does not seem to be substantially compromised when the amount of questions prompted increases, so with a bigger access to computational resources, it might be possible to prompt the full test-set at once. The removal of fine-tuning greatly improves the ease of use if one only needs to verify a few claims. While we are hesitant to make any conclusion with the small sample size, we believe that the results serve as an approximate benchmark of how difficult the dataset is.

6 Conclusion and Future Work

Our results show that with simple, yet efficient methods for subgraph retrieval, our models were able to improve fact verification with knowledge graphs with respect to both performance and efficiency. The fine-tuned BERT model with single-step subgraphs clearly achieves the best performance, while the QA-GNN models are more efficient to train.

This indicates that complex models can work well with simple subgraph retrieval methods. Since the single-step subgraphs mostly contain information not relevant for the claims, the models are themselves able to filter away irrelevant information, and complex subgraph retrieval methods may hence not be necessary for accurate fact verification. Additionally, since the best performing model performed the poorest with multi-hop claims, future research could explore simple subgraphs retrieval methods allowing for bigger depths than one. Additionally, future work should also be directed towards running similar experiments on other datasets.

We also encourage researchers that have access to bigger computational resources to further explore the performance of LLMs for fact verification. A core limitation of our ChatGPT prompting was the inability to use the full test-set, and we consider this crucial for further development. We also think it would be especially interesting to make LLM and KG hybrid models. Since our results indicate that simple single-step subgraph retrievals outperform more complex methods, a promising path of future research would be to simply use both the claims and the single-step subgraphs as input to the LLM. If possible, the LLM could also be fine-tuned on

Task:
Determine the truth value (True or False) of the following claims based on information verifiable from Wikipedia, as represented in the DBpedia knowledge graph. Provide your answers without using real-time internet searches or code analysis, relying solely on your pre-trained knowledge.
Instructions:

- You will evaluate the following claims, presented one per line.
- Base your answers solely on your knowledge as of your last training cut-off.
- Provide answers in Python list syntax for easy copying.
- Respond with `True` for verifiable claims, and `False` otherwise.
- Include a brief explanation for each answer, explaining your reasoning based on your pre-training.
- If the claim is vague or lacks specific information, please make an educated guess on whether it is likely to be True or False.

Output Format: Format your responses as a list in Python. Each entry should be a tuple, formatted as (claim number, answer, explanation).
Example Claims:
1. The Atatürk Monument is located in Izmir, Turkey, where the capital is Ankara.
2. Yes, Eamonn Butler's alma mater is the University of Texas System!
3. I have heard 300 North LaSalle was completed in 2009.
4. The band Clinton Gregory created an album in the rock style. ...

Example output:
[
(1, True, "The Atatürk Monument is indeed located in Izmir, and the capital of Turkey is Ankara."),
(2, False, "Eamonn Butler did not attend the University of Texas System; he is a British author and economist whose educational background does not include this institution."),
(3, True, "300 North LaSalle in Chicago was indeed completed in 2009."),
(4, False, "Clinton Gregory is primarily known as a country music artist, not rock."),
...
]
Here are the actual claims you should answer:

Figure 3: **Final prompt used to get truth values from ChatGPT 4o.** The actual questions are not included, but were in the format of the **Example Claims**. The **Example Claims** are from the training set, and the **Example Output** is copy pasted from an actual ChatGPT answer.

the dataset. We also encourage future work to create fully reproducible results with LLMs, which we were unable to do.

7 Limitations

Our experiments with ChatGPT were done on a small sample of test questions, with a model that was not possible to seed, and therefore is not reproducible. Due to the small sample size, we are not able to directly compare the performance to other approaches. The lack of reproducibility, which stems from the state-of-the-art model that was available to the author is not fully publicly available, makes it impossible for other researchers to completely verify our findings. Additionally, the process for creating prompts were not standardized, we simply tried different configurations based on our own experience with using LLMs until we could not increase the validation accuracy further. Due to these limitations, one should therefore be very hesitant to make any confident conclusions based on the experiments we performed with ChatGPT.

Because our intention was to specifically explore different language models' abilities of fact verification with knowledge graphs on the FACTKG dataset, we did not conduct any experiments on other datasets. It is possible that our results will not be consistent with other datasets.

Additionally, our selection of models and hyperparameter settings could be more diverse. Due to computational constraints, we did not perform a grid search for hyperparameters, but tuned hyperparameters one by one. Which parameters we searched for were not decided in advance. A predefined grid search might lead to a fairer and more reproducible approach. We did not experiment with different orderings of the knowledge triples for the fine-tuned BERT models, which could influence the performance.

References

Josh Achiam, Steven Adler, Sandhini Agarwal, Lama Ahmad, Ilge Akkaya, Florencia Leoni Aleman, Diogo Almeida, Janko Altenschmidt, Sam Altman, Shyamal Anadkat, et al. 2023. Gpt-4 technical report. *arXiv preprint arXiv:2303.08774*.

Giannis Bekoulis, Christina Papagiannopoulou, and Nikos Deligiannis. 2021. A review on fact extraction and verification. *ACM Computing Surveys (CSUR)*, 55(1):1–35.

Steven Bird, Ewan Klein, and Edward Loper. 2009. *Natural language processing with Python: analyzing text with the natural language toolkit.* " O'Reilly Media, Inc.".

Jiangui Chen, Ruqing Zhang, Jiafeng Guo, Yixing Fan, and Xueqi Cheng. 2022. Gere: Generative evidence retrieval for fact verification. In *Proceedings of the 45th International ACM SIGIR Conference on Research and Development in Information Retrieval*, pages 2184–2189.

Wenhu Chen, Hongmin Wang, Jianshu Chen, Yunkai Zhang, Hong Wang, Shiyang Li, Xiyou Zhou, and William Yang Wang. 2019. Tabfact: A large-scale dataset for table-based fact verification. *arXiv preprint arXiv:1909.02164*.

S Cohen, C Li, J Yang, and C Yu. 2011. Computational journalism: A call to arms to database researchers, 148-151. In *5th Biennial Conference on Innovative Data Systems Research, CIDR*.

Jacob Devlin, Ming-Wei Chang, Kenton Lee, and Kristina Toutanova. 2018. Bert: Pre-training of deep bidirectional transformers for language understanding. *arXiv preprint arXiv:1810.04805*.

Sushant Gautam. 2024. Factgenius: Combining zero-shot prompting and fuzzy relation mining to improve fact verification with knowledge graphs. *arXiv preprint arXiv:2406.01311*.

Andreas Hanselowski, Avinesh PVS, Benjamin Schiller, Felix Caspelherr, Debanjan Chaudhuri, Christian M Meyer, and Iryna Gurevych. 2018. A retrospective analysis of the fake news challenge stance detection task. *arXiv preprint arXiv:1806.05180*.

Charles R Harris, K Jarrod Millman, Stéfan J Van Der Walt, Ralf Gommers, Pauli Virtanen, David Cournapeau, Eric Wieser, Julian Taylor, Sebastian Berg, Nathaniel J Smith, et al. 2020. Array programming with numpy. *Nature*, 585(7825):357–362.

Naeemul Hassan, Bill Adair, James T Hamilton, Chengkai Li, Mark Tremayne, Jun Yang, and Cong Yu. 2015. The quest to automate fact-checking. In *Proceedings of the 2015 computation+ journalism symposium*. Citeseer.

Christopher Hidey, Tuhin Chakrabarty, Tariq Alhindi, Siddharth Varia, Kriste Krstovski, Mona Diab, and Smaranda Muresan. 2020. Deseption: Dual sequence prediction and adversarial examples for improved fact-checking. *arXiv preprint arXiv:2004.12864*.

Matthew Honnibal and Ines Montani. 2017. spaCy 2: Natural language understanding with Bloom embeddings, convolutional neural networks and incremental parsing. To appear.

Sergey Ioffe and Christian Szegedy. 2015. Batch normalization: Accelerating deep network training by reducing internal covariate shift. In *International conference on machine learning*, pages 448–456. pmlr.

Jiho Kim, Sungjin Park, Yeonsu Kwon, Yohan Jo, James Thorne, and Edward Choi. 2023. Factkg: Fact verification via reasoning on knowledge graphs. *arXiv preprint arXiv:2305.06590*.

Jens Lehmann, Robert Isele, Max Jakob, Anja Jentzsch, Dimitris Kontokostas, Pablo N Mendes, Sebastian Hellmann, Mohamed Morsey, Patrick Van Kleef, Sören Auer, et al. 2015. Dbpedia–a large-scale, multilingual knowledge base extracted from wikipedia. *Semantic web*, 6(2):167–195.

Yinhan Liu, Myle Ott, Naman Goyal, Jingfei Du, Mandar Joshi, Danqi Chen, Omer Levy, Mike Lewis, Luke Zettlemoyer, and Veselin Stoyanov. 2019. Roberta: A robustly optimized bert pretraining approach. *arXiv preprint arXiv:1907.11692*.

Ilya Loshchilov and Frank Hutter. 2017. Decoupled weight decay regularization. *arXiv preprint arXiv:1711.05101*.

Shreyash Mishra, S Suryavardan, Amrit Bhaskar, Parul Chopra, Aishwarya N Reganti, Parth Patwa, Amitava Das, Tanmoy Chakraborty, Amit P Sheth, Asif Ekbal, et al. 2022. Factify: A multi-modal fact verification dataset. In *DE-FACTIFY@ AAAI*.

Yixin Nie, Haonan Chen, and Mohit Bansal. 2019. Combining fact extraction and verification with neural semantic matching networks. In *Proceedings of the AAAI conference on artificial intelligence*, volume 33.01, pages 6859–6866.

Open AI. 2024. Hello gpt 4o. `https://openai.com/index/hello-gpt-4o/`, Accessed 30.05.2024.

Jungsoo Park, Sewon Min, Jaewoo Kang, Luke Zettlemoyer, and Hannaneh Hajishirzi. 2021. Faviq: Fact verification from information-seeking questions. *arXiv preprint arXiv:2107.02153*.

Adam Paszke, Sam Gross, Francisco Massa, Adam Lerer, James Bradbury, Gregory Chanan, Trevor Killeen, Zeming Lin, Natalia Gimelshein, Luca Antiga, et al. 2019. Pytorch: An imperative style, high-performance deep learning library. *Advances in neural information processing systems*, 32.

Tal Schuster, Adam Fisch, and Regina Barzilay. 2021. Get your vitamin c! robust fact verification with contrastive evidence. *arXiv preprint arXiv:2103.08541*.

Tal Schuster, Darsh J Shah, Yun Jie Serene Yeo, Daniel Filizzola, Enrico Santus, and Regina Barzilay. 2019. Towards debiasing fact verification models. *arXiv preprint arXiv:1908.05267*.

Nitish Srivastava, Geoffrey Hinton, Alex Krizhevsky, Ilya Sutskever, and Ruslan Salakhutdinov. 2014. Dropout: a simple way to prevent neural networks from overfitting. *The journal of machine learning research*, 15(1):1929–1958.

James Thorne and Andreas Vlachos. 2018. Automated fact checking: Task formulations, methods and future directions. *arXiv preprint arXiv:1806.07687*.

James Thorne, Andreas Vlachos, Christos Christodoulopoulos, and Arpit Mittal. 2018. Fever: a large-scale dataset for fact extraction and verification. *arXiv preprint arXiv:1803.05355*.

University Of Oslo University Centre for Information Technology. 2023. Machine learning infrastructure (ml nodes).

Petar Veličković, Guillem Cucurull, Arantxa Casanova, Adriana Romero, Pietro Lio, and Yoshua Bengio. 2017. Graph attention networks. *arXiv preprint arXiv:1710.10903*.

Thomas Wolf, Lysandre Debut, Victor Sanh, Julien Chaumond, Clement Delangue, Anthony Moi, Pierric Cistac, Tim Rault, Rémi Louf, Morgan Funtowicz, et al. 2020. Transformers: State-of-the-art natural language processing. In *Proceedings of the 2020 conference on empirical methods in natural language processing: system demonstrations*, pages 38–45.

Michihiro Yasunaga, Hongyu Ren, Antoine Bosselut, Percy Liang, and Jure Leskovec. 2021. Qagnn: Reasoning with language models and knowledge graphs for question answering. *arXiv preprint arXiv:2104.06378*.

Jie Zhou, Xu Han, Cheng Yang, Zhiyuan Liu, Lifeng Wang, Changcheng Li, and Maosong Sun. 2019. Gear: Graph-based evidence aggregating and reasoning for fact verification. *arXiv preprint arXiv:1908.01843*.

Dimitrina Zlatkova, Preslav Nakov, and Ivan Koychev. 2019. Fact-checking meets fauxtography: Verifying claims about images. *arXiv preprint arXiv:1908.11722*.

A Hyperparameter Details

We used an AdamW optimizer (Loshchilov and Hutter, 2017) with a linear learning rate scheduler with 50 warm up steps, and used the model from the epoch with lowest loss on the validation set. The hyperparameters were tuned in a line search, first testing different learning rates, and then testing all the other hyperparameters with the best learning rate. We searched for learning rates in $\{1e-3, 5e-4, 1e-4, 5e-5, 1e-5\}$ for all models. We initially set the batch size to 32, except for the BERT models with large subgraphs, which were set to 4 due to memory constraints. After finding the learning rate, we tried batch sizes in $\{32, 64, 128, 256\}$. For the QA-GNN model, we initially set the GNN dropout and the classifier dropout to 0.3, and tried values in $\{0, 0.1, 0.3, 0.5, 0.6\}$. We also tried to freeze some of the layers in the base model, and to use a RoBERTa (Liu et al., 2019) instead of BERT (Devlin et al., 2018), but neither of these approaches improved the validation loss.

The final hyperparameters can be found in Table A.

Model	Learning Rate	Batch Size	Best Epoch
BERT (no subgraphs)	1e-4	32	6
BERT (direct)	1e-4	32	7
BERT (contextual)	5e-5	8	7
BERT (single-step)	5e-5	4	7
QA-GNN (direct)	1e-4	128	8
QA-GNN (contextual)	5e-5	64	17
QA-GNN (single-step)	1e-5	128	20

Table 5: **Final hyperparameters for the different models.** The direct QA-GNN model used GNN and classifier dropout rates of 0.3 and 0.3, while the two other QA-GNN models used 0.1 and 0.5, respectively.

B Scientific Artifacts

We conducted the experiments using several python libraries, including PyTorch version 2.0.1 (Paszke et al., 2019) with CUDA version 11.7, HuggingFace Transformers (Wolf et al., 2020), NumPy (Harris et al., 2020), SpaCy (Honnibal and Montani, 2017) and NLTK (Bird et al., 2009).

Author Index